To my husband, Jerry

Merchandise Buying
Principles and Applications

Maryanne Smith Bohlinger

Coordinator, Retail Management Program
Community College of Philadelphia

WM. C. BROWN COMPANY PUBLISHERS
Dubuque, Iowa

CONTENTS

The Environment of the Buying Specialist 1   SECTION 1

1 The Role of the Buyer: Yesterday and Today 3

Part 1 will (1) review the development of basic merchandising activities, (2) relate how retailing developed in the United States, and (3) discuss the development of the buying activity in different types of retail stores. Part 2 will discuss the buying activity of today. Topics to be considered are (1) major forces that the buyer should be aware of when planning the buying activity, (2) techniques the buyer may use to meet the challenge of today's retail environment, and (3) the need for the buying activity in modern merchandise management.

2 The Buyer's Responsibilities in Merchandise Management 41

Part 1 will (1) describe the retail specialist who is responsible for performing the buying-selling activity in different types of retail stores, (2) outline the duties and responsibilities required of this individual, and (3) discuss the job of the buyer as a manager. Part 2 will discuss buying as a career. Topics to be considered are (1) the challenge of merchandise management, (2) personal requirements for a career in merchandising, (3) the availability of college training programs as well as executive development programs offered by most retail stores, and (4) the role of the assistant buyer in merchandise management.

3 Organizing the Buying-Selling Activity 69

Part 1 will (1) define retail buying, (2) discuss the necessary essentials in organizing a retail business, (3) determine how various types of retail organizations are organized, and (4) identify current trends in store organization. Part 2 will (1) discuss how buying is controlled in various types of retail stores, (2) identify various methods of central buying, and (3) discuss the advantages and disadvantages of each method.

4 The Resident Buying Office 111

Part 1 will discuss (1) the development of resident buying offices, (2) the different types of resident buying offices, (3) how to determine which type of resident buying office is suitable for a particular store, and (4) the organization of various types of offices. Part 2 will discuss numerous services offered by typical resident buying office. Topics to be considered are (1) the merchandising function, (2) the promotion function, (3) the ancillary function, and (4) the research function.

The Merchandise Assortment 141   SECTION 2

5 The Importance of Fashion 143

Part 1 will (1) outline and explain basic fashion terminology, (2) discuss why fashions change, and (3) discuss fashion origins and trends. Part 2 will (1) discuss who is responsible for fashion coordination, (2) show how fashion coordination is organized in different types of retail stores, (3) discuss the role of the buyer in fashion coordination, and (4) discuss the planning of the fashion season.

Part 1 will discuss (1) steps in the negotiation process, (2) order placement, (3) the kinds of orders available, and (4) some hints for retail buyers. Part 2 will discuss the vendor's responsibility to the buyer. Topics to be discussed are (1) the conduct of the vendor, (2) legal aspects of the buyer's order, (3) causes of friction between vendors and buyers, and (4) establishment of good vendor-buyer relations.

Part 1 will discuss how the wholesale price is determined by (1) developing a thorough knowledge of prices, (2) determining elements in the wholesale price, and (3) understanding the legal aspects of pricing. Part 2 will discuss how the retail price is determined. Topics to be considered are (1) its importance in merchandise selection, (2) various factors in pricing for retail, and (3) formulas used to determine the retail price.

Part 1 will (1) discuss the importance of effective communication and the role of nonpersonal selling, (2) identify the main types of retail advertising, (3) discuss the psychological aspects of advertising, and (4) determine how advertising is planned and the importance of ethics in advertising. Part 2 will discuss (1) the importance of personal selling, (2) various types of personal selling, (3) the buyer's job in managing retail salespeople, and (4) the duties and responsibilities of sales personnel.

Merchandise Buying: Principles and Applications has been written as a basic textbook for two types of students: (1) those who want some knowledge of the activities involved in the buying-selling function of the retail store, and (2) those planning a career in merchandising as buying specialists. What students of each type need most as beginners in the field of merchandising is a well-rounded course that provides maximum exposure to the function of retail buying. To achieve this purpose, *Merchandise Buying: Principles and Applications* presents both an overview of the retail system and a detailed description of the major functions concerned with the buying-selling activity in various types of retail institutions. It also relates the function of merchandising to the business environment by examining the responsibilities of all types of buying specialists to our society as well as to consumers.

This text was specifically designed for the college student. It provides a comprehensive, up-to-date presentation of information vital to the beginning student of merchandising as well as theoretical knowledge necessary for retail middle management employment, the level many graduates enter upon completion of the academic degree. Mid-management opportunities available in merchandising are stressed throughout this text.

Merchandising mathematics used by the buying specialist and his or her assistant is presented in a simplified matter to facilitate decision making and problem solving for student and teacher alike. The importance of electronic data processing (EDP) is also stressed throughout various chapters; the computer and its application to specific merchandising activities are emphasized throughout the text. Performance objectives, chapter organization, illustrations, printed store forms, photographs, and end-of-chapter activities combine to show the application of classroom theory to real-life work situations.

The material in this text has been structured to permit maximum teaching flexibility. It may be used in an introductory course in the field of retailing, or it may be used in a specialized course such as one in retail buying or in other courses such as marketing, management, salesmanship, fashion merchandising, advertising, and wholesaling.

Performance Objectives

Merchandise Buying: Principles and Applications is a performance-oriented text. For the student to achieve a position in merchandising at the mid-management level, he or she must be equipped with the skills, knowledge, and concepts required of those entering such positions. Each chapter will contain a set of performance objectives at the beginning which are intended to bring about increased learning and understanding. The students should read the statement of objectives before reading the chapter and then refer to them as they proceed through the text. Review of performance objectives is necessary if the student is to gain as much as possible from each chapter.

Organization

Merchandise Buying: Principles and Applications is organized into four major sections, which are further subdivided into fifteen chapters. An outline at the beginning of each chapter provides the student with an overview of chapter material. Each chapter is broken down into two parts to facilitate learning and comprehension. Review boxes also occur throughout each chapter. These boxes will provide the student with an opportunity to recall important merchandising principles and also serve as study aids.

End-of-chapter Activities

Each chapter concludes with a series of activities that require thought, application, and interpretation. These activities consist of the following:

Trade Terminology. A list of business terms commonly used in the field of merchandising. Each trade term is referred to in the chapter and will be identified by being printed in italics. A glossary of trade terminology appears at the end of the text in alphabetical order with complete definitions to serve as a ready reference.

Questions for Discussion and Review. A series of review questions will be given. They will require an understanding of chapter material and the application of such material to present-day situations.

Case Studies. Presentation of typical retail situations will test the student's awareness of business problems as well as his or her ability in decision making and problem solving. Case studies are omitted from chapter 1, since this chapter presents a general introduction to and review of merchandising principles.

Retailing Activities to Stimulate Student Interest and Participation. These are designed to stimulate the student by providing an opportunity to research retailing activities through a variety of practical experiences.

Retail Student's Reference Library. A list of available books, pamphlets, and trade sources will assist the student in research work and enlighten him or her as to the vast sources of material available in specific subject areas.

Supporting Materials

An *instructor's manual* will be provided. This manual contains specific suggestions for planning a fifteen-week course and for teaching each chapter in the text. It contains answers for all review questions, problems, and cases.

ACKNOWLEDGMENTS

This textbook would not have been possible without the encouragement and advice of many dedicated individuals in the field of retailing. I am most grateful to Ms. JoAnne DiSanto of the John Wanamaker Department Store and Mr. Richard Dallas of the Strawbridge & Clothier Department Store, both in Philadelphia, for their generous assistance and cooperation. I would also like to express special thanks to the National Retail Merchants Association, the Pennsylvania Retail Merchants Association, Frederick Atkins Resident Buying Office, Korvettes, O'Shea's Department Store, Duckwall Stores, Inc., Sears, Roebuck and Co., the Bailey, Banks & Biddle Company, Lord & Taylor, Avon Products, the NAWCAS Guild, Sperry & Hutchinson Company, Pantry Pride/Food Fair Supermarkets, Brown Shoe Company, Dante's Inferno, Retail News Bureau, Homer Hoyt Associates, R. H. Macy & Company, George Jacobs, Mr. Paul M. Mazur, and to the many other retail executives who have made significant contributions.

I am most grateful to my many colleagues at Community College for their helpful suggestions and comments, and especially to my students, whose desire for knowledge of and enthusiasm for the retail industry have inspired me to write this book.

Finally, I wish to thank Mr. Steve Hawkins for his excellent photography, Ms. Anne Smith for her typing skills, and Mr. Benjamin Cutler of the Bronx Community College, Ms. Charlene Bomrad of Onondaga Community College, Mr. Jack Rittenberg of the Fashion Institute of Technology, and Ms. Ruth Cressman of Milwaukee Technical College, who patiently reviewed this manuscript.

The Environment of the Buying Specialist

The Role of the Buyer:
Yesterday and Today

1

Performance Objectives

PART 1

The Buying Activity:
An Introduction

A Review of Basic Concepts

And in the Beginning

Merchandising Activities in the United States

Development of Different Types of Stores

Trading Post and Wagon Peddler
General Store
Specialty Store
Limited-Line Store
Chain-Store Operation
Department Store
Supermarket
Discount House
Franchise
Cooperative Chain Store
Voluntary Chain Store
Shopping Center

Non-Store Retailing

Mail-Order House
Catalog Sales
Vending Machines
Door-to-Door Selling

PART 2

The Role of the Buyer:
Today

Never a Dull Moment

Social Environment
Economic Environment
Technological Environment
Competitive Environment
Governmental Environment

Meeting the Challenge

Response to Social Changes
Response to Economic Changes
Response to Technological Changes
Response to Competitive Changes
Response to Governmental Changes
Antitrust Laws
Unfair Trade Practice Laws
Price Competition Laws
Laws Affecting Customer Relations
Extension of Credit
Product Safety
Consumer Protection
Packaging, Labeling, and Advertising

The Buying Activity in a Changing Society

Chapter Summary
Trade Terminology
Questions for Discussion and Review
Retailing Activities to Stimulate Student Interest and Participation
The Retail Student's Reference Library
References

PERFORMANCE OBJECTIVES

As a result of reading this chapter, the student should be able to accomplish the following:

1. Discuss the development of basic merchandising activities.

2. Relate how retailing developed in the United States.

3. Discuss the buying activity and its development in different types of retail stores.

4. Define marketing, retailing, retailing institution, and twig store.

5. Outline and explain four types of nonstore retailing.

6. Become aware of external factors within the retail trade that may affect the buyer's performance as a merchant. Five external factors to be studied are: social environment, economic environment, technological environment, competitive environment, and governmental environment.

7. Explain in detail how the retail buyer has responded to the challenges resulting from each environmental influence.

8. Define merchandise scrambling and one-stop concept.

The Role of the Buyer: Yesterday and Today

The Buying Activity: An Introduction

This book is concerned with the buyer and the role the buyer plays in merchandise management. What does this statement bring to mind? Different types of retail stores? Retail trade? Marketing? Mass merchandising? The buying-selling activity? All of these basic concepts relate in one way or another to the retailer in the role of buying specialist.

A Review of Basic Concepts

For the student to complete a course in retail buying successfully, there must be an awareness of the development of those concepts that are characteristic of the environment of the retailer. The objective of this chapter, therefore, will be to present these concepts in a logical and informative manner. Part 1 will (1) review the development of basic merchandising activities, (2) relate how retailing developed in the United States, and (3) discuss the development of the buying activity in different types of retail stores. Part 2 will discuss the buying activity of today. Topics to be considered are (1) major forces that the buyer should be aware of when planning the buying activity, (2) techniques the buyer may use to meet the challenge of today's retail environment, and (3) the need for the buying activity in modern merchandise management.

And in the Beginning

If you had the opportunity to trace business transactions throughout the course of history, you would be interested to discover that such activities occurred as early as the Stone Age of the prehistoric period. Records show that during that time, the caveman would trade his goods for other goods that would provide the basic necessities of his very primitive life-style. The business transaction was indeed a very simple one, since producer met face to face with consumer to accomplish an exchange. That meeting was the beginning of what is known today as retail trade.

References to retail trade and the many business transactions involved have been found in the numerous writings of the ancient Egyptians, about 3000 B.C. They are said to have been the first people to have a well-developed system of trade. They floated barrels of precious oils, bags of linen, and sacks of wheat down the Nile River on barges. The chief Egyptian exports were cotton, linen, oils, fruit, honey, wax, and precious metals. In return, Egyptian traders imported goods that they were unable to produce themselves. It would be interesting to visualize the Egyptian trader in the marketplace drawing up business contracts, negotiating for a loan, formalizing a trade agreement, and extending credit to his customers.

During the Middle Ages, which historians place between the fall of Rome in A.D. 476 and the fall of Constantinople in 1453, populations expanded and provided more opportunities to sell goods. The town became the center of distribution for craftspeople and traders alike. Here the skilled worker organized a business in a small dwelling and began producing goods by hand and manufacturing them to order. He was called a handcraft manufacturer. He was self-employed and was responsible for the activities of the entire business operation.

Business expansion continued through what is often referred to as the Age of Exploration (1295–1620). Merchants with money were continuously seeking new market potentials in which to invest their finances. The Florentines, the Spaniards, and the Portuguese turned their attention to exploration. New trade routes to India, Africa, and the Americas were discovered. The explorers could not have left their harbors if it had not been for the merchant capitalists, who lent money on the promise that goods found in the New World would be received as payment. Preparing the ship for its long voyage, as well as the search for goods throughout the world, lent itself to large-scale wholesaling by the merchants. As a result of such business ventures, merchant capitalists gained control over materials and markets. These wholesalers were the only people who knew the origin of the goods as well as the market destination.

Populations continued to expand, and more goods were in demand. It soon became apparent that the handcraft manufacturer was unable to produce enough goods to meet this demand, while continuing to sell and advertise products. Farmers were also affected by the growth in population. Since agricultural products were necessary for basic subsistence, farmers had to expand production and, consequently, had to spend most of their time on the farm and less time traveling to and from the market square. It was becoming increasingly difficult for both the handcraft manufacturer and the farmer to produce or manufacture goods as well as to transport and sell such commodities to the consumer.[1]

Merchandising Activities in the United States

It was not until the late 1700s, with the Industrial Revolution, that enough goods were produced to satisfy the ever-increasing demand. This revolution within industry was very important to the development of retail trade, since, for the first time, a commodity surplus was provided. Due to technological innovations such as the steam engine, the telegraph, and the cotton gin, employment was provided to men and women that raised the level of economic output. The handcraft manufacturer who sold the goods produced in his or her own shop gave way to mass production in the factory. Merchants and moneylenders continued to accumulate the necessary capital to finance the equipment, machinery, land, and buildings required. Mass production led to standardization and simplification of production.

The United States was the first nation to accommodate itself to the Industrial Revolution. As a result of innovative methods of transportation, particularly in the West, and the availability of capital from European investors, industry and people spread across the country. The building of railroads influenced the growth of many towns and provided means of transportation to the various trade or market centers, as well as communication. European merchants looked upon the early colonies as providers of raw materials to European markets, as well as consumers of European finished goods. The colonies provided merchants with the opportunity for organizing shipping ventures for the importation and exportation of goods.[2]

With the continued development of new production methods and the rapid growth of towns into cities, a very specialized and complex communication system soon developed. This system, which links the markets of production with the markets of demand, is called *marketing*. It was the mass production of the Industrial Revolution that paved the way for mass marketing. When goods arrived at their destination, it was necessary to provide markets to disperse them. However, the technology capable of producing the commodities and the transportation network that moved the goods were not sufficient. Trading centers or marketplaces were needed to facilitate trade.

Retailing provides the consumer with the merchandise assortment at the right time and at the best price; it is the last stage of the marketing system. Retailing, therefore, is not only a vital part of the trade system; it is also the segment of marketing with which we are most familiar. When we speak of marketing, we almost automatically think of retailing and retail institutions. The *retail institution* or *store*, therefore, became identified as the trading center or marketplace that provided for the last activity in the marketing system—getting the goods to the consumer.

The marketing system links markets of
production with markets of demand.

Manufacturers ⟶ Middlemen ⟶ Retail stores ⟶ Final consumers

Retailers soon found it necessary to specialize in selling commodities and services to the ultimate consumer, since they were the vital force within the marketing system that linked the manufacturer and the ultimate consumer. They performed an important marketing function in that they stimulated the sale of commodities, thus creating a demand for manufactured goods.

During this period of industrial expansion, retail merchants discovered that a division and greater specialization of labor was needed. The buying activity, which had been performed by the store owner, soon was delegated to a particular individual within the store. This individual was made responsible for deciding what to buy, where to buy, how much to buy, and what price to ask. Such a person was called a *buyer.* He or she became the specialist within the retail institution who was responsible for getting the merchandise into the hands of the ultimate consumer.

Development of Different Types of Stores

Trading Post and Wagon Peddler

As the population of the eastern United States continued to grow, the frontier was extended farther west. Two very popular forms of retailing were found in the frontier settlements: the trading post and the wagon peddler. The trading post was usually located on a main route of travel and was eagerly sought by wagon trains as they crossed an often hostile frontier. It provided an opportunity for trade and exchange of information. The peddler's wagon was often a trading post on wheels. The existence of roads made it possible for the peddler to carry a variety of merchandise and travel greater distances to supply the needs of the sparsely populated frontier. Thus, the wagon peddler or trader became the forerunner of the traveling salesperson.

General Store

The general store of the eighteenth century became a popular form of retailing in small communities and rural areas. The owner of the general store provided a greater selection of products and better service to his customers than did his predecessor, the trading post owner. The merchandise of the general store was not separated according to type of goods, particular style, or size, but was placed in a haphazard manner throughout the store. These stores provided a variety of staple goods, such as sugar, flour, coffee, salt, dried meat, tools, cloth, gunpowder, whiskey, hides, and clothing, which was purchased from traveling salesmen or peddlers. The general store was conveniently located between the nearest city and the farmlands; the farmer who patronized it accepted the merchandise selection and usually did not question the prices. Credit was often extended, with payment for goods due "when the crops came in." Not only did the general store provide much-needed merchandise, but it also often served as a social center where people would congregate and discuss politics or catch up on local gossip.

Specialty Store

By the middle of the nineteenth century, the Industrial Revolution had found its way to the American city. As a result of technological developments within industry, an increase in the labor market, and the mass production of commodities, new and more progressive types of retail outlets developed. Such a variety of goods were being produced in the United States that the general store concept, which placed merchandise haphazardly throughout the store, was no longer tolerable. The unlimited offerings of the manufacturers necessitated the specialization of goods by retailers; thus we have the beginning of the specialty store. This retail establishment carried a few lines of closely related items. Millinery shops, fashion-accessory shops, and leather-goods stores are examples of specialty retail businesses. As a result of industrialization and the increased purchasing power of the consumer, these specialty stores became more and more common. They were usually located in larger cities or towns.

Merchandise buyers soon began to specialize in the marketplace by seeking new markets and price information. These specialty store retailers were responsible for providing the customer with a selection of merchandise as well as services, and were concerned with the activities of their competition. Competition among specialty store owners became quite evident during the late 1800s. To meet the competition, some merchants offered services, such as credit, delivery, and gift wrapping to attract the customer. The specialty store owner was usually a sole proprietor. Many of these stores have grown into the well-known retail stores of today.

Limited-Line Store

The limited-line store also became popular during this period. However, unlike the specialty store, the limited-line store sold only one kind of merchandise, such as bakery goods, tobacco products, or hardware items. The limited-line store may be found selling all kinds of merchandise lines, from home furnishings to lumber. This type of business is dominated by small stores or "mom-and-pop stores."

Chain-Store Operation

The chain store, a new and original type of retailing, had its beginnings during the latter part of the nineteenth century. The owner of the specialty store or the limited-line store now purchased two or more stores that were similar in merchandise offerings and were controlled by one individual. Among early chain-store operations were the Great Atlantic and Pacific Tea Company, Incorporated (A & P, 1859), the food giant; the J. C. Penney Company, Incorporated (1902), dry goods; and F. W. Woolworth Company (1879), variety stores. The chain-store organization is credited with being the first to venture into large-scale retailing in the United States. The merchandise buyer was now responsible not only for purchasing goods for one store but perhaps also for several stores located throughout the country. The new chain-store buyers encountered difficulties with manufacturers who had not perfected the art of mass production and who were uncertain as to the buyers' intentions. Production was limited, transportation inadequate, and goods had to be distributed rapidly to meet consumer demands.[3]

Figure 1.1. On April 25, 1875, Dennis and John O'Shea began a dry goods operation. In December of that year, the brothers expanded their operation, adding ready-made clothing. By 1878, O'Shea's had become the largest retailer in the state of New Hampshire. (Courtesy of O'Shea's, Laconia, New Hampshire.)

Department Store

Towards the end of the nineteenth century and at the beginning of the twentieth, a departmentalized type of retailing emerged. Interestingly, however, the department store began as early as the sixteenth century. The early colonists imitated their English ancestors by providing small booths or stands, all under the same roof and each carrying a line of merchandise. During the 1880s, however, the department technique of merchandising took on a more sophisticated appearance and became more complicated as a result of increased competition. The department-store operation developed, whereby a wide variety of hard and soft goods were contained each within its own unit or department. The departments were located under the same roof and had common ownership. Department-store buyers brought together many specialty operations under one roof, with each department managed by its own buying specialist. The typical offerings of the department store in the hard-goods lines were furniture, large and small appliances, and tools, while in the soft-goods area, fashion accessories and articles of clothing were typical. More buying specialists were needed to cover the many different market centers, so buyers sought wholesalers or vendors who could offer the best prices, merchandise assortment, and service. The department store also provided services for the customer, such as custom tailoring, alterations, delivery service, and credit arrangements. The consumer was provided with luxury items as well as necessities. As a result of this expansion of goods and services, the *one-stop concept* of retailing developed. The one-stop concept boasts of providing all the merchandise needed under one roof.

Figure 1.2. John Wanamaker of Philadelphia opened a men's and boys' clothing store in 1861. By 1877, the store carried over 38 different lines of separate departments of merchandise. (Courtesy of John Wanamaker, Philadelphia, Pa.)

Many of the retail stores of the nineteenth century are still in existence today. John Wanamaker of Philadelphia opened a men's and boys' clothing store in 1861. By 1877, the store carried more than thirty-eight different lines or separate departments of merchandise, ranging from carpeting to ladies' hair ribbons. Wanamaker's was one of the first retail stores to adopt a one-price policy, which set the example for others in the field. This retail policy discontinued consumer bargaining and reduced credit; thus, many retail outlets began to operate on a cash-only basis. Other early department stores were R. H. Macy and Company, Incorporated (1858), in New York, and Marshall Field & Company (1881) in Chicago.[4]

The department-store method of retailing spread rapidly after 1900. Many department stores expanded or followed population growth into particular areas and opened "branch stores." These branch stores were smaller units carrying a representative selection of the goods offered in the "mother store," or main store. The merchandise buyer, besides purchasing goods for a department in the main store, was also responsible for forecasting the needs and

Figure 1.3. R. H. Macy and
Company, Incorporated, opened
its doors in New York City in
1858. Today, Macy's at Herald
Square is the world's largest
retail store. (Courtesy of R. H.
Macy and Co., Inc., New York,
N.Y.)

wants of consumers in the branch stores. As a result of the increase in retail
trade, resident buying offices that represented the buying activity of many retail
stores developed. Major responsibilities of the resident buyer are to seek the
latest information concerning market trends, to locate manufacturers, and to
negotiate the best price for member stores.

Supermarket

The supermarket had its beginnings during the depression era of the 1930s. Up
to that period food was sold in small neighborhood stores that offered a limited
selection and charged high prices. During the depression, incomes were extremely low, and promoters of the supermarket concept used low prices to
appeal to the consumer. The supermarket was primarily a self-service store;
it was departmentalized and carried a full line of food products, including fresh

meats, vegetable produce, and dairy products. In addition, it carried drugs, hardware, and accessories. The supermarket, like the department store, provided the one-stop concept for the consumer, who now had the opportunity of purchasing all needed foodstuffs at one location instead of making separate trips to various food markets. Food buyers or brokers were responsible for the movement of goods from distribution centers into the supermarket.

The early supermarket was located in low-rent areas, had a minimum of displays and decor, and offered limited personal service. It provided a means for independent retailers to meet the competition of the chain store. However, large food chains such as A & P also turned to this innovative method of food service to reach new consumer markets. The supermarket concept had a tremendous impact on the distribution methods of the retail trade. The impact was felt not only in the food trade but in the whole area of retailing.

Discount House

A recent innovation in retailing has been the discount house, which became popular during the 1940s. The principal retailing philosophy of the discount house has been low overhead, low prices, and rapid turnover. The mass-merchandise buyer offers limited service in return for lower prices. This method of selling has found its way into all types of retail establishments, for example, the department store, the supermarket, and the specialty shop. The early discount-house buyer purchased primarily hard goods, such as furniture and kitchen appliances. After World War II the discount-house concept spread rapidly as a result of changes in economic and social conditions. These cut-rate retailers expanded their operations on a large scale into the soft-goods or fashion-apparel line. One of the largest discount houses was E. J. Korvette, founded in New York City in 1948.

Problems faced by the discount buyer are primarily a result of an increase in first-rate competition in the discount field, consumer resistance to crowded store conditions, and sloppy presentation of soft-goods lines; in healthy economies customers tend to be drawn to retail stores with better decor.

Franchise

The franchise, which dates back to the 1890s, became a popular method of retailing during the 1950s. In franchising, a business firm or sponsor, called a *franchisor,* grants operating rights to a given business, called a *franchisee.* A key ingredient in franchising is the working relationship between the franchisor and the franchisee.

Five types of franchises can be identified. In the first type, wholesalers offer franchise contracts to independent retailers in such trades as hardware, grocery, drugs, and auto supply. This type of franchise provides small retailers with the benefits of volume buying as well as other operating assistance. A second type of franchise involves manufacturers and wholesalers. The soft-drink industry is perhaps the best example, since syrup manufacturing companies such as Pepsi-Cola, Seven-Up, and Coca-Cola will franchise local bottlers, who in turn sell the bottled drinks to retail outlets. A third type is the manufacturer-retailer franchise, in which manufacturers, for example, appliance and television producers, will grant franchises to dealers to cover their line of products. Individual dealers can have several manufacturers' franchises; for instance, they can carry Whirlpool, Magnavox, and other products. A manufacturer-retail franchise that covers the entire business outlet is the fourth type. In this type the manufacturer franchises the total business operation. For example, General Motors and other auto makers, as well as Mobil and Shell petroleum refiners, will determine the retailer's marketing strategy and business operations. The franchisee will manage the business operation on a daily basis in return for a salary and a share of the profits. The fifth type of franchise is the service franchise, in which the major component is a service arrangement. Examples may include food (McDonald's, Dairy Queen); employment (Kelly Girl); income-tax preparation (H & R Block, Inc.); automobile rental (Hertz, Avis); and motel/hotel accommodations (Howard Johnson, Holiday Inn). The service franchise is the most common type of franchise today.[5]

Cooperative Chain Store

Two popular types of retailing are the cooperative chain store and the voluntary chain store. The cooperative chain store is owned by a group of independent retailers who have organized their own wholesale company with its own warehouse and offices. The wholesaling activity is owned on a cooperative basis, thus providing its member stores with an opportunity to partake in group buying activities to meet competition from large chain stores. However, unlike the chain-store operation, cooperative chain stores are still independently operated and owned. The cooperative chain store is most common in the food industry. Examples are Associated Grocers and Certified Grocers.

Voluntary Chain Store

The voluntary chain store, in contrast, is owned by the wholesaler. Individual stores will remain independent in ownership; however, they surrender most of their operating control to the wholesaler. They will agree to operate under the name of the chain and offer the wholesaler's private brands of merchandise. In return, the stores will receive assistance, such as lower wholesale prices, store displays, advertising copy, and marketing information. Examples of voluntary chain stores are Independent Grocers Alliance (IGA), Supervalue, Rexall, Walgreen, and Ace Hardware stores.

Shopping Center

The shopping center has been a most influential retailing innovation since World War II. With the movement of people from the city to the suburbs, the deterioration of urban shopping districts, availability of transportation, the habit of leisurely family shopping, and traffic congestion in the city, the shopping center has become popular. It offers the advantages of convenient location and parking.

Shopping centers vary in size and type. There are large regional shopping centers with 500,000 to 1,000,000 square feet of building area on 50 to 100 acres of land in the larger metropolitan areas. These contain branches of one to three major department stores, women's and men's clothing stores, shoe stores, a variety store, restaurants, a bank, a supermarket, a drugstore, and other specialty stores. Usually 100,000 families are required in the immediate trade area to support this type of shopping center.[6] Next down the scale is the community shopping center, which usually contains a junior department store, specialty stores, a supermarket, and a drugstore. The community shopping center serves the needs of smaller cities, as well as drawing customers from isolated neighborhoods. Oftentimes, however, the community shopping center will suffer from the competition of large regional centers, since the larger stores can offer a greater merchandise assortment. The neighborhood center or "baby shopping center" is the smallest type. It usually contains a supermarket, a drugstore, some specialty shops, beauty and barber shops, and a variety of "Mom-and-Pop" stores. Neighborhood shopping centers draw their customers from a neighborhood of 5,000 to 10,000 families.[7] In addition to the regional, community, and neighborhood shopping centers, a new kind of shopping center has developed. Large discount stores such as Woolco, Korvette, and K-Mart will, with their own supermarkets or affiliated supermarkets, become complete shopping centers in themselves, consisting of about 100,000 square feet of store area on approximately 10 acres of land.[8] There is no exact information available on the number of each of the different types of shopping centers discussed; however, it is estimated that there are probably not over 250

Explain the development of each of the following types of retail institutions.

How was the buying-selling activity performed?

Trading post; Wagon peddler	General store
Specialty store	Limited-line store
Chain-store operation	Department store
Supermarket	Discount house
Franchise	Cooperative chain; Voluntary chain

Regional shopping center
Community shopping center
Neighborhood shopping center
Discount shopping center

Table 1.1. *Number of new regional shopping centers in selected U.S. metro-politan areas supported by new household growth 1968–1978.*

Area	Added Genl. 1973	Mdse. Sales 1978	Number of 1973	New Centers 1978	Date First New Center
New York-N.E. New Jersey	$206,200,000	$491,800,000	4	9	1970
Los Angeles - Orange County	321,400,000	773,000,000	6	12	1969
Chicago - Gary	136,800,000	327,200,000	2	6	1970
Washington, D.C.	157,100,000	377,100,000	3	6	1973
Miami - Ft. Lauderdale	85,000,000	203,500,000	1	4	1973
Philadelphia	65,900,000	158,800,000	1	3	1973
San Francisco - Oakland	106,600,000	254,700,000	2	5	1970
Seattle - Everett - Tacoma	84,300,000	202,300,000	1	4	1970
Detroit	78,200,000	178,400,000	1	3	1973
Atlanta	55,900,000	133,900,000	1	2	1973
Boston	51,600,000	123,200,000	1	2	1973
Houston	50,600,000	119,300,000	1	2	1973
Minneapolis	44,300,000	106,500,000	1	2	1973

Source: Homer Hoyt Associates, 2939 Van Ness Street, N.W., Washington, D.C. 20008.

large regional centers in the United States. The majority of the 9,300 shopping centers in the nation are smaller neighborhood centers.[9] Table 1.1 illustrates the number of new regional shopping centers in selected United States metro-politan areas.

Nonstore Retailing

A retailing transaction may occur without the customer's actually visiting the store. This type of retailing is called *nonstore retailing.* Examples are: (1) the mail-order house, (2) catalog sales, (3) vending machines, and (4) door-to-door selling.

Mail-order House

Towards the end of the nineteenth century and the period of the general store, such houses as Montgomery Ward and Sears Roebuck, began to offer a variety of merchandise by catalog. General-store owners were rather unconcerned about the activities of the mail-order houses, since they were convinced that people would not purchase merchandise they had never seen or inspected. However, with the development of the postal service and newer methods of mail delivery, these goods could be delivered inexpensively and efficiently. People soon realized the importance of the mail-order house. This concept of merchandising is still very much in existence today and has become firmly entrenched as a type of retailing.

Catalog Sales

Due to the popularity of mail-order retailing, many retail stores provided their customers with catalogs of available merchandise and information on how to order, particularly during the Christmas season and major sales promotions. Some chain stores like Sears also provided telephone facilities, whereby customers could simply telephone an order rather than sending it by mail.

Figure 1.4. Catalog sales have proven to be a popular form of nonstore retailing. Some chain stores, for example, Sears Roebuck and Company, provide store areas where customers can select merchandise from catalogs and place orders. (Courtesy of Sears Roebuck and Co.)

Vending Machines

Vending machines are fairly new on the retail scene; however, they play an important role in the sale of certain merchandise lines. They are used primarily to sell cigarettes, candy bars, soft drinks, and numerous accessory items. They account for approximately 1 percent of total retail sales. This form of nonstore retailing has found its way into cafeterias, college dormitories, hospital waiting rooms, and other areas where people want fast, convenient service.

The greatest advantage of vending machines is their convenience; however, they are high-cost operations. They require accurate and efficient stocking, and equipment repairs are frequent. Also, the prices charged for goods sold in this way are often 20 to 25 percent higher than the same products purchased elsewhere.

Door-to-Door Selling

Door-to-door selling had its beginnings with the wagon peddler of frontier days. It is still a popular form of retailing, especially in the cosmetics, toiletries, housewares, and home furnishings lines. Companies that have successfully used door-to-door selling are Avon, a cosmetics company; Tupperware, a company selling kitchenwares; and Fuller Brush, a company selling housewares.

Explain how the following are examples of nonstore retailing

1. The mail-order house
2. Catalog sales
3. Vending machines
4. Door-to-door selling

PART 2

The Role of the Buyer: Today

Never a Dull Moment

Supplying the needs and wants of consumers has been the job of the merchant since the beginning of time.

Today, however, the student of retailing will discover that many factors have a pronounced effect on the buyer in his or her performance as a retailer. Since the overall objective is to provide goods and services wanted by the consumer, the merchant must be aware of various elements external to the retail trade that may affect performance and, thus, success. The retail buyer is influenced by (1) the social environment (2) the economic environment, (3) the technological environment, (4) the competitive environment, and (5) the governmental environment.[10]

Social Environment

The retail buyer must be aware of the nature and number of potential customers who will patronize his or her store or department. The buyer must know the immediate trading area or business community and recognize its needs. Government publications on population growth and distribution are often helpful. For example, according to the Bureau of the Census, the United States has witnessed a population explosion. In 1970 it was estimated that our total population was over 204 million; projections for the next two decades were over 225 million by 1975 and 270 million by 1985. In recent years, however, the birthrate has been declining. The buyer should also be aware of the increase in the number of households and families. In the United States the number of households has been increasing at a rate of about 950,000 a year, and it is probable that by 1980 the total number may reach 90 million or more.

Population growth in certain age groups is also of interest to the merchant. For example, by 1970 there were more than 99 million persons aged under 25 in a population of approximately 210 million. It has also been estimated that the group aged 20 to 64 increased by 40 percent during the 1970s, which is more than twice the increase of any other age groups. This has important implications for the youth-oriented retailer. However, the over-65 age group has been expanding and will probably increase by 55 percent by 1985. The senior citizen may well become an important market to the alert retail buyer. We are getting older as a society, with the median age rising from 28.8 in 1975 to a predicted level of 31.1 by 1985. One reason may be attributed to the falling birthrate, with the under-5 group declining; the same is true for the 5–13 age group. It is expected that 28 million people will live on retirement benefits by 1985. Table 1.2 further illustrates the changing patterns in the United States population by age group.

There are other changes in the social environment that the retailer should recognize, such as the mobility of people and the shifting of populations from the cities to the suburbs, the emergence of a better-educated and well-informed consumer who is demanding better-quality merchandise, more conveniences, and more service. The consumer wants to shop in pleasant surroundings, with soft music and personal sales attention. In recent years there has been more

Table 1.2. *United States population by age group.*

Age Group	1965	1970	1975	1980	1985
			Projections[*]		
All ages	194,583	208,615	227,929	250,489	274,748
Under 5 years	20,434	21,317	27,210	31,040	33,288
5 to 13 years	35,888	37,224	37,884	45,215	53,497
14 to 17 years	14,118	15,808	16,896	16,005	19,006
18 to 24 years	20,186	24,589	27,535	29,612	28,956
25 to 34 years	22,358	25,315	31,423	36,998	40,699
35 to 44 years	24,431	22,961	22,458	25,376	31,384
45 to 54 years	22,045	23,326	23,532	22,147	21,705
55 to 64 years	16,966	18,490	19,831	21,032	21,236
65 to 74 years	11,487	12,097	13,191	14,457	15,570
75 yrs. & over	6,669	7,488	7,968	8,606	9,407

Source: U.S. Bureau of the Census.
*Figures in thousands.

emphasis on leisure living, which may lead to a reduction of the work week to four or perhaps even three days; long weekends have provided additional shopping hours and the opportunity for the whole family to shop together. People in general are more knowledgeable and more aware of the environment in which they live.

Economic Environment

Since the Industrial Revolution of the eighteenth century, mass production has raised the level of employment, increased consumer purchasing power, and improved the standard of living. An increase in the personal income level, particularly in the middle class, has led to a greater spending capacity for many consumers, which in turn affects total retail sales. For example, experts have predicted that by 1980 the average income per household will exceed $11,500 and that the number of families of two or more persons with real purchasing power of more than $10,000 should grow to 30 million by 1980. Refer to Table 1.3 for a more detailed presentation of the annual growth in number of households and median income of households from 1968 to 1978.

The economic recession of the mid-1970s had a tremendous impact on retail buyers and their merchandising methods. Due to high unemployment, the increase of small-business failures, the energy crisis, high food prices, and a high rate of inflation, consumers became cautious about the way they spent their money. Retailers encountered many problems, since they found themselves catering to a price-conscious consumer trade that became more selective when making purchases. Also, more demands were placed on retailers to provide a variety of merchandise as a result of the easy availability of consumer credit afforded by retailers and financial institutions alike.

There are other elements within the economic structure that affect the retail buyer's success. The presence of labor unions may force the employees of a store to strike, which leads to a loss of thousands of dollars in sales as well as a loss in store patronage. Retailers may also be affected by business conditions in other firms. For example, if a source of supply were to go out of business, change its product line, raise prices, or relocate, the retailer would have to seek comparable alternatives.

Technological Environment

Over the past several decades tremendous strides have been made in technology, particularly in the field of electronic data processing (EDP). This has many implications for the progressive retailer. For example, the computer has provided speedy, reliable, and accurate information that facilitates managerial decision making. It is used by buyers for internal store operations such as inventory control, payroll, credit and collections, and order processing. More reliable information on returns, markdowns, and exceptionally fast- or slow-

Table 1.3. *Annual growth in number of households and median income of households 1968–1978 in the twenty-six U.S. metropolitan areas with a population of 1,000,000 or over on January 1, 1968. (Ranked in order of household growth).*

Standard Metro. Area	Estimated Population Jan. 1, 1968	Estimated Number Households Jan. 1, 1968	Estimated Annual Growth Households	Total Household Growth Increase 1968–1973	1968–1978	Median Household Income After Federal Income Taxes 1968	1973	1978
Los Angeles - Orange County	8,686,000	2,900,000	83,700	418,500	837,000	$ 9,300	$11,600	$13,950
New York-N.E. New Jersey	15,671,000	5,084,000	65,000	325,000	650,000	8,700	10,900	13,000
Chicago - Gary	7,740,000	2,347,000	40,300	201,500	403,000	8,950	11,200	13,400
Washington, D.C.	2,691,000	824,300	34,000	170,000	340,000	10,400	13,000	15,600
San Francisco - Oakland	3,288,000	1,105,000	28,500	142,500	285,000	9,025	11,300	13,500
Miami - Ft. Lauderdale	1,815,000	607,000	26,375	131,875	263,750	6,875	8,600	10,300
Seattle - Everett - Tacoma	1,769,000	591,500	24,000	120,000	240,000	8,500	10,625	12,750
Philadelphia	4,844,000	1,443,000	20,800	104,000	208,000	7,850	9,800	11,800
Detroit, Michigan	4,200,000	1,210,000	20,000	100,000	200,000	8,900	11,125	13,350
Atlanta, Georgia	1,415,000	409,800	17,500	87,500	175,000	7,525	9,470	11,350
Houston, Texas (Harris County)	1,668,000	489,000	15,000	75,000	150,000	7,375	9,200	11,000
Boston, Mass.	2,778,000	854,000	14,925	74,625	149,250	8,700	10,875	13,000
Minneapolis - St. Paul	1,800,000	536,000	13,200	66,000	132,000	8,250	10,300	12,375
Dallas, Texas	1,584,000	469,000	12,000	60,000	120,000	7,300	9,125	11,000
Tampa - St. Petersburg	1,004,000	352,200	11,300	56,500	113,000	5,850	7,300	8,775
St. Louis	2,300,000	703,000	10,000	50,000	100,000	8,000	10,000	12,000
Baltimore	1,961,000	553,500	9,950	49,750	99,500	8,470	10,600	12,700
Cleveland	2,048,000	623,100	9,650	48,250	96,500	8,750	10,950	13,125
Denver	1,211,000	373,000	9,300	46,500	93,000	8,100	10,000	12,150
Kansas City	1,300,000	414,000	9,000	45,000	90,000	7,500	9,375	11,250
New Orleans	1,130,000	327,000	8,700	43,500	87,000	6,950	8,700	10,400
San Diego	1,250,000	380,000	8,500	42,500	85,000	8,650	10,800	13,000
Milwaukee	1,400,000	415,000	6,050	30,250	60,500	9,375	11,700	14,000
Pittsburgh	2,517,000	749,400	5,333	26,667	53,333	7,400	9,250	11,100
Cincinnati	1,200,000	365,000	4,850	24,250	48,500	7,800	9,750	11,700
Buffalo	1,400,000	419,000	4,250	21,250	42,500	7,950	9,900	11,900
Total	78,760,000	24,543,800	512,183	2,560,915	5,121,830			

Source: Homer Hoyt Associates, 2939 Van Ness Street, N.W., Washington, D.C. 20008.

Figure 1.5. Tremendous strides have been made in the field of electronic data processing (EDP). The computer is used by buyers for internal store operations such as inventory control, payroll, credit and collections, and order processing.

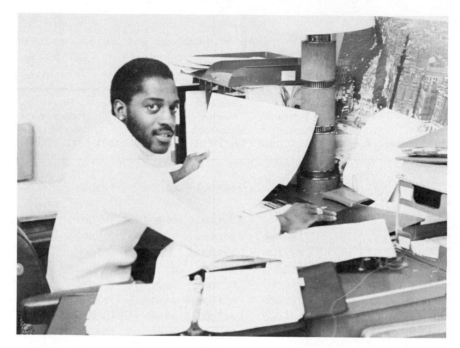

moving items, and prompt exchange of relative sales data among branches are some advantages of using a computer.

Sears Roebuck has been experimenting with a new computerized device that will expedite the input of various data into the company's existing computerized system. The system uses an optical scanning device to read computerized sales tickets by passing a "wand" over digits of a certain style. It also involves the use of tape strips. This device could expedite handling of credit-card purchases and could receive computerized input on merchandise numbers, colors, and costs; cash and credit transactions; the name of the sales clerk closing the transaction; and merchandise chain receipts by departments. If the transaction is a credit sale, a specific tape strip records the purchase for input. A major advantage on the selling floor would be quicker handling of purchase transactions and less waiting time for customers.[11]

Another example of technology is ADP (automatic data processing). This is an accounts-receivable system that enables a merchandise supplier (manufacturer, vendor, or wholesaler) to make collections from retailers, as well as making accurate credit decisions. The ADP accounts-receivable system includes a customer ledger card that shows the complete life-span of a transaction, from the creation of an invoice to the receipt of the payment and all that has occurred in between. A separate aging schedule provides the names and addresses of the accounts, the amount owed, and the amount past due. This information is useful in following up delinquent accounts and helps to speed up the collection of the money. The system is useful in an uncertain economy such as that of the mid-1970s.

Other examples of technology are vending machines, movable sidewalks, revolving ramps, and audiovisual telephones. All have contributed to the changing environment in which the retailer must operate.[12] You will note that electronic data processing (EDP) and its application to various phases of retailing will be stressed throughout this textbook.

Competitive Environment

Competition is an ever-present element in retailing. Characteristics of the competitive environment are the numerous types and sizes of retail stores, their various locations, the overlapping or scrambling of merchandise, and the wide range of services being offered to the consumer. In the mid-1970s retailers had to develop new merchandising techniques, more innovative methods of distribution, and more intensified sales promotions to coax consumers into the stores.

Governmental Environment

Over the years increased attention has been given to legislation governing the retailer's locations, methods of distribution, the hours during which the store may operate, and methods of advertising merchandise. More than ever before the consumer is demanding guarantees of product quality, product safety, protection, and satisfaction in products purchased. The old saying "buyers beware" has been reversed to the point where retailers have become very defensive and the saying "seller beware" has become more applicable.

As you will learn in chapter 14, "Pricing Merchandise for Resale," federal legislation affecting retailers began with the Sherman Antitrust Act of 1890, the Clayton Act of 1914, and the Federal Trade Commission Act of 1914. These antitrust laws, which have an indirect effect upon consumers, were designed to protect against monopoly in business and unfair methods of competition. The Robinson-Patman Act, a landmark law that has been on the books since 1935, primarily prohibits price discrimination among competing customers except for certain limited situations. This act was originally de-

---

How have the following affected the retailer's business environment?

1. Society
2. The economy
3. Technological advancements
4. Competition
5. The federal government

signed to protect small retail firms from the cutthroat competition of big business. There have been attempts to amend or repeal the act; small business groups have opposed this.

Meeting the Challenge   How, then, has the retail buyer met the challenges resulting from the social, economic, technological, competitive, and governmental environments present in the field of merchandise management?

Response to Social Changes

In responding to social changes, the retail buyer has had to cater to the needs and wants of the consumer in a variety of ways. For youth market there are merchandise assortments with youthful styles, bright colors and patterns, as well as a variety of fashion accessories. The merchant also continues to cater to the middle-aged market, since established money is more predictable despite the uncertain economy. For the over-65 age group, however, the factor of the fixed income must be considered. Buyers have used promotional senior-citizen discounts in combination with existing senior-citizen discounts on transportation. This type of "icing-on-the-cake" sale can add valuable sales dollars to the overall profit.

When populations shift from urban areas to the suburbs, the retailer follows, building branch stores and locating in shopping centers. Since people are more mobile and will drive from one shopping center to another, the retailer has to provide a wider merchandise assortment, pleasant and clean surroundings, and knowledgeable sales help to draw the customer away from the competition. However, higher fuel prices have recently curtailed consumer driving to the point where retailers have had to intensify sales promotions.

A popular concept in department-store expansion is the development of the twig store. The *twig store* is representative of one line of merchandise or price line carried by a main store. It is usually found in or near a major shopping center. The twig store provides the opportunity to acquire a smaller segment of the market without investing in the large overhead characteristic of a branch operation. The retail buyer must carefully survey a potential consumer market to determine which prices and lines of merchandise will be most successful.

Leisure living, characterized by shorter working hours and more time for recreation, has encouraged the retailer to lengthen the business day by two or more night openings a week. Some stores are opened seven days a week, unless prohibited by blue laws (laws of a religious nature that prohibit Sunday sales), while food stores may stay open twenty-four hours a day. Additional store space is designed to fill leisure time—tea gardens, snack bars, and even baby-sitting services. The merchandise assortment also reflects leisure living. Sportswear, particularly tennis, skiing, and fishing wear, has dominated the recreational-clothing market. Sporting goods such as golf clubs, bowling balls, and diving suits are widely used throughout store displays. Some stores have added travel bureaus and ticket offices to appeal to the consumer's leisure-living style.

Response to Economic Changes

Since the consumer has the potential to increase his or her spending power, the retailer is constantly working to bring the consumer into the retail store. Advertising campaigns on television, radio, and newspaper; special events; additional store promotions; and emphasis on service and uniqueness of imports are but a few of the techniques employed by the buyer. Easy credit terms, coupons and trading stamps, and special charge accounts are promotional methods utilized by the merchandise buyer to attract the customer to the particular store or department.

During the mid-1970s, however, the buyer had an especially difficult business period. As a result, merchants had to deplete inventories, reduce sales personnel, take heavy markdowns, offer a better selection of merchandise, and become more discriminating when making purchases. Advertising and promotional methods were re-evaluated in relation to costs and sales. Some department-store and chain operations had to consolidate their operations by closing marginal-profit stores as well as abandoning expansion activities. Retail buyers had to make adjustments. Some merchandise, especially fashion goods, became more difficult than usual to obtain because manufacturers were not producing without firm orders; however, the lower inventories planned by many buyers created more reorders and in the long run minimized the shortage problems. The merchandising practice of buyers during that period was to hold on, avoid overextending, and keep a careful watch on receivables.

3 Steps to Recession Survival

1 - Sharpen your selling effort. Turn your order takers into salesmen. Use old fashioned prospecting.

2 - Cut every frill and expense that does not impair operating efficiency. Make your employees cost conscious about little things, as well as big ones.

3 - Reduce your income tax to retain more of your profit. This step is easy; use the Association's SMALL BUSINESS TAX CONTROL service at just $3.00 per month. Order now and start saving tax dollars in a few days.

Figure 1.6. Advice to retailers on recession survival. Source: *The Merchant,* published monthly by the Pennsylvania Retail Merchants Association, February, 1975.

Trading-stamp giveaways are no longer as common at big supermarket chains and gas stations as formerly, but they are beginning to make a comeback with employee-incentive plans and small-town retailers. Trading-stamp industry experts say incentive plans among companies like General Motors, Dow Chemical, International Telephone & Telegraph, Coca-Cola, and Holiday Inns now represent $50 million annually in sales in this category, and that figure is expected to double by 1980.[13]

Response to Technological Changes

Despite the developments of technology, there seems to be a gap between the advantages of electronic data processing (EDP) and its use by retail buyers. Often a great deal of technical training is required on the part of retail management to change over efficiently to the use of EDP equipment. Time and money are also required. A great deal of experience goes into training of store personnel to use the equipment efficiently and capitalize on the investment. However, EDP has been used successfully for such activities as merchandise planning, pricing, credit and collections, accounting statements, and inventory control. Electronic equipment still poses a host of questions in terms of cost, obsolescence, and consumer acceptance.

Examples of technological development may also be seen in automatic merchandising, where a vending machine may provide anything from a hot roast beef sandwich to a fifty-dollar bill!

Response to Competitive Changes

The buyer as well as the suppliers need to be aware of changing trends in merchandising. Merchandising trends may be classified as follows: (1) discounting, (2) merchandise scrambling, (3) franchising, (4) private labeling, (5) catalog presentations, and (6) new store images.

Discounting. Discounting has changed from its original philosophy of low overhead, mass merchandising, and little service. The discount buyer of today has had to provide more attractive displays, add fashion merchandise, and offer additional service. During the past decade, discounting has become a major method of retailing in all types of stores.

Faced with this fact of life, the buyer of high-quality fashion merchandise who takes a normal markup has had to meet the challenge. He or she may join this fast-growing part of the retail community by lowering the initial markup and purchasing some off-price goods to lower prices. Such a practice may enable the buyer to continue to appeal to the taste level of regular customers, or it may prove disastrous. The size of the retail operation is an important consideration here. A merchant who can cut expenses to make up for the lower gross profit may make a profit. However, since the whole theory of discounting is vast buying power and a small cost-sales ratio, the small retailer is immediately at a disadvantage, and an attempt to compete with a discount chain may be self-destructive. The buyer must respond to the discounting thrust in a positive sense, without alienating established customers. In addition, the buyer must make an attempt to win back those customers who are drifting away to the discount competitor.

Merchandise Scrambling. Merchandise scrambling may be defined as the overlapping of one or more lines of different types of merchandise in a given type of retail store. Merchandise overlapping may take different forms, such as: the addition of nonfood items in supermarkets; addition of snack bars to gasoline stations; addition of auto-supply departments to department stores; and addition of coin-operated laundries to supermarkets. Many retail buyers have adopted this merchandising technique because it affords the opportunity to increase company profits through the introduction of an item that needs little or no extra marketing effort and takes up little or no valuable selling space. The buyer will seek unusual items as well as convenience goods that will appeal to regular customers. The only real danger is that such items may detract attention from the store's main line of business as well as detracting from the store's image.

Franchising. As stated in part 1 of this chapter, a franchise contract is a legal agreement to conduct a given business in accordance with prescribed operating methods. Franchising is already well established in auto and gasoline sales, fast-food service, and dry-cleaning establishments. A new feature in the franchise picture is the addition of soft goods such as fabrics, junior fashion apparel, and children's wear. The franchisor usually offers the franchisee a number of services such as management aids, location and site layout, fixtures, discounts, market research, suppliers, and credit arrangements.

Since the franchise operation may be considered a type of chain-store retailing, many small retailers, especially in the field of food service (restaurants), have given a great deal of attention to this type of competitor. The franchise has the opportunity to make volume purchases that result in a lower cost price to the consumer. Since a local franchise outlet is usually a member of a nationally recognized chain, it is able to offer a variety of conveniences, especially fast service. The small restaurant has had to offer special luncheon and dinner menus, more attractive decor, and fast, friendly service. Small service establishments must rely on quality and reputation to meet the competition of the franchise operation.

Private Labeling. Private labeling or branding occurs when a store decides to carry its own line of merchandise, which it sells under its own name. Private brands give a store a certain distinction and free it from direct competition. Most buyers will participate in private labeling since it provides an opportunity to maintain a balanced assortment of merchandise offerings, increase customer loyalty, build up a better trade within particular merchandise lines, and offer lower prices. Private labeling allows the buyer to add new lines of merchandise as well as a new image to his department or store.

Catalog Presentations. The influences of the early mail-order houses are still prevalent today. Sears Roebuck, Montgomery Ward, Spiegel, and J. C. Penney remain the leaders in the field of mail-order selling. The consumer who lives in the small city or town may go into a catalog store, examine the samples on display, and fill out an order blank. Mail-order stores will send catalogs to the homes of customers, provide outlets from which they may telephone, or provide catalogs from department-store counters. One example of a department store that has entered this fastest-growing and most competitive area of retailing is the May Company, based in St. Louis, Missouri. It opened the first of many showrooms in Eatontown, New Jersey, and has since opened showrooms on the West Coast. Customers browse through catalogs either in the showroom or at home. However, unlike other catalog operations, the company maintains a large stockroom to provide faster service and delivery. In most cases, prices are discount.

New Store Images. The traditional discount house such as Korvette has improved its store image through dressier decor, professional signs, more expensive fixtures, improved lighting, the addition of credit, and the offering of a wider assortment of merchandise. Korvette claims it deserves the title of "promotional department store."

J. C. Penney, long limited to soft goods, has balanced its merchandise presentation through the addition of hard goods. It is also trying to create a department-store image by offering services that are typical of the traditional department store.

Mass merchandise buyers have applied the merchandise-scrambling technique to the point where it is often difficult to determine the exact type of retail

---

How have the following trends in merchandising helped the buyer respond to competitive changes?

1. Discounting
2. Merchandise scrambling
3. Franchising
4. Private labeling
5. Catalog presentations
6. New store images

operation of a particular store and the market it is attempting to serve; the store image is blurred. Discounters and low-margin retailers of the 1970s have found themselves faced with lower-margin "warehouse" and "factory-outlet" types of retail stores. New and innovative types of retail establishments probably will continue to challenge the more traditional forms of retailing as the special needs of consumers continue to grow.[14]

Response to Governmental Changes

Today the federal government is making increased efforts to provide fuller protection for consumers. More recent federal legislation has been directed specifically to the relationship between retailers and consumers. The Federal Trade Commission (FTC), the Food and Drug Administration (FDA), the Federal Communications Commission (FCC), and the Consumer Products Safety Commission (CPSC) are some government agencies that have become active in protecting consumers in regard to advertising claims, price discrimination, fabric quality, guarantees and warranties, consumer credit, flammable products, poisons, and allergenic ingredients (see Figure 1.7). It is imperative that retail buyers have an understanding of federal legislation, since the deci-

Figure 1.7. Today, the federal government is making increased efforts to provide fuller protection of consumers. More recent federal legislation has been directed specifically to the relationship between retailers and consumers.

FEDERAL TRADE COMMISSION

TRADE REGULATION RULE

CARE LABELING
OF
TEXTILE WEARING APPAREL

Effective July 3, 1972

Federal Trade Commission

GUIDE CONCERNING
USE OF THE WORD "FREE"
AND SIMILAR REPRESENTATIONS

Promulgated November 16, 1971

Federal Trade Commission

GUIDES AGAINST

BAIT ADVERTISING

Adopted November 24, 1959

Federal Trade Commission

GUIDES AGAINST

DECEPTIVE PRICING

Effective January 8, 1964

sion on the part of governmental agencies to continue this consumer-protection movement will depend in part on the willingness of merchants to regulate their own trade activities and to operate with integrity. This section lists some federal legislation that affects retailers and consumers.

Laws Regulating Competition. The government tries to ensure that no one group gains too much economic power and that consumers continue to have a wide variety of choice. There are three categories of laws used by the government to regulate competition: (1) antitrust laws, (2) unfair trade practice laws, and (3) price-competition laws.[15] Some of these laws will be discussed in detail in chapter 14, "Pricing Merchandise for Resale."

Antitrust Laws

The Sherman Antitrust Act, 1890. The first important legislation designed to combat monopolies.

The Clayton Act, 1914. The Clayton Act amended the Sherman Antitrust Act, which proved too vague to be effective. This act supplemented existing laws against unlawful restraints and monopolies.

Unfair Trade Practice Laws

Federal Trade Commission Act, 1914; Amended 1938. This act was passed to create a Federal Trade Commission (FTC), and to define its powers and duties. The Wheeler-Lea Act of 1938 amended the Federal Trade Commission Act. It stated that unfair methods of competition in commerce are illegal.

Export Trade Act, 1918. The FTC has the power to enforce the provisions of the Export Trade Act, which was passed to promote export trade. The meaning of "export trade" was defined, as well as the meaning of "trade within the United States." This act also prohibited unfair methods of competition in export trade.

Lanham Trademark Act, 1946; amended 1962. This act was passed to provide for the registration and protection of trademarks used in commerce. The FTC may apply to cancel a trademark on certain grounds, as specified by the law.

Price-competition Laws

The Robinson-Patman Act, 1936. The act amended Section 2 of the Clayton Act. It was passed to supplement existing laws against unlawful restraints and monopolies.

Miller-Tydings Act, 1937. The act amended Section 1 of the Sherman Act and legalized the practice of resale price maintenance in interstate commerce.

Laws Affecting Customer Relations

The government is making increased efforts to provide fuller protection of consumers. Legislation has been passed to protect consumers in the following areas: (1) extension of credit, (2) product safety, (3) consumer protection, and (4) packaging, labeling, and advertising.[16]

Extension of Credit

Truth in Lending Act, 1968 (Consumer Credit Protection Act). This law was passed to protect the consumer in the use of credit. The law requires a full disclosure of the terms and conditions of finance charges in credit transactions. The Consumer Credit Protection Act created the National Commission on Consumer Finance to study and make recommendations on the need for further regulation of the consumer finance industry.

Fair Credit Billing Act, 1974. The act amended Section 102 of the Truth in Lending Act and increased consumer credit protection by adding provisions against inaccurate and unfair credit billing and credit-card practices.

Equal Credit Opportunity Act, 1974. The act amended the Truth in Lending Act by prohibiting discrimination on the basis of sex or marital status. The purpose of this law is to require that financial institutions and other firms engaged in the extension of credit make that credit equally available to all credit-worthy customers without regard to sex or marital status.

Product Safety

Wool Products Labeling Act, 1939. This law was passed to protect producers, manufacturers, distributors, and consumers from the unrevealed presence of substitutes and mixtures in spun, woven, knitted, felted, and other manufactured wool products. The FTC has the responsibility for enforcing the law.

Fur Products Labeling Act, 1951. The act was passed to protect consumers and retailers against misbranding, false advertising, and false invoicing of fur products and furs.

Flammable Fabrics Act, 1953; amended 1967. This law was passed to regulate the manufacture of highly flammable clothing. The act prohibits the introduction or movement in interstate commerce of articles of wearing apparel and fabrics that are highly flammable. In 1967 this act was amended to cover a wider range of clothing and interior furnishings.

Consumer Products Safety Act, 1972. This law established a new independent federal regulatory agency, the Consumer Product Safety Commission (CPSC). The Commission's primary goal is substantially to reduce injuries associated with consumer products. The responsibilities held by the Flammable Fabrics Act were transferred to the Consumer Product Safety Commission. Federal standards may be applied to the following areas:

General wearing apparel, effective 1954
Large carpets and rugs, effective 1971
Small carpets and rugs, effective 1971
Mattresses and mattress pads, effective 1973
Children's sleepwear, sizes 0–6X, effective 1972
Children's sleepwear, sizes 7–14, effective 1975

Textile Fiber Products Identification Act, 1958; amended 1965. The act was passed to protect producers and consumers against misbranding and false advertising of the fiber content of textile fiber products. The FTC has the responsibility for the enforcement and the policing of this law.

Consumer Protection
Magnuson-Moss Warranty—Federal Trade Commission Improvement Act, 1975. The act provided minimum disclosure standards for written consumer product warranties. It also defines minimum federal content standards for such warranties and amended the Federal Trade Commission Act to improve its consumer-protection activities.

Postal Reorganization Act, 1960. This act prohibited the mailing of unordered merchandise except for free samples that are clearly and conspicuously marked, as well as merchandise mailed by a charitable organization soliciting contributions.

Guide Concerning the Use of the Word "Free" and Similar Representations, 1971. The FTC has adopted a guide to encourage those merchants who make "free" and similar offers in connection with the sale of a product or service to comply voluntarily with the Federal Trade Commission Act. The guide defines the meaning of the word "free," establishes conditions for the use of the term, and identifies the supplier's responsibilities.

Packaging, Labeling, and Advertising
Fair Packaging and Labeling Act, 1966; Amended 1968. The intent of this act is to regulate interstate and foreign commerce by preventing the use of unfair or deceptive methods of packaging or labeling of certain consumer products distributed in commerce.

Federal Cigarette Labeling and Advertising Act, 1965. This act was passed to regulate the advertising of cigarettes as well as to regulate packages of cigarettes that are manufactured, imported, or packaged for export from the United States.

Food, Drug, and Cosmetic Act, 1938. This law requires that a cosmetic be labeled without false or misleading representation and with information regarding the product, its manufacturer or distributor, and the quality of its contents. Four regulations have been issued by the Food and Drug Administration (FDA) in 1972 and 1973 that will afford consumers greater protection.

> Regulation 1: A voluntary registration with FDA by cosmetic firms. As of 1974 a total of 771 manufacturing establishments out of an estimated 1,000 had registered. The cosmetics marketed by those companies represent approximately 85 percent of the cosmetic products now on the market.
> Regulation 2: A call to cosmetic companies to submit formula information. As of 1974, only 50 percent out of 486 firms had submitted this information.
> Regulation 3: The industry is asked to report to FDA any product experiences it learns about from consumers.
> Regulation 4: This regulation requires cosmetic ingredients to be listed on the label, effective January 1, 1976.

Care Labeling of Textile Wearing Apparel, 1972. The FTC has ruled that it is an unfair method of competition and an unfair or deceptive act or practice to sell in commerce any textile product in the form of a finished article of wearing apparel that does not have a label or tag permanently affixed or attached by the manufacturer of the finished article. The label or tag must clearly inform the consumer on instructions for the care and maintenance of the article.

Guides Against Bait Advertising, 1959. The FTC has adopted guides to protect consumers against bait advertising and related switch practices. Such practices are declared unlawful and unfair methods of competition in commerce.

Guides Against Deceptive Pricing, 1964. The FTC has adopted guides to aid businesspersons who seek to conform to business practices that meet the requirements of fair and legitimate merchandising. The basic objective of these guides is to enable the retail buyer to advertise his goods honestly and to avoid offering the consumer nonexistent bargains that will be misunderstood.

Guides Against Deceptive Advertising of Guarantees, 1960. The FTC has adopted guides to be used in the evaluation of the advertising of guarantees. In general, any guarantee in advertising must clearly inform the consumer of

Explain how the retail buyer will meet the challenge of federal legislation. How will the acts listed affect the business environment?

Laws regulating competition

Price Competition Laws

Unfair Trade Practice Laws

Antitrust Laws

The Sherman Antitrust Act, 1890
The Clayton Act, 1914
Federal Trade Commission Act, 1914,
    Amended 1938
Export Trade Act, 1918
Lanham Trademark Act, 1946, Amended 1938
The Robinson-Patman Act, 1936
The Miller-Tydings Act, 1937

Laws affecting customer relations

Extension of Credit

Product Safety

Truth in Lending Act (Consumer Credit Protection
    Act), 1968
Fair Credit Billing Act, 1974
Equal Credit Opportunity Act, 1974
Wool Products Labeling Act, 1939
Fur Products Labeling Act, 1951
Flammable Fabrics Act 1953, Amended 1967
Consumer Products Safety Act, 1972
Textile Fiber Products Identification Act, 1958,
    Amended 1965

Consumer Protection

Packaging, Labeling, Advertising

Magnuson-Moss Warranty—Federal Trade
    Commission Improvement Act, 1975
Postal Reorganization Act, 1960
Guide Concerning the Use of the Word "Free" and
    Similar Representations, 1971
Fair Packaging and Labeling Act, 1966,
    Amended 1968
Federal Cigarette Labeling and Advertising Act, 1965
Food, Drug, and Cosmetic Act, 1938
Care Labeling of Textile Wearing Apparel, 1972
Guides Against Bait Advertising, 1959
Guides Against Deceptive Pricing, 1964
Guides Against Deceptive Advertising of Guarantees,
    1960

the nature and extent of the guarantee, the way in which the guarantor will perform, and the identity of the guarantor.

Retail merchandising is always in a state of flux, and those persons involved in the operations of a retail store are active and continually on the go. Social, economic, technological, competitive, and governmental factors are ever present and will continually challenge the merchant in his or her attempts to make a profit for the store or department. The buyer must keep pace with these factors by meeting the challenge of competition, keeping abreast of innovations in distribution, being constantly aware of federal legislation affecting retailers and consumers, and developing an awareness of the socioeconomic forces that are inherent in the retailer's environment. The merchant is constantly dealing with large numbers of people with different desires, changing economic statuses, changing tastes, and different life-styles. The one thing the retail buyer must be prepared for is to accept and anticipate change if he is to maintain his place in the competitive marketplace.

The Buying Activity in a Changing Society

The essential task of retail buying is to translate consumer needs into products and services that will satisfy consumers. The buying activity, however, involves far more than determining consumer needs and wants. It also involves formulating effective buying policies, selecting the best sources of supply, determining the suitability of the merchandise offered for sale, negotiating terms of sale and transfer of title, and pricing merchandise for resale. Since the success or failure of a retail store will depend upon how well the buying activity is performed, it is the purpose of this text to discuss in detail the various activities of the retail buyer. Major topics to be covered in this text are: (1) the environment of the retail buyer, (2) planning the merchandise assortment, (3) selecting merchandise resources, (4) preparing merchandise for resale, and (5) the buying activity of the small business. The important functions involved in the buying activity will be outlined in detail and will comprise the remaining chapters of this text.

Chapter Summary

For the student successfully to complete a course in retail buying, he or she must be aware of the development of those concepts that are characteristic of the environment of the retailer. The student should review the development of basic merchandising activities as well as the development of retailing in the

United States. This review should include a knowledge of the development of the following types of retail stores: (1) the trading post and the wagon peddler, (2) the general store, (3) the specialty shop, (4) the limited-line store, (5) the chain-store operation, (6) the department store, (7) the supermarket, (8) the discount house, (9) the franchise operation, (10) the cooperative chain store and the voluntary chain store, and (11) the shopping center.

Nonstore retailing may occur without the customer actually visiting the store. Examples are the mail-order house, catalog sales, vending machines, and door-to-door selling.

The overall objective of the retail buyer is to provide goods and services wanted by consumers. However, the retailer must be aware of environmental elements that may affect his or her success as a merchant. The retail buyer is influenced by the social environment, economic environment, technological environment, competitive environment, and governmental environment. The student should review each and be able to discuss how the buyer will meet the challenges resulting from these external influences.

Retailing is always in a state of flux; therefore, the one thing the retail buyer must be prepared for is to accept and anticipate change to maintain his or her place in the competitive market.

Trade Terminology

DIRECTIONS: Briefly explain or discuss each of the following trade terms:

1. Marketing
2. Merchandise scrambling
3. Nonstore retailing
4. One-stop concept
5. Retailing
6. Retail institution or store
7. Twig store

Questions for Discussion and Review

1. Compare retailing transactions of the early days in the United States with those of the twentieth century. What changes have occurred?

2. Trace the development of various types of retail institutions in the United States and discuss factors that fostered the development of each.

3. What types of retail stores are still in existence today? To what do you attribute the success of these retail outlets?

4. Define marketing; retailing. Why is retailing considered the last stage in the marketing system?

5. Compare the discount house of the 1940s with the discount house of today. What changes have taken place? What are the reasons for such changes?

6. The retail buyer has had to face many challenges that are ever present in the retailing environment. Discuss each of the following: socioeconomic influences, competitive influences, and technological influences.

7. How will the retail buyer meet the challenge presented by increased federal legislation? Name and explain five examples of federal legislation of which the buyer should be aware.

8. What is meant by the term "nonstore retailing"?

9. Select an article from your local newspaper or business magazine dealing with the topic of economic conditions and their effect on retailing. How can the subject matter of this topic be used by a retail buyer in a specialty store in your own town or neighborhood?

10. How have the following patterns of distribution helped the buyer respond to competitive changes: merchandise scrambling; private labeling; new store image; discounting; franchising; catalog presentations?

Retailing Activities to Stimulate Student Interest and Participation

1. Using the yellow pages of your telephone directory, make up a list of discount stores in your area. What conclusions can you make concerning the amount and kind of competition faced by each? Visit two stores of the same type. What types of services are offered by the discount retailers to attract customers to their stores? What types of store images are projected by each?

2. Survey your nearest shopping center to determine the kinds of stores occupying the area. How many discount stores are in the shopping center? Department stores? Specialty stores? Supermarkets? Variety stores? What conclusions can you make concerning competition?

3. Identify the social, economic, technological, competitive, and governmental factors that have affected retail stores in your closest neighborhood shopping center since 1976.

REFERENCES   **The Retail Student's Reference Library**

Ashton, Thomas S. *The Industrial Revolution: 1760–1830.* New York: Oxford University Press, 1968.

"Avon Products: Is Its Beauty Only Skin-Deep?" *Forbes,* July 1, 1973.

Boserup, Ester. *Women's Role in Economic Development.* New York: St. Martin's Press, 1970.

Brown, M. P.; Applebaum, W.; and Salmon, W. J. *Strategy Problems of Mass Retailers and Wholesalers.* Homewood, Ill.: Richard D. Irwin, Inc., 1970.

"Census of the Industry: Total Vended Dollar Volume." *Vend,* May 1, 1974.

Dickman, Robert A. *Personnel Implication for Business Data Processing.* New York: Wiley-Interscience, 1971.

Duncan, D. J., and Hermanson, Rober H. *Retailing: Modern Concepts and Practices.* Homewood, Ill.: Learning Systems Company, 1970.

Duncan, D. J., and Hollander, S. C. *Modern Retail Management.* Homewood, Ill.: Richard D. Irwin, Inc., 1972.

Engel, James F. *Cases in Promotional Strategy.* Homewood, Ill.: Richard D. Irwin, Inc., 1971.

Ferry, John William. *A History of the Department Store.* New York: Macmillan, Inc., 1960.

Fulweiler, John H. *How to Promote Your Shopping Center.* New York: Chain Store Publishing Corporation, 1973.

Grupenhoff, John. *Federal Laws: Health, Environment, Manpower.* Washington, D.C.: Science & Health Communications Group, 1972.

Herndon, Booton. *Satisfaction Guaranteed.* New York: McGraw-Hill Book Company, 1972.

Krieger, Murray. *Decision Making in Retailing and Marketing.* New York: Fairchild Publications, Inc., 1969.

Lebhar, Godfrey. *Chain Stores in America 1859–1962.* New York: Chain Store Publishing Corporation, 1963.

Mahoney, T., and Sloane, L. *The Great Merchants.* New York: Harper & Row Publishers, Inc., 1966.

Michman, Ronald D. "Union Impact on Retail Management." *Business Horizons,* Spring, 1967.

Miller, Donald B., and McLaughlin, Lois I. "Markets Today—Gone Tomorrow: Customer Profit is Changing." *Direct Marketing,* March, 1972.

Mulhern, Helen. *Facts About Department Stores.* New York: National Retail Merchants Association, n.d.

"1974 Survey of Buying Power." *Sales Management,* July 8, 1974.

"Organic Shops Move into the Big Stores." *Business Week,* July 10, 1971.

Orlicky, Joseph. *The Successful Computer System.* New York: McGraw-Hill Book Company, 1969.

Orr, John. *Economics in American Society.* Belmont, Calif.: Wadsworth Publishing Company, 1971.

Phillips, C., and Duncan, D. J. *Marketing Principles and Methods.* Homewood, Ill.: Richard D. Irwin, Inc., 1973.

Poe, Jerry B. *An Introduction to the American Business Enterprise.* Homewood, Ill.: Richard D. Irwin, Inc., 1972.

Porter, Glenn. *Merchants and Manufacturers.* Baltimore: Johns Hopkins Press, 1971.

"Pretty Penney." *Forbes,* March 15, 1972.

Retailer's Guide to Guarantees. New York: National Retail Merchants Association, 1969.

Richert, Meyer, and Haines, Harris. *Retailing Principles and Practices.* Hightstown: McGraw-Hill Book Company, 1974.

Story of Sears Roebuck and Company, The. New York: Fairchild Publications, Inc., 1961.

"Suburban Malls Are Trying Harder." *Business Week,* March 9, 1974.

"Troubled Avon Tries a Face-Lifting." *Business Week,* May 11, 1974.

"Vendors Pull Out All Stops." *Business Week,* August 15, 1970.

References

1. Miriam Beard, *A History of Business* (Ann Arbor: University of Michigan Press, 1938), pp. 1–52.
2. T. Ashton, *The Industrial Revolution,* pp. 1–12.
3. Benjamin C. Butcher and James R. McAnelly, *Fundamentals of Retailing* (New York: Macmillan, Inc., 1973), pp. 12–14.
4. Ibid., pp. 6–9.
5. D. L. James, B. J. Walker, and M. Etzel, *Retailing Today* (New York: Harcourt Brace Jovanovich, Inc., 1975), pp. 542–545.
6. Homer Hoyt, "Changes in Retail Land Investment and Locations of Retail Stores 1910–1968 and Prospects for the Coming Ten Years," in *An Economic Evaluation of Retailing's Future* (New York: National Retail Merchants Association, 1968), pp. 36–37.
7. Ibid.
8. Ibid.
9. Ibid.
10. D. J. Duncan and C. Phillips, *Retailing Principles and Methods* (Homewood, Ill.: Richard D. Irwin Inc., 1969), pp. 10–26.
11. John Osbon, "Sears 'exactly on schedule' for Computerized System," *Apparel Retailer,* June, 1975.
12. "Data Processing Aids Collections in an Uncertain Economy," *Apparel Retailer,* June, 1975.
13. "Trading Stamps Making Big Comeback," *The Merchant,* June, 1975.
14. C. A. Bearchell, *Retailing: A Professional Approach* (New York: Harcourt Brace Jovanovich, Inc., 1975), pp. 220–222.
15. Federal Trade Commission, *The Statutes* (Washington, D.C.: The Commission, December, 1971).
16. Ibid.

The Buyer's Responsibilities in Merchandise Management

2

Performance Objectives

PERFORMANCE OBJECTIVES

As a result of reading this chapter the student should be able to accomplish the following:

1. Define: retail buyer; assistant buyer.

2. Relate similarities and differences in buying responsibilities in the small shop; the department store; a specialty shop; a chain-store operation; a discount house; a variety store.

3. Become aware of the responsibilities of the assistant buyer.

4. Identify basic qualities that make a buyer a good manager.

5. Explain the personal qualifications representative of many fields of management.

6. Prepare a chart listing the numerous merchandise categories that require buyer responsibilities.

7. Discuss the cooperative work-experience plan used by many colleges.

8. Discuss the executive development plan used by most retail stores to assist graduates who are interested in pursuing a career in merchandising.

The Buyer's Responsibilities in Merchandise Management

What the Buyer Does

PART 1

Retailing Specialists

The previous chapter reviewed basic merchandising activities, related how retailing developed in the United States, and discussed the development of the buying activity in different types of retail stores. The purpose of Part 1 of this chapter will be (1) to identify the retail specialist who is responsible for performing the buying-selling activity in different types of retail stores, (2) to outline the duties and responsibilities required of this specialist, and (3) to discuss the job of the buyer as a manager. Part 2 will discuss buying as a career. Topics to be considered are (1) the challenge of merchandise management, (2) personal requirements for a career in merchandising, (3) the availability of college training programs as well as executive development programs offered by most retail stores, and (4) the role of the assistant buyer in merchandise management.

In most types of retail stores, the individual responsible for carrying out the buying-selling activity is called a *buyer,* although in some types of stores the buyer may also be called a *department manager.* The *retail buyer* may be identified as the key individual in the retail institution who is responsible for providing merchandise that will meet the needs of consumers. Therefore, for the purpose of this text, the individual who performs the buying-selling activity will be called a retail buyer.

Buying Responsibilities in Different Types of Stores

The buyer is the key person in the retail store who is responsible for the movement of goods into the hands of the ultimate consumer; therefore, it is important to be aware of all the tasks that the buyer performs in the completion of the buying-selling activity. A more detailed discussion of this topic will be found in the next chapter; this chapter will discuss buyer responsibilities. The following types of retail establishments will be considered: (1) the small shop, (2) the department store, (3) the specialty shop, (4) the chain-store operation, (5) the discount house, and (6) the variety store.

In a Small Shop

In a small retail store the owner-manager is usually responsible for all the merchandise sold. He or she is, therefore, not only responsible for the management activities of the entire business, but the buying-selling activity as well. As the buyer, the owner-manager visits the local markets and arranges to visit major market centers, with the number of buying trips dependent upon his or her time, energy, and finances. While visiting manufacturers, he or she is responsible for the selection of the merchandise assortment, the breadth and depth of the selection, and the placement of orders with vendors.

In a Department Store

In the department store, several individuals—for example, merchandise managers, buyers or department managers, and assistant buyers—are assigned the responsibility of buying merchandise for one or more departments. Since the department-store philosophy of merchandising emphasizes close selling contact with its clientele, good buying techniques are essential.

The department-store buyer works closely with the merchandise manager to select merchandise for the department with enthusiasm and confidence. He or she must make merchandise plans for the department in terms of dollars and convert the dollar plan into units of merchandise that will make a profit for the department and the store. The buyer must develop a balanced merchandise assortment and plan for the line, always considering customer acceptance or rejection of the many items available in the market. The buyer must be sensitive to changes in customer demand and familiar with the peculiarities of the wholesale market. He or she is responsible for communicating with market and trade specialists, visiting local as well as foreign markets, keeping abreast of current fashion trends, working effectively with merchandise resources (vendors, manufacturers, jobbers), developing good inventory control techniques, working with branch stores, and supervising department selling activities.[1]

In a Specialty Shop

The specialty-shop buyer may be a member of a large chain operation (see "Buying Responsibilities in a Chain-Store Operation") or of a small operation (two to four stores). In a small operation, the buying responsibilities are similar to those of the department-store buyer. The specialty-shop buyer must adjust buying activities to meet the needs of the immediate trade area, since business depends to a great degree on the patronage of local customers. Since a specialty shop usually deals with single types of merchandise such as women's apparel and fashion accessories, its buyers will specialize in those particular markets when planning the store's merchandise assortment. The specialty-store buyer will visit local as well as central markets and, if the budget permits, foreign trade centers. He or she will work with the manager of each store in determining the merchandise assortment; assist in the formulation of effective buying policies; locate and negotiate with vendors and manufacturers who offer the best prices, service, and quality goods; forecast future trends that may affect sales; and keep current and accurate records. Since the entire store operation is oriented towards a particular line of goods, the specialty-store buyer is an expert in that particular area and does not necessarily have the vast market coverage usually required of the department-store buyer.

In a Chain-Store Operation

A chain-store operation consists of many units that are similar in merchandise offerings and widespread over a particular geographical region. The buying activity, therefore, is centralized. Since each unit in the chain offers similar types of goods, it is more practical and more economical for one buyer to purchase goods for all the units of the chain rather than to have separate buyers for each member store.

The chain-store buyer or central buyer is located at a main headquarters, which is found in the major market center. For example, if the buyer is responsible for buying fashion apparel and accessories, he or she may be located in New York City; if responsible for purchasing sportswear, in Los Angeles; or, if responsible for purchasing home furnishings, in Atlanta or Chicago.

The chain-store buyer becomes an expert in the area of specialization because he or she is centrally located in the major market. The buyer must give close attention to market changes, take advantage of quantity and off-season purchases, make special arrangements with manufacturers for private labeling or branding, locate new manufacturers and vendors, and make accurate forecasts concerning supply conditions, production, and distribution. Being responsible for the movement of large quantities of merchandise, he or she must be constantly alert to changes in consumer demand and market trends, must effectively communicate with store managers about local consumer buying trends, and, if a buyer of fashion goods, must keep abreast of changes in fashion. These responsibilities can be overwhelming, and for this reason the chain-store buyer is usually a seasoned merchandiser who possesses a wealth of background and experience in a particular area of specialization.[2]

In a Discount House

The discount-house operation may consist of a few stores or may be part of a large chain operation. If it is part of a chain operation, buying activity is centralized in a main headquarters located in the major market center. Whether the operation is a small one or a centralized one, the discount-house buyer will have many of the duties and responsibilities previously discussed. However, because low prices have been and still are the appeal of the discount house, the discount-house buyer will continuously comb the market for the best prices, the best deals, convenient service, and merchandise lines that will appeal to the majority of customers. The buyer will concentrate on vendors and manufacturers who will offer "special buys," even though this may cause an imbalance in already existing lines of merchandise.

Most discount houses concentrate on selling home furnishings and related types of hard goods, with limited offerings in soft goods such as clothing and accessories. The discount-house buyer will usually purchase only those soft goods that have been proved to be successful. Being responsible for the movement of low-priced merchandise in large quantities, the discount-house buyer must be constantly aware of supply and distribution conditions, changes in consumer demand, the state of the economy, and the amount of competition in the marketplace. He or she will work closely with market and trade specialists and remain in constant contact with store managers. If possible, the buyer will visit sevseral stores in the operation to determine how well the merchandise is selling or not selling.[3]

In a Variety Store

Today, although the small five-and-dime or variety store still exists, most variety stores have grown into large chain operations (for example, F. W. Woolworth Company). The buyer for a variety store is located at a central headquarters and provides merchandise that appeals to the basic needs of the customers and lends itself to a self-service type of operation. Since the usual variety store provides hard goods (for example, pots and pans, kitchen utensils, hammers and nails), as well as soft goods (children's wear, linens and towels, curtains and drapes), buyers are appointed to cover specific markets to procure the best buys at the best prices. The variety-store buyer also assumes many of the responsibilities characteristic of the chain-store buyer.

Similarities and Differences

As you review the buying responsibilities just discussed, you will notice similarities in responsibilities as well as differences in performance and technique. Table 2.1 is a summary of buyer responsibilities in differnt types of retail stores. As you read this table, consider the following questions: In what types of retail stores are the responsibilities of a buyer similar? How do responsibilities differ according to type of store?

A Job in Management

Successful buying depends a great deal on team play—the ability of people to work together for a common objective or goal. The buyer has constant contact with salespeople, merchandise managers, staff personnel, other store buyers, and customers. He or she has the responsibility of running a good department, attracting consumers to the store, and, of course, maximizing profit. To fulfill these basic responsibilities, the buyer must have the ability to function as a manager. He or she must accept and discharge executive responsibility for carrying out company policy in and out of the store and must have the ability of getting people to work together.[4]

Table 2.1. *A summary of buying responsibilities.*

1. Formulating effective buying policies
2. Understanding the retail consumer; determination of the goods that consumers need and want
3. Effectively communicating with market and trade specialists
4. Continuously visiting local markets as well as central trade markets
5. Keeping abreast of market trends, economic conditions, competition, supply conditions, and methods of distribution
6. Developing an awareness of fashion trends and their influence on fashion merchandise as well as on other merchandise lines
7. Planning for effective merchandise control
8. Planning and selecting the merchandise assortment
9. Working with merchandise resources (vendors, manufacturers, suppliers)
10. Pricing merchandise for a profit
11. Advertising, displaying, and selling merchandise for resale
12. Employing good management techniques when working with trade specialists as well as store executives and personnel
13. Working as a liaison between the parent store and branch stores; between store managers and department managers

Figure 2.2. Successful buying depends a great deal on team play—on the ability of people to work together for a common objective or goal.

With so many activities and responsibilities, the buyer is an important link in management's communication network. For example, the divisional merchandise manager communicates store policies down to the buyer. In turn, the buyer communicates with the assistant buyer, sales personnel, vendors, manufacturers, and customers. The buyer must also be alert to changes in personnel attitudes and values, market and supply conditions, and consumer buying habits. Such changes should be communicated upwards to top management through the divisional merchandise manager.[5]

What makes a buyer a good manager? What qualities must a buyer possess to foster team spirit and enthusiasm?

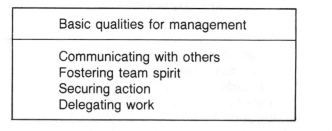

Basic qualities for management
Communicating with others Fostering team spirit Securing action Delegating work

Communicating with Others

The most important quality for an individual considering a management position in any type of organization is the ability to communicate. This is especially true in an organization as complex as the retail store, which may have as few as two or as many as a thousand employees, and which has contacts with middlemen and consumers on a daily basis.

Communication is a daily job for the retail buyer. Some policies are formulated by top management and may remain as long as the store is in business, while other policies may last only briefly. The buyer must be aware of changes in policy and must communicate store philosophy to customers, to employees, and to new personnel.

Fostering Team Spirit

The buyer is responsible for getting people to work together as a team, and so must communicate enthusiasm and spirit to others. To accomplish this, the buyer must communicate his or her own enthusiasm for the store, the merchandise, and the customers. Since nothing is quite so contagious as enthusiasm and love for the job, individuals, whether they be the sales force, the vendors in the marketplace, or the store's customers, will be influenced and exert themselves willingly in the buyer's behalf. Remember: *buyers are selected for their managerial ability; however, the difference between a strong buyer and a weak buyer is the ability to build a team and foster enthusiasm!*

Securing Action

Since good management begins with the individual, the buyer who wants to secure action from others should first consider his or her own personality. A buyer who is indifferent and lacks purpose and direction can expect the same lack of interest in subordinates. The buyer must, therefore, delegate work that is planned in advance and well organized, and must consider the feelings of others. Then he or she can be assured that subordinates will take pride in their work and do their jobs competently and enthusiastically.

Delegating Work

Deciding who will do what job is an important phase of management. Today, so many buyers are responsible for more than one selling location (for example, the branch store), that proper delegation of work must be carefully and thoughtfully planned. The proper delegation of work responsibility involves three steps: (1) selecting the right person for the job, (2) assigning duties and responsibilities that are exact, and (3) following up to see that the job is executed properly.

1. *Selecting the right person for the job.* When selecting an individual for a particular job assignment, care must be taken that each person is placed in a position that will develop his or her talents and provide worthwhile experience. In selecting individuals as midmanagement trainees, heads of stock, or assistants, their work habits, abilities, and experience must be considered. A person who is very successful doing

one kind of job may be totally unsuccessful in another. Special care and consideration should be given to those individuals who will be responsible for the department in the absence of the buyer. A thoughtful executive will select the strongest possible subordinates and then continue to train them for increasing responsibility.

2. *Assigning duties and responsibilities that are exact.* An individual who is to work properly and efficiently must completely understand what is expected of him or her. The buyer must communicate directions in such a way that they are completely understood by subordinates. Direct and explicit instructions will decrease the likelihood of error and wasted time and energy. Subordinates should be encouraged to ask questions if they do not understand their assignments, and the buyer must have the patience and understanding to teach proper store methods and techniques.

3. *Following up to see that the job is executed properly.* When the buyer follows up, he or she must be careful not to embark upon a faultfinding mission or to discourage people's incentive and initiative. Follow-up, when accomplished properly, will encourage the worker to continue progress and provide satisfaction in a job well done. If fault is found, the buyer should be constructive in criticism and should attempt to determine the reason for the error, should offer suggestions for improvement, and assist the person in accomplishing it. This, however, may only be done through good human relations and a thorough understanding of individual differences.

Explain how the following are important in
the delegation of work responsibility

1. Selecting the right person for the job
2. Assigning duties and responsibilities that are exact
3. Follow-up

The Buyer's Assistant   A retail buyer, whether a buyer for a department store, a chain operation, or a discount house, is basically in business for himself or herself. The buyer is responsible for the operation of the entire department and for making a profit for the department or store. Duties and responsibilities are far-ranging and often complex. With such broad responsibilities, the buyer must have the ability to delegate authority to subordinates, thus gaining needed time and energy to go about the business of buying.

In the department-store operation the buyer is out of the store much of the time; therefore, responsibilities are delegated to an assistant or understudy. The *assistant buyer* is an individual who has been selected for managerial potential and is capable of assuming the managerial functions of the department in the absence of the buyer. Table 2.2 lists the responsibilities of the assistant buyer.

Table 2.2. *Responsibilities of the assistant buyer.*

1. Managerial functions of the department when the buyer is out of the store
2. Paperwork involved with the movement of merchandise onto and off of the floor
3. Receiving, marking, and stock-keeping activities, and invoice and order checking problems
4. Presentation of new merchandise for display, coordinating promotion ads with the merchandise, and department housekeeping
5. Store communications; supervising salespeople; knowledge of merchandise trends and promotions; establishment of good communications among the merchandise staff and with management; visits to branch stores or other stores in the unit and maintenance of good telephone contacts

The position of assistant buyer is of interest to many college graduates. This is usually the first position in mid-management in the retail store, particularly in the department store; it provides the graduate with the experience and training necessary for upper management positions, especially the position of retail buyer. Part 2 of this chapter will discuss assistant buyer training in the retail department store.

Buying as a Career   PART 2

Usually, when retailing students are asked about their future plans and aspirations, a great number respond that they would like to be retail buyers. The merchandising function seems to be the most glamorous aspect of the retail operation, since it is directly involved with the public. Also, it affords opportunities for advancement in many areas of merchandising and in a variety of types of retail organizations.

The student who is interested in pursuing a career in retail buying will

The Challenge of Retail Buying

Figure 2.3. The merchandising function affords many opportunities for advancement in retailing. The student who is interested in pursuing a career in retailing will discover a great personal challenge.

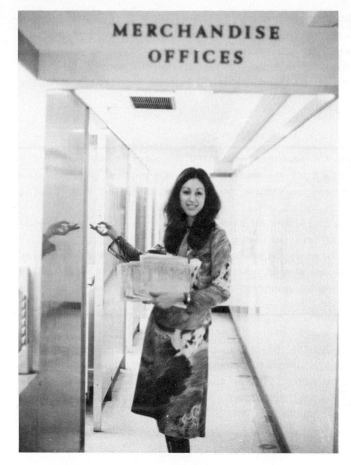

discover a great personal challenge. As a result of changes in consumer demand and changes brought about by the computer, the buyer's role is increasingly demanding. Retailers are extremely dependent on all kinds of changes. They must be both imaginative and analytical if they are to meet the challenges brought about by change and must take advantage of the opportunities it presents if they are to serve the consumer well.

For the most part, a career in retailing demands *a keen interest in merchandise, an equally keen interest in people, and an understanding of the world of fashion.* A unique element of retailing is that there is scarcely a career goal that cannot be reached through a retail organization.

What It Takes

When attempting to discuss personal qualifications for a position in any profession, it is important to remember that each person is a unique individual with unique characteristics. Guidelines may be developed to assist students in the choice of a career or field of endeavor; however, it is the responsibility of the individual to determine what best meets his or her goals and aspirations. The following presents a listing of those personal qualifications that are needed not only in retailing but also in many of the fields of management. Special skills required depend on the responsibilities of the particular position. The responsibilities and qualifications of a buyer and those of the assistant will be discussed throughout this book. Generally, the following characteristics may be considered: (1) educational background, (2) attitude, (3) dedication to hard work, (4) dedication to long hours, (5) knowledge of the trade, (6) enthusiasm, and (7) managerial ability.[6]

Educational Background

Today a great deal of emphasis is placed upon the college degree, whether from the four-year college or the two-year college. What is the reason for this emphasis? Generally, the educational system develops discipline in learning, sharpens intellectual abilities, and provides a frame of reference that may guide the student in the choice of a career. For students interested in pursuing careers as a buyer, the following core business subjects should be considered.

Retailing Math. A knowledge of the basic mathematical process required for business calculations is essential. The fundamentals of arithmetical operations and business problem-solving techniques are basic mathematical skills needed in retailing. The student will be surprised at the extent to which business judgments depend upon accurate figures.

Management. An introductory course in the field of management will present an organized body of knowledge applicable to various management situations. As stated previously, the buyer and the assistant buyer are responsible for communicating company policy both in and out of the store and, therefore, are vital links in management's communications network.

Marketing. Marketing is the process by which trading relationships are established and maintained in a complex and specialized economy. Learning the role of the marketing function as a social institution and understanding consumer characteristics and buying habits and the relationship of various marketing systems to the American economic system will assist the retail buyer in the decision-making process.

Advertising. Communications within the marketplace will provide the consumer with the necessary information to find the right goods at the right place and for the best price. Advertising is the basic persuasion tool utilized by retail firms to sell their products. An understanding of advertising will familiarize the student with the social, psychological, economic, and governmental constraints involved in the development of such a communications system.

Retail Management. The functions of management as specifically related to the retailing industry are of paramount importance to a student pursuing a career in the retail trade. A course in retail management will discuss the basic principles of retailing, the organization of management, and the layout and organization of a store, as well as many of the problems involved in the retail industry.

Textiles. A basic course in textiles will provide information concerning different types of fabric construction, fabric weaves, the various types of dyes, and fabric finishes. With rapid technological changes occurring in the textile industry and the related needle trade industry, the buyer and his assistant are continuously deluged with new types of fabrics, finishes, and fibers.

Fashion Merchandising. The fashion industry is perhaps the prime force that influences the consumer in making purchases. A knowledge of the language of fashion and an in-depth study of the tools of fashion such as color, line, and design, and of the influences of the fashion designers and fashion leaders, provide the student with information that is of vital importance in selecting merchandise for the consumer.

Electronic Data Processing (EDP). The influence of the computer was discussed in Chapter 1. In a retail store, information on such business activities as sales transactions, credit and collections, charge accounts, and inventory turnover is provided by the computer. An introductory course with a managerial approach will give the student an understanding of the importance, advantages, uses of, and problems with, the computer and of its future in the business environment.

Economics. A course in economics will present an overview of the American economy, a study of the determinants of level of income and employment, and an analysis of business and its various resources. The student of retailing will learn how the state of the economy can affect the spending power of the individual consumer and thus influence buying decisions.

Retail Buying. A course in retail buying will provide the student with a knowledge of the problems, policies, and techniques necessary for successful buying and selling activities in different types of retail stores. Such a course does not qualify an individual for an immediate position as a buyer; however, upon graduation many students are qualified to join junior executive trainee programs and work towards a position in upper management. Such programs will be discussed in detail later in this chapter.

Other Academic Subjects. Retailing is directly related to many other subjects that are a part of the business college curriculum, such as accounting, statistics, personnel management, business law, and report writing. Retailing draws freely from sociology; the buyer as a member of society must have an understanding of the social nature of human beings of the social world in which they live. Retailing is related to psychology, which is the study of the basic ideas and principles of human behavior. Course work in psychology will assist the buyer in attempting to determine what motivates the consumer during the selection process.

Liberal Arts Subjects. Course work in English composition that emphasizes sentence structure, the mechanics of punctuation and grammar, and paragraph development will help the student to achieve clear expression in writing. Course work in science, history, and philosophy will also broaden the student's intellectual scope, so that he or she will be a well-rounded individual on entering the realistic, complex world of business.

Attitude

Attitude is a person's mental position or feeling towards an object. Attitude or "spirit" is of vital importance to the student who is considering retailing as a profession—a strong desire for the field of retailing, with its long hours and hard work, criticism, and dejection—for the opportunity to do something for other people and to provide goods that satisfy a need—a feeling for what is new and exciting. This is the job of the retail buyer! This is the job of the assistant buyer!

Dedication to Hard Work

Dedication to hard work is dedication to standing on your feet for eight hours a day, continuously listening to people complain, confusion and turmoil, delayed deliveries, misplaced merchandise, goods marked incorrectly, and so on and so on. Hard work perhaps is in the eyes of the beholder. It is what you consider hard work that matters, but also what you consider exciting and challenging!

Dedication to Long Hours

The buyer, like most people in business, has a minimum of time that needs to be spent in accomplishing his or her work. However, when most people are relaxing, having fun and enjoying a holiday, the buyer is working. The buyer is responsible for providing all the merchandise and conveniences to encourage the shopper to return to the particular department or store. Not only is the buyer responsible for providing consumer conveniences; he or she also spends many hours doing routine paperwork, planning merchandise assortments, evaluating market conditions, and traveling to various market centers, branch stores, or store units.

Knowledge of the Trade

As a result of your experiences as a mid-management trainee or as an assistant buyer, your knowledge of the trade will develop. A knowledge of which merchandise vendors are providing the best service, the best prices, and the best merchandise lines for your particular market is essential. Trade knowledge can only come with experience, sensitivity, and confidence. As an assistant, you are exposed to the marketplace; with the guidance of knowledgeable buyers, you will soon learn your way around.

Enthusiasm

A keen interest in the field of retailing is an excellent ingredient for success. Enthusiasm for the job will bring you to work before starting time and often keep you on the job after your co-workers have gone home. It is your enthusiasm that brings you to work on Saturday morning and perhaps on the day right after a holiday. Dedication to the job and sincerity in doing a good job are all qualities basic to a good manager and, consequently, to a good retail buyer.

Managerial Ability

The scope of managerial responsibilities delegated to the new junior executive is dependent upon his or her background and experience. For a recent graduate working in the capacity of a mid-management trainee, managerial responsibilities are limited. However, handling the responsibilities delegated will provide the trainee with the necessary experience to handle more complex management decisions.

Types of Available Buying Positions

A student who states that he or she is interested in pursuing a career as a retail buyer is often unaware of the many types of merchandise within a retail store that require buyer responsibilities. Most individuals think in terms of the department-store buyer who covers the fashion market in women's apparel or in men's wear. However, buyers are also required in the area of furniture, for example, occasional and modern furniture, bedding, springs, and mattresses; in the home areas of radios and accessories, major appliances, linens and towels, china and glassware; in the budget area, for example, linens and domestics, gifts, infants' apparel and furniture, and luggage; and in the areas of pictures and picture frames, paints and artist supplies, cameras, sporting goods, and of sewing machines and piece (fabric) goods. Table 2.3 shows the merchandise categories of one type of store. The graduate should carefully

Table 2.3. *Merchandise categories that require buyer responsibilities.*

Fashion Division

SHOES
Children's shoes
Women's shoes (designer)
Casual shoes
Men's shoes

CHILDREN'S WEAR
Children's accessories
Infants' wear
Toddler boys' wear
Little girls' wear
Boys' and girls' outerwear
Boy and Girl Scouts
Underwear and sleepwear

INTIMATE APPAREL
Foundations
Robes and loungewear

Junior intimate apparel
Daytime lingerie
Sleepwear

FASHION ACCESSORIES
Costume jewelry
Rainwear
Ladies' belts
Sunglasses
Handkerchiefs
Moderate-priced handbags
Small leather goods
Millinery
Gloves
Hosiery
Slippers

MEN'S FURNISHINGS
Made-to-order
Hats and Caps
Better-priced clothing
Tailored sports clothing
Shirts and ties
Furnishings and accessories
Active sportswear

**SPORTSWEAR
AND JUNIOR
SPORTSWEAR**
Better Junior coats
Junior coats and suits
Better Junior dresses
Junior dresses
Blouses

Active sportswear
Misses' sweaters
Contemporary

DESIGNER CLOTHING
Tribout accessories
Couturier shop

WOMEN'S CLOTHING
Better dresses
Inexpensive dresses
Bridal salon
Moderate-priced
Better knits
Casual dresses
Coats and Suits
Aprons and uniforms

Home Furnishings Division

FURNITURE
Bedding
Upholstered furniture
Case goods
Occasional furniture
Summer furniture
Colonial furniture
Springs and mattresses
Dual sleep furniture
Modern furniture
Interior design

DOMESTICS
Blankets, comforters,
  spreads
Towels
Linens
China
Glassware
Major appliances
Color TV

Black-and-white TV
Stereo-combination
Phonographs
Radios and accessories
Records, cabinets and
  players

MISCELLANEOUS
Notions, closet accessories
Laces, ribbons, trimmings
Drugs
Fine jewelry and clocks
Precious jewelry
Silverware
Books
Stationery
Greeting cards
Candy
Gourmet shop

BUDGET
Linens, domestics
Gifts

Infants' apparel and furniture
Little girls' wear
Little boys' wear
Men's clothing
Luggage
Curtains, draperies
Aprons, housedresses
Misses' dresses
Women's dresses
Junior dresses
Gloves and umbrellas
Hosiery
Millinery

HOME
Art needlework
Oriental rugs
Carpets and broadlooms
Domestic rugs
Lamps
Custom fabric
Draperies

Curtains
Trim-a-tree
Pictures, frames
Gift shop
Candle and flower shop
Contract department
Hostess shop
Small electrics
Housewares, furniture
Cookware and pantry
Bath shop
Paints
Toys
Artist supplies
Hobby
Cameras
Sporting goods
Luggage
Sewing machines
Storm windows

investigate the merchandise breakdown of the particular store in which he or she intends to pursue a career in retailing as an assistant buyer.

Opportunities for Retail Training Provided by Educational Institutions

High-school and college students often serve as an excellent source of employees for retail organizations. As a result of the availability of large sums of money from the federal government, many high schools, community colleges, and four-year colleges and universities have become more interested in vocational or career education programs. They have come to realize that many young people want and need to begin work early in life. Therefore, educational institutions throughout the United States have developed cooperative work-study programs for students interested in careers in distribution, retailing, marketing, and management.

Cooperative work-study programs vary with the objectives of the educational institutions. Two-year colleges and senior colleges usually implement their cooperative work-experience programs in the following way: the student is employed for a specific time period (one to three semesters) during the school year with a retail organization selected by the college coordinator. The student usually receives academic credit while working. At the same time, he or she is employed by the retail organization and is receiving a planned work experience and an opportunity to apply classroom theory to on-the-job training. At the end of the training period, the student returns to college for the completion of studies. Other kinds of cooperative work-study programs permit the student to continue classroom studies while being trained in job skills on a part-time basis. The cooperative plan will vary with the educational institution and the

Figure 2.4. Cooperative work experience programs permit the student to continue classroom studies while being trained on the job. (Courtesy of John Wanamaker, Department Store, Philadelphia.)

particular retail firm. Figure 2.4 illustrates a cooperative program offered by the John Wanamaker department store in Philadelphia.

The success of these occupational programs is based on the cooperation that exists between the school and the retail firm. It is during the cooperative work-study experience that many young people have an opportunity to investigate the multitude of positions available in retailing. Here the student may begin training for the position of assistant buyer.

Table 2.4. *A cooperative work experience plan used by one type of retail store.* [*]

First week	Training	Store orientation, learn sales techniques, store procedure, cash register, training and development
Second week		Apply basic selling techniques, develop good work habits, handle customer
	Sales	
Third week		problems, develop product knowledge, learn display work, learn how to take orders, follow directions, give orders
Fourth week	Stock	Learn stock procedure, receiving, checking, marking, shipment to branch stores
Fifth week	Adjustments and complaints	Learn process involved in handling customer complaints, and returned merchandise
Sixth week	Control	Learn to handle vendor returns, defective merchandise, lost or stolen merchandise, shipments to branch stores
Seventh week	Credit	Observe techniques in credit and collections, interview new accounts, check credit references
Eighth week		Assist in clerical work, engage in telephone contacts with vendors and branch
Ninth week	Buyer's office	stores, learn purchase journal procedure and inventory control, depart-
Tenth week		ment housekeeping, scheduling of sales force, handling customer
Eleventh week		complaints, returned merchandise, and exchanges, develop good personnel relations, handle special
Twelfth week		events, learn sales promotion

*Length of time spent in each work experience is dependent upon the experience of the student as well as upon the needs of the store.

Opportunities for Executive Development Provided by Retail Institutions

Retail organizations provide store management training programs since most of their personnel is actively employed in the management of the store operations. However, with growth and expansion of many retail stores, management has found it necessary to provide training programs for individuals interested in pursuing careers in merchandising.

Figure 2.5 is representative of a typical pattern used by a retail store for preparing new recruits for executive positions in merchandising.

Figure 2.5. A typical pattern for preparing new recruits in merchandising.

Trainee

The graduate who has limited or no previous retailing experience goes through a planned training program. The length of time may vary from one to three weeks, depending on the policy of the store. The trainee is introduced to store procedure and policy, employee benefits, and cash register control, as well as other activities involved in the movement of merchandise. Trainees are usually required to work on the selling floor for a period of time to learn basic merchandise and to gain experience in meeting and working with people.

Junior Assistant Buyer

Depending on the size of the department, some buyers have more than one assistant, who in turn has helpers. The junior assistant will remain in that position long enough to prove his or her capabilities, and is then usually promoted to the next level, that of assistant buyer.

Assistant Buyer

By this time the student should have a good idea of the merchandise category that interests him or her. As stated previously, the assistant buyer is responsible for performing numerous clerical duties, managing sales personnel and stock people, keeping good telephone contacts with branch stores or other store units, following up with vendors and manufacturers, and planning neat, well-organized merchandise presentations. The assistant buyer will usually remain in this position from one to three years. However, this will vary with individual potential as well as the needs of the store. (Review Table 2.1, "A Summary of Buying Responsibilities.")

A Manager

After an appreciable amount of time the assistant buyer, if working in a department store, may achieve a position in a branch store as a group manager. In a chain operation, the assistant buyer may achieve a position as a department manager. As manager of one or more departments, he or she is responsible for organizing the sales force, communicating with the buyer, analyzing consumer needs and wants, handling customer complaints, and preparing merchandise for the selling floor. In this capacity the manager learns firsthand the problems faced by retail buyers in determining consumer preferences, the problems with deliveries and lost or stolen merchandise, and the results of poor communications.

Retail Buyer

The position of retail buyer may be achieved in less than five years in most types of retail stores. The new buyer has been exposed to many of the responsibilities concerned with buying and selling, advertising, display, stock keeping, and vendor relations, as well as having experience in management. He or she is now prepared to take on the duties, responsibilities, and prestige that have been justly earned and now are deserved. (Review Table 2.1 again.)

Merchandise Manager

The individual usually found at the head of the merchandising division is commonly called the *merchandise manager.* The merchandise manager may have a number of divisional merchandise managers working under him or her, each of whom is a specialist in a particular line of merchandise. The divisional merchandise managers are responsible for the activities of the buyers of the various selling departments under the merchandise manager's jurisdiction. The buyer will consult with the divisional merchandise manager as to the seasonal merchandise plan, the amount of merchandise to purchase for a selling season, the best method of promoting sales, future market trends, and so forth. In many retail stores, the divisional merchandise manager must also sign the buyer's order form before it is sent to the vendor or manufacturer. The job of merchandise manager is considered a top executive position and one that requires a great deal of experience in the retail trade.

Advice to the New Assistant Buyer

As stated previously, the job of assistant buyer is usually the first position in mid-management in a retail store that will provide the graduate with the experience and training necessary for an upper management position. As a fresh recruit in the field of retailing, the new assistant buyer is immediately challenged by an entirely new set of problems and by new situations that will stimulate learning and growth. He or she is supported by the knowledge of being well enough thought of by superiors to be promoted to this new job, which is a giant step forward in a retailing career. However, this confidence should not lead the new assistant buyer to seek self-sufficiency in decision making too soon. It would be well to avoid "coming on too strong." Since inexperience is to be expected on a new job, the assistant should not be embarrassed to ask questions and should not ignore methods and procedures that have been established. The new assistant buyer will no doubt find some problems left by the previous assistant. The newcomer should accept these negative conditions without complaint and instead learn from both the errors and the achievements of those who have gone before.

The new assistant will immediately be snowed under by the attention of store employees, particularly those in the same department, of merchandise suppliers, of the customers, and of the buyer. The newcomer should listen carefully to the suggestions of peers and, most importantly, to the advice and direction of the buyer.

The buyer was chosen for both professional experience and ability as a manager. A good buyer will take the time and effort to train and instruct a new assistant properly and will provide learning experiences that will prove beneficial to buyer, assistant, and company. It is important for the assistant and the buyer to establish a good working relationship early and develop the ability to effectively communicate.[7]

Chapter Summary

The retail buyer is the key individual within the retail institution who is responsible for providing merchandise that will meet the needs of consumers. Buying responsibilities will differ, depending on the size and type of the retail store. The student should review buying responsibilities in a small shop, department store, specialty shop, chain-store operation, discount house, and variety store. In reviewing the buying responsibilities of retail buyers in different types of stores, the student will notice similarities in responsibilities, as well as differences in performance and technique. (Review the list in Table 2.1.) Successful buying depends a great deal on the ability of a buyer to work as a manager. Basic qualities a buyer must possess to be a manager are the ability to communicate, to foster team spirit, to get action, and to delegate work responsibility. Deciding who will do what job is an important phase of management. The proper delegation of work responsibility involves three steps: (1) selecting the right person for the job, (2) assigning duties and responsibilities that are exact, and (3) following up to see that the job is executed properly. The assistant buyer is an individual who has been selected for managerial potential and who is able to assume the managerial functions of the department in the absence of the buyer. This is usually the first position in mid-management in the retail store.

The merchandising function seems to be the most glamorous aspect of the retail operation and affords opportunities for advancement in many areas. For the most part, a career in retailing demands a keen interest in merchandise, an equally keen interest in people, and an understanding of the world of fashion. The student considering a job in retailing will need to have the following characteristics: a suitable educational background, a good attitude, dedication to hard work, dedication to long hours, knowledge of the trade, enthusiasm, and managerial ability. The student should be aware of the many merchandise categories in different types of retail stores that require buying responsibilities. Table 2.3 lists a number of these merchandise categories. Opportunities are provided by educational institutions for retail training through cooperative work-study plans. Retail institutions also provide executive development programs for graduates, especially in the area of merchandising.

Trade Terminology

DIRECTIONS: Briefly explain or discuss each of the following trade terms:

1. Retail buyer
2. Assistant buyer
3. Merchandise manager

Questions for Discussion and Review

1. Define retail buyer; assistant buyer.

2. List the responsibilities of the buyer; of the assistant buyer.

3. Why is the buying activity considered a function of management?

4. Discuss the basic qualities a buyer must possess to foster team spirit and

enthusiasm. In addition to those mentioned, what qualities do you feel are important? Why?

5. What is the cooperative work-study plan? Do you feel that such plans have any value? Explain your answer.

6. If you were asked to speak to a group of high-school students on the value of a college education in the field of retailing, what would you tell them?

7. Students often wonder why they are required to take course work in science and humanities along with their business subjects. How would you explain this requirement?

8. Refer to Table 2.3. As an assistant buyer, which merchandise category would you be interested in? Why?

9. After reading "Advice to the New Assistant Buyer," what problems would you anticipate as a fresh recruit in the field of retailing? How would you overcome these problems?

10. Explain how the job of buying goods for resale is similar in the following types of retail stores: the chain operation; the department store; the small shop. How will the buying responsibilities differ?

Case Study Number One

Handling Salespeople   You have been appointed assistant buyer for the small electric appliances department. After some months you discover that three full-time salespeople who have worked for the store several years are lax in regard to employee regulations. They take extended lunch hours and unscheduled coffee breaks and are late for work. You are aware that this situation has prevailed for the past year or so under your predecessor. The buyer, although aware of the problem, is unable to give it much attention, being out of the store most of the time, so has asked you to deal with it. Since you want to maintain good relations with the salespeople and also show that you can take care of the department in your buyer's absence, you have been waiting on customers in the absence of salespeople as well as doing your own work. You recognize that this situation cannot continue, since your own duties and responsibilities are beginning to suffer. As a new recruit on the job, you want to show your buyer that you can handle the situation; yet you do not want to cause friction with the salespeople. Be prepared to discuss the alternatives available in class and justify your statements.

Case Study Number Two

Bill Smith, a college student majoring in retail management, was placed in a cooperative work-study position as a mid-management trainee at Reed and Dunn's Department Store, located in a small city on the West Coast. Bill had studied retail theory and was very excited about having an opportunity to apply classroom theory to on-the-job training.

Too Many Smiths

During the first two weeks, Bill attended classes on sales training, store systems procedure, customer services, and merchandise policies, adjustments, and procedures. While attending classes he was given his department assignment and was informed that he would be the junior assistant trainee to Mr. Jackson, the toy buyer. Bill and Mr. Jackson hit it off immediately. Mr. Jackson had gone through a similar type of program when he attended college and was, therefore, an excellent teacher to his new recruit.

Things were going very well for Bill Smith. He enjoyed working in the toy department, since it was the Christmas season and there was always an interesting assignment that provided a new challenge and the opportunity to learn more about the duties and responsibilities of a store buyer. He got along well with his peers, and Mr. Jackson felt he was a very capable and enthusiastic young man.

One day Mr. Jackson asked Bill to wear a pair of old trousers and an old shirt to work the next day, since he was going to be doing a great deal of heavy stock work. The following morning, according to procedure, Bill reported to the personnel office, where he punched his time card. As Bill was leaving the office to go to his department, he heard Mr. Case, the store's new personnel manager, loudly refer to his unbusinesslike attire and sloppy appearance. Mr. Case called Bill over to his desk, where he reprimanded him in front of other store employees, two of whom worked with Bill on the same floor. He said that he had been informed of Bill's sloppy appearance on numerous occasions and that he was tired of sending him notices regarding his attire on the selling floor. Mr. Case fired Bill Smith.

Bill was so surprised by the reprimand, as well as by the fact that he was fired, that he was visibly shaken. All he said to Mr. Case was that he did not understand what was going on and that he had been told to dress in jeans and an old shirt. Mr. Case, however, was shouting so loudly that he did not hear what Bill Smith was attempting to say.

Bill went to his department and informed Mr. Jackson that he had been fired because of the way he was dressed. Mr. Jackson did not understand, since he had often asked his personnel to wear casual clothing when a great deal of heavy stock work had to be done. Bill was so embarrassed and disturbed by the incident that he decided to go home.

Later that day Mr. Jackson finally caught up with Mr. Case. Mr. Case informed Mr. Jackson that he had had numerous complaints about Bill

Smith's appearance on the selling floor and that several notices had been sent reminding him of the store's dress code. Now Mr. Jackson was totally confused! He was quite certain that his trainee had never received notices regarding dress code. Also, Mr. Jackson had noted that Bill had always dressed very neatly and was well groomed. Mr. Jackson insisted that some mistake had been made.

Indeed, a mistake had been made. The following day Mr. Case learned there were two Bill Smiths: one was a coop work experience trainee assigned to Mr. Jackson in the toy department; and one was a part-time salesperson. Needless to say, Mr. Case had fired the wrong Bill Smith.

Both Mr. Case and Mr. Jackson agreed that a terrible mistake had been made.

What methods would you use to solve this problem?

Retailing Activities to Stimulate Student Interest and Participation

1. Interview an assistant buyer or department manager in a local department store; discount house; variety store. Make a list of the duties and responsibilities of each. How are they similar? How do they differ?

2. Make a list of the stores that you patronize on a regular basis. What kind of stores are they? Explain how the buying-selling activity is performed in each store.

3. Visit a women's specialty shop that is composed of only a few stores and a women's specialty shop that is part of a chain operation. Interview the store manager of each to determine how the buying activity is accomplished.

REFERENCES

The Retail Student's Reference Library

Albers, Henry H. *Management: The Basic Concepts.* New York: John Wiley & Sons, Inc., 1972.

Appraising Retail Executive and Employee Performance. New York: National Retail Merchants Association, 1968.

Bloom, H. N., and Longenecker, J. G. *Small Business Management.* Cincinnati: South-Western Publishing Company, 1971.

Davenport, Lawrence. *Minorities and Career Education.* Columbus, Ohio: ECCA Publications, 1973.

Drucker, Peter F. *Careers in Retailing.* New York: National Retail Merchants Association, 1969.

The Essential Challenge—The Sources of Management for Retailing. New York: National Retail Merchants Association, 1967.

Executive Compensation In Retailing. New York: National Retail Merchants Assoc., 1971.

Helfant, Seymour, and Judelle, Beatrice. *Management Manual for Independent Stores.* New York: National Retail Merchants Association, n.d.

Job Finding Techniques for the Mature Woman. Washington, D.C.: U.S. Government Printing Office, 1970.

Judelle, Beatrice. *The Branch Manager's Manual.* New York: National Retail Merchants Association, 1968.

Kreger, Murray. *Decision Making in Retailing.* New York: Fairchild Publications, Inc., 1969.

Lazarus, Sy. *Developing the Retail Executive.* New York: National Retail Merchants Association, 1971.

Livingston, J. S. *Managerial Effectiveness—The Impact of Management Style on Store Performance.* New York: National Retail Merchants Association, 1969.

Management By Objectives In Retailing. New York: National Retail Merchants Association, 1967.

Olsen, R., and Wotruba, T. R. *Readings in Sales Management.* New York: Holt, Rinehart & Winston, Inc., 1971.

A Personal Checklist For Retail Top Management. New York: National Retail Merchants Association, 1971.

Personnel Policies Guidebook. New York: National Retail Merchants Association.

Schwartz, Irving. *Personal Qualities Needed to Manage a Store.* Washington, D.C.: U.S. Government Printing Office, 1970.

Stadt, Ronald W. *Managing Career Education Programs.* Englewood Cliffs, N.J.: Prentice-Hall, Inc., 1973.

Thomas, Robert. *Management Training.* Columbus, Ohio: Distributive Education Materials Laboratory, 1970.

Wilinsky, Harriet. *Careers and Opportunities in Retailing.* New York: National Retail Merchants Association, 1970.

Your First Branch Store. New York: National Retail Merchants Association, 1967.

References

1. K. Gillespie and J. C. Hecht, *Retail Business Management* (New York: Gregg/McGraw-Hill Book Company, 1970), pp. 150–152.
2. Donald L. Belden, *The Role of the Buyer in Mass Merchandising* (New York: Chain Store Publishing Corporation, 1971), pp. 1–7.
3. D. J. Duncan and C. F. Phillips, *Retailing Principles and Methods* (Homewood, Ill.: Richard D. Irwin, Inc., 1969), pp. 15–18.
4. K. Gillespie and J. E. Hecht, Retail Business Management (New York: Gregg/McGraw-Hill Book Company, 1970), p. 150.
5. David Blumenthal, "The Buyer as a Manager of People," in *The Buyer's Manual* (New York: National Retail Merchants Association, 1965), pp. 37–45.
6. J. W. Wingate, and J. J. Friedlander, *The Mangement of Retail Buying* (Englewood Cliffs, N.J.: Prentice-Hall, Inc., 1963), pp. 13–18.
7. T. W. Johnston, "You're The New Buyer—Now What," in *The Buyer's Manual,* pp. 440–448.

Organizing the Buying-Selling Activity

3

Performance Objectives

PERFORMANCE
OBJECTIVES

As a result of reading this chapter the student should be able to accomplish the following:

1. Define retail buying.

2. Explain the importance of good organization.

3. Recall how the following types of stores are organized: the small store, the departmentalized store, the chain-store organization.

4. Discuss current trends in store organization.

5. Explain how the buying-selling activity is controlled in a small business, the traditional department store, a specialty store, a general-merchandise chain, a discount chain store, a variety chain store.

6. Define local buying; central buying.

7. Discuss the various forms of central buying.

8. Relate the advantages and disadvantages of the central merchandising plan; the warehouse-and-requisition plan; the price-agreement or catalog plan.

Organizing the Buying-Selling Activity

Organization in Different Types of Stores

PART 1

The retail buyer is the key individual primarily responsible for the movement of merchandise from the retail store into the hands of the final consumer. However, duties and responsibilities required of the buyer will differ according to the size and type of retail organization.

The Buying Activity

    The purpose of Part 1 of this chapter will be to (1) define retail buying, (2) discuss the necessary essentials in organizing a retail business, (3) determine how various types of retail organizations are organized, and (4) identify current trends in store organization. Part 2 will (1) discuss how buying is controlled in various types of retail stores, (2) identify various methods of central buying, and (3) discuss the advantages and disadvantages of each method.

Generally speaking, the term *buying* simply connotes the act of purchase. However, as used by the retail trade, the term includes far more. Buying may be defined as the purchase of consumer goods in relatively large or wholesale quantities for subsequent resale in smaller (retail) lots to the ultimate consumer.[1] The buying function may take on different forms, depending on the size of the retail store, the type of merchandise carried, or the type of clientele the store is trying to please. For example, in a department store the buying activity is performed by a store buyer who is located in the main or "mother" store and makes buying decisions for that store as well as for the various twigs and branch stores. In contrast, in a large chain operation the buying activity is transferred from a local to a central location; that is, buying decisions are made by central buyers who are located in central or divisional offices. In a small shop the buying activity is performed by the owner-manager, who purchases goods either from manufacturers' representatives who visit his or her place of business or from vendors and manufacturers located in the central market. Or the department-store buyer, the central buyer, and the small-shop buyer may work with an outside agency called a *resident buying office*. This office provides a merchandising consulting service; it is staffed by resident buyers who will assist and advise its client or member stores in merchandising

Buying Defined

decisions. The resident buying office will be discussed in detail in the next chapter.

Essential Factors in Organization

The retail buyer should keep in mind that good organization is an essential ingredient in any type of business if the firm's goals and objectives are to be realized. Some business firms are better organized than others and thus better able to accomplish their objectives. Those firms that operate on a shoestring may find themselves in serious difficulties, particularly when economic conditions are uncertain and consumer spending power is hampered. Therefore, before we consider the organizations of various types of retail institutions, let us look at those factors that are essential in developing the organizational structure of a business firm. The factors included for discussion are: (1) responsibility-authority relationships, (2) staffing, (3) departmentalization, and (4) line-staff relationships.

Responsibility-Authority Relationships

Responsibility is closely related to accountability. Managers, assistant managers, and supervisors at all levels of business are given responsibility and are held accountable for the men and women who work under their direction. They know that responsibility for getting the work accomplished rests on their shoulders, and that they are held responsible by top management. However, managerial personnel often voice the complaint that they are not given the authority in decision making that is equal with their responsibility. In other words, responsibility for results should not be separated from the power to make the necessary decisions to achieve those results.[2]

Authority is the power to make business decisions. An important aspect of responsibility-authority relationships is the delegation of authority to subordinates. A manager cannot delegate a responsibility as such to an assistant; however, he or she can delegate authority, thus creating a new responsibility relationship between the assistant and the manager. This type of authority delegation does not lessen the manager's responsibility to the superior, but it does make more efficient work assignments possible. Such assignments will assist the manager in achieving the overall objectives of the business enterprise.[3] For example, a store manager has the responsibility for the work activities of many salespeople and other personnel in sales-related activities. This responsibility does not lessen when the store manager divides the total work efforts into separate sections and appoints a manager for each section. Each section manager has been delegated the authority to do the job and is held responsible for the accomplishment of work activities. The store manager does not give up or lessen his or her responsibility for the results of the sections, but instead is able to obtain valuable managerial assistance.

Staffing

Staffing of an organization requires finding the right managerial talent for the right position. Top management should provide a good staffing program to ensure that an adequate system of management succession is developed as well as executed. Proper staffing is very important in a small or medium-sized business, since proportionately there will be fewer competent managers in these types of businesses as compared to large organizations.

Managerial or executive talent may be found within the organization, that is, individuals may be promoted from lower management positions or from nonmanagement positions; or management talent may be brought in from the outside. The business organization should provide some kind of management training program to prepare new management for the duties and responsibilities of a given position. Formal training programs may include special training classes, discussions, lectures, and management seminars. Apart from formal training programs, the business may rotate or transfer individuals through a series of different types of positions to acquaint them with the different aspects of the business operations. Or a person may be given special assignments where he or she will have responsibility for a project. This will show what special talents and abilities this person has. For example, as you read in the previous chapter, an individual who is preparing for the position of assistant buyer may do so either through a cooperative work-study program (review Table 2.4) or through the store's junior executive development plan (review Figure 2.5). Both plans will provide the new recruit as well as the individual who was promoted from within the organization with the opportunity to learn the skills necessary to perform the job successfully.

Departmentalization

In departmentalization the various operations and activities of a business are compartmentalized and individuals are assigned the responsibility to see that the various activities within each department are carried out. Departmentalization can easily be seen in a retail store where many kinds and types of merchandise are found in various departments, each headed by a buyer and assistants, all working together to achieve their own objectives as well as the objectives of the company as a whole.

Line-Staff Relationships

The line function in the business firm includes those activities that are directly related to the achievement of the goals of the business. Thus, the line activities in a merchandising division of a department store would be those relating to the buying and selling of merchandise for profit. The staff function, therefore, would include those activities that assist the line in meeting the company's objectives. Activities such as personnel, store operations, and finance would be considered elements of staff function because they support the line activity in meeting the store's profit objective. However, what constitutes a staff function in one business operation may be a line function in another. For example, the buying activity in a retail store is considered a line function, but for a manufacturing company the buying or purchasing activity may be considered a staff function.

Organization in Various Types of Retail Stores

Traditional organization of a business firm becomes necessary whenever it expands to more than a one-person operation. The various activities that are necessary to carry out the company's goals and objectives must be systematically arranged and assigned to ensure maximum use of time and energy. Formal written organization charts are used by many retail firms to define duties and responsibilities as well as to show the lines of authority.

Different retail businesses seldom have exactly the same organizational system. The type of operation, size of the retail firm, different types of merchandise lines, and different consumer emphasis lead to somewhat different organizational systems. However, there are similarities in the organizational patterns used. We shall now turn our attention to the organization of various types of stores and examine the similarities and differences that exist. The following types of stores will be considered: (1) the small store, (2) the depart-mentalized store, and (3) the chain-store operation.

The Small Store

The small store has been in existence since human beings first began retail transactions. It is usually owned and operated by one individual, with family members assisting the owner-manager when necessary. The corner grocery, the beauty salon, the men's wear specialty shop, the local flower shop, and children's favorite candy store are all small businesses providing goods and services for their customers. In fact, many young people first learn about retailing from working in a small business on a part-time basis while attending school. Such an experience often provides valuable training to the individual who later considers a career in merchandise management.

As the small store grows, one person can no longer handle all the necessary tasks. The owner-manager will hire employees and designate certain duties and responsibilities to them. Figure 3.2 illustrates how employees are assigned sales, stock, clerical, and maintenance duties, with the owner-manager still continuing to handle the merchandising activity as well as other management functions. As you can see, some specialization does occur.

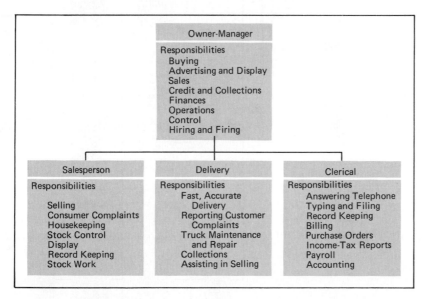

Figure 3.2. Organization chart of a small business. SOURCE: Adapted from Paul M. Mazur, *Principles of Organization Applied to Modern Retailing* (New York: Harper & Row Pub., 1927, frontispiece).

The Departmentalized Store

As the business continues to expand, the owner will need to hire a manager to assist in the performance of store activities as well as in the supervising of employees. It is at this point that the manager may have to make a decision

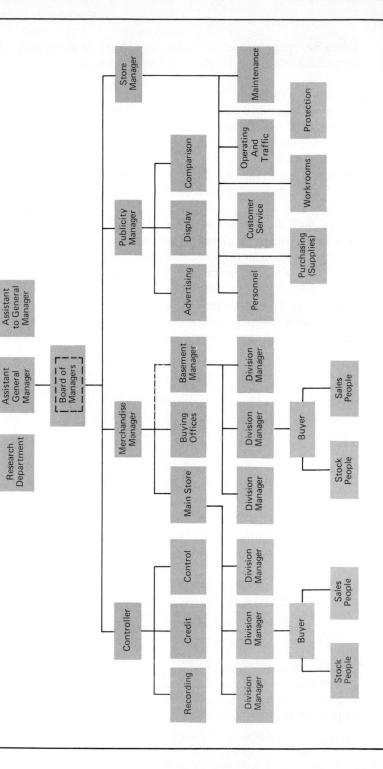

Figure 3.3 The Mazur Plan or Four-Function Plan. Source: Adapted from Paul M. Mazur, *Principles of Organization Applied to Modern Retailing* (New York: Harper & Row Pub., 1927, frontispiece).

Function	Chain of Command	Responsibilities	
The merchandising division is responsible for the buying-selling activities of the store. Other divisions are designed to supplement and assist this division, since it is often considered the "heart" of the retail store.	*Merchandise Manager* *Buyers* *Assistant Buyers* *Junior Executives* *Trainees*	*Buying* *Selling* *Controlling Stocks* *Supervision*	**Merchandising**
This division may also be called the advertising and sales promotion division. It is responsible for all selling efforts that are not classified as personal selling. The primary responsibility of this division is to attract customers to the store.	*Publicity or Advertising Manager* *Assistants* *Copywriters*	*Advertising* *Display* *Sales Promotion* *Public Relations*	**Publicity**
This division is charged with the responsibility of those activities *not* directly associated with buying and selling.	*Store Manager or Store Superintendent* *Assistants* *Security*	*Store Maintenance* *Customer Service* *Warehouse Activities* *Purchasing* *Store Security*	**Store Management or Operations**
The primary function of this division is to provide adequate working capital, protect the company's assets, and keep a watchful eye on the company's treasury.	*Controller or Treasurer* *Assistants* *Accountants* *Clerks*	*Expense Planning* *Accounting Control* *Credit* *Collections*	**Accounting and Control**

on how to divide work activities and still accomplish the primary goals and objectives of the business. Since organizing the business enterprise into departments is a conventional method of business organization, departmentalization is used by many types of retail firms.

Departmentalizing may be defined as organizing different activities and functions into departments or compartments, with individuals assigned to each department to see that the various activities and functions are carried out. This is a very important aspect of the retail store organization, since it will enable store management to locate and eliminate weaknesses in various departments as well as to make improvements.

The best example of departmentalizing can be seen in the merchandise division of a department store. Here, various lines of merchandise are divided into a number of groups, with each group called a department and operated more or less as a separate unit. This is why you will see "Sweaters," "Electrical Appliances," "Linens," "Shoes," or "Misses' Better Dresses" listed in a store directory or on a lighted panel in the elevator. This tells the customer where to find specific types of merchandise, gives an indication of price ("Better Dresses," for example), and helps to simplify the returned goods process.

However, once the decision is made to departmentalize, how is this task accomplished? What methods may be used in departmentalizing? The usual ways of organizing a business into departments are by (1) functional departmentalization, (2) product-line departmentalization, (3) geographical departmentalization, and (4) a combination of these.

Functional Departmentalization. In *functional departmentalization* activities of a similar nature are grouped together in the same department.[4] Most department stores, unless they have expanded into multiunit operations, are departmentalized according to function. The theory of functional departmentalization was clearly demonstrated by Paul M. Mazur in his book *Principles of Organization Applied to Modern Retailing,* where he wrote, "In the long run, the man must be suited to the job, for the job is created and imposed by the rigorous competitive struggle for sales and profits. The principle of fitting jobs to men can be applied with safety only in a most limited way."[5] Mazur set forth the four-function or four-pyramid plan, which is still widely used today. As Figure 3.3 illustrates, department-store activities are classified into the following four functions: (1) merchandising, (2) publicity, (3) store management or operation, and (4) accounting and control.[6]

Many department stores have adopted the four-function organization; however, some retail firms use a five-function organization. The five-function system developed as a result of department-store growth and expansion. The store operations function was divided into two separate activities: store operations and personnel. A personnel function was added for a number of reasons: (1) more and more qualified personnel had to be recruited to staff the new

Figure 3.4. The five-function organization.

stores; (2) new salespeople had to be trained; (3) methods of selecting personnel had to be developed, for example, tests and interviews; (4) methods of compensation had to be developed; (5) working conditions such as hours of work, vacations, and number of days per week had to be determined, and (6) consideration had to be given to employee complaints, unions and labor organizations, employee discounts, and promotions, transfers, and terminations. As Figure 3.4 illustrates, the five-function organization includes personnel as a separate function.

Many department stores have expanded to the suburbs, which has resulted in the addition of units or branches and twigs. Figure 3.5 illustrates a partial organization chart of a department store with several branches.

Figure 3.5. A partial organization chart of a department store with branches.

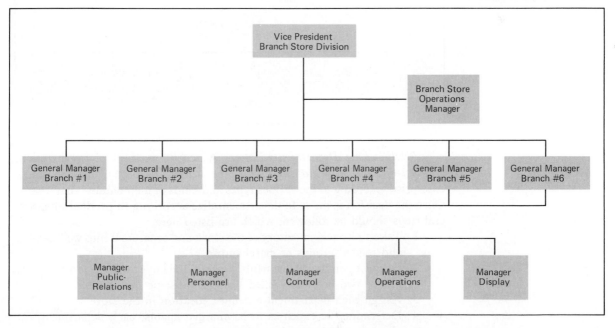

There are other variations of functional departmentalization. For example, it is rare that a department store does not have some leased or franchised departments. A leased department may be a service department, for example, a shoe-repair service or a dry-cleaning service, or a merchandise department, for example, a leather-goods department or a wig department. In a leasing operation an outside firm will operate under the name of the department store, which takes the responsibility for providing sales personnel, advertising, and displaying the goods or services, and financial responsibility for inventory, as well as other merchandising activities. A franchised department may be run as a small store within the department store, using the store's name. However, the franchisor will assist in sales planning, manage the department, and provide trained demonstrators to stimulate sales. Many cosmetic and toiletries departments are actually franchised operations.[7]

If the store has added branch stores outside of its immediate geographical location, it may also add a research and marketing division. This division will provide valuable information concerning sales potential and consumer spending power in a particular area and conduct in-store and out-of-store surveys, as well as assisting the retail buyer to determine consumer preferences in a particular trade area (see Figure 3.6).

Figure 3.6. A six-function organization. The addition of a research and marketing division will provide valuable information regarding the store's trading area.

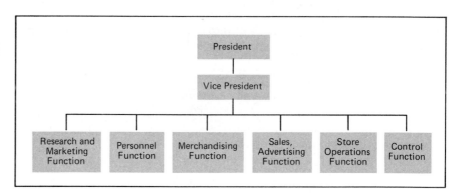

Product-Line Departmentalization. A second method of organization, *Product-line departmentalization* may be defined as organizing a business enterprise according to the various types and kinds of merchandise that it sells. Once the decision is made to departmentalize according to product-line, several steps should be followed, which are listed here.

1. Take a physical inventory of the stock and separate it into well-defined and related groups of merchandise.
2. Decide upon the departments. Usually the buyer will place a complete line or two or more related lines in the same department.
3. Assign each department a definite location in the store.
4. Determine the expenses to be charged against each department, for

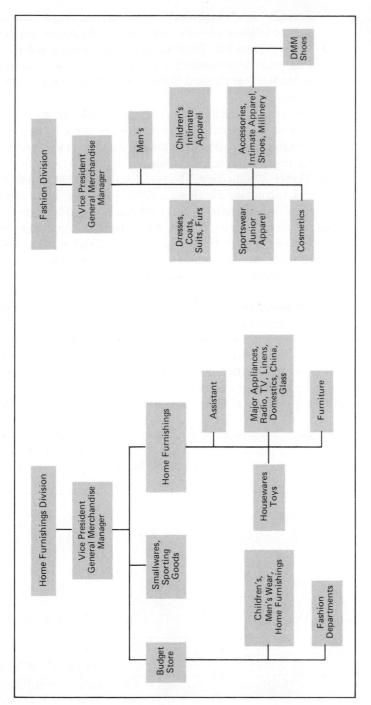

Figure 3.7. The merchandising division may be departmentalized into two major divisions: a fashion division and a home-furnishings division.

example, direct expenses such as salaries, wages, and advertising, as well as indirect expenses such as rent, heat, and utilities.

5. Gross margin (the difference between net sales and the cost of goods sold) must be computed for each department, with consideration given to the fact that all items in the department will not yield the same gross margin.

6. Record all purchases, vendor returns, sales returns, and markdowns, as well as customer and employee discounts by departments.

7. Assign the department a number or some other type of identification for ready reference and control.

As Figure 3.7 illustrates, the merchandising division may be departmentalized into two major divisions, a fashion division and a home-furnishings division. The fashion division may be further subdivided into various kinds of clothes and shoes, and the shoe division, for example, is further subdivided into children's shoes, women's shoes, casual shoes, and men's shoes. This type of departmentalization is especially helpful in coordinating the many details and activities for which the buyer is responsible.

Geographical Departmentalization. In *Geographical departmentalization,* activities are departmentalized on a territorial or geographical basis. This type of departmentalization is used when different markets or territories are assigned across the country. For example, a chain-store operation (see Figure 3.8) will use this method of departmentalization, since it has units in various cities spread across the country. The merchandising activity is departmentalized on a geographical basis because of the importance of having the buying

Figure 3.8. An example of geographical departmentalization used by a typical chain operation. This type of departmentalization is used when different markets or territories are assigned across the country.

Figure 3.9. An example of geographical departmentalization used by a typical department store with branches located in several cities.

activity centrally controlled (central buying) to keep abreast of market changes in the immediate trade area. The department store may also use geographical departmentalization, particularly if it has expanded into several branches located in several cities (see Figure 3.9).

Departmentalization Combined. In many large stores, combinations of the various types of organization are common. For example, a department store that is basically organized according to function (merchandising, personnel, store operations, advertising display, accounting and control) will organize its merchandising division according to product-line (fashion division and home-furnishings division) and will also organize on a geographical basis (branch store #1, branch store #2, etc.) (See Figure 3.10).

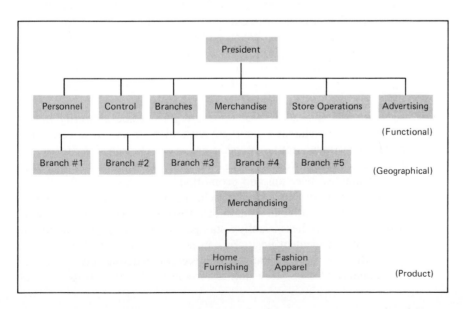

Figure 3.10. An example of departmentalization combined. A department store that is basically organized according to function (merchandising, personnel, store operations, advertising, accounting, and control) will organize its merchandising division according to product line (fashion division and home-furnishings division) and will also organize on a geographical basis (branch store #1, branch store #2, etc.).

> How will a knowledge of the following methods of business organiza-
> tion help the retail buyer in performing the merchandising activity?
>
> 1. Functional departmentalization
> 2. Product-line departmentalization
> 3. Geographical departmentalization
> 4. A combination of these

The Chain-store Operation

The *Chain-store operation* may be defined as having two or more centrally
owned and managed outlets that operate on the same plane of distribution and
handle the same or similar lines of merchandise.[8] Examples of chain stores are
Sears, Montgomery Ward, J. C. Penney, Korvette, and Safeway.

In contrast to department stores, which emphasize local management,
centralized management is emphasized in a chain-store operation. The primary reason for a centralized organization is control. Since chain stores can
be very large, with hundreds and even thousands of stores under a single
organization, the organizational structure must permit flexible growth as well
as close control. Chain stores will vary not only in size and numbers of stores
but in types of operation. A chain operation may be a general-merchandise
chain such as J. C. Penney (see Figure 3.11), a discount chain such as Korvette,
or a food chain such as the Great Atlantic and Pacific Tea Company (A & P).
Despite these differences, there are a number of characteristics common to
many chain operations.

1. The chain-store organization is broken down into a greater number of
   functions than the department store. A chain operation may have
   separate divisions for warehousing and transportation, manufacturing,
   real estate, and electronic data processing.
2. Major responsibilities are centralized in the headquarters or home
   office. The exception is the selling activity, which is performed on a
   local level.
3. Store managers of individual units are given some authority in the
   selection of merchandise for their particular stores. However, some
   major department-store ownership groups, such as Allied Stores and
   Federated Stores, give each store unit a large amount of independence
   in merchandise selection and promotion.
4. The personnel division is emphasized. A personnel manager is considered a major executive in a chain operation, in contrast to the department store, where he is usually a staff person. The hiring of individuals
   for upper management positions comes under the control of the personnel division, which is located in the central headquarters. However,
   the manager of each store unit is responsible for the hiring of local

Figure 3.11. The organizational structure of a typical chain operation.

personnel who make up the work force, as well as for the employment of middle-management trainees.

5. The merchandising activity is centralized (central buying) in contrast to the department store, where the buying activity is performed in the main store (local buying). The purpose of central buying is to provide greater control and specialization and better merchandise emphasis. (We will discuss central buying in detail in Part 2 of this chapter.)

6. Centralized management will employ and train executives to direct each of the divisions or functions into which the chain operation is divided.

7. Effective control methods are established by the use of electronic data processing and other forms of information retrieval, whereby the central headquarters is continuously and accurately informed of all the activities for which it is responsible. Provision is made for supervision and follow-up of all activities performed by the individual store units.

Review the organization charts presented in this section. How is the organization used by the following types of stores similar? Where does it differ?

1. A small store
2. A departmentalized store
3. A chain-store operation

Current Trends in Store Organization

A question often asked by retailers today is "Should we centralize management activities in a central headquarters, or should we delegate it to store buyers located in the main or parent store?" This question is asked not only by the management of chain-store operations, but also by the management of department stores with branches and twigs, as well as by managers of small stores who are perhaps considering opening another store in a new shopping center. How much authority should be delegated? What kind and amount of control is required to ensure the success of the retail operation?

To Centralize or Decentralize?

Organization in the field of merchandising is continuously changing. Many chain stores appear to be moving away from centralization to decentralization, with department stores and some specialty shops moving towards a more centralized management organization. For example, Sears, a typical centralized chain operation, has determined that the best way to grow and continue to meet the competitive challenge of the marketplace is to decentralize. According to Sears, the key to decentralization is to delegate as much decision-making responsibility as possible to lower management, in this case a group manager who is responsible for twenty to thirty stores. The group manager has the responsibility of seeing that the objectives of the group's store managers are consistent with Sears' policies regarding merchandise selection, pricing policies, and advertising and promotion practices.[9] In contrast, department stores that have merged into ownership groups, such as Federated Department Stores, Inc., Allied Stores Corporation, and Hawley Hale Stores, while still retaining their original names and maintaining their own merchandising and operating procedures, seem to be moving in the direction of a more centralized management organization.

To Separate the Buying Activity from the Selling Activity?

There is really no agreement as to what is the best form of organization. The decision to centralize or decentralize must be carefully weighed by the management team. However, an important development that is closely related to the centralization program is the increasing desire to separate buying and selling activities. As we have seen, chain-store operations have long separated buying-selling activities, with the buying activity being done in a central headquarters by a central buyer and the selling activity occurring in each store unit. You have also read that the buying-selling activities of a department store are the responsibilities of the department buyer and the buyer's assistants. There are arguments for maintaining the present system of combining the buying-selling activity, and there are arguments for the separation of the buying-selling activity. The pros and cons are listed here.[10]

Advantages of Combining the Buying-selling Activity:
1. The individual who purchases the merchandise for resale, the buyer, should also be responsible for selling the goods.
2. The buyer is in the best position to communicate enthusiasm and interest to the selling force.
3. As the store's buying representative, the buyer can best communicate necessary product information to the sales force and store executives.
4. The buyer must have direct consumer buying information to effectively interpret consumers' needs, wants, and desires.
5. A great deal of expense is involved in attempting to develop selling-department heads, since buyers will be required anyway.

Disadvantages of Combining the Buying-selling Activity:
1. Since the buying activity involves a great deal of time and effort, the selling activity should be designated to a separate individual.
2. Buying and selling are different jobs, therefore, require different training, ability, talent, and personality.
3. When buying-selling activities are combined, the buying activity often takes precedence over the selling activity.
4. Effective selling can only occur when it is given the proper emphasis.
5. Separating buying from selling has been proven to be a successful method in chain stores.

Organizing for the Separation of Buying and Selling

If a store decides to separate the buying-selling activity, various organizational forms may be used. For example, Figure 3.12 shows that a store may divide the buying-selling activity into two separate and distinct functions, with each division headed by a manager, that is, a merchandise or buying manager and a sales manager. Or the buying-selling responsibilities may remain the responsibility of the merchandising division, with a separation of the two functions occuring at a lower level. As Figure 3.13 illustrates, the merchandise manager may delegate buying responsibilities to buying specialists who are supervised by upper management, and delegate selling responsibilities to salespersons who are supervised by a sales manager.

The organizational structure followed will depend on the goals and objectives of the retail store, personal preferences of the store's top executives, future expansion plans, and the ability of management to experiment to find the most efficient organizational plan.

Figure 3.12. Organizational structure for the separation of the buying-selling activity. A store may divide the buying-selling activity into two separate and distinct functions, with each division headed by a manager.

Figure 3.13. Organizational structure for the separation of buying and selling at a lower level. The merchandise manager may delegate buying responsibilities to buying specialists who are supervised by upper management, and delegate selling responsibilities to salespersons who are supervised by a sales manager.

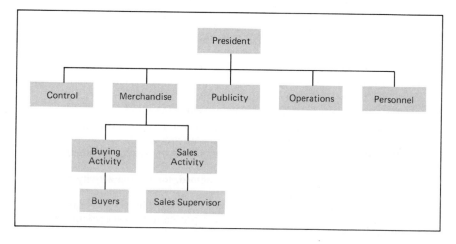

How the Merchandising Activity is Controlled

Retail institutions act as purchasing agents for consumers. Those activities associated with the planning and control of merchandise assortments are, therefore, of primary importance. You will recall that retail stores separate various business activities into major functions (store operations, control, advertising and sales, personnel, buying-selling, and so forth), and that there are similarities as well as differences in the type of organization used by stores, depending on their size, type, and the customers they are trying to please. You will see similarities and differences in organizational structure in a department store with branches (John Wanamaker); a department store with branches and twigs (Lit Brothers); a specialty chain store (Lane Bryant); a general merchandise chain (Sears,); or a food chain (A & P). The buying-selling activity, or merchandising function, as it is also called, may be combined, as in the small store and the department store, or may be a separate activity, as in the discount house or variety-store chain operation. However, whether a combined activity or a separate one, merchandising (buying-selling activity) is responsible for the selection, arrangement, and sale of goods, and all other store functions are dependent upon the merchandising activity of the store. Let us closely examine how merchandising is organized and how it is controlled in various types of stores.

The Importance of the Merchandising Function

Organization and Control in a Small Business

In a small business, the owner-manager may be totally responsible for purchasing all the merchandise sold. As a buyer, he or she determines the needs and wants of customers and visits manufacturers or vendors in the major markets, or has manufacturers' representatives come to the store. Since the owner-manager is usually in the store for most of the day, he or she also supervises the activities involved with incoming merchandise. For example, the owner-manager checks the condition of the shipment, prepares records for incoming merchandise, checks contents against the vendor's invoice (bill), checks the shipment against the buyer's (purchase) order, marks the merchandise, moves it to a storage point, or places it on shelves or on racks. Once the merchandise has been moved onto the floor, the selling activity can begin. The owner-manager is literally a "one-man band" and is primarily responsible for the success of the business.

With growth and expansion, the owner-manager may delegate some of the buying responsibilities to an assistant. The assistant may accompany the owner on market trips, or the owner may leave the assistant in charge of the store during trips. It is often very difficult for the owner to delegate authority to other individuals, since he or she has become so used to doing all the work. However, an intelligent and successful businessperson will know when and how to release responsibilities to subordinates.

Figure 3.14 illustrates how the buying-selling activity is organized in a small furniture store. As you will note, the owner-manager has an assistant who, among other things, is responsible for sales, assists in buying, and supervises employees. Rather than have detailed written job descriptions, the owner-manager will communicate orally to the assistant, who in turn will communicate with the various employees. It is not unusual for employees to know their fellow employees' responsibilities as well as they know their own. Occasionally, another employee will assist an employee who is overburdened with work. It should be noted that the primary responsibility of all the employees in a small business is to sell merchandise. Thus, if the store is busy,

Figure 3.14. Organization chart of a small furniture store. In a small business the buying-selling activity will be combined, since there would be no advantage to separating it.

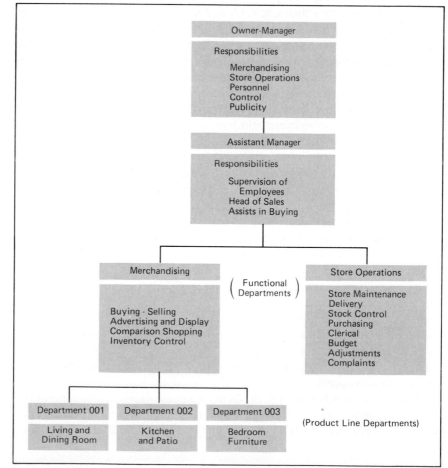

as during the Christmas season, other duties may be put aside until all customers have been served.

The store has been divided into two major functions: merchandising and store operations. In a small business the buying-selling activity will be combined, since there would be no advantage to separating it. You will note also that the furniture store has been departmentalized according to product-line: Department 001, living and dining room furniture; Department 002, kitchen and patio furniture; and Department 003, bedroom furnishings. (The student should review the section on "Buying Responsibilities in a Small Shop" in chapter 2).

Organization and Control in a Traditional Department Store

A *traditional department store* may be defined as a retail store that employs twenty five or more people and is engaged in selling merchandise in the areas of home furnishings, fashion apparel, linens, and dry goods.[11] Examples of traditional department stores are Strawbridge & Clothier, Gimbel's, Bamberger's, J. L. Hudson Company, and May Department Stores.

The definition of a department store will vary with the type of merchandise it sells and the type of customer to which it caters. For example, *a discount department store* may be defined as a departmentalized retail store that offers hard goods and major appliances along with fashion apparel and soft goods, but at discount or cutrate prices.[12] An example of a discount department store is J. M. Fields. A *departmentalized specialty store* may be defined as a departmentalized retail store that concentrates its merchandise offerings in one broad category such as fashion apparel or home furnishings.[13] Levitz Furniture is an example of a departmentalized furniture specialty store, Loehmanns is an example of a women's fashion apparel store.

As you recall, the vast and varied collection of merchandise in a traditional department store is offered for sale in separate departments, each of which is administered by a buyer who is a specialist in his or her field. The buying and selling division is called the merchandising division, which is set off from the operation, control, personnel, advertising and display, and branch store development divisions. Many department stores have added branch stores that offer a similar assortment of goods. Branch stores are usually located in profitable shopping centers outside the metropolitan area, as well as in other large cities. Or the department store may add a twig store that contains merchandise of one category or price line.

Figure 3.15 illustrates how buying is organized in a traditional department store. The merchandising division is responsible for both buying and selling. This division is sometimes headed by a vice-president of merchandising, followed by the merchandise manager, who is responsible for the supervision and coordination of buying activities for each major line of goods. Much of the time of the merchandise manager is given to the merchandising activity, with the execution of the plan left largely to the buyers.

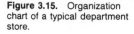

Figure 3.15. Organization chart of a typical department store.

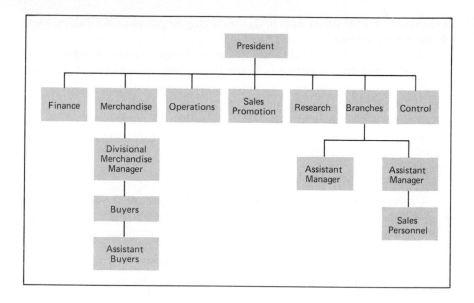

The buyers are located in the main store (this is called local buying) and perform the buying-selling activity for both the main store and the branch stores. The number of merchandise categories assigned to each buyer depends on his or her capabilities, the volume of each line, and the type of merchandise handled. For example, a small department store may have only one buyer for men's sportswear, while a larger department store may have a separate buyer for different categories of men's sportswear such as men's tailored sports clothing and men's better tailored sports clothing.

The department-store buyer must be able to predict the needs and wants of the clientele of the main store as well as of the branch or twig store. He or she must be able to forecast the additional merchandise needed to stock the branch store and make the necessary purchases. The assistant buyer is responsible for the activity within the department in the main store while the buyer is visiting the branches. However, the buyer's job may become very complicated with the continuous addition of branch stores, since they are often located out of the geographical region of the main store and may require separate and distinct types of merchandising. With just one or two branches, the buyer is able to visit each store and to oversee the selling activity of the branches, so that the buying and selling activity remains combined. However, as more are added, the time required to go to and from each branch from the main store becomes so great that visits are often minimized. In this case the selling activity may become a separate one, with the responsibility of selling granted to branch store managers. This separation would result in a better concentration of merchandise in the right place, at the best price, and in an assortment the customers are willing to accept. (The student should review "Buying Responsibilities in a Department Store" in chapter 2.)

Organization and Control in a Specialty Shop

The specialty shop is organized in much the same manner as the department store, except that it does not carry as complete a range of merchandise. It usually deals with one merchandise category—for example, women's apparel and accessories. At one time the specialty shop catered primarily to the well-to-do fashion-conscious clientele; however, today some specialty shops may cater to the middle- and lower-income consumer. Specialty shops may also find themselves competing in merchandise categories other than women's apparel, for example, infants' and children's wear, millinery, shoes, and intimate apparel. They may cater to size and age groups, for example, tall men, big women, juniors, boys, or teens; or they may sell home furnishings, for example, linens and towels or curtains and draperies.

The specialty shop is also departmentalized, and for this reason it is much like the department store in its merchandising organization. In fact, it is usually thought of as a department store by its customers. The popularity of this type of store lies in its distinctive merchandise, its prestige, and its fashion appeal. Many customers find their self-esteem enhanced in dealing with this type of store.

Depending on the size of the store, the merchandising division may or may not be set apart from other major divisions. As Figure 3.16 illustrates, the merchandising division is headed by a manager who is responsible for the

Figure 3.16. Organizational chart of a typical specialty store.

buying-selling activities of buyers in the fashion apparel division and the fashion accessories area. Since the store in this example is a relatively small women's specialty shop (two to three stores), the buying activity is conducted from one store (local buying), with the buyers responsible for the selling activity as well. However, with store expansion, the buying-selling activity may become separated, with store managers responsible for selling; and, if the specialty store develops into a chain operation, the buying activity may become a centralized one rather than being done on a local basis. We will talk more about central buying later in this section. (The student should review "Buying Responsibilities in a Specialty Shop" in chapter 2.)

Organization and Control in a General-merchandise Chain Operation
As you recall, the chain operation contains a group of two or more stores, usually under a single ownership and managed from a central headquarters. A *general-merchandise chain* will offer merchandise in both the soft-goods and fashion-apparel lines, as well as in the hard-goods or staple-goods area. The merchandising philosophy will be the same for all store units, with the central or main headquarters responsible for setting store policies and procedures, pricing, and merchandising, as well as other managerial decisions. In a chain operation, merchandising is conducted from a central headquarters (central buying) and the selling activity is separated, with selling responsibilities granted to the manager of each store unit.

The buyers for the chain operation are located at the central headquarters, which is located in a major trading area, and are responsible for supplying merchandise to all the members of the chain. As a result of this mass purchasing power, chain-store buyers may purchase the complete output of certain manufacturers and offer the merchandise under their store's own private label. Chain stores are able to offer goods at a lower price than the department store or the independent merchant. However, since this price advantage is based upon mass purchasing, chain operations, such as J. C. Penney, Sears, and Montgomery Ward, usually concentrate on merchandise for which there is a steady, predictable demand. The risk factor is minimized as a result of not offering exotic or high-fashion merchandise (see Figure 3.17). (The student should review "Buying Responsibilities in a Chain-Store operation" in chapter 3.)

Organization and Control in a Discount Chain Operation
Low prices have been and still are the appeal of the discount house. Most discount houses sell both home furnishings and clothing, with accessories. Their philosophy, like that of the traditional department store, is to provide a one-stop shopping convenience for their clientele. Some examples of discount chain operations are J. M. Fields, Inc., Two Guys, K-Mart, King's Department Stores, and Almart stores.

While the discount house has the wide variety of merchandise associated

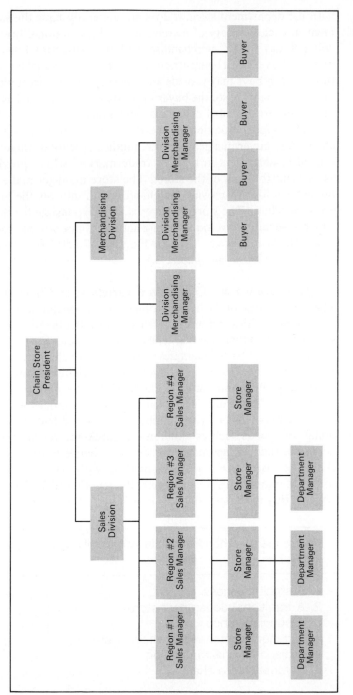

Figure 3.17. Organization of merchandising in a chain operation.

with the department store, it does not generally have the same broad assortment in each category of merchandise. Many national brand manufacturers will not have their merchandise sold in a discount house. Therefore, the discount buyer must concentrate on shopping for special buys of all kinds, even though such buys may provide an imbalance in the already existing merchandise assortment. Also, the buyer must shop for merchandise that may be sold under the private label of the discount house.

The buying function in the discount house is much like that of the chain-store buyer in a general-merchandise operation. Buyers are located in a central headquarters in a major trade market, which provides merchandise assortment for each of the stores. The store manager makes suggestions and predictions for fast-moving merchandise and informs the buyer which goods are slow sellers. The store manager is also responsible for the selling activity, which is separated from the buying activity, since buyers are centrally located in a main headquarters. (Review Figure 3.17 and "Buyer Responsibilities in a Discount House" in chapter 2.)

Organization and Control in a Variety-store Chain Operation

The merchandise of the five-and-dime store or variety store was once confined to basic necessities and novelty items in a particular price range. This type of store offers merchandise that lends itself to a quick sales transaction, usually on a self-service basis. Examples of variety-store chains are F. W. Woolworth, J. J. Newberry, and S. S. Kresge. The merchandise must be geared to the customer's budget and must be the kind that he simply "picks up" and does not have to "shop for." The usual variety store stocks everything from hard goods such as pots and pans, kitchen utensils and television sets, to the traditional soft goods such as children's apparel, scarves, and bathing suits, and domestics such as rugs, draperies, curtains, blankets, and sheets. Variety-store chains also use the central buying method, with the selling activity the responsibility of individual store managers. Review Figure 3.17. (The student should review "Buying Responsibilities in a Variety Store" in chapter 2.)

How is the merchandising activity controlled in the following types of stores?

1. A small business
2. A traditional department store
3. A specialty shop
4. A general-merchandise chain operation
5. A discount chain operation
6. A variety-store chain

Do you recall the buying responsibilities of each type of buyer?

Let's review for a moment. *Local buying* or *department-store buying* has been explained as a method of buying that is accomplished by a retail specialist who works out of the main store and procures the necessary merchandise for the main store and its various branches and twigs. This method of buying is commonly used by small shops, boutiques, specialty shops (those that are not members of a chain operation), and various types of departmentalized stores. Recall, also, that the buying-selling activity is combined; thus, the responsibility for buying and selling merchandise remains with the buying specialist. However, in contrast, central buying—a method used by chain operations such as discount chains, specialty-store chains, general-merchandise chains, and variety-store chains—occurs in a main or central headquarters, with buying decisions left to central buyers who procure merchandise for all the units in the chain. The selling activity is separate, with the responsibilities for selling granted to the manager of each unit. Thus, *central buying* may be defined as the centralization of all buying activities from a central headquarters that is located in a market center, with the authority and responsibility for the selection and purchase of merchandise limited to buyers of particular merchandise categories. Remember, however, that central buying should not be confused with a chain-store operation; central buying is merely the way chain operations usually organize to procure their goods faster and more cheaply. Also, not all large chain operations use central buying; it may be adopted by small specialty stores, hardware businesses, drugstores, and food stores. Finally, a chain operation may use central buying for certain price lines, particular types of merchandise, and certain staple items. In this case you will see a combination of local buying and central buying.

> **Central Buying**

Central buying may take one of three forms: (1) the central merchandise plan, (2) the warehouse-and-requisition plan, and (3) the price-agreement plan.

Central buying may take one of three forms
The central merchandise plan The warehouse-and-requisition plan The price-agreement plan

Central Merchandise Plan

The *central merchandise plan* may be defined as a form of central buying whereby the central buying authority assumes complete responsibility for buying the assortment of goods, pricing, warehousing, and distribution to the many store units.[14] This is the most popular form of central buying for multiunit operations, especially in the area of fashion merchandise. Examples of stores using this method are J. M. Fields, Two Guys, and Kings.

Since merchandise is usually purchased in manufacturers' lots, the goods may be placed in warehouses located in or near the market. Central buyers will make their purchases and have the merchandise delivered to the warehouse. Here the central buyer has an opportunity to check the goods to be sure they have been shipped as ordered according to size, color, style, and so on. Also, merchandise for several departments of one store may be consolidated and shipped at one time, minimizing freight charges. Warehousing helps ensure that goods will be available when needed by individual stores.

All multiunit operations do not have warehouses, however. If they do not, merchandise may be shipped directly to each store by the vendors or manufacturers. Problems may arise, since the goods may not be delivered on time or be the quality, size, color, or style ordered by the central buyer.

A variety of the central merchandising plan is the *automatic open-to-buy plan,* which may be defined as a plan whereby a predetermined portion of funds is allotted to the central buyer after the month's purchases have been planned, with the balance allotted to the store manager. For example, if the purchases for the month of December are planned at $20,000, $8,000 may be available to the central buyer and $12,000 to the store manager. The central buyer would use his money to keep the store supplied with new and popularly priced merchandise. The store manager would use his quota for reorders of fast-selling merchandise and for ordering merchandise of special interest to his customers. The store manager will use past sales records to determine the monthly open-to-buy for the central buyer, as well as specifying quantities and price lines. The central buyer selects the styles, but the store manager usually determines the limits. With this method the store manager is given some responsibility and "say" over the selection of his inventory. We will discuss open-to-buy in detail in chapter 8.

The central merchandising plan offers many advantages as well as disadvantages.[15]

Advantages of the Central Merchandising Plan
1. The central merchandising plan provides a steady flow of merchandise. Since the central buyer spends a great deal of time in the marketplace, he is able to ensure frequent deliveries, a large stock of merchandise, and popular lines, and minimize problems that may arise as a result of delays, inaccurate counts, etc. The buyer must be aware of market trends to supply merchandise that will sell and, therefore, will be readily accepted and sold in the retail stores.
2. Advance planning by each unit is eliminated. Unlike the local store buyer, central buyers purchase goods in large volume without necessarily considering the needs of each individual unit. The goods are placed in the warehouse and shipped to individual stores as they are in demand. The central buyer is not always totally accurate in forecasting future needs for the members of the organization; however, this method will succeed far better than forecasting for each individual unit.
3. The central merchandising plan allows for more accurate forecasting. As a result of the gigantic size and scope of the multiunit operation, the central buyer is better able to make accurate predictions concerning fashion trends, styles, colors, fabrics, etc. Since chain stores are located throughout the

country, the central buyer may gather information regarding the sale of a particular style in every unit in different parts of the country. This rapid assembling of information at a central location promptly reveals how acceptance or rejection of a new style at one location may compare with the norm. In comparison, a small number of sales in one particular unit could not provide for quick and accurate decision making regarding the selling life of a particular style.

4. The central merchandising plan provides for specialists in each merchandise category. Since the central buyer is concerned only with his particular merchandise category, he becomes thoroughly familiar with his market center. He becomes knowledgeable about particular vendors and manufacturers, as well as new items in his category of merchandise. As a result of this concentration, he is able to select merchandise more wisely, gather merchandise of high quality, and seek a price advantage as a result of volume buying.

5. Goods are inspected before delivery to the stores. The central buyer may inspect the merchandise while it is still in the possession of the manufacturer or at a distribution center maintained by the central headquarters. Those goods that are defective may be promptly returned; thus, a great deal of time, money, and aggravation for individual store units is minimized.

6. The central merchandising plan allows better stock control with attention on selling. Each store in the unit is provided with a well-balanced stock assortment. Since the individual store is not concerned with the buying function, it is able to concentrate its attention on the selling activity. Detailed records of merchandise that is selling may be kept by each store and some merchandise transferred to another store, which eliminates the need for numerous markdowns. This plan enables the central buyer to test merchandise and keep inventory new and fresh-looking to customers in a particular unit.

Disadvantages of the Central Merchandising Plan

1. Adjustment to local conditions is difficult. Since the chain operation is spread all over the country, it is more than likely that the central buyer has not had an opportunity to study the market or business environment in each city where stores are located. The individual store is merely a number on a page, and the buyer's world tends to become a vast computer printout rather than a realistic world of stores and customers. The central buyer must be careful to recognize that people have different likes and dislikes, needs and wants. He or she should attempt to: (a) visit each store occasionally; (b) meet with store managers and discuss the special requirements of each trading area; (c) maintain a store record book that contains up-to-date information about each store, the community it serves, its particular type of clientele, and proved merchandise lines; (d) analyze styles that have been readily accepted as well as those that have been rejected; and (e) determine when to move particular fashions into a store so that they will arrive neither too early nor too late.

2. Cooperation may be lacking. A system of merchandising whereby the store manager and the central buyer must work together may prove difficult, particularly when certain styles do not sell. An apathetic attitude may develop on the part of the store manager, since he does not have an opportunity to make decisions in the selection of the goods. The people at central headquarters may also be at fault, because they did not take the time or consideration to include the store manager in some of the decision making. Such friction can only lead to poor results. Cooperation is important in central-merchandising planning because of the nature and the diversity of the functions. Clear-cut under-

standing of the division of functions should be achieved at the outset to avoid misunderstandings in the future.

3. An enthusiastic selling force may be lacking. Since the buyer is absent from the selling floor, the sales force is often uninformed and lacking in knowledge of the merchandise it is asked to sell. The salespeople may be critical of the merchandise sent to the store and be totally lacking in enthusiasm about the goods. The central buyer is often needed to explain the merchandise, particularly today, when so many new products and new manufacturing techniques are flooding the market. Central buyers will frequently send bulletins to the sales force explaining the selling points of the merchandise. Weekly or daily fashion forecasts are sent to store managers, who in turn pass the information on to the salespeople. However, the printed word is hardly a good substitute for a direct presentation!

The advantages and disadvantages of the central merchandising plan

Advantages

1. It provides a steady flow of merchandise
2. Advance planning by each unit is eliminated
3. It allows for more accurate forecasting
4. It provides for specialists in each merchandise category
5. Goods are inspected before delivery
6. It allows better stock control with attention on selling

Does local buying offer the same advantages?

Disadvantages

1. Adjustment to local conditions is difficult
2. Cooperation may be lacking
4. An enthusiastic selling force may be lacking

Does local buying offer the same disadvantages?

The Warehouse-and-Requisition Plan

The second form of central buying, the *warehouse-and-requisition plan,* may be defined as a form of central buying whereby the central buyer arranges for the initial stock assortment and has the merchandise shipped to the individual stores. This plan is usually used by multiunit organizations in the procurement of staple merchandise or what is often referred to as "never-out" goods. Staple goods may include office supplies, housewares, paint, wallpaper, sheets, pillowcases, and numerous other items that people will purchase continuously. Stores using this type of central buying are Sears and J. C. Penney. Drug companies and food chains also use this plan in buying staple goods. This type of merchandise can be purchased in large quantities and stored in a warehouse until requisitioned by the store manager.

The plan works like this! The store manager is provided a list of the stock that is inventoried in the warehouse. He or she checks off the required merchandise in the proper quantities and sends a requisition to the warehouse, where the central buyer will see that it is promptly filled. The store manager has the responsibility for ordering enough merchandise to carry the store through the buying season. As previously mentioned, Sears is steadily turning over buying authority to its store managers (group managers) with a number of distribution centers to provide merchandise as quickly and economically as possible when requests are made.

The warehouse-and-requisition plan offers advantages as well as disadvantages.[16] The advantages are as follows:

1. The plan gives the store manager some responsibility in merchandise selection. The store manager may requisition fill-in stock as needed from a warehouse.
2. The store manager is usually assured of receiving the requested items. Since the central buyer also has the responsibility of maintaining the required inventory in the warehouse, the store manager is usually assured of receiving the merchandise he requests, or at least a reasonable substitute.
3. Reorders or fill-ins are usually filled promptly. The store manager may reorder merchandise by sending his requisition directly to the central buyer or to a warehouse. The central buyer will follow up and expedite store orders to ensure that the manager will have an adequate merchandise selection throughout a given season or selling period.
4. There is an advantage to buying large quantities of merchandise. Since staple goods are usually in demand throughout the year, it is economically advantageous to purchase such goods in quantity and store them in a warehouse until needed by various stores. Quantity buying offers a price advantage that in turn may be passed on to individual store managers to help meet lower prices offered by competition.

The disadvantages of the warehouse-and-requisition plan may be listed as follows:

1. There is little control over the composition of the merchandise selection. Since the merchandise selection is the decision of the central buyer, the store manager has little say as to the nature and type of goods offered to him. He must fill in his stock with the merchandise that is listed on the check list. However, a buyer may make an arrangement with a local wholesaler to provide items that are in demand in particular areas.
2. Poor warehouse control may lead to an imbalance in store inventory. If the central buyer does not maintain a safe level of inventory in the warehouse, requisitions cannot be filled promptly. This may lead to an imbalance in the merchandise offerings of the individual store. The central buyer must analyze the sales of various merchandise categories in each store to improve and maintain profitable levels of stock turnover.

The advantages and disadvantages of the warehouse-and-requisition plan

---

Advantages

1. Gives the store manager some responsibility in merchandise selection
2. The store manager is usually assured of receiving the requested items
3. Reorders or fill-ins are usually filled promptly
4. There is an advantage to buying large quantities of merchandise

Does local buying offer the same advantages?

Disadvantages

1. There is little control over the composition of the merchandise selection
2. Poor warehouse control may lead to an imbalance in store inventory

Does local buying offer the same disadvantages?

The Price-Agreement Plan

A third form of central buying is the *price-agreement plan,* whereby a central buyer working with vendors and manufacturers will agree on the retail price, color, size, style, and assortment of staple types of merchandise as well as the terms of shipping. The merchandise is then illustrated and described adequately in a catalog. Thus, the price-agreement plan is sometimes referred to as the *price-agreement* or *catalog plan.* This method of buying is used primarily by variety-store operations, for example, S. H. Green, F. W. Woolworth, and J. J. Newberry, as well as by other types of chain operations. The central buyer is responsible for prearranging the minimum amount of goods to be purchased by the entire chain, keeping the store catalog up to date, adding new items, seeking new merchandise resources (vendors, manufacturers), canceling old items, instructing the store manager when to take markdowns, and transferring merchandise from one store to another.

The store manager has complete authority for the composition of his stock. He places orders directly with the vendors concerned. Vendors are willing to carry reserve stocks, since the goods usually are staple goods that have a long selling life. Since arrangements have been previously negotiated by the central buyer, the store manager is assured of a supply of everything listed in the catalog.

The Advantages and Disadvantages of the Price-agreement or Catalog Plan[17]

The advantages of the price-agreement plan are listed as follows:

1. The plan develops a feeling of responsibility on the part of the store manager. Since the store manager may place orders directly with the vendors concerned, he is given responsibility for the selection of merchandise to be sold in his store.
2. It reduces the expense of a warehouse. Since previous arrangements have been made by the central buyer, the vendors or manufacturers concerned have adequate amounts of merchandise on hand, so goods can be shipped directly to the store when requested. This eliminates the expense of having to store the merchandise in a warehouse.
3. It reduces the necessity of keeping detailed records for each unit. Since the store manager has control over his merchandise inventory, detailed record keeping is reduced. The store manager will communicate directly with the vendors or manufacturers listed in the catalog and place orders as they are required.

The disadvantages of the price-agreement or catalog plan are as follows:

1. Problems arise with tardy deliveries. Since a warehouse facility is not used, the store manager is often faced with the problem of tardy or late deliveries. He must compensate for this by placing orders well in advance with vendors, thus providing ample time for late shipments.
2. Problems arise with high transportation costs. Even though vendors are willing to store reserved stocks and make direct shipments to the store units, problems often arise with high transportation costs. If this is the case, the central buyer may send the order to a different resource or find a substitute who is in a position to do a better job.

The advantages and disadvantages of the price-agreement or catalog plan

Advantages

1. It develops a feeling of responsibility on the part of the store manager
2. It reduces the expense of a warehouse
3. It reduces the necessity of keeping detailed records of each unit

Does local buying offer the same advantages?

Disadvantages

1. Problems arise with tardy deliveries
2. Problems arise with high transportation costs

Does local buying offer the same disadvantages?

Central Buying Takes on Different Forms

As you now realize, central buying takes on different forms depending upon the merchandising arrangements of various types of retail stores. A combination of local buying and central buying may be used by a chain-store operation. However, local buying becomes an impossible task for department stores. They have to centralize their buying activity in a main headquarters and separate the selling activity, with this responsibility delegated to branch store managers.[18] Thus, department stores will use the central buying method. Remember: retail stores will differ in their organizational pattern depending upon their objectives and philosophies and their ability to remain flexible in an ever-changing, highly competitive business environment.

Chapter Summary

Buying may be defined as the purchase of consumer goods in relatively large or wholesale quantities for subsequent resale in smaller (retail) lots to the ultimate consumer. The buying function may take on different forms, depending on the size of the retail store, the type of merchandise carried, or the type of clientele the store is trying to please. The retail buyer should keep in mind that good organization is an essential ingredient in any type of business if the firm's goals and objectives are to be realized. The student should review responsibility-authority relationships, staffing, departmentalization, and line-staff relationships. There are similarities as well as differences in the organizational pattern of retail firms. The following types of stores show similarities as well as differences in organizational structure: the small store, the departmentalized store, and the chain-store operation. Once the decision is made to departmentalize, various methods are used to organize a business into departments. They are functional departmentalization, product-line departmentalization, geographical departmentalization, and a combination of these. The four-function or four-pyramid plan is still widely used by many department stores. The student should review the organization charts presented throughout the chapter. The chain store may be defined as having two or more centrally owned and managed outlets that have the same plan of distribution and handle the same or similar lines of merchandise. The primary reason for a centralized organization is control. The student should review the characteristics common to many chain operations that use the central buying method. What are the current trends in store organization? To centralize or decentralize? To separate the buying activity from the selling activity? How is the separation of the buying-selling activity organized?

It is important to learn how the merchandising activity is controlled in a small business, a traditional department store, a specialty shop, a general-merchandise chain operation, a discount chain operation, and a variety-store chain operation. Central buying is the centralization of all buying activities from a central headquarters that is located in a market center, with the authority and responsibility for the selection and purchase of merchandise limited to buyers of particular merchandise categories. Central buying may be accomplished in one of three forms: the central merchandising plan, the warehouse-and-requisition plan, and the price-agreement plan. The student should review the advantages and disadvantages of each.

Trade Terminology

DIRECTIONS: Briefly explain or discuss each of the following trade terms:

1. Buying
2. Departmentalizing
3. Functional departmentalization
4. Product-line departmentalization
5. Geographical departmentalization
6. Chain-store operation
7. Traditional department store
8. Discount department store
9. Departmentalized specialty store
10. General-merchandise chain
11. Local buying or department-store buying
12. Central buying
13. Central merchandise plan
14. Automatic open-to-buy plan
15. Warehouse-and-requisition plan
16. Price-agreement or catalog plan

Questions for Discussion and Review

1. How does store organization differ in a small business, a department store, and a chain operation?

2. Why is good organization important to the success of a retail business?

3. Discuss the relationship between authority and responsibility; between line and staff.

4. How does local or branch store buying differ from central buying?

5. What types of stores use local buying? Central buying?

6. What are the various forms of central buying that may be considered by a retail business? Discuss the advantages and disadvantages of each.

7. What is the automatic open-to-buy? What advantages does it offer the store manager?

8. What type of central buying would be used by a variety store? A discount chain operation? A women's specialty shop? A general-merchandise chain?

9. What is departmentalizing? Illustrate how function, product-line, and geographical departmentalization may be used by a department store.

Case Study Number One

Meeting the Competition

The policy of your traditional department store is that you will meet your competition's price on all types of merchandise. A customer complains that a handbag your store is selling is also being sold at a nearby discount house for much less. You know the markup on the merchandise is fair, since your comparison shopping bureau has supplied you with weekly figures on market activity. You realize, however, that your competitor uses the services of a central buyer; therefore, he is in a better position to obtain merchandise at lower prices. However, the customer insists that you live up to your store's policy of "not being undersold." How would you handle the customer's complaint? How would you protect yourself from having the same situation occur in the future?

Case Study Number Two

The Terror of the Third Floor

Mitchells' was a leading department store located in a large city in the midwest. It had expanded to eleven branch stores located in several suburban shopping centers. It had an excellent reputation for high-fashion and quality merchandise, especially in the misses' better dresses department. The buyer of this profitable and prestigious department was Mrs. Sophie Potter. She had an excellent background in women's fashions and had been the buyer of misses' better dresses for the past nine years. Since her arrival at Mitchells', she had built the department into one of the most profitable in the store. Store management was very pleased with her merchandising abilities.

However, Mrs. Potter had the reputation for being a very difficult, temperamental, and demanding person to work with. She made unreasonable demands upon her salesladies and stock people. She would exclude her assistant buyer from important department activities and then criticize the assistant for not doing her job. She was often heard reprimanding her assistant and salesladies in front of other employees and store customers. As a result, the misses' better dresses department had the highest employee turnover in the entire store.

The personnel department was aware of the situation. The director, Mr. Naples, had on numerous occasions spoken with Mrs. Potter about the high rate of turnover and the difficulty in finding junior assistants who were willing to work in her department. He informed her that she was getting the reputation of "the terror of the third floor" and employees were refusing work assignments to her department.

Mrs. Potter always promised that she would be more considerate and make a serious attempt to consider the feelings of her subordinates. However, her conduct continued. Finally, the fifth assistant buyer she had had in one year went to Mr. Naples and informed him that she could not tolerate the degrading and demoralizing treatment she was getting from Mrs. Potter. Mr. Naples decided the situation could not continue. He took up the matter with the merchandise manager and carefully related the numerous complaints that he had been receiving. The merchandise manager, Mr. Jackson, listened attentively. He then reminded Mr. Naples that Mrs. Potter was one of the store's best buyers and that her department was one of the most profitable. He suggested that perhaps the personnel division should do a better job in providing a high-caliber assistant capable of working with an aggressive, hardworking, and successful buyer. Mr. Jackson politely reminded Mr. Naples that "keeping employees happy" was the function of the personnel division, while merchandising was the merchandise manager's responsibility. In short, Mr. Jackson put the problem back into Mr. Naples' hands.

What should Mr. Naples do?

Retailing Activities to Stimulate Student Interest and Participation

1. Survey your local community and determine what type of store expansion has occurred. Classify each new store according to the types of stores discussed in this chapter, for example, traditional department store, specialty store, general-merchandise chain, etc. What type or types of stores are widely represented? How do you account for the presence of these stores in your community?

2. Visit a traditional department store, a variety chain operation, and a boutique. Determine the buying method (local or central buying) used by each store. Is the selling activity combined with or separated from buying?

3. Interview the store manager of a branch store, a discount house, and a drugstore. Obtain an organization chart for each store. Compare each store with regard to functional organization and product-line departmentalization. How is the merchandising activity organized?

REFERENCES

The Retail Student's Reference Library

Barnhill, I. A. *Sales Management: Contemporary Perspectives.* Glenview, Ill.: Scott, Foresman & Company, 1970.

Bear, R. D. *Mass Merchandising: Revolution and Evolution.* New York: Fairchild Publications, Inc., n.d.

Belden, Donald L. *Role of the Buyer in Mass Merchandising.* New York: Chain Store Publishing Corporation, 1971.

The Buyer's Manual. New York: National Retail Merchants Association. 1970.

Chisholm, Robert F. *The Darlings: The Mystique of the Supermarket.* New York: Chain Store Publishing Corporation, 1970.

The Convenience Food Store. Chicago: The Quaker Oats Company, 1970. *Department Store and Specialty Store Merchandising and Operating Results of 1969.* New York: National Retail Merchants Association, 1970.

England, Wilbur. *Modern Procurement Management.* Homewood, Ill.: Richard D. Irwin, Inc., 1970.

Fundamentals of Men's Wear Retailing. New York: Fairchild Publications, Inc., 1972.

Gillespie, Karen. *Apparel and Accessories for Women, Misses and Children.* Washington, D.C.: U.S. Government Printing Office, 1965.

Goodman, Charles S. *Management of the Personal Selling Function.* New York: Holt, Rinehart & Winston, 1971.

Greenwood, William T. *Issues in Business and Society.* Boston: Houghton Mifflin Company, 1971.

Guide to Fashion Marketing and Merchandising. Bronx, N.Y.: Milady Publishing Corporation, 1974.

Johnson, Rossall J. *Executive Decisions.* Cincinnati: South-Western Publishing Company, 1970.

Judelle, Beatrice. *The Fashion Buyer's Job.* New York: National Retail Merchants Association, 1971.

Koeninger, J., and Koeninger, G. *The Retail Buyer.* Austin: University of Texas Press, 1972.

Leased Department Rates, Policies and Expenses in Department and Specialty Stores. New York: National Retail Merchants Association, n.d.

Leed, Theodore; and German, Gene. *Principles of Food Merchandising.* New York: Chain Store Publishing Corporation, 1973.

Levinson, R. E. *Small Marketers Aid No. 127.* Washington, D.C.: U.S. Government Printing Office, 1970.

Mallowe, C. A.; and McLaughlin, D. *Food Marketing and Distribution.* New York: Chain Store Publishing Corporation, 1971.

Newman, W. H., and Logan, J. P. *Strategy, Policy, and Central Management.* Cincinnati: South-Western Publishing Company, 1971.

Profitable Merchandising of Men's Clothing. New York: National Retail Merchants Association, n.d.

Putting Classification Merchandising to Work. New York: National Retail Merchants Association, n.d.

Sisk, Henry L. *Management and Organization.* Cincinnati: South-Western Publishing Company, 1973.

Smith, Samuel. *Organization of Branch Stores.* New York: National Retail Merchants Association, 1969.

Strietelmeier, J. *Franchising.* Columbus: Distributive Education Materials Laboratory, 1972.

Telchin, C. S., and Helfant, S. *Planning Your Store for Maximum Sales and Profit.* New York: National Retail Merchants Association, 1969.

Thomas, Robert. *Management Training.* Columbus: Distributive Education Materials Laboratory, 1970. *To Multiply A Buyer.* New York: National Retail Merchants Association, n.d.

Wienslaw, Arthur. *Jewelry Retailing.* Washington, D.C.: U.S. Government Printing Office, 1965.

Women's Ready-to-Wear, 1970. Austin: University of Texas Press, 1970.

Your First Branch Store. New York: National Retail Merchants Association, 1967.

References

1. Wingate, J. W., and Friedlander, J. S., *The Management of Retail Buying* (Englewood Cliffs, N.J.: Prentice-Hall, Inc., 1963), p. 1.
2. Poe, Jerry B, *An Introduction to the American Business Enterprise* (Homewood, Ill.: Richard D. Irwin, Inc., 1972), p. 140.
3. Ibid.
4. Ibid., p. 134.
5. Mazur, P. M., *Principles of Organization Applied to Modern Retailing* (New York: Harper and Bros., 1927), as cited by Bond, Richard C., "Department Store Organization," in *The Buyer's Manual* (New York: National Retail Merchants Association, 1965), p. 12.
6. Mazur, *Principles of Organization,* frontispiece.
7. Bond, "Department Store Organization," p. 16.
8. Stanton, William J., *Fundamentals of Marketing* (New York: McGraw-Hill Book Company, 1971), p. 293.
9. "How Giant Sears Grows and Grows," *Business Week,* December 16, 1972, pp. 52–57.
10. Duncan, D. J., and Phillips, C. F., *Retailing Principles and Methods* (Homewood, Ill.: Richard D. Irwin, Inc., 1967), pp. 206–207.
11. Gillespie, Karen, and Hecht, Joseph C., *Retail Business Management* (New York: Gregg/McGraw-Hill Book Company, 1970), pp. 80–81.
12. Ibid., p. 79.
13. Ibid.
14. Wingate and Friedlander, *Management of Retail Buying,* p. 41.
15. Ibid., pp. 44–48.
16. Ibid., pp. 50–58.
17. Ibid., p. 52.
18. Ibid., p. 41.

The Resident Buying Office

4

Performance Objectives

PERFORMANCE OBJECTIVES

As a result of reading this chapter the student should be able to accomplish the following:

1. Define resident buying office; resident buyer.

2. Trace the development of the resident buying office from the early days of retailing to the present.

3. Outline the two major types of resident buying offices and discuss each.

4. Give in his or her own words the important qualifications that should be considered when selecting a resident buying office.

5. Relate the similarities that exist between the resident buying office and a client store; between the resident buyer and the store buyer.

6. Describe how each type of resident buying office is organized.

7. Evaluate the many and varied services offered by most resident buying offices.

8. Explain the responsibilities of a resident buyer.

The Resident Buying Office

Organization of a Resident Buying Office

In chapter 3 we discussed three basic types of central buying used by buyers in single and multiunit retail organizations. However, buyers, whether of staple goods or fashion goods, cannot rely on occasional market trips or visits by manufacturers' representatives alone, since such activities are often inadequate, time-consuming, and expensive. Many stores must seek the services of an outside agency that will provide a steady flow of market information on a local as well as a national basis. The purpose of Part 1 of this chapter, therefore, will be to discuss (1) the development of resident buying offices, (2) the different types of resident buying offices, (3) how to determine which resident buying office is suitable for a particular store, and (4) the organization of various types of resident buying offices. Part 2 will discuss the numerous services offered by the typical resident buying office. Topics to be considered are the merchandising function, the promotion function, the ancillary function, and the research function.

An Outside Agency

A *resident buying office* (RBO) is an outside agency whose primary responsibility and specialization is coverage of the various trade markets it represents. Those individuals who represent the resident buying office are called resident buyers.

A *resident buyer* is a buying specialist who works in the capacity of advisor or assistant to those stores represented by the office and who is responsible for all phases of merchandising and promotion. Resident buying offices, unlike retail stores, are located "in residence," or in the heart of the wholesale district. They become market representatives for the client stores.

A great majority of resident buying offices are located in New York City, since this city is the primary market for fashion apparel, soft goods and related accessories, hard goods, home furnishings, and appliances. Miami serves as a center for stores interested in southern fashion markets, while Los Angeles serves as a center for stores interested in West Coast fashions. Chicago, Rocky Mountain, and Atlanta serve as centers for home furnishings and hard goods. Resident buying offices are also scattered in a few other major cities.

Resident buying offices represent many types of client stores. These stores are usually fairly similar in size and type of trade, but since they are located in different towns and cities, they do not compete with one another. Some offices may represent only large-volume department stores, while other offices represent both large and medium-sized department stores, giving complete coverage of both soft and hard lines. Some offices serve only specialty stores providing a single line of merchandise, such as furs or infants' and children's wear, or even a single department, such as millinery.

Buying offices are of all sizes. Some are literally one-person offices with only a few store accounts, while other offices may revolve around a single individual and yet have several buyers specializing in fashion or soft-goods lines. Still other offices represent several hundred stores and maintain large staffs with separate divisions for various types of goods, for example, men's and boys' wear, housewares, piece goods, and domestics. This concentration gives the retail store access to a team of buyers it could not possibly employ itself.

The resident buying office serves as an important link between stores and manufacturers by offering a variety of services. Buying offices play a major role in store merchandising and distribution. They give the retail-store buyer an opportunity to carry out his or her duties and responsibilities in a particular department with the security of knowing that someone is constantly scanning the principal markets for new merchandise, new resources, and favorable prices.

The Development of Resident Buying Offices

Resident buying offices first developed during the early days of retailing. The early resident buyer would travel to the central marketplace and purchase goods for a store owner who could not leave the store. The primary objective was the placement of orders.

Resident buying offices have continued to develop for many reasons. First, the small retailer found it was necessary to be represented in the marketplace, especially in the apparel and home-furnishing lines, since he or she was responsible not only for the buying-selling activity but also for the management of the entire retail store. Retailers soon realized that the "I'd-rather-do-it-myself" attitude was depriving them of dollar savings and often found themselves unaware of current customer demands and without popular lines of merchandise.

A second reason for the continued development of resident buying offices was the growth of multitudes of new products and the continuous changes in old products. The retail buyer found it difficult to keep up with new manufacturing techniques, new fibers and fabrics, and modifications of already existing product lines.

A third reason was to obtain assistance and advice in the selection of key resources and to maintain good working relations with these resources. Since retail buyers only visited the marketplace occasionally, it was necessary to provide a representative who would act as an agent between the source of supply and the retail store, ensuring an adequate, reliable communications system.

A fourth reason was to strengthen the trading position and purchasing power of individual stores. A retail store, unlike a chain store, does not have the opportunity to take advantage of volume discounts or private labeling, since it does not have the facility or the demand for the volume necessary for discount purchasing. However, by pooling purchasing power with noncompeting stores, the retail outlet has an opportunity to partake in volume buying or group buying and thus can better meet the competition from large chain-store operations.

In recent years resident buying offices have added a wide variety of services to their original function of placing store orders. They have become merchandising consultants, serving approximately 90 percent of the nation's department and specialty stores, small apparel businesses, and large discount and chain operations.[1]

How does a store determine which type of resident buying office is suitable and reflects its image? What types of resident buying offices are available?

Types of Resident Buying Offices

There are two major classifications of resident buying offices: (1) the independent office, including the salaried office or the merchandise broker, and (2) the store-owned office, including the private buying office, the associated buying office, and the syndicated or chain-owned buying office.

The classification of resident buying offices	
The Independent Office	**The Store-owned Office**
1. Salaried or fixed-fee office 2. Merchandise broker or commission office	1. Private office 2. Associated office 3. Syndicated or chain-owned office

Independent Buying Office

The *Independent buying office* is privately owned and operated, and continuously seeks stores as clients. Some of these independent buying offices represent large department stores, while others represent small apparel shops, specialty stores, home-furnishing stores, and other types of stores that require market representation. The office serves member stores with similar merchandise lines, so that the resident buyer can scout the marketplace for as many as 100 or more member stores carrying similar merchandise. Since noncompeting stores are members of the same resident office, the resident buyer has an opportunity to work with the buyers from each member store to develop private branding, encourage volume buying, and offer a variety of promotional aids. The majority of buying offices fall into this category. Examples are Felix Lilienthal and Company; Kirby Block and Company; Arkwright; Independent Retailers Syndicate; Werring and Howell; Mutual Buying Syndicate; and Atlas Buying Corporation.

There are two types of independent buying offices: (1) the salaried or fixed-fee office and (2) the commission or merchandise-broker office.

Salaried or Fixed-Fee Office. The salaried office is paid a fixed fee directly by the client stores it represents. Contractual arrangements are made between the salaried office and the client store. The typical fee ranges from 1/2 percent to 1 percent of a store's annual sales volume for the past year, payable in equal monthly installments.[2] The relationship of the buying office to the client store is that of a private professional offering service to a client. For example, a department-store buyer of hard goods may seek information and advice regarding new sources of supply, product changes and obsolescence, and special buying problems.

Commission or Merchandise-Broker Office. This type of independent office receives its fee directly from the manufacturers or vendors it represents and is found primarily in the fashion apparel trade. The commission is based on the percentage of orders placed in client stores. The merchandise broker receives a commission from the manufacturer or vendor rather than from the client store, and thus is considered a "special type" of resident buyer; however, he or she offers many services similar to those offered by other resident buyers. The fee ranges from 2 to 4 percent of the sale. The merchandise broker usually represents many lines of manufacturers, and thus is often called a manufacturers' representative.

Merchandise brokers have an opportunity to broaden the market to boutiques and other small apparel shops that could not be contacted directly by manufacturers. For example, a manufacturers' representative may call on a small shop to show a line of merchandise, or may display merchandise in local hotel rooms and invite several retailers to view it. In this case, the merchandise is modeled informally, and ideas for display and promotions are also provided. This type of service can be an advantage to the smaller retailer who cannot afford the monthly installments asked by the salaried office. One disadvantage, however, is that the service is confined to the manufacturers and vendors that pay a commission on the orders brought in by the office. The broker is not an employee of the store, not even its agent. There is often conflict of interest between the client store and the manufacturers. The merchandise broker must be careful to give the best service possible to his or her customers to ensure continued business.[3]

The Store-Owned Office

The *store-owned office* is owned by the store or stores that it represents and is organized to provide buying services for them. Very large department and specialty stores are generally represented by their own offices. This type of buying arrangement provides the least conflict of interest. There are three types of store-owned offices: (1) the *private office,* (2) the *associated buying office,* and (3) the *syndicated* or *chain-owned office.*

The Private Office. Some large retail organizations maintain their own private buying offices in major market centers such as New York City. However, due to the large investment involved and the lack of an opportunity to exchange information with noncompeting stores, this type of resident buying office is not very common nowadays. The buyers in these offices perform the same functions as those in the independent offices; in fact, some stores maintain private offices on the premises of an independent office. This enables them to have access to all the services of the large resident buying office and yet to maintain an office for a market representative who is directly responsible to them. Examples of stores owning private buying offices are Neiman-Marcus and Marshall Field, who own offices in New York City. These stores restrict their merchandising activities to their own buying offices.

The Associated Buying Office. Associated buying offices are owned and operated by a group of stores. They are also called cooperative offices, since their expenses are distributed among the member stores. Fees are based upon the size of each store and the amount of service each requires. Associated offices are more expensive than salaried offices. They must represent all their members and are, therefore, difficult to join and to leave. Since the member stores share similar business interests, they are willing to exchange confidential information and to assist one another in the development of various types of merchandising techniques, promotional buying assists, control and operations, and store management. Associated offices are restricted in choice of membership, as compared to the independent buying office; however, they have the advantage of developing a greater assortment of brand-name merchandise and of operating wholesaling activities that are more difficult to maintain in independent offices. The best-known buying offices are the Associated Merchandising Corporation (AMC), which serves thirty to forty large department stores, for example, Bloomingdale's, Bullock's, Dayton-Hudson, Rich's, Abraham & Strauss and Capwell; Frederick Atkins, Inc., with some forty to fifty department stores, for example, John Wanamaker's; and the Specialty Store Association, which represents women's apparel stores and has a membership of approximately twenty stores.[4] A buyer who makes a trip to the market, for example, New York City, is accompanied by the office's resident buyer on visits to vendors and manufacturers; the resident buyer arranges fashion shows and provides office space and clerical assistance in the resident buying office. The store buyer who becomes familiar with the services of the store's resident buying office and learns to use its facilities intelligently can make market trips more productive and the entire operation more successful.[5]

The Syndicated or Chain-Owned Office. Syndicated buying offices differ from the associated buying office in that they are divisions of a corporation that owns a chain of department stores. Therefore, most chain stores have central buyers in the stores as well as resident buyers in the principal markets. The syndicated buying office functions in much the same manner as the associated office; however, the syndicated office is better able to maintain a dominant position and can force adoption of its recommendations on stores because of the common ownership. For example, the syndicate office may insist that its stores maintain certain merchandising policies, whereas the associated office may offer suggestions but cannot force a member store to adopt them. Examples of the syndicate buying office are Allied Purchasing Corporation (APC), which serves more than 100 stores, an example of which is Jordan Marsh and Co.; and Associated Dry Goods Corporation (ADG), which serves Lord and Taylor, Inc. Other examples of syndicated buying offices are Gimbels Central Buying Office, Macy's Corporate Buying Division, and May Department Stores.[6] Once central buyers have determined the needs of their individual stores, they will request the resident buyer to go into the marketplace and make the necessary buying arrangements. A major advantage of such an affiliation, even for the central buyer, is the market feedback that is provided. Since central buyers handle large volumes of merchandise, they require fast, accurate information on fashion trends, market conditions, "best sellers," "hot items," and prices. A central buyer may request a resident buyer to place orders, follow up on deliveries, and handle special orders, adjustments, and complaints.

Selection of the Resident Buying Office

How does the retail buyer narrow the possibilities and avoid buying offices that do not reflect his or her type of store? The following is a list that should be considered when selecting a resident buying office:[7]

1. What will be the cost of using a resident buying office? Is a minimum monthly fee required?
2. What kind of contract arrangements are required? Are there arrangements for canceling them?
3. What is the extent of the office market coverage? Its fashion knowledge? Its merchandising judgment?
4. What kind of merchandise lines are represented by the resident buying office? Popular-priced merchandise? Promotional merchandise? Higher-priced merchandise? Discount-priced merchandise?
5. Does the office maintain buyers with separate divisions for various types of

goods? Or does it specialize in one line of merchandise? Does the resident buying office give full coverage to both hard goods and soft goods?

6. What kind and scope of services are offered by the resident buying office?
7. Do the retail policies of the resident buying office basically agree with yours?
8. Would your type of retail operation be too limited to be serviced properly?
9. Do the executives and staff of the resident buying office provide an atmosphere of work compatibility? What is the size of the staff? What are their abilities?
10. What other clients are represented by the resident buying office? Are most of them similar to your type of retailing operation?

The retail buyer must be careful in the selection of a resident buying office, because this resident office becomes the store's market representative. The buyer should speak frankly with the executives of the buying office and should ask for references, speak to some of the members, get their opinion of the buying office, and discuss its method of operation with them. Also, the buyer should speak with manufacturers and vendors, since they are aware which offices have competent resident buyers and give good reliable service.

Organization of the Resident Buying Office

The organization of the resident buying office generally corresponds closely to that of the member or client store or stores. Like the member store, the resident buying office usually has one or more buyers for each classification of merchandise. Depending on the size of the market, however, larger resident offices may have as many as twenty buyers for a particular merchandise line, who cover certain size ranges and price lines intensively.

It is the responsibility of the resident buyer to thoroughly cover the entire market that he or she has been assigned. This requires constant checking and evaluation of vendors and manufacturers, seeking new merchandise resources, and in turn, alerting the client store to changes. The resident buyer must be constantly aware of styles and must be able to meet the needs of all the visiting store buyers. The staff of the resident buying office must keep stores informed of current market trends by using a variety of communications techniques (see figure 4.1).

Table 4.1 shows the similarities in organization between the resident buying office and a client office.

Resident buying office		Client store
Divisional department head	Similarities that exist	Divisional merchandise manager
Resident buyers		Store buyers

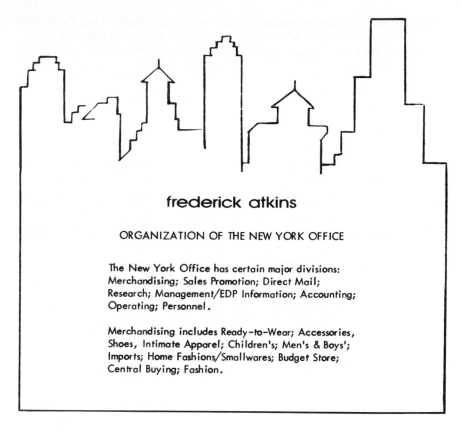

frederick atkins

ORGANIZATION OF THE NEW YORK OFFICE

The New York Office has certain major divisions: Merchandising; Sales Promotion; Direct Mail; Research; Management/EDP Information; Accounting; Operating; Personnel.

Merchandising includes Ready-to-Wear; Accessories, Shoes, Intimate Apparel; Children's; Men's & Boys'; Imports; Home Fashions/Smallwares; Budget Store; Central Buying; Fashion.

Independent Buying Office

The independent resident buying office and its member stores enjoy mutual freedom in setting their own merchandise policies. "Across-the-board offices" serve clients who handle both hard goods and soft goods. Their organization is similar to that of their client stores, who also offer "across-the-board" merchandise coverage.

Private Resident Buying Office

As you recall, the private office is owned by and run for a single store. Its organization, therefore, will closely correspond to that of the store that owns and operates it. Merchandise lines represented by the resident buying office will be the same as that represented by the retail store.

Associated Resident Buying Office

Because the associated buying office is owned by several stores, it must organize in such a way that all its members are represented in the formulation of business policies and philosophies. In such offices there is usually a board of

Table 4.1. *Similarities in organization between resident buying office and client store.*

RESIDENT BUYING OFFICE	CLIENT STORE
Divisional Department Head ⟷	Divisional Merchandise Manager

1. Work closely together, disseminating market information to their staff.
2. Both have the primary function of directing and supervising the activities of their buyers, who report to them. Together they are responsible for organizing and directing divisional meetings.
3. Work with store steering committees in developing group purchases and private brand promotions.
4. Maintain good vendor relationships.

Resident Buyers ⟷	Store Buyers

1. Work closely togeter in determining current trends, consumer needs, pricing policies, and quality merchandise.
2. Locate new merchandise resources and communicate with store buyers.
3. Maintain sample rooms where, at scheduled hours or by appointment, store buyers may visit the resident office to see lines of merchandise or confer with buyers.

directors whose members are executives of the owning stores. The board members determine policy, merchandising techniques, and services, which will in turn benefit all the member stores. The merchandise classification, the scope of merchandise carried, and the price lines offered will depend upon the member stores and their particular interests.

Syndicated or Chain-Owned Buying Office

Since the syndicated buying office is a division of the corporation that owns it, it is organized to serve only the domestic member stores of the corporation. Because it is owned by the stores, it is less flexible in policy formulation than other types of offices and can insist that its rules be followed.

Cooperation between Buyers is a Must

Unless there is complete cooperation between the resident buyer and the retail-store buyer, the many advantages offered by the resident buying office may not be realized. A good, strong working relationship must be developed. The store buyer should take the resident buyer into his or her confidence about business problems, seek the resident buyer's advice, and adopt the suggestions offered.

A typical example of good cooperation between buyers occurs when the store buyer notifies the resident buying office well in advance of plans to visit the market. This will give the resident buyer an opportunity to prepare for the visit by scouting the market for particular store needs, which will save market time for the store buyer. Most resident buying offices require that store buyers make appointments ahead of time to ensure a more productive market trip.

Services Offered by the Resident Buying Office

The Buyer's "Right Arm"

Resident buying offices are organized to save the retail buyer time and money and to provide professional assistance. As the buyer's "right arm" in the market, the buying office eliminates unnecessary market trips, saves money, and offers a variety of services.[8]

Most resident buyers restrict their activities to the women's and children's apparel trades, although many also offer service in the purchase of men's wear, furs, millinery, and home furnishings, to name but a few. Some resident buying offices are organized to serve only a limited number of stores in a few lines of merchandise, while others are organized to offer a complete line of service encompassing many fields.

A typical well-staffed buying office has four major functions: (1) the merchandising function, (2) the promotion function, (3) the research function, and (4) the ancillary function. Table 4.2 provides a more detailed description of each.

Table 4.2. *Services offered by the typical resident buying office.*

Merchandising Function	Promotion Function
1. Order placement, adjustment, follow-up	1. Providing buyer information
2. Preparation for buyer's visit	2. Promotion of goods
3. Ordering for stores	3. Preparation of advertising
4. Group buying	4. Fashion service
5. Central buying	
6. Private branding	
7. Jobbing service	**Ancillary Function**
8. Purchasing	1. Buying clinics
	2. Divisional meetings
Research Function	3. Foreign service
1. Research and analysis	
2. Management marketing information	

Merchandising Function

The merchandising function assists the store buyer in obtaining merchandise.

1. Order placement, adjustments, follow-up
   a. Merchandise is ordered from the vendor with the approval of the store buyer.
   b. Adjustments such as returns and cancellations are handled, as

well as reorders on successful numbers and special orders. Most store buyers will send copies of their orders and reorders through the resident buyer, since this enables the market representative to keep careful checks.

    c. The resident buyer will followup the client's orders to ensure prompt delivery of merchandise.

2. Preparation for the buyer's visit

    a. The best source of merchandise is located in advance, and advice on the most favorable terms of sale and service available is provided.

    b. The resident buyer publishes a notice of the store buyer's arrival in the trade papers in advance and arranges appointments with manufacturer's representatives in the office or in vendors' showrooms.

    c. The resident buyer accompanies the store buyer on visits to vendors and manufacturers.

Figure 4.2. A market representative may arrange for store buyers to view a manufacturer's showing. (Courtesy of Pacific Northwest Apparel Association, the NAWCAS Guild.)

    d. The office provides office facilities for store buyers when they are in the market; this includes telephone service, mail service, a telephone message center, and secretarial help.

3. Ordering for stores
    a. The resident buyer may be called upon to handle "open-to-buy" for the client stores. The store buyer sends in an open order to the resident buyer, which specifies price lines and the amount of money to be spent. However, the choice of the resource and of the type of merchandise is left to the resident buyer's judgment.
    b. To do this successfully, the resident buyer must be familiar with the retail store, the type of merchandise it sells, and its particular merchandising problems.

4. Group buying. The resident buying office, because of its many market contacts, is able to arrange for some or all of the member stores to participate in group buying. *Group buying* is a method of buying in which a number of stores participate to secure better prices, ensure high standards of quality, and obtain goods more readily. For example, the resident buyer will notify its member stores of an opportunity to make a group buy. Store buyers will meet with the resident buyer and discuss the price and quality of the merchandise available, determine consumer needs, consider the manufacturer's specifications, and analyze how the merchandise is best suited to the needs of the individual store. Each store will decide whether or not it wishes to go along with the group; however, it usually is advantageous to do so.

5. Central buying
    a. The resident buying office may organize a form of central buying for certain lines of merchandise, for example, women's sportswear. Figure 4.3 illustrates how a resident buying office will assist the buyer of moderately-priced sportswear in purchasing goods.
    b. In central buying, the small independent store is provided with an opportunity to be competitive with large chain operations offering similar merchandise. For example, the resident buyer will send a few pieces of merchandise to each of the member stores. In turn, the stores will report on how the merchandise is selling. The resident buyer, through an efficient system of unit control, can quickly spot trends, facilitate reorders, and determine which pieces of merchandise are not selling.
    c. Under this arrangement the retail store buyer turns over buying authority to the resident office buyer.

6. Private branding
    a. Many resident buying offices have developed private branding programs to assist their member stores to meet competition and provide store individuality.
    b. The resident buyer will work closely with a committee of store

buyers who have developed specifications for the product under consideration.

    c. The resident buyer has the responsibility for finding the best resource, having samples made, and communicating any necessary changes.

    d. Once the item is approved, the resident buyer will make suggestions for store advertising and promotion.

7. Jobbing service

    a. Some resident buying offices provide a jobbing service whereby they make purchases, usually of staple items, in their own name and warehouse the merchandise.

    b. The merchandise is then shipped to the client stores on request, or perhaps dropped-shipped directly from the manufacturer to the store.

    c. The resident buyer will sell the merchandise to its client stores at a nominal profit. In some cases nonmember stores are permitted to take advantage of this service for a fee.

    d. The jobbing service provides an opportunity for off-season purchases and quantity purchases, the savings from which are passed on to the member stores.

8. Purchasing service

    a. Quantities of goods are purchased by the resident buyer at special price concessions on overstocks or on merchandise lines that have been reduced.

    b. This type of merchandise is usually used by a retail store for special promotion activities.

    c. A great deal of cooperation is required between the resident buyer and the store buyer for the purchasing service to be successful.

Promotion Function

The promotion function assists the store buyer in selling the merchandise by:

1. Providing buyer information

    a. The resident buying office keeps its stores informed of market developments through periodic reports and bulletins.

    b. Reports may forecast fashion trends, styles, colors, and fabrics for the coming season, closeouts and job lots, promotional items and best sellers.

    c. The report may be given orally at meetings held by the resident office for buyers of fashion accessories, men's wear, children's wear, etc., or it may take the form of an attractive booklet that is sent to the stores in advance of the season.

2. Promotion of goods

    a. A buying office may work out arrangements with manufacturers to sell certain styles exclusively to member stores.

Figure 4.3. The merchandising function will assist the store buyer in obtaining merchandise. A resident buying office may organize a form of central buying for certain lines of merchandise—for example, women's sportswear. The resident buying office will provide market information to the buyer of moderately-priced sportswear to assist in decision making. (Courtesy of Frederick Atkins, Inc.)

FREDERICK **Atkins**, INC

●*READY-TO-WEAR*

TO: BUYER – MODERATE SPORTSWEAR

COPY TO: MERCHANDISE MANAGER – READY-TO-WEAR

FROM: PENNY DOLARA
              ETHEL NEWBOLD

Route to:	

MARKET NEWS

WHAT'S SELLING?

I. COORDINATES – Spring basic Polyester groups has proven once again to be of major importance. Reorders are being placed on:

    1. Russ Togs – Active group   #4440R.
    2. Queen Casuals – Polyester Enclosure group   #100R
    3. Fire Islander –Polyester Yellow/Black/White group   #5100R

For the updated missy customer, 'What's Happening' Cotton patchwork group in natural, #038R, has received great over-the-counter action. Strong reorders are being placed.

II. SEPARATES – HOT SELLERS

    1. Jumpsuits from Ira Joyce. Their Calcutta zip front belted jumpsuit – #25301/$14.75, continues to receive super reorders. The look is great for your updated department.

    2. Sweaters – The best sellers are wraps in short and long sleeve, in solid, stripe and Aztec prints. The already proven multi color stripe pullovers continue to receive super reaction. The latest look in sweaters are Ponchos. Penrose's Aztec print poncho, #751/$12.75 has just started to check. Reorders are being placed.

    3. Tee Tops are selling and selling. The basic in Cotton, Polyester and Nylon with muscle and short sleeve are the best sellers. Also checking are the lace and embroidered trim tees.

    4. Big Tops and Tunics are just beginning to check. The belted look in stripes and solid gauzes are the major sellers.

    5. Pants – Polyester basic pants continue to be the top seller with continued interest in Calcutta. For Spring/Summer Chino and Duck cloth have great selling potential for the updated missy customer.

RESOURCE: IRA JOYCE
1407 Broadway

Sizes: 8 – 16
Colors: Natural, Peach,
Lilac, Powder Blue

#25302
$14.75

Delivery: A/R complete
4 weeks

b. This merchandise may be used for store promotions, special sale days, or special events.

c. Since this merchandise was purchased at a lower cost, the goods may be sold at lower prices and thus entice people into the store for the sale. Figure 4.4 is an example of promotion information provided a home-smallwares division in a department store.

3. Preparation of advertising

a. Promotional departments of the resident buying office will assist their stores in planning and executing promotional events.

b. The resident buying office will provide suggested advertising calendars, prepare illustrations, write copy, and suggest interior and window displays.

Figure 4.4. (Courtesy of Frederick Atkins, Inc.)

FREDERICK

Atkins, INC.

● *HOME SMALLWARES*

TO: BUYER—LUGGAGE

COPY TO: MERCHANDISE MANAGER—HOME SMALLWARES

Route to:

HOLIDAY "TRI—STRIPE"

JANUARY — PROMOTION

Holiday Luggage has announced their January promotion on the Holiday "Tri—Stripe" deluxe nylon series. The attached catalog sheet will show the new color combination of black with tan trim and the original combination of navy with red trim.

A 12" petite tote (JL12) and a cosmetic case (JL14) have been added to the collection since the consumer demand for these items is on the upswing.

We feel action should be taken on this line due to its proven success. A number of major department stores have carried this line and done extremely well with it. Recent success stories were reported by John Wanamaker in Philadelphia, Abraham & Strauss and Bloomingdale's in New York, Bamberger's in New Jersey, and Rich's in Atlanta.

Listed below are the regular costs and sale costs:

STYLE	DESCRIPTION	REGULAR COST	SALE COST
JL 12	Petite tote	$ 9.50	$ 8.75
JL 15	Shoulder tote bag	13.75	12.50
JL 14	Cosmetic Case	15.75	14.50
JL 22	Underseat Carry-on	15.75	14.50
JL 24	Jr. Pullman	19.75	18.30
JL 26	Pullman	21.75	20.00

c. Mailing pieces, Christmas catalogs, and special sale catalogs may be purchased from the resident buying offices at a low price, with the store's name imprinted on them.

4. Fashion service

a. Most large resident buying offices provide a fashion director and staff to supply merchandise information to soft-goods or fashion-apparel buyers. The information may be presented in the form of a fashion show, usually held during market week, or bulletins devoted to fashion trends, or color and fabric promotions may be planned with cooperating stores.

CHILDRENSWEAR ————————• from the fashion office

FREDERICK *Atkins*, INC.

Gauze top, print insert
15520/6.00
Matching calcutta cloth
pants. 33316/5.50
DALE

Gauze dress with peasant
embroidery and ric-rac
trim. 17877/6.50
TINY TOWN

Figure 4.5. A resident buying office provides a fashion director and staff who will supply merchandise information —in this case, to the buyer of children's wear. (Courtesy of Frederick Atkins, Inc.)

b. The resident buying office may offer fashion clinics twice a year to assist buyers in merchandise selection and planning and in store promotions, and to offer suggestions on fashion themes. Figures 4.5 and 4.6 illustrate the kind of fashion information provided by a resident buying office.

Research Function

The research function will assist the store buyer in obtaining up-to-date market information to aid in decision making:

1. Research and analysis
   a. Statistical information concerning economic trends, consumer buying habits, new methods of operation, and changes in market conditions is sent to the member stores to assist them in planning and in selling merchandise.
   b. The resident buying office becomes a clearinghouse of information

Figure 4.6. The fashion coordinator of a resident buying office will provide bulletins on current fashion trends—in this case, accessories—to assist the fashion-accessories buyer in planning the merchandise assortment. (Courtesy of Frederick Atkins, Inc.)

by continuously collecting data on recent federal legislation, training systems, supplier costs, manufacturer's expenses, markdowns, and other such items of interest to top management. Figure 4.7 illustrates the kind of research information provided by a resident buying office.

2. Management information. Research information may be passed on to top management through management seminars that emphasize proper operational procedure and facilitate fast, accurate decision making.

Ancillary Function

The ancillary function offers additional services to the retail buyer, which will vary with the resident buying office:

1. Buying clinics. During the mid-1970s, as a result of the fuel shortage, store buyers found it increasingly difficult to travel to the marketplace as often as they would have liked. Resident buying offices offered clinics to discuss more efficient methods of obtaining and selling merchandise. Buying clinics also assist buyers in solving merchandising problems, locating new sources of merchandise, and developing new selling techniques.

2. Divisional meetings. The scheduling of seasonal divisional merchandise meetings is a very important service to merchandisers. During these meetings the market is reviewed for new lines, special offerings, and price concessions.

3. Foreign service
   a. The resident buying office usually has a specialist who provides information on the complexities of buying abroad (see Figure 4.8).
   b. This specialist may have a display of items available from foreign sources. This gives the store buyer the opportunity to actually view and handle particular items of interest.

The services offered by the resident buying office are many and varied, depending on the nature of the buying office and the stores it represents. The major advantage is that time and money may be conserved by the retail buyer. Resident buying offices have the facilities for providing a continuous flow of market information. They have many "ears and eyes" with which to locate new merchandise, new resources, and favorable prices.[9]

The services offered by a resident buying office are many and varied. What activities are included in each of the following?	
The merchandising activity The promotion activity	The research activity The ancillary activity

Figure 4.7. The research function will assist the store buyer in obtaining up-to-date market information. The resident buying office becomes a clearinghouse of information by continuously collecting data on recent market trends of interest to client stores. (Courtesy of Frederick Atkins, Inc.)

MARKET SURVEY

STATE OF NEWBURGH INC.

At the last April market, this firm entered the Contemporary upholstered business under the "I Love You" banner.

They are now expanding this category with the addition of 4 new sofas, 2 love seats, 6 chairs and a modular sofa and love seat components.

...brics, in which colorful

...dular seating system, a ...new fabrics are included,

current selling trends

RESOURCE	STYLE/COST	DESCRIPTION	REORDERS	
Trissi	097/6.60	Polyester Ponti basic petite	A. & S.	724
			J. L. Hudson	554
			Wieboldt's	528
			Gimbels, Pa.	375
			Kaufman	138
			Meier & Frank	144
	197/6.60	Polyester Ponti basic	A. & S.	1143
			Gimbels, Pa.	975
			Wieboldt	972
			J. L. Hudson	1167
			Thalheimer's	377
			Kaufman's	224
			Meier & Frank	216
Eccobay	1200/6.25	Polyester basic pant – petite	Gimbel's, N. Y.	1212
			Rich's	1150
			Foley's	1000
			Crowley Milrun	835
			Hecht Co.	654
			Dayton Co.	522
			Sibley's	462
			Joseph Horne	360
			Wm. H. Block	304
			Shillito's	368
	1201/6.25	Polyester basic pant average	Gimbel's, N. Y.	1168
			Crowley Milner	558
			Dayton	522
			Sibley's	385
			Shillitos	368
			Jos. Horne	360
			Wm. H. Block	306
			Famous Barr	264
Pants – Polyester Knit – Fashion				
Eccobay	1210/7.75	Polyester zipper front with hidden elastic	Bamberger	673
			Famous Barr	340
			Emporium	76
	1206/7.75	Polyester tab pant with belt	J. L. Hudson	2204
			May Co., La.	400
			Bamberger's	673
			Rich's	363
			Capwell's	200
			F. R. Lazarus	225
			Milwaukee Boston stores	232
			Gimbel's, P.H.	168
			Davisons	120

Figure 4.8. The ancillary function offers additional services or assists to the retail buyer. The resident buying office usually has a specialist who provides information on the complexities of buying abroad. (Courtesy of Frederick Atkins, Inc.)

Accessories are as important as the
is a TOTAL LOOK. The LONG S
shown with everything from sweate
solid or tweed, and may match a s
Total Look, and should be include
is BODY JEWELRY, and decorativ
of Class" to sportswear, leisurewe
cuff bracelets, soft-link bracelets,
all meant to be worn in multiples.
popular, but the gold look is stagi
headwear is the finishing touch, e
tweed cap and small, soft brim lea
many with coordinated mufflers an

For Forward Fashion. . . watch for
and LESS CONSTRUCTION, as th
proportions.

GO VIA *Europa!*

The European Shape-Up

YVES ST. LAURENT
Ralph/21874/67.50
Flannel two-button
shaped suit.

YVES ST. LAURENT
St. Honore/77.50
Sharkskin shaped
three-button suit.

frederick atkins inc.

**The Responsibilities of
the Resident Buyer**

The resident buyer, much like the retail store buyer, has many responsibilities and, therefore, must develop the talent and ability to carry them out. He or she deals with many types of personalities from the member stores and must be able to get along with these people. He or she is not only constantly in touch with store buyers but also with salespeople, vendors, and manufacturers. The resident buyer must have the ability to communicate new ideas, new styles, and new fashion trends, and must possess the ability to conduct merchandising meetings that will generate the enthusiasm and interest of members. This individual usually has had a great deal of experience in the merchandising trade before embarking on a career as a resident buyer.

Chapter Summary

The resident buying office is located in a major trading area and provides highly specialized experts, called resident buyers, who work in the capacity of assistants or advisors to the stores their office represents. A great majority of the resident buying offices are located in New York City, since this city is the primary market for fashion apparel, soft goods, and related accessories, as well as for hard goods, home furnishings, and appliances. Resident buying offices are also located in Los Angeles, Chicago, Rocky Mountain, and Atlanta. There are two major classifications of resident buying offices. They are the independent office, which includes the salaried office and the merchandise broker, and the store-owned office, which includes the private office, the associate office, and the syndicated or chain-owned office. The student should review Part 1 of this chapter. A retail store buyer must be careful to select an office that will reflect his or her type of store. There are many qualifications that should be considered. The list given in "Selection of the Resident Buying Office" provides information that should be considered when selecting an office.

The organization of resident buying offices usually corresponds closely to that of the member stores. There usually are one or more buyers for each classification of merchandise. The student should review Table 4.1.

The resident buying office provides numerous services to save the store buyer time and money. These services may be classified as follows: merchandising function, promotion function, research function, and ancillary function. The student should review Table 4.2. The resident buyer, like the retail-store buyer, has many responsibilities and must develop the talent and ability to carry out those responsibilities. He or she should have a great deal of retailing experience in a particular area of expertise before embarking on a career as a resident buyer.

Trade Terminology

DIRECTIONS: Briefly explain or discuss each of the following trade terms.

1. Resident buying office
2. Resident buyer
3. Independent buying office
4. Salaried or fixed fee office
5. Commission or merchandise-broker office
6. Store-owned office
7. Private office
8. Associated buying office
9. Syndicated or chain-owned office
10. Group buying

Questions for Discussion and Review

1. Define resident buying office; resident buyer.

2. Why are the majority of resident buying offices located in New York City?

3. In what major trade market/markets would you locate if you were a resident buyer of home furnishings? Of misses' sportswear? Of furniture and furnishings? Of hardware?

4. How does the resident buying office serve as an important communications link between stores and manufacturers?

5. Why did the first resident buying office develop? Why have they continued to be so popular?

6. Explain the differences among the following: private resident buying office; merchandise broker; chain-owned office.

7. Briefly explain the differences in responsibilities between the department-store buyer and the resident buyer; between the central buyer and the resident buyer.

8. Compare the organization of the following: the chain-owned office and the associated office; the salaried office and the commission office.

9. What major types of service are provided by the resident buying office? Select one major service and explain how this service would assist the boutique buyer; the children's wear buyer of a department store; the infants and toddlers' buyer in a discount house.

10. You are considering opening a bath and linen shop. How would you go about finding a suitable resident buying office? What factors would you consider before making a decision?

Case Study Number One

Sivard's, Inc.

Sivard's, Inc. is a full-line department-store chain containing five department-store units. It is located in the southeastern part of the United States; top management operates from the main store in West Palm Beach, Florida. The organization has always been under the control of its original founders, the Sivard family. Store policies over the years have been rather conservative, and sales are beginning to decline. After a complete analysis of the buying system, it was recommended by retail specialists that Sivard's affiliate with other stores to organize a type of private buying office or form its own separate buying office. It was also recommended that Sivard's join a large resident buying office to take complete advantage of merchandise offerings in both the hard-goods and fashion-goods lines.

The board of directors have met for several months. They are convinced that they must use some type of resident buying affiliation if they are to provide a merchandise assortment that will increase sales and profits. However, they have not been able to reach a decision as to which type of resident buying office they need.

Keeping in mind that Sivard's is still controlled by a very conservative management team, what course of action would you suggest? Develop a list of alternatives. After considering all alternatives, which type of structure would you recommend? Why?

Case Study Number Two

Mr. Phillips and Laurie Jackson

Paul Phillips was the costume-jewelry buyer for Bryant's department store, which was located in a large New England city. He ran a large department in the main store and its ten branches. In fact, Bryant's was now in the process of opening its eleventh branch store.

One afternoon the resident buyer for costume jewelry, Laurie Jackson, called to inform Mr. Phillips that Dalmer Jewelry Company, one of Mr. Phillips' principal resources, was offering a new line of jewelry for $1.98 retail. She felt that this line would be excellent for the store's forthcoming pre-Christmas promotion and advised Mr. Phillips to come to the market to view it. She emphasized that Mr. Phillips should "grab hold" of the opportunity to be one of the first in the area to handle the line.

As usual, Mr. Phillips was very involved in his daily activities, and now even more so with the opening of a new branch store; however, he felt that this advice should be followed up. Laurie Jackson and he had a very good working relationship, and he had a great deal of confidence in her ability to select merchandise that met the taste and price range of Bryant's customers. Therefore, he instructed Miss Jackson to take another look at the line and, if she was still impressed with it, to place an order.

She later called Mr. Phillips to inform him that the order was placed and also provided information regarding delivery date, discounts, display fixtures, and the opportunity for a cooperative advertising arrangement.

Three weeks later the merchandise arrived from Dalmer Jewelry Company. When Mr. Phillips saw it, he was horrified. He was shocked that such junk had been ordered and immediately told his assistant to return the merchandise to the jewelry company. When Laurie Jackson was informed of this action, she argued with Mr. Phillips, insisting that the merchandise had excellent sales potential, especially if it was advertised and displayed properly. She also argued that to return the merchandise was a breach of contract and would seriously jeopardize future business dealings with the jewelry company.

If you were the resident buyer, how would you handle this situation?

Retailing Activities to Stimulate Student Interest and Participation

1. Interview a retail buyer in a department store; a chain store; a specialty store. Prepare a list of questions based on the topic "What services are offered by the resident buying office with which you are affiliated?" Are there similarities in the methods used by each? How do they differ?

2. Select three small apparel shops similar in merchandise offerings in your neighborhood and arrange an interview with the store manager. Discuss the various techniques used in selecting the merchandise assortment. What role does the resident buying office play in selection?

3. Select three small businesses that carry primarily hard goods and arrange

an interview with the store manager. Discuss the techniques used in selecting the merchandise assortment. What is the role of the resident buying office?

REFERENCES

The Retail Student's Reference Library

Been, Eugene L. "Retailing in the 1980's," *Marketing Insights,* November 18, 1968.
Belden, Donald L. *The Role of the Buyer in Mass Merchandising.* New York: Chain Store Publishing Corporation, 1971.
Brown, M. P., Applebaum, W., and Salmon, W. J. *Strategy Problems of Mass Retailers and Wholesalers.* Homewood, Ill.: Richard D. Irwin, Inc., 1970.
Butcher, Benjamin C., and McAnelly, James R. *Fundamentals of Retailing.* New York: Macmillan Company, 1973.
The Buyer's Manual. New York: National Retail Merchants Association, 1965.
China and Glassware Merchandiser. New York: National Retail Merchants Association, n.d.
A Department Store in the Classroom. Chicago: Sears, Roebuck & Company, 1969.
The Do's and Dont's of Bra and Girdle Buying. New York: The Lovable Company, n.d.
Duncan, D. J., Phillips, C. F., and Hollander, S. C. *Modern Retailing Management: Basic Concepts and Practices.* Homewood, Ill.: Richard D. Irwin, Inc., 1972.
Everhardt, Richard. *Men's Furnishings.* Columbus: Distributive Education Materials Laboratory, 1971.
Fashion Buyer. Indianapolis: ITT Educational Publishing Company, n.d.
Fashion Merchandising. Albany: State University of New York Press, 1969
Fried, Eleanor. *Is the Fashion Business Your Business?* New York: Fairchild Publications, Inc., 1970.
Fundamentals of Men's Wear Retailing. New York: Fairchild Publications, Inc., 1972.
Hartley, Robert F. *Retailing Challenge and Opportunity.* Boston: Houghton Mifflin Company, 1975.
Hoffman, E., Buck, E. F., and Small, V. *Fairchild's Dictionary of Home Furnishings.* New York: Fairchild Publications, Inc., 1972.
How to Buy Sheets and Pillow Cases. New York: Consumer Buying Series, n.d.
How to Select A Resident Buying Office. Washington, D.C.: U. S. Government Printing Office, n.d.
James, Don L., Walker, Bruce J., and Etzel, Michael J. *Retailing Today.* New York: Harcourt Brace Jovanovich, Inc., 1975.
Judelle, B., and Troxell, M. *Fashion Merchandising.* Hightstown: Gregg/McGraw-Hill Book Company, 1971.
Leather Sales Tactics. New York: Leather Industries of America, n.d.
Levine, Albert R. *How to Sell Domestics and Linens.* New York: Fairchild Publications, Inc. 1962.
Menswear. Austin: University of Texas Press, 1970.
Phelon, J. S. *Phelon's Resident Buyers Book.* New York: Phelon-Sheldon Publications, Inc., 1963.
Profitable Merchandising Techniques. New York: Fairchild Publications, Inc., 1970.
Promoting New Merchandise Areas. New York: Fairchild Publications, Inc., 1971.
Reich, E., Feldman, R. Q., and Levy, L. *Basic Retailing and Distribution.* New York: Pitman Publishing Corporation, 1970.
Siber, Alan. *A Complete Guide To Retail Management.* Baltimore: Penguin Books, Inc., 1972.
Slom, Stanley. *How To Sell Furniture.* New York: Fairchild Publications, Inc. 1971.

References

1. Adele C. Elgart, "The Contribution of the Resident Buying Office," in *The Buyer's Manual* (New York: National Retail Merchants Association, 1965), p. 400–1.
2. *How to Select a Resident Buying Office* (Washington, D.C.: U.S. Government Printing Office, n.d.), p. 1.
3. Ibid., p. 2.
4. "Amc's Power on 7th Avenue: Peanuts or High Pressure?" *Women's Wear Daily,* April 27, 1964, pp. 1–18.
5. Elgart, "Contribution of the Resident Buying Office," p. 400.
6. B. Butcher and J. R. McAnelly, *Fundamentals of Retailing* (New York: Macmillan Company, 1973), p. 257.
7. *How to Select a Resident Buying Office,* p. 2.
8. Ibid., p. 3
9. Elgart, "Contribution of the Resident Buying Office," p. 400.

The Merchandise Assortment

The Importance of Fashion

5

Performance Objectives

PERFORMANCE
OBJECTIVES

As a result of reading this chapter the student should be able to accomplish the following:

1. Define: fashion, style, fad, silhouette, detail, good taste, classic, haute couture.

2. Explain how fashions differ, according to: age groups, geographic location, ethnic groups, vocational or occupational groups.

3. Discuss human tendencies that condition fashion.

4. Explain the reasons for changes in fashion.

5. Illustrate the six stages every fashion passes through as it rises in response to consumer demand and then eventually declines.

6. Explain how fashion coordination is organized in the chain store, the department store, the boutique, the specialty store, the small shop, and the resident buying office.

7. Outline the merchandising responsibilities of the fashion coordinator.

8. Define: fashion department; fashion trend.

9. Discuss the role of the buyer in fashion coordination.

10. Outline the activities that should be considered by the fashion coordinator when planning a store's fashion calendar.

The Importance of Fashion

The Language of Fashion

The fashion director for a leading department store was asked, "What departments within a retail store are influenced by fashion?" Reply: "All departments."

A knowledge of fashion is of vital importance to the retail buyer, since all merchandise lines are affected in one way or another by the fashion influences of the time. Fashion is everywhere. It is found in the clothing apparel industry (the most obvious representative of fashion influences), in home furnishings, in appliances, in automobiles, in education, and in recreation, to name but a few.

Fashion has existed since the beginning of time. When man first added colored beads and fancy ornaments to his wardrobe of hides and skins, he was,

Figure 5.1. Fashion has existed since the beginning of time. . . .

perhaps, feeling a desire for change; he wanted to try something new; he was giving way to the fundamental human desire for originality. If this early caveman was a leader among his tribesmen, he was emulated and copied by the members of his village. Thus he became a "fashion leader."[1]

Fashion is a powerful force that affects us not only as individuals but also as members of society. It satisfies our desire for conformity, for status and prestige, for security, and for distinctiveness. Since fashion influences what we wear, what we eat and drink, the way we decorate our homes, and the environment in which we live, it is important to understand the workings of fashion. The purpose of Part 1 of this chapter will be to (1) outline and explain basic fashion terminology, (2) discuss why fashions change, and (3) discuss fashion origins and trends. Part 2 will discuss (1) who is responsible for fashion coordination, (2) how fashion coordination is organized in different types of retail stores, (3) the role of the buyer in fashion coordination, and (4) planning the fashion season.

Basic Fashion Terminology

In studying such a complex and exciting topic as fashion the student needs to be aware of the various terms that are used over and over within the retail trade. Such terms may seem simple, yet their use by different people at different times may affect their meanings. If the student is to acquire an understanding of fashion, he must learn the following basic terminology. Basic fashion terminology includes: (1) fashion, (2) style, (3) fad, (4) silhouette, (5) detail, (6) good taste, (7) classic, and (8) haute couture.[2]

Fashion

Fashion may be defined as a distinctive method of expression that has been accepted and adopted by a number of people as the result of common thought. It is what the majority of people have accepted at a given time in a particular consumer market.

Fashion is not a universal phenomena. What is accepted as a fashion in one geographic area is not necessarily a fashion in another geographic area and perhaps is not even acceptable. For example, the short skirt of the 1960s was

Figure 5.2. Fashion is everywhere. Different fashions exist for different age groups. Fashion may be found in apparel and accessories for children, juniors, women, and men. (Courtesy of Frederick Atkins, Inc.) See facing page.

Fashion is not universal.

Fashions differ according to:

1. Geographic location
2. Age groups
3. Ethnic groups
4. Occupational or vocational groups

Juniors

Flannel BigTop with shoulder tucking and cinch belt, corduroy pants.
GLENORA

Womenswear

The layered dress, this one a gentle smock in rust "suede", worn over a giant hooded turtleneck sweater.
CONCEPT V11

Childrenswear

Patch print tuck front dress.
BOW AGE

Multi-patch crawler and hooded jacket.
THOMAS TEXTILES

Menswear

ARTHUR RICHARDS SPORT
Bush/35.00
Poplin Bush Coat, flannel lining.

frederick atkins inc.

popular with women in most metropolitan cities; however, in more conservative areas of the country women wanted longer skirt lengths.

Different fashions exist for different age groups (see Figure 5.2). For
example, during the early 1970s some prevailing styles in the youth market
were the ankle-length skirt, argyle knee socks, raglan-sleeved sweaters, and
high platform shoes. Mature women, on the other hand, found conformity and
self-assurance in pantsuits, the double-breasted blazer, body shirts, and medi-
um-heeled shoes. The coordinated look of the pantsuit, worn with a variety
of accessories and accented with interesting color combinations, was so popular that it has since found a place in the wardrobes of the career woman, the
housewife, and the mother.

The menswear industry has also experienced the influence of fashion in
different consumer markets. The young men of the early 1970s were attired
in multicolored shirts accented with three-inch-wide bow ties and worn with
baggy trousers. However, businessmen of the period found the myriad colors,
textures, and accessories unacceptable to the more conservative business environment.

Not only do fashions differ according to geographic location and age
groups but also according to ethnic groups. Members of different ethnic groups
often wear clothes that are representative of their native countries. For example, the natural hair style of black people during the late 1960s, the corn-row
hair style of the early 1970s, and the caftan dress decorated with African prints
had tremendous impact on this particular ethnic consumer market. Other
ethnic fashions, such as the sari from India, the kimono from the Orient, the
fringed suede vest from the American Indian, have found their way into the
apparel trade; and their design motifs and fabrics have influenced other trades
as well. Madras fabric, batik prints, and Oriental and African designs have
been used in automobile interiors, wallpaper design, art objects, and kitchen
appliances.

Different vocational or occupational groups, such as students, teachers,
hairdressers, doctors, and lawyers, have been influenced by fashion. Cotton
denim jeans have dominated the college campuses of the 1970s. Jeans or
denims have been tie-dyed and bleached, patched and embroidered, and stud-
ded with rhinestones.

Since different groups have different fashion tastes, fashions may be divided according to the group to which they appeal. Therefore, *high fashion*
may be defined as high-priced fashion, usually created by a famous designer,
in limited editions and accepted by an elite group of consumers who are the
first to accept the new style. In contrast, a *mass fashion* is a style or design
that is mass-produced at a moderate price and is widely accepted by the
majority of consumers.

Being "in fashion" indicates conformity, social adaptation, and a certain
feeling of superiority or self-assurance. Fashion helps the individual to fulfill
many emotional and practical needs. Fashion is influenced by such aspects of

Figure 5.3. Fashions will differ according to ethnic groups. A fashion popular with black women is the African print worn with the wrapped turban. (Photograph by Steve Hawkins.)

human behavior as the desire to be alike and the tendencies to act in common, to have the same or similar tastes, to have similar instincts or desires, and to respond in similar ways to the same impulses.

Fashion, therefore, has the power to satisfy many of the buying motives that you will study in detail in Chapter 6, "Understanding the Retail Consumer."

Human characteristics that influence fashion
1. The desire to be alike
2. The tendency to act in common
3. The tendency to have the same or similar tastes
4. The tendency to have similar instincts or desires
5. The tendency to respond in similar ways to the same impulses

Style

Since fashion is an art form, *Style* may be defined as the characteristic of one fashion that makes it different from another. Style is the distinctive quality of an art form that makes it different from other art forms in the same category.

There are styles in architecture, styles in home furnishings, styles in writing, and styles in speech. A fashion style is distinctive enough to express the tastes and feelings of the majority of people and to become associated with a particular fashion period. For example, dresses worn by women during the early 1970s were worn in various lengths, ranging from floor length to six inches above the knee. Skirt styles included the wraparound skirt, the accordion-pleated skirt, the bias-cut skirt. Each was a different fashion style that appealed to a variety of consumer markets.

Since styles are often associated with a particular fashion period, their return as a fashion influence is often recognized. For example, the flapper style of the 1920s with the skirt worn above the knee influenced fashion again during the mid-1960s. However, *it is important to remember that when a style returns to a new fashion period, some details of the style are changed to meet the needs and tastes of the new period in which it appears.* Also, unless the style is accepted and adopted by a number of people, it is not a fashion. For instance, a style adopted by you or me alone has no influence on fashion.[3]

Fad

Fad may be defined as a minor fashion that has been adopted by a group of people for a short period of time. A fad is usually taken up with exaggerated zeal and quickly abandoned. Fads, like fashion, have also invaded every field. There are fads in children's toys (skate boards), in furniture (the water bed), and in works of art (pop art). For brief periods of·time we are interested in pet rocks and mood rings, such hobbies as macramé and decoupage, and natural foods. Then we lose interest and go on to cross-country skiing, karate, quadraphonic sound, or acupuncture.

The youth market is especially vulnerable to fads, since fads originate as novelty fashions that stimulate and excite the young consumer. In recent years, we've had fads of Mickey Mouse wrist watches, rhinestone-studded T-shirts, bubble umbrellas, and hotpants.

Many fashions that begin as fads continue for many seasons. The length of time the fad is popular is dependent upon (1) the type of fad, (2) the market to which it appeals, (3) the amount of market saturation that has occurred, and (4) the strength of other fads prevalent at the time. *What is important to remember, however, is that a fashion is far-reaching and includes many consumer markets, whereas that which is insignificant and includes few consumer markets is a fad.*

How long is a fad popular?	
It depends on:	
1. Type of fad	3. Amount of market saturation
2. The market	4. Strengths of other popular fads

Silhouette

The overall shape or contour of a costume is called the *silhouette.* It is the basic ingredient that changes slightly with each new season. The silhouette or general outline of both men's and women's garments is one of the dictates of fashion that progresses from one standard of beauty to another over a period of from five to ten years (see Figure 5.4). Silhouette is also revealed in home furnishings, in which it seems to last for several years, and in architecture, where the popularity of particular shapes or silhouettes may last for decades.

Shetland and rayon pullover worn over tweed turtleneck and divided skirt. CAROL HORN'S HABITAT

THE BIG BUILD-UP

Wool flannel jumper worn over plaid cotton flannel blouse. BEENE BAG

frederick atkins inc.

Figure 5.4. The overall shape or contour of a costume is called the silhouette. It is the basic ingredient that changes slightly with each new season. (Courtesy of Frederick Atkins, Inc.)

It is oftentimes difficult to determine the start of a particular fashion silhouette, since its beginnings are almost always overlapped by preceding fashions and its endings are lost in the oncoming new fashion wave. For example, the fashion tendency to shorter skirts was apparent during the 1920s. However, the movement was influenced twenty-five years previously with the growing popularity of the bicycle in about 1895. Bicycling costumes for women had skirts shortened to provide utility and comfort. Such costumes soon led to the development of "short," comfortable walking skirts. The mod period of the mid-1960s also gave us the short-skirt silhouette, with skirts ranging in length from the micro-mini to the midi-length of the 1970s. In recent years, because of technological innovations and numerous external environmental influences, the time-period of a silhouette has become shortened, in the apparel industry and in other industries as well.

Detail

The design lines that are held within the silhouette are the *details* of the silhouette (see Figure 5.5). The features or cut of the design may include waist, neckline, or bodice treatment and trimmings and decoration. These individual segments that make up the silhouette may gradually lead to changes in silhouette. For example, skirt lengths in the mid-1960s were extreme in brevity, to the point where the silhouette reversed itself and lengths dropped to the ankle during the early 1970s. Such changes are predictable; however, the time period involved and the particular markets that will be affected are oftentimes unpredictable. For example, women wore ankle-length skirts and skirts three to six inches above the knee during the day. During the 1970s short skirts were predicted for evening wear. As a result, long skirts were worn to the office, while short dresses were worn to the theater. The silhouette was beginning to reverse.

Variations in design line offer variety and change to both the consumer and the retail merchant. Unlimited opportunities for individuality may be offered to the customer, while the retailer is able to meet competition by offering many variations of an accepted fashion silhouette.

Good Taste

Good taste is essential to an understanding of fashion. *Good taste* implies a knowledge of the proper use of materials, design, and color. For some people good taste comes naturally, while other people may have to learn or struggle to attain it.

Good taste may be influenced by common sense. Good taste is understanding of when and where it is appropriate to wear a fashion, as well as of the correct way to accessorize the garment. Good taste is a concept that changes from year to year; consequently, it is necessary to recognize such changes within the retail environment as well as changes within ourselves.

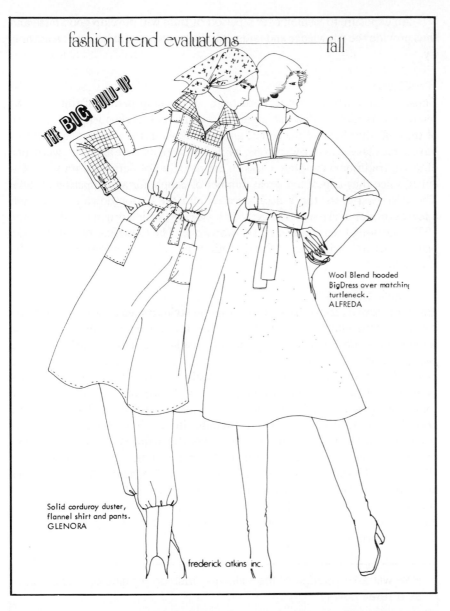

fashion trend evaluations————fall

THE BIG BUILD-UP

Wool Blend hooded
BigDress over matching
turtleneck.
ALFREDA

Solid corduroy duster,
flannel shirt and pants.
GLENORA

frederick atkins inc.

Figure 5.5. The design lines that are held within the silhouette are the details of the silhouette. (Courtesy of Frederick Atkins, Inc.)

What is considered in good taste one year may be considered the wrong thing or in poor taste another year. For example, a new style is considered daring when first introduced; therefore, it may be in doubt in considerations of good taste. The more people who accept the style and the more "fashionable" it becomes, the more it will be considered in good taste.

An exposure to fashion over a period of time will develop good taste and thus provide the knowledge and understanding necessary to become an authority.

Classic

Those styles which remain in good taste over a long period of time may be referred to as *classic.* Minor changes may occur, such as skirt length, the width of the cuff, the shape of the collar, and variations in the neckline. Most of us have some classics in our wardrobe, while others of us have an entire wardrobe of basic, traditional clothing. Classics are usually not derived from fad influences, since they appeal to a great number of people for a long period of time. The shirtwaist dress, the V-neck sweater, and the button-down shirt are but a few examples of classics. The crewneck sweater, which originated during the 1920s, has long been a classic of the wardrobe. The crewneck returned to the fashion picture during the 1970s with minor neckline variations influenced by the period.

Haute Couture

Haute couture refers to an expensive original style created by a French fashion designer or manufacturer in limited editions for a group of people considered leaders of fashion. Such designs are usually in advance of mass-market fashions and, therefore, appeal to a limited number or elite group of fashion-conscious people. The retail buyer is usually interested in viewing the couture openings in Paris and other European cities, since high fashion is representative of something new and different. However, many high-fashion designs usually never become accepted as mass-merchandise items, since they are usually far in advance of the needs, wants, and desires of the majority of fashion consumers. For example, the French designer Courrèges influenced the look of the 1960s with the short white boots that he designed. Madame Chanel gave us her famous "Chanel suit"; Yves Saint-Laurent gave us the "Crusader Cross." Bill Blass, Bonnie Cashin, Betsy Johnson, and many other American designers have a tremendous influence on the American mass market, perhaps more so than the European designers.

How will a knowledge of the following fashion terminology help you as a retail buyer?

Fashion	Detail
High fashion	Good taste
Mass fashion	Classic
Style	Haute couture
Fad	Silhouette

Fashion, as stated previously, is conditioned by the human tendencies to be alike, to act in common, to have the same or similar tastes, to have similar instincts or desires, and to respond in similar ways to the same impulses. A question that should be considered at this point is, "What causes changes in fashions?" Why are short white boots fashionable during one period and out of fashion the next? Social historians relate that fashion in clothing and accessories, home furnishings, food and drink, and other merchandise classifications reflects the economic, political, and social feelings of the time. That we as consumers create a fashion by accepting it; and we end or cause a fashion to change by rejecting what we actively dislike. For example, most women refused to accept the midi-length style created by designers during the early 1970s. As a result, manufacturers were forced to abandon the style and continue to produce shorter lengths. Reasons for changes in fashion, therefore, may be classified as follows: (1) boredom, (2) outstanding and dominating events, (3) dominating ideals, and (4) dominating social groups.[4]

Reasons for fashion change
1. Boredom 2. Outstanding and dominating events 3. Dominating ideals 4. Dominating social groups

Boredom

The most simple explanation for desiring something new in fashion is boredom. We become tired of looking at the same old thing hanging in the closet or on the wall or furnishing the dining room. In other words, we find those sensations tiring that are constantly experienced. Clothing that has been worn throughout a season has tired the senses of sight and touch and has aesthetically fatigued the wearer. Fashion designers continue to create styles or variations of styles that cause already existing fashions to become obsolete and tiresome. Naturally, a demand for something new develops. Expensive items (and the definition of expensive depends on our own value concepts) will remain fashionable longer than inexpensive items. Accessory items are usually worn more often and, therefore, we grow tired of them sooner. Shoes, jewelry, ties, shirts, hats, scarves, sweaters—the list is unending—are worn frequently and soon become monotonous and uninteresting.

Another consideration that affects the development of boredom is that apparel and accessories of bright colors, busy or outstanding designs, popular or "in" fabrics, will bore or fatigue the wearer sooner than muted or soft colors, fabrics, and textures will.

Outstanding and Dominating Events

Examples of outstanding and dominating events that may influence the character and direction of fashion movements may be events such as wars, world's fairs, art exhibits, technological innovations, and scientific explorations, to name but a few.

The Vietnam conflict influenced the fashion industry with jump suits, battle jackets, and bullet belts. The space explorations of the 1960s and early 1970s gave us shiny metallic fabrics, brightly colored geometric-shaped jewelry, and bubble silhouetted hats and helmets. The moon walk influenced furniture departments to display transparent tables and chairs in a variety of colors and patterns. Art exhibitions influence fabric designs, the use of texture, and new color combinations.

All phases of retailing are affected by such occurrences. The meat shortage of the 1970s created a demand for fish-poaching pans and other types of gourmet cooking utensils. The fuel shortage of the mid-1970s encouraged the manufacture of small economy cars by the automobile industry. Thus, the fashionable autos of the time became American Motors' Pacer, Ford's Maverick, Chevrolet's Chevette, and Cadillac's Seville.

Dominating Ideals

Ideals or philosophies that tend to blend the thoughts and actions of a large number of people also affect fashion movements. Many examples of people's ideals during the 1960s may be cited. President John Kennedy emphasized youth, physical fitness, and freedom. Such ideals were reflected in youthful looking styles in men's and women's apparel, in homes with brightly colored appliances and gayly printed wallpaper. The Vietnam conflict generated ideals of love and peace. Lovebeads, smocked dresses, sandals, and long hair—all portrayed the feeling of freedom and the urge to "do your own thing."

Women's greater activity outside the home affected the textile industry's successful development of carefree, drip-dry, wrinkle-resistant fabrics. The food industry capitalized on this movement with advertisements of timesaving convenience foods. Not only were the textile industry and the food industry influenced by the new role of women but the garment, automobile, appliance, and home furnishings industries also geared themselves to producing an easy, free environment for the working mother and wife.

The environmental crisis of the 1970s and the problems with air pollution, noise pollution, water pollution, and energy shortages had an effect on fashion. Among other things, the use of recycled paper in magazines and books, increased interest in electric-battery-powered automobiles, and a return to use of natural fibers were brought about by the rising respect for the natural environment.

Dominating Social Groups

Society is dominated by particular groups of people or fashion leaders who influence the rest of society. Such groups may include a particular economic group, such as the very wealthy. Normally, new styles first appear among the wealthy, then filter down to the lower income levels. Because of complex, advanced marketing systems and well-developed techniques in mass-production, fashions of quality are made available to all consumer markets in a wide range of prices.

Other groups who influence fashion may be of a religious, ethnic, or political nature. Today, many fashions start among young people, who influence their elders. For instance, the youth market influenced the automobile industry in its choice of such names as "Pinto," "Charger," and "Maverick." The buyer, manufacturer, and designer need to be constantly alert to those fashion leaders who inspire fashion trends.

Fashion Trends

What happens to a fashion after one season? two seasons? a year? Does it return to fashion? Do we ever see it again? Such questions are often asked, and the best way to answer them is to study the trends in fashion. A *fashion trend* is the direction in which a style or fashion is moving. Fashions move continuously through their life cycles at varying, individual speeds. The art of predicting what the current fashions are, estimating how popular they are, and estimating future demands requires careful recognition of fashion trends.

Every fashion passes through definite stages as it rises in response to consumer demand and then eventually declines. Fashion goes through a series of six stages to complete a "life cycle." The stages are: (1) the rise of a fashion, (2) acceptance or rejection, (3) style becomes popular, (4) mass production, (5) decline in popularity, and (6) fashion abandonment. This life cycle may be called the *fashion cycle*[5] (see Figure 5.6).

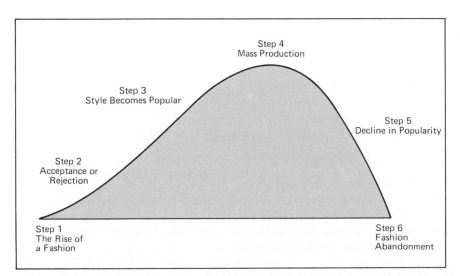

Figure 5.6. The life cycle of a fashion. Source: Wingate, J. W. and Weiner, J. D. *Retail Merchandising* (Cincinnati: South-Western Publishing Company, 1963), p. 177.

Feminine apparel and accessories have a high fashion turnover. Consumer appeal, price, and aesthetic qualities all affect how fast a style will pass through each stage. For example, some fashions are abandoned shortly after they are introduced and never reach the mass consumer market. Fashions in accessory items, such as jewelry, scarves, and handbags, have short life cycles. Styles of suits, coats, and jackets may appeal to consumers for longer periods of time. Home furnishings, appliances, and linens, as well as other products, follow the same cycle; however, the length of the fashion cycle may be a year or longer because of the nature of the goods. The life cycles of fashions in carpeting, china, glassware, utensils, and upholstered goods may take several years to complete.

Steps in the Fashion Cycle

Step 1—The Rise of a Fashion

Where do fashions originate? Fashions begin with designers or manufacturers, who are usually the first to introduce the new fashion influence. New designs may be presented at the European couture openings; however, since the fashion life expectancy in the market is still untried, these fashions are very expensive.

Step 2—Acceptance or Rejection

Once the styles are introduced to manufacturers, decisions are made concerning the style, color, or texture that will appeal to a majority of people. Acceptance of the design by an increasing number of people will lead to steadily increasing sales. Rejection of the design is evidenced by a lack of sales.

Step 3—Style Becomes Popular

After the style has been accepted in the marketplace, its popularization with consumers follows rapidly. The fashion is in demand. Buyers will place their orders with those manufacturers who are able to supply the merchandise quickly.

Step 4—Mass Production

As a result of consumer demand, certain styles are mass-produced by the manufacturers. Once the fashion is mass-produced, it is mass-distributed and sold at prices within reach of a majority of the people in particular consumer markets.

Step 5—Decline in Popularity

In time, consumer boredom, outstanding and dominating events, changes in ideals, and the influence of the "Beautiful People" or fashion leaders will bring about a decline in demand for the fashion. Consumers start experimenting with new styles that have been introduced.

Step 6—Fashion Abandonment

A style is totally abandoned when it is no longer manufactured and cannot be sold at any price. The item has saturated the market to the degree that it is of no interest to the consumer. As buyers would say, "You can't give it away!"

One can conclude that fashion is a never-ending, continuous process.[6] It influences the clothes we wear, when we wear them, and how we accessorize them. There are fashions in home furnishings, fashions in food, and fashions in recreational activity.

A Continuous Process

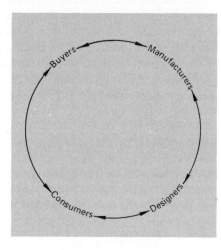

Figure 5.7. Fashion—a continuous process.

Fashion influences the designer, the manufacturer, the retail buyer, and the consumer. We all interact with one another in creating a fashion. As consumers we reveal our feelings about a particular style by buying or not buying. We learn to discriminate and compare. As retail buyers we determine whether or not particular goods will sell, depending upon consumer reactions. The retail buyer passes the information on to the manufacturer, who, in turn, communicates with the designer. The designer then creates a style that will have a psychological, aesthetic appeal to the consumer. Thus, the process begins again.

Fashion Coordination in Retail Stores

PART 2

A *fashion department* may be defined as a department that sells masculine or feminine outer apparel and accessories. The merchandise offerings of a fashion department must be timed to coincide with peak fashion demands if the merchandise is to sell. Not only must fashion departments be coordinated with each other but also with departments not usually considered "fashion departments; for example, children's clothing and intimate apparel must offer merchandise of the "right type." This takes a great deal of teamwork and coordination. If the store's customers are to be able to find fashionable merchandise, a store must provide a suitable merchandise assortment, adequately train salespeople to sell fashion goods, effectively display and advertise the merchandise, and offer promotional events that will develop a favorable store image. The individual usually responsible for such activities is called a fashion coordinator. Therefore, a *fashion coordinator* may be defined as an individual who is responsible for promoting the sale of fashion merchandise throughout the entire store.[7] Since a store's fashion story must be carried to the merchandise manager, who, in turn, passes the information down to the buyer and his assistant and so to the salespeople, it is important to consider the various duties and responsibilities of the fashion coordinator.[8]

Responsibilities of a fashion coordinator
1. Analyze current fashion trends in terms of the store's merchandising policies, fashion image, and customers.
2. Be aware of fashion trends in the store's immediate trade area, as well as of those across the country and abroad.
3. Attend fashion shows presented by manufacturers and fashion designers in the major national markets as well as abroad, if the budget permits.
4. Alert the merchandise managers, retail buyers, and other store executives to up-and-coming fashion influences as well as to those fashions no longer considered popular.
5. Correctly interpret fashion trends in relation to the needs of individual store buyers.
6. Assist store buyers in coordinating their merchandise offerings with those of other departments of the store.
7. Promote fashion throughout the store through fashion-show presentations, news bulletins, and attractive displays.
8. Continuously visit all major markets to get a clear picture of currently popular fashions.
9. Maintain close contacts with textile and accessory representatives to obtain opinions about upcoming trends.
10. Regularly visit the offices of trade publications and consumer fashion magazines.
11. Conduct merchandising seminars to explain the store's fashion calendar and upcoming promotional events.
12. Work with merchandise managers and buyers in planning the store's seasonal fashion themes.
13. Maintain close contacts with fashion coordinators from other retail stores and resident buying offices.
14. Promote the store's fashion image by conducting fashion shows and fashion seminars for sales personnel as well as for store customers.
15. Promote the store's fashion image by conducting out-of-store fashion shows for charitable organizations, women's groups, and high schools and colleges.

Regardless of the size or type of retail store, the objective of the fashion coordinator is the same, that of coordinating and promoting the sale of fashion merchandise throughout the entire store. However, the manner in which this objective is achieved and the methods used will vary with the store type and size. For example, the approach used in a chain operation will differ from that used in a department store, which, in turn, will differ from the approach of the boutique. Since the retail buyer is directly affected by the efforts of the fashion coordinator, the approach used in the following types of retail firms will be discussed: (1) the chain-store approach, (2) the department-store approach, (3) the boutique approach, (4) the specialty-store approach, (5) the small-shop approach, and (6) the resident-buying-office approach.[9]

Organizing for Fashion Coordination

The Chain-store Approach

The fashion coordinator of a large chain operation has the duty and responsibility:

1. To work closely with the firm's merchandise executives, central and regional buyers, marketing experts, and trade specialists.
2. To be responsible for market trips to both domestic and European markets to view major collections.
3. To make arrangements to purchase original designs that the coordinator feels could be incorporated into the fashion assortments to be featured by the firm.
4. To arrange to have famous fashion designers create exclusive models, which would eventually be manufactured by the firm under its own label.
5. To be responsible for providing current information to chain-store personnel on current trends, style changes, and future market potentials.
6. To attempt to pinpoint customer preferences as well as determine the best methods for coordinating fashion presentations in each store throughout the chain.
7. To insure that fashion merchandise will be distributed en masse on the basis of consumer interest, good taste, moderate price, and fashion appeal.

Since the chain operation is usually national in scope, the fashion coordinator will restrict the fashion assortment to proved and accepted styles; that is, each style will be considered from the viewpoint of fashion popularity, quality, price, and whether or not it will meet the fashion image projected by the store. The fashion coordinator of large chain operations has recognized the power of fashion and its ability to move huge volumes of apparel and accessories. Evidence of this is revealed in the catalogs of large chain operations, such as J. C. Penney Company, Montgomery Ward and Company, and Sears,

Roebuck and Company, who have made tremendous efforts toward upgrading both the breadth and quality of their fashion assortments and, thus, their images as fashion stores.

The Department-store Approach

The fashion coordinator in a department store also has an awesome job, which, however, does not require as much experience or training as the job of fashion coordinator in a large chain operation. The fashion coordinator of a department store may have been a former buyer or a former assistant to a large store's fashion coordinator. The department-store fashion coordinator has the responsibility:

1. To provide fashion information for the main store as well as its various branches. The fashion assortment presented in the branches must represent the fashion image of the store as a whole, as well as meet the diverse needs of consumers in the different local trade areas. To accomplish this task, the fashion coordinator will attend all market openings, both at home and abroad, maintain close contact with market specialists, and attend social gatherings usually frequented by fashion leaders to determine what is "in" for the upcoming season.
2. To carefully observe fashion trends, since any decision on trend directions will affect the development of the store's seasonal fashion themes.
3. To be responsible for (1) communicating fashion trends to store executives and buyers, (2) conducting fashion shows and merchandise seminars, (3) assisting buyers in all departments in merchandise planning, (4) working with advertising and display departments to develop store-wide fashion themes, and (5) training salespeople and new store personnel by providing pertinent fashion information about the various kinds of merchandise they have been hired to sell.

Depending on the size of the department store, the job of the fashion coordinator may be divided among several assistants, with a fashion coordinator for each major fashion division within the store. For example, a large department store may have one fashion coordinator for women's, children's, and accessories departments; another for home furnishings departments; and yet another for men's and boys' fashions. In this type of organization the store's top fashion executive is called a "fashion director" (see Figure 5.8).

The Boutique Approach

Boutique is a French word that means "shop." The boutique has come to be associated with unique and distinctive types of fashion goods usually presented in dramatic displays. Oftentimes, once a fashion offered by a boutique becomes popular, the boutique will abandon it and go on to newer fashions. The fashion

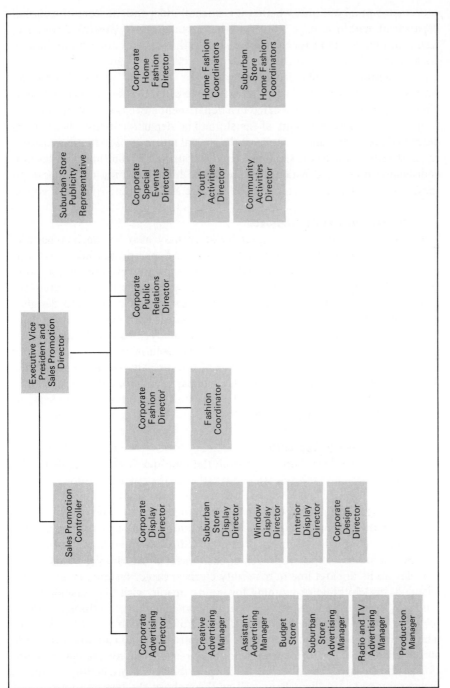

Figure 5.8. Organizational structure of the sales promotion division of a typical department store.

coordinator in a boutique, whether it is a small independent store or a special department within a large store, has the opportunity to present distinctive, well-coordinated, and expensive merchandise that consumers can purchase in a single visit. The fashion coordinator will seek apparel and accessories that are representative of the more "avant-garde" or "way-out" tastes of well-to-do women, as well as goods that represent newness, exclusiveness, and one-of-a-kind designs. The boutique located in a department store is strikingly different from other sales departments of the store. The department-store boutique is decorated and merchandised to meet the special interests of particular customers, in the same way as the small independent business is. The boutique fashion coordinator must be constantly aware of the higher fashion that appeals to these consumers and continuously seek unique and distinctive kinds of goods.

The Specialty-store Approach

The fashion coordinator of a specialty store may also be the merchandise manager of the women's apparel and accessories department who has worked up from a buyer's position and who enjoys working closely with fashion specialists. Like the fashion coordinator of larger stores, the specialty-store coordinator will visit the market centers, view manufacturer and designer collections, plan the store's fashion seasons, consult with executives and fashion buyers from other stores, and continuously analyze current fashion trends in terms of the store's merchandising policies, fashion image, and customer demand. Since the merchandise offerings of the specialty store are not as vast as those of the chain operation or the large department store, the merchandise-manager–fashion coordinator is able to offer well-stocked, well-balanced, and distinctive fashion assortments.

The Small-shop Approach

The small independent shop differs from the boutique in not being dedicated primarily to new and exclusive styles but rather to the current fashion demands of the store's clientele. The fashion coordinator of the small shop is usually the owner-manager, who is responsible for the management of the entire store as well as for the buying function. As in the boutique, the fashion coordinator of the small shop will attempt to present coordinated apparel and accessories to meet the needs of special groups of customers. For example, a small shop may devote its apparel line to maternity clothes; career fashion, country, and leisure-living clothing; or clothing for young people with high fashion tastes but ready-to-wear budgets. In this case, the owner-manager–fashion coordinator must visit local markets, attend fashion shows, consult with trade specialists, train salespeople, and be continuously aware of the fashion interests of the store's clientele. The store owner is not only responsible for the entire operation of the business but also has the responsibility for projecting the shop's fashion image to its clientele as well as throughout the community.

Figure 5.9. The fashion coordinator of the small shop is usually the owner-manager, who attempts to present coordinated apparel and accessories to meet the needs of special groups of people.

The Resident-Buying-Office Approach

As stated in Chapter 4, the resident buying office has the same or similar personnel that a retail store has. There is a buyer working with each department in the retail store; there is a merchandise manager who directs the activities of the buyers; and there is a fashion coordinator who pulls together all fashion activities of the resident buying office and its member stores. The fashion coordinator is sometimes called the fashion director in a resident buying office, and is solely responsible for covering the ready-to-wear, the sportswear, the casual, and the accessories markets. Therefore, the coordinator may have a number of assistants to help cover the numerous and varied markets. It is the fashion director's duty:

1. To bring together the entire fashion operation through careful planning, organizing, researching, and follow-through.
2. To coordinate the buyer's efforts for both the resident buying office and its member stores.
3. To act as a clearinghouse for fashion information regarding current fashion trends, colors, popular fabrics and textures, silhouettes, and styles (see Figure 5.10).

Figure 5.10. The fashion coordinator of a resident buying office will supply its client stores with current fashion news. (Courtesy of Frederick Atkins, Inc.)

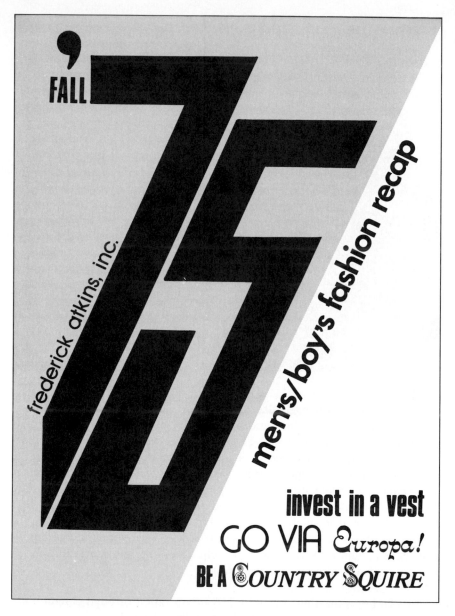

4. To be responsible for arranging fashion shows for the major seasons: a January fashion show to present spring merchandise, and a June fashion show to present fall fashions.
5. To discuss with individual buyers the fashion trends and promotions for the coming season.

6. To visit textile mills, fabric houses, and manufacturers to determine the most popular fashion trends.
7. To send fashion bulletins to member stores containing information on selling techniques, fashion forecasts, the best fashion sellers, new display techniques, fashion show themes, important fashion accessories, and fashions that are slow sellers.

The fashion coordinator of a resident buying office is usually a seasoned buyer or merchandiser and has had a wealth of experience in the retailing business.

In each of the following stores the fashion coordination approach differs. In what respects do they differ? What are their similarities?

The department store	The small shop
The boutique	The resident buying office
The specialty store	The chain store

The Role of the Buyer in Fashion Coordination

Unlike buyers in large, departmentalized stores, fashion buyers in small stores are responsible for merchandising several related classifications of merchandise. A single buyer may have to purchase goods for several accessory departments, for example, jewelry and belts; wigs, scarves, and hats; ties and socks. In a large chain operation several buyers may be responsible for buying fashion accessories. For example, there may be separate buyers for jewelry, for scarves and neckwear, for rainwear, for wigs and hairpieces, and so on. The fashion buyer must plan purchases, promotions, displays, and special sales events.

Special problems arise in buying fashion merchandise. How long customers will continue to purchase certain fashions or fads is oftentimes a guess. As a result of the unpredictable tastes of the retail consumer, the individual fashion buyer must work with market specialists, especially those in the buyer's particular area of expertise; must analyze fashion trends in terms of the store's merchandising policies, customer reactions, and fashion image. If several buyers are working as a team, it is a relatively simple matter to get them together to work out a coordinated fashion picture for the store. In coordinating the small-store operation, the owner-buyer-coordinator will display entire outfits that are easily viewed and compared by the shop's customers. In addition, it is easier for salespeople in a small store to keep one another informed about the likes and dislikes of their customers and to communicate such information to the owner-buyer.

Planning the Fashion Season

The fashion coordinator, whether a buyer, merchandise manager, or owner-manager, must plan the fashion season for the store or department. To accomplish this task, the fashion coordinator must plan a consumer or retail calender as well as be aware of the trade calendar of events that will affect the planning of the store's seasonal fashion theme. A basic consumer calendar is important to a retail operation because it provides information regarding the time period when fashion merchandise must be in the store; a trade calendar is important because it informs the buyer of trade activities that occur throughout the fashion season. The outline below includes the basic consumer calendar as well as a calendar of trade activities.[10]

Outline for Planning the Store's Fashion Calendar

Merchandise that must be in the Store	*Trade Activities*
JANUARY	**JANUARY**
Cruise and resort wear Sportswear, swimsuits Casual clothing	Spring ready-to-wear market opens Summer collections are shown to buyers Boutique market opens Sportswear market opens
FEBRUARY	**FEBRUARY**
Lightweight coats New spring knits Colorful spring suits and dresses	Fall shoe market opens Fall collections are shown Fall knitwear and sweater market opens
MARCH	**MARCH**
Fashionable spring coats Spring suits, dresses, and coordinates Spring accessories: shoes, millinery, handbags and leather goods, belts, hosiery, jewelry, scarves, gloves Spring lingerie and intimate apparel	Fall men's and boys' market opens Junior sportswear market opens Boutique market opens
APRIL	**APRIL**
Presentation of summer colors and fabrics Summer dresses, active sportswear, and accessories Swimwear and beach accessories	Missy sportswear market opens Ski apparel market opens
MAY	**MAY**
Transitional cottons, linens Cocktail dresses, long dresses, evening gowns Bridal fashions Summer coordinates	Major fall ready-to-wear market opens Dresses, coats, suits, ensembles market opens Fall bridal market opens
JUNE	**JUNE**
Summer sportswear and accessories Special sports costumes	Couture fall ready-to-wear market opens Fall sportswear market opens

JULY

Fall bridal fashions
Transitional cottons, lightweight woolens
Fall knitwear
Fall ensembles and costumes
Transitional sweaters, jackets, coats

AUGUST

Childrenswear, dresses, shoes, accessories
Back to school
Casual and career clothing
Early winter jackets
Mediumweight jackets and coats
Fall accessories: shoes, handbags, hats, gloves

SEPTEMBER

Fall ready-to-wear; coats, suits, dresses, ensembles, costumes

OCTOBER

Leather and suede accessories, coats, jackets
Ski apparel and accessories
Medium to heavyweight tweed suits and coats

NOVEMBER

Holiday fashions and accessories
Cruise and resort wear and accessories

DECEMBER

Holiday dresses, evening gowns
Accessories: jewelry, scarves, handbags, leather accessories, notions, shoes, winter coats, fur coats, dresses, accessories

JULY

Fall and winter accessories market opens
Manufacturers' showings: coats, dresses, suits, sportswear

AUGUST

Holiday and resort market opens
Cruise and resort market opens
Spring shoe market opens

SEPTEMBER

Early spring market opens
Spring knitwear market opens

OCTOBER

Swimsuit market opens
Spring ready-to-wear market opens

NOVEMBER

Spring bridal market opens

DECEMBER

Little activity in the market due to the Christmas season

When fashion coordinators are aware of what is happening at both the retail and the trade levels, they can plan their work accordingly. Fashion coordinators must work with top store executives, as well as with buyers of various departments, and continuously supply up-to-date fashion information that will assist fashion buyers when selecting merchandise for resale. It is the fashion coordinator's job to provide interesting and exciting fashion themes that will promote a store's fashion image, stimulate sales, and provide customers with quality fashion assortments.

Chapter Summary

A knowledge of fashion is of vital importance to the retail buyer, since all merchandise lines are affected in one way or another by the fashion influences of the time. In studying such a complex and exciting topic as fashion the student needs to be aware of the various terms that are used over and over within the retail trade. The student should review the following basic fashion terminology: fashion, high fashion, style, fad, mass fashion, silhouette, detail, good taste, classic, and haute couture.

Fashion is not a universal phenomenon. It will differ according to age groups, geographic location, ethnic groups, and occupational or vocational groups. Being "in fashion" indicates conformity, social adaptation, and a certain feeling of superiority or self-assurance. The student should review the human tendencies that condition fashion. Fashions reflect the economic, political, and social feelings of the times. Reasons for changes in fashion, therefore, may be boredom, outstanding and dominating events, dominating ideals, and dominating social groups.

The direction in which a style is moving is called a fashion trend. Fashions move continuously, but at varying and individual speeds, through life cycles. The student should review the six stages through which every fashion must pass as it rises in response to consumer demand and then eventually declines. Fashion is a never-ending and continuous process. The student should review how fashion influences the designer, the manufacturer, the retail buyer, and the consumer.

A fashion department is one that sells feminine outer apparel and accessories. The fashion coordinator is the individual responsible for promoting the sale of fashion merchandise throughout the entire store. The student should review the numerous merchandising responsibilities of a fashion coordinator as they are listed in Part 2 of this chapter. The job of the fashion coordinator will vary with the type and size of the retail firm. The student should review the approach used by the following types of stores: the chain store, the department store, the boutique, the specialty store, the small shop, and the resident buying office. The buyer of fashion merchandise must work closely with the fashion coordinator to determine the unpredictable tastes of the retail consumer. The fashion coordinator, whether a buyer, merchandise manager, or owner-manager, must plan the fashion season for the store or department. The student should review the basic consumer calendar and the trade calendar that are used by the fashion coordinator when planning the store's fashion season.

Trade Terminology

DIRECTIONS: Briefly explain or discuss each of the following trade terms:

1. Fashion
2. High fashion
3. Mass fashion
4. Style
5. Fad
6. Silhouette
7. Detail
8. Good taste
9. Classic
10. Haute Couture
11. Fashion trend
12. Fashion cycle
13. Fashion department
14. Fashion coordinator
15. Boutique

Questions for Discussion and Review

1. Do you agree with the statement that "fashion is everywhere"? Explain your answer by citing examples.

2. Select a popular fashion and trace it through the six stages in the fashion cycle. In what stage is the fashion currently? How long do you predict it will remain in stage five? stage six?

3. Who are the fashion leaders in your particular age group? ethnic group?

4. What fashions are popular in your particular occupational group? geographic area?

5. What is the difference between a fashion and a fad? Cite an example of each.

6. How does the fashion coordination approach differ for each of the following stores: the chain operation, the boutique, the specialty store?

7. By referring to the "Outline for Planning the Store's Fashion Calendar" in Part 2 of this chapter, develop a fashion theme for the months of February, April, July, and September. What kinds of information should be considered when planning the fashion theme for each month?

8. What is the difference between a fashion department and a nonfashion department?

9. What is the role of the fashion buyer in fashion coordination?

Case Study Number One

Too Much Conservatism?

The women's specialty shop in which you are employed has maintained a policy of taking as few risks as possible in purchasing fashion merchandise. The store does not purchase the more popular lines of merchandise until other stores have tested them and found them to be acceptable by customers. As a result, your store's fashion image has become less appealing and your more fashion-conscious clientele are going elsewhere. You have been promoted to the position of fashion coordinator for the entire store. Your store manager has informed you that you may have a free hand in the development of the store's fashion image. However, you must be careful not to offend the existing clientele. The manager has also emphasized the fact that the store must upgrade its fashion image so that it will attract the more fashion-conscious customer. Be prepared in class to outline the merchandising responsibilities of a new fashion coordinator in a specialty shop.

Case Study Number Two

The New Look

Henson's is a twelve-store large volume discount chain that specializes in women's fashion apparel and accessories. It is an aggressive company that caters to the middle- to low-income groups in a large metropolitan area. During the past year, however, it was decided that Henson's was going to "trade-up"; that is, offer fashion apparel and accessories that would attract the upper middle class and wealthy class type of clientele.

Mr. Blackmore, Henson's divisional merchandise manager, met with Ms. Skinner, the merchandise manager of the store's resident buying office, to discuss the change in Henson's merchandise policy. Mr. Blackmore felt that it was necessary to improve the store's fashion image to attract the higher-income clientele. He felt that Henson's would have to initiate an ambitious merchandising program to achieve its goal. Ms. Skinner suggested that Mr. Blackmore seek the advice of Mrs. Alexander, the fashion coordinator of the resident buying office. Mr. Blackmore agreed.

Mrs. Alexander was informed of Henson's intent to offer higher-priced fashion merchandise and of the store's intent to upgrade its fashion image. Mrs. Alexander immediately went to work. She consulted with various fashion buyers and developed a list of manufacturers and vendors who supplied high-fashion merchandise. She developed promotional themes that would tie in store advertising and display, sales events, fashion shows, and special public relations events. She developed a seasonal fashion calendar and made suggestions for special in-house fashion shows. This she felt was necessary to provide sales personnel with up-to-date information.

A meeting was called for the following week. Mr. Blackmore, Ms. Skinner, several store buyers, several resident buyers, and Mrs. Alexander met to discuss the development of Henson's new look. All agreed that improvement of store image was a number-one priority. They also agreed that store advertising and promotion campaigns should be coordinated to give the store a total fashion picture.

However, when Ms. Skinner asked Mr. Blackmore when he was going to hire additional buyers for the new high-price fashion departments, trouble started. Mr. Blackmore stated that the store's regular buyers would also buy for the new fashion departments. The entire room was silent. Ms. Skinner and Mrs. Alexander insisted that such a task was impossible because the regular store buyers were totally unfamiliar with the new resources. Mr. Blackmore insisted that the resident buying office had the responsibility for providing assistance in seeking new resources. Ms. Skinner agreed, but only to the extent that store buyers were able to come into the market and view the lines. This, she said, was extremely important due to the nature and price of the goods. Ms. Skinner further suggested that the regular store buyer would be too busy with existing buying responsibilities and would not have the time or the energy to view the additional vendors and manufacturers who offered high-fashion goods. In fact, she further stated that the fashion accessories markets alone would require the work of two or three store buyers. Mr. Blackmore disagreed. He stated that the store did not have the money to go out and hire additional buyers and that a good fashion coordinator would be able to provide the necessary fashion information. Mrs. Alexander agreed, but only to the degree that adequate market coverage on the part of store buyers was available. The meeting ended.

Considering the facts just stated, do you think that Henson's will accomplish its new merchandising objectives?

Retailing Activities to Stimulate Student Interest and Participation

1. Interview the fashion coordinator of a department store; a boutique; a chain store operation. Prepare a list of questions based on the topic, "How do you predict fashion trends for the coming season?" Are there similarities in the methods used by each? How do they differ?

2. Interview a buyer of fashion merchandise; a buyer of nonfashion goods. Determine the techniques used by each in determining the life-cycles of the merchandise they handle.

3. Develop a list of the fads that are currently popular on your college campus. Are these fads popular as a result of ethnic influence? geographic location? age group? occupational or vocational group?

REFERENCES

The Retail Student's Reference Library

American Footwear Industry Association. Arlington, Virginia: American Footwear Industry Association Press, 1973.

Axlerod, Nathan. *Selected Cases in Fashion Marketing.* New York: ITT Educational Services, Inc., 1970.

Cummings, James. *Making Fashion and Textile Publicity Work.* New York: Fairchild Publications, Inc., 1971.

Curtis, Frieda. *How to Give a Fashion Show.* New York: Fairchild Publications, Inc., 1972.

Everhardt, Richard. *Men's Furnishings.* Columbus: Distributive Education Materials Lab., 1971.

Evolution of Fashion. Bronx: Milady Publishing Corp., 1970.

Fashion Buying. New York: ITT Educational Services, Inc., 1970.

Frank, Bertrand. *Progressive Apparel Production.* New York: Fairchild Publications, Inc., n.d.

Fried, Eleanor. *Is the Fashion Business Your Business?* New York: Fairchild Publications, Inc., 1970.

Fundamentals of Menswear Retailing. New York: Fairchild Publications, Inc., 1972.

Garland, Madge. *Fashion.* Baltimore: Penguin Books Inc., 1962.

Gawne, Eleanor. *Fabrics for Clothing.* Peoria, Ill.: Chas. A. Bennett Co., Inc., 1973.

Goodman, S., and Winter, A. *Fashion Sales Promotion.* New York: ITT Educational Services, Inc., 1970.

Gore, Budd. *How to Sell the Whole Store as Fashion.* New York: National Retail Merchants Association, 1969.

Great Developments in Fashion. New York: Fairchild Publications, Inc., 1972.

Guerin, Polly. *Fashion Writing.* New York: ITT Educational Services, Inc., 1972.

Guide to Fashion Marketing and Merchandising. Bronx: Milady Publishing Corp., 1974.

Guide to Fashion Merchandise Knowledge. Bronx: Milady Publishing Corp., 1974.

The History of the Menswear Industry: 1899–1950. New York: Fairchild Publications, Inc., n.d.

Judelle, B., and Troxell, M. *Fashion Merchandising.* New York: McGraw-Hill Book Company, 1971.

Kolodny, Rosalie. *Fashion Design for Moderns.* New York: Fairchild Publications, Inc., 1970.

Mullikin, Eleanor. *Selling Fashion Apparel.* Cincinnati: South-Western Publishing Company, 1971.

Oerke, Bess V. *Dress—The Clothing Textbook.* Peoria, Ill.: Chas. A. Bennett Co., Inc., n.d.

Paris Couture I, II. New York: Fairchild Publications, Inc., 1970.

Peltz, Leslie R. *Color Line, and Design.* New York: ITT Educational Services, Inc., 1971.

Rowe, Patricia. *Shorthand Fashion Sketching.* New York: Fairchild Publications, Inc., 1970.

Sixty Years of Fashion. New York: Fairchild Publications, Inc., n.d.

Swimwear Merchandising. Washington, D.C.: National Education Association, n.d.

What Every Woman Should Know About Men's Fashions. New York: The Van Heusen Co., n.d.

Women's Ready-To-Wear, 1970. Austin: University of Texas Press, 1970.

References

1. George Simmel, "Fashion," *The American Journal of Sociology,* 57, no. 6 (May 1957), pp. 541–43.
2. Paul Nystrom, *Economics of Fashion* (New York: The Ronald Press Company, 1928), pp. 3–7.
3. Bernice G. Chambers, *Color and Design* (Englewood Cliffs, N.J.: Prentice-Hall, Inc., 1951), pp. 160–61.
4. M. D. Troxell and B. Judelle, *Fashion Merchandising* (New York: McGraw-Hill Book Company, 1971), pp. 20–28.

5. John W. Wingate and J. Dana Weiner, *Retail Merchandising* (Cincinnati: South-Western Publishing Company, 1963), pp. 176–78.
6. Troxell and Judelle, *Fashion Merchandising,* pp. 71–74.
7. *Fashion Coordination,* (New York: ITT Educational Services, Inc., 1969), pp. 5–7.
8. Troxell and Judelle, *Fashion Merchandising,* pp. 318–22.
9. Ibid., pp. 323–30.
10. *Fashion Coordination,* pp. 12–23.

Understanding the Retail Consumer

6

Performance Objectives

PERFORMANCE OBJECTIVES

As a result of reading this chapter, the student should be able to accomplish the following:

1. Define: retail consumer.

2. Outline and explain five major characteristics of retail consumers that affect consumer buying behavior.

3. Discuss how social psychologists use social class, family interactions, and membership groups to study consumer social behavior.

4. Compare the six social classes as classified by Warner.

5. Explain how population characteristics will assist the buyer in determining consumer behavior.

6. Analyze the five levels of needs that affect personal characteristics that influence buying motives.

7. Explain the most common patronage motives important in store selection.

8. Discuss seven techniques that may assist retail buyers to recognize their customers.

9. Become familiar with trade sources of information, government sources of information, and business sources of information.

Understanding the Retail Consumer

Consumer Buying Motives

How can a retail buyer predict which items in a given group of goods and services will be purchased by consumers? in what quantities? Why does a consumer purchase a particular item?

An Important Responsibility

A most important responsibility of retail buyers is to forecast, as accurately as possible, the needs and wants of those customers they expect to serve. When buyers decide on merchandise selections they are going to offer to retail customers, they must be certain that the merchandise offered will appeal to that particular consumer market. A retail store, no matter how small or how large, cannot be all things to all people. A profitable store becomes reputable in the marketplace only by thoroughly understanding its customers, by learn-

Figure 6.1. The consumer is an important element in retailing. Buyers must forecast as accurately as possible the needs and wants of those customers they expect to serve. (Courtesy of Sears, Roebuck and Company.)

ing its clientele's needs, wants, and desires. The retail buyer, therefore, has the responsibility to study the consumer and interpret consumer demands, as they apply both to the general objectives and policies of the retail store and to the particular department. The buyer's success in consumer forecasting will not only enhance the prestige and reputation of the retail organization but also build his or her own department through an increase in sales and profit.

Since the consumer is such an important element in retailing, the buyer must study characteristics that influence consumer buying motives. Part 1 of this chapter, therefore, (1) discusses the importance of understanding the retail consumer, (2) defines the retail consumer, and (3) discusses factors that influence the retail consumer when selecting goods or services. Part 2 discusses the numerous methods buyers may use to help them learn about their customers; that is, methods they may use to determine the sex, age, income level, habits, occupations, and aspirations of each man, woman, or child who enters a retail establishment.

Who Is the Retail Consumer?

The *retail consumer* is an individual who attempts to satisfy physical and psychological needs and wants, through the purchase of goods and services. Marketing experts, manufacturers, wholesalers, and retailers attempt to analyze the current needs of consumers by forecasting their potential needs as well as determining the prices they will pay. The manufacturer, the wholesaler, and the retail buyer find that it may indeed be difficult to decide what type of merchandise assortment or services consumers will accept or reject.

Factors that Influence Buying Behavior

Let us now turn our attention to those factors that influence the retail consumer when selecting goods or services. Consumer characteristics discussed in this chapter are (1) psychological consumer behavior, (2) sociological consumer behavior, (3) population characteristics, (4) personal characteristics, and (5) patronage motives.

Major factors that affect consumer buying motives

1. Psychological consumer behavior
2. Sociological consumer behavior
3. Population characteristics
4. Personal characteristics
5. Patronage motives

Psychological Consumer Behavior

The consumer buys things for many reasons, whether in the soft-goods line, the hard-goods line, or the foods line. Today's consumer is not only concerned with basic needs, such as food, clothing, and shelter, but also strongly motivated by psychological needs to acquire a different variety of goods. Consumers not only seek to satisfy so-called basic wants, but also construct new wants or needs based on their own life-styles.[1]

According to Melvin T. Copeland,[1] a pioneer in the psychological approach to classification of consumer motives, consumer buying motives may be divided into two categories: (1) emotional buying motives and (2) rational buying motives.[2]

Emotional Buying Motives. Emotional buying involves little logical thought. Buying decisions come from an individual's feelings rather than from thinking or rationalizing. Examples of emotional motives are many; however, some of the more common are (1) courtship and marriage, (2) care for one's offspring, (3) satisfaction of the five senses, (4) fear and anxiety, (5) rest and recreation, (6) social acceptance, (7) curiosity, (8) personal pride, and (9) distinctiveness.

Examples of emotional buying motives

1. Courtship and marriage
2. Care for one's offspring
3. Satisfaction of the five senses
4. Fear and anxiety
5. Rest and recreation
6. Social acceptance
7. Curiosity
8. Personal pride
9. Distinctiveness

Courtship and Marriage. The desire to appeal to the opposite sex is strong in most people. Consumer products make endless appeals to masculinity and femininity, to beauty and strength. Hair tonics, perfumes, deodorants, shampoos, fashion clothing, and automobiles—all appeal to our emotions. Newlyweds are appealed to by presentation of an array of merchandise—china, silverware, kitchen utensils, appliances, and cookbooks—that supposedly promises wedded bliss and conjugal harmony.

Care for One's Offspring. Since parental love is strong in most human beings, many products make appeals to this motive. For example, the use of vitamins "will protect your child through his formative years"; or "Wise mothers never take chances, so feed your family cereal every morning." Oftentimes, we are reminded of our responsibility to care for our offspring through such advertising subtleties as "Don't let your family down, buy . . ." or "Do you know where your children are?"

Satisfaction of the Five Senses. Appeals to the five senses—touch, taste, sight, smell and hearing—are important influences on consumer buying habits. A TV commercial may appeal to the sense of taste through such descriptive terms as "finger-lickin' good" or "thirst-quenching." Advertisements for paper products may appeal to the sense of touch through such boastings as "squeezably soft," "tender, loving care," or "baby smooth."

Fear and Anxiety. The emotions of fear and anxiety are exploited by appeals to the instincts of self-preservation and protection. We buy seat belts, burglar alarms, fire extinguishers, and vitamin pills to protect ourselves, our family, and our friends. Future uncertainties, the possibility of accident, and the occurrence of death concern us to the point where we indulge in the acquisition of insurance policies, home safety equipment, and the latest in health-care products.

Rest and Recreation. Since the need for rest and recreation is basic to us as individuals, the desire to lighten the work load or perhaps to eliminate work altogether leads to a strong desire for leisure living. Today, innovations within industry have presented us with automation, power machinery, and assembly lines. As a result of these technological advances, the physical work load has been reduced; we find we are able to turn our attention to a more leisurely life-style. The three-day weekend and the four-day workweek have become popular with many businesses.

Since leisure time creates a need for activities, many appeals are designed to provide for such activities; for example, goods associated with camping and sports activities, do-it-yourself kits, indoor games and hobbies.

Social Acceptance. We are strongly motivated by the desires to escape rejection and loneliness and to win approval and acceptance from our family and peers. Therefore, we, as individuals, are strongly motivated to become a part of a group. We belong to clubs, associate with a particular peer group, and live in a particular neighborhood so that we may gain confidence, security, and acceptance. We conform to particular norms to avoid being embarrassed, humiliated, or laughed at. Advertisers tell us, for example, that we should "care enough to send the very best," or "join the Pepsi generation." Such ads appeal to our need to belong.

Curiosity. Many of us are curious individuals, and we have the desire to try things that are new, different, and exotic. That which is mysterious or enticing stimulates our sense of curiosity and tugs at our imagination. What interests other people often arouses our own curiosity. For example, a motorist "gaper-block" on the freeway often creates more problems than the accident itself. We read advertisements that suggest "romance and excitement in faraway places." Signs may read "adults only," "it's new and improved," or "more to come." We find it difficult to resist the "try it, you'll like it," appeal found in many consumer products.

Personal Pride. Pride in ourselves, in the way we look, in the way we feel, have been popular retailer appeals. We have a basic desire to maintain our dignity without necessarily feeling that we must impress those around us. We have the desire to look neat and clean, to smell "fresh as an Irish spring," or to have a "kissing-sweet breath." If our home has "house-a-tosis," we have neglected our homemaking responsibilities; if the toilet bowl does not contain a blue liquid, it is unsanitary. We have been made "germproof," "wrinkle-resistant," "drip-dry," "longer lasting," "curl-free," "shined and waxed," and "underarm safe"!

Distinctiveness. To be distinctive or to express individuality in some socially accepted way is a desire that provides strong motivational appeal. We may express the desire to be different through the clothes we wear, the food we eat and drink, or the automobiles we drive. During the fuel crisis of the mid-1970s, the socially acceptable "thing to do" was to drive a small, economical car or ride a bicycle to work. We became leaders in our communities and set good examples by not using Christmas-tree lights and by keeping thermostats turned down.

In the quest for distinctiveness we also seek to become specialists or to become superior in particular areas. We seek, perhaps, to become an expert or to become "number one." Perhaps the best illustration of this point is the boasting of a famous prizefighter, "I am the greatest!"

Retailers provide merchandise that appeals to the vanity of consumers. Such merchandise may "cause you to be the envy of your friends," "build a better you," or change you into the girl "girl watchers watch."

Rational Buying Motives. In contrast to emotional buying motives, *rational* or *economic motives* involve people's ability to reason or learn and to give consideration to making the most effective use of limited resources. The consumer who is rationally motivated thinks in terms of logic and gives attention to the effective use of economic resources.

Retailers who advertise merchandise that is top quality and low cost will appeal to the rational consumer. Differences in size and weight, dollar savings, and other measurable characteristics may be emphasized. Terms such as "economic," "savings," "reliable," "worthy," "practical," and "durability" are frequent appeals used by retailers to increase sales. Rational buying motives, therefore, may be classified as follows: (1) economy, (2) efficiency and durability, (3) dependability and reliability, (4) financial security, and (5) property enhancement.

Examples of rational buying motives
1. Economy 2. Efficiency and durability 3. Dependability and reliability 4. Financial security 5. Property enhancement

Economy. During the 1970s shoppers were faced with the problems of power shortages, fuel cutbacks, and a scarcity of food products. Since consumers had less money to spend, they would carefully shop and compare prices and would seek the best value for their money. As consumers became more budget-conscious, more retailers promoted "moneysaving coupons," "special sales days," or "super bargains." Or, as a well-known appliance ad read, "Come and get it while it lasts!"

Efficiency and Durability. Since the Industrial Revolution in the nineteenth century, industry has been producing and manufacturing products in volume. Automation has provided society with the ability to mass-produce goods in highly efficient ways. As a result of this highly mechanized method of production, we have learned not only to become efficient ourselves but also to expect efficiency in the products we purchase. Warranties and guarantees provide bulwarks against dissatisfaction; labels and instruction booklets provide product information necessary to ensure the life and efficient operation of the product. We expect manufacturers to live up to their "promises," if the product does not perform satisfactorily. We look for guarantees when we purchase automobiles, appliances, home furnishings, and clothing, to name but a few products. As retailers we can appeal to the customer's desire for efficient living by emphasizing product "ease of handling" or "fast, effective performance."

Product durability is also an important motivation factor. Durability determines both how well the product will perform under certain conditions and the life expectancy of the product. Instructions for care may emphasize "hand wash in lukewarm water," "dry clean only," "do not use bleach," etc. Retailers and manufacturers are responsible for advising consumers about the care and maintenance required for merchandise. For instance, after July 1972, clothing manufacturers were required to provide information regarding the care of garments. Since that time, the consumer needs only to read the garment label, which contains specific care instructions. The consumer is now better able to extend the life of the garment. Today, if uncertain about how to care for a product, the consumer usually hesitates to purchase the item.[3]

Dependability and Reliability. "You can be sure if it's Westinghouse!" Such is the promise of an appliance manufacturer. When finances become limited, the consumer may hesitate and, thus, "shop around." Wise advertisers will appeal to the consumer's cautious nature, particularly in the purchase of red-ticket or more expensive items. Not only do consumers want to purchase items which are long-lasting, but they also desire products that are of good quality. Consumers dislike surprises. They do not wish to be inconvenienced by having to return an item. The consumer becomes more expert in the purchase of retail products, and at the same time becomes more discriminating and more selective. The consumer desires the "best for the money" and, in addition, desires to purchase the best in the "least amount of time." Thus, advertisements may read, "This is a top quality store," "We aim to please," or "Buy right and you'll only have to buy once."[4]

Financial Security. The American culture has long fostered the concept that money in the bank will provide us with security, peace of mind, and financial independence. As consumers, therefore, we spend money with the idea that we want enough left over to guarantee us a "nest egg" for a happier tomorrow. Banks tell us that pennies saved today will increase our financial security for the future. We join Christmas Clubs to ensure the availability of cash during the holiday season. We join vacation clubs to have "a little something extra" for next year's family excursion. We give our children piggy banks and encourage the teenager to open a savings account when the first paycheck is received. As one TV commercial says, "My kid is smarter than I was at his age; he's opened a savings account at Federal Savings . . . !" Service institutions encourage us to save at their banks, purchase their insurance, buy through their real-estate offices, or buy stocks from their brokerage houses. Why? Because each one knows the "best way of increasing your money!"

Property Enhancement. Improvement or upkeep of personal property has a rational appeal to the consumer. Our neighbors "paint up, fix up, and clean up" during the spring of the year and, usually, so do we. We know that property value is best insured by yearly maintenance and repairs. However, as stated earlier, since we desire freedom from work, we turn our attention to economical worksaving devices. During the spring, retailers provide window displays and newspaper advertisements that demonstrate "no-peel paint," "longer-lasting window screens," "maintenance-free aluminum siding," "quick-drying cement," or "easy-to-install screen doors."

An understanding of psychological motives, both emotional and rational, may assist the retail buyer to interpret and explain why consumers buy certain kinds of products or various product lines. However, we know less about why people buy *specific* merchandise and *specific* brands. Consumers in different trading areas may purchase goods for a variety of different reasons, depending on their needs and the influence of others. Since each consumer is influenced by a wide range of different buying motives, emotional motives may be strongest in one consumer, while rational or economic motives predominate in another. For example, one consumer may elect to "put himself into debt," ignoring the desire "to save" and, instead, fulfilling a stronger emotional motive.

By understanding consumer buying motives, the retail buyer can enhance the abilities to better serve the retail consumer and to provide a successful merchandise assortment. A buyer's own initiative and insights about how particular consumers behave in determining their wants, coupled with retailing experience, can foster development of a distinctive marketing strategy that will be far superior to the average plan utilized by competitors.

Up to this point we have been discussing approaches to the understanding of consumer buying behavior that can be developed from psychology. However, consumer buying attitudes may be determined not only by psychological drives but also by relationships with others. Therefore, we will turn our attention to sociological factors that motivate consumer buying.

Sociological Consumer Behavior

Sociological factors are a second major influence that affects consumer selections of goods or services. As previously stated, the consumer is a most important element in retailing, although perhaps the least understood, both individually and collectively. Retail buyers are most anxious to understand their customers better, but they have difficulty in gathering, sorting, and utilizing available data. Knowledge of human behavior that has been gathered by social psychologists and sociologists will certainly prove helpful in studying consumer behavior in terms of social interactions arising from (1) social class, (2) family interactions, and (3) membership or reference groups.

Social Class. Social class has long been identified as part of American society. Much consumer behavior may be explained in terms of social class. This is not to say that an individual is superior or inferior because he or she is in a particular social class. But social standing and social aspirations do motivate buying behavior. Some people aspire to enter a higher class, since they find its values more to their liking; others prefer the standards of their own group and are happy to remain there.

One of the goals of retailers should be to learn the characteristics and typical behavior patterns of each social class. Such knowledge will help retailers to better serve their customers and thus enable development of unique marketing strategies oriented toward particular markets.

W. Lloyd Warner, a social psychologist, developed a class system for cities in the 10,000 to 25,000 population range.[5] *Social class* refers to groups of people who share the same goals and attitudes toward life. Members of the same social class are more or less equal to one another in income, prestige, and community standing, and interact formally or informally, readily, and regularly.

Warner's classification is based on source of income, type of occupation, house type, and residential area.

The six social classes are, starting from the highest, (1) upper-upper class, (2) lower-upper class, (3) upper-middle class, (4) lower-middle class, (5) upper-lower class, and (6) lower-lower class (see Table 6.1).

Upper-Upper Class. Often referred to as "the elite," individuals from this group are very wealthy, come from prominent families, live in the finest homes, and buy the most expensive clothing. This is the smallest of the six classes and represents approximately one percent of the total population.

Table 6.1. *The Warner Social Class System — an Overview.*

Social Class	Characteristics	Percent of Population
Upper-Upper Class	Very wealthy; old wealth; prominent families; expensive clothing and home	Approximately 1% of the total population
Lower-Upper Class	Nouveau riche; first generation wealth; professional, educated	Approximately 2% of the total population
Upper-Middle Class	Reflect value of leisure living, fairly successful in top management	Aproximately 10% of the total population
Lower-Middle Class	White-collar workers; highly paid blue-collar workers; strive for right neighborhood; save money; practical	Approximately 35% of the total population
Upper-Lower Class	Semiskilled; labor unions; enjoy life day to day; uninterested in future savings	Approximately 40% of the total population. Represents the largest class.
Lower-Lower Class	Unskilled workers; unemployed ethnic groups; fatalistic, apathetic attitudes; little concern for self-improvement	Approximately 10–15% of the total population

Lower-Upper Class. This class consists of individuals who have achieved first-generation wealth or who are "nouveau riche." Families are composed of professional people, such as doctors and lawyers, who desire a leisurely lifestyle and work successfully to achieve it. This class represents approximately two percent of the total population.

Upper-Middle Class. This social class is composed of fairly successful individuals who have achieved top-management positions in business. This group reflects the value of leisure living as reflected in the first two classes. This social class represents approximately ten percent of the total population.

Lower-Middle Class. Individuals within this group are white-collar workers—teachers, office workers, entrepreneurs, and most salesmen—and some highly paid blue-collar workers. Members of this class are essentially practical people. Respectability, living in the "right neighborhood," saving for a college education, and saving money are important. This group represents approximately thirty-five percent of the total population.

Upper-Lower Class. These are assembly line workers, members of labor unions, the semiskilled, and those employed by small service establishments. Members of this group are interested in enjoying life on a day-to-day basis rather than in saving for the future. This group represents the largest class, accounting for approximately forty percent of the total population.

Lower-Lower Class. This class consists of many unskilled, unemployed ethnic groups. Its members are frequently fatalistic, apathetic, and show little concern for self-improvement or planning for the future. This group represents approximately ten to fifteen percent of the total population.[6]

Significance of Social Class

What does social class mean to the retail buyer? Since social class is based on source of income, type of occupation, house type, and residential area, it is often quite significant in attempts to analyze consumer buying habits, store preferences, and communications media and product likes and dislikes. The various classes patronize different stores, buy different merchandise lines, and have different cash or credit attitudes. Various classes may read quite different meanings into a single retail advertisement. One advertisement for plastic automobile seat covers showed the plastic covers on the seats of a new Cadillac. Unhappily for the advertiser, the lower class associated plastic seat covers with less-expensive and used cars. The "prestige image" of the Cadillac did not spur the consumer to buy plastic seat covers; and the owners of Cadillacs felt that if they could afford the car, they could afford to keep it clean![7]

Class differences may also affect the type of merchandise carried by the retailer. For example, members of the more affluent classes, such as the upper and upper-middle classes, may prefer period or traditional furniture, hand-crafted and expensive, whereas members of less-affluent classes may prefer mass-produced, lower-priced furniture, selected strictly for function rather than style. Lower-class buyers may be confused by the variety of furniture styles available and look to the retailer for advice in furniture selection. On the other hand, upper-class buyers are usually more knowledgeable and, even if they are not, have often had the advice of an interior decorator; they are likely to be more confident when making a selection.

It is important for the retail buyer to carefully analyze his or her particular consumer market before planning marketing strategies. Consideration should be given to the type of occupation, source of income, educational achievement, and family goals and aspirations. All may affect the social-class standing of various members. Therefore, the retailer may have problems distinguishing among individual consumer needs within each social class.

Family Interactions. Understanding family interactions is a second aid to the retailer in efforts to understand consumer social behavior. Since many buying decisions are made within the structure of the family, individual family members are often influenced by the rest of the family in their selections of products and services. Often, the family is consulted before a buying decision is made. The family, therefore, provides a frame of reference that guides its members in the purchase of goods that will benefit most of the family members. A significant fact is that one person in the family usually makes most of the purchases. The retail buyer needs to learn the identity of the decision maker who is the most influential in selection of goods and services.

Traditionally, the housewife was considered the chief decision maker of the family. Today, however, due to increased emphasis on leisure living and to growth of shopping centers in or near outlying residential areas, more and more men make purchases. Such shopping centers enable whole families to participate in buying decisions. The head of a family, however, is usually consulted when expensive, or "red ticket," items are considered. Perhaps both husband and wife may share in the decision-making process.

The buyer must be aware of the different roles of each family member in regard to various buying responsibilities (not to mention the great variation in reaction among separate families when faced with choices among merchandise).

It would be valuable for the retail buyer to know a family's present and past shopping experience and its future goals and aspirations in relation to society and the family social position.

Membership or Reference Groups. A third help in studying consumer social behavior is knowledge of a consumer's *membership* or *reference group, the group of people that the individual looks to when formulating concepts, beliefs, opinions, and attitudes.* Reference groups may be organized according to age, sex, religion, ethnic background, occupation, income, life-style, or likes and dislikes.[8] An individual may be a member of many reference groups, depending on what he or she finds appealing and comfortable. Retailers need to be aware of the kinds of reference groups within their particular consumer markets since buying decisions may be based upon "what the rest of the crowd is wearing (eating, or driving)." Automobile advertisements appeal to the youth market with such automobile names as "Maverick," "Pinto," and "Charger"—all representative of the "footloose, fancy-free" spirit symbolic of the youth market. Different ethnic groups may be reached by promoting Indian cottons, African caftans, natural hairstyles, or Peruvian embroidery. Convenience foods appeal to the large group of working wives and mothers, who hear radio commercials describing food products that may be prepared by just "adding water at breakfast time," " 'adding to' at lunchtime" or " 'mixing into' at dinnertime." She can cook food in a microwave oven, pop it into a toaster, or serve it precooked from the can!

In summary, human beings' interactions with those around them, with their families, and with particular groups of individuals have far-reaching effects upon their buying decisions and thus upon retailers. Information about people, their ability to purchase, and what influences their motivation to buy is necessary if retailers are to identify their consumer markets.

The consumer may be studied in terms of social interactions

1. A knowledge of social class
2. Family interactions
3. Membership groups

How will information about these help the retail buyer?

Population Characteristics and Income Data

A third major factor that affects consumer buying motives is the population with which the retailer must work—and average income of that population. The retailer must be constantly aware of changes in population, such as shifts in population from the urban to the suburban market or changes in age distribution within a population. A sudden growth in one area may create a demand for new shopping centers, while existing facilities may be more than adequate in other areas. A change in age distribution of a population may alert the retailer to the necessity to increase stocks of merchandise that will appeal to the dominant age groups.

Populations are composed of people, and people are consumers. Retailers must know where people are today and where they will be tomorrow. Population figures for only a single year fail to reveal the full potential of consumer markets. For example, the U.S. population has been growing continuously since the founding of the country, and it more than doubled from 1910 to 1970. However, the population did not increase equally over the entire nation. Some states have grown rapidly; others have grown at a slower rate. Since it is certain that the U.S. population will continue to grow (for example, experts predict that the population will be nearly 250 million by 1990), retailers must ask themselves "how much, how fast, and where?" As a result of present-day attitudes toward marriage, women working, educational opportunities, family planning, and family size, population trends should be watched carefully. Figures 6.2, 6.3, 6.4, and 6.5 have been prepared by the U.S. Department of Labor, Bureau of Labor Statistics, and are examples of source material a retailer may use to determine population characteristics.

Figure 6.2. The population will grow to nearly 250 million by 1990. Source: U.S. Department of Labor, Bureau of Labor Statistics.

If the members of the population are going to purchase products, they must have money to spend. Income data should be studied by retailers, since the amount of money available will affect the type of goods consumers are likely to purchase. Also, unless a person has money or the assurance of acquiring it, he cannot be regarded as a potential customer. Income is an important ingredient in purchasing power.

Income, which is measured in money, is derived from producing and selling goods or services in the marketplace.

Figure 6.3. Predicted population growth. Source: U.S. Department of Labor, Bureau of Labor Statistics.

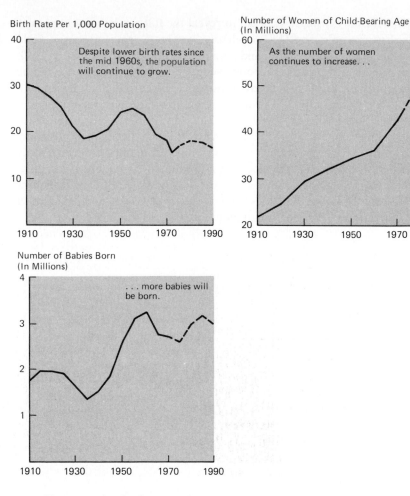

Birth Rate Per 1,000 Population

Despite lower birth rates since the mid 1960s, the population will continue to grow.

Number of Women of Child-Bearing Age (In Millions)

As the number of women continues to increase. . .

Number of Babies Born (In Millions)

. . . more babies will be born.

Four standards that may be used to measure the output and the growth of the economy are:

1. *Gross national product (GNP),* which represents the total output of goods and services produced in a year;
2. *National income (NI),* the sum of employees' earnings, proprietors' income, corporate profits, rental income, and net interest for a given year;
3. *Personal income (PI),* calculated by first subtracting undistributed corporate profits, taxes on profits, and social security taxes from national income and then adding to it all transfer payments (payments unrelated to current production, such as social security benefits and pensions);
4. *Disposable personal income (DPI),* the income that persons have avail-

able for saving or spending; the most useful measure of income for retailers. Disposable personal income may be determined by subtracting personal taxes from personal income.

Disposable income refers to that part of income that may be spent by the consumer. However, since most families do not have to spend their entire disposable income, a distinction needs to be made between disposable income and actual expenditures. Many households allocate a portion of their income to necessities, such as food, rent, and household furnishings. A family's purchase of luxury items comes from what remains, called the discretionary income. Discretionary income is important because its availability increases purchasing power for luxury items. If the consumer lacks discretionary income, sales of luxury items suffer.

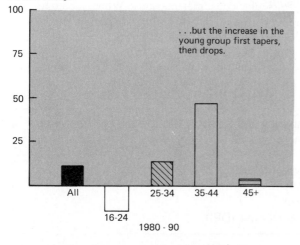

Figure 6.4. Shift in proportion of the younger work force. Source: U.S. Department of Labor, Bureau of Labor Statistics.

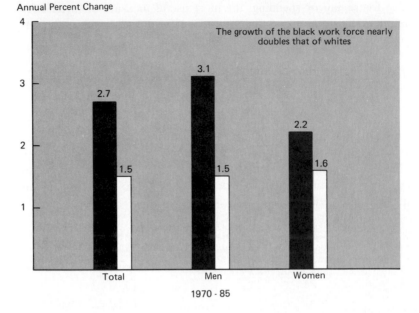

Annual Percent Change

An important point to remember is that individuals' needs for necessities may continue to grow, perhaps to a point where needs exceed purchasing power. Once a retail buyer has determined total expenditures in his or her particular trading area on goods that he or she stocks, then that buyer's particular share of the business must be estimated. The buyer must consider the possibility of attracting both new customers and customers presently shopping the competition.

Consumer expenditure patterns are closely related to population characteristics. Population and income data are pertinent because such information assists retailers to identify particular consumer markets. When such data are evaluated, a clearer picture of consumer life-styles and spending habits will provide better insight into present as well as future buying activities. This provides the retailer with information on how different kinds of consumers live and spend their money, thereby guiding the retail buyer in the decision-making process.[9]

> How will information about the following help the buyer in determining consumer spending power?
>
> 1. Gross national product (GNP)
> 2. National income (NI)
> 3. Personal income (PI)
> 4. Disposable personal income (DPI)

Personal Characteristics

A study of personal characteristics, the fourth major factor that affects spending, will provide information on that part of the consumer personality concerned with preservation of "the self." Each of us has a mental image of "ourself," and these ego-related images are of great importance in attempts to understand consumer buying behavior. A majority of consumer purchasing decisions are related in some way or another to the questions, "What will this do for me?" or "How will this impress those about me?" Many of us need the approval of those around us to give us self-confidence and, thus, reinforce our self-concept.

We all have certain needs and wants. Some needs may be physiological, concerned with an individual's physical body, while others are psychological or sociological. The presence of unsatisfied needs or wants leads to efforts to obtain satisfaction. Psychologist A. S. Maslow proposed five levels of needs, in ascending order of importance to the individual. They are:

1. Physiological needs: hunger, sex, thirst, etc.
2. Safety needs: the need for security, protection, order or routine.
3. Love needs: the need for affection and belonging.
4. Esteem needs: the need for self-respect, prestige, success.
5. Self-actualization needs: the need for self-fulfillment.[10]

Individual consumers attempt to satisfy, first, the needs they regard as most important to them. However, the *total* needs of each consumer are both partially satisfied and partially unsatisfied. That is, certain needs are given high priority, but not to the complete exclusion of other needs. For example, the need for food may be given high priority, but not all of the consumer's income will be spent on food. Once an adequate food supply has been purchased, the consumer will allocate money to satisfy another high priority need, such as housing, clothing, entertainment, or whatever else is important at that time. An important point to remember is that one product may satisfy several needs at the same time.

Consumers are pictured as wanting to improve their self-images. Some social psychologists view individuals as having several "selves": (1) the way an individual really is, (2) the way the individual sees himself, (3) the way the individual would like to be, and (4) the way the individual thinks others perceive him. Each consumer, therefore, is trying to develop a better "self." It goes without saying that products and services that offer means of self-image improvement will be very successful in the marketplace.

Retail buyers will find that there are problems when trying to study consumer personality.

1. Not all psychologists agree on the same set of theories, nor are the theories developed necessarily compatible.

2. One psychological theory might not be helpful in explaining the behavior of a particular type of consumer.

3. Consumers may not be willing to discuss or perhaps may not even be

aware of the motivations that drive them to strive to meet particular needs, wants, and desires.

4. Consumers may act at three levels of awareness: conscious, preconscious, and unconscious. At the conscious level consumers are aware of their motivations and are willing to talk to their neighbors about them. At the preconscious level consumers may be aware of motives but would rather not discuss them. At the unconscious level consumers are not even aware of what forces are driving them. Keep in mind that several motives may be affecting consumer buying simultaneously, perhaps at different levels of awareness.

Patronage Motives

Why do consumers favor one store over another? What influences where they will buy? Up to this point we have been discussing buying behavior in terms of why individuals buy *what* they do. Let us now turn our attention to why they buy *where* they do.

The fifth major factor in consumer buying behavior is *"patronage motives,"* which may be emotional or rational. Patronage motives explain why a consumer purchases products or services from one retail store rather than from another. This, needless to say, is a matter of great concern to the retail buyer, since he must first get the customer into his store before he can sell merchandise.

Figure 6.6. Why do consumers favor one store over another? Patronage motives explain why a customer purchases products or services from one retail store rather than another. (Courtesy of O'Shea's, Laconia Mall, Laconia, New Hampshire.)

Retailers must ask themselves, "What can we do to get customers into our stores?" "How can we make our stores more attractive than the competition?" The motives listed below are the most common.[11]

Price. The value received for merchandise sold may be the single most important factor in store patronage, particularly during poor economic periods. The discount revolution has emphasized "low prices" and has influenced pricing policies of all types of stores, from department stores to specialty shops. Where have you not seen such signs: "discount bakery," "discount furs," "discount gasoline," or even "last sale day before Christmas." Since there is no simple formula for determining the most attractive price, retailers must keep abreast of economic forecasts, rates of unemployment in their particular trading areas, consumer spending, and income levels of their consumers.

Convenience. The location of your store may be a decisive factor in influencing the consumer to shop at your store instead of at your competition. Large shopping centers contain branches of chains and large department stores, supermarkets, discount operations, specialty stores, and many small businesses. A shopping center emphasizes the one-stop concept by providing a variety of merchandise under one roof. The consumer may drive to the shopping center, find plenty of parking space, and leisurely select merchandise from a number of stores that provide various assortments of merchandise in varying price lines. A good location is essential to the retailer, particularly one merchandising food, gasoline, or other basic consumer goods.

Integrity. The store's reputation for fair dealing may influence the consumer, particularly when the product is an intangible or service, such as banking, shoe repair, dry cleaning, or food. To build repeat business and develop store loyalty, retailers must establish a record of honest dealings with consumers.

Quality and Assortment of Goods. Quality of the merchandise line is often the basis for many appeals made by retail buyers. Such appeals as "We sell only name brand lines," "Quality is the only consideration!" "Shop here for the best!" will attract consumers, since quality is equated with dependability. As consumers become more experienced shoppers, they tend to become more selective shoppers. Quality becomes an important factor in store patronage.

The *assortment of goods offered by a particular store* is often a reason why consumers patronize a store. However, with new products, new styles, and new adaptations saturating the market, consumers often become confused and hesitate to spend. Retailers must be careful to supply a merchandise assortment that will appeal to but not confuse the customer. Such appeals as "See our special line from Paris!" or "Your choice of three colors," or "We have the best selection in town!" may be used in advertisements. A merchandise assortment provides more convenience for the consumer because fewer stops need to be made while shopping for particular items.

Services Offered. A service is *an intangible offered by the retailer to encourage patronage.* Services may include credit, delivery, gift wrapping, a baby-sitting service, tailoring and alterations, or a return policy. Service is a technique used by retailers to distinguish their stores from competitive stores. In good economic conditions, when consumers have more money to spend, they will often patronize stores with liberal service policies. Service often increases the price of the merchandise sold; however, some consumers want a great deal of service and are, therefore, willing to pay.

Courteous Personnel. Consumers will shop in retail establishments where personnel are likable, friendly, and courteous. Particular products may require advice and explanation from sales help; if such advice is not available, the retail buyer has found that consumers will not purchase. Courteous personnel are a part of the store's reputation for integrity and of its overall image. Therefore, the more courteous and helpful the store's personnel, the more likely it is that customer spending will increase.

Retailers may use such advertising appeals as "Fast, friendly, courteous service awaits you!" or "You're number one!" or "You're the only one who counts."

How will a knowledge of patronage motives help explain why consumers shop at one store rather than at another?
1. Price
2. Convenience
3. Integrity
4. Quality and assortment of goods
5. Courtesy of personnel

PART 2

Recognizing the Customer

Up to this point, we have discussed factors that influence consumer buying behavior and how an understanding of those factors will greatly assist buyers in selecting merchandise assortments. Let us now discuss techniques a retail buyer may utilize in recognizing a particular customer that will patronize a particular store.

How can the buyer learn about the customer? How does a buyer determine the sex, age, income level, habits, occupations, and aspirations of each man, woman, or child entering his or her retail establishment? The following seven techniques may help retail buyers to recognize customers.

Customer-Recognition Techniques

Techniques the buyer may use in recognizing customers
1. Personal contacts 2. Basic sources of information 3. Trade sources of information 4. Observations and counts 5. Competition 6. Reporting services 7. Electronic systems

Personal contacts

Whenever possible, the buyer should attempt to be on the selling floor to personally evaluate buying-selling activity. As a result of talking to sales personnel and consumers, a buyer may gain insight into why merchandise offered for sale is or is not selling. For instance, customer complaints that a particular brand of swimsuit is vulnerable to fading and will not hold up for one season's wear may be overheard. This may indicate that such merchandise is low quality and will be difficult to sell. A customer may return a pair of men's slacks because the seams fell apart after one washing; later, other customers may come into the store with the same complaint. The buyer may then suspect that that particular shipment of men's slacks was defective and that the goods will have to be returned to the manufacturer. Since consumers are usually free with their opinions about merchandise offered for sale, the buyer may hear clues about the kinds of styles, colors, and fabrics that are popular with his or her particular market. It is an advantage to have personal knowledge of what customers like and dislike.

The buyer is responsible for personal contacts with salespeople, not only in the main store but also in the branch stores. A major problem with personal-contact activity, however, is that the buyer is so completely absorbed with merchandising activity that it is difficult to get out onto the selling floor. In these circumstances the assistant buyer may prove invaluable in assisting the buyer by gathering valuable market information.

Basic Sources of Information

Basic consumer information is readily available to the retail buyer from a variety of federal government and business publications. Table 6.2 represents

Table 6.2. *Federal government sources.*

Federal Government Sources	
Alphabetical	Census of Business
Index of	County Business Patterns
Occupations	Retail Trade Area Statistics
and Industries	Small Business Administration Pamphlets

Business Sources	
Barrons National Business &	Newsweek
Financial Weekly	New York Times
Business Horizons	Occupational Index
Business Week	Sales Management: The
Dun's	Marketing Magazine
Fortune	Time
Franchise Journal	U.S. News & World Report
Journal of Marketing	The Wall Street Journal

a partial listing of sources. These basic sources of business information provide consumer data by states, cities, counties, and specific trading areas. By reading such material, retail buyers may gather data about population growth and projections, population age groupings, population shifts, employment, family income and expenditures, and family life-styles. For example, a daily newspaper, such as *The Wall Street Journal,* relates current economic trends, consumer spending patterns, and environmental conditions that affect business in general. The buyer may apply basic business information to his or her particular retail market.

Trade Sources of Information

This information serves the common interests of firms in the same business on a local or national basis. Sources of trade information are (1) resident buying offices, (2) noncompeting stores, (3) vendors and manufacturers, and (4) trade papers and trade associations.

Trade sources of information	
1. Resident buying offices	3. Vendors and manufacturers
2. Noncompeting stores	4. Trade papers

Resident Buying Offices. Resident buying offices, described in Chapter 4, are responsible for providing buyers with information about market trends, styles, sizes, and assortments available; conducting consumer surveys; and forecasting seasonal trends. Resident buying offices not only inform buyers of demands in their particular trading areas but also of demands in different parts of the country. Resident buying offices offer a variety of services that may prove effective in assisting buyers to identify their customers.

Noncompeting Stores. Noncompeting stores are frequently organized into groups for purposes of quantity buying. Since buyers from such stores are not in direct competition with one another, they are often willing to exchange information about the types of merchandise that sold successfully or unsuccessfully in their particular stores. Information from noncompeting stores provides a buyer with knowledge of what is selling in other areas and what may soon be in demand locally.

Vendors and Manufacturers. Vendors and manufacturers are in close contact with designers of new merchandise lines and usually possess knowledge of sales results in stores to which they sell. Sales figures from vendors are likely to be accurate, because vendors' success is based upon their ability to obtain orders, and such orders require accurate record keeping. Buyers may obtain information from vendors' and manufacturers' salespersons, catalogs, fashion bulletins, and fabric swatch cards; or information may be issued directly from vendors' and manufacturers' showings. Vendors may inform buyers about which styles other retail stores have ordered, and they are particularly anxious to pass on information about "best sellers." Reorders are usually an indication of customer acceptance; therefore, reorder information is important to the buyer.

Trade Papers and Trade Association. There are different types of buyers for various merchandise lines. Since nearly every line of merchandise has its particular trade paper or magazine, each buyer will subscribe to those trade journals that provide the most interesting and accurate information in his or her particular field of interest. Trade papers provide information regarding the newest styles or trends and what is selling in particular markets in different parts of the country, as well as vendor advertisements, notices of market showings, and arrivals of buyers in the marketplace, to name but a few types of information. Examples of various trade papers and trade publications are listed in Tables 6.3 and 6.4.

Observations and Counts

A fourth technique used by buyers to aid recognition of customers is observing individuals and groups in the immediate trading area. For instance, if a men's shirt buyer is interested in learning about styles, colors, and patterns popular in the immediate trade area, the cut and style of shirts worn by men at business meetings, social gatherings, and sporting events may be observed, and also the

Table 6.3. *Various trade papers and publications.*

Fashion and Fashion Accessories

Boot and Shoe Recorder	Daily News Record	Leather and Shoes
Boutique Fashions	Fabric and Fashion Maker	Men's Wear
California Apparel News	Footwear Forecast	New England Apparel
California Men's Stylist	Fur Age Weekly	Retailer
Clothes	Jewelers' Circular	Women's Wear Daily

Home Furnishings

Bedding Magazine	Hardware Merchandising	New England Furniture News
Casual Living Magazine	Home Furnishings Daily	Pacific Marketeer
Contract Magazine	Home Goods Retailing	Professional Furniture
Decorating Retailer	Interior Design	Merchant
Furniture Field	Interiors	Small World
Furniture and Furnishings	Juvenile Merchandising	Southwest Furniture
Furniture Methods	Market Place	Western Furniture
and Materials	National Hardwood	Manufacturer
Furniture World	Magazine	Western Merchandiser Inc.

General Trade Sources

American Druggist	Discount Merchandiser	Merchandising Week
American Vocational Journal	Drug Topics	Modern Retailer
Chain Store Age	Journal of Retailing	Progressive Grocer
Department Store	Journal of Marketing	Stores
Management		Supermarket News

age, social class, and life-style of the men wearing particular colors, patterns, and price lines. In addition, trade papers may print detailed reports of costumes worn by men considered to be leaders of fashion, which may give some indication of future popular demand.

A buyer of lamps and accessory items may notice that a particular kind of lamp or style of lampshade is in demand. Observations of shoppers, in both main and branch stores, may indicate shopper merchandise preferences, as well as regional differences in preferred merchandise items. For example, some items that are not selling well in urban stores may be showing good sales results in branch stores. This difference may arise from differences in shopper types: the shopper typically found in the suburban shopping center is a more affluent, leisurely shopper than the urban customer, who may feel pressed for time, more hurried and concerned with meeting specific needs.

Table 6.4. *Trade associations also provide useful information to retail buyers.*

American Advertising Federation	International Association of	National Glove Manufacturers
American Hardware Manufacturers	Clothing Designers	Association
Association	Intimate Apparel Associates	National Handbag Association
American Millinery Manufacturers	Knitted Outerwear Foundation	National Hand Embroidery
Association	Lingerie Manufacturers Association	and Novelty Manufacturers Assn.
American Printed Fabrics Council	Master Furriers Guild of America	National Knitwear Manufacturers
Association of Buying Offices	Men's Fashion Association of America	Institute
Chamber of Commerce of the	Men's Tie Foundation	National Neckwear Association
Apparel Industry	Menswear Retailers of America	National Outerwear and Sportswear
Clothing Manufacturers Association	Merchandise Mart Apparel Association	Association
of the U.S.A.	Millinery Displayer's Association	National Retail Hardware Association
Cosmetic, Toiletry, Fragrance	Millinery Institute of America	National Retail Merchants Association
Association	National Association of Blouse	National Skirt and Sportswear
Costume Designers Guild	Manufacturers	Association
Cotton Council	National Association of Daytime	National Women's Neckwear and
Council of Fashion Designers of	Dress Manufacturers	Scarf Association
America	National Association of Hosiery	Silk and Rayon Manufacturers
Custom Tailors and Designers	Manufacturers	Association
Association of America	National Association of Men's	Sportswear Salesman's Association
Daytime Apparel Institute	and Boys' Apparel	Textile Association of Los Angeles
Fashion Group, Inc.	National Association of Men's	Undergarment Accessories Association
Fur Brokers Association of America	Sportswear Buyers	Underwear-Negligee Associates
Fur Information and Fashion	National Association of Textile	United Better Dress Manufacturers
Council	and Apparel Wholesalers	Association
Greater Blouse, Skirt and Under-	National Association of Women's	United Infants' and Children's Wear
garment Association	and Children's Apparel Salesmen	Association
Handkerchief Industry Association	National Costumers Association	United Fur Manufacturers Association
Industrial Association of Juvenile	National Dress Manufacturers	Upholstery and Decorative Fabrics
Apparel Manufacturers	Association	Association of America
Infants' and Children's Wear	National Fashion Accessories	
Salesmen's Guild	Salesmen's Guild	

Competition

Study of merchandising techniques used by competing stores is a fifth technique in customer recognition. Buyers may study competition advertisements, which will give a base for price and quality comparisons and represent the competitor's judgment about what people will buy. Buyers may observe competitors' window displays, since they indicate what the competition thinks may be best sellers, as well as showing how the merchandise relates to other style trends. Buyers may also "shop" competition by actually going into a particular store and looking over the merchandise assortment, talking to salespeople, observing the number of items sold or not sold, and perhaps even buying merchandise to compare price and quality. Buyers or their representatives may shop many competing stores during "rush hours" to observe which counters or departments are doing the most business. Such observations may indicate items that customers are *not* interested in purchasing as well as items for which there is great popular demand. Buyers may find that stocked merchandise would move faster if it were displayed differently or perhaps marked down or, unhappily, that merchandise they do not even carry is in demand. Buyers who are responsible for much of the activity in their own stores often do not have time to visit competitors. Therefore, assistant buyers, department managers, salespeople, comparison shopping bureaus, and resident buying offices may provide the needed information.

Along with observations of competitors' merchandise, buyers must compare the merchandising *policies* of their own stores with those of the competition. Often a store emphasizes quality and service along with price. A buyer may recognize that the competition is only interested in selling cheaply, forsaking customer service. The buyer who emphasizes quality merchandise with top-quality service may still "beat out" the competition despite the price difference.

Reporting Services

Buyers may receive assistance from reporting services responsible for predicting styles and trends in the consumer market. A number of trade papers, fashion magazines, resident buying offices, consumer magazines, and special reporting bureaus undertake market research valuable to retail buyers. Such information may be analyzed and published weekly or monthly in specific trade papers or sent directly to buyers. Contents of these trade papers include announcements of the arrival of the latest fashions from Europe, reports on conditions of manufacturing facilities in Hong Kong and economic conditions in South American markets, announcements of the newest fabrics and textures or of new colors and coordinates. Perhaps the most useful trade service is the type that reports specific items that are selling well in leading stores throughout the country. The following list is representative of retail reporting services:

Retail News Bureau. Provides reports on current promotions of New York City retailers. This reporting agency also provides advanced market reports from Seventh Avenue. Figure 6.7 is an example of the kind of information available to retail buyers who use this service.

Retail Memo. The American Newspaper Publishers Association offers news of particular interest to retailers on a weekly basis.

ATT: CONTEMPORARY DRESS BUYER

DI NOTTE
Room 1265
1411 BROADWAY, NEW YORK CITY 10018
SIZE RANGE: 5/6-13/14
PRICE RANGE: $13.75-$26.75
DELIVERY: OCTOBER 15 COMPLETE

THIS RESOURCE IS ONLY TWO SEASONS OLD AND
OFFERS HIGH STYLED, WELL PRICED CHIFFON FOR
EVENINGS. THE FEELING IS SOFT, FLOWING AND
HAS A LADYLIKE "SENSUOUS" LOOK. THERE ARE
SEVERAL DRESSES. A GREAT MAJORITY OF THE
LINE IS PRESENTED IN SEPARATES. WE HAD A
LOVE AFFAIR WITH THE HANDKERCHIEF HEMMED
SKIRTS AND THE EVENING PANTS.

COLORS OFFERED ARE BLACK, SILVER, SAND, RED,
WHITE AND RUST. ALL COLORS WILL BE SMASH-
ING FOR SPECIAL OCCASIONS AND HOLIDAY EVE-
NINGS. MANY OF THE BLOUSES HAVE LACE IN-
SERTS OR ROMANTIC RUFFLES. SEVERAL OF
THESE STYLES ARE AVAILABLE SHEER OR LINED
AT THE SAME PRICE. THERE IS ONE BASIC
SHEER SHIRT WITH ONLY TWO POCKETS COVERING
THE "BARE ESSENTIALS".

SOME OF THE STORES WHO HAVE BOOKED ARE SAKS
FIFTH AVENUE AND GIMBELS-PHILADELPHIA.
FRANKLIN SIMON WAS THE FIRST STORE TO RE-
CEIVE THIS MERCHANDISE. THEY REORDERED
DURING THE FIRST WEEK AFTER DELIVERY.

STYLES TO NOTE ARE: #2042R at $22.75 a v-
neck slip dress with fabric flower at bust.
This dress falls below the knee and is done
in tiers of handkerchief treatment. (Also
available long as #2045R at $26.75) Style
#2018R at $23.75 is a long tiered skirt
with long/short hemline. This style says
fantastic with #2021R an unlined wrap
blouse with curved front and back, ruffle
hem and V-neck at $13.75.

RETAIL NEWS BUREAU 232 MADISON AVENUE · NEW YORK, N.Y. 10016

A Confidential REPORTING SERVICE . . . ITEMS . . . IDEAS . . . RESOURCES

NEW YORK REPORTS · CALIFORNIA REPORTS

Errors subject to corrections.
Reproduction in whole or in part
in any form whatsoever forbidden.

Figure 6.7. A retail news report. (Courtesy of Retail News Bureau.)

Tobe Service. An independent fashion consulting service, Tobe Service issues bulletins reporting fashion trends and market activities that are of interest to the fashion trade.

Beryl Tucker Young Trends. An independent fashion consulting service that provides current information to those who specialize in children's fashions.

Ram Services, Inc. A reporting agency that provides data on how particular styles of misses' dresses are selling in department stores representative of a particular region.

The Use of Electronic Systems

Electronic systems cannot be overlooked as an excellent source of information to assist retail buyers in fast, accurate decision making. For example, the electronic cash register (ECR) is a sophisticated version of the traditional cash register designed primarily for checkout systems such as those found in discount stores and other self-service types of retail establishments. This type of electronic system calculates and automatically adds in taxes, voids errors, and records multiple transactions. It can keep track of sales of several departments at one time, and it provides information of value for both department and overall store sales reports.

When the electronic cash register (ECR) is combined with a computer, an electronic point-of-sales (POS) system is developed. This system automati-

Figure 6.8. The electronic cash register is a sophisticated version of the traditional cash register. It is designed primarily for checkout systems such as those usually found in discount stores and other self-service types of retail establishments. (Courtesy of Pantry Pride/Food Fair Supermarkets.)

cally reads or scans special labels on merchandise, verifies prices, and registers sales. This and similar systems will help the buyer, who can more readily obtain information about peak sales periods, take accurate customer counts, and determine amounts and types of merchandise that are "best sellers." (See Figure 6.8.)

Chapter Summary

A most important responsibility of the retail buyer is to forecast as accurately as possible the needs, wants, and desires of customers he or she expects to serve. Retail consumers are individuals who attempt to satisfy physical and psychological needs, wants, and desires through the purchase of goods and services. Students should review psychological consumer behavior, sociological consumer behavior, population characteristics, personal characteristics, and patronage motives; and also the lists provided in Part 1 of this chapter.

What factors influence retail consumers when selecting goods or services? There are emotional buying motives and rational buying motives. Examples of emotional motives are courtship and marriage, care for one's offspring, and satisfaction of the five senses. Examples of rational buying motives are economy, efficiency and durability, and dependability and reliability. Buying motives may also be studied in terms of social interactions by social class, family interactions, and membership groups. Population characteristics affect consumer buying motives. Retailers must continuously ask themselves "how much, how fast, and where is the population growing?" A study of income data goes hand in hand with the study of population characteristics. Four standards may be used to measure the output and growth of the economy: gross national product (GNP), national income (NI), personal income (PI), and disposable personal income (DPI). Important in consumer motivation is that part of the consumer personality concerned with preservation of "the self." In relation to this, psychologist A. S. Maslow proposed five levels of needs: physiological, safety, love, esteem, and self-actualization needs. Patronage motives, which may be emotional or rational, explain why a consumer purchases products or services from one retail store rather than another. Examples of patronage motives are price, convenience, integrity, quality and assortment of goods, and courtesy of personnel.

There are a number of sources of information that retail buyers may use to assist in recognizing customers: personal contacts, federal government and business publications, trade sources of information, observations and counts, competition, and reporting services. A representative list of federal and business publications is included in this chapter. There are a number of trade sources of information that will assist buyers in recognizing customers, such as resident buying offices, noncompeting stores, vendors and manufacturers, and trade papers. A list of general trade sources of information is provided, as well as a list of trade associations that may provide useful information. Reporting services also provide market information, and students should review the examples of reporting services in this chapter.

Trade Terminology

DIRECTIONS: Briefly explain or discuss each of the following trade terms.

1. Retail consumer
2. Emotional buying
3. Rational or economic motives
4. Social class
5. Membership or reference groups
6. Income
7. Gross national product
8. National income
9. Personal income
10. Disposable personal income
11. Patronage motives

Questions for Discussion and Review

1. Why is it important for buyers to know what motivates consumers to purchase particular items?

2. Develop a list of characteristics that may be referred to when determining consumer buying motives. Explain.

3. What is the difference between a rational motive and an emotional motive?

4. What is the Warner Social Class System? Describe the characteristics of each class in Warner's system. Do you feel this system is applicable today?

5. What is a reference group? Name five reference groups that buyers may find in an urban consumer market.

6. How can the four standards used to measure economic output and growth help buyers to determine consumer purchasing power?

7. How can retail buyers apply Maslow's five levels of needs when selecting merchandise assortments?

8. Develop a list of ten patronage motives that may influence consumers to

shop at one store instead of another. Why have you selected these particular patronage motives?

9. How do personal contacts help buyers to a better understanding of their customers?

10. To what business sources would you refer to predict consumer income level? economic trends? an area buying trend?

11. What trade sources of information are popular in the fashion apparel trade? home furnishings trade? menswear industry? footwear trade?

Case Study Number One

The women's boutique at Hoffman's Department Store is one of the store's most profitable departments. One reason is the great ability of the boutique buyer; another is that the store is located in an area occupied by many firms that employ large numbers of female employees. During the past several months, however, while the rest of the store continues to meet its past year's sales figures, the women's boutique has been plagued with slow sales, high inventory, and numerous markdowns. The boutique buyer, realizing she was overconfident in her sales projections, is uncertain of how to correct the situation. She realizes, however, that she must keep the boutique customer in mind while attempting to solve her problem.

The Women's Boutique

Be prepared in class to discuss the methods you would use in this buyer's place to secure information about your customers. What additional information would you require to help you solve the problems of slow sales, high inventory, and numerous markdowns?

Case Study Number Two

Kittering & Blake operated a high-quality, profitable women's specialty shop in Society Hill, a fashionable shopping and cultural section of Philadelphia. Since K & B was located in this high-rent area, it concentrated on offering well-known national brands of merchandise, with price emphasis upon the moderate to upper income groups. The store offered a well-rounded assortment of both classic types of merchandise, and currently popular fashions. Its philosophy of business was to provide personalized selling in attractive and pleasant surroundings.

Should Uptown Shoppers Go Downtown?

Mr. Kittering, one of the store's owners, learned that the city was planning to provide a special "cultural loop" bus, which would carry business people, shoppers, and out-of-town visitors for a minimum fee to visit various historical and cultural centers throughout the city. The route, of course, included Society Hill. Upon examining the store's charge account records, he discovered that many of K & B's customers came from the immediate residential area, composed of townhouses, condominiums, and high-rise apartments. He discussed his findings with Mr. Blake; together they decided that a new advertising campaign should be developed to encourage shoppers from uptown to come to Society Hill and shop at K & B, especially since transportation was readily available.

However, there were some factors to consider.

First, Kittering & Blake's advertising efforts had been limited to local newspapers and magazines with an occasional ad appearing in one of the city's larger newspapers. A major problem was that K & B was operating on a limited advertising budget; therefore, it advertised only in smaller, less-expensive newspapers and magazines.

Second, since K & B was a small specialty shop, it had limited purchasing power in the marketplace; it often had difficulty in obtaining exclusives and other specials when dealing with merchandise sources. As a result, Kittering & Blake might not be able to provide a merchandise assortment that could meet demands of customers from such a variety of socioeconomic backgrounds.

Finally, K & B would have to offer merchandise in heretofore unrepresented price ranges. This would require locating new merchandise sources. Since the business was small, locating new sources was likely to prove difficult.

Considering the above factors, do you think K & B should develop a new advertising campaign to attract more customers?

Retailing Activities to Stimulate Student Interest and Participation

1. Select a store advertisement from local newspapers for each of the following types of stores: a men's and boys' specialty shop; a discount house; a department store; a variety store; a chain-store operation. Evaluate each advertisement to determine the consumer appeal of each ad. Do you feel that each store's advertising reflects the social-class values of its potential customers?

2. Refer to the list of trade publications in this chapter. What trade publications would you subscribe to if you were a buyer of furs and fur accessories? of curtains and draperies? of hardgoods, such as kitchen utensils, pots and pans, and small electrical appliances? of children's furniture and accessories? of expensive furniture and furnishings?

3. Refer to the list of trade organizations in this chapter. What trade organizations would you join if you were a buyer of fabrics (piece goods) and sewing notions? of cosmetics, toiletries, and perfumes? of millinery, scarves, and neckwear? of lingerie and intimate apparel? of men's sportswear?

The Retail Student's Reference Library

Aaker, D. A., and Day, G. S. *Consumer Search for the Consumer Interest.* New York: The Free Press, 1971.

Anderson, W. T. *The Convenience Oriented Consumer.* Austin: University of Texas Press, 1971.

Canfield, James. *Teaching a Course in Personal Economics.* New York: Joint Council on Economic Education, 1971.

Consumer Buying Guide Reprints. New York: J. C. Penney Co., Inc., n.d.

Consumer Decides, The. New York: J. C. Penney Co., Inc. n.d.

Curtis, George, and Mattingly, John. *Course Outline for Retail Induction Into Self-Service Stores.* Columbus, Ohio: D. E. Materials Lab, 1970.

DeCamp, Catherine. *Money Tree.* New York: The New American Library Inc., 1972.

Decision Making for Consumers. New York: J. C. Penney Co., n.d.

Downing, G. D. *Basic Marketing—A Strategic Systems Approach.* Columbus, Ohio: Charles E. Merrill Publishing Company, 1971.

Ehrenberg, A. S. C., and Pyatt, F. G. *Consumer Behavior.* Baltimore: Penguin Books Inc., 1971.

Faria, A. J.; Johnstone, D. C.; and Nulsen, R. O. *Compete: A Dynamic Marketing Simulation.* Dallas: Business Publications, Inc., 1973.

Helitzer, M., and Heyer, C. *The Youth Market.* New York: Media Projects, Inc., 1970.

Hughes, C. D. *Attitude Measurement for Marketing Strategies.* Glenview, Ill.: Scott, Foresman and Company, 1971.

Kangun, N. *Society and Marketing.* New York: Harper and Row, Publishers, 1972.

Lankfort. *Consumer Mathematics.* New York: Harcourt Brace Jovanovich, Inc., 1971.

Levy, L.; Feldman, R. Q.; and Sasserath, S. *Consumer in the Marketplace, The.* New York: Pitman Publishing Corporation, 1970.

McEvilla, J. D. *Small Business Bibliography.* Washington, D.C.: U.S. Government Printing Office, 1970.

Montgomery, D. B., and Urban, G. L. *Application of Management Science in Marketing.* Englewood Cliffs, N.J.: Prentice-Hall, Inc., 1970.

Personal Finance. Homewood, Ill.: Learning Systems Company, 1972.

Retailing Services the Consumer. New York: J. C. Penney Co., n.d.

Sanford, David. *Who Put the Con in Consumer?* New York: Liveright, 1972.

Siber, Alan. *Complete Guide to Retail Management.* Baltimore: Penguin Books Inc., 1972.

Spitz, A. E. *Product Planning.* Philadelphia: Auerbach Publishers Inc., 1972.

Still, R. R., and Cundiff, E. W. *Basic Marketing—Concepts, Decisions and Strategies.* Englewood Cliffs, N.J.: Prentice-Hall, Inc., 1971.

Wanous, E. E., and Wagner, G. *Fundamentals of Data Processing.* Cincinnati: South-Western Publishing Company, 1971.

References

1. Melvin T. Copeland, *Principles of Merchandising* (New York: A. W. Shaw Co., 1924), pp. 155–67.

2. Ibid., p. 162.
3. John G. Udell, "A New Approach to Consumer Motivation," *Journal of Retailing,* 40, no. 4 (Winter 1964–1965), pp. 6–10.
4. Ibid., pp. 8–9.
5. W. Lloyd Warner, "Classes Are Real," *Issues in Social Inequality,* ed. Gerald W. Thielbar and Saul D. Feldman (Boston: Little, Brown and Company, 1972), pp. 8–9.
6. W. Lloyd Warner, Marchia Mecker, and Kenneth Eels, *Social Class in America* (Chicago: Science Research Associates Inc, 1949).
7. Sidney J. Levy, "Social Class and Consumer Behavior," in *On Knowing The Consumer,* ed. J. W. Newman (New York: John Wiley & Sons, Inc., 1966), p. 154.
8. Calvin Hall and Gardner Lindzey, *Theories of Personality* (New York: John Wiley & Sons, Inc., 1957).
9. Pierre Martineau, "The Personality of the Retail Store," *Harvard Business Review,* 36, no. 1 (January–February 1958), pp. 47–55.
10. A. H. Maslow, "A Theory of Human Motivation," *Psychological Review,* 50 (1943), pp. 370–96.
11. Martineau, "The Personality of the Retail Store," pp. 47–48.

The Buyer and Merchandise Controls

7

Performance Objectives

Chapter Summary
Trade Terminology
Questions for Discussion and Review
Case Study Number One; Number Two
Retailing Activities to Stimulate Student Interest and Participation
The Retail Student's Reference Library
References

As a result of reading this chapter the student should be able to accomplish the following:

1. Evaluate the elements contained in a control system.

2. Discuss the requirements of a good control system.

3. Explain two methods of merchandise control.

4. Illustrate the formula used to determine the periodic inventory system.

5. Demonstrate how the retail value of stock on hand may be reduced to a cost basis.

6. Define: merchandise inventory, perpetual inventory system, periodic inventory system.

7. Determine the figure for net sales under the physical inventory system.

8. Explain inventory systems for use in unit control other than the periodic system and the perpetual system.

9. List the advantages and limitations of merchandise control.

10. Identify characteristics that differentiate retail inventories from inventories carried by most other types of businesses.

11. Explain the reasons for taking a physical inventory.

12. Outline the procedure used in taking a physical inventory.

13. Write the formulas for the following: The cost method of inventory, the book method of inventory value, and the retail method of investment value.

The Buyer and Merchandise Controls

The Use of Merchandise Controls

It is evident from the material in Chapter 6 that an awareness of consumers' needs, wants, and desires will greatly assist buyers when purchasing merchandise assortments. Buyers, however, must also be aware of certain control measures that will assist in purchase planning, ensure prompt reordering of goods, and prevent additional purchases of merchandise that has proved unacceptable to the consumer.

The Last Stage of Management

Control is often thought of as the fifth stage in the management process of planning, organizing, staffing, directing, and controlling. However, a good control system will be built into management's business objectives during the initial planning stage. Control provides a way to inform top management if established standards are or are not functioning according to plan. Control also provides a basis for making changes to correct problems that are already present. Although the buyer plays an important role in the control function, the merchandise manager and other store executives are usually responsible for the overall development and practice of effective control measures.

Today, complexities of multistore operations, the rapid expansion of department stores into branches and twigs, and the expansion of small businesses into shopping centers have intensified the need for the rapid provision of accurate, complete data for buyers, merchandise managers, store managers, and small shop owners alike. Retailers can no longer depend upon their memories of past buying and selling experiences to guide their present and future merchandising activities. For this reason, they must be aware of the control process and its application to merchandise management. Therefore, Part 1 of this chapter discusses (1) elements of a control system, (2) requirements of a good control system, (3) application of control systems to merchandising, and (4) types of inventory systems. Part 2 discusses (1) the advantages and limitations of merchandise controls, (2) characteristics of the merchandise inventory, (3) reasons for and major steps necessary in taking a physical inventory, and (4) methods used to determine the value of the closing inventory.

Elements of a Control System

No matter what activity is being controlled in the retail establishment, whether it is personnel, operations, finance, or merchandise, there are certain elements that should be present in every control system. Three elements important to a good control system are (1) establishment of control standards, (2) measurement of performance, and (3) analysis and correction of deviations from planned standards.[1]

Establishment of Control Standards

Every type and size of retail establishment has certain goals and objectives it is striving to attain. *Control standards* represent a business firm's objectives and goals. A retail store will establish certain *monetary standards* or goals for each department, for example, the quota that the average sales department must attain during certain selling periods, such as special sales promotions, Mother's Day, and the Easter season. Another example of a monetary control standard is the number of sales required of each salesperson; a monetary standard may include cost of store overhead, such as labor, utilities, and rent, in ratio to the amount of profit earned by each department.

A retail store will also have certain *physical standards.* For example, if a chain store opens a new unit, there will be certain physical characteristics —the design of the store exterior and interior, window displays, store signage —that will readily identify the store as a member of a particular chain operation. A franchise operation emphasizes certain physical standards (for example, McDonald's golden arch) throughout all its franchises.

Finally, a retail store will establish certain *intangible standards,* such as "quality" service, "good performance," or store "loyalty." Intangible standards, however, are often difficult to measure because they cannot be precisely stated in either monetary or physical terms. We cannot necessarily see, touch, or feel such factors as "loyalty," "good performance," or "quality."

Measurement of Performance

If control standards have been properly established and communicated to store personnel, then the measurement of performance resulting from application of these standards should be a relatively simple task. A department manager may measure the performance of a management trainee by using a rating form based on ratings of good, average, or poor (see Figure 7.1). The performance of a store executive may be rated according to such descriptions as needs improvement, average expected for position, or above average (see Figure 7.2). Performance measurement, however, is not as simple as it appears. For example, definitions of terms such as "good," "average," and "poor" may differ. One evaluator may have a very strict standard regarding what constitutes a good performance, whereas another evaluator may be much more lenient.

If past records are available and information regarding department sales, inventory turnover, purchases, and expenses are provided, then fulfillment of

Date Sent to Department _____ Date to be Returned to Personnel _____

EXECUTIVE DEVELOPMENT TRAINEE
Progress Review
(six and twelve months)

Date _____

Name _____ No. _____ Department _____

Starting Date: _____ Age _____ Education _____

Department Manager _____

Department Manager: Please evaluate the above trainee by answering the following questions. After you have completed this review of your trainee's progress, discuss your evaluations with him and then *forward the review to the Divisional Merchandise Manager for his comments.*

1. Please evaluate your trainee on the following factors:

	Good	Average	Poor			Good	Average	Poor
Dependability					Maturity			
Initiative					Aggressiveness			
Appearance					Cooperation			
Tact					Loyalty			

2. What responsibilities has your trainee been given? Please describe briefly below.
   Supervising Salespeople: _____

   _____

   Handling Classifications: _____

   _____

   Meeting resources: _____

   _____

   Advertising and/or Display: _____

   _____

   Responsibility for department while you are away: _____

   _____

Figure 7.1. A department manager may measure the performance of a management trainee by using a rating form based on such factors as good, average, or poor.

monetary standards may be measured more accurately. The department manager or store buyer can plan department sales, purchases, and expenses based on past performance and use this information as a guide through selling seasons. In some departments, such as notions, greeting cards, gift wrapping, and stationery, monetary standards have been established for certain selling

Figure 7.2. An example of a form used to rate a store executive. (Courtesy of John Wanamaker Department Store, Philadelphia, Pa.)

seasons, and sales projections for staple types of merchandise become fairly routine.

Analysis and Correction of Deviations from Planned Standards

What happens when the owner-manager of a small variety store does not make the sales quota for the Christmas season and has to take several markdowns? What does a department manager who has not requested enough sales help for the week-long "Founder's Day Sale" do when the store is swamped by customers? Obviously, the owner-manager overestimated sales potential, and the department manager underestimated the need for sales personnel. Why? How will each correct the situation?

A good control process will include as part of its system the ability to analyze and correct any deviations from established standards. For example, the owner-manager will have to refer to projected sales goals and determine corrective action to prevent the same mistake from recurring. The department manager may have to take another look at the budget and determine how to correct the understaffing situation in light of past information.

There are certain elements that should be present in every control system.

Review each of the following.
Why are they necessary?

1. Establishment of control standards
   a. Monetary standards
   b. Physical standards
   c. Intangible standards
2. Measurement of performance
3. Analysis and correction

The kind of control system required by a retail business will depend upon its merchandising policy, the size of the store, and the clientele it serves. However, there are certain requirements that should be a part of any control system. A good control system should (1) call attention to deviations, (2) suggest a means of solving the problem, (3) be accurate and timely, (4) be understood by the members of the organization, and (5) be economical.[2]

Requirements of a Good Control System

A good control system should:

1. Call attention to deviations
2. Suggest a means of solving the problem
3. Be accurate and timely
4. Be understood by the members of the organization
5. Be economical

Call Attention to Deviations

Well-planned control systems will be applied to those store activities with which management is most concerned. For example, inventory control is watched carefully by large and small retailers alike. In the large departmentalized store, merchandise inventory is usually controlled by the use of electronic data processing (EDP), since EDP has proved to be an excellent method of fast, accurate, efficient information retrieval. In contrast, the owner of a small hardware store may use "eyeball" checks to determine the amount of merchandise sold, the amount of goods left in the stockroom, and the amount and type of inventory that must be reordered.

A good control system should be able to determine errors, mistakes, and any other problems that require the immediate attention of the store manager or buyer. A good control system should be able to locate problem areas before a complete breakdown occurs in some part of the system. Suppose that a salesperson working in a greeting-card shop sees a reorder card appear in the bin or on the rack. When this occurs, the reorder card should be turned over to the department manager or store buyer so that merchandise can be reordered promptly; or the department manager or buyer should alert the manufacturer's representative to the necessity of reorders when the agent visits the store.

Suggest a Means of Solving the Problem

Once attention is called to a problem, a good control system should provide a means of solving it. The store's EDP system may have corrective measures built in for some types of variations from standards. The manager of a variety store that is a member of a large chain operation may receive a computer-prepared stock list indicating that a particular stock item has been discontinued; however, the stock list also suggests a reasonable substitute. As a result the store manager will be able to maintain both a continuous flow of stock and a balanced stock assortment. Even less automated systems should alert management to areas that require improvement.

Be Accurate and Timely

A good control system should provide accurate corrective information in time to allow effective decision making. Often, however, it is difficult to achieve a balance between accuracy and time. For instance, the manager of a cosmetic and perfume department may wish to offer a new line of fragrance. However, uncertainty about the success and, therefore, the profitability of the fragrance causes the manager to hesitate. Trade journals are read, manufacturing representatives consulted, and buyers in noncompeting stores are sought out for advice. While all this information accumulates, the competition may enter the market with the new line. Needless to say, if the new line proves successful, and if the merchandising philosophy of the manager's store is based upon being a leader in offering new lines of merchandise, this manager has "missed the boat." When accuracy and time come into conflict, store management must ask which is more important. The answer will depend on the merchandising philosophy of the store and the time pressure under which retailers are working. One store may offer only items that are well established and proved to be profitable, while another store may wish to be a leader when it comes to offering new lines of merchandise.

Be Understood by the Members of the Organization

Even the most sophisticated control system is worthless if it is not understood by those who must use the information it provides. Management must carefully explain both the purposes and objectives of the control system and how to use it. If a new credit procedure is introduced, the data-processing division must inform store managers or merchandise managers and buyers about the new procedure, and they, in turn, will pass the information on to members of their staff. Perhaps the store's personnel division will offer special training sessions, to sales personnel especially, to instruct them about the procedures involved in implementing the new credit procedure. When the control system is understood by the members of the organization who must use it, it is likely to increase managerial effectiveness and improve profitability.

Figure 7.3. Even the most sophisticated control system is worthless if it is not understood by those who must use the information it provides.

Be Economical

A good control system will remain consistent with the overall profit objectives of the retail firm. The amount of money spent on a control system will depend on both the relative importance of the division or system to be controlled and the size of the operation. Sophisticated computer systems used by many retail organizations require not only elaborate installation, maintenance, and repair but also intensified training sessions for those who will operate them. All of this is expensive; the necessity for such complex systems should be thoroughly considered before implementation. Management should not spend more money collecting and analyzing data than they will save by improvements that result from the addition of the control system.

A Key Device in Management Control

An important tool used by management in planning, coordinating, and controlling various control systems is the budget, a plan that forecasts specific merchandising activities for a specified period of time. Owner-managers, divisional merchandise managers, and other top executives will begin the budgeting process by outlining the needs of the business enterprise in broad terms. Necessary data are collected from various staff divisions, such as marketing and research, advertising, personnel, and finance, and are translated into budgets that make up the store's overall financial plan. Budgeting is the method by which management translates its goals and objectives into quantitative terms. It is a key device in management control because it provides guidelines (monetary standards) for the various departments to use in doing their part to attain the overall profit objectives of the retail business. (We will discuss the subject of budgeting in detail in Chapter 8.)

Control Systems Used in Merchandising

Up to this point, we have discussed general characteristics of control systems. Let us now turn our attention to the specific application of control systems to merchandising divisions of retail stores. An important control measure used by store managers, buyers, and small business managers alike to assist them in data collection is called merchandise control. *Merchandise control* may be defined as the maintenance of a stock of merchandise that is adjusted to the needs of consumers and prospective consumers.[3]

The type of merchandise control system that a retail store uses will depend upon the type and size of the business, the kind and amount of data required, the methods employed by the store's competition, and the store's business objectives. The owner-manager of a small retail store may determine the amount of stock on hand by simply inspecting or counting items on the shelves and in the stockroom. Because the business is small, this visual count of merchandise will help to determine which items are selling and which are not, as well as which items should be reordered. In a large department store, the buyer may seek the assistance of salespeople and stock personnel, who are assigned to specific areas or departments. The buyer will use more formal means of stock control because of the amount and value of the stock and the need for more detailed information concerning particular stock units. In a chain operation, the central buyer will refer to both reorder requests from store managers and supply information from warehouse managers to determine the amount and kind of merchandise on hand as well as items of merchandise that need to be replenished.

There are two major forms of merchandise control: (1) dollar control and (2) unit control.

Dollar Control

Dollar control may be defined as the amount of dollars at retail prices invested in the merchandise inventory. Dollar control usually involves maintaining records designed to provide accurate information in terms of retail prices by answering the question, "How much?" This information can be used as a guide to buying and reordering. The small store buyer will usually use this method of control throughout the entire store. If the small store grows and expands, however, the dollar control method becomes more specific; that is, the dollar control method may be applied (1) to departments, (2) to classifications, or (3) to specific price lines.[4]

Departmental Control. Departmental control refers to the use of dollar control on a departmental basis. Through the use of sales records, customer returns, returns to vendors, markups and markdowns, physical inventory counts, and rate of stockturn, the buyer or department manager can determine his or her department's profit picture in comparison with other store departments and with the profit objectives of the company. Departmental dollar control will assist store management to determine weaknesses and strengths in each department and thus lead to the development of measures that will improve individual department operations.

However, depending on the size of the store, many retailers have found that dollar information compiled at the department level is inadequate. "Over" and "under" conditions of sales, purchases, markdowns, stock, and open-to-buy are grouped together, thus concealing information that may be vital for effective management decision making. These retailers, therefore, use a more detailed analysis called classification control or classification merchandising.[5]

Classification Control. Classification control or *classification merchandising* refers to the use of dollar control based upon classifications of related types of merchandise within individual departments. For instance, in a ladies sportswear department information regarding dollar investment may be recorded separately for each classification of merchandise, such as active sportswear, casual sportswear, and spectator sportswear. Because this type of control is so popular today, many retailers have shown a tendency to subdivide broad classifications of merchandise into even smaller groups based on "consumer end-use"! Activity sportswear, for example, may be further subdivided into tennis wear, boating attire, or golf clothing.

According to the National Retail Merchants Association, there are ten basic steps that a retail store should follow when preparing for implementation of a merchandise classification control system. The steps that follow are applicable whether the system is operated manually or with sophisticated electronic equipment.

1. Designate the executive responsible for the installation and operation of the program.
2. Select the departments in which the system is to be started.
3. Define the classification descriptions, codes, and merchandise contents of the classes to be adopted in each of the departments selected for the initial installation.
4. Begin to use the new classification codes on purchase orders and price tickets.
5. Review internal systems, procedures, equipment, and forms, and determine the method to be used for accumulating and compiling the data necessary for preparing classification reports.
6. Select and contract for any equipment and/or services necessary for operation of the system.
7. Establish a timetable for installing the new system in stages, in terms of the depth of report sophistication, including the actual beginning date of the new system.
8. Prepare the store personnel through orientation and training.
9. Establish plans and schedules for entering class number on tickets of the merchandise on hand.
10. Develop a follow-through program to monitor the use of classification information and measure the success of the program against its cost.[6]

Price-Line Control. *Price-line control* refers to the use of dollar control based upon a single retail price. A department or a classification of merchandise may be broken down by particular price lines, such as $5.99 for a certain classification of men's shirts or $19.95 for all men's shirts sold in the men's furnishings department. In some cases, a buyer or department manager may use price-line control in place of merchandise control; furthermore, price lines may also be broken down according to size, style, fabric, or some other desired category.

Unit Control

Unit control, a second major form of merchandise control, may be defined as an organized method of recording the individual units or pieces of merchandise found in the inventory. This type of control is usually concerned with purchase orders, inventories, and sales. It involves the maintenance of records designed to provide accurate information in terms of physical units rather than in terms of dollars. Unit control attempts to answer the question "What?" This type of control is usually considered a supplement to dollar control; therefore, both types of formal control are essential in stock maintenance and in regulating stocks to consumer demand. According to Beatrice Judelle, an expert in the field of fashion merchandising, unit control guides the buyer toward an ideal assortment by:

1. Mapping the flow of merchandise in and out of a department.
2. Identifying fast and slow sellers.
3. Indicating the prominence that should be given in the assortment to various prices, sizes, colors, etc.
4. Keeping sections of the stock within predetermined maximum and minimum quantities.[7]

Explain the major forms of merchandise control

---

1. Dollar control
   Answers the question "how much?"
   May be applied to:
   a. Department—departmental control
   b. Classifications—classification control
   c. Price—price-line control
2. Unit control
   Answers the question "what?"
   Considered a supplement to dollar control

Types of Systems That Regulate Dollar Control and Unit Control

Dollar control and unit control may be achieved either through a perpetual inventory system or a periodic inventory system. A *perpetual inventory system* may be defined as a system where sales figures are derived from sales and purchase records of merchandise on hand—reported at regular intervals, such as every day, week, or month—in terms of goods that have been received and goods that have been sold. Tally records kept by salespeople on control cards or computer tape that is punched when the cash register is operated are two examples of sales records that yield information that will provide a basis for a perpetual, or ongoing, inventory system. This system is suitable for high-priced and fashion merchandise, since such merchandise is subject to high risk because of the short selling season. Inexpensive staple merchandise generally does not require sales information on a daily basis, since this type of merchandise has a longer selling period.

The *periodic inventory system* may be defined as an inventory method that derives sales figures from inventory and purchase data by periodically adding opening inventory and purchases and subtracting the sum of the closing inventory and markdowns. This is the commonly used method for staple goods and may be illustrated as follows:

SALES = OPENING INVENTORY + PURCHASES – CLOSING INVENTORY AND MARKDOWNS

Dollar Control and the Perpetual Inventory System

When using the perpetual inventory system in dollar control, it is necessary (1) to use the retail inventory method of accounting (discussed in detail in Part 2 of this chapter) for the store as a whole and for each department, classification, and price line, or (2) to analyze sales data and inventories without attempting to determine initial markup or gross margin. A major problem under the perpetual inventory method is to obtain complete and accurate information. To solve this problem, many retailers have installed EDP equipment. However, some retail stores, particularly smaller stores, still use clerical help to obtain necessary information. Whether done with clerical assistance or with electronic equipment, the perpetual inventory method provides a cumulative record of stocks on hand, sales for a particular period, and reorder periods.

Dollar Control and the Periodic Inventory System

When using the periodic inventory system in dollar control, three important records must be kept, whether the system affects the store as a whole, individual departments, classifications, or price lines. Records which must be kept, all at retail prices, are (1) records of inventory, (2) records of purchases, and (3) records of markdowns. These records will provide valuable information either on a semiannual basis or at other designated intervals.

Sales from retail inventories, retail purchases, and markdowns may be analyzed on a semiannual basis as follows:

Retail Stock on Hand—May 1	$25,000
(whole store, department, classification, or price line)	
Retail Purchases—May 1–October 31	+ 50,000
Total Retail Stock on Hand—October 1	$75,000
Retail Stock on Hand—October 31	– 30,000
Sales and Markdowns—May 1–October 31	$45,000
Markdowns—May 1–October 31	– 5,000
Derived Sales (including stock shortages)	$40,000

When an average rate of stock shortages for the store, department, classification, or price line is known, actual sales may be determined. For example, the derived sales may be divided by 100% plus the shortage percentage to determine the estimated net sales. If the shortage percentage is 2% of net sales, $40,000 may be divided by 102% to give estimated sales of $39,215.

Actual or net sales = Derived sales ÷ (100% + shortage percentage)
$39,215 = $40,000 ÷ 1.02 (100% + 2%)

The periodic inventory method may also be used to determine the maintained markup, the difference between cost price and final selling price. A markup percentage may be obtained by recording opening inventory and retail purchases at both cost price and retail price. By calculating the cost percent, which is 100 –markup percent, the retail value of the stock on hand may be reduced to a cost basis. The gross cost of merchandise sold and the gross margin figures may be obtained by this procedure; however, stock shortages must be closely estimated. An example follows:

	At Cost	At Retail	Markup %
Retail Stock on Hand–May 1	$15,000	$25,000	
Retail Purchases, May 1–October 31	+ 30,000	+ 50,000	
Total Retail Stock on Hand	$45,000	$75,000	40.0%
Retail Stock on Hand–October 31		–$30,000	
Cost Stock on Hand–October 31	$18,000		
Sales and Markdowns, May 1–October 31		$45,000	
Markdowns, May 1–October 31		– 5,000	
Sales and Shortages		$40,000	102.0%
Estimated Sales ($40,000 ÷ 1.02)		$39,215	100.0%
Gross Cost of Goods Sold	–$27,000		
Maintained Markup	$12,215		31.1%

A major advantage of the periodic inventory method of dollar control is that it is simple to use. Unfortunately, its usefulness is limited, since information is provided only at designated intervals.

Unit Control and the Perpetual Inventory System

As a result of using the perpetual inventory system in unit control, a continuous feedback of information on merchandise moved into and out of a department is readily available. To obtain this information, however, the buyer must establish a method of recording sales, receipts of merchandise, and merchandise returns based on a unit control system. Because the buyer receives this information on a weekly or even daily basis, inventory levels can be adjusted accordingly. This method of control also helps the buyer to determine stock shortages at the time inventories are taken.

The perpetual inventory system in unit control is commonly used for merchandise of high unit value that has a short selling season, such as women's apparel, fashion accessories, and men's clothing. This type of merchandise must be watched carefully to avoid taking high markdowns because of obsolescence. The method is practical because sales are easily recorded by units and reorders are common; however, the method is not practical where units of merchandise are small, for example, cosmetics and notions. The system enables the buyer and other store officials to keep a close watch on the progress of a specific line of merchandise or a specific merchandise classification.

In most department stores and chain operations the perpetual system of unit control is electronically operated. The computer issues daily, weekly, or monthly sales reports on styles, colors, sizes, price lines, vendors, and merchandise classes. However, for smaller stores other methods may be more practical. For example, the owner-manager of a small women's boutique keeps track of merchandise by using style cards. A separate style card is used for each style represented in the assortment. Each style card contains information on all transactions involved—orders, returns, markdowns, damages, price changes, colors, and sizes. The style card is kept either in a file box or on a rack. With this system the store owner can see at a glance what styles are selling fast; what styles need to be reordered; what styles are slow sellers; and what colors, fabrics, and sizes are popular.

Unit Control and the Periodic Inventory System

The periodic inventory system in unit control is based upon periodic inventory counts, which may be taken as frequently as desired (for example, weekly, monthly, or semiannually). This is the basic system used for the control of staple, low-value merchandise and of items with a long selling life that are replaced as they sell out, such as men's underwear, classic sweaters, men's socks, and women's hosiery. When using the periodic system, buyers or store managers should make frequent counts of fast-moving items, especially at the beginning of a season when they are watching for trends. Classic and basic merchandise items are counted less frequently but at regular intervals. Special attention should be given to merchandise that often sells out between counts. This system can be a basis for decisions about dropping merchandise lines that show little or no sales activity between counts. The buyer should continually check past sales figures, because even basic merchandise categories can show upward or downward trends.[8] Staple merchandise is usually in continuous demand; consequently, markdowns are less likely.

Another approach to the periodic system of unit control is the "physical inventory system." Under this system *a figure for net sales is obtained by adding the former physical inventory to the purchases received from vendors minus the ending physical inventory.*

Former Physical Inventory	$15,000	
+ Purchases Received from Vendors	+ 30,000	
Total	$45,000	
– Ending Physical Inventory	–$ 5,000	($15,000-$10,000)
Net Sales	$40,000	(Physical inventory minus merchandise sold)

For control purposes, information about stock is obtained by analyzing the rate at which merchandise is being sold and by comparing the stock in the previous inventory with that remaining in the current inventory. Purchases are also analyzed in this manner.

Unit Control and Other Types of Inventory Systems

Other types of inventory systems, in addition to perpetual or periodic systems, have been developed for use in unit control: (1) visual control, (2) tickler control, (3) warehouse control, (4) checklist control, (5) want-slip control, and (6) electronic control. These systems are used when visual inspection indicates that stock will soon be in short supply. They are designed to minimize lost sales caused by merchandise being out of stock and to maintain adequate assortments of stocks based on consumer demand. Selection of one or all of these inventory systems depends upon the special needs of the individual business.

Visual Control. Visual control is used when there is a reserve quantity of stock that has been separated from the rest of the stock by a divider or a banding device. When it becomes necessary to break into the reserve, a control ticket attached to the reserve stock is forwarded to the buyer for his evaluation on whether or not to reorder. In visual control, stock people or salespeople simply make a notation of the need to reorder whenever they observe that stock is low or depleted. This system is usually used for staple merchandise with a steady turnover.

Tickler Control. Under this type of control, lists of items to be counted (usually staples, such as drugs and cosmetics) are kept in a tickler file. A *tickler file* may be defined as a system that serves as a reminder and is arranged to **bring matters to timely attention. For example,** lists of cosmetic items to be counted each day are kept in a tickler file. They are so arranged that the list for any given day appears at the front of the file on that day and, thus, automatically comes to the attention of the buyer. The advisability of reorder is determined at this point. This system is most useful for goods having a steady turnover.

Warehouse Control. Merchandise commonly displayed in the store only in the form of floor samples, such as furniture, refrigerators, and washing machines, with delivery to the customer made from warehouse stock, may be controlled from the retail store, from the warehouse, or from both places. When the sale is made, a copy of the sales check is sent to unit control, where the transaction is entered into the control book. Control information is readily available to buyers, salespeople, and warehouse personnel alike to help eliminate overselling with consequent inability to deliver merchandise.

Checklist Control. Under the checklist system, stock on hand is checked against a basic or a model stock list at regular and frequent intervals. The basic stock includes the minimum assortment and quantities of stock; the model stock consists of a complete, well-balanced assortment of merchandise, which includes basic stock. The inventory is counted periodically by salespeople when the merchandise is on the floor and by stock people when the merchandise is in the stockroom. To avoid counting all items of merchandise on the same day, the counts are spread over a four-week period. Thus, a specified portion of stock is counted every day. Care is taken to count all stock purchased from a single vendor or manufacturer on the same day.

For this system to reveal overstocked and understocked merchandise effectively, care must be taken when checking merchandise on hand against the stock list. In addition, salespeople must be careful not to permit any item to be completely sold out, since it is difficult to determine what merchandise belongs in an empty space. It is important to maintain a uniform arrangement of goods, so that anyone counting the stock can readily identify the merchandise.

Want-Slip Control. A want slip is a simple form filled out by salespeople regarding either out-of-stock items or items not sold by the store but requested by customers. It is a method of unit control that tells the buyer or store manager of sales that might have been made. A want-slip system may indicate to a buyer that a new trend is starting, a particular fad is developing, or a particular color or fabric is becoming popular. Chapter 9 discusses how want slips can guide buyers in making decisions about planning merchandise assortments.

Electronic Control. Many small businesses, general merchandise operations, department stores, variety stores, specialty shops, and food stores have turned to electronic controls (EDP) to facilitate counting procedures. The computer is used by retail executives in many aspects of retailing; however, it is especially suited to the control of merchandise inventories. For example, most large department stores and specialty shops are using sales registers which record on tape the department number, classification, style number, amount of sale, and number of the salesperson for each sales transaction. At the end of the day, register tapes are taken to the computer center, where they are processed. The following day, the store buyer is furnished with a detailed report of the previous day's sales. Daily information concerning net sales, customer returns, fast-selling items, slow sellers, and merchandise on hand will assist buying specialists to make decisions affecting markdowns, reorders, vendor returns, and consumer demand. The computer also issues a list of all stock items to be counted on any given day, and by means of an optical scanner, it will provide a complete list of merchandise in stock. Provision of fast, accurate data retrieval to ensure correct merchandising decisions has been achieved by the use of EDP equipment.

The National Retail Merchants Association (NRMA) has developed a group EDP service, whereby small businesses may make arrangements to send register tapes of sales and inventory data to the NRMA computer service bureau. The NRMA computer sorts the transactions into merchandise classifications and sends back printed sales and inventory reports for classifications and departments as well as for the entire store.[9]

In the multiunit chain operation, EDP is a more elaborate, sophisticated procedure. A variety store chain may use an automatic replenishment system that keeps track, by means of a special tape, of each order placed by each store in the chain. The computer keeps a record of each item shipped and from the monthly on-hand reports it knows how many items are sold. By correlating each store's merchandise history with its monthly on-hand reports, the data-processing center can forecast and order shipment of the quantities of each item (usually staple goods) that will be required by each store over a certain period of time. It is important for each store to accurately record merchandise on hand, so that the store will not overstock or run out of an item. An inventory should be taken at least every two weeks; oftener, if needed. At inventory time, the store manager or the staff will check to see how many units of merchandise are on hand, both on the selling floor and in the stockroom. A report is then sent to the data-processing center, where items will be either reordered or canceled.

In between the monthly on-hand reports, the store manager or the staff may notice that the store is out of an item, very low on an item, or, upon receipt of a shipment, has more of an item than it needs. If this is the case, another report will be prepared to tell the EDP center that figures for store totals of that item need adjustment. Once this report is sent to the EDP center, immediate action is taken to adjust the store's stock by changing the amount of merchandise that will be shipped in the future.

As you recall, a good control system must be accurate, timely, and understood by the members of the organization if it is to be an effective tool in managerial decision making. Thus, an EDP center should issue guidelines that store personnel may use for reference and as reminders when filling out various EDP forms. Guidelines may include instructions to write numbers legibly; refrain from stapling, folding, or tearing reports; and record numbers accurately.

Types of inventory systems that regulate merchandise controls

Dollar control	Visual control
Perpetual inventory system	Tickler control
Periodic inventory system	Warehouse control
Unit control	Checklist control
Perpetual inventory system	Want-slip control
Periodic inventory system	Electronic control

How will each of the above assist the buyer or store manager in making effective merchandising decisions?

PART 2

Merchandise Controls Continued

**Advantages and
Limitations of
Merchandise Controls**

The purpose of a good control system has already been stated: (1) to assist store managers, department store buyers, and small-store owners to make effective purchases, (2) to ensure prompt reordering, and (3) to prevent purchase of merchandise that is unacceptable to the consumer. However, retail stores have found that control measures also offer limitations along with their many advantages, and close attention must be given to both when determining which control system is best for the individual store or department. The following list of advantages and limitations should be consulted by all retailers when considering the adoption of merchandise controls.

Advantages of merchandise controls	Limitations of merchandise controls
1. Ensure meeting consumer needs, wants, desires 2. Improve profits 3. Minimize inventory investment 4. Reduce slow sellers 5. Reduce the cost of selling 6. Provide buying information	1. Require frequent reviews 2. No substitute for experience 3. Expensive to operate 4. Require follow-up 5. Require thorough understanding

Advantages of Merchandise Controls

Ensure Meeting Consumer Needs and Wants. An important responsibility of retailers is to provide merchandise that consumers need and want, at a price they are willing to pay, in a convenient location. Since consumer demand may change from day to day, season to season, and year to year, a merchant often has difficulty in determining such demands. Merchandise controls that are effectively implemented will assist the buyer by indicating stock items that are fast moving and slow selling, as well as items that have proved unsatisfactory and have been returned by customers.

Improve Profits. A well-balanced stock will usually lead to greater sales and, thus, fewer markdowns. Good merchandise controls will improve profits by indicating trends and conditions that may affect the balance of stock. Such controls may focus attention on fast- and slow-moving stock items, assist the buyer in reorders, and help keep stocks up to date through sales promotion and advertising.

Minimize Inventory Investment. It is usually desirable to keep the investment in merchandise inventory at the lowest possible level consistent with fulfillment of consumer demand. This also results in a better rate of stockturn. Merchandise controls tell the buyer when it is necessary to reorder merchandise, take markdowns, order new stock items, and eliminate merchandise that has proved unappealing.

Reduce Slow Sellers. Slow-selling merchandise will decrease profits when not handled properly. Therefore, a store manager or buyer continuously seeks feedback information regarding stock turnover from salespeople, department managers, and assistant buyers. Merchandise controls provide accurate information, usually on a daily basis, and facilitate buyer decisions about items that should be marked down, transferred, or returned to vendors.

Reduce the Cost of Selling. Since good merchandise controls provide information about stock turnover, slow-moving merchandise, and popular stock items, the cost of selling may be reduced. Unnecessary markdowns will be eliminated, warehousing and transportation costs reduced, and popular or new items can be moved onto the selling floor into space that might otherwise have been occupied by marked down merchandise. Good controls make selling easier and lead to a well-balanced stock assortment.

Provide Buying Information. For buyers to make accurate decisions regarding the merchandise assortment, they must receive up-to-date selling information. Merchandise control really begins *before* goods are purchased from vendors and manufacturers. Before entering the marketplace, therefore, buyers should be aware of sales trends, customer returns, defective merchandise, popular types and prices of merchandise, current fashion trends, markdowns taken to sell goods, and other information of a similar nature. Good merchandise controls provide information to serve as a guide in making purchasing commitments.

Limitations of Merchandise Controls

Require Frequent Reviews. Since merchandise control systems are set up to provide specific types of information under a given set of circumstances, they should be reviewed frequently. Retailing is always changing; its people and its systems must keep pace. All too often, control systems that provide important merchandise information are continued long past the time when the information they provide becomes obsolete. The merchandise manager, central buyer, or store manager must frequently review the types of merchandise controls in use and to determine if they are effective under new sets of circumstances.

No Substitute for Experience. Merchandise controls should never be used to substitute for experience, knowledge, or decision making. They should be looked upon only as supplementary to management know-how. Whether a buyer deals with staple goods or fashion goods, merchandise information should always be analyzed and interpreted in the light of new situations. A good retail executive will not depend totally on a computer printout, since such information has been supplied indirectly by human beings and is, therefore, subject to inaccuracies.

Expensive to Operate. Merchandise control systems are not only costly to install but also expensive to operate and maintain. Since they need to be revised frequently, additional expense is incurred in retraining personnel to use the new methods. Retailers often hesitate to install newer electronic devices, and then find that their competition is already one jump ahead of them. Other retailers fail to recognize the many benefits of newer control systems. However, the decision as to which type of control system to implement in a business is based upon the finances available and the size and type of the retail operation.

Require Follow-up. Some retail stores, aware that competition is using highly sophisticated control systems, have adopted similar systems, thinking that good control systems would result automatically. However, a good control system exists only when the information received is interpreted and translated into meaningful action. Buyers must learn to accurately interpret information if it is to help them select merchandise assortments that will meet the needs of their customers and, thus, make profits for their stores.

Require Thorough Understanding. For merchandise control systems to operate effectively, merchandise managers, central buyers, assistant buyers, salespeople, and stock personnel—in other words, the entire work force—must thoroughly understand the operating procedures involved in a good merchandise control system. For example, salespeople must properly record returned or damaged merchandise, stock personnel must take accurate counts during inventory periods, and assistant buyers must accurately record merchandise that has been transferred to a branch store or returned to the vendor. All involved in the merchandising activity of the retail store should be made aware of the purposes and objectives of merchandise control systems.

> How will the advantages and limitations of merchandise controls affect merchandising activities in:
>
> | A small men's wear business? | A specialty chain operation? |
> |---|---|
> | A discount department store? | A medium-sized furniture store? |

In most retail stores, the largest monetary investment is usually in the *merchandise inventory*, merchandise that is available for sale to the ultimate customer. Unlike inventories of merchandise carried by most other types of businesses, inventories carried by retail stores have certain differentiating characteristics.

Characteristics of the Merchandise Inventory

Merchandise Inventories:

1. Constitute an exceptionally large part of the assets, usually more than 50%
2. Fluctuate daily, monthly, or seasonally
3. Are constantly changing as new items are added and old items deleted
4. Contain only the most appealing and up-to-date lines of merchandise
5. Contain large numbers of many different types of items
6. Are perishable; that is, they will deteriorate as soon as new items enter the market
7. Are subject to stock deterioration; therefore, markdowns become a major consideration
8. Are vulnerable to shoplifting and pilferage
9. Are difficult to safeguard, since they are displayed and stored in many locations
10. Must be readily available to meet consumer demands

Because the merchandise inventory is so varied, the problems of inventory planning and control become major ones for store managers and buyers. A physical inventory, therefore, becomes a necessity. A *physical inventory* may be defined as the actual counting and recording of the merchandise or stock on hand at a specified time, together with the cost or the retail price of each item.[10] There are several reasons for taking a physical inventory:

Why Take a Physical Inventory?

First: Preparation of Financial Statements. A retailer must take a physical count of merchandise on hand to determine the total value of his stock. This information is necessary for the preparation of financial statements, such as the profit-and-loss statement. Business statements provide management with a detailed analysis of the financial condition of an individual department or of the store as a whole. We discuss financial statements and other important business records in greater detail in the next chapter.

Second: To Familiarize Personnel with the Stock Assortment. By taking a physical count of stock on hand, all personnel—merchandise managers, central and local buyers, assistants, salespeople, and stock people—will have an opportunity to know what merchandise is in stock. Since the merchandise inventory contains thousands of many different types of items, merchandise may often remain unnoticed or "lost." Think, for example, of the number of items you can find in a variety store, a hardware store, or a discount house! By taking a physical count, items are brought to the attention of salespeople, who, in turn, will adapt selling techniques to selling that merchandise.

Third: Inventory Analysis. At a specific time, the physical inventory relates the quantities, kinds, and values of the items found in stock in the entire store and in individual departments. If there are branch operations, an inventory analysis is also taken of the stock in each branch store. In a chain operation, a count is taken of all merchandise in each individual unit. In a storewide inventory, stock is analyzed according to merchandise classification, price line, and physical units by season or age group. With this information, buyers or store managers can adjust stock on hand according to consumer demand by marking down old stock that has accumulated or by shipping that merchandise to a branch store or unit where the merchandise has proved more appealing.

Fourth: Determine Stock Shortages and Overages. By taking a physical count of merchandise in stock, buyers may compare actual counts with stock records to determine the amount of stock shortage or overage. This information will help buyers to take corrective measures. It provides a basis for checking and correcting unit control and other stock records.

Fifth: Sales Determination. Sales records are usually kept for the entire store, for individual departments, and for each merchandise classification for each store and its branches (if a branch operation) or for each unit in the chain (if a chain-store operation). The physical count may be taken for subgroups, for price lines, or for special stock items. If a count is taken by these breakdowns at specified periods and if purchase records are maintained for each, valuable sales data may be obtained that will assist buyers or managers to determine slow sellers, best sellers, markdowns, and so forth.

Steps in Taking the Physical Inventory

If you ever worked in a retail store, large or small, you were probably involved either directly or indirectly in taking a physical inventory. However, methods used by different stores and the time periods involved vary with the type and size of the retail establishment. Some types of retail operations require little advance preparation (for example, the grocery store where stock personnel simply count merchandise on the shelves and in the stockroom and record the counts on special forms). However, in a department store and chain operation the procedure of taking a physical inventory is far more complex. The procedure discussed in the following pages is the one used primarily by these stores. The inventory procedure may be broken down into five steps.[11] (1) The times of the inventory—annually or semiannually; (2) The planning stage—careful advance planning is a *must;* (3) Counting, recording, checking—must be thorough to insure accuracy; (4) Calculating the stock value—the cost method, the book method, the retail method; (5) The use of inventory reports—daily sales records, style reports, vendor summary, and so forth.

The Times of the Inventory

In most retail stores, it is the practice to take two inventories a year. In fashion apparel stores and in general merchandise chain operations these inventories are usually taken during the months that are considered to be the end of selling seasons, for example, January and July. In stores where inventory is taken only once a year (an annual inventory) the complete inventory is usually taken at the end of January. Management must consider when counting times will occur during the specified inventory period and determine whether to close down the store during the period in which inventory is taken, to take the inventory after business hours or on weekends, or to conduct the inventory during store hours and close the store early. Most retail store managements decide to conduct inventory counts during business hours and, in some cases, close the store early to complete the physical inventory procedure. Many times a store notifies customers of a store inventory through such advertisements as "We will close today at 3:00 P.M. to take our annual inventory" or "Early closing due to storewide inventory."

Planning Stage

Careful advance preparation is a must if accuracy in recording and thoroughness in counting are to result. Advance preparation includes six types of activities: (1) classifying and grouping merchandise by type, price, and style; (2) placing all merchandise information on the price ticket; (3) planning sales to reduce stock; (4) preparing a layout chart; (5) obtaining the necessary forms; and (6) issuing inventory instructions to sales and stock personnel.

> Careful advance preparation is a must if accuracy in recording and thoroughness in counting is to occur.

Classifying and Grouping Merchandise by Type, Price, and Style. By this means, the speed of the count will be increased and the buyer will be sure that all merchandise is included. For example, the buyer or department manager of the handbag department will direct assistants and sales and stock personnel to group the merchandise according to shoulder bags, clutch bags, evening bags, etc. Once merchandise is classified, the counting procedure may proceed with counts recorded according to the specified merchandise classification. This also assists the buyer by increasing his or her own information regarding what is in stock.

Placing All Merchandise Information on the Price Ticket. If an accurate count is to occur, the buyer must be certain that all merchandise information is on the price ticket. Ticket information should include price, department, classification, style, season and size (where applicable), and vendor number. Figure 7.4 illustrates the kind of information found on most price tickets.

Figure 7.4. Price ticket information should include price, department, classification, style, season, size (where applicable) and vendor.

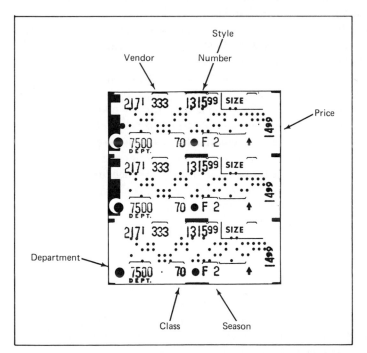

Planning Sales to Reduce Stock. As a result of classifying and grouping merchandise by type, price, or style, the buyer may discover that certain stock items may be included in special sales-promotion activities, for example, an "Inventory Clearance Sale." In this way, the buyer may clear out unwanted, slow-moving merchandise before the actual inventory count begins.

Figure 7.5. Inventory sheet. (Courtesy of John Wanamaker Department Store, Philadelphia, Pa.)

223-3B (Rev. 10-73)

INVENTORY SHEET

Location __Stockroom__	STORE or WAREHOUSE	
Fixture No. __10__	__1__ __Phila.__	__97-00__
Shelf/Bin No. __6__	No. Name	Dept. No.

FASHION DEPTS. ONLY	0 to 3 Months	4 to 6 Months	PRIOR					
SEASONAL CODES	S-1 to S-6	R-1 to R-6	All Other					
ALL OTHER DEPTS.	0 to 6 Months	7 to 12 Months	PRIOR					
DESCRIPTION, STYLE, NO., OR MANUFACTURER'S NO.	QUANT.	DEDUCT.	QUANT.	DEDUCT.	QUANT.	DEDUCT.	UNIT EACH DOZ., FAIR, ETC.	UNIT RETAIL PRICE DOLLARS | CENTS
1 Hairpins	150	~~174~~					pkg.	10
2 Shoes #2601	2		4	2	6		pr.	16 | 95
3 Saucepans			13				2 for	5 | 50
4 Handkerchiefs	13						pkg.	5 | 00
5 Handkerchiefs	3						6 for	5 | 00
6 ~~Tablecloths~~	~~14~~						~~ea.~~	~~6 | 95~~
7 Tablecloths			16				ea.	6 | 95
8 Shirts - Medium			21	18			ea.	4 | 99
9 Shirts - Large			23	15			ea.	4 | 99
10								
11								
12								

AGE OF STOCK	DOLLARS	CENTS	DOLLARS	CENTS	DOLLARS	CENTS	TOTALS DOLLARS | CENTS
RETAIL	DO NOT SUMMARIZE HERE						
COST							

Listed by __A. Alpha__

Counted by __B. Bravo__

Recounted by __C. Charley__

FOREIGN

№ 035453

Classification No. __20__

1. Deductions are accumulated; there are 146 packages remaining.
2. The merchandise is from three different seasons.
3. List loose multiple items.
4. List packages or boxed multiple items.
5. List of a broken package, originally containing 6 items.
6-7. Errors are corrected and additions are made.
8-9. Large quantities may be accumulated in the description column and then summarized in the quantity column.

Preparing a Layout Chart. The buyer or department manager should prepare a layout chart of the entire department that indicates the position of each fixture that contains stock items. This information is sent to the controller who, in turn, issues inventory sheets that mark specific sections in each department. This is one way to ensure that all merchandise is included when the count is taken.

Obtaining the Necessary Forms. Three types of forms may be used by a store for recording and listing stock: (1) the inventory sheet, (2) the inventory tag or ticket, and (3) the punch card.

The *inventory sheet* allows recording a large number of items on one sheet and includes such information as description, quantity, price, style or lot number, season letter, classification, vendor, and other desired information. If selling continues while the count is being taken, a special deduction sheet is made out. (The deduction sheet is the same as the regular inventory sheet but is clearly marked to differentiate it.) Salespeople must carefully fill out the deduction sheet as sales are made; otherwise inventory figures will not agree with information obtained from previous inventory records (see Figure 7.5).

The *inventory tag* or ticket is not as popular as the inventory sheet. The information required is similar, but a separate tag is required for every different style or lot number and for the same article in different locations. Since these tags are filled out in advance of the inventory period, deductions are made between the time the tag is filled out and the time the inventory is completed. Figure 7.6 illustrates an inventory tag that can be attached to merchandise in the furniture department.

Since electronic data processing has become so popular, some retail stores

Figure 7.6. An illustration of an inventory tag that can be attached to merchandise in the furniture department. (Courtesy of John Wanamaker Department Store, Philadelphia, Pa.)

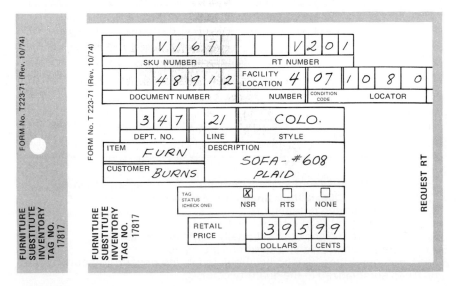

have adopted *punch cards* or tape to facilitate inventory computations. A punching machine may be used, and while one person calls out the description and quantity of each stock item, another person operates the machine, which punches a card for every item (see Figure 7.7).

Issuing Inventory Instructions to Sales and Stock Personnel. It is important for sales personnel to understand completely the technique of inventory taking. Usually the merchandise manager or store manager issues instructions to department assistants, salespeople, and stock personnel before the inventory period begins and carefully explains the importance of accuracy and thoroughness when counting and recording stock items. Figure 7.8 illustrates the first page of instructions issued to merchandise personnel that explain the entire procedure involved in taking a physical inventory of, in this case, a furniture department.

Why are each of the following planning activities important when taking a physical inventory?

1. Classifying and grouping merchandise by type, price, and style
2. Placing all merchandise information on the price ticket—style, vendor, price, class, season, size, department
3. Planning sales to reduce stock—"Inventory Clearance Sale"
4. Preparing a layout chart—the position of each fixture that contains stock
5. Obtaining the necessary forms—the inventory sheet, the inventory tag or ticket, the punch card
6. Issuing inventory instructions to sales and stock personnel—explain the entire procedure to merchandise personnel

---

Figure 7.7. An example of a punch card. The punch card is punched by the computer with an identifying mark before it is attached to the merchandise or its ticket. (Courtesy of John Wanamaker Department Store, Philadelphia, Pa.)

Figure 7.8. Issuing inventory
instructions to salespeople.

TO: Furniture Divisional Merchandise Manager
         All Furniture Buyers, Assistant Buyers
         Branch Store Furniture Divisional Merchandise
             Managers
         Branch Store Furniture Group Managers
         All Branch Store Operations Managers

FROM: Arthur Kimmel *AK*

> **Furniture Inventory Instructions
> For Taking Inventory on the
> Selling Floor—All Locations**

Inventory will be taken on January 31, 1977, in all selling locations for the following furniture departments:

51-21   51-23   51-26   51-28   51-24   51-22   51-25

A. *Preparation for Inventory*

1. Prepare a floor plan of the area to be inventoried.
2. Divide the floor into area of responsibility and assign same to individuals.
3. Beginning immediately, individuals assigned to an area must inspect each piece of furniture in his assigned area to be sure that the appropriate tag with at least one stub is affixed to each piece of furniture.
4. For pieces of furniture without the appropriate tag with at least one stub, a request must be made. This request is to be made by contacting the terminal control area.
5. The following information must be available:

    a. Department Number
    b. Line
    c. Manufacturer's Style
    d. Article
    e. Description

6. Issuing inventory instructions to sales and stock personnel: explaining the entire procedure to merchandise personnel.

Counting, Recording, Checking

The third step in taking a physical inventory involves counting the merchandise (both on the floor and in the stockroom), recording the counts on the inventory sheets, and checking for accuracy. Before counting begins, it is

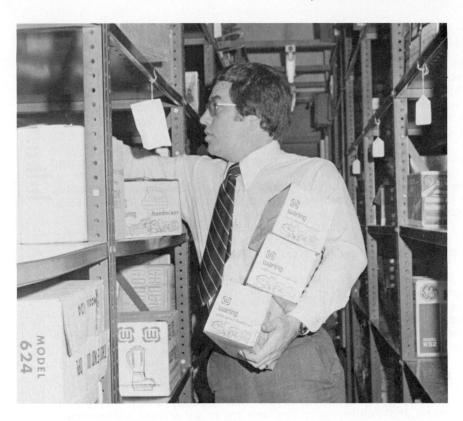

Figure 7.9. The actual counting of merchandise, both on the floor and in the stockroom, is an important step in taking a physical inventory.

important to ensure that no merchandise will be moved onto the selling floor from the stockroom. Movement of merchandise during the inventory count increases the possibility of double counting; that is, counting the same item, both in the stockroom and on the selling floor.

Some stores count their complete forward stock (that is, stock on the selling floor) in advance to avoid difficulties in handling sales during inventory. Warehouse and reserve-stock inventories may also be taken in advance, and careful records must be kept of all goods sent to the selling floor or received in the stockroom or warehouse. Addition and deduction sheets are used, along with the regular counting forms, such as inventory sheets, inventory tags or tickets, or punch cards. Employees usually work in pairs with one person calling and one recording. To ensure accuracy, the person recording the count may change places with the person counting and do a recount. However, because this method slows down inventory taking, spot checks or partial recounts are frequently taken. Unless spot checks indicate the existence of many errors, the inventory count is assumed to be correct. Figure 7.10 illustrates a list of instructions issued by a control division to counters and listers for all departments except furniture.

1. List all entries legibly and in the correct columns.
2. List on consecutive lines—**Do not skip lines when listing.**
3. List only **ONE** classification of merchandise on any one inventory sheet.
4. List directly from the merchandise and its price ticket to the inventory sheet. **Copying from memoranda to an inventory sheet is absolutely forbidden.**
5. List the total quantity only in the quantity columns.
6. List quantities in the correct season column. (A listing of season letters, and the columns in which they are to be listed has been included in the Inventory Books.)
7. List multiple items that are loose at the multiple price shown on the tickets. It is not necessary for you to divide or to multiply. Just count the items as indicated and enter the information in the proper columns. 13 Pants selling for 2 for $5.50 would be listed as follows:

   Example: Pants   13   2 for $5.50

8. List items that are multiples, but in a standard package or box, as a unit. 13 packs of handkerchiefs packaged 6 in a package for $5.00 would be listed as follows:

   Example: Handkerchiefs   13   pkg. $5.00
   Not: Handkerchiefs   78   6 for $5.00

9. List the multiple quantity (2 for or 6 for etc.) in the unit column only when the merchandise is loose.
10. **Ditto marks are not permitted** except in the description column.
11. **Do not erase** an entry if any error has been made. Cross out errors with a single line and make the correct entry on another line.
12. If merchandise that has already been listed is sold or removed, the quantity must be entered in the **deduct column** to the right of quantity column. Do not use strokes, use whole numbers.
13. When you finish inventorying a fixture, review the inventory sheet. Make sure that all season letters and months, quantities, and prices are entered in the correct columns and that none are omitted. Then sign the sheet on the appropriate line.
14. If any fixture where an inventory sheet is laid is empty, write **"No Merchandise"** on the inventory sheet.

Recounting the Inventory

1. You cannot recount an inventory sheet that you originally counted.
2. When recounting an inventory sheet always count the merchandise, and check to see if it is listed correctly on the sheet. Never check from the sheet and try to find the merchandise.
3. When a mistake is found, call it to the attention of the buyer or divisional, and then make the correction by crossing out the wrong line and rewriting the information correctly on the next blank line. Remember to check the deduction column if you find the count short as the merchandise may have been removed. If the missing pieces are listed in the deduction column, no correction is necessary.
4. After you have verified the entire sheet, and it is correct, sign your name on the "Recounted by" line.

The sincere cooperation and interest of all concerned will assure a proper and accurate inventory.

Controller's Office

Calculating Inventory Value

The fourth step in taking a physical inventory is calculating the value of the inventory. Three methods may be used to determine inventory value: (1) the cost method, (2) the book method, and (3) the retail method.

Methods used to determine the value of closing inventory

---

1. The cost method—goods are recorded at cost price
2. The book method—a record of inventory
    book inventory = stock on hand + purchases – goods sold
3. The retail method—a combination of the cost method and book method at retail prices

---

The Cost Method. In the *cost method of inventory,* goods are recorded at cost price and the ending inventory values are determined by actually counting the merchandise in stock and recording values at cost prices. The cost price of each item is usually recorded in code on the price ticket. Most codes are expressed in such a way that the value is not apparent to customers or even to those employees who do not need to possess such information.

This valuation of inventory is based on the assumption that present in-stock goods have the same worth as they had when they were bought. However, this may not always be true, since some inventories can depreciate in value. For example, factors that may contribute to merchandise depreciation are (1) obsolescence, (2) damaged merchandise, (3) a drop in wholesale price, (4) change in consumer demand, and (5) the type of goods (that is, staple or fashion). The inventory, therefore, should be evaluated at less than cost or at the current market value. For example, if a toy buyer bought bicycles at $50 and priced them at $150, they may have to be sold for $105 if they are still on the selling floor when new models appear. The inventory value of the bicycles can be determined as follows:

Original Cost Price	$ 50.00	
+ Markup Price	+100.00	(200% Markup)
Original Retail Price	$150.00	
New Cost Price (at Cost or Market, whichever is lower)	$ 35.00	(devalued due to obsolescence)
+ New Markup Price	+70.00	(200% Markup)
New Price (Markdown)	$105.00	

The inventory value or new cost price is $35.00. Note that the same markup of 200% is maintained.

Figure 7.10. Counters and listers inventory instructions for all departments except furniture. See facing page.

If prices remained constant, there would be little, if any, problem concerning valuation of inventory. However, when changes occur with no relationship to cost of initial purchases, buyers and store managers have a difficult task when they attempt to place values on inventory at cost or market price, whichever is lower. There are two methods that may be used to calculate inventory value: (1) the First-in First-out Method (FIFO) and (2) the Last-in First-out Method (LIFO).

Under the FIFO method of inventory evaluation, larger profits result during periods of rising prices because higher values are placed on ending inventories than on the merchandise on hand at the beginning of the year. The difference is added to profits. For example, a buyer of children's toys will usually attempt to sell items that were bought earliest because they have been in stock for the longest period of time and they initially cost less than merchandise purchased later. Thus, goods included in the beginning-of-the-year inventory would be the first units sold. The FIFO method is one way of keeping stocks fresh and up to date. It is also used to keep profits high due to price increases of end-of-year inventories.

A second method of inventory valuation, the LIFO method, assumes that those goods purchased recently are sold first. Once a retail organization decides to use this method of inventory valuation, it must do so continuously. This method also requires that total markdowns must be deducted from the retail sales figure in calculating the net markup figure. This method of inventory is gradually being accepted by most retail organizations, primarily because of the continued upward trend of retail prices.

The following illustration compares the FIFO method and the LIFO method in a period when costs are increasing.

A buyer purchased 100 items at $5 each and 100 additional items at $7 each, a total of 200 items at $1,200. During the season, 100 items were sold, leaving 100 items remaining in stock. The 100 items that were sold brought a retail price of $10 each.

	FIFO		LIFO	
Retail Sales				
100 items @ $10	$1,000		$1,000	
Cost of Goods Sold				
100 items @ $5	− 500;	100 items @ $7 −	700	(increased
Profits Before Taxes	$ 500		$ 300	costs)
Ending Inventory Value				
100 items @ $7	$ 700;	100 items @ $5 $	500	

The student should note that under the FIFO method, profits are $200 higher and ending inventory values are $200 higher. Under the LIFO method, profits before taxes are $200 lower, which leads to lower taxes, and ending inventory values are $200 lower.

When costs are decreasing, the above illustration is reversed. The LIFO method shows inflated profits, taxes, and ending inventory, and the FIFO method results in lower profits before taxes and lower ending inventory. Needless to say, during a period of steady costs, the buyer will not gain from either the FIFO method or the LIFO method.

The Book Method. Many stores, such as discount houses, specialty chain operations, variety stores, and drugstores, require continuous information about the value of the merchandise inventory, even though it is impractical to take a physical inventory more than twice a year. This information may be obtained by using the book method of inventory. The *book method of inventory* is the record of stock that should be on hand in terms of what has been purchased and what has been sold. What should be on hand is called the closing book inventory. No actual counting of the merchandise is required for the book inventory; however, what is counted twice a year is called the physical inventory. The book inventory method, if calculated every day, week, or month, is called a perpetual inventory. It may be kept either in terms of dollar value or in terms of units of merchandise. The excess of book inventory at the end of every six months over physical inventory is the merchandise shortage. In recording information for a book inventory, values may be recorded at either cost or retail prices. Most retail stores employ the book method of inventory at retail prices. An example follows:

	At Retail
Physical Inventory, August 1	$10,000
Purchases, August–January	+ 15,500
Total Merchandise Handled	$25,500
Goods Sold, August–January	− 15,000
Book Inventory, January 31	$10,500
Physical Inventory, January 31	− 10,000
Merchandise Shortage	$ 500

The retail buyer will subtract from the book inventory those markdowns he may have taken before he compares it with the physical inventory.

The Retail Method. The *retail method of inventory* is a combination of the cost method of inventory with the book method of inventory at retail prices. When inventory is calculated at retail prices rather than at cost prices, it is necessary to subtract the cost or market price from the total retail value to figure profit or loss. Every six months all purchases are recorded at both cost and retail prices. The markup on all purchases, including the opening inventory, is determined. This markup is applied to the closing inventory at retail to arrive at the cost or market value. An example of this procedure follows.

	At Cost	At Retail	Markup %
Beginning Inventory	$3,050	$ 5,000	40%
Purchases	+ 5,950	+10,000	
Total Merchandise Handled	$9,000	$15,000	
Closing Physical Inventory at Retail		2,500	
Closing Physical Inventory at Cost or Market Value ($2,500 × 60%)	$1,500		

Eventually, the merchandise in the entire store must be physically counted. It is highly unlikely that a physical count will show agreement of the book inventory and the physical inventory. When the physical inventory is greater than the book inventory, there is a *merchandise overage;* when the physical inventory is less than the book inventory, there is a *merchandise shortage.*

A merchandise shortage usually indicates an actual loss of inventory in the department, whereas a merchandise overage probably indicates an error in the physical count.

Analyzing Inventory Reports

The last step in taking a physical inventory is analyzing and summarizing all information derived from the various inventory forms (inventory sheets, tags, punch cards) and from perpetual and periodic inventory counts. Reports are drawn up that analyze the inventory by price, by classification, by season, and by department in relation to sales.

If the punch-card method is used to take inventory, sorting by department, classification, season, and price line is accomplished automatically. If inventory sheets or tags are used, the information is sent to the computer center, where a card is punched for each item appearing on the inventory sheet or on each inventory tag. These cards are then fed into the computer, which issues a typed, classified report. When department totals are added, the result gives the dollar value of merchandise in the entire store. The buyer can then determine whether he should reduce his present inventory.

If a number of slow sellers are discovered, an effort is made to clear out old stock by listing these items on special slow-selling sheets. An inventory is taken of slow-selling merchandise, either daily, weekly, or monthly. Additional markdowns may be necessary to move the stock. (Markdowns and the reason for taking them are discussed in detail in chapter 14.)

Sales and stock reports assist buyers or store managers in making decisions regarding inventory conditions. The following list is representative of the kinds of reports buyers and managers receive on a daily, weekly, or monthly basis.

> Reports used by buyers and store managers
> to assist in decision making regarding
> inventory conditions
>
> 1. Daily sales reports
> 2. Sales by style, vendor, best seller, classification, color and size,
>   price line
> 3. Exception reports

Daily Sales Reports. The daily sales report shows how rapidly or how slowly inventory is being converted to sales. It is a day-to-day indication of progress toward the department's or store's sales goals and serves as a reminder to adjust inventory. It informs store management of possible changes in consumer demand, either throughout the entire store or in particular departments. If daily sales figures are high or low for several days running and there is no obvious explanation, such as unusual weather conditions, special sales promotions, or changes in economic conditions, then store management should carefully search for possible reasons. Beatrice Judelle tells us that

> If sales are unusually high, look for:
> 1. An unnoticed "natural"—a style or item that attracts customers spontaneously and that should be exploited promptly
> 2. Colors, styles, textures, that have suddenly become strong because of the fashion coordination story your store is presenting
> 3. Price lines, classifications, etc., that have become suddenly strong because of a shift of consumer interest or a weakening of competition
> 4. Something you are doing right and should do more in briefing your salespeople, presenting your merchandise, etc.
>
> If sales are unusually poor, look for:
> 1. Unnoticed "duds" and slow sellers that need action to get them moving
> 2. Colors, styles, texture, etc., that are out of step with the storewide fashion story
> 3. The absence from stock of wanted styles, sizes, prices
> 4. Prices that are too high or too low for present customer demands
> 5. New or strengthened competition
> 6. Something you are not doing but should be doing to brief salespeople, improve your merchandise presentation, etc.[12]

Sales by Style, Vendor, Best Sellers, Classification, Color and Size, Price Line. A type of reporting system used by some department stores is a computerized system called the SABRE System. It provides sales activity reports to buyers or group managers on a weekly basis, both in the parent store and in the branches. Figure 7.11 is an example of a Weekly Buyers Style Status Report that shows unit sales for the entire week, one week ago, month to date, and season to date. Sales totals in units are given by style, class, subclass, and department. Within each classification, the percentage of each store's weekly unit sales is compared to the total corporate unit sales.

The buyer or manager may also receive a Vendor Summary Report (Figure 7.12), which provides unit sales information for all styles of each vendor within a department by location. The frequency of the report is predetermined by the buyer, and the report may be received once a week, twice a week, quarterly, or upon request of the merchandise manager. Unit sales by vendor are provided for the week to date (WTD), one week ago (1WA), month to date (MTD), and season to date (STD). The Vendor Summary Report contains information by classification, selling price, vendor, style, and branch store.

In many cases the selling activity of the parent store tends to outweigh

Figure 7.11. Weekly Buyers Style Status Report shows unit sales for the entire week, one week ago, month to date, and season to date. Sales totals in units are given by style, class, subclass, and department. (Courtesy of John Wanamaker Department Store, Philadelphia, Pa.)

Figure 7.12. Vendor Summary Report provides unit sales information for all styles of each vendor within a department by location. (Courtesy of John Wanamaker Department Store, Philadelphia, Pa.)

Figure 7.11.

Figure 7.12.

each branch store's selling activity; therefore, the buyer will request a Suburban Store Best Seller Report (Figure 7.13). This report isolates the ten best selling styles by dollar volume by department for each separate branch or suburban store. Sales in units are provided for this week (T.W.), last week (L.W.), and two weeks ago (2 wks. ago). The report may be distributed once a week, usually on Monday morning, to the divisional merchandise manager, the buyer, and the general manager for all departments for each branch store. The report contains information according to classification number and name, vendor number and name, style number, single unit price, and total store dollars.

Figure 7.13. Suburban Best Seller Report. This report isolates a suburban store's ten best selling styles by dollar volume by department for each separate branch or suburban store. (Courtesy of John Wanamaker Department Store, Philadelphia, Pa.)

REED - LEISURE RECR		WYNNEWOOD	BEST SELLERS REPORT		WEEK ENDING	03/15/75		FMSPR06B

DPT NO CLASS	DESCRIPTION	VENDOR NAME	VEN NO.	STYLE NO.	UNIT PRICE	TOTAL DOLLARS	U N I T S		
							T.W.	L.W.	2 WKS AGO
075-00	LUGGAGE	WYNNEWOOD			BEST SELLERS REPORT			WEEK ENDING	03/15/75
60	CANVAS LUGGAGE	YORK LUGGAGE CORP	015	0526	55.00	110	2		
21	WOMENS LUGGAGE	ATLANTIC PRODUCTS	054	8824	43.99	88	2		
21	WOMENS LUGGAGE	AMERICAN TOURISTER	001	1027	72.50	73	1		
22	WOMENS LUGGAGE	LARK LUGGAGE	020	0021	54.00	54	1		
21	WOMENS LUGGAGE	SAMSONITE	002	5629	45.00	45	1		
21	WOMENS LUGGAGE	YORK LUGGAGE CORP	015	1220	42.50	43	1		
40	BRIEF CASE ATTACHE	SAMSONITE	002	0443	42.00	42	1		
31	MENS LUGGAGE	SAMSONITE	002	2133	42.00	42	1		
31	MENS LUGGAGE	SAMSONITE	002	3352	40.00	40	1		
21	WOMENS LUGGAGE	YORK LUGGAGE CORP	015	1214	40.00	40	1		
		TOTALS				577	12		

In addition to the Suburban Store Best Seller Report, buyers and merchandise managers receive a Weekly Classification Sales Report (Figure 7.14), which summarizes unit and dollar sales by class on a weekly basis and is used as an input into the classification "open-to-buy." It is usually distributed once a week. The report contains regular unit and dollar sales and percent to classification and markdown unit and dollar sales and percent to classification, as well as total department regular and markdown dollar sales. The percentages are comparisons of each store's *class* units and dollars with each store's *department* total units and dollars.

For departments (usually fashion) where unit control is based on color and size, the Unit Control-Color/Size Posting Report (U/LC) shows unit sales at these levels by store. This report may be distributed twice a week, with one copy sent to the unit control office. The form contains information on vendor, style, color, size, class, and price. Unit control keeps a daily record of basic merchandise, of deductions, and of what has been received into inventory.

Besides the Unit Control-Color/Size Posting Report, the buyer and merchandise manager receive a monthly Classification Price Line Report, which provides information in units for each department by location for each price

		REGULAR					MARKDOWN					TOTAL SUBCLASS			
		UNITS	%	DOLLARS	%	/ UNITS	%	DOLLARS	%	/	UNITS	%	DOLLARS	%
S-CLASS 000	04	1	100	36	100	/				/	1	100	36	100
SUBCLASS TOTAL		1	100	56	100	/				/	1	100	56	100
S-CLASS 010	02	2	100	65	100	/				/	2	100	65	100
SUBCLASS TOTAL		2	100	65	100	/				/	2	100	65	100
S-CLASS 020	01	1	4	48	6	/				/	1	4	48	5
WOMENS LUGG	03	1	11	30	8	/				/	1	11	30	8
	11	1	20	50	26	/				/	1	20	50	26
SUBCLASS TOTAL		3	4	128	4	/				/	3	4	128	4
S-CLASS 021	01	12	57	462	59	/ 1	100	30	100	/	13	59	492	61
	03	8	88	337	91	/				/	8	88	337	91
	04	5	83	251	83	/				/	5	83	251	83
	05	7	70	290	67	/				/	7	70	290	67
	06	3	75	109	70	/				/	3	75	109	70
	07	4	100	284	100	/				/	4	100	284	100
	08	1	33	25	34	/				/	1	33	25	34
	11	3	60	114	61	/				/	3	60	114	61
SUBCLASS TOTAL		43	68	1,872	72	/ 1	100	30	100	/	44	68	1,902	72
S-CLASS 022	01	8	38	263	34	/				/	8	36	263	32
	02	1	100	25	100	/				/	1	100	25	100
	04	1	16	50	16	/				/	1	16	50	16
	05	3	30	138	32	/				/	3	30	138	32
	06	1	25	45	29	/				/	1	25	45	29
	08	2	66	47	65	/				/	2	66	47	65
	11	1	20	22	11	/				/	1	20	22	11
SUBCLASS TOTAL		17	26	590	22	/				/	17	26	590	22
CLASS 020	01	21	40	773	41	/ 1	100	30	100	/	22	41	803	42
WOMENS LUGG	02	1	12	25	9	/				/	1	12	25	9
	03	9	60	367	67	/				/	9	60	367	67
	04	6	40	301	52	/				/	6	40	301	52
	05	10	43	428	46	/				/	10	43	428	46
	06	4	80	154	95	/				/	4	80	154	95
	07	4	44	284	62	/				/	4	44	284	62
	08	3	42	72	38	/				/	3	42	72	38
	11	5	71	186	72	/				/	5	71	186	72
CLASS TOTAL		63	43	2,590	48	/ 1	100	30	100	/	64	43	2,620	68

Figure 7.14. Weekly Classification Sales Report. This report summarizes unit and dollar sales by class on a weekly basis for Regular and Markdown Dollar Sales. (Courtesy of John Wanamaker Department Store, Philadelphia, Pa.)

line within each classification. The report contains information on class number, price, store, unit sales for each month of a season, and total dollar sales for price line by classification for each store.

Exception Reports. It is important that the retailer locate problems as well as opportunities in stock-sales relationships to ensure effective merchandise replenishments. Most stores use a computerized system that simplifies the problem of locating exceptions; hence, the use of exception reports. Once certain sales and inventory standards have been planned for a specific period in a department, the information is sent to the computer center. The computer periodically prints out information on stock items that do not meet predetermined standards and are, therefore, exceptions. When an exception report is received, the buyer carefully reviews why sales are low or why sales are high on certain items. Immediate action should be taken to rid the department of merchandise items that are slow sellers by using new display techniques, markdowns, store transfers, special sales promotions, and so forth. The exception report that shows best sellers is important to the buyer because it enables prompt identification of fast-selling sections of the assortment for the purpose of determining specific areas in which consumer demand is strong (color, size, style, etc.) and can possibly be made stronger. (Review Figure 7.13, Suburban Best Seller Report.) A fashion buyer will carefully determine the direction the demand is taking, so that other fashions in the same color, fabric, or silhouette or with similar design lines can be added to the stock. The buyer does not necessarily have to reorder the same best seller but instead may promote garments that have characteristics similar to the best seller. According to Beatrice Judelle, the fashion buyer should:

1. At least once a week pull all fast-selling numbers from stock and place them on a rack together
2. Examine them for a common factor
3. When they are segregated from the rest of the assortment in this way, that factor usually stands out—new lengths, silhouette, neckline, sleeve treatment, fabric, color, texture, or whatever.[13]

How will the following information assist the buyer or store manager in making fast, accurate decisions regarding the condition of the merchandise inventory?

1. Daily sales reports
2. Buyer's style status report
3. Vendor summary report
4. Suburban store best seller report
5. Weekly classification sales report
6. Unit control-color/size posting report
7. Classification price line report
8. Exception reports

Chapter Summary

Control provides a means to inform top management whether or not established standards are functioning according to plan, and it provides a basis for changes to correct problems that have already occurred. There are three elements important to a good control system: (1) the establishment of control standards, (2) the measurement of performance, and (3) the analysis and correction of deviations from planned standards. The kind and type of control system required by a retail business will depend upon its merchandising policy, the size of the store, and its clientele.

There are certain requirements that are characteristic of any control system. A good control system should (1) call attention to deviations, (2) suggest a means of solving the problem, (3) be accurate and timely, (4) be understood by the members of the organization, and (5) be economical. An important tool used by management in planning, coordinating, and controlling various control systems is the budget, a plan that forecasts specific merchandising activities for a specified period of time.

Merchandise control may be defined as maintenance of a stock of merchandise that is adjusted to the needs of customers and prospective customers. There are two major forms of merchandise control that store management may consider: (1) dollar control and (2) unit control. Dollar control may be defined as the amount of dollars at retail prices invested in the merchandise inventory. Dollar control answers the question "How much?" It may be applied to departments, to classifications or to specific price lines. Unit control is an organized method of recording the individual units or pieces of merchandise found in the inventory; it answers the question "What?"

Dollar control and unit control may be operated either through a perpetual inventory system or a periodic inventory system. The perpetual inventory system derives sales information from sales and purchase records that record merchandise on hand in terms of what has been received and what has been sold at regular intervals, such as every day, week, or month. In contrast, the periodic inventory system derives sales information from inventory and purchase data by periodically adding opening inventory and purchases and subtracting the sum of the closing inventory and markdowns. The student should review how dollar control and unit control may be operated through either system.

There are other types of inventory systems used in unit control: visual control, tickler control, warehouse control, checklist control, want-slip control and electronic control. The selection of one or all of these inventory systems depends upon the special needs of the business operation.

There are advantages as well as limitations to merchandise controls. The **student should review the chart on page 232. The merchandise inventory is the** assortment of goods available for sale to the ultimate consumer. Unlike inventories of merchandise carried by most other types of businesses, inventories carried by retail stores have certain differentiating characteristics. The student **should review the list on page 235.**

A physical inventory is the actual counting and recording of the amount of merchandise or stock on hand at a specified time together with the cost or retail price of each merchandise item. There are several reasons for taking a physical inventory: (1) to help in the preparation of financial statements; (2) to familiarize personnel with the stock assortment; (3) to aid inventory analysis; (4) to determine stock shortages and overages; (5) sales determination.

Some types of retail stores require little advance preparation. However, in a department store or chain operation the procedure for taking a physical inventory is far more complex. The inventory procedure may be broken down into the following five steps: the times of the inventory, the planning stage, counting, recording, checking, calculating the stock value, and the use of inventory reports.

Trade Terminology

DIRECTIONS: Briefly explain or discuss each of the following trade terms:

1. Control standards
2. Merchandise control
3. Dollar control
4. Departmental control
5. Classification control
6. Price-line control
7. Unit control
8. Perpetual inventory system
9. Periodic inventory system
10. Tickler file
11. Merchandise inventory
12. Physical inventory
13. Cost method of inventory
14. First-in first-out method (FIFO)
15. Last-in first-out method (LIFO)
16. Book method of inventory
17. Closing book inventory
18. Retail method of inventory
19. Merchandise overage
20. Merchandise shortage

Questions for Discussion and Review

1. What is meant by the statement "A good control system will be built into management's business objectives during the initial planning stage"?

2. What elements should be present in every control system?

3. Discuss how a good control system can accomplish the following: call attention to deviations, be accurate and timely, be economical.

4. Prepare an outline of the steps you would follow when taking a physical inventory. Could this procedure to used in a small retail business? Explain.

5. You have been asked to write a paper on the topic "The use of electronic data processing in merchandise replenishment." What topics would you cover and why?

6. Summarize the essential differences between unit control and dollar control.

7. Under what conditions would you recommend the use of the following inventory reports: daily sales reports; unit control—color/size posting report; exception report; and vendor summary report? Why?

8. At the start of a six-month period a men's shirt department had an inventory of $59,200 at retail. Purchases during the period amounted to $96,400 at retail. Sales for the period were $88,000, and markdowns were $5,000. Find the book inventory.

9. What information must be provided so that you can determine the cost or market value of inventory? What is the retail method of inventory?

10. Define: periodic inventory system; perpetual inventory system. What other types of inventory systems may be used in unit control?

11. Why is a knowledge of the average rate of stock shortages necessary to determine actual sales? Illustrate the formula used to determine actual or net sales.

12. What advantages and limitations should the buyer or store manager consider before implementing merchandise control systems?

Case Study Number One

A Father-and-Daughter Business

Mr. Stevens has been successfully running his medium-sized children's shoe business for the past twenty years. He decided, however, to pass the business on to his daughter, Elizabeth, who had worked in the store while attending college. His daughter was enthusiastic about taking over her father's business and was eager to institute many changes. For example, she was very concerned about the growth of the children's shoe market and the necessity of broadening the stock assortment to meet consumer demand. To accomplish this, it was necessary to take a closer look at inventory control methods presently in use. Inventory was taken twice a year. The stock assortment was broken down according to price, style, size, and classification, and value was based on the amount of dollars at retail prices. A visual count was taken when "someone had the time," and reorders were placed when the stockroom inventory was depleted. Clerical help was used to tabulate the results of the inventory. Mr. Stevens felt that his method of inventory control was very efficient and resisted the idea of changing an inventory method that had worked well for twenty years. If you were Elizabeth Stevens, how would you convince your father that changes were necessary? Be prepared in class to discuss the changes you would suggest.

Case Study Number Two

Lloyd & Burns, located in a large New England city, has always catered to a well-to-do, conservative clientele. This large women's specialty store does an annual volume of approximately 35 million dollars and prides itself on being a high-quality, personal-service type of retail establishment.

Inherited Inventory Problems

As a conservative business, however, L & B never really enjoyed the reputation of real fashion leadership. The management determined that a number of the store's competitors were using the "boutique approach" in merchandising to add a high-fashion image to their stores. Management decided that Lloyd & Burns would try its hand at this new merchandising approach in an effort to gain higher fashion recognition.

Shortly thereafter, the "Royal Garb Boutique" was opened, with a buyer responsible for purchasing exclusive, high-fashion types of merchandise. The buyer was provided with an assistant, two full-time salespeople, part-time sales help, and stock personnel.

The "Royal Garb Boutique" was a success. Store volume increased as a result of the addition of the boutique, and L & B was gaining an image as a high-fashion store. After three years the buyer was rewarded with a promotion and took over the buying responsibilities of a much larger department, the women's better coat department.

When Gwen Franklin, an assistant buyer in fashion costume jewelry, heard that a buyer's position was available, and in the Royal Garb Boutique, at that, she immediately applied for the position. After several interviews, she was informed that she was to be the new buyer for the boutique. However, Gwen was soon to discover that along with a successful department she was also about to inherit serious inventory problems.

For various reasons, Gwen's predecessor had allowed a large amount of old merchandise to accumulate in the stockroom. The merchandise consisted of expensive blouses, handbags, sweaters, and other accessory items. When Gwen checked the price tickets for the seasonal code, she was amazed to learn that some of the merchandise was more than two years old. She immediately realized that she must take a physical count of all merchandise on hand to determine the condition of the merchandise assortment. She soon discovered that over 25% of her dollar stock was tied up in old or slow-moving merchandise. For some reason, her predecessor had allowed old merchandise to accumulate in stock while new items were being sold.

The Christmas season was rapidly approaching. Gwen realized that almost half of her sales volume would occur between November and January. However, she was overloaded with old and out-of-style goods, a limited open-to-buy, expensive markdowns, and limited storage and selling space. She was in trouble inventorywise, budgetwise, seasonwise. The department's fashion image was in jeopardy.

Outline a plan of activities that Gwen could follow to help her solve her inventory problems. How could she avoid the recurrence of these problems in the future?

Retailing Activities to Stimulate Student Interest and Participation

1. Interview the store manager of a variety chain operation; a discount chain; a department store branch. Prepare a list of questions based on the topic "How will the use of EDP improve merchandise replenishment systems?" Develop a list of future computer applications in areas other than merchandising.

2. Interview the manager of a small hardware store; a small variety store. What forms of merchandise control are used by each store? What kinds of problems has each store manager had to deal with when initiating good control procedures?

3. You have been asked to write a term paper on the topic "Why is control an important management activity?" Referring to the list of references that follow, develop an outline of the important points you wish to emphasize.

REFERENCES

The Retail Student's Reference Library

Bearchell, C. A. *Retailing—A Professional Approach.* New York: Harcourt Brace Jovanovich, Inc., 1975.

Belden, Donald. *The Role of the Buyer in Mass Merchandising.* New York: Chain Store Publishing Corporation, 1971.

Codner, Bernard. "Retail Management Systems—The Present and the Future." *Retail Control,* April–May 1970, pp. 3–11.

Curtis, Bob. *Security Control—Internal Theft.* New York: Chain Store Publishing Corporation, 1973.

Fleisher, David T. "Poor Marks for Computer in the Merchandising Area." *Retail Overview,* Summer 1970, pp. 33–41.

Fruman, Emanual K. "The Automated Way to Mail Order Merchandise Profits." *Marketing Insights,* III (January 27, 1969):15.

Gillespie, K., and Hecht, J. *Retail Business Management.* Hightstown: Gregg/McGraw Hill Book Company, 1970.

James, D. L; Walker, J. B.; and Etzel, M. J. *Retailing Today.* New York: Harcourt Brace Jovanovich, Inc., 1975.

Judelle, Beatrice. *The Fashion Buyer's Job.* New York: National Retail Merchants Association, 1971.

McConaughy, David. "An Appraisal of Computers in Department Store Inventory Control." *Journal of Retailing,* 46 (Spring 1970): pp. 3–19.

Mulhern, Helen. *Facts about Department Stores.* New York: National Retail Merchants Association, n.d.

National Cash Register Company. *Register Enforced Automated Control Technique for Total Merchandise Control.* Dayton, Ohio: National Cash Register Company, n.d.

National Retail Merchants Association. *Operations Research in Retailing—Case Studies and Electronic Data Processing for Retailers.* New York: NRMA, n.d.

———*Retail Inventory Method in Practical Operation, The.* New York: NRMA, n.d.

———*Status of EDP in Retailing.* New York: NRMA, 1970.

———*Want Slip Policies and Systems in Department Stores.* New York: NRMA, n.d.

Palcho, Fred K. *Receiving Controls.* Columbus, Ohio: Distributive Education Materials Lab, 1971.

Reeser, Clayton. *Management Functions and Modern Concepts.* Glenview: Scott, Foresman and Company, 1973.

Scher, Jay. *Department Store and Specialty Store Merchandising and Operating Results of 1970.* New York: National Retail Merchants Association, 1971.

Siber, Alan. *The Complete Guide to Retail Management.* Baltimore: Penguin Books, 1972.

Sisk, Henry L. *Management and Organization.* Cincinnati: South-Western Publishing Company, 1973.

Smith, S. B. "Automated Inventory Management for Staples." *Journal of Retailing,* 47 (Spring 1971): pp. 55–62.

Wanous, E. E.; Wanous, S. J.; and Wagner, G. *Fundamentals of Data Processing.* Cincinnati: South-Western Publishing Company, 1971.

References

1. Jerry B. Poe, *An Introduction to the American Business Enterprise* (Homewood, Ill.: Richard D. Irwin, Inc., 1972), pp. 158–61.
2. Ibid., pp. 162–64.
3. Delbert J. Duncan and C. F. Phillips, *Retailing Principles and Methods* (Homewood, Ill.: Richard D. Irwin, Inc., 1969), p. 366.
4. Ibid., pp. 371–72.
5. Albert I. Schott and Herbert A. Turetzky, *Retailer's Guide to Merchandise Classification Control* (New York: National Retail Merchants Association, 1969), p. 1.
6. Ibid., pp. 3–4.
7. Beatrice Judelle, *The Fashion Buyer's Job* (New York: National Retail Merchants Association, 1971), p. 51.
8. Ibid., p. 55.
9. Bernard Codner, "Retail Management Systems—The Present and the Future," *Retail Control,* April–May 1970, pp. 3–5.
10. Duncan and Phillips, *Retailing Principles and Methods,* pp. 382–83.
11. Ibid., p. 385.
12. Judelle, *The Fashion Buyer's Job,* p. 51.
13. Ibid., p. 53.

The Planning Function and the Merchandising Activity

8

Performance Objectives

Chapter Summary
Trade Terminology
Questions for Discussion and Review
Case Study Number One; Number Two
Retailing Activities to Stimulate Student Interest and Participation
The Retail Student's Reference Library
References

As a result of reading this chapter, the student should be able to accomplish the following:

1. Discuss three components that make up the planning process.

2. Describe types of records used in planning.

3. Define merchandise budget.

4. List the elements that are essential to a good merchandise budget.

5. Outline the factors considered important when planning the merchandising budget.

6. Discuss the top-down plan; the bottom-up plan.

7. Calculate the following equations: BOM stock method; the percentage-variation (or deviation) method; the weeks' supply method; the stock-sales ratio method.

8. Write three formulas that may be used to compute stock turnover.

9. Calculate the average inventory.

10. Discuss the advantages and limitations of rapid stock turnover.

11. Define merchandise shortage; merchandise overage; employee discount.

12. Calculate the markdown; the markdown percent.

13. Explain why markdowns are necessary, as well as the reasons for taking them.

14. Calculate the initial markup; the markup percent; the maintained markup.

15. Write the formula for computing gross margin; for net profit.

16. Write the formula used when planning purchases.

17. Explain open-to-buy control.

The Planning Function and the Merchandising Activity

Preparing the Merchandise Budget

As previously discussed, the control system provides a means that management may use to determine whether a business is functioning according to pre-established plans. A good control system will be built into management activities from the beginning, that is, during the planning stage. Planning, therefore, is a very important part of the merchandising activity.

Why Plan?

In a new business, the planning activity is the first stage (the stages are planning, organizing, staffing, directing, and controlling). In the established retail store, planning is still considered a primary activity; it is a continuous process and an integral part of the management system. Without adequate planning, the store manager, buyer, or small-business owner is frequently making merchandising decisions that deal only with immediate problems and do not have a meaningful relationship to future needs. The means used to achieve the planning objectives are based upon the philosophy and objectives of the particular retail institution. Differences in merchandising philosophies are not only the result of external influences, but also the result of differences in retailing methods and in the ability of each retail store to plan ahead in a systematic, organized way.[1]

Until recently, retailing has been primarily a day-to-day business. Plans have been based on short-range seasonal activities and monthly sales promotions. Buyers were concerned with beating last year's sales figures *today*. However, population shifts, urban redevelopment, the shortage of natural resources, and other environmental factors have forced retailers to take a second look at their merchandising policies and philosophies. Retail merchants must plan ahead if they are to survive and maintain their position in a complex, highly competitive, and aggressive business environment.

The purpose of Part 1 of this chapter, therefore, will be (1) to discuss the essentials of good planning, (2) to discuss the importance of record keeping, and (3) to discuss the importance of the budget and the different types used. Part 2 will deal with the planning of the merchandise budget. Topics to be covered are planned sales, stocks, reductions, markups, gross margin and operating profit, expenses, and purchases. Each will be discussed in detail.

The Planning Process   When planning the business enterprise, the manager should give consideration
to the three components that make up the planning process: (1) objectives, (2)
policies, and (3) procedures.[2]

Objectives

Objectives provide the framework for business planning; therefore, the formulation of business objectives during the early stages of planning is a must. A
business objective may be defined as the goal toward which the management
activities of the business establishment are directed. Business objectives may
be stated in broad terms, that is, they may present a general picture of what
the company hopes to achieve; or they may be stated in very specific terms.
It is important to remember that all of those involved in retailing, whether a
chief executive, a mid-management trainee, or a first-line supervisor, must give
attention to company objectives and the methods used to achieve them.

Management objectives will change. According to John B. Joynt, in a
speech presented to the National Retail Merchants Association on the topic
Management by Objectives in Retailing:[3]

> When we turn the clock back to the turn of the century, our first objective
> pointed upward to the topic management level. As time went on, we became
> more people conscious. The objective was directed towards getting more involve-
> ment of people down the line, in connection with what we were trying to achieve
> in terms of production. More recently we are talking about management by
> objectives or result-oriented management.
> . . . Now, where do we start? Ideally, we start with the chief executive and the
> operation as a whole, and we move down the organization. We should have
> objectives for the corporation and we should have objectives for each organiza-
> tion unit—the unit you head up, the unit you are part of. At all management
> levels we want to establish objectives. . . .

Examples of business objectives may be illustrated as follows: a retail store
may wish to offer exclusive or unique products, such as handcrafted items or
imports not usually carried by other retailers; it may provide store customers
with the newest, high-fashion styles and, therefore, will step up its foreign
buying program; or it may wish to have the "dependable-store" image. Another specific store objective may be to appeal primarily to upper-middle and
upper price bracket customers. This could be accomplished through store
advertising and promotion appeals. Or, the store may have a policy of only
selling merchandise that will be consistent with its objectives regarding quality
and dependable merchandise offerings.

Policies

Business policies provide management with a frame of reference for decision
making that is consistent with planned objectives. If policy statements are
written clearly and concisely, they will provide the necessary guidelines for
dealing consistently with problems and issues. Policies may be broadly stated

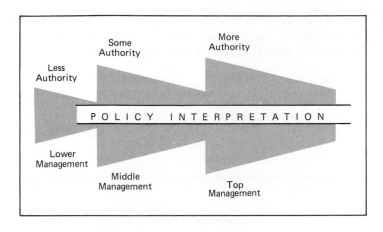

Figure 8.1. Breadth of policy interpretation.

to provide latitude to upper management, or they may be stated in specific terms. Usually more authority will be granted in policy interpretation to those in upper management, for example, members of the corporate board, store managers, and merchandise managers, while less latitude in policy interpretation is granted to those holding lower management positions. See Figure 8.1.

Figure 8.2 is an example of one store's merchandising philosophy and

Figure 8.2. An example of one store's merchandising philosophy and policies.

We in Merchandising have the fundamental objective of developing "Maximum Sales Volume at a Maximum Rate of Profitability."

We, therefore, in Merchandising, perform the functions of planning our stocks and assortments aimed to satisfy our customer's demands—to then buy this merchandise—to promote it through advertising and display— and to have it sold at a price that will give us a sufficient gross margin which, after expenses, will return a net profit.

How we are to arrive at that goal and how our Company should accomplish the profitable volume and growth result we wish to obtain is set forth in the "Merchandising Philosophy and Policies" manual which was distributed to all executives as well as all of our associates. I am sure that you have all received a copy and I trust you have read it carefully. Our Merchandising Philosophy and Policies as to the kind and type of store that we wish to be are clearly set forth. It is the responsibility of all of us in merchandising to implement these objectives and policy statements.

policies as presented to an executive training group by the vice-president of merchandising. As you will note, the store's broad objective is developing "maximum sales volume at a maximum rate of profitability."

Procedures

Procedures are necessary steps that must be followed to implement a given policy. When management sets up procedures for implementing store policies, it should emphasize whether or not the particular procedure is a *rule,* that is,

Figure 8.3. An illustration of the importance of store regulations that must be observed by employees, since a violation of these rules can result in immediate dismissal.

Important Store Regulations!

You can understand and recognize the importance of a retail store as large as ours providing rules of conduct both for your protection and for the protection of our customers. We ask your full cooperation and understanding in observing all store regulations for a violation can result in immediate dismissal.

1. Use of intoxicating liquor or illegal drugs during store working hours or reporting to work under their influence.
2. Excessive tardiness or absences, or failure to report absences promptly.
3. Unauthorized presence in freight elevators, stock rooms and other areas unless authorized.
4. Unauthorized personnel are prohibited from entering the receiving and marking areas unless specifically authorized.
5. Handling merchandise in departments other than that to which they are assigned is prohibited.
6. Registering time for anyone other than yourself or permitting anyone else to register time for you is a violation of store rules which is cause for dismissal.
7. Improper procedures in handling cash or cash registers. You are responsible, particularly at the end of the day, to prevent not only the theft of cash but leaving the day's receipts and bank funds in a department overnight.
8. Gambling.
9. Violation of other Company rules and policies.

Thank You

IT'S A WANAMAKER CUSTOM

TO SMILE Everyone agrees that we're all more attractive when we smile. A gracious smile is the easiest way to make friends for Wanamaker's. This applies to all personnel, for no matter what your line of duty, you are a public relations representative for Wanamaker's. Of course the public can see your smile on the selling floor. But the public can feel your smile in a letter or from behind the telephone. So let's smile more and more: when we talk, when we write, and when we phone.

TO BE TELEPHONE CONSCIOUS Telephone business is big business. You'll be making good impressions if you answer promptly, in a clear, interested voice, give correct and complete information, eliminate side tone noises, and hang up carefully . . . without that bang in the ear. And remember, seconds seem like minutes when someone is left holding the line.
Automatic phones are used for intra-store communication in order to keep Bell phones free for customer service.

TO BE HOST TO THE PUBLIC "Make every visitor feel like a welcomed guest in your home." John Wanamaker said that. Just remember your manners, for they are always showing. When you use the passenger elevator stand aside to permit customers to enter first. You are permitted to use the passenger elevators for all purposes, except to carry freight and while in an elevator it's wise to refrain from shop talk, eating, or loud talking. Escalators should be used wherever possible so that the public can be served more efficiently.

TO GIVE SERVICE Of course selling merchandise is Wanamaker's principal service. But there are additional services that create good will. To give direction and information accurately and graciously also pays off. When you don't know the right answers, just ask. There are information centers in all stores. Our public is important. Without it, we wouldn't be here. The impressions we make keep the doors open for all of us. So let's always remember to treat each day as though it were our first . . . in this way we are bound to make it our best.

TO TALK UP THE STORE Make Wanamaker history. Rouse your customers, your relatives, your friends. Spread the news about the store. Talk current and coming store events. Let the people know . . . *THE EAGLE SPEAKS*, your publication, tells you regularly about the store family and its activities.

8

Figure 8.4. An illustration of how a store guides its employees in the performance of their duties. (Courtesy of John Wanamaker Department Store, Philadelphia, Pa.)

a statement that must be obeyed, or a *guide,* which is a statement that recommends an action be taken and is not necessarily mandatory. For example, Figure 8.3 illustrates the importance of store regulations that *must be observed* by employees, since a violation of these rules can result in immediate dismissal. Figure 8.4 illustrates how one store provides information to employees to *guide* them in the performance of their duties. The store suggests that employees "smile," "be telephone-conscious," "be host to the public," "give courteous service," and "talk up the store."

Planning Requires Accurate Record Keeping

A primary objective of any business is to make a profit. However, to determine whether or not the business is profitable, management must set specific policies for effective record keeping. Specific policies will be set for the following types

What type of stores will plan the following objectives, policies, and procedures?

Objectives	Policies	Procedures
Provide mass-produced goods at discount prices	No cash refund; credit only	All employee packages must be checked before leaving the store
Provide one-stop shopping for food items, hard goods, soft goods	Cash and carry; no charges accepted	Smile and be courteous when on the selling floor
Offer exclusives and imported merchandise assortments	"The customer is always right"	Use authorized employee exits
Provide special services not found in competing stores	Personal and friendly service	Never ring anyone else's time card

of records used in most retail establishments: (1) cash receipts and disbursements, (2) credit, (3) expenses, (4) sales, (5) purchases, (6) stocks and inventories, and (7) profit-and-loss statements.

Cash Disbursements and Receipts

Cash disbursements refers to the amount of cash paid out by a business. A retailer will keep a record of all cash paid out for expenses such as inventory, sales help, clerical items, advertising, display, and so forth. *Cash receipts* refers to the amount of money taken into the business throughout the day. Usually, cash receipts come from sales and from payment on account by customers. Store management will set policies regarding the amount of money a buyer or department has to spend, as well as the amount of money or profit the department is responsibile for earning. Top management will provide a *cash budget,* which is an estimate of the department or store's cash receipts and cash disbursements over a specified period of time. The cash budget, as well as other types of budgets, will be discussed later in this chapter.

Credit

The decision as to the amount and kind of credit that will be extended to store customers will depend on the overall merchandising policies of the business. Management may decide that sales will be made on a cash-only basis and thus eliminate the problem of credit and collections. This may be the credit policy of a small businessperson who must have adequate amounts of working capital to buy stock and inventory. A specialty shop may adopt a conservative credit policy to provide a service to its clientele as well as to keep up with competition. A discount house may offer a liberal credit policy to encourage shopping as well as to keep up with the merchandising techniques used by similar stores.

The store will maintain its own credit records and set up its own type of credit system. For example, Figure 8.5 and Figure 8.6 illustrate a charge system used by a department store. You will note the various types of charge systems available. The customer may wish to charge and carry the merchandise (Charge Take Salescheck); she may wish to charge but does not have her charge plate (Charge Take Without Charge Card); the customer may wish to charge merchandise and have it sent elsewhere (Charge to One-Sold to Another); or a store employee may wish to charge and take the merchandise (Employee Charge Take-With Tax). The store issues specific instructions (policies) to employees to ensure that proper charge procedures are followed.

It should also be noted that many stores now accept major credit cards. For example, American Express, Bank Americard, Master Charge, and others are accepted by many retail stores, large and small, as a convenience to their

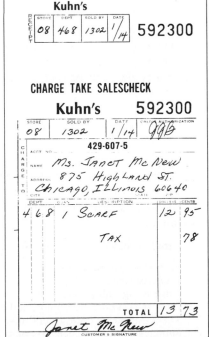

Figure 8.5. Examples of charge stystems used by a department store. The customer may wish to charge and carry the merchandise (charge take salescheck); she may wish to charge but does not have her charge plate (charge take without charge plate).

Figure 8.6. The customer may wish to charge merchandise and have it sent elsewhere (charge to one-sold to another); or a store employee may wish to charge and take the merchandise (employee charge take-with tax).

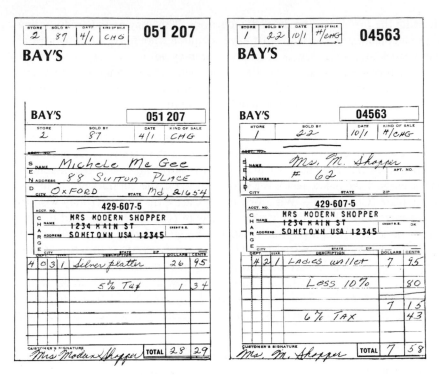

customers. Stores usually advertise the acceptance of various credit cards by displaying a symbol of the credit card company near the cash register. Many customers prefer this method of charging merchandise, since it eliminates carrying a credit card for each individual store.

Expenses

Records are kept of the expenses incurred by the store or department. The merchant will keep records of those expenses that involve direct cash outlays; however, those records do not provide information about all expenses. One way to classify retail expenses for monthly, semiannual, or annual analysis is to set up expense categories. The chart that follows is an illustration of "natural" expense classification as recommended by the National Retail Merchants Association.[4]

Retailers may classify expenses according to a "natural" expense category

Payroll—salaries, wages
Property Rentals—all property used in the business
Advertising—all payments for various media used
Interest—on borrowed funds, and assets
Taxes—all local, state, federal taxes
Supplies—wrapping, delivery, office, repairs

Services Purchased—purchase of cleaning, repair, delivery, light, heat, power
Travel—transportation and hotel accommodations
Unclassified—cash shortages, supper money, etc.
Communications—postage, telephone, telegrams
Pensions—retirement allowances
Insurance—fire, public liability, etc.
Depreciation—building, equipment, fixtures
Professional Services—legal, accounting, resident buying office
Donations—charitable, welfare, educational
Losses from Bad Debts—bad checks, etc.
Equipment Rentals—cash registers, computer, delivery trucks

Expenses may also be classified as direct and indirect expenses.

Direct expenses are paid out directly for the benefit of the department; the department manager or buyer is responsible for keeping control of these expenses. Examples are the payroll of full-time and part-time salespeople; the department manager's and assistant's salary; advertising, promotions, and special events expenses; selling materials and supplies; travel expenses and hotel accommodations; and miscellaneous expenses.

Indirect expenses are those that serve the whole store. Examples are utilities (heat, light), rent, taxes, insurance, and the payroll of sales-supporting departments. Thus, if a department's expenses are $20,000, the cost of goods sold is $14,000, and direct expenses are $4,000, the department will be responsible for contributing $2,000 to the store as a whole to help cover the store's indirect expenses as well as contributing to the store's profit. The following example illustrates how a department will contribute to the store's overall expenses:

Department Expenses	$ 20,000
Cost of Goods Sold	– 14,000
Total	$ 6,000
Direct Expenses (salaries, promotions, advertising, etc.)	– 4,000
Total	$ 2,000

Sales

Sales records will tell the merchant how much is sold each day, according to classification, style, price, size, color, and so forth; how much is sold each week and during a particular season; and how much is sold in branches or other store units. Some buyers, especially during storewide sales, will take hourly sales readings to determine whether or not their predetermined sales goals will be reached.

As you recall from our previous discussion of sales reports, sales analysis may be accomplished manually or electronically. A small business will usually use a manual type of control system. For example, at the end of the day, the owner-manager or assistant will count the day's receipts (cash and charge) and total the sales. Thus a sales total is derived for the entire store, with little consideration given to merchandise classification, style, price, color, size, etc. As the store expands, however, the owner-manager may determine sales by classification, style (remember the discussion of style cards), and so forth.

Most chain operations, department stores, variety stores, and other types of retail stores with more than one unit will use electronic controls to obtain sales information. The sales-control process may work like this. A cash register will punch holes in a register tape for cash and charge sales each time a transaction is made. Every sale is automatically recorded by price, department number, salesperson, date sold, and other information deemed necessary by the store. The register tapes are periodically (usually at the end of the working day) sent to the data processing center, where sales information is sorted in the order determined by buying specialists or managers. The information is printed out in a sales report and made available to store managers, buyers, assistants, or to whomever has a need for the reports.

Purchases

The department-store buyer or central buyer will keep a record of merchandise purchased from vendors, suppliers, and manufacturers for the department for which he is responsible. This record is called the *purchase journal.* Each department keeps a separate record *(billing record)* of all invoices (bills) received from various merchandise resources. The purchase journal and billing record contain invoices that provide information on department transfers, vendor returns, short shipments, damages, lost merchandise, and other claims. The buyer usually also keeps his or her own record of such transactions to compare with the store's overall accounting records.

Figure 8.7. A purchase journal.

Department Name	Girls' wear											

Department Number __476__　　　　　Month __Oct. 1__　　　Year __77__　　　　　　　Page Number __2__

VENDOR	Vendor No.	Invoice Date	Style No.	Quant.	Cost per Unit	Cost at Retail	Apron No.	Total Cost	Total Retail	Disc.	Balance Paid	Balance Due
Sweet and Sour, Inc.	17	10/3	75	432	8.95	17.95	1103	3,866.40	7,754.40	80.17	3,517.28	
Lemon Twist	12	10/5	12	108	7.85	15.00	1301	847.80	1,620.00	90.03	572.31	
Big Girl, Inc.	6	10/9	80	95	11.94	22.50	1400	1,134.30	2,137.50	50.41	1,410.10	
Four Foot Two	10	10/12	14	230	12.50	25.00	1403	575.00	5,750.00	82.71	2,826.32	

As Figure 8.7 illustrates, the purchase journal will contain the following information: vendor's name, invoice date, style number, quantity, cost per unit, unit retail cost, the receiving apron number, total cost, total retail discounts, and balance paid or owed. The purchase journal is a most important record, since it is used to compare dollar amounts of merchandise receipts against planned purchase figures. This information will tell the buyer what has been received and what is on order, so that he or she can decide whether to increase or slow down the inventory turnover to conform to the merchandise budget. Also, the purchase journal will assist the buyer in determining the accuracy of the invoice figures charged to the department. Finally, the buyer can use the figures shown in the purchase journal, together with his or her own record of unfilled orders, for immediate and current information when planning the department's open-to-buy. (We will talk more about open-to-buy later in this chapter.)

Stocks and Inventories

The retailer may take a physical inventory, that is, actually count the goods on hand (merchandise on the shelves, on racks, and in bins, both on the selling floor and in the stockroom). This may be done semiannually or annually. In this way old, lost, or damaged merchandise may be found and thus eliminated from the inventory through preinventory clearance sales. (We shall discuss opening and closing inventories in the section "Profit-and-Loss Statements.")

As Figure 8.8 illustrates, stock and inventory records show the amount of inventory on hand, on order, actual sales results, planned sales and stocks, and the sales and stocks for the same period of the previous year. If EDP is used, figures are recorded not only for department totals but also for totals according to merchandise class and subclass. A buyer, therefore, can use stock records to determine those merchandise classifications that are above or below the merchandise plan. Also, stock records will show the individual needs of branch stores or store units; thus, the buyer can either replenish the merchandise assortment or transfer goods to another store.

Profit-and-Loss Statements

The department *profit-and-loss statement,* also called the *income statement* and the *operating statement,* may be defined as a summary of the transactions conducted by a business during a specific period of time such as one month, six months, or a year. It shows the relationship that has prevailed for the period among sales, cost of goods sold, and expenses.[5] The buyer will receive reports on the financial standing of each department, which includes information on actual and planned dollar sales figures for all phases of merchandising operation. As Figure 8.9 illustrates, the buyer will obtain information on gross sales, customer returns and adjustments, markdowns, purchases, gross margin of profit, operating expenses, cash discounts, and so on.

You will notice that the profit-and-loss statement starts with net sales and

Figure 8.8. An EDP report will provide information on inventory turnover. Figures are recorded not only for department totals but also for totals according to merchandise class and subclass. The buyer can use stock records to determine those merchandise classifications that are above or below the merchandise plan. (Courtesy of John Wanamaker Department Store, Philadelphia, Pa.)

```
              WEEKLY CLASS SUMMARY REPORT
    DIV 29 DEPT 517 WEEK 4 ENDING 11/03 PERIOD 09    PG.    1

              S A L E S          $       S T O C K    S A L E S  L Y
                UNITS                      UNITS          UNITS
      C     THIS   PER TO    TOTAL    THIS WEEK    THIS   NXT   FOLL
      L     WEEK   DATE      PER      OH     00    PER    PER   PER

  090 P
      W                                                            1
  TOTAL                                                            1

  100 P
      A                                                            1
      N          1         22
      EH                                             2             3
  TOTAL          1         22                        2             4

  110 P    8     25        538                      23     20     49
      A    1     2         30                                      9
      J          2         24                       13     42     80
      W    1     6         111                      14     31     96
      C          1         22                       32     53    202
      SP   5     17        256                      16     31     70
      PL   1     5         584                      22     89    101
      N    4     7         115                       7     23    107
      EH   3     8         117                       7     56     88
      EX   2     5         72
  TOTAL   25     78        1869                     134    345    802

  117 P                                              2
      C                                              1      3      1
  TOTAL                                              3      3      1

  120 P   11     51        1014                     110    173    306
      A    4     20        405                       13     35    153
      J    4     28        566                      103     72    319
      W    6     20        405                       43     73    220
      C    3     48        940                       72     93    471
      SP   7     48        963                       83    152    473
      PL   7     33        655                       78    116    429
      N    8     43        843                       79    201    340
      EH   5     48        941                       33    128    331
      EX   7     33        656
  TOTAL   62    372        7388                     614   1043   3042
```

deducts cost of goods sold. The result is called *gross margin*. From gross margin the operating expenses are deducted, and the result is *net profit*. Each term will be discussed individually as follows:

Net Sales. *Net sales* is the difference between gross sales (all the sales that were made) and customer adjustments or returns. For example, the profit-and-loss statement for the women's blouse department shows net sales of $10,890. The following example illustrates how net sales were calculated.

Gross Sales	$11,259.00
Returns and Adjustments	– 369.00
Net Sales	$10,890.00

Cost of Goods Sold. The *cost of goods sold* is the amount of money paid for merchandise sold during a particular period covered by the profit-and-loss statement. The $25,290 figure was calculated as follows: at the beginning of June all the blouses in stock were counted and the cost value of the stock was figured. This cost value of stock is called the *opening inventory*. Thus, the

Figure 8.9. Profit-and-loss statement, women's blouse department, month ending October 31.

INCOME			
Gross sales		$11,259.00	
Customer returns and adjustments		− 369.00	
Net sales		$10,890.00	$10,890.00
COST OF GOODS SOLD			
Open inventory (cost value)		$18,990.00	
Purchase costs	$6,000.00		
	+		
Shipping costs	300.00		
Total purchase costs	$6,300.00	+ $ 6,300.00	
Total purchases		$25,290.00	
Closing inventory (cost value)		− 17,400.00	
Gross cost of goods sold		$ 7,890.00	
Cash discount		− 60.00	
Net cost of goods		$ 7,830.00	−$ 7,830.00
Gross margin			$ 3,060.00
OPERATING EXPENSES			
Buyer's salary		$ 600.00	
Sales help salaries		1,200.00	
Advertising and promotions		240.00	
Rent		450.00	
Utilities		+ 150.00	
Total operating expenses		$ 2,640.00	−$ 2,640.00
NET PROFIT			$ 420.00

opening inventory at cost is $18,990. However, purchases were made during the month that were added to the inventory value. For example, 500 blouses were purchased at $12 each. Thus the purchase cost is $6,000. Also, there was a shipping cost on the blouses. This amounted to $300. The total cost of purchases may be calculated as follows:

Cost of Goods Sold:

Opening Inventory (cost value)		$18,990.00	
Purchase Costs	$6,000.00		
Cost of Shipping	+ 300.00		
	$6,300.00	+$ 6,300.00	
Total Cost of Purchases		$25,290.00	

Once a determination is made of what was in stock at the beginning of the month (opening inventory $18,990) and what was added during the month (purchase costs plus shipping $6,300), it is important to determine what is left at the end of the month (closing inventory). A closing inventory figure of $17,400 is assumed. Thus, if we take the total cost of purchases ($25,290) and deduct the closing inventory, $17,400, the result is the *gross cost of goods sold,* which includes what was sold during the month as well as merchandise lost, damaged, stolen, or worn. This may be calculated as follows:

Opening Inventory (cost value)		$18,990.00
Purchase Costs	$6,000.00	
Shipping Costs	+ 300.00	
	$6,300.00	+ 6,300.00
Total Cost of Purchases		$25,290.00
Closing Inventory (cost value)		−17,400.00
Gross Cost of Goods Sold		$ 7,890.00

However, the buyer is allowed cash discounts for paying his bills within a certain period of time. Therefore, if the buyer was granted a 1 percent discount for paying the invoice (bill) within 20 days after receipt, he may deduct the following amount:

Cash Discount = Cash Discount % of Purchase Costs
$60 = 1% of $6,000

Since the entire purchase cost of $6,000 is figured in total goods handled, it is now necessary to deduct the cash discount to determine the net cost of goods sold. Net cost of goods sold may be calculated as follows:

Opening Inventory (cost value)		$18,990.00
Purchase Costs	$6,000.00	
Shipping Costs	+ 300.00	
	$6,300.00	+ 6,300.00
Total Cost of Purchases		$25,290.00
Closing Inventory (cost value)		−17,400.00
Gross Cost of Goods Sold		$ 7,890.00
Cash Discount		− 60.00
Net Cost of Goods Sold		$ 7,830.00

Gross Margin. *Gross margin* is the amount of profit before operating costs are deducted. It is determined by subtracting the net cost of goods sold ($7,830) from the net sales ($10,890). Thus:

Income

Gross Sales	$11,259.00	
Returns and Adjustments	− 369.00	
	$10,890.00	
Net Sales		$10,890.00
Cost of Goods Sold		
Opening Inventory		
(cost value)	$18,990.00	
Purchase Costs $6,000.00		
Shipping Costs + 300.00		
$6,300.00	+ 6,300.00	
Total Cost of Purchases	$25,290.00	
Closing Inventory	−17,400.00	
Gross Cost of Goods Sold	$ 7,890.00	
Cash Discount	− 60.00	
Net Cost of Goods Sold		− 7,830.00
Gross Margin		$ 3,060.00

Operating Expenses. As previously stated, expenses may be classified as *direct* and *indirect.* The two together make up *operating expenses,* which may appear in the profit-and-loss statements as follows:

Operating Expenses	
Buyer's Salary	$ 600.00
Sales Help Salaries	1,200.00
Advertising and Promotion	240.00
Rent	450.00
Utilities	+ 150.00
Total Operating Expenses	$2,640.00

Net Profit. *Net profit* is determined by deducting operating expenses from gross margin.

Now, let's review for a moment. There are five key factors important in the formulation of the profit-and-loss statement: net sales, cost of goods sold, gross margin, operating expenses, and net profit. The student should determine how a profit-and-loss statement is developed by reviewing each step in the procedure. Refer to Figure 8.9 again for a complete picture of what the profit-and-loss statement looks like.

Key factors important in the formulation of the profit-and-loss statement are:

1. *Net Sales*
   Net sales = Gross sales (–) Customer adjustments or returns
2. *Cost of Goods Sold*
   Opening inventory + purchase costs and shipping costs = total purchases (–) closing inventory = gross cost of goods sold (–) cash discount
3. *Gross Margin*
   Gross margin = net sales (–) net cost of goods sold
4. *Operating Expenses*
   Total operating expenses = direct expenses + indirect expenses
5. *Net Profit*
   Net profit = net sales (–) net cost of goods (–) total operating expenses

Planning requires accurate record keeping.

How will the following types of records assist you in merchandise planning?

Records of cash receipts and disbursements
Credit records
Expense records
Sales reports
Purchase journal
Stocks and inventory records
Department profit-and-loss statement

Planning the Budget

As you recall from the previous chapter, the budget is an important tool used by management in planning and controlling business systems. It is a document that outlines in quantitative terms the planned operations of the retail business for a specified period of time.[6] However, the size and type of retail establishment will determine the number and the extent of budgetary controls used. The procedure involved in setting up the budget will occur during the planning stages. The retailer, therefore, will plan different types of budgets even before the merchandising activity begins. The important types of budgets used by most retail establishments, regardless of size or type, are: (1) operations budget, (2) cash budget, (3) capital budget, and (4) merchandise budget.

Operations Budget

The *operations budget* may be defined as a forecast of expected sales along with expected costs for a specified time period. The operations budget is sometimes referred to as the revenue-and-expense budget. This type of budget is usually made up a year in advance, though estimates may be made for as long as three to five years. The revenues portion of the budget is based on estimated sales for the coming year, especially in a retail operation where the sale of goods and services constitutes the chief source of operating income.

The buyer, store manager, and merchandise manager, as well as other store executives, will hold several meetings throughout the year (called division meetings) to determine if present sales figures are keeping pace with sales projections. For example, the buyer and merchandise manager of a department store will refer to daily sales and stock reports to guide them in determining whether they will be able to meet planned sales objectives in the parent store and in branches during a particular selling season, such as the Easter season. In a chain operation the central buyer and corporate executives will also utilize daily sales and stock reports to tell them how much merchandise is selling in each unit throughout the chain. If a certain style of women's coats is reported to be a slow seller in one unit, the buyer will arrange with the store manager either to mark down the goods or have them transferred to a unit where that style of coat is a popular selling item. The discount buyer will give close

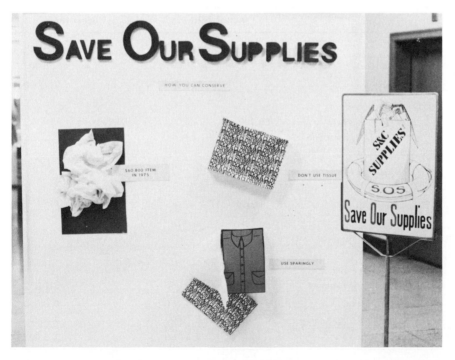

Figure 8.10. The merchant must be aware of changes in the business environment. For example, one retailer encouraged employees to avoid wasting paper when packing merchandise for store customers because of diminished natural resources and increasing cost of paper. (Courtesy of Strawbridge & Clothier Department Store, Philadelphia, Pa.)

attention to daily sales figures, since he must depend on rapid turnover to make his profit. If men's sandals are a popular selling item in a store unit located in a shopping center, the discount buyer will make certain that reorders are on time, and carefully watch the development of trends not only for the sandals but for a reasonable substitute.

Merchants must pay close attention to daily flash reports, sales analysis, inventory turnover, exception reports, and so forth when determining if sales figures are meeting projected goals. However, they must also consider internal as well as external business factors that may affect the accomplishment of sales goals. For example, the small business owner may fall ill, which may require that the business be closed for a few days, so that customers go elsewhere to purchase goods. This is an internal business factor. Other factors include labor strikes, poor morale, inefficient management, poor control systems, and so forth. External business factors are always present in the retailer's environment. As you recall from chapter 1, the merchant must be aware of economic conditions, changes in consumer spending patterns, changes in federal legislation, income and age levels of the population in the immediate trading area, population shifts, urban redevelopment, the prevalence of crime, and so forth. Retailers should read trade journals and daily newspapers, consult with marketing specialists, be aware of the methods used by competition, and "keep

Figure 8.11. An example of an operations budget for the Fabric for Fashion shop for the year 1976–1977.

		Actual 1976		Budget 1977
Sales		$35,000		$42,000
Cost of goods sold		– 21,000		– 25,000
Gross profit		$14,000		$17,000
Operating expenses				
Salaries of sales help	$5,100		$5,200	
Advertising & promotion	1,200		1,800	
Miscellaneous	200		250	
Total selling expenses	$6,500		$7,250	
Rent	$1,200		$1,200	
Utilities	450		500	
Taxes	350		450	
Insurance	150		150	
Miscellaneous	600		800	
Total general expenses	$2,750		$3,100	
Total operating expenses		$ 9,250		$10,350
Operating profit		$ 4,750		$ 6,650
Income taxes		$ 600		$ 1,050
Net profit		$ 4,150		$ 5,600

their own house in order" at all times. These methods will help them determine how closely actual results are conforming and will continue to conform to the projected budget.

Estimated costs or expenses, as you recall, may be classified as direct or indirect expenses. Usually, expenses are controlled and fixed throughout the budgetary period. Controllable expenses are those expenses directly attributed to a specific department. If a department is discontinued, these expenses end. Fixed expenses are continuing storewide expenses, which will remain even if one or two departments within the store close down.

Figure 8.11 is an example of an operations budget for the Fabric for Fashion Shop for the year 1976–1977.

Cash Budget

The *cash budget* is an estimate of the retail business' cash receipts and cash disbursements for a specified period of time. The cash budget will tell management how much cash is required during future periods. In a small business, this is a useful tool in determining the need for a short-term loan for a forthcoming selling season. Depending on the size of the business, the cash budget may extend over a year, with cash receipts and disbursements estimated on a monthly basis. If cash balances are very large, as in chain operations, discount houses, and department stores, closer and more sophisticated controls are used, for example, EDP. Figure 8.12 is an example of the cash budget for the Fabric for Fashions Shop for one month.

Figure 8.12. An example of a cash budget for one month for the Fabric for Fashion shop for the year 1976–1977.

	JANUARY	FEBRUARY	MARCH	APRIL	MAY	JUNE	JULY	AUGUST	SEPTEMBER
Cash receipts									
Cash sales	$1,500	$1,000	$2,000	$3,000	$1,500	$1,000	$1,000	$1,500	$2,500
Credit & collections	3,000	2,000	1,000	2,000	3,000	1,500	1,000	1,000	2,000
Total receipts	$4,500	$3,000	$3,000	$5,000	$4,500	$2,500	$2,000	$2,500	$4,500
Disbursements									
Purchases	$3,500	$5,500	$1,000	$1,000	$3,500	$2,000	$1,250	$3,500	$2,000
Wages	400	400	500	500	400	400	400	400	500
Rent	100	100	100	100	100	100	100	100	100
Utilities	75	75	75	50	50	50	75	75	75
Taxes			600			600			600
Total disbursements	$4,075	$6,075	$2,275	$1,650	$4,050	$3,150	$1,825	$4,075	$3,275
Monthly cash flow									
Cash in; cash out	+$ 250	–$3,175	+$ 675	+$3,150	+$ 300	–$ 750	+$ 100	–$1,695	+$1,325
Beginning cash	$ 750								
Cash minimum	$ 750								
Cash overage; cash shortage	–$ 500	+$2,925	–$2,250	+$ 900	+$1,200	–$ 450	+$ 550	–$1,125	+$ 400
Anticipated monthly loans	$2,925		$2,250				$1,125		

Capital Budget

The *capital budget* will plan for the investment of assets that will last longer than a year. It contains a list of future investment projects, with a justification for each proposal listed next to each item. For example, a department store may propose to open two new branch stores during the year 1976, one in 1977, and one in 1978. The plan would include a careful analysis of the geographical region, income level, competition, and the number of support businesses (banks, food markets, shoe repair stores, drug stores, etc.) also estimated for the area. Capital budgets are usually planned by the store's research division. However, the buyer has additional responsibilities for merchandising each time a new branch is added, and therefore must be included in a store's future plans.

Merchandise Budget

The *merchandise budget* is planned by the buyer (local or central) together with other store executives. Since the maintenance of an inventory that meets the needs and wants of customers and is within the financial plan set by management is a primary responsibility of store buyers, this topic will comprise the second part of this chapter.

Why are the following types of budgets used by most retail establishments?

What kind of information is contained in each?

Operations budget
Cash budget
Capital budget
Merchandise budget

PART 2   **Planning the Merchandise Budget**

The Merchandise Budget

A successful retail operation requires a merchandise assortment of the right type, in the right place, and at the right price. To accomplish this, factors such as profit and loss, sales, inventory, purchases, markups, markdowns, and expenses must be planned at least six months in advance by buyers and managers. This plan is called the merchandise budget. A *merchandise budget* may be defined as a plan that forecasts specific merchandising activities for a department or store for a specified period of time.

The buyer will work with numerous store executives in developing a plan to guide him or her in the various phases of the merchandising activity. For example, the control manager will provide detailed information on previous years' sales activities for the parent store and branches in a department store or for each store unit in a chain operation. The financial manager will provide information regarding the availability of funds, future cash needs, and figures on cash receipts and disbursements. The merchandise manager will provide valuable guidance based on company objectives and procedures, and will maintain a proper balance among the departments under his or her jurisdiction with regard to departmental opportunities and needs. A buyer who is also the owner-manager, as in the small independent business, will rely on past experience and on his or her ability as a manager and merchandising objectives when planning a workable merchandise budget.

The fundamental purpose of a merchandise budget is to provide a clear-cut plan of action for a specific time period (usually six months); it includes the appropriate methods by which results may be accomplished. The merchandise budget is a control measure that enables the buyer to follow a definite course of action, as well as an evaluation of current activities. Without it a buyer would have no guide, and management would have no way to estimate income, disbursements, and other financial needs from month to month and from one selling period to the next.

Certain elements must be present for the merchandise budget to accomplish its objectives. They are listed as follows:

1. The budget should be planned in advance of the specific date.
2. It should be simple, yet complete.
3. It should represent the judgment of both buyers and managers.
4. It should cover a time period for which reliable estimates can be made.
5. It should be flexible enough to permit necessary adjustments.

What the Merchandise Budget Includes

Once all available information regarding business conditions, consumer trends, market and supply conditions, competition, business philosophies, and future forecasts are gathered, actual planning for the period ahead may begin.

The small store will usually adopt a six-month plan that is very simple. For example, the desired results of the various merchandising activities for a specific period are put down on paper in the form of dollar figures, and comparisons and adjustments are made at frequent intervals in relation to the actual performance. The budget items may consist solely of sales, purchases, expenses, and stocks. However, in the department store or chain operation, a separate merchandise budget is made for each department and will contain, in addition to those items mentioned, markdowns, employee discounts, stock

Figure 8.13. Example of six-month merchandise budget, a plan that forecasts specific merchandising activities for a department or store for a specified period of time.

Department Number:	714

The Six-Month Merchandise Plan

Department Name: Junior Sportswear

Profit Goal	$12,000	Actual Profit Goal	
Operating Expenses	$10,000	Actual Operating Expenses	

Fall 1977	AUG.	SEPT.	OCT.	NOV.	DEC.	JAN.	SEASON
Last Year's Sales	$13,400	$20,200	$23,400	$19,000	$17,400	$13,000	$106,800
Planned Sales	15,400	20,200	26,000	21,000	19,000	13,400	115,000
Actual Sales							
Stock Last Year	$24,000	$34,000	$40,000	$32,000	$22,000	$18,000	$ 25,000
Planned Stocks	13,000	33,000	36,000	31,000	24,000	20,000	28,300
Actual Stock							
Reductions	$ 220	$ 320	$ 440	$ 300	$ 420	$ 400	$ 2,100
Planned Reductions	220	320	300	400	400	400	2,040
Actual Reductions							
Markup Last Year	45%	33%	50%	53%	40%	50%	
Planned Markups	45%	33%	45%	50%	45%	50%	
Actual Markups							
Profit Last Year	$ 2,500	$ 1,500	$ 2,000	$ 2,000	$ 1,500	$ 3,500	$ 12,000
Planned Profit	2,000	1,500	2,500	2,500	1,500	2,000	12,000
Actual Profit							
Expenses Last Year	$ 420	$ 480	$ 600	$ 480	$ 340	$ 280	$ 2,600
Planned Expenses	500	540	660	540	420	340	3,000
Actual Expenses							
Purchases Last Year	$23,400	$26,200	$15,400	$13,000	$13,800	$ 9,000	$100,800
Planned Purchases	22,400	23,700	21,000	18,000	15,000	9,400	109,000
Actual Purchases							
Comments	Rainy Month	Turned Cool	News-paper Strike	Sales Pro-motion	Fair Weather	Snow Storm	

Merchandise Manager	Buyer	Store Controller
L.L. Allen	M.S. Smith	H.I.

shortages, stock turnover, customer returns, gross margin, net profit, and average sales. Thus the buyer and the store executives will develop a merchandise budget based on planned: (1) sales, (2) stocks, (3) reductions, (4) markups, (5) gross margin and operating profit, (6) expenses, and (7) purchases.

It is important to note that management plans the budget in terms of dollar figures, since dollar figures formulate the store's overall profit objective. Also, buyers will plan in units, that is, they will estimate what they expect to sell during a season or period according to merchandise classification, subclass, size, color, price, or whatever, and determine inventory needs based on this plan. Once unit needs are determined, dollar figures are arrived at by multiplying the number of units times prices.

Figure 8.13 is an example of a six-month merchandise budget. You should refer to the illustration to understand the relationship among the factors discussed on the following pages.

Important factors to consider when planning the merchandise budget

1. Planned sales
2. Planned stocks
3. Planned reductions
4. Planned markups
5. Planned gross margin and operating profit
6. Planned expenses
7. Planned purchases

Planned Sales

Sales planning is the first step in the merchandise budget and is the key element in planning. Most plans span the time from February 1 to July 31, and from August 1 to January 31. Sales are planned first because it is easier to adjust stocks, markups, and expenses to sales potentials than to attempt to plan these factors and to reach a sales goal consistent with them.

The first step in planning sales is to consider the overall past sales performance of the store or chain operation as a whole, as well as sales trends for each department in individual branches or units. Consideration should be given to factors within the store that may aid or hinder sales activity. For example, a store may decide to upgrade its fashion image, add a new branch, close two store units, develop a discount merchandising philosophy, or change to a self-service operation. Next, the buyer must consider outside factors that may affect sales, such as economic trends, the rate of employment and unemployment, the growth of shopping centers, competitive conditions, etc. For example, management may determine that a 7 percent gain in sales storewide is necessary to meet rising costs due to increased fuel expenses, scarcity of building supplies, demands of labor unions, and changes in overhead and operations, to name but a few. Management may determine that the unpainted furniture department could increase its sales activity by 6 percent, whereas the kitchen appliances department offers little opportunity for increased sales activity. Therefore, only a 2 percent sales increase would be planned for the kitchen appliances department.

After considering the store's sales opportunities as a whole, the buyer must next consider how the department or departments will achieve the sales goals based on the store's overall projections. The buyer must consider sales planning according to each classification, price line, size, color, or other subdivision that is felt to be important. The following records will be helpful when planning sales for the department.

Department sales records. The buyer will gather information concerning sales activity for the past year and longer, take notice of trends (fads), variations in sales growth (unseasonable weather, labor strikes), or unusually high profits (upturn in economic activity).

The buyer's diary. The buyer will usually keep a diary of conditions outside the business that affect sales activity. The diary may include information regarding fashion trends, price increases, population trends in the store's trading area, changes in consumer spending, market activities, availability of suppliers, changes in competition, and world trade activities.

Store policies and procedures. The buyer must be aware of existing store policies as well as those likely to be adopted in the foreseeable future. For example, policies regarding store renovations, addition of new merchandise lines, the elimination of departments, changes in store hours, opening of branches or units, revision of credit policies, and changes in store image will all have an effect on sales planning.

The Monthly Sales Plan. To plan the six-month budget realistically, buyers and management must first plan for each of the six months on a monthly basis. Sales goals will be set for each month, since all months will not contribute equally to the six-month plan. For example, the months of November and December will have a higher sales goal than the months of July and August, due to changes in seasonal demand patterns. Easter and the back-to-school period are peak periods for most fashion departments; therefore, the sales goals for the corresponding months (March and April; September) will be higher. Or a store may plan a preinventory clearance sale during the month of January, which would account for a higher sales goal then as opposed to goals for a month where no significant sales promotion was planned. Finally, a department that sells seasonal goods, for example, patio and outdoor furniture, will plan for higher sales activity during the months of June and July due to weather patterns.

As stated previously, management will plan in terms of dollar figures, and the buyer will plan in terms of units. As a buyer, you will plan units of merchandise according to classification, price line, size, color, or other breakdowns that are applicable to your particular department. For example, if you are a buyer of men's sweaters, you may find that the classic crew neck sweater is featured as an important fashion look for the fall season. You will plan your stock in units with the crew neck classification given priority, while less popular styles are offered in a limited selection. Or you may plan sales according to price line. For example, if the previous year's sales were low due to poor economic conditions, you may note an upswing in the economy that may lead you to offer higher-priced goods.

Methods Used in Planning Departmental Sales. Buyers and managers will not only consider the points just discussed but also will plan in general terms, that is, in terms of store needs and individual departmental needs. Two methods used in planning departmental sales are (1) the top-down plan and (2) the bottom-up plan.

Top-down planning may be defined as the planning of overall sales management based on economic trends, external conditions, and changes in store policies. Sales goals are further broken down into plans for each department in the store, and if the store is a branch or chain system, into plans for each department or each store. If there is a central buying system, the departmental sales plans will include the sales in all the selling units within each store. In this case, buyers have their sales goals planned for them by top management and can only make suggestions for adjustments in the sales figures presented to them.

Sales plans made by this approach may prove very close to the actual sales volume for the entire store; however, they are frequently inaccurate for individual departments within the store. Top management is often too far removed from individual departments and cannot predict the external forces that may affect sales.

Bottom-up planning may be defined as the planning for a specific department, whether it is located in one store or in many units. In this method, the initial planning is accomplished by those directly responsible for implementing the sales plan, and storewide plans are primarily built up from the plans formulated from within each department and selling unit. This is the most favored plan used by retail stores; however, flexibility and realistic thinking are prime requisites for its success. For example, after the buyer has formulated the sales plan for the coming season, he must confer with the merchandise manager, who is aware of the goals and objectives set by top management. If the buyer's plan falls short of the overall objectives of the store, research is required to establish how a particular department may increase sales.

The best approach to planning department sales is a realistic one. Sales should be forecasted as close to actual sales as possible. This will ensure the proper merchandise assortment, help minimize markdowns, ensure adequate sales coverage, and cut down expenses.

How will the following techniques help the buyer when planning department sales?

Department sales records
The buyer's diary
Store policies and procedures
The monthly sales plan
Top-down planning
Bottom-up planning

Planned Stocks

The second step in the merchandise plan is to maintain a balanced stock in relation to anticipated sales. It is interesting to note, however, that inventory costs are closely linked to economic booms and recessions. Buyers tend to overstock when prospects of increased sales are good and to understock when prospects are bad. Often, a relatively small increase in sales leads to excessive buying and excessive production. For example, during the economic recession of the mid-1970s, surplus of stock made it necessary for retail buyers to take sharp markdowns until inventories were depleted.

The buyer will plan the stock in terms of the specific items of merchandise he believes will serve his customer's needs and wants. However, stock planning also includes: (1) an understanding of the various methods used to plan needed stocks, (2) the computation of stock turn, (3) computation of the average inventory, (4) an understanding of methods of increasing stock turn, (5) an understanding of the different rates of stock turn, and (6) stock planning for branches and store units.

Various Methods Used to Plan Needed Stocks. A most important responsibility of all types of buyers is to plan stock accurately and efficiently, whether for the forthcoming season or for merchandise replenishment at any time. Four methods may be used when planning stock: (1) the basic stock method (BOM), (2) the percentage-variation (or deviation) method, (3) the weeks' supply method, and (4) the stock-sales ratio method.

The basic stock method (BOM) shows the necessity of having a *basic stock* (which in this case refers to the difference between the average stock and the average amount sold monthly) on hand at all times. Beginning-of-the-month (BOM) stock is determined by the following equation:

BOM = Planned Sales for the Month + (Average
Stock at Retail – Average Monthly Sales)

For example, during the six-month period, season sales may be planned at $57,000; planned turnover, 3; June sales may be estimated at $15,000 and July sales at $17,000.

Stock, June 1 $15,000
  Average Stock at Retail
  = $57,000 ÷ 3
  = $19,000
  Average Monthly Sales
  = $57,000 ÷ 6
  = $ 9,500
  Stock, June 1 = $15,000 +
  ($19,000 – $9,500)
  = $15,000 + $9,500
  = $24,500

Stock, July 1 $17,000
  Average Stock at Retail
  = $57,000 ÷ 3
  = $19,000
  Average Monthly Sales
  = $57,000 ÷ 6
  = $ 9,500
  Stock, July 1 = $17,000 +
  ($19,000 – $9,500)
  = $17,000 + $9,500
  = $26,500

The student will note that this plan increases and decreases stock at the first of each month in approximately the same amount of dollars as sales increase or decrease. In the example, July sales are approximately $2,000 higher than June sales, and stocks are also $2,000 higher. Since the basic stock is constant throughout the season, stocks for the first of the month may be found by adding the sales for the month to the basic stock.

A second method of stock planning, *the percentage-variation (or deviation) method,* is based on the premise that BOM stock is increased or decreased from the planned average stock by approximately 50 percent of the sales variations from the average monthly sales. The formula may be expressed as follows:

$$\text{BOM Stock} = \text{Average } \frac{\text{Yearly Sales}}{\text{Turnover}} \times$$

$$\left[\frac{1}{2} \left(1 + \frac{\text{Sales for the Month}}{\text{Average Monthly Sale}} \right) \right]$$

For example, the planned yearly sales may be $48,000; the planned sales for the month of September, $2,500; and the planned yearly turnover, 6.

Then:
Retail Stock September 1
   (BOM Stock)

$$= \frac{\$48,000}{6} \times \frac{1}{2} \left(1 + \frac{\$2,500}{\$48,000} \div 12 \right)$$

$$= \$8,000 \times \frac{1}{2} \left(1 + \frac{\$2,500}{\$4,000} \right)$$

$$= \$8,000 \times \frac{1.625}{2}$$

$$= \$8,000 \times .8125$$

$$\text{BOM Stock} = \$6,500$$

The week's supply method of stock planning is to plan stock on a weekly basis and to set stocks equal to a predetermined number of weeks' supply, depending upon the stock turn desired. For example, if approximately eight turns a year are desired, the stock should equal approximately six weeks' supply. The calculations are as follows:

$$\begin{aligned}
\text{Weeks' Supply} &= 52 \text{ Weeks} \div \text{Desired Stock Turn} \\
&= 52 \div 8 \\
&= 6.1
\end{aligned}$$

Estimates are made, therefore, to cover sales about six weeks ahead.

A fourth method of stock planning, known as the *stock-sales ratio method,* uses the monthly stock-sales ratio as the basis for stock planning. With this method, the planned sales volume for the month is multiplied by the planned BOM stock-sales ratio to determine the planned BOM stock. The formula may be written as follows:

BOM Stock = Planned Monthly Sales Volume × Planned BOM Stock-Sales Ratio

The stock-sales ratio is the BOM stock expressed as a ratio of sales. It shows the number of months that would be necessary to dispose of BOM stock at the rate of the sales for that month. The formula may be written as follows:

$$\text{Stock-Sales Ratio} = \frac{\text{Beginning Stock}}{\text{Sales}}$$

For example, it may be found that the January stock-sales ratio for a shoe department is 5. This means that the stocks on the first of January are usually 5 times the January sales. Thus, if the department sales forecast is $15,000 for January, this figure is multiplied by the stock-sales ratio of 5 to determine planned stocks of $75,000 for January 1.

$$\text{Stock-Sales Ratio} = \frac{\text{BOM Stock}}{\text{Month's Sales}}$$

$$\text{Stock-Sales Ratio} = \frac{\$75,000}{\$15,000}$$

Stock-Sales Ratio = 5

BOM Stock = Planned Monthly Sales Volume × Planned BOM Stock-Sales Ratio

BOM Stock = $15,000 × 5

BOM Stock = $75,000

The Computation of Stock Turnover. Stock turn or stock turnover is the rate at which stock is disposed of or depleted and replaced in a given period of time. Every buyer should understand stock turnover to make more profitable use of his capital investment, control inventories, and maximize profits. Stock turn may be computed by one of the following formulas:

1. $$\frac{\text{Stock Turn}}{\text{Retail Basis}} = \frac{\text{Net Sales}}{\text{Average Stock at Retail Price}}$$

2. $$\frac{\text{Stock Turn}}{\text{Cost Basis}} = \frac{\text{Cost of Goods Sold}}{\text{Average Cost of Stock}}$$

3. $$\frac{\text{Stock Turn}}{\text{Unit Basis}} = \frac{\text{Number of Units Sold}}{\text{Average Number of Units in Stock}}$$

For example, if the retail store keeps records of the retail value of the stock, then the retail basis for computing stock turnover is used. When information regarding stock is available only in terms of cost, the cost basis of computing stock turnover is preferred. The unit basis is useful in studying the number of items or units carried in relation to the number sold.

Stock turn may be computed for any period, such as a year, a month, or a week. However, when the term *rate of stock turn* is used, a period of one year is understood.

Average inventory. To find the average inventory, you would find the sum of all the inventories in a period and divide by the number of inventories. Many buyers use the average of the actual stocks as determined by a physical inventory at the beginning and at the end of the year. For example:

Inventory on Hand at Retail

January 1	$ 30,000
February 1	17,000
March 1	22,000
April 1	25,000
May 1	+ 23,000
Total Inventory =	$117,000

$$\text{Average Inventory} = \frac{\text{Total Inventory}}{\text{Number of Inventories}}$$

$$\text{Average Inventory} = \frac{\$117,000}{5}$$

$$\text{Average Inventory} = \$ 23,400$$

It must be remembered, however, that the stock remaining at the end of a selling period is not an accurate reflection of the average stock carried throughout the year. For example, stock at the end of the year (December 31) is usually below the true yearly average because more goods have been disposed of, primarily through store inventory clearance sales. A more accurate method of determining the average inventory is by dividing the sum of the stocks on the first of every month, plus the ending stock, by 13. The number 13 is used because the retailer is starting with the beginning-of-the-month inventory and there will be an additional 12 times (each month throughout the year) when inventory is counted. A physical inventory is not necessary because a monthly book inventory may be utilized. An example follows:

Inventory on Hand at Retail

January 1	$ 30,000
February 1	$ 27,000
March 1	$ 26,500
April 1	$ 22,000
May 1	$ 25,500
June 1	$ 19,500
July 1	$ 24,000
August 1	$ 21,400
September 1	$ 27,000
October 1	$ 22,600
November 1	$ 25,000
December 1	$ 23,000
December 31	+$ 20,000
Total Inventory	=$313,500

$$\text{Average Inventory} = \frac{\text{Total Inventory}}{\text{Number of Inventories}}$$

$$\text{Average Inventory} = \frac{\$313,000}{13}$$

$$\text{Average Inventory} = \$24,076$$

Increasing stock turn. The buyer who maintains a small, clean inventory will find this the fastest method of increasing stock turn. Since profit is not realized until the inventory is turned back into money, the higher the stock turnover, the greater the profit returned on the dollars invested. The following is a list of methods the buyer may use to keep inventory to a minimum without jeopardizing sales.

Stocks may be kept to a minimum by:
1. Reducing the number of price lines carried
2. Limiting the number of brands carried
3. Reducing duplicate styles
4. Carrying smaller reserve stocks
5. Avoiding the accumulation of unsalable goods
6. Eliminating unsalable goods
7. Closely following the buying plan

Advantages of Rapid Stock Turnover
1. Markdowns and depreciation are reduced because merchandise sells faster.

2. Sales are stimulated because of the availability of new goods.
3. Interest expenses on merchandise investment is reduced, since less merchandise is required.
4. Less storage space is required, since fewer goods are needed.
5. The use of capital is maximized, since less inventory is needed.
6. Expense of selling and promoting is reduced since fresh, new merchandise will sell with less effort.

Limitations of Rapid Stock Turnover
1. Merchandise costs may increase due to a loss of quantity discounts.
2. Sales may be lost if the store or department is out of stock.
3. Internal problems may result due to an increase in clerical work—for example, correspondence, vendor follow-up, and periodic inventory checks.

Different Rates of Stock Turn. Another major consideration in the planning of stock is the different rate of stock turn. The rate of stock turnover will depend on certain factors, which are listed here.

1. Different lines of merchandise have different rates of stock turn. The rate of stock turn for a gourmet food department is faster than the rate for a small-appliance department due to the nature of the goods.
2. Type of goods also influences stock turn. Convenience goods will have a faster rate than shopping goods. Convenience items are articles for which there is an immediate need or which are bought on impulse. Shopping goods, because they cost more and are less frequently needed, require more careful consideration and selection.
3. Type of retail institution influences stock turn. Discount stores will have faster rates than traditional department stores. Discounters concentrate on the fastest-moving merchandise, even though stock assortment may be thrown out of balance. Department stores, on the other hand, will provide a full line of merchandise to offer the customer a variety of choices in each category.

Planning Stock for Branches and Store Units. A final major consideration in planning stock is the number of branches or units for which you are responsible. For example, if you are a local buyer for a department store, you may have to purchase goods for your department in the parent store and for the same department in a number of branches, depending on the size of the operation. If you are a central buyer for a chain-store operation, you may have to purchase large quantities of merchandise for your particular department in many store units, perhaps 30 to 40 or 300 to 400. Or you may be a resident buyer offering assistance and advice to a number of client stores that require goods for the particular department or departments you represent. The following points should be considered when planning stock for more than one store branch or unit:

1. Plan stock separately. Be mindful of differences in individual branches or units regarding consumer spending patterns, such as ethnic needs, price lines, popular merchandise classification, discount or high quality sportswear and childrenswear, and peaks and lows in sales-stock ratio.

2. Seek the advice of store managers and department managers, since they work closely with the store's clientele and have firsthand experience and knowledge of the merchandising needs of the store and its departments.

3. Recognize that each branch store or unit has its own set of unique characteristics. Do not underestimate sales and stock potential simply because the store unit is located in a rural area, for example, and not in a suburban shopping center. A common fault is to provide merchandise that is not well balanced with regard to classification, style, color, size, or price line. Fashion merchandise especially requires careful inventory planning, since most customers will shop where they find a completely accessorized and well-balanced assortment. (We will talk more about merchandise assortment in the next chapter.)

A primary responsibility of the buyer is to provide a merchandise assortment that reflects the needs and wants of the store's clientele. How will the following factors assist the buyer in accomplishing this task?

Various Methods Used to Plan Needed Stocks
The basic stock method, the percentage-variation (or deviation method), the week's supply method, and the stock-sales ratio method

---

The Computation of Stock Turnover
Retail basis, cost basis, unit basis

Average Inventory

$$\text{Average inventory} = \frac{\text{Total inventory}}{\text{Number of inventories}}$$

Increasing Stock Turn
Advantages and disadvantages

Different Rates of Stock Turn
Rates according to different merchandise, the types of goods carried by the department and the type of retail institution

---

Planning Stock for Branches and Store Units
Plan stock separately, seek advice, recognize that each branch or unit has its own set of unique characteristics

Planned Reductions

The third step is to plan retail reductions. *Retail reduction* may be defined as the allowance for the difference between the original retail value of merchandise and the actual final sales value of the merchandise. It consists of three major factors: (1) merchandise shortages and overages, (2) employee discounts and discounts for other special groups, and (3) markdowns.

Merchandise Shortages and Overages. As previously explained, a *merchandise shortage* is the difference between the book inventory and the physical inventory when the book inventory is larger. In most stores today, merchandise shortages exceed 1 percent of the store's sales; and since the buyer is the person responsible for the inventory, his competence as a merchandiser is in question when inventory shortages are high. Also, the gross margin of the department will suffer because shortages will cut into the buyer's profit, and gross margin is one of the important factors by which management judges the buyer's performance.[7]

The buyer and his manager require sound facts to determine the extent of merchandise shortages as well as their causes. A most important step toward improving the shortage problem is to make sure that all records are kept as accurate as possible. For example, if a handbag department receives 10 units of handbags and the report lists 12 units, 2 units may be presumed to be lost. It is important that all personnel within the department, from the stockboy upward, be trained to count and recount actual merchandise units against the figures recorded. For instance, if a buyer decides to transfer 20 dresses at $35.95 each to a branch store or another unit, the assistant buyer or department manager should check the count, price tickets, style number and whatever else is necessary to ensure that the right merchandise in the right amount is going to the right place. And, in turn, someone at the branch or store unit should check and count the incoming merchandise to make sure that the right goods in the right amount have been received. According to the National Retail Merchants Association, there are at least six common sources of errors in receiving and shipping of merchandise:[8]

1. Failure to count the number of pieces received from or returned to vendors, or transferred from one store or branch to another
2. Failure to check the actual count against the figure entered on the form covering the receipt or transfer of merchandise
3. Failure to check the prices marked on the merchandise against the prices marked on the form covering the movement of that merchandise
4. Failure to check the department or classification number on the form against the merchandise itself
5. Failure to make an entry covering movement of merchandise or changes in price
6. Failure to watch prices and extensions on invoices and chargebacks to vendors

If accuracy in record keeping is maintained, methods may be developed that will assist the buyer in pinpointing the source of the shortage problem and thus serve to discourage carelessness, dishonesty, and waste. (The subject of shoplifting will be covered in detail in Chapter 15.)

The formula used to determine inventory shortage is illustrated as follows:

Merchandise Shortage = Book Inventory − Physical Inventory

For example:

Net Sales	$150,000
Purchases	70,000
Opening Inventory	160,000
Physical Inventory	70,000

Then:

Opening Inventory	$160,000
+ Purchases at Retail	70,000
Total Handled	$230,000
− Net Sales	150,000
Book Inventory	$ 80,000

When comparing the physical inventory with the book inventory, we find:

Book Inventory	$ 80,000
Physical Inventory	70,000

Apply the formula:

Merchandise Shortage = Book Inventory − Physical Inventory = $80,000 − $ 70,000
Merchandise Shortage = $ 10,000

A *merchandise overage* is the difference between the book inventory and the physical inventory when the physical inventory is larger. In this case there has usually been an error in the physical count. The formula is as follows:

Merchandise Overage = Physical Inventory − Book Inventory

For example:

Net Sales	$150,000
Opening Inventory	160,000
Purchases at Retail	70,000
Physical Inventory	70,000

Then:

Opening Inventory	$120,000
+ Purchases at Retail	70,000
Total Handled	$190,000
− Net Sales	150,000
Book Inventory	$ 40,000

When comparing the physical inventory with the book inventory, we find:

Book Inventory	$40,000
Physical Inventory	70,000

Apply the formula:

Merchandise Overage = Physical Inventory − Book Inventory
= $70,000 − $40,000
Merchandise Overage = $30,000

Employee and Other Discounts. The *employee discount* is a price reduction granted to store employees. Such discounts are also granted to other groups, such as charitable organizations and various religious orders. The dollar amount of discounts for the period may be illustrated as follows:

Net Sales for May $200,000
Employee Discounts for the Month 2,000

Employee Discount % =

$$= \frac{\text{Employee Discounts for the Month}}{\text{Net Sales}}$$

$$= \frac{\$\ 2,000}{200,000}$$

Employee Discount % = 1%

Markdowns. The retail buyer will mark down his merchandise in an effort to keep his prices at a level that will reflect consumer demand. A reduction in price from the original retail price is called a *markdown*. The markdown equation may be written as follows:

Original Retail Price	$5.00
− Markdown Price	4.00
Dollar Markdown	$1.00

The *markdown percent* is the difference between the net dollar markdown and the original retail price divided by the net sales. The markdown equation may also be expressed in terms of a percent (%). The formula is as follows:

$$\text{Markdown \%} = \frac{\text{Net Dollar Markdown}}{\text{Net Sales}}$$

$$\text{Markdown \%} = \frac{\$1.00}{\$5.00}$$

$$\text{Markdown \%} = 20\%$$

Why Markdowns Are Necessary. The buyer will plan markdowns because it is frequently necessary to reduce the price of items to sell them (see Figure 8.14). This is particularly true of fashion goods that have become slow sellers. There are two major reasons for markdowns: (1) to sell merchandise to which customers have not satisfactorily responded, and (2) to induce customers to come to the department or store seeking bargains and thus stimulate sales for regularly priced goods.

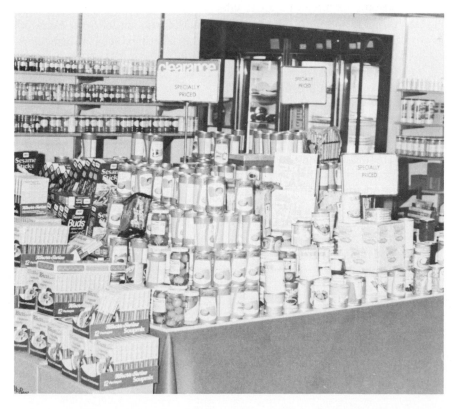

Figure 8.14. A retail buyer will plan markdowns because it is frequently necessary to reduce merchandise to sell it. Clearance sales will induce customers to come to the store seeking bargains.

Why markdowns are necessary
1. To sell merchandise to which customers have not responded 2. To induce customers to seek bargains, thus stimulating sales

There are many reasons why goods must be sold at a price lower than the retail price. For example, buying errors may occur, such as purchasing too many goods in one size, price, fabric, or color; careless selling may result in return of merchandise; pricing errors may occur, as when goods are priced too high. The following is a list of the causes of markdowns.

1. Buying errors—purchasing the wrong sizes, styles, fabrics, prices, colors, etc.
2. Selling errors—careless selling, neglect of slow sellers, and old inventory
3. Pricing errors—offering goods at a higher price than the consumer is willing to pay
4. Special promotion sales—reducing goods to stimulate sales, for example, special after-Christmas sales
5. One-day specials—offering special markdowns on leftover, damaged, and soiled pieces, and special vendor offerings such as irregulars, seconds, or job lots
6. Prestige goods—price reduction due to poor judgment in determining the value of a prestige item
7. Store policy—reducing goods to meet competition, to stimulate sales, and to maintain inventory until late in the selling period

How are the following formulas used when planning reductions?
Merchandise shortage formula Merchandise overage formula Employee discount percent Markdown equation Markdown percent

Planned Markups

The fourth step in the merchandise plan is to plan markups. A retail buyer must sell merchandise at a price that will cover the cost of the goods and the expenses incurred as a result of acquiring the goods and that will yield a profit. The term *markup* may be defined as the difference between the cost price and the retail price of an item. The formula may be written as follows:

Dollar Markup = Retail Price − Cost Price
Dollar Markup = $20.00 − $10.00
Dollar Markup = $10.00

Most retail buyers think of markup in terms of percent. The markup equation as expressed in percent *(markup percent)* may be written as follows:

$$\text{Markup \% at Retail} = \frac{\text{Markup}}{\text{Retail Price}}$$

$$\text{Markup \% at Retail} = \frac{\$10.00}{\$20.00}$$

Markup % at Retail = 50%

The markup percent is usually calculated as a percent of retail price because all operating costs and profit or loss are determined as a percentage of net sales.

The buyer should seek the following information to plan a satisfactory markup:

1. Total amount of sales for the planned selling season
2. Planned expenses for the season
3. Planned reductions such as markdowns, shortages, and employee discounts
4. Profit goal planned for the season

Markup may apply to individual pieces of merchandise, to a group of items, or to the entire stock.

In addition, the buyer should give consideration to the initial and maintained markup. *Initial markup* (also known as mark-on or original markup) is the difference between the cost price and the retail price of goods. *Maintained markup* is the difference between the cost price and the final retail price. For example, if a pair of shoes costs $10 and is retailed for $20, the difference between the retail and the cost is $10; this is the initial markup. However, if the shoes do not sell at $20 but instead sell at $15, the difference between the cost price and the final selling price is $5; this is the maintained markup. The $20 price may be called the original retail selling price and the $15 price the sale price.

When planning the initial markup, the buyer must also consider consumer demand. The initial markup must be set at a point at which the merchandise will readily be accepted by customers. If this markup is too low to cover expenses and costs, the buyer may consider selling at a loss temporarily. However, he must soon adjust to a realistic markup figure or he will eventually go out of business.

The type of clientele the store is serving and the competition have an important influence on markup. If the buyer is serving the needs of a well-to-do community, a high markup may be acceptable. On the other hand, if the members of the community are price-conscious, a low markup may be necessary. The markup taken by competing stores is also important.

Markups will also vary with the kind of merchandise and the kind of store. For example, department stores usually use an initial markup of 43–50%; discount houses, 38–45%; specialty stores, 48–60%. Those stores that depend primarily on their low-price policy take lower markups than do retail stores that attract customers with a stock of service, convenience, and specialty items.

Considerations when planning the initial markup

1. To cover costs and expenses and to make a profit (the initial markup formula)
2. Consumer demand: how high or how low to attract customers?
3. Types of store clientele: low-income group? average-income? well-to-do?
4. Kind of merchandise carried by the store: top quality? discount? prestige item?
5. Type of retail store: discount house? traditional department store? boutique?
6. Competition: what kind of a markup does my competition take?

How are the following formulas used when planning markup?

Markup equation
Markup percent
Initial markup
Maintained markup

Planned Gross Margin and Operating Profit

The fifth step in the merchandise plan is to plan gross margin and operating profit. Gross margin, as previously explained, is the difference between net sales and the cost of goods sold. Gross margin represents what is available for operating expenses and profit. It is what is left after costs have been deducted but before operating expenses have been considered. The formula is as follows: Net Sales – Cost of Goods Sold = Gross Margin. For example:

Net Sales	$5,549.00
− Cost of Goods Sold	1,320.00
Gross Margin	$4,229.00

Operating profit may be defined as that part of the gross margin which remains AFTER operating expenses have been deducted. As you recall, operating expenses are the expenses incurred during the operation of the department or store. For example:

Operating Expenses:

Buyer's Salary	$ 400
Sales Help Salaries	350
Asst. Buyer's Salary	200
Sales Promotions	100
Rent	200
Utilities	+ 100
Total Operating Expenses	$1,350

Once operating expenses have been planned for the month, the *net profit* may be computed by deducting the total operating expenses from the gross margin. For example:

Gross Margin	$4,320
− Total Operating Expenses	1,350
Net Profit	$2,970

The retail buyer is always faced with the task of determining how best to forecast a realistic gross margin figure that will yield, after expenses have been deducted, a satisfactory and reasonable net profit. Planning techniques should include not only the buyer's previous experience, but also all pertinent information that is available. (Review Figure 8–9, illustrating a profit-and-loss statement.)

Planned Expenses

The sixth step in planning the merchandise budget is to plan expenses for the store as a whole and for each department. Expense planning is a most important activity for all buyers in all types of stores, since it provides a control system that assists in analyzing and forecasting the costs involved in merchandising and thus safeguards the store's profit objective. Expense planning consists of a series of dollar estimates of the various expenses a retail business will incur in a specified (budgeted) period. The primary objective of expense planning is to make careful and accurate forecasts of expenses so that proper controls can be established to meet them. Top store management and buying specialists have the responsibility for estimating future expenses and thus preparing the expense plan or budget. However, management will plan for all store units and branches, while buying specialists (local or central) will plan for departmental needs. The following procedures should be considered when planning expenses for the store or department:

1. Plan expenses for the whole store and for each branch or unit in the retail operation. Top store executives, such as the controller, finance manager, director of research, store operations manager, vice-president of branch stores, and vice-president of merchandising, are responsible for this activity. To estimate expense control figures, however, two kinds of basic data should be used: first, overall total expense figures must be set, and second, a breakdown of the expense figure according to major accounts—for example, merchandising, operations, personnel, advertising, and display—is necessary. Control figures should also be broken down by individual stores and by departments. Even the small business plans expenses; however, the plan may be restricted to a few major expense activities (operations and merchandising). The owner-manager or his assistant will prepare monthly reports comparing actual expenses with those planned.

2. Once figures are set for the store's overall expenses plan, as well as for individual branches or units, and for individual departments, the buyer or department specialist may estimate future needs. The store's control manager or budget committee is responsible for providing all available, pertinent information regarding sales analysis, stock turn, cash receipts and disbursements, salary policies, personnel recruitment practices, changes in competition, price guidelines, supply or market conditions, and economic forecasts, as well as anticipated changes in store policy. In addition, information regarding the sales-stock activity in each store unit or branch, the number of sales transactions in relation to the number of store personnel, and advertising and promotion plans are also important. And, where applicable, the buyer or department head will be informed of the amount of general overhead of the store that is to be charged against the department budget.

3. Once detailed data are provided, the department executive is in a position to estimate direct expenses for his department for the six-month merchandise budget. Monthly expense estimates may include:

- Payroll requirements for full-time and part-time personnel
- Advertising and special promotional events
- Clerical assistance and record keeping
- Expenses for buyer market trips, transportation, hotel accommodations, meals
- Telephone and telegraph expense
- Miscellaneous office supplies

A major advantage of expense planning is that remedial action may be taken where and when required. For example, the department executive may need additional sales help as a result of increased sales activity due to an upswing in the economy. He will submit a sales help request to his merchandise manager, who will approve or disapprove the request, depending on the status of the expense budget and the relationship to anticipated sales.

Review the methods used to plan expenses

1. Plan figures for the store's overall expenses
2. Plan expenses for individual units or branches
3. Estimate expenses for each department

Planned Purchases

The last step in planning the merchandise budget is to plan the dollar amount of goods that can be brought into the department or store during a specified period or season. The buyer can determine planned purchases by adding together planned sales, planned reductions, and planned stock (stock planned for the end of the month or for the beginning of the next month) and subtracting from the total needs for this month the planned stock at the beginning of the month. The formula is as follows:

Planned Sales
+ Planned Reductions
+ Planned End-of-Month Stock
= Total Needs for the Month
− Beginning-of-the-Month Stock
= Planned Purchases

For example:

Planned Stock, October 1	$100,000
Planned Sales, October 1–31	140,000
Planned Markdowns, October 1–31	70,000
Planned Stock, October 31	120,000

What are the planned purchases?

Then:

Planned Sales	$140,000
+ Planned Reductions	70,000
+ Planned End-of-Month Stock	120,000
= Total Needs for the Month	$330,000
− Beginning-of-the-Month Stock	100,000
= Planned Purchases	$230,000

Purchases are planned at retail prices and then converted to cost value by applying the planned markup percent.

For the buyer to control purchases effectively, a device called the *open-to-buy* (abbreviated OTB) is used. The OTB, as previously stated, may be defined as the amount of merchandise, either at cost price or at retail, that the buyer is open to receive into inventory during a certain time period based on the plans formulated. It contains figures agreed upon by store executives in consultation with finance and control personnel and is based on the expectations of the merchandising division. It may be prepared weekly or monthly, and provides a method of allocating purchases so that planned stock levels may be maintained. It may be broken down according to separate merchandise categories within a department or into specific quantities of individual items of merchandise. The breakdown depends on the amount and extent of control that management feels is necessary. For example, a large discount chain operation would use EDP replenishment controls to keep stock replenished and balanced according to sales, classification, style, size, color, or whatever.

The OTB may be calculated either in dollars or in units. For example, let us say that a woman buyer has planned purchases for the month of August at $2,000. By August 20, she has spent $1,500 for merchandise that has been received or that will be received into the department before the end of the month. This leaves $500 for her to spend during the remaining time; therefore, she is open to buy $500 worth of merchandise on August 20. The dollar open-to-buy formula may be calculated as follows:

Planned Purchases	$2,000
− Merchandise on Order	1,500
= Open-to-buy	$ 500

In practice, however, the open-to-buy formula is far more complicated than this illustration shows. Adjustments are often necessary due to fluctuations in reductions, sales, and availability of goods. Also, merchandise ordered but not yet received may further complicate the open-to-buy figure. For example:

Planned Sales	$ 50,000
+ Planned Reductions	10,000
+ Planned End-of-month Stock	40,000
= Total Needs for the Month	$100,000
− Beginning-of-the-month Stock	25,000
= Planned Purchases	$ 75,000
− Merchandise on Order	30,000
= Open-to-buy	$ 45,000

The OTB figure shows how much merchandise may be received into a particular department or merchandise classification during the course of a month without exceeding the planned inventory at the end of the month.[9]

For the OTB to be an effective control measure, however, careful checks must be made concerning all orders placed with vendors; therefore, merchandise must be ordered on the appropriate form or purchase order. One copy of

A well-planned merchandise budget will assist store managers and buying specialists in meeting the profit objectives of the business. How will the following information be useful in meeting this objective?

I Planned sales	
Departmental sales records	The monthly sales plan
The buyer's diary	Top-down planning
Store policies and procedures	Bottom-up planning

II Planned stocks	
Various methods used to plan needed stocks	Increasing stock turn
Computation of stock turnover	Different rates of stock turn
Average inventory	Planning for branches and store units

III Planned reductions
Merchandise shortages and overages
Employee discounts and special groups
Markdowns

IV Planned markups	
Markup equations	Initial markup
Markup percent	Maintained markup

V Planned gross margin and operating profit	
Gross margin	Total operating expenses
Net profit	

VI Planned expenses
Figures for the store's overall expense plan
Expenses for individual units or branches
Estimated expenses for each department

VII Planned Purchases
Equation for determining purchases
Open-to-buy formula

this form is submitted to the store's computer center at the time the original is sent to the vendor. In turn, the vendor will send an invoice or bill to the store upon shipment of the merchandise. The buyer will keep a file of all unpaid invoices in a journal or on a billing sheet. Once an invoice is paid, it will be removed to a "paid" file. The total remaining in the unpaid-invoice file represents the amount of outstanding orders as well as the amount due to creditors. Outstanding orders are usually totaled every week or ten days to obtain the number of outstanding orders (the dollar figure) which is used to calculate the merchandise-on-order figure in the OTB.

Not only must orders be filled out properly, but also merchandise should be delivered to the department before it is needed. The buying specialist should set delivery dates that are realistic and should inform resources that merchandise arriving after the agreed delivery date will be returned. Also, since shipping costs are charged against the OTB, the buyer should make it a practice to know each resource's shipping point and specify shipping instructions that will prove consistent with costs.

The OTB is often tied up with unfilled or partially filled orders. For this reason, the buyer will check the order file on a regular basis to follow up on wanted merchandise, cancel overdue orders and unwanted balances on unfilled orders, check for clerical errors, and settle any problems or disputes with resources regarding price changes, style substitutes, and size or color shortages.

Finally, the OTB should be carefully checked against the inventory on hand. If the inventory is larger than the planned OTB figure, the OTB is reduced by the difference between the actual goods on hand and the planned purchases. The buyer should check all inventory figures regarding vendor returns, check all invoices charged to the department, correct prices, take markdowns when needed, eliminate slow sellers, and build assortments based on seasonal needs.[10]

Chapter Summary

Planning is a very important function of the buying activity. However, the means used to achieve the planning objectives are based upon the business's objectives, policies, and procedures. Planning requires accurate record keeping. Specific policies will be set for the following types of records used in most retail establishments: (1) cash disbursements and receipts, (2) credit, (3) expenses, (4) sales, (5) purchases, (6) stocks and inventories, and (7) profit-and-loss statements. The student should review the discussion of each in Part 1 of this chapter.

There are several types of budgets used in a business; however, the plan used by the buyer to guide him in the merchandising activity is called the merchandise budget. This is a control measure that enables the buyer to follow a definite course of action as well as to evaluate current activities. Certain elements should be present for the merchandise plan to accomplish its objectives. The student should review the list under "The Merchandise Budget" in Part 2. A merchandise budget may be planned for a week, a month, or six months. Referring to the six-month merchandise plan illustrated, we see that seven important factors should be considered when planning: (1) sales, (2) stocks, (3) reductions, (4) markups, (5) gross margins and operating profits, (6) expenses, and (7) purchases.

Sales planning is the first step in the merchandise plan and is the key element in planning. Sales are planned first because it is easier to adjust stocks, markups, and expenses to sales potentials, rather than attempt to plan these factors and then to reach a sales goal consistent with them. The buying specialist should review several kinds of records used when planning sales. Two methods may be used in planning department or store sales: (1) the top-down plan, and (2) the bottom-up plan.

The second step in the merchandise plan is to maintain a balanced stock in relation to anticipated sales. Stock planning includes an understanding of the various methods used to plan needed stocks, the stock turn, the average inventory, increasing stock turn, and the different rates of stock turn. Four methods are used when planning needed stocks: (1) the basic stock method (BOM), (2) the percentage-variation (or deviation) method, (3) the week's supply method, and (4) the stock-sales ratio method.

Planned reductions is the third step in the merchandise plan. Retail reductions consist of three major factors: (1) merchandise shortages and overages, (2) employee and other types of discounts, and (3) markdowns. A reduction in price from the original retail price is called a markdown. The markdown percent is the difference between the original retail price and the markdown price. The buyer will plan markdowns because it is frequently necessary to reduce merchandise for various reasons.

Planned markups is the fourth step in the merchandise plan. Most retail buyers think of markup in terms of percent. The markup percent is usually calculated as a percent of the retail price because all operating costs and profits or loss are determined as a percentage of net sales. The buyer should review several kinds of records when planning the markup. Initial markup, also known as mark-on or original markup, is the difference between the cost price and the retail price of the goods. The maintained markup is the difference between the cost price and the final selling price. Consumer demand, initial markup formula, store clientele, etc., should also be considered when planning the initial markup.

The fifth step in the merchandise plan is to plan gross margin and operating profit. Gross margin is the difference between net sales and the cost of goods sold. Profit is that part of the gross margin that remains after operating expenses have been deducted. Once operating expenses have been planned for the month, net profit may be computed by deducting the total operating expenses from the gross margin.

The sixth step in the merchandise plan is to plan expenses. There are two types of operating expenses: (1) direct expenses, and (2) indirect expenses. Expense planning is a method of control that will help safeguard the store's profit objective. The student should review the procedure listed under "Planned Expenses." A major advantage of expense planning is that remedial action may be taken where and when needed.

The last step in planning the merchandise budget is to plan the dollar amount of goods that can be brought into the department or store during a specific period or season (planned purchases). The buyer can determine planned purchases by adding together planned sales, planned reductions, and planned stock and subtracting from the total needs for the month the planned stock at the beginning of the month. To control purchases effectively, a device called the open-to-buy (OTB) is used. The OTB is the amount of merchandise, either at cost price or at retail price, that the buyer is open to receive into inventory during a certain time period, based on the plans formulated. For the OTB to be effective, careful checks are made of all orders placed with vendors. The buyer will keep a file of all unpaid invoices; once an invoice is paid, it will be removed to a "paid" file. The total remaining in the unpaid-invoice file represents the amount of outstanding orders as well as the amount due to creditors. Outstanding orders are usually totaled every week or ten days to obtain the dollar figure used to calculate the merchandise-on-order figures in the OTB.

Trade Terminology

DIRECTIONS: Briefly explain or discuss each of the following trade terms:

1. Business objectives
2. Business policies
3. Procedures
4. Cash disbursements
5. Cash receipts
6. Direct expenses
7. Indirect expenses
8. Purchase journal or billing record
9. Profit-and-loss statement
10. Net sales
11. Cost of goods sold
12. Gross margin
13. Operating expenses
14. Net profit
15. Operations budget
16. Cash budget
17. Capital budget

18. Merchandise budget
19. Top-down planning
20. Bottom-up planning
21. Retail reduction
22. Merchandise shortage
23. Merchandise overage
24. Employee discount
25. Markdown

26. Markdown percent
27. Markup
28. Markup percent
29. Initial markup or mark-on
30. Maintained markup
31. Operating profit
32. Open-to-buy

Questions for Discussion and Review

1. It has been stated that the tempo of retailing has accelerated. Do you agree with this statement? Cite specific examples of forces that have affected the planning activity of merchandisers.

2. Explain the differences among objectives, policies, and procedures. How would each be applied to: a small independent pet-supply store; a women's specialty chain operation; a general store?

3. What are the functions of the following types of records used by most retail stores: cash disbursements and receipts, credit, expenses, profit-and-loss statement?

4. Summarize the seven steps you would follow when preparing the merchandise budget. Explain why "sales planning" is considered the first step in budget planning.

5. As the new buyer for an electrical-appliance department, how would you proceed to estimate your stock needs for the next six months?

6. Assume that you have recommended the use of the merchandise budget to a buyer in a small retail store who has not used this method previously. What words of caution would you give this buyer? What results might he or she expect from using the merchandise budget?

7. What is the difference between initial and maintained markup?

8. Write the formula for each of the following: finding the retail price; finding the stock turn at cost price; finding the average inventory.

9. Would it be wise for the buyer to adopt a policy of taking approximately the same markup percent on all kinds of merchandise? What would be the pros and cons of such a practice?

10. How does the open-to-buy operate as a control feature of the merchandise budget?

11. Why is it common to recalculate the planned purchases and the open-to-buy every week to ten days?

Case Study Number One

Problems with Inventory

As assistant buyer in the children's shoe department, you have been concerned with the problem of too much inventory remaining in stock at the end of the selling season. This situation has resulted in an imbalance in stock assortment, several markdown periods, and an increase in merchandise costs. You have also noticed that, due to faulty vendor deliveries and the lack of adequate follow-up, merchandise has not been received into the department when requested. The buyer has had difficulty in determining how much open-to-buy is available and is unable to meet the steady flow of consumer demand. Your buyer has invited you to attend a meeting with the merchandise manager to discuss the problems with inventory. Develop a list of suggestions you would recommend to help solve the problems. Be prepared to discuss your recommendations in class.

Case Study Number Two

Stock Turn in a Small Business

As an independent businessman, Jerry Grover felt very strongly about maintaining a competitive yet well-balanced stock assortment. In the first three years of operating his small sporting-goods business, he went through many periods of trial and error while attempting to merchandise the store. He quickly learned the importance of careful and accurate inventory planning and control and was especially concerned with stock turnover. Jerry's business was primarily a discount type of operation; therefore, rapid turnover and low markup were his basic business objectives. He had limited capital and was always concerned with increasing sales volume on the same or smaller stock investment. Often he had to take a short-term loan for additional inventories, particularly during the Christmas season.

Jerry's assistant Bob Meyer was attending college on a part-time basis as a retail-marketing major. Jerry felt that Bob might be of some assistance in the area of good inventory control. One day he expressed to Bob his problems in determining stock turn. He stated that he could not accurately estimate how much merchandise was disposed of or depleted and replaced during certain selling periods. He further stated that in the past he had had to take short-term loans to have enough money to invest in inventory. He felt this was a definite disadvantage, since the cost of the loan was cutting into his profits and, as a discounter, he was working on a low markup to begin with. He asked Bob to make some suggestions regarding the situation.

Bob told Jerry that a retail store may use three methods to compute stock turn. It can determine stock turn on a retail basis, where net sales at retail is divided by the average stock at retail; it can determine stock on a cost basis, where the cost of the goods sold is divided by average cost of stock; or it can determine stock on a physical unit basis, where the number of units sold is divided by the average number of units in stock.

There were other problems in determining the stock turn. Jerry had a problem in determining his average inventory. Bob informed him he could take his actual stock at the beginning of the year and the end of the year, add them, and divide by two. However, as in most stores, 60 percent of the sales occurred during the Christmas season; therefore, the average inventory carried through-out the year would not be accurate and the stock turnover figure too high. Bob suggested that Jerry calculate the inventory at the beginning of the year, during the middle, and at the end. He could sum the three inventories and divide by 3 to determine the average inventory. Or a more accurate method of determining average inventory might be to divide the sum of the stocks on the first of every month, plus the ending stock, by 13 (since he would start out with one month's inventory).

Before Jerry begins to determine the best method of stock turn, what kind of information should be available? When determining average inventory, what method of calculation would you suggest? Do you agree that there are advantages to rapid stock turnover?

Retailing Activities to Stimulate Student Interest and Participation

1. Contact a general-merchandise chain store and interview the store manager on the problems of inventory replenishment. What methods does the store use to communicate control information to its employees? Be prepared to discuss your findings in class.

2. Referring to the reference material listed in "The Retail Student's Reference Library," prepare a paper on the topic "High overhead and its effect on retail profits."

3. Visit three small businesses that deal in different types of merchandise lines, for example, a hardware store, a greeting-card shop, and a jewelry business. Discuss with the owner-manager methods used to determine stockturn for particular selling seasons.

REFERENCES

The Retail Student's Reference Library

Annual Survey of Operating Expenses for Men's Wear Stores. Washington, D.C.: The National Association of Retail Clothiers and Furnishers, n.d.

Baron, H., and Steinfeld, Solomon. *Clerical Record Keeping.* Cincinnati: South-Western Publishing Company, 1971.

Bacon, Jeremy. *Managing the Budget Function.* New York: National Industrial Conference Board, 1970.

Belden, Donald A. *The Role of the Buyer in Mass Merchandising.* New York: Chain Store Publishing Corporation, 1971.

The Buyer's Manual. New York: National Retail Merchants Association, 1970.

Established Cash Discounts to Retailers. New York: National Retail Merchants Association, n.d.

Expenses in Retail Businesses. Dayton: National Cash Register Company, n.d.

Fisher, William. "Expense Planning and Control Other than Payroll." *Retail Control,* January 1970, pp. 35–39.

Internal Control and Documentation of EDP. New York: National Retail Merchants Association, n.d.

Judelle, Beatrice. *The Fashion Buyer's Job.* New York: National Retail Merchants Association, 1971.

Kieta, Ed. "Records for Profitable Retailing." *Hardware Retailer,* June 1970.

Krieger, Murray. *Creative Markdown Practices for Profit.* New York: Fairchild Publications, Inc., 1971.

———. *Merchandising Math for Profit: An Executive Handbook.* New York: Fairchild Publications, Inc., 1972.

Let the Expert Tell You About Electronic Data Processing. New York: National Retail Merchants Association, n.d.

Lewis, Diffy R. *How to Keep Merchandise Records.* New York: Fairchild Publications, Inc., n.d.

198 Ways to Control Markdowns. New York: The National Retail Merchants Association, n.d.

Operating Results of Furniture Stores. Chicago: National Retail Furniture Association, n.d.

Profitable Merchandising Techniques. New York: Fairchild Publications, Inc., 1970.

Retail Control. New York: National Retail Merchants Association, n.d.

The Retail Inventory Method in Practical Operation. New York: National Retail Merchants Association, n.d.

Retail Inventory Method Made Practical. New York: National Retail Merchants Association, 1971.

Siber, Alan. *Complete Guide to Retail Management.* Baltimore: Penguin Books, Inc., 1972.

Status of EDP in Retailing. New York: National Retail Merchants Association, 1970.

Will, R. Ted. "Causation of Gross Margin Percentage Difference between Intra-Firm Discount Stores." *Journal of Retailing,* Spring 1970.

Your Business Records. Englewood Cliffs, N.J.: Prentice-Hall, Inc., 1971.

References

1. Jerry B. Poe, *An Introduction to the American Business Enterprise* (Homewood, Ill.: Richard D. Irwin, Inc., 1972), pp. 127–128.
2. Ibid., pp. 128–132.
3. *Management by Objectives* (New York: National Retail Merchants Association, 1967), pp. 4–5.
4. I. Wingate and J. D. Weiner, *Retail Merchandising* (Cincinnati: South-Western Publishing Co., 1963), pp. 448–449.

5. D. J. Duncan and C. F. Phillips, *Retailing Principles and Methods* (Homewood, Ill.: Richard D. Irwin, Inc., 1969), pp. 661–662.

6. Poe, *American Business Enterprise,* p. 164.

7. *The Buyers Manual* (New York: National Retail Merchants Association, 1965), p. 248.

8. Ibid., p. 250.

9. Beatrice Judelle, *The Fashion Buyer's Job* (New York: National Retail Merchants Association, 1971), p. 74.

10. Ibid., p. 74–77.

Planning the Merchandise Assortment

9

Performance Objectives

Chapter Summary
Trade Terminology
Questions for Discussion and Review
Case Study Number One; Number Two
Retailing Activities to Stimulate Student Interest and Participation
Retail Student's Reference Library
References

As a result of reading this chapter, the student should be able to accomplish the following:

1. Become aware of six factors a buyer must consider when planning the merchandise assortment.

2. Relate five sources the buyer can use to obtain information about customers.

3. Describe a want slip.

4. Discuss internal as well as external sources of information that will help the buyer in planning.

5. Define fashion goods, staple goods, seasonal goods, convenience goods, shopping goods, specialty goods.

6. Plan a model stock that includes a staple assortment, a fashion assortment, and a seasonal assortment.

7. Calculate the formulas used in determining periodic fill-ins for staple goods; for fashion stocks; for home furnishings.

8. Become aware of the advantages and disadvantages of private branding.

9. Cite information necessary to plan staple stocks.

10. Refer to five predictable characteristics of a fashion assortment when planning the model stock.

11. Plan a seasonal assortment for soft goods based on fashion apparel seasons.

Planning the Merchandise Assortment

Merchandise Characteristics

As you have already learned, the buying specialist, regardless of the type and size of the employing store, must know customer preferences, must be aware that different types of stores have different target markets, and must decide which category of merchandise to offer, as well as being aware of lines that may prove unsuccessful. The buying specialist must exercise careful control measures when selecting the merchandise assortment and at the same time attempt to meet the ever-changing demands of customers. All store buyers will find that careful assortment planning will provide (1) a balanced stock in terms of units and retail dollars; (2) the kinds of merchandise lines typically carried in their departments or stores; (3) information regarding the kind of space available for inventory in the warehouse, branch store, or store unit; and (4) merchandise that will meet the sales and profit potential planned for in the six-month merchandise budget. Part 1 of this chapter discusses (1) characteristics important to the merchandise assortment, (2) factors that must be considered during the planning process, and (3) problems encountered by different types of store buyers. Part 2 discusses development of assortment plans and covers (1) the development of basic stock lists, (2) the model stock plan, and (3) formulas used to determine periodic fill-ins of staple goods and fashion stocks.

PART 1

Assortment Planning

The merchandise assortment must be planned and controlled by the store buyer in conjunction with top store executives. A term that best describes this function of buying is *merchandising*. A broad definition, approved by the American Marketing Association (AMA), describes *merchandising* as the planning and supervision involved in marketing the particular merchandise or service at the places, times, and prices, and in the quantities that will best serve to realize the marketing objectives of the business.[1]

By the terms of this definition, a well-planned assortment must contain merchandise (1) of the right type, or those goods and services that customers will readily purchase because they meet their sociopsychological needs; (2) of the right quality, or those goods and services that meet the expectations of the

What a Well-Planned Assortment Should Contain

consumer; (3) of the right price, which will reflect the image of the store and the consumer; (4) in the right quantities, which are adequate to satisfy the demands of the consumer; (5) at the right time, so that the goods may be purchased when the consumer wants them; and (6) at the right place, which from the consumer's point of view is most convenient.[2]

What should a well-planned assortment contain?	
Merchandise of the:	
Right type	Right quality
Right price	Right quantity
Right time	Right place

These six characteristics of a well-planned merchandise assortment lead to sales opportunities by providing for a balanced inventory, which will help the buyer to maintain a markup that adequately covers costs and expenses. A well-planned assortment, therefore, is advantageous to both the customer and the merchant.

In assortment planning, the merchandise manager and the buyer together must determine where to place the greatest emphasis. Should they emphasize merchandise classifications, subclasses, price range, specific price lines, style variations, number of styles, number of sizes, number of colors, or what? Decisions must also be made about what to deemphasize or drop from the assortment. Just as no one retail store can carry all products available in the market, so no one store can offer all available merchandise categories. Therefore, decisions about which merchandise assortments to carry are not left to chance but are based on a number of important factors: (1) the type of retail institution, (2) past sales records, (3) a determination of consumer wants, (4) a study of internal and external sources of retail information, (5) the types of goods offered for sale and (6) the elimination of merchandise lines.[3]

The Type of Retail Institution

Needless to say, a discount house usually will not offer high-priced, one-of-a-kind types of merchandise, a variety chain will not stock Oriental rugs, and a department store usually will not carry landscaping and gardening supplies. Customers usually expect to find merchandise consistent with a store's image, merchandise that meets their individual needs and interests and reflects the store's reputation in the business community. Since no single store can be all things to all people, the buyer must work within certain limitations set up by top store management. Such limitations as (1) the availability of capital resources, (2) the particular trading area served by the store, (3) the nature of the goods carried, and (4) the amount and kind of competition represented in the trading area may affect the buyer in attempting to plan the merchandise assortment.

Capital Resources Available. A retail store must have sound financing, since it often takes time to gain consumer acceptance for new lines of merchandise. Ample capital resources permit the heavy promotion campaigns necessary to hasten product recognition and, eventually, acceptance. Sound financing will absorb the costs of increased inventories and markdowns that may occur during the introduction period. Retailers with limited capital may adopt a merchandise plan that leads to fast turnover of stocks, offers limited service, and offers a narrow merchandise assortment, such as the kind usually found in a discount house.

Particular Trading Area. No store can cater to all people in all areas; differences in consumer tastes, occupations, incomes, and life-styles make this impossible. Wise management will realize that the general character of a particular trading area may be self-limiting. For example, the trading area may be either very rich or very poor; consequently, the merchandise assortment offered may be either lower-priced staple goods or high-priced fashion goods. Most stores, however, attempt to cater to that considerable portion of middle-class consumers who are price-conscious yet who are willing to make discretionary expenditures. Many stores located in urban environments cater not only to middle-class consumers but also to those of lesser economic means, perhaps even to those who are dependent upon public assistance. Urban stores often expand into suburban shopping centers in attempts to draw more affluent, fashion-conscious shoppers.

Nature of the Goods Carried. A merchandise plan that calls for a fashion assortment is certainly more important to a women's specialty store than it is to a variety store. A wide selection of staple merchandise is more important to a department store than it is to a discount house. The nature of the merchandise assortment offered, whether it be fashion goods or staple goods, will clearly depend upon the character of the retail institution and the type of consumer it caters to.

Competition Represented in Trading Area. Every type of retail store has some kind of competition. Not only is there competition among similar stores, but also among different types of stores. For example, department stores soon realized that they had to offer special promotion sales to offset the sales of discount houses. As mentioned in chapter 1, a great deal of merchandise scrambling has occurred among department stores, discount houses, variety stores, and specialty shops. If a store is going to continue to attract customers and build its trade, its merchandise plan must include the successful offerings provided by its competition.

Explain how the following limitations will affect the buyer's merchandise plan.

1. Capital resources available
2. Particular trading area
3. Nature of the goods carried
4. Competition represented in the trading area

Past Sales Records

The second factor the buyer must consider when planning the merchandise assortment is records of past sales. Sales records provide valuable information about sales made and lost, about returned goods, and about customer complaints. There are numerous records available that can supply the sales information, such as unit control records, special promotion records, want slips, charge accounts, and files from the adjustment office. Personal observations on the selling floor, as well as conversations with salespeople, will also prove helpful.

Because sales of different product lines fluctuate from year to year and from season to season, the wise buyer will examine records of the previous year or, perhaps, of the past two or three years and use the information as a basis for planning sales in any given season. The buyer's sales records should contain notes that refer to weather conditions, economic trends, labor strikes, supply conditions, market opportunities, and whatever else affected sales activity in a particular period.

For past sales records to be useful, however, they must contain a detailed breakdown of specific information. For example, a department-store buyer of men's shirts will keep detailed records of those sizes, styles, colors, and patterns that are meeting consumer acceptance, in the main store and in each branch. The central buyer will keep similar records for each store unit in the operation. The small shop owner will also keep sales records of the sizes, styles, price lines, and colors of goods that are accepted or rejected by customers. The buyer of bedroom furniture, for example, will have more repeat sales, since bedroom furniture styles change less frequently. It is easier to plan the merchandise assortment when repeat sales are likely. On the other hand, the fashion buyer is less likely to have repeat sales, since fashions change from one season to the next and from year to year. Fashion buyers have to analyze past sales records carefully. For example, the buyer of women's coats and suits may derive some indication of demand for the next selling period by examining sales records according to price lines, sizes, and the type of style that has sold best, such as the "professional look," "sporty look," or "youthful look."

The buying specialist will be helped not only by analyzing his or her own sales records and those of the store, but also by examining various reports available through market sources. Market surveys can provide the buyer with information regarding actual sales of particular merchandise lines in the store's trading area as well as in various parts of the country. Retail trade papers will conduct their own surveys and provide information about "hot items" or "best sellers." They may also rank each product by sales and show the number of different items needed to meet the consumer demand for a particular merchandise category. A limitation to sales surveys, however, is that they must be carried out in a merchandise category that is staple enough to make the findings useful. For example, soaps and detergents could be measured just as effectively as bicycles, whereas the short fashion life of women's costume jewelry and millinery would not lend itself to a realizable sales survey. The buyer will learn to weigh and judge the results of surveys as they are provided. He will talk to vendors and suppliers, note the activity of his competition, and compare the results prepared by professional market analysts. Needless to say, when the buyer has reliable, accurate information available to him, his job in assortment planning is greatly simplified.[4]

Determination of Consumer Wants

A third factor a buyer must consider when planning the merchandise assortment is the consumer. With the growth of the middle-income group, we have developed into a more affluent society. Thus, there has been a demand for a greater assortment of goods, which has led to quicker product replacement and an increase in impulse buying. Today, the consumer can afford new and attractive variations of a particular item or product. The modern shopper does not wait until a set of dinnerware is cracked and chipped before purchasing a new set, but will purchase a new set of dinnerware to improve the appearance of the dinner table as well as taking advantage of new designs and patterns. As a result of having more money to spend and an increase in consumer education, the modern shopper is more critical in merchandise selection. Shoppers read labels carefully, check the warranty or guarantee, and compare before buying.

Most consumers, however, given the financial means, will yield to impulse buying when purchasing fashion apparel and accessories. The buyer must provide just the right selection of merchandise, at the right time, in the right quality, at the right price, in the right quantity, and in a convenient location to sell these items.

The buyer is the purchasing agent for store customers. The goods purchased for resale will reflect the buyer's judgment and ability to forecast what customers will like. Information regarding those people who patronize the store or department is needed. The buyer will: (1) analyze past purchase records, (2) offer new items, (3) refer to want slips, (4) conduct customer surveys, and (5) personally observe customers.

How can a buyer get information about customers?
1. Analysis of past purchases 2. Offerings of new items 3. Want slips 4. Customer surveys 5. Personal observations

Analysis of Past Purchases. What customers have purchased in the past will tell a great deal about customer wants for the future. Past sales records, if notated properly, should provide information about colors, sizes, prices, quantities, and the kinds of merchandise that were popular or unpopular. Past records are often an indication of recurring consumer demand. For example, the buyer may get a clear picture of best-selling and slow-selling items for a particular season by referring to the "Best Sellers Report" or the "Exception Report" (see Chapter 7, "Analyzing Inventory Reports"), which will usually list sales for the previous season and year. If merchandise was returned, it is important to know why. Usually, when an item is returned, the salesgirl or department supervisor will ask the customer what was wrong. Was the merchandise the wrong color? Too small? Too expensive? Of inferior quality? A wise buyer will take all of this information into account when reordering or planning assortments for the next selling season.

Offer New Items. A smart buyer will not be content continuously to offer those items that have proved to be popular for a particular season. He or she must spend a great deal of time planning a merchandise assortment that offers new products and new promotional items. The buying specialist must be continuously alert to economic conditions and environmental changes. Stores cannot progress by providing only those goods that have been sold in the past. A buyer, as well as store management, must keep pace with changes in the environment.

New items are often thought of as the lifeblood of the retail store. The more innovative and imaginative a store's assortment can be, usually the more successful that store is. However, the introduction of new items must be a continuing process, thus part of the store's overall merchandising policy.[5]

What is a new item? Is it a style of blouse that was popular during the spring season in cotton denim and returns for the summer season in an Indian cotton fabric? Is it the leisure suit of the fall season which returns the following spring in a "newer" color and texture? Or are the two items mentioned here simply replacements for those previously carried? In other words, items that have been restyled are not necessarily new items, particularly as we discuss them here. A *new item* may be defined as one that introduces certain new and different characteristics that are not yet available in merchandise of a similar type.[6] New items are usually substitutes, adaptations, or redesigns of articles already in use. For example, consider the changes that have occurred in bicycles: from the single-speed balloon tire, to the five-speed narrow tire and thence to the bicycle of today, the ten-speed narrow-tire racing bike. An item may be considered new as a result of the material of which it is made, the design or the construction, or the uniqueness of the color, design, and texture used.

Since the market for new items is wide and varied, the buyer must skillfully evaluate and select new items he is about to add to his assortment. Needless to say, not every new item is going to be a success in every department, in all branches, in all store units, in all parts of the country. Before adding a new item the buyer must consider the type of clientele served, store policy, and the amount of competition in the immediate trade area. The buyer must also consider whether the new item will become an established fashion or simply a passing fad. These and other questions will be considered in detail in the next chapter, where we will learn how this information is applied to the selection of the assortment.

Refer to Want Slips. As you recall, a want slip is a form filled out by salespeople regarding items not sold by the store but requested by customers (see Figure 9.1).

Date ___ July 1, 1977 ___   Department No. ___ 320 ___

Employee No. ___ 62 ___   Department Name ___ Shoes ___

DIRECTIONS: Keep this slip in your salesbook. Whether an item is called for that is not in stock, whether carried regularly or not, record that fact at once on this form. Be sure and record every request.

ITEM REQUESTED	STYLE	COLOR	SIZE	PRICE	MODEL	SUBSTITUTE	PRICE	OTHER
Sandal	flat heel	blue	8½	4.99	—	Sandal	3.95	—
Slippers	reg.	black	7	8.95	—	—	—	—
Oxford	low heel	red	5	10.95	63T	Oxford	10.95	grey

Figure 9.1. A want slip for a typical store department.

Salespeople may forget details of the merchandise requested; therefore, the want slip will help the recording process and facilitate communications between customer and store. You will note that the list of items requested in Figure 9.1 includes descriptions, such as style, color, size, price, or model. Each column will be filled out, depending, of course, on the nature of the item requested. If the salesperson succeeds in selling an article other than the one requested, the substitution is also reported on the want slip. By studying want slips every day, a buyer may determine whether or not there is a definite demand for a particular item, as well as the most popular prices, styles, sizes, and colors. By studying the report of substitutes sold, the buyer can readily determine goods that will sell in place of the commodity requested. This may also indicate to the buyer that good salesmanship will sell products already offered for sale and eliminate the need to purchase articles that are not strongly sought after by the customer. Some want slips include the customer's name, address, and phone number so that the buyer may inform him or her when the merchandise becomes available.

Customer Surveys. Many buyers have found that records of past purchases and information contained on want slips are not enough to forecast what the customer will purchase the following season. The store research division will attempt to conduct surveys for particular departments to help them determine consumer buying habits. A saleslady may ask questions about popular shoe brands, styles, and prices, or the customer may be asked to fill out a questionnaire as he or she enters the store. The questionnaire may contain information regarding favorite colors, brand preference, price, store atmosphere, service policy, and treatment by sales personnel. This information may be used by the department to help the buyer plan the merchandise assortment.

Personal Observations. An observant buyer will soon realize that people often reveal what they are thinking. The buyer must learn to interpret and read these signs provided by the customer. By listening to and watching the consumer throughout the decision-making process, the buyer may learn about life-styles, interests, and hobbies. He or she will soon be able to discriminate the more conservative shopper from the liberal shopper; the housewife from the career woman; the professional man from the laborer. How can a buyer get information about consumer wants? Consumers tell the buyer what they want.

Internal and External Sources of Information

A fourth factor the buyer must consider when planning the merchandise assortment is internal as well as external sources of information, such as: (1) salespeople, (2) vendors and manufacturers, (3) trade sources, (4) comparison shopping bureaus, and (5) consumer publications.

> There are other sources of information which help the buyer in planning
>
> 1. Salespeople
> 2. Vendors and manufacturers
> 3. Trade sources
> 4. Comparison shopping bureaus
> 5. Consumer publications

Salespeople. Because salespeople are in daily contact with customers, they are continuously receiving information about consumer wants that are not reflected in sales. *Salespeople, therefore, become an important source of buying information.* They are typical customers themselves, and their reactions to new items may be an indication of sales potential. They often know their customers and can accurately judge sales possibilities correctly. However, the buyer must be careful in weighing the judgment of the salespeople, since they may lack the ability to distinguish clearly between their personal likes and dislikes and those of the store's customers.

Vendors and Manufacturers. Retail buyers soon realize that market offerings and consumer wants must be similar. Unless a product is available in the marketplace, the buyer cannot offer it for sale. Information about the success of certain articles sold to stores in other cities can be a guide to the store buyer. Vendors and manufacturers are in close contact with designers and new merchandise developments, and are aware of sales results in stores in similar trade areas. They function as an important reporting service. Also, they frequently issue catalogs and price lists, which contain information of value to the buyer. Many small stores do most of their buying from catalogs.

Trade Sources. As mentioned previously, trade papers provide a great deal of information to the retail buyer. A *trade paper* or *journal* may be defined as a publication containing information that is of importance and interest to people dealing within a specific trade or line. For example, *Women's Wear Daily,* published by Fairchild Publications, Inc., contains valuable information for those interested in women's apparel and fashion accessories. *Home Furnishings Daily,* another Fairchild publication, provides information to those in the home furnishings and decorating field, and *Hardware Merchandising,* a MacLean-Hunter publication, provides information for the hardware trade. Chapter 6 contains a list of available trade papers and their respective trades.

Trade papers inform the buyer on what is new in the market, what is selling fast, what items will yield the most profit, and in what sections of the country an item is selling best.

Comparison Shopping Bureau. Another source of information that will help the buyer in planning is the amount and the type of competition faced by the store. Retail stores usually want to learn about their competition's stock conditions, price lines, special promotion merchandise, and so forth. Most retail stores provide a comparison shopping bureau (usually located in the sales and advertising division) to assist store buyers in merchandise planning. A *comparison shopping bureau* may be defined as a special bureau whose objective is to shop competing stores and determine if the competition is selling the same merchandise at the same price and quality or merchandise of an inferior quality at a lower price. Comparison shoppers may tell the buyer what type of merchandise is selling well, the location of the merchandise in the competing store, and the selling techniques used by the salespeople, as well as the kind of advertising and display employed. For example, a comparison shopper in a department store will learn of a special promotion to be held by a competitor located nearby. The shopper will go to the store, visit the department, purchase several items, and return to the office. There he or she will determine if the price and the quality are similar to the merchandise offered by a similar department in the shopper's own store. In this way, the buyer will have firsthand information regarding the activities of the competition. In turn, he or she must then decide whether to mark down the merchandise, display it in a more appealing manner, transfer it to another store, return it to the vendor, or let it remain the way it is. Or the buyer or assistant buyer may visit competing stores and check out the merchandising activity of departments that are similar. Finally, the small-shop owner will occasionally visit department stores, chain stores, and other small businesses to see the kind of merchandise offered for sale. However, due to limited finances, the owner-manager usually will not purchase the items in question.

Consumer Publications. The buyer of fashion goods in particular may find help in planning the merchandise assortment by referring to consumer publications such as fashion magazines, financial reports, or business magazines, as well as the daily and Sunday newspapers. Some of these publications may report on fashion trends through their fashion columns, while others may have a special section that covers the retail trade. Since there are so many consumer publications available, a good retail buyer must determine the best source of information that will enable him or her to make accurate decisions.

The Type of Goods Offered
A fifth factor the buyer must consider when planning the merchandise assortment is the type of goods offered for sale to the retail consumer. As stated previously, the type of goods offered will depend upon the merchandise policies of the store. A discount house will offer fashion goods; however, they will differ

from those offered by a specialty store or a boutique in that they will cost less and have less high-fashion appeal. Department stores and general merchandise chains will offer a broad assortment of goods in most price lines, while the small shop will be more discriminating.

From the point of view of the buyer, merchandise can be categorized as: (1) fashion goods, (2) staple goods, and (3) seasonal goods. The buyer may also classify merchandise according to the manner in which consumers purchase goods such as convenience goods, shopping goods, and specialty goods. The way merchandise is classified will be introduced in Part 1 of this chapter; however, the way each classification is used in assortment planning will be discussed in Part 2.

How merchandise may be classified	
By the buyer	By the consumer
1. Fashion goods	1. Convenience goods
2. Staple goods	2. Shopping goods
3. Seasonal goods	3. Specialty goods

Fashion Goods. Fashion goods may be defined as new merchandise that appeals to consumers for a short period of time and has a relatively short life cycle. When the buyers of fashion apparel or accessories plan the fashion merchandise assortment, they must be aware of current fashion trends and the consumer's willingness to invest in new items, and determine a markup that will cover risks, yet still be within the reach of the consumer's pocketbook. Since fashion merchandise must be moved out quickly, the fashion buyer must have a good inventory control system and be constantly aware of changes in the fashion markets. The fashion buyer will usually communicate frequently with the store's fashion office and with trade sources such as the resident buying office to keep abreast of both fast-selling and slow-selling items. However, as you recall, a buyer may deal in high-fashion merchandise (a specialty shop), mass fashions (a discount chain), current fashions and fads (a boutique), and proven types of fashion (a general merchandise operation).

We said earlier that "fashion is everywhere," and this is undoubtedly true. However, the degree of fashion influence will depend upon the merchandise and the target market to be served. Fashion may be seen in kitchen appliances, furniture, stereo equipment, and food items; however, buyers who purchase these lines of goods will not be influenced by seasonal changes as much as the buyer of soft goods. As you will read later in this chapter, fashion apparel and accessories will change with each new season, that is, every three to four

Figure 9.2. When the buyers
of fashion apparel plan the
fashion merchandise
assortment, they must be
aware of current fashion trends
and the consumer's willingness
to invest in new items.

months, while the buyer of hard goods will have two market seasons, that is,
one every six months.

Staple Goods. *Staple goods* may be defined as goods that should always
be in stock, since they are demanded by consumers year in and year out.
Never-out goods is a term used synonymously by the buyer for such goods.
Unlike the fashion buyer, however, buyers for staple merchandise lines, such
as housewares, domestics, small electrical appliances, notions, luggage, pictures and frames, and lamps and table accessories can estimate demand by
checking on sales for the previous year and by keeping abreast of current
trends and conditions in the marketplace. The life cycle of staple goods will
vary from one merchandise classification to the next; however, it is usually
from one to two years. As you recall from reading about the warehouse-and-
requisition plan in chapter 3, staple merchandise may be ordered well in
advance and stored in a warehouse until needed. For example, a variety store
will sell primarily staple types of merchandise such as stationery supplies,
paints, kitchen utensils, toys, sewing notions, china and glassware, paper prod-

Figure 9.3. Goods that are always in stock, or *never-out* goods, are demanded by consumers year in and year out. (Courtesy of Duckwall Stores, Inc., Abilene, Kansas.)

ucts, and so on, because merchandise of this type is in constant demand, is practical and functional, meets an immediate need, and is considered a necessity by the customer. Thus, the goods may be placed in a warehouse without endangering the product life cycle. You will find staple goods in many types of retail stores, such as the discount house, the department store, the general merchandise chain, the variety store, and even the small business. Staple goods are a very important part of a merchant's assortment; therefore, the buyer must plan for items that will appeal to old customers as well as attracting new ones.

Seasonal Goods. Seasonal goods may be defined as merchandise that is in demand only at certain times of the year or for particular seasons of the year. Seasonal goods may include both staple goods and fashion goods. For example, Christmas-tree trimmings and Christmas cards may be considered staples, since they are not fashion-oriented and may be stored until the following year. However, fashion apparel provided for the Christmas shopper must be sold or marked down soon after the New Year, since this merchandise will be out of style the following year. Nearly all departments in all types of retail stores are affected by the Christmas season, so buyers of soft goods, hard goods, and food items must be aware of merchandise that will appeal to Christmas shoppers.

Buyers will also plan assortments for other seasons such as fall, back to school, spring, summer, transitional, and resort. Assortments may be planned for special promotional events such as Mother's Day, Father's Day, Columbus Day, Washington's Birthday, Valentine's Day, and so forth.

A firm's seasons will depend upon the merchandising policies of the store. For example, most department stores will have some type of "founder's day sale" or "anniversary sale." A discount operation may have a "special bargain days sale" or "big values sale." The small shop owner may have a "Mother's Day specials sale" or a "back-to-school event," and a variety store may feature "Halloween specials." Regardless of the season, however, the buyer must plan the assortment carefully to include special events and seasonal merchandise lines that will enable him to have a full share of the market.

Convenience Goods. Convenience goods may be defined as those goods consumers expect to have readily available at a convenient location. These goods are usually inexpensive and may include such products as candy, notions, small housewares, drug items, hardware items, beauty and medical aids, and so forth. Depending on the merchandise line carried, a buyer will usually plan for such items. These goods are goods that are either needed immediately by the consumer or are purchased on impulse because they are so appealing.

Figure 9.5. Have you ever noticed the kind of merchandise found alongside the checkout counter of a self-service store? (Courtesy of Duckwall Stores, Inc., Abilene, Kansas.)

Have you ever noticed the kind of merchandise found alongside the checkout counter of a food market or a variety store? There you will find chewing gum, assorted types of candy, razor blades, film, deodorant, magazines, pocket lighters, and, for a special season such as the Fourth of July, picnic supplies, colored crepe paper, sparklers, and other decorations. Often as you are standing in line, you will pick up a number of items, primarily because you are bored with having to stand and such items occupy your time while you are waiting to be served. Usually, convenience items are attractively displayed and placed on racks or stands that are easily accessible.

Shopping Goods. Shopping goods may be defined as those products for which a consumer will accept no substitute and about which the consumer does not have a thorough knowledge. This includes merchandise for which there is no replacement or no alternative in the mind of the customer. Since

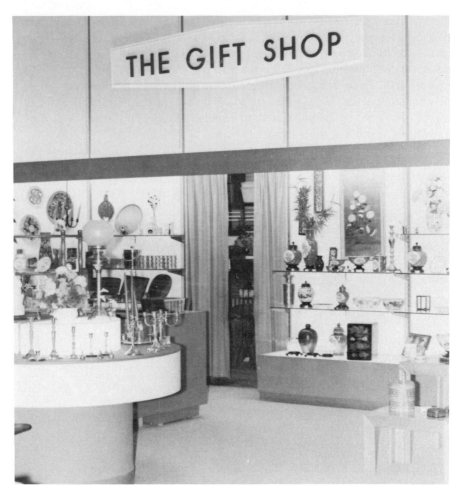

the consumers usually do not have a thorough knowledge of the item, they will
go from store to store and compare the different prices, colors, product features, styles, guarantees, and warranties, as well as other characteristics. Usually, the consumer will decide on a brand of merchandise to purchase; thus,
the retail buyer will make an effort to provide the customer with specific
information and advice on the product sought, as well as offering deals, customer service, prompt delivery, and credit terms. Examples of shopping goods
are television sets, stereo equipment, radios, cameras, automobiles, small appliances, gift items, and furs.

Specialty Goods. Specialty goods may be defined as those products of
which the consumer will usually accept only a well-known brand and of which

the consumer has full knowledge. For example, a buyer of fine china is providing specialty merchandise. The consumer may wish to increase a set of chinaware and will return to the store for the particular pattern or design. Buyers of specialty goods will plan to have as wide an assortment as possible, since consumers will surely be satisfied once they locate the specific item. Examples of specialty goods are brand-name items, silverware, furniture, pianos, watches, kitchen appliances, household appliances, and cosmetics.

Table 9.1 presents an overview of how merchandise may be categorized.

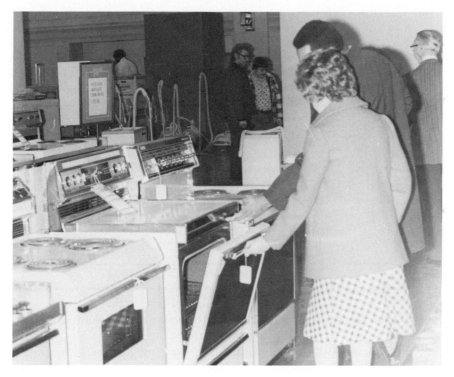

Figure 9.7. A buyer of specialty goods will plan to have as wide an assortment as possible, realizing that customers will be satisfied once they locate the specific item.

Eliminating Merchandise Items

The final factor the buyer must consider when planning the assortment is the elimination or dropping of certain items from the merchandise plan. As more items are added to the assortment, a limit to what can be carried by the store or department, considering the financial investment involved and the amount of space required to store the goods, becomes evident. Therefore, the buying specialist must include in the assortment plan the elimination of certain items. The buyer must also consider whether or not the items to be dropped are fashion goods, since, due to their short selling life, such goods must be eliminated before they become out of style. If the goods to be dropped are staple

Table 9.1.   *An Overview of How Merchandise May be Categorized.*

FASHION GOODS	STAPLE GOODS	SEASONAL GOODS
New merchandise that appeals to consumers for a short period of time and has a relatively short life cycle.	Goods which are always in stock—never-out goods.	Merchandise in demand at certain times of the year.
EXAMPLES ARE:	EXAMPLES ARE:	EXAMPLES ARE:
Women's wear	Housewares	Easter candy
Women's fashion accessories	Domestics	Christmas decorations
Men's wear	Small electrical appliances	Halloween costumes
Men's fashion accessories	Notions	Washington's Birthday
Children's wear	Luggage	Valentine's Day
Boys' wear	Pictures	Mother's Day
Girls' wear	Frames	Father's Day
	Mirrors	Fall
	Lamps	Back-to-school
	Table accessories	Spring
	Stationery	Summer
		Cruise and resort
		Transitional

BY THE BUYER

types of merchandise, they must be eliminated before they become obsolete or outdated.

Mistakes in assortment planning are made by many retailers, but are more common in the small business, since the entrepreneur does not have the facilities (electronic data processing), the team of management experts or the market specialists (for example, the resident buying office) to assist in assortment planning. However, retailers large and small have a tendency to stock too many similar brands or types of merchandise. Often one item is simply a substitute for another; therefore, it is not necessary to stock both. How, then, does the buying specialist or manager determine which items should be eliminated from stock?

1. The buyer will give close attention to stock turnover and the rate of sales for each item found in the assortment. Large retailers are provided with sales and exception reports on a daily basis, for branch stores as well as for each store in the unit. Sales reports will inform the buying specialist what items, price lines, styles, colors, or sizes are selling in a particular merchandise

CONVENIENCE GOODS	SHOPPING GOODS	SPECIALTY GOODS
Goods consumers expect to have readily available.	Consumers will accept no substitute. Products about which the con- sumer does not have a thorough knowledge.	Consumers will usually accept only a well- known brand and have full knowledge of the product.
EXAMPLES ARE:	EXAMPLES ARE:	EXAMPLES ARE:
Candy	Television sets	Silverware
Cigarettes	Stereo equipment	Furniture
Drug items	Radios	Pianos
Beauty supplies	Cameras	Watches
Notions	Automobiles	Kitchen appliances
Medical supplies	Small appliances	Household items
Magazines	Gift items	Cosmetics
Razor blades	Furs	

BY THE CONSUMER

classification as well as subclass. The reports will also tell the buyer how similar types of merchandise sold during the previous year or years. If the item has not been selling, it will usually be dropped from the plan.

2. The buyer may discover that a substitute has been developed that offers better merchandising opportunities. This often occurs in the area of hard goods or staple goods, where innovations or improvements have taken place in the design, material, construction, or usefulness of the products. Many consumers have the financial ability to throw away the old and try the new. Recognizing this fact, the buying specialist must be aware of new products, changes in consumer demand, and the availability of substitutes. The fashion buyer must pay close attention to changes in demand, since fashion goods have a short selling life to begin with. The occurrence of fads, changes in fashion trends, the desire to try the new and exotic—all are ever-present elements that keep the fashion buyer alert to changes when planning the fashion assortment for a department or store.

3. Items may be eliminated from the line if changes in merchandising

efforts have failed to improve the sale of goods. For example, a buyer may learn from daily sales reports that a style of cashmere sweaters is not selling. He or she will visit branch stores, talk to department managers, and perhaps decide that the merchandise should be displayed differently and moved to better selling locations. However, the buyer may be informed that the sweaters are too expensive for the clientele patronizing the department. As a result, several markdowns may have to be taken to sell the merchandise before the season ends. The buyer will take this into account when planning the assortment for the same season the following year.

4. The buyer will eliminate items from the assortment that contribute little or nothing to the sales of other products. That is, the items do not "tie in" or relate to those items already available. A certain style of costume jewelry may be obsolete in design, of inferior quality, out of place, or too expensive for the rest of the line. Thus, it will be eliminated from the assortment plan.

Explain why the buying specialist should consider the following factors when planning the merchandise assortment.

1. Type of retail store
2. Past sales records
3. Determination of consumer wants
4. Study of internal and external sources
5. Types of goods offered for sale
6. Elimination of merchandise items

PART 2

How Assortment Plans are Developed

Plans Used in Assortment Development

Let us review for a moment. From the point of view of the buyer, merchandise can be categorized as fashion goods, which appeal to consumers for a short period of time; as staple goods, which should always be in stock, since they are demanded year in and year out; and as seasonal goods, which are in demand only at certain times of year. Goods may also be classified according to the manner in which they are purchased by consumers. Such a classification divides the assortment into convenience goods, which consumers expect to have readily available at a convenient location; shopping goods, which are more costly, less frequently needed, and require more careful selection by the customer; and specialty goods, for which a consumer will accept no substitute. Shopping goods, convenience goods, and specialty goods may also be identified as fashion, staple, or seasonal merchandise. The buyer's planning of the merchandise assortment is based on the merchandising policies of the retail store, the needs and wants of the store's clientele, and the scope and type of the store. A well-defined, systematic approach to planning the appropriate assortment of merchandise is needed. Let us now turn our attention to the methods used by buying specialists when planning the merchandise assortment and see how various types of merchandise are considered during the planning process.

Assortment plans are developed in one of two ways. The first method is through the use of a basic stock list; the second method is through the use of a model stock plan. All merchandise assortments can be planned by using either of these methods; however, the method used depends on the kind of merchandise under consideration.

Assortment plans may be developed by two methods

Method 1. Through the use of a basic stock list
Method 2. Through the use of a model stock plan

In a retail store, basic stock lists are composed of staple types of merchandise. For example, in a variety store, staple goods may include toothpaste, deodorants, socks, underwear, detergents, light bulbs, and shoelaces. The central buyer will develop a basic stock list for goods of this kind. The list will specify in detail the items to be carried in stock. As Figure 9.8 illustrates, a basic stock list will include the following information: the name of the item, stock number,

Planning a Basic Stock List

Figure 9.8. An example of a basic stock list used by a buyer in a notions department.

MC 7			STAPLE LIST			Date April 1						
Sheet No.:												
Item					Description			Retail	Min.	Quarters			
No.	Item	Brand	Manufacturer	Type	Color	Size	Price	Stock	1st	2nd	3rd	4th
1	Cotton thread	Cordo	Cordo	Mercer	All	Fine	59	100	25	50	20	5
2	Silk thread	Cordo	Cordo	Fine	All	Fine	69	100	25	25	25	25
3	Nylon thread	Cordo	Cordo	Fine	All	Fine	49	100	25	25	25	25
4	Linen thread	Cordo	Cordo	Medium	Red, Wh	Med.	59	200	50	50	50	50
5	Elastic thread	Cordo	Cordo	Medium	White	Med.	59	200	75	25	50	50
6	Darning thread	Elso	Elso	Fine	All	Fine	29	300	100	100	50	50
7	Carpet thread	Gruner	Gruner	Thick	Black	Thick	89	100	25	50	20	5
8	Buttonhole thread	Finely	Finely	Thick	All	Thick	49	200	50	50	50	50
9												
10												
Class Sewing Notions-Sewing Thread							Dept. 428-Notions					

size, price at cost and at retail, color, brand name, weight, sales from the previous year, sales to date, projected sales, and so forth. The central buyer will send each store manager a list of staple items, usually in the form of a notebook, that must be carried by the store. Often there will be a picture of the item for easy identification.

In a department store the local buyer will develop a basic stock list for the particular department. For example, the buyer of boys' wear will include such items as handkerchiefs, underwear, socks, and pajamas on a basic stock list and make certain that the merchandise is distributed as needed to all the branch stores. Daily sales and stock reports will inform the buyer of the status of staple goods in all branch stores.

The small independent shop owner will also develop a list of staple items. For example, the owner-manager of a bicycle shop will keep daily records on such staples as tires, handlebar grips, chains, bicycle seats, wire baskets, and so forth. A certain level of inventory, based on past sales experience and anticipated sales, will be maintained.

The techniques used by buyers in all types of stores are basically the same. An analysis of past sales reveals items that have sold in sufficient quantities, peak demand periods, and items that show an active demand. In central merchandising, for example, the joint sales experience of all the store units is used to develop a master list of goods to be carried regularly throughout the year. Once the staple list has been developed, the buyer may readily determine what to buy by checking the actual stock assortment against the list. Additions to and subtractions from the original stock list may be made by watching sales carefully. For example, if certain types of goods are selling well but salespeople reveal that customers want particular colors and sizes, additions may be made. If some items sell slowly or only during certain seasons, they may be dropped. Or, if certain items are always in demand, they may be put on a special list to ensure reordering.

When planning staple merchandise assortments, buying specialists should consider (1) brand preference, (2) private brands, (3) homogeneous and heterogeneous staples, (4) seasonal and nonseasonal staples, and (5) periodic fill-in of staple stocks.

When planning staple merchandise assortments, the buyer should consider:

1. Brand preference
2. Private brands
3. Homogeneous and heterogeneous staples
4. Seasonal and nonseasonal staples
5. Periodic fill-ins of staple stocks

Brand Preference

Brand preference is an important consideration in the consumer's choice of staple merchandise. A difficult task for the buyer is to determine the number of brands to carry.

In most lines of merchandise there are many competing brands. The buyer must not be tempted to carry many brands, since this practice may create heavy stock assortments. The best policy would be to carry a few popular brands that will give satisfaction to the majority of customers. Most stores have learned through trial and error which brands have proved successful or unsuccessful.

Today, however, brand selection is becoming more scientific. Chain-store operations, large department stores, and discount houses utilize the services of research bureaus that determine the popularity of different brands in the community.

Private Brands

A second factor the buyer should consider is private branding. Private brands may give a store distinction and free it from direct competition, and may also be purchased for less. Department and specialty stores often carry their own private brands of merchandise along with the leading national brands. Private branding permits goods to be made to the specifications of the retail buyer and of consumer needs.

Private branding may cause a variety of problems and obligations for the buyer, however. Often it costs more to advertise and promote private brands than to sell leading national brands. Also, the stock turnover may be less, since the buyer may have to place larger orders with the vendors and carry larger reserves. Of course, if the brand is successful, a repeat business is assured. The advantages and disadvantages of private branding are shown in Table 9.2.

The small business operator has difficulty in making private branding arrangements with suppliers. Since the small business does not have the inven-

Table 9.2. *When considering private branding the buyer must remember.*

Advantages	Disadvantages
1. Usually costs the buyer less	1. Higher advertising and promotion costs
2. Builds repeat retail business	
3. Avoids direct competition	2. Involves making commitment for large orders
4. Allows goods to be made to buyer specification	3. Unadvertised brands may lead to customer resistance
5. Store may carry exclusives	4. Goods may not meet high standards of quality

tory turnover, investment capital, and market potential of the large business, vendors and manufacturers are hesitant to set up special production facilities, make packaging arrangements, or offer price concessions. Thus, the small businessman will compensate by offering special services and seek unique staple assortments to encourage the customer to enter his store.

Homogeneous and Heterogeneous Staples

A third factor the buyer should consider when planning staple merchandise is the kinds of staples that are available. *Homogeneous staples* may be defined as staple goods that are all of the same size, color, fabric, and style ("homogeneous" means "the same or similar"). For example, light bulbs are manufactured by Westinghouse and General Electric. The 100-watt bulbs produced by each company are alike in that they are the same size, provide the same amount of light, and fit into standard light-bulb sockets. Another example is the glass used in picture frames. The glass looks the same and performs the same function, yet it is produced by different manufacturers, for example, Pittsburgh Plate Glass and Corning Glass.

Heterogeneous staples may be defined as staple goods that are alike but not identical ("heterogeneous" means "containing dissimilar elements"). For example, shoelaces of the same length and width will come in assorted colors, patterns, and textures, though they all perform the same function. Hairpins or bobby pins of the same size come in different colors, to be worn by blondes, brunettes, or redheads. The buyer must plan the staple stock according to the similarities that exist among the staple goods available, as well as the differences.

Seasonal and Nonseasonal Staples

A fourth factor the buyer should consider is seasonal and nonseasonal staples. Items offered in the staple category should be available at all times of the year or at least during recurring seasons of demand. For example, some staples may be in demand regularly for years and not be affected by seasonal variations. This is true for hardware, foodstuffs, and toiletries. On the other hand, many staples tend to be seasonal, since sales will vary throughout the year or during specific times of the year in a manner that is predictable. For example, Easter egg decorations may be staples only during the Easter season, Christmas tree trimmings during the Christmas season, Halloween costumes during the fall season, and ski poles during the winter season.

Periodic Fill-Ins of Staple Stocks

To ensure a well-balanced assortment of merchandise, it is essential that staples be reordered periodically. However, the buyer must have certain information available before reorder formulas can be applied. The necessary information is outlined in the list that follows. The student should review this list carefully, since the information it presents is necessary for calculating the formulas that follow.

Information Necessary in the Planning of Staple Stocks[7]
1. *Rate of sale* (S)
   Calculated as follows:
   Previous inventory count plus receipts, minus current inventory counts. Usually determined from the past rate and expressed on a weekly basis.
2. *Re-order period* (RP)
   The time period between planned inventory counts. The inventory which remains is the expected sales volume during the reorder period.
3. *Delivery period* (DP)
   The interval time between the time a reorder is determined and the time the stock is made ready for sale.
4. *Lead time* (LT)
   A sum of the delivery period and review periods.
5. *Review inventory period* (RIP)
   The time period at which the inventory is checked. It may be the same as the reorder period.
6. *Reserve* (R)
   A safety factor is included to allow for sales variations from normal sales activity occurring during the delivery and the review periods.
7. *Maximum* (M)
   The maximum amount of stock which results from the inventory on hand plus the merchandise on order. The expected sales which result during the normal reorder and delivery periods plus a reserve.
8. *Minimum order* (MO)
   The stock level including stock on hand and on order at which a reorder should be placed.
9. *Outstanding orders* (O)
   The unshipped quantity of goods not yet received since placement of the last order.
10. *On-hand orders* (OH)
    The goods in stock while the reorder is being calculated.
11. *Unit open to buy* (OTB)
    The quantity of stock to be reordered when the minimum stock is opened.

To summarize, the information necessary for reordering staple merchandise is:

1. The normal sales rate expected during the delivery and reorder periods
2. The delivery period
3. The reorder period
4. The reserve
5. Stock on hand
6. Merchandise on order

When stock is checked between the normal reorder dates, the length of the review inventory period should also be known. The unit of measurement used in calculating stocks, orders, and sales is usually expressed as the number of pieces. Or it may be expressed in terms of cases or dozens where the stock value is large.

The following formulas best illustrate how this information is used when determining the periodic fill-in of staple stocks.

The first formula may be used to determine the maximum or total amount of staple goods to be on order and on hand:

Maximum = (Reorder Period + Delivery Period) Rate of Sales + Reserve

$\quad$ M $\qquad\qquad$ RP $\qquad\qquad$ DP $\qquad\quad$ S $\qquad\quad$ R

or:

Maximum = (Lead Time) Rate of Sales + Reserve

$\quad$ M $\qquad$ (LT=RP + DP) $\qquad$ S $\qquad$ R

For example, you want to determine the total number of goods on order and on hand, or the *maximum*. You know that the item is selling at 100 items per week (S), with 58 units left in reserve (R). To ensure that you will have an ample supply of stock to cover the reorder period of four weeks and the delivery period of two weeks, you must have enough goods to carry you through the six-week (RP + DP) period; also, you must continue to carry an additional 58 units in reserve (R) for unexpected sales fluctuations.

Thus:

$$
\begin{aligned}
M &= (RP + DP)\,S + R \\
&= (4 + 2)\,100 + 58 \\
&= 6 \times 100 + 58 \\
&= 600 + 58 \\
&= 658
\end{aligned}
$$

The total number of staple goods on order and on hand, or the maximum amount, is 658 items.

The second formula is used to determine the unit open-to-buy (OTB), or the quantity of stock that needs to be reordered when minimum stock is opened:

Unit open-to-buy = Maximum – On-hand orders – Outstanding orders

$\quad$ OTB $\qquad\qquad$ M $\qquad\qquad$ OH $\qquad\qquad\qquad$ O

That is:

Unit open-to-buy = Maximum – (On-hand + Outstanding orders)

$\quad$ OTB $\qquad\qquad$ M $\qquad\qquad$ OH $\qquad\qquad$ O

Let us say you know that you have 200 units on hand (OH) and 58 units still on order (O) from your supplier. Your total number of goods on hand, or the maximum (M), is 658 units.

Thus:

$$
\begin{aligned}
OTB &= M - (OH + O) \\
&= 658 - (200 + 58) \\
&= 400
\end{aligned}
$$

The quantity of stock that needs to be reordered, or the unit open-to-buy, is 400 units.

Another formula may be used when you wish to determine the reserve period or safety time period required to maintain a maximum reserve level. Management considers this method a 99–100% protection against reserve depletion:

$$
\underset{R}{\text{Reserve}} = 2.3 \times \sqrt{\underset{(LT = RP + DP)}{\text{(Lead Time) Sales}} \quad S}
$$

For example, you want to determine the number of items you must have in reserve to cover unexpected sales. The Poisson distribution table of probability reserves,[8] which is based on estimates of 99%, states that reserves should be 2.3 times the square root of the reorder period (RP), which in your case, we will say, is four weeks, added to the delivery period (DP), which is two weeks, multiplied by the rate of sales (S), which you know to be 100 units per week.

Thus, 99–100% protection:

$$
\begin{aligned}
R &= 2.3 \times \sqrt{(LT)\ S} \\
&= 2.3 \times \sqrt{(\ 6)\ 100} \\
&= 2.3 \times \sqrt{600} \\
&= 2.3 \times 25 \\
&= 57.5 \text{ (rounded to 58)}
\end{aligned}
$$

The number of items you must have in reserve, based on the 99–100% protection to cover unexpected sales, is 58 units.

A fourth formula may be used when managment feels that 95% protection is adequate to maintain a maximum reserve level:

$$
\underset{R}{\text{Reserve}} = 1.6 \times \sqrt{\underset{(LT = RP + DP)}{\text{(Lead Time) Sales}} \quad S}
$$

Ninety-five percent protection means that one lost sale in 20 reorder periods will occur.

Thus, 95% protection:

$$R = 1.6 \times \sqrt{(LT)\ S}$$
$$= 1.6 \times \sqrt{(6)\ 100}$$
$$= 1.6 \times \sqrt{600}$$
$$= 1.6 \times 25$$
$$= 40$$

The number of items you must have in reserve, based on the 95% protection to cover unexpected sales, is 40 units.

How do the following formulas assist the buying specialist when determining the periodic fill-in of staple stocks?

$M = (RP + DP)\ S + R$
$OTB = M - (OH + O)$
$R = 2.3 \times \sqrt{(LT)\ S}$
$R = 1.6 \times \sqrt{(LT)\ S}$

Planning the Model Stock

The model stock plan is the second method a buyer may use to develop the assortment plan. A *model stock* may be defined as the desired assortment of stock broken down according to predictable factors, such as classification, price, material, color, and size, based on consumer demand. The model stock plan is used by buyers of fashion goods to plan fashion assortments since, unlike staple goods, fashion items are identified by general characteristics rather than by specific details. In planning a model stock, accurate sales and stock information is necessary to achieve maximum sales from the merchan-

---

What the model stock includes

An assortment of staple goods
    Goods always in stock
    Goods in demand year in and year out

An assortment of fashion goods
    Goods that appeal for a short period of time
    Goods that have a short life cycle

An assortment of seasonal goods
    Goods in demand only at certain times of the year
    Goods that have a life cycle as long as the season

dise assortment. The buyer of fashion apparel and of home furnishings must be guided by current trends as well as by previous sales patterns. As you will learn in the next chapter, the buying specialist will develop a specific buying plan that gives consideration of what to buy, when to purchase, and when to have merchandise delivered for the model stock plan to be fulfilled.

The model stock plan is used to plan the ideal assortment; thus, it will include an assortment of staple goods, fashion goods, and seasonal goods.

An Assortment of Staple Goods

The amount and kinds of staple items found in the model stock plan will differ. For example, the buyer of boutique fashions may develop a different basic stock list from that developed by the buyer of mass fashions. The boutique buyer may consider tie-dyed scarves, jeweled sweaters, and plastic jewelry to be part of the basic stock assortment, whereas the buyer of mass fashions may consider such items too innovative, fad-oriented, or expensive; the basic mass-fashion assortment may include plain silk scarves, basic sweaters, and proved styles of costume jewelry. The staple fashion assortment is used for the normal stocking of fashion items that the customer expects to find available (convenience items). (See Figure 9.9.)

Figure 9.9. Model stock plan, women's blouse department.

Department Stock in Dollars		
Total, April 1		$30,000
Major Breakdown		
Special promotional stock		3,500
Stock left over		1,500
Model stock		25,000
Total		$30,000
Distribution of Model Stock Based on Classification		
Short-sleeved	35%	$10,000
Printed silks	25%	6,250
Evening prints	20%	3,750
Suit blouses	15%	1,250
Sporty knits	5%	1,250
Total	100%	$22,500

An Assortment of Fashion Goods

The model stock plan will include a fashion assortment. Fashion stock in both apparel and home furnishings is the most difficult of all classes of merchandise to plan for because of the many choices of styles, colors, materials, vendors, and manufacturers, and the many new items available. Since fashion goods have a short life cycle, the risks in fashion buying are high. Five characteristics of fashion merchandise will assist the buyer in determining the fashion assortment. They are (1) classification, (2) price, (3) size, (4) material, and (5) color.

Planning the fashion assortment
Characteristics of the fashion assortment that are predictable:
1. Classification   4. Material 2. Price   5. Color 3. Size

Classification. In planning by *classification,* the buyer will break each general line of merchandise down into subdivisions. Examples are as follows:

Furs	*Lamps*	*Rugs*
Fun furs	Modern lamps	Oriental rugs
Expensive furs	Contemporary lamps	Hooked rugs
Fur accessories	Terrarium lamps	Axminster rugs
Fur stoles	Lamp shades	Chenille rugs

The consumer demand for merchandise in each classification is usually predictable by the buyer, who therefore can determine fairly accurately the quantity of merchandise to buy. Often further subdivisions may be used if the subdivision becomes too cumbersome (for example, fur stoles may be further subdivided into expensive, medium-priced, and low-priced within the fur classification).

Price. Since most retail stores attempt to cater to consumers representing many income levels, a variety of price lines is found within each classification of fashion goods. The buyer will plan the fashion assortment to include at least three price lines tailored to the income brackets of the customers who patronize the store. Such planning will enable the customer to have a choice in the price of the item bought. Once the price norm in each classification is determined, the buyer can predict with considerable accuracy future demands in lower and higher price ranges as well as a specific price range. We will discuss pricing in detail in Chapter 14.

Size. Size is an important factor with most fashion merchandise. This is true not only of fashion apparel but also of many home furnishings. The buyer must determine the customer demand for each size and buy accordingly. The size distribution of the items sold during the past season is usually an indication of future demands.

Material. A knowledge of textiles and the kinds of materials available will help the buyer determine customer wants. For example, wide customer acceptance of cotton denim during the mid-1970s caused retail store buyers to stock fashion apparel such as jeans, hats, swimsuits, and handbags all made of denim. The automobile industry followed the trend by using the "denim look" in automobile seat covers; the furniture industry was influenced by the popularity of the fabric and used denim as an upholstery fabric. Knowledge of customer acceptance of materials will assist the buyer in stocking a well-balanced fashion assortment with proper emphasis given to particular materials in demand.

Color. Color plays an important role in the selection of fashion goods. Since each new season popularizes specific color combinations, the buyer can predict the color or color combinations most consumers will seek. Basic colors usually account for the majority of sales; however, fashion colors or seasonal colors have promotional value and are used to attract fashion-conscious customers into the department. The buyer must be careful not to overstock that which is new and popular while neglecting the standard and more conventional colors.

The five characteristics listed here are mostly predictable on the basis of past experience. However, consumer acceptance or rejection of an individual fashion or of a particular style is often not predictable. Once the predictable elements are identified, the buyer is able to plan the fashion assortment of model stock.

An Assortment of Seasonal Goods

Finally, the model stock plan will contain an assortment of seasonal goods. Many staple stocks and fashion stocks will also reveal a pattern of seasonal variations, whereby goods are in demand only at certain times of the year and their life cycle is only as long as the season. Good planning will provide for seasonal coverage, whether on a six-month basis or broken down into monthly or weekly subdivisions. For example, fashion apparel may be broken down into fashion seasons. Table 9.3 illustrates this.

Major seasons usually include showings by the majority of manufacturers in the fashion apparel and accessory trades. Manufacturers who specialize in certain types or lines of products participate in minor season showings.

Staple products and home furnishings also have seasons. They are the fall season, from August until March, and the spring season, from April until July. Manufacturers' openings are generally held in January and July.

Table 9.3. *Fashion apparel seasons.*

SEASON	TYPE	LENGTH OF TIME	MERCHANDISE LINE AFFECTED
Fall season	Major	Late August to December	Sportswear, coats, dresses, suits, accessories
Holiday season	Minor	November to December	Eveningwear, dresses, special Christmas merchandise
Cruise and resort	Minor	January to March	Sportswear, swimwear, casual clothing
Spring season	Major	March to April, depending on occurrence of Easter Sunday	Coats, dresses, suits
Summer	Major	May to June	Sportswear, coats, suits, dresses, accessories
Transitional	Minor	July to August	Casual wear in lightweight fabric in dark colors
Back to school	Minor	Late August to October	Children's wear, casual clothing, and accessories

Planning Fill-Ins for the Model Stock Plan

Both staple and fashion stocks require accurate assortment planning and careful controls. However, the control measures used differ in two respects: first, fashion assortments must be reviewed more frequently, usually on a weekly basis, whereas most staple or basic stocks require review only every three to four weeks. Second, fashion reorders are generally based on the heterogeneous assortment, such as a style, price line, or size within a classification, whereas in the staple stock assortment each different item may require a separate control measure.

Formulas may be used to determine periodic fill-ins of fashion stocks. The following formula may be used when a particular style becomes popular and needs to be reordered several times during the selling season. (As you recall, this formula was also used for reordering staple goods.)

Maximum = (Reorder Period + Delivery Period) Rate of Sales + Reserve

M   RP   DP   S   R or:

Maximum = (Lead Time) Rate of Sales + Reserve

M   LT = RP + DP   S   R

Suppose that you want to determine the total number of women's blouses on order and on hand, or the maximum. You know that the blouses are selling at 100 pieces per week (S), with 58 units left in reserve (R). To ensure that you will have an ample supply of blouses to cover the reorder period of four weeks and the delivery period of two weeks, you must have enough goods to carry you through the six-week selling season (RP + DP); also, you must continue to carry an additional 58 pieces in reserve (R) for unexpected sales fluctuations. Thus:

$$
\begin{aligned}
M &= (RP + DP) \, S + R \\
&= (2 + 4)100 + 58 \\
&= 6 \times 100 + 58 \\
&= 600 + 58 \\
&= 658
\end{aligned}
$$

The total number of women's blouses on order and on hand, or the maximum amount, is 658.

There are several other methods that may be used to control the periodic fill-ins of fashion stock. As you recall from reading chapter 7, the buyer specialist will use various types of reports. These are listed in Table 9.4.

Table 9.4. *Reports the buyer will use to control the periodic fill-ins of fashion stocks.*

1. Vendor Summary Report

   This report may be prepared weekly or monthly. It will show the activity of all styles purchased from each vendor. (Review Figure 7.12.)

2. Buyer's Style Status Report

   This report is prepared on a weekly basis and gives the sales history of each style with size and color breakdowns as well as the sales activity of each style. (Review Figure 7.11.)

3. Daily Sales Reports

   The daily sales report is prepared on a daily basis and will give the class, style, color, size, and store in which the items are selling, along with other information.

4. The Unit Open-to-Buy

   The OTB report is prepared on a weekly basis. It will list the department's current open-to-buy figures by period. It also lists the following information at retail: merchandise in stock at the beginning of the period, a running total of merchandise received, total amount of merchandise sold, total markdown, total current merchandise in the department, and total amount on order to date. This report may be used to plan orders for styles that are frequently reordered, and also for popular colors, sizes, and price lines. (See Figure 9.10.)

Figure 9.10 An example of an
open-to-buy report.

Plan Sales This Week	Actual	Plan	I O D	Original Plan O-T-B	On Order To Date	Overbought Last Period	Net Open-To-Buy
1. Beginning Stock* O/S	443.2 9.6	410.0	(FEB) I				
Claims 2. Plus Receipts	2.2 37.7		(MAR) II				
3. Total	488.3		(APR) III				
4. Less: Sales Period to Date	16.3		(MAY) IV				
5. Total	472.0		(JUNE) V				
6. Less: Markdowns	.11		(JULY) VI				
7. Actual Current Stock	471.9		(AUG) VII				
8. Plus: Current on Order**	4.0		(SEPT) VIII				
9. Total Commitment	475.9		(OCT) IX				
10. Less: Planned Sales Bal. Per.	20.7		(NOV) X	115.0	48.4	45.2	21.4
11. Total	455.2		(DEC) XI	80.0	9.0		71.0
12. Less: Planned BOM Stock Next Per	410.0		(JAN) XII	13.0	—		13.0
13. Open-To-Buy this Period	45.2						

*   Inc. O/S Bills of _____

**   Inc. No. Order of _____

     & Foreign Orders of _____

Current Period	Sales	Retail Purchase	M.D.	BOM Stock Next Per.
Original Plan	37.0	37.0	1.0	410.0
Revised Plan				

Department   Luggage

Department No.   75-00

Along with various kinds of reports, a popular technique used by buyers to determine periodic fill-ins of fashion goods is the style-out. The *style-out technique* may be defined as a method used to detect trends in customer preferences. The technique works like this: the buyer of, for example, handbags and leather goods will select from stock some of the best-selling items—for example, three popular styles of handbags in each classification, such as shoulder bags, clutch bags, and pouch bags. He or she will carefully examine each to determine a feature that is characteristic of all. For example, the common denominator may be the color, fabric, type of closing, shape, or whatever. Once the feature is noted, for example, the type of closing, the buyer will confer with the buyer of better handbags and the budget-store buyer to seek their opinion. As a result, each buyer may reorder handbags with this particular feature for the store's forthcoming pre-Christmas sales promotion.

In the home furnishings field there are many types of merchandise, for example, bedroom furniture, dinette sets, living-room furniture, bedding, and major appliances, to name but a few, that are sold largely from samples. Since many of these products must often meet specific consumer requirements, such as fabric covering or addition of extra parts, they need not be reordered periodically. Instead, the finished product is shipped to the customer directly from the manufacturer's warehouse. However, if the merchandise is stocked in the store's warehouse, then a periodic control system must be maintained among the store, the particular selling department involved, the vendor, and the customer. Samples on the selling floor will usually carry tickets that report the current stock availability, particular fabrics and colors available, or whatever. The ticket will also note the length of time required to prepare the merchandise to meet customer specifications, as well as the delivery date.

Periodic Fill-Ins and Home Furnishings

How will the following information assist the buyer when planning periodic fill-ins for fashion goods and home furnishings?

$M = (RP + DP) S + R$
Vendor selling reports
Buyer's style status report
Daily sales report
The unit open-to-buy
The style-out technique
The periodic fill-in of home furnishings

Chapter Summary

The buying specialist must exercise careful control measures when selecting the merchandise assortment and at the same time must attempt to meet the ever-changing demands of customers. The term that best describes this function of buying is *merchandising*. Thus, a well-planned assortment will contain merchandise of the right type, the right quality, the right price, and the right quantities, at the right time and in the right place. Decisions as to which merchandise assortments to carry are not left to chance, but are based on a number of important factors. The student should review each of the following: (1) the type of retail institution, (2) past sales records, (3) determination of consumer wants, (4) a study of internal and external sources of retail information, (5) the types of goods offered for sale, and (6) the elimination of merchandise lines.

The buyer will work within limitations set forth by store management. The limitations to consider are: (1) the availability of capital resources, (2) the particular trading area served by the store, (3) the nature of the goods carried, and (4) the amount and kind of competition represented in the trading area.

Sales records may be used as a basis for planning sales in any given season. However, to be effective, they must contain a breakdown of specific information. When attempting to analyze consumer demands, the buyer will (1) analyze past purchases, (2) offer new items, (3) refer to want slips, (4) conduct customer surveys, and (5) personally observe the store's clientele. There are a number of internal and external sources of information that will also help the buyer in planning. These sources may include salespeople, vendors and manufacturers, trade sources, comparison shopping bureaus, and consumer publications.

The type of goods offered in the merchandise assortment will depend upon the type of retail store. From the point of view of the buyer, merchandise can be categorized as (1) fashion goods, (2) staple goods, and (3) seasonal goods. The buyer may also classify merchandise according to the manner in which consumers purchase goods: convenience goods, shopping goods, and specialty goods. The student should review the definition of each.

The plan for the merchandise assortment may be developed in one of two ways. The first method is through the use of a basic stock list; the second method is through the use of a model stock plan.

Basic stock lists are composed of staple types of merchandise. When planning the staple merchandise assortment, the buyer should consider (1) brand preference, (2) private branding, (3) homogeneous and heterogeneous staples, (4) seasonal and nonseasonal staples, and (5) periodic fill-ins of staple stocks. When determining the periodic fill-in, certain information is necessary to calculate the formulas. Review the list under "Periodic Fill-Ins of Staple Stocks." The student should study carefully the formulas listed in the same section.

The model stock plan is the second method a buyer may use to develop the assortment plan. It is used to plan fashion assortments, since, unlike staple goods, fashion items are identified by general characteristics rather than by specific detail. The model stock will include an assortment of staple goods, an assortment of fashion goods, and an assortment of seasonal goods. The student should review the sections on fill-ins for fashion goods and home furnishings to determine how the buyer will plan.

Trade Terminology

DIRECTIONS: Briefly explain or discuss each of the following trade terms:

1. Merchandising
2. New item
3. Trade paper or journal
4. Comparison shopping bureau
5. Fashion goods
6. Staple goods
7. Seasonal goods
8. Convenience goods
9. Shopping goods
10. Specialty goods
11. Homogeneous staples
12. Heterogeneous staples
13. Model stock
14. Classification
15. Style-out technique

Questions for Discussion and Review

1. What is merchandising? Is this definition applicable to the supermarket trade? Discounters? Variety stores? Chain stores? Specialty shops? Why?

2. What is the importance of good planning? What should a well-planned assortment contain?

3. The merchandise plan a buyer adopts for a particular store or department may depend on four factors. What are they? What else should the buyer consider?

4. Suppose you are a buyer of sporting goods in a department store. What sources of information are available concerning your customers' likes and dislikes, incomes, life-styles, education, and so on? How would you apply this information to help increase sales in your department?

5. Why must a buyer consider eliminating goods when planning the assortment?

6. Define fashion goods, staple goods, seasonal goods, convenience goods, shopping goods, and specialty goods.

7. What is the difference, if any, between a basic stock list and a model stock plan?

8. Describe a homogeneous and a heterogeneous staple stock. Cite examples of each.

9. Why is fashion planning more difficult than staple planning? What are the predictable characteristics of a fashion assortment?

10. What are the fashion apparel seasons? Why are there more seasons in fashion apparel than in home furnishings? In staple goods? Explain.

Case Study Number One

The Best-made Plans

You have recently been hired to manage The Closet Shop, a specialty store selling linens, towels, bath accessories, and related merchandise. Your previous experience has been with a department store. You feel that The Closet Shop needs to improve its merchandising planning. You have noticed that merchandise is not planned well enough in advance; there is an excess of goods in the bath accessories classification, and not enough merchandise is available in the linen classification. Also, customers have been asking for the season's popular color combinations, and the merchandise assortment of items in these colors is not complete.

From your experience and knowledge of merchandise planning, what course of action would you suggest? Outline a merchandise plan you feel is appropriate for this type of store.

Case Study Number Two

Peter's Place

A large men's specialty shop located downtown in a Midwestern city, called Peter's Place, did over a million dollars' worth of sales last year and is likely to go higher this year. The clientele are predominantly upper middle class and purchase primarily conservative clothing and accessories. Business peak periods for Peter's Place occur at Christmas and Father's Day and at the beginning of each season.

Peter Leaman, owner of Peter's Place, recently decided to relinquish part of his buying responsibilities and hired Alan Michaels as buyer of men's furnishings. Peter Leaman assured Alan when he was hired that he would have ample opportunity to "act on his own initiative" when buying merchandise for his area of responsibility, men's coats and suits.

One of the first decisions Alan had to make related to his largest merchandise classification, men's suits. Specifically, the problem revolved around the brand or brands of suits upon which to place major emphasis. Alan, who had been a men's wear buyer for eight years, knew that if he ordered a particular well-known brand of men's suits, they would sell well because of the strength of the brand name. Also, the particular brand manufacturer advertised all year round, which assured the store of ample sales opportunities; with the manufacturer advertising, stable price, Alan would be assured of at least a 50% markup on sales.

Alan decided to consider an alternative to this buying practice, however. He knew that if Peter's Place could provide a suit of equal quality and at a lower cost, it would sell well. Alan also knew that if he could place a quantity order with a manufacturer on a long-term contract, he could purchase and market a suit of superior quality to that sold under the leading brand name. The private brand label would be purchased at a lower cost and offered at a slightly lower retail cost, with a higher markup—55% to 60%. In other words, Alan, new in his present position, knew that he could order the leading brand, or go ahead and attempt to commit Peter's Place to private branding.

What course of action should Alan Michaels take?

Retailing Activities to Stimulate Student Interest and Participation

1. Interview the store manager of a discount supermarket in your local area. Make a list of nonfood items handled by the store. Ask the store manager how many new items are added to the basic stock list every six months.

2. Interview the buyer of fashion merchandise in a junior department store; a buyer of fashion merchandise in a women's specialty shop. Determine the techniques used by each in determining the periodic fill-in of the fashion assortment; of the seasonal assortment.

3. Interview the owner of a small boutique and a buyer for a boutique department in a specialty shop. Prepare a list of questions based on the topic "How is a model stock assortment planned for boutique types of merchandise?" You may refer to the Retailing Student's Reference Library for additional reference information.

REFERENCES

The Retail Student's Reference Library

Belden, Donald L. *The Role of the Buyer in Mass Merchandising*. New York: Chain Store
    Publishing Corporation, 1971.
Brown, M. P., Applebaum, W., and Salmon, W. J. *Strategy Problems of Mass Retailers and
    Wholesalers*. Homewood, Ill.: Richard D. Irwin, Inc., 1970.
The Buyer's Manual. New York: National Retail Merchants Association, 1970.
China and Glassware Merchandiser. New York: National Retail Merchants Association, n.d.
Day, George. *Buyer Attitude and Brand Choice Behavior*. New York: Free Press, 1970.
Duncan, D. J., Phillips, C. F., and Hollands, S. C. *Modern Retailing Management—Basic Con-
    cepts and Practices*. Homewood, Ill.: Richard D. Irwin, Inc., 1972.
Duncan, D. J., and Hermanson, R. H. *Retailing, Modern Concepts and Practices*. Homewood, Ill.:
    Learning Systems Company, 1970.
Fairchild's Financial Manual of Retail Stores. New York: Fairchild Publications, Inc., 1971.
Fashion Buying. New York: ITT Educational Publishing Company, 1970.
Fundamentals of Men's Wear Retailing. New York: Fairchild Publications, Inc., 1972.
Furniture Chart. New York: Good Housekeeping Service, n.d.
Gillespie, K., and Hecht, J. *Retail Business Management*. Hightstown: McGraw-Hill Book Com-
    pany, 1970.
Guide to Fashion Marketing and Merchandising. Bronx, N.Y.: Milady Publishing Corporation,
    1974.
Judelle, B. *The Fashion Buyer's Job*. New York: National Retail Merchants Association, 1971.
Judelle, B., and Troxell, E. *Fashion Merchandising*. Hightstown: McGraw-Hill Book Company,
    1971.
Mulhern, Helen. *Facts about Department Stores*. New York: National Retail Merchants Associa-
    tion, n.d.
Operations Research in Retailing: Case Studies. New York: National Retail Merchants Associa-
    tion, n.d.
Profitable Merchandising Techniques. New York: Fairchild Publications, Inc., 1970.
Promoting New Merchandise Areas. New York: Fairchild Publications, Inc., 1971.
Reich, E., Feldman, R. Q., and Levy, L. *Basic Retailing and Distribution*. New York: Pitman
    Publishing Corporation, 1970.
Retailer Visits the Market. New York: National Retail Merchants Association, n.d.
Slom, Stanley. *How to Sell Furniture*. New York: Fairchild Publications, Inc., 1971.
Swimwear Merchandising. Washington, D.C.: National Education Association, n.d.
Taylor, Charles G. *Merchandise Assortment Planning*. New York: National Retail Merchants
    Association, n.d.
Verbatim Report: Successes to Date in Classification Merchandising. New York: National Retail
    Merchants Association, n.d.
Walker, H. S., and Mendelson, N. H. *Children's Wear Merchandiser*. New York: National Retail
    Merchants Association, n.d.
Women's Ready to Wear, 1970. Austin: University of Texas Press, 1970.

References

1. E. Jerome McCarthy, *Basic Marketing: A Managerial Approach* (Homewood, Ill.: Richard D.
    Irwin, Inc., 1971), pp. 44–45.
2. Ibid.
3. *The Buyer's Manual* (New York: National Retail Merchants Association, 1970), pp. 240–241.

4. Donald L. Belden, *The Role of the Buyer in Mass Merchandising* (New York: Chain Store Publishing Corporation, 1971), pp. 54–55.
5. *The Buyer's Manual,* pp. 275–276.
6. Ibid.
7. J. W. Wingate, E. O. Schaller, and F. L. Miller, *Retail Merchandise Management* (Englewood Cliffs, N.J.: Prentice-Hall, Inc., 1972), pp. 338–339.
8. *Handbook of Probability and Statistics.* New York: McGraw-Hill Book Company, 1953.

Selecting the Merchandise Assortment

10

Performance Objectives

PERFORMANCE
OBJECTIVES

As a result of reading this chapter, the student should be able to accomplish the following:

1. Relate eight factors a buyer should consider in assembling stock.

2. Define merchandise quality.

3. Determine the qualifications a buyer should consider when selecting a new item.

4. Illustrate and explain the life cycle every product goes through.

5. Define product line; product mix.

6. Recall eight important points the buyer must consider when determining a balanced merchandise assortment.

7. Discuss four advantages of buying foreign products.

8. Define buying committee.

9. Describe four points a buying specialist should consider when determining the quantity of goods to purchase.

10. Review the open-to-buy formula.

11. Become aware of conditions that may affect the desired merchandise at the end of the inventory period.

12. Review the market agenda usually followed by small shop owners and department-store buyers while visiting the wholesale markets.

Selecting the Merchandise Assortment

What Merchandise to Buy

PART 1

In the preceding chapter you read that the objective of merchandise planning is to make available to the retail customer a suitable selection of merchandise and a well-balanced merchandise assortment. To accomplish this task, the buying specialist must select merchandise that has proved to be in constant demand by the store's clientele; add new merchandise lines that have become popular through changing fashion trends; and delete merchandise lines or assortments that do not contribute to the overall profits of the retail institution.

Where to Begin

As the buyer, store manager, or small business operator plans purchases, he or she must consider not only what kind of merchandise will meet consumer needs but also how many dollars are available. Since this information has been carefully worked out in the six-month merchandise plan, the buying specialist can now set about the task of selecting the merchandise assortment. What guidelines are available for this task? How can the buyer determine the number of brands to offer? How many colors of men's sweaters or styles of children's shoes should be ordered? The purpose of Part 1 was to discuss (1) those factors a buyer should consider in determining what merchandise to buy; (2) the importance of foreign buying; and (3) buying for different types of merchandise categories, special promotions, and special departments. Part 2 discusses (1) the quantity of merchandise to purchase; (2) problems encountered by different types of stores; and (3) preparing for the buying trip.

No aspect of retailing is more subject to close and constant scrutiny than is the selection of merchandise assortments. The buyer must not only determine the selection of a particular merchandise classification or category, but also must decide whether or not to offer the classification at all. The buyer must determine the quality of the merchandise, the price range, and the number of brands as well as the number of lines within each classification. Other important factors are: (1) the quality of the merchandise offered for sale; (2) price range; (3) choice of national brands or private store brands; (4) good taste; (5) proper timing; (6) life cycle of the product; (7) variety of product lines; and (8) depth vs. breadth vs. common assortment.[1]

Under Close and Constant Scrutiny

> Factors the buyer should consider in assembling stock
>
> 1. The quality of the merchandise offered for sale
> 2. Price range that will meet consumer demand
> 3. National brands or private (store) brands
> 4. The essence of good taste
> 5. Proper timing
> 6. The life cycle of the product
> 7. Variety of product lines
> 8. Depth vs. breadth vs. balanced assortment

Assembling the Merchandise Assortment

Quality of the Merchandise Offered for Sale

Merchandise Quality may be defined as the best or finest material available, or superior to that of lesser quality or standards. Usually a high-quality merchandise line will boast a higher price range, while merchandise of low or inferior quality may be found in the lower price ranges. However, with the merchandising evolution brought about by the discount house, good-quality merchandise may be offered at lower prices.

Figure 10.1. In selecting the merchandise assortment, the buyer must be careful to exercise good judgment as to the quality of merchandise that will appeal to the customer and must keep in mind the merchandise policies of the store.

Merchandise quality will reflect the image of the store. Those stores that cater to clientele in the upper income bracket will offer merchandise representative of high standards and excellent quality. Such merchandise will "wear well," "last longer," or "never wear out," as we say. On the other hand, you may have walked through a store and felt its merchandise presentation to be "junky," "low-quality," or "not worth the money." Perhaps you felt this retail store was offering merchandise that was not consistent with your standards of quality.

As the buyer selects the assortment, he or she must be careful to exercise good judgment as to the quality of merchandise that will appeal to the type of consumer served and uphold the merchandising policies of the store. Merchandise of well-known brands may exceed standards of quality in a number of areas and be below those standards in other aspects. Here the buyer must rely on past experiences and decision-making ability to select merchandise of a quality that reflects the image of the store and the good taste of the consumer.

Price Range

Price range and quality usually interact with each other during the selection process. There is no specific correlation between price and quality; however, a general correlation does exist. Better-quality merchandise is usually offered at a higher price, whereas lower-quality or inferior merchandise is usually found in lower price ranges. Since a store normally cannot offer merchandise of all price ranges, management must determine particular price lines and suitable quality. The buyer must follow the pricing policies of the store when selecting the merchandise assortment. A detailed discussion of the formulation of pricing policies will appear in Chapter 14, "Pricing Merchandise for Resale."

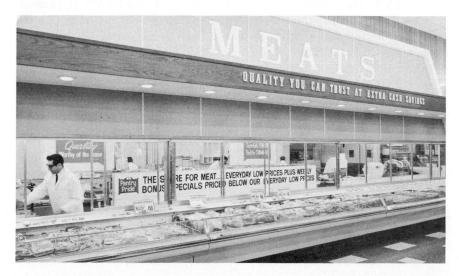

Figure 10.2 Price and quality usually interact with each other during the selection process. (Courtesy of Pantry Pride/Food Fair Supermarkets.)

National Brands or Private (Store) Brands

The established store policy may call for offerings of national brands as well as store or private brands. As you recall from Chapter 9, there are pros and cons that must be considered when deciding between standard offerings and exclusives (Review Table 9.2.). Private brands give the buyer an opportunity to be exclusive, to offer a variety of different goods, and to avoid direct competition. National or standard brands, however, are usually easily recognized by the store's customers and, therefore, readily accepted. Today most stores have adopted the policy of offering a selection of popular-brand items along with private-brand items that are consistent with store standards of quality and price.

Good Taste

Good taste is not easily defined. What is in good taste for one individual may be in poor taste for another. The buyer must determine what will be esthetically pleasing to all customers. Buyers are responsible for providing a selection of goods that will be appropriate in design, express the moods and feelings of the season, and appeal to the majority of people. Trade papers and journals in both the hard-goods line and the fashion apparel markets are usually able to predict trends in consumer preferences. However, many buyers will tell you of costly mistakes resulting from inaccurate prediction of consumer likes and dislikes. Remember the Nehru jacket, hot pants, the midi, and bullet belts? The stores couldn't even give them away!

Proper Timing

Timing is of vital importance, especially when introducing a new item. Some new items become staples, others convenience goods, while still others may become important fashions. The buyer, therefore, not only has the problem of deciding what to offer; the best time to introduce new items must also be decided. Does the store want to become a leader in the market or wait until the new item has been accepted? Each department must develop policy guides as to how often new items will be experimented with and at what risk, and how soon previously existing merchandise lines should be dropped from the stock.

There are certain questions the buyer should consider when selecting a new item. They are listed as follows:

1. What type of goods is it? A staple? A fashion? A seasonal item? Shopping goods? A convenience item? An impulse item?
2. To what type of consumer does it appeal? Youth market? Senior citizen? Ethnic group? Working wife? Career girl? Professional?
3. Will it fit into already existing price ranges? $12.95–16.95? $8.95–10.95? $3.00–6.00?
4. Does this item meet the image of the department or store? Discount image? Specialty store? Chain operation? Boutique?

5. Will this new item build up the profit picture of the department? A lead item? High-profit item? Convenience item? Shopping item?
6. What kind of performance or service will this new item fulfill?
7. Will customers be able to afford the item? Are they middle-income? Welfare recipients? Upper-income? Senior citizens? The unemployed?
8. Does the new item add interest and variety to the existing stock in color? Texture? Fabric? Style?
9. Is the item properly labeled and packaged? Easily identified? Already boxed? See-through package?
10. How will I promote the new item? Is it worthy of special sales promotion? Will the manufacturer assist in the promotion plans?

An important point to remember when buying a new item is that it should not simply be placed into stock in the hope that it will sell. It should be properly promoted and advertised to make people aware of its availability. Also, since the buying and selling activities are so closely related, a good selling plan should be decided upon before a final decision is made to purchase the new item.

Life Cycle of the Product

Maintaining a regular stock assortment is important to most types of goods. For example, staple convenience goods, shopping goods, and specialty items must be available for ample replenishment. Even fashion lines must be available to ensure continuity of individual colors, styles, sizes, and prices. However, factors such as changing consumer wants and needs, a higher standard of living, the growing youth market, and the mass media have all contributed to a constantly changing retail environment. These factors, as well as others, have affected the life cycle of individual products.

A product's life cycle may be divided into seven stages. They are: (1) product research and development; (2) introduction into the market; (3) product growth; (4) product maturation; (5) product saturation; (6) product decline; and (7) product abandonment.[2]

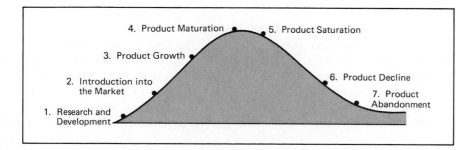

Figure 10.3. Every product goes through a life cycle.

The length of the life cycle will depend upon the product. As you recall from Chapter 5, "The Importance of Fashion," a fad may last only a few weeks, while a fashion may last two to three seasons or even several years. Staple goods may last for several decades. A product will usually yield the greatest amount of profit for the department or store late in the growth stage and will decline in profit yield late in the maturation stage of its life cycle. The buyer must be aware of the fact that, while there is little competition during the early stage of product growth, as a product becomes more popular competitors will enter the market, thus lowering the price. The buyer must also keep abreast of market trends, consumer preferences, and product demands. This information will be useful in planning reorder periods for stock replenishment.

Variety of Product Lines

A *product line* may be defined as a broad category of products having reasonably similar characteristics and similar end uses. The variety of product lines offered may be limited, as in the specialty store, which offers only a few lines of merchandise, or may be numerous, as in the department store. The buyer must be informed whether the "sky is the limit" or if buying must be done within the confines of only a few related lines of merchandise. Such information will help determine where to place greatest emphasis as to type, variation, sizes, colors, and styles. Also, decisions about lines to be de-emphasized must be made.

Over the past several years there has been a rapid expansion of product lines, which has made the buyer's selection process more complex. Consumers are always willing to purchase products that are more innovative, more attractively designed, and offer more advantages. With the increased interest of consumers in fashion apparel and home furnishings and the desire to try something new each season, manufacturers and retailers have increased their sales. In the area of housewares, the housewife has become more interested in kitchen appliances that are fashionably decorated and in electrical appliances that are not only useful but also tie in to the color and decorating theme, such as early American, Spanish, or contemporary, of the kitchen or dining area. Merchandising teams have had to work harder to provide a merchandise assortment that is both fashionable and has the quality wanted at a price customers are willing to pay.

Depth vs. Breadth vs. Balanced Assortments

The last factor the buyer should consider is the breadth and depth of the assortment. Working with the money available in the inventory budget, the buyer must make a decision about the width of the assortment with respect to its depth, and vice versa. The balanced assortment must also be considered.

Assortment depth may be defined as a characteristic of an inventory assortment offering limited versions of proved popular styles. This kind of assortment is spoken of as a "narrow and deep assortment." Mass merchandisers usually use this method of stock inventory, since it has been proved the most efficient from a cost point of view. Its advantages are: (1) it has a faster turnover; (2) it is easier to stock; (3) it uses less room and display area; (4) it is easier to reorder, check, and receive; (5) counting is simplified; and (6) markdowns are easier to avoid. A major disadvantage, however, is that consumers are not offered a wide selection of products and may have to shop in competing stores to find what they want.

Let us suppose that you walk into a discount house to purchase a pair of slacks. You find three styles of slacks: the flared look, the straight look, and the tapered look. However, each of these styles is available in several sizes, numerous colors, and different patterns. You do not have a large selection of styles to choose from, but you do have a good selection of color and patterns, and you will more than likely find your size. If you are satisfied with the styles offered, you will probably make a purchase.

Assortment breadth may be defined as a characteristic of an inventory assortment offering a large number of different categories or classifications, but not a large stock of any one style. This is a "broad and shallow assortment." Stores and departments catering to middle- to upper-income consumers usually use this kind of inventory assortment. The advantages of this type of assortment are: (1) presentation of a wide variety of goods; (2) a high degree of stopping and pulling power; and (3) slant to those customers of discriminating taste. The major disadvantage is that, due to shallowness of the assortment, alert and frequent reordering is needed to keep everything in stock. Consequently, this is a costly method of inventory.

If you are a woman, you may walk into a women's specialty shop or small boutique to purchase a long evening dress. You will find several styles of long dresses—a style with long, flowing sleeves, the clinging look, the long dress with a jacket, the gathered-waist style, and so forth. However, you may discover that the style you select is only available in one or two colors, in a limited size range, and in the same type of fabric. Thus, you may not find your size or color, or you may find that the fabric is unsuitable to your needs (perhaps it must be dry cleaned). You will shop elsewhere.

The *balanced assortment* may be defined as an inventory assortment using both assortment breadth and depth to develop an assortment that is balanced. For example, broad assortments are used early in the season, when new styles are still being tested for consumer acceptance; however, narrow and deep assortments are used later in the season, when demand is clearly defined. The balanced type of assortment may be used by mass merchandisers as well as by stores boasting a high-fashion image. In fact, this may be considered a normal compromise. Breadth and depth comprise a retailer's *product mix,* which may be defined as all the products and services offered for sale.

A well-balanced stock assortment will be maintained by all types of stores to provide an assortment of goods that is attractive to consumers. However, there are several considerations the buying specialist should keep in mind when determining stock balance. These are listed as follows:

1. Type of retail store
2. Demand factor in the seasonal selling cycle
3. Cost of inventory control
4. Amount of time and room required for storage
5. Rate of turnover and reorder period
6. Degree of stopping and pulling power
7. Kind of clientele
8. Amount and kind of competition in the marketplace

Type of Retail Store. In big chain operations such as variety stores, food chains, and drug chains, standardization of merchandise assortments has been an important merchandising objective. Chain operations cannot compete favorably if they are frequently out of stock of well-known brands of merchandise such as aspirin, toothpaste, razor blades, nail-polish remover, deodorants, or mouthwash. The central buyer who decides to yield to the temptation to broaden the stock assortment must eliminate inventory elsewhere to ensure turnover and control inventory investment. Since most chain operations are recognized for balanced assortments in staple merchandise categories, the addition of lines should be aimed at the particular socioeconomic level of the clientele, while maintaining a store image that reflects the types of goods promoted by the store.[3]

The department store will best serve its customers and achieve maximum sales and profits by providing balanced assortments throughout all departments. A weak department assortment can weaken the assortment offerings of the entire store, while, when a store strengthens all of its departments, the store's total sales and profit performance will be improved. It is important that the merchandise manager and buyer clearly understand and agree upon the breadth and depth of the assortment as well as the nature of the goods that the store should carry in each department. For example, a store's merchandising team must break down department offerings into major classifications, subclasses, and price lines.

It is also important to coordinate the assortments of the various departments. The merchandise manager will usually direct the coordination activities. Storewide coordinated assortment planning will ensure that a senior citizen, college student, homemaker, or professional at all income levels can find items in one department that "go with" those bought in another.

Other departmentalized types of stores provide balanced assortments. The discount house will offer discount prices as well as an assortment that meets the needs of those who patronize this type of store. The assortment is usually limited in breadth, since, as stated earlier, the philosophy of a discount house is rapid turnover; thus, the assortment will come in versions of proved styles. The discounter will offer more styles early in the season, when they are still being tested for consumer acceptance or rejection; toward the end of the season, limited versions of popular styles will be made available.

The specialty shop will also offer balanced assortments based on price line, classification, and subclass. However, the price line (in this case the better price line) will be coordinated throughout all departments. The specialty shop will offer a number of different categories but in limited sizes, colors, patterns, etc. It, too, will offer a broader assortment early in the season, with the assortment becoming narrow and deep when the demand for certain styles is clearly seen.

The small shop owner will employ the same merchandising techniques, depending on the nature of the stock, when planning a balanced assortment. When adding new lines, the merchant must carefully judge consumer demand throughout the particular selling season. He or she may decide to drop certain items to develop narrow and deep assortment offerings. Since capital is usually limited, the entrepreneur must carefully watch stock-sales turnover and coordinate assortment plans throughout the entire store. Thus, the owner of a children's wear business may offer two price lines (moderate-price and better-price) and provide a complete selection of children's clothing—dresses, coats, hats, underwear, play clothes, and so forth.

Demand Factor in the Seasonal Selling Cycle. As you recall from reading Chapter 5, fashion apparel and accessories pass through very definite stages as they rise to consumer demand and then eventually decline. This life cycle is also called the fashion cycle. Fashions begin with designers or manufacturers, who are usually the first to introduce the new fashion influence. Since such designs may be presented at the European couture openings, the fashion itself is still untried; thus, such fashions are very expensive. Those who shop at the specialty shop or boutique and desire the unique and "far out" will be willing to pay more for this type of fashion merchandise. Thus, the small boutique or specialty shop will stock an assortment of new items, usually at higher prices due to the risk involved, at the beginning of the season, and will later drop those styles that have proved to be unsatisfactory.

The mass merchandiser will place orders with manufacturers who are able to supply merchandise quickly once a style has been accepted in the marketplace and is in demand by a majority of people. The retail price is usually less than that of similar merchandise found in department stores and specialty shops, since mass merchandisers purchase in large quantities. However, the discount buyer is careful to watch fashion trends at the beginning of the season to determine which stock items will be continued, reordered, or eliminated.

The general merchandise chain and variety chain will provide certain styles that are in demand by a majority of people. Such proved styles of stock are mass produced, mass distributed and sold at prices within the reach of a majority of people in a particular consumer market. Already proved styles may comprise the buyer's staple stock list; thus, they are in demand all season long.

The small business manager will carefully note changes in consumer demand as the particular selling season comes to an end. He or she will be aware of new items and new styles that are being introduced and will give close attention to consumer demand, as well as to factors that may influence the rise of new fashions and the decline of some already existing.

All types and sizes of retail stores will take notice of items that have saturated the market and have been totally abandoned by manufacturers, thus cannot be sold at any price. Such items may be part of a store's "storewide clearance sale," marked down at the end of the season, or stored in the stockroom (as in the case of staple items) until the following year. However, "sitting on the merchandise" is not recommended to most retail stores, since inventory capital is tied up until the following year and there is always the risk of obsolescence or damage resulting from storage.

Figure 10.4. Staple types of goods will be in demand during particular seasons of the year. For example, the buyer of a toy department will build up the merchandise assortment at the beginning of the Christmas season.

Staple types of goods will also be in demand during particular seasons of the year. However, staple items usually have a longer selling cycle than fashion goods, since they are considered necessity items and serve a different type of need. For example, garden supplies, lawn mowers, landscaping equipment, and other related items are usually in peak demand during the spring season. Air conditioners are in demand at the beginning of the summer season; paint supplies and home improvement equipment are wanted during the spring season; small electrical appliances, bicycles, and fur coats, among other things, are in heavy demand during the Christmas season. The demand for such items is usually great at the beginning of the season and causes a higher price; however, as the season progresses, demand drops off and the price may decline. Thus, merchants of staple types of goods will also provide a balanced assortment based on the demand factor in the seasonal selling cycle.

Cost of Inventory Control. Most large retailers employ some form of electronic data processing. Inventory control will inform the buying specialist of stocks that need to be reordered, of best sellers, of slow sellers, of stocks that should be marked down, and of stocks that should be transferred to another branch store or store unit. The expense involved in using a computerized system may be offset by the increased profits and sales potential that result from balanced stock assortments. The small business proprietor must keep careful checks and maintain accurate records to provide balanced assortments. However, the implementation of a computerized system of inventory control is usually too costly for the small businessperson.

Amount of Time and Room Required for Storage. The buying specialist has an important role in the transportation and warehousing of merchandise. Since no buyer will know all the best methods to ship specific goods to specific points, buyers must consult specialists in the field to assist them in the planning and timing of deliveries and to obtain the lowest possible transportation costs. They must be aware of the time required to ship merchandise to various store locations so that goods will arrive in all store units simultaneously. Poor planning can result in a shipment of women's blouses arriving the day after Mother's Day, special promotion merchandise arriving after the advertisement appears in local newspapers, or fast-selling Christmas goods arriving after December 25.

Most large retail stores (chain operations, discount houses, general merchandise chains, variety stores, specialty houses) own warehouse facilities. The buyer has the responsibility of maintaining a complete warehouse stock to make all items available to individual store units as requested. Since many new store units and branches have limited storage space, the store's warehouse plays a very important role in merchandise replenishment. Through automatic electronic devices, the warehouse can be mechanized to break down large shipments into smaller quantities required by individual units. The buyer with warehousing facilities can be assured of adequate merchandise controls that will permit the department manager or store manager to maintain balanced assortments as required.[4]

Rate of Turnover and Reorder Period. Fashion merchandise usually has a faster turnover and more reorder periods than staple goods. However, buying specialists of both types of merchandise must be aware of the rate of stock turn and the number of reorder periods required to maintain a balanced assortment of goods. For example, the store manager of a variety store may reorder merchandise by sending his requisition directly to the central buyer or to a warehouse. The central buyer will follow up and expedite store orders to ensure that the manager will have an adequate merchandise selection throughout a given season or selling period. (Review "The Warehouse- and Requisition Plan" in Chapter 3.) The department-store buyer of home furnishings must make accurate predictions concerning trends, styles, colors, fabrics, etc., to determine the rate of turnover and the number of reorder periods required to maintain a balanced assortment.

Degree of Stopping and Pulling Power. A balanced assortment of stock will contain merchandise that consumers need and want. Depending on the merchandising policies of the store, the assortment will contain a variety of different goods in an adequate quantity to minimize stock shortages and lost sales, and a supply of merchandise that is within the financial capabilities of the retail organization. If the merchandise assortment is composed of fad-type fashions, the retailer can expect a great deal of consumer interest; thus, we say that the merchandise has a high degree of stopping and pulling power. The buying specialist will have to reorder this merchandise continuously to maintain a balanced assortment. In contrast, however, staple types of goods usually have a slow but steady demand, hence less stopping and pulling power.

Kind of Clientele. Since the buyer is trying to please store customers, he will make every attempt to purchase goods that will reflect the life-styles, tastes, interests, and habits of those who patronize his store and department. For example, a buyer of high-fashion merchandise will cater to customers who desire service and quality. The buyer of discount goods will offer limited assortments at cut-rate prices; the department-store buyer will attempt to offer a complete line of goods at various prices. The type of clientele who patronize a store will determine the nature of the goods offered for sale and thus the type of assortment planned.

Amount and Kind of Competition in the Marketplace. A balanced assortment will help build a repeat sales business. Since the one-stop concept has proved popular with customers, merchants have attempted to provide a complete line of goods in various classifications, colors, sizes, styles, and prices. A number of retailers have begun to analyze already existing merchandising policies and store image and identify types of store customers to determine how to meet competition. As a result, assortment planning, number of reorders, and determination of which items to add as well as eliminate from the assortment are based on the amount and kind of competition faced by the retailer.

Many retailers have found it profitable to offer their customers foreign goods. Carved statues from Africa, chocolate candy from France, ski boots from Austria, cuckoo clocks from Switzerland, lace scarves from Spain, marble tabletops from Italy—all help to provide an assortment that is unusual, competitive, and different. The kind of imported merchandise offered, however, will depend on the merchandising policies of the store, the size of the store, the store's target market, and the amount and kind of competition in the marketplace. There are four major reasons for buying foreign products: (1) they afford an opportunity for larger markup; (2) they provide the unusual and different; (3) they add prestige and leadership; and (4) they help meet direct competition.

Buying Foreign Goods

An Opportunity for Larger Markup

As a result of competition in the domestic market, retail specialists have had to turn to foreign markets for products that yield a reasonable markup. During the past three decades, however, there have been many fluctuations in the use of foreign markets as a source of supply. For example, years ago few retail stores carried foreign items; thus, the foreign goods selected were often sold for many times their cost. Today, however, this has changed. Many retailers, both large and small, are taking the opportunity to purchase from foreign sources, and as a result, competition has affected the markup price. This has limited the opportunity for a higher than usual markup. A buyer must be careful not to offer imported merchandise at an abnormally high markup, thus running the risk that customers may find the identical merchandise offered elsewhere at a lower price.

Providing the Unusual and Different

A second reason the buyer will balance the assortment with foreign goods is that imported merchandise provides an opportunity to round out the stock. The merchandise is considered to be unusual and different because it cannot be found in domestic markets. For example, the product may involve skilled workmanship or unusual dyes or fabrics or may combine textures and colors that are native to the country of origin. Usually imported merchandise is made by hand; in the United States, products are mass-produced, which restricts product individuality and exclusiveness. Since the buyer is using imported merchandise to round off his stock, he may place small orders with foreign producers and be assured that his orders will be filled.

The buyer may also purchase goods not for resale but to copy and then resell at a lower price. A buyer of women's dresses may attend the couture openings in Rome and purchase dresses ranging in price from $1,500 to $2,000. The store may have the originals copied and in turn sell the copies for $250. The originals were purchased at a loss; however, the loss will serve its purpose if the copies sell well.

Adding Prestige and Leadership

A third reason for adding foreign goods to the assortment is that a store will enhance its image by selling imported merchandise. When the buyer assembles the rare and the unusual, he builds a reputation for leadership. A store may continuously build an image of prestige and leadership by holding storewide promotions of merchandise imported from a single foreign country such as Ireland, Brazil, or Great Britain.

Helping Meet Direct Competition

Since there are many foreign resources available, a merchant has an opportunity to provide imported goods that are different from those offered by his competition. The uniqueness in product offerings will help a department store, chain store, small business, or whatever to maintain an image and be readily identified as a distinct type of retail store offering a balanced selection of merchandise.

How will foreign buying help the buyer provide a balanced merchandise assortment?

1. An opportunity for larger markup
2. Providing the unusual and different
3. Adding prestige and leadership
4. Helping meet direct competition

PART 2

How Much Merchandise to Buy

The Quantity to Purchase

The buyer who has decided *what* merchandise to purchase for resale then faces the question of *how much* merchandise should be purchased for particular time periods. The buyer may utilize the judgment of a *buying committee,* which is a three- to eight-person committee that acts in behalf of a single buyer and assists in decision-making policies regarding the procurement of specific merchandise categories. However, if the buyer has complete responsibility for the buying-selling activity, as do the department-store buyer or the small business owner-manager, decisions may rest on four important factors: (1) the period for which purchasing is done; (2) estimated sales for the period; (3) merchandise on hand and on order; and (4) the desired merchandise at the end of a particular period.

When determining the quantity of goods to purchase, the buyer should consider these important factors:

1. Period for which purchasing is done
2. Estimated sales for the period
3. Merchandise on hand and on order
4. Desired merchandise at the end of a particular period

Period for Which Purchasing is Done

The time period for which purchasing is done may differ with the type of goods sold, the type of store in which the goods are sold, and the nature of the period itself. For example, a fashion goods buyer may purchase winter coats for the winter season, which is approximately three months long; a buyer of contemporary furniture may make purchases based on a six-month selling plan; while a buyer in a gourmet food department may work on a buying period of one to seven days. There are six factors that may influence the period for which purchasing is done: (1) the open-to-buy; (2) hand-to-mouth buying; (3) speculative buying; (4) quantity discounts; (5) supply conditions; and (6) storage facilities.

The Open-To-Buy

The open-to-buy (OTB), as stated previously, is the amount of retail dollars that a buyer is permitted to spend for merchandise inventory within a certain time period based on formulated plans, for example, the six-month merchandise budget. The buyer's objective in using open-to-buy planning is to avoid having too much money tied up in inventory, which may require a large amount of capital and add to the rise of markdowns. Nor does the buyer wish to have too little merchandise available, which will lead to out-of-stock conditions and lost sales. The open-to-buy is based on a broad dollar scale, rather than on individual units or even small groups of units, which may help in preventing such problems. It involves a given budget period and estimations concerning planned sales, planned ending inventory, and a planned beginning inventory, and can be calculated either in dollars or in units of merchandise. The dollar figure automatically shows the buyer whether or not the proposed purchases are within the financial limits of the budget. The unit figure may be used as a check against merchandise that still remains in the inventory assortment. Often open-to-buy figures are estimated several months into the next season or period, especially if the buyer expects to make commitments in advance of expected merchandise sales. As you recall from chapter 8, the formula for determining open-to-buy is as follows:

Planned Sales	$ 50,000
+ Planned Reductions	10,000
+ Planned End-of-month Stock	40,000
= Total Needs for Month	$100,000
– Beginning-of-month Stock	25,000
= Planned Purchases	$ 75,000
– Merchandise on Order	30,000
= Open-to-buy	$ 45,000

Thus, the open-to-buy formula may be written as:

Open-to-buy = Planned Sales + Planned Reductions + Planned End-of-Month Stock
= Total Needs for the Month – Beginning of the Month Stock
= Planned Purchases – Merchandise on Order

It is important to remember, however, that planned figures are estimations of future needs. Often actual results will differ from what was planned. This will necessitate either plus or minus adjustments in planned purchases at frequent intervals, usually at the end of each week.[5]

An example of how interim open-to-buy is calculated is illustrated in *The Buyer's Manual*[6] as follows. Suppose the following data represent the condition of a department on May 15 (all amounts at retail):

Initial Mark-on Percentage	40%
Planned Purchases for May	$ 7,000
Planned Stock, May 1	$ 9,000
Planned Sales for May	$ 8,000
Actual Stock, May 15	$10,500
Actual Sales, May 1–15	$ 4,500
Merchandise in Transit	$ 1,100
Unfilled Orders for May Delivery	$ 2,000

Note that sales are $500 ahead of planned figures, as $4,500 has been sold during the first half of the month, while the plan was for only $8,000 for the entire month. This means that the purchase allotment may be increased $500 at retail. Also note that the actual stock is $1,500 at retail, above the planned amount ($10,500 minus $9,000), and the purchase allotment must be decreased by this amount.

The calculation at retail of the open-to-buy adjustment is:

Planned Purchases for May		$ 7,000
Add Variation of Sales from Plan		+ 500
		7,500
Deduct Variation of Stock from Plan		–$ 1,500
Adjusted Planned Purchases		$ 6,000
Less: Merchandise in Transit	$ 1,100	
Unfilled Orders	2,000	–3,100
Open-to-Buy, May 15		$ 2,900

Hand-to-Mouth Buying. This will also affect the period for which the purchasing is done. *Hand-to-mouth buying* may be defined as the practice of limiting orders to immediate needs and ordering goods for immediate delivery rather than well in advance. The practice of limiting orders to current needs rather than placing them on a basis of future sales usually occurs during periods of price fluctuations in the marketplace. For example, a buyer of men's expensive suits will delay buying as long as possible if there is evidence that the longer buying is delayed, the lower the wholesale price will be. Also, the practice of letting orders go until the last minute will increase the vendor's risk, because a vendor must carry a reserve that is subject to price fluctuations and may require warehouse expenses.

Hand-to-mouth buying also suggests the trend towards carrying minimal stocks, which may lead to a loss in sales. The buyer must be constantly alert to market conditions when using this buying method. There must always be an up-to-date inventory count to ensure an ample reserve, which will take care of possible sales variations as well as problems resulting from faulty deliveries. Needless to say, this buying practice would be curtailed during periods of rising prices, since the buyer who purchased early would get the best prices.

Speculative Buying. *Speculative buying* may be defined as the decision to purchase goods based on an expected rise or fall in the price level. The buyer who expects rising prices will place large orders in anticipation of reselling at the higher prices. The buyer who expects falling prices will adopt the policy of hand-to-mouth buying. Speculative buying may help the buyer obtain a larger gross margin; however, a buyer is not in business to speculate, but rather to purchase goods for the purpose of making a merchandising profit and not a speculative profit.

Quantity Discount. Quantity discount is a reduction in wholesale price based upon a specific quantity of merchandise purchased from the vendor or wholesaler. For example, the buyer may be informed that purchases in lots of 100 or more will get a 2 percent discount off the regular wholesale price. Quantity discounts are often used by vendors and manufacturers to encourage advance ordering. Usually, the buyer of staple merchandise is able to take advantage of quantity discounts, since such a buyer is able to stock the merchandise for longer periods of time with a minimum of concern for risk due to obsolescence. The fashion buyer will also take advantage of quantity discounts, especially if the department is included in a special store promotion. A fashion buyer will order promotional goods before they are needed, store them in a warehouse, and thus take advantage of a quantity discount offering.

Supply Conditions. If delivery periods are uncertain, the buyer will place orders early to ensure receiving merchandise on time. Vendors, trade journals, resident buyers, and newspapers serve as excellent sources of information on the conditions of supply in the marketplace. The time required to have merchandise delivered will, therefore, affect the period for which purchasing is done.

Storage Facilities. The retailing specialist must consider whether or not there are adequate storage facilities when considering the length of the purchasing period. If a warehouse is available or if there is adequate storage space within the store itself, the buyer may place the order in advance and have the merchandise delivered before the actual selling period. However, if warehousing is costly and in-store storage space is limited, the buyer may have to plan carefully the delivery period to avoid storage problems. Thus, lack of storage facilities may restrict the length of the period for which the retail buyer can purchase.

Explain how the following factors may affect the period for which purchasing is done

1. The open-to-buy	4. Quantity discounts
2. Hand-to-mouth buying	5. Supply conditions
3. Speculative buying	6. Storage facilities

Estimated Sales for the Period

A second important factor the buyer should consider when determining the quantity of goods to purchase is the estimated sales for the particular selling period.

Sales planning for the coming period is fundamental to any kind of retail plan. There are probably as many different methods of sales planning as there are retailers. However, most sales plans will contain one or all of the following:

1. Sales volume of the preceding year
2. Sales volume of the preceding season
3. Economic conditions, both nationally and locally
4. Fashion predictions for the coming season
5. Action taken by competition in the marketplace
6. Planned sales promotions, both for the department and the store
7. Fluctuations in price
8. Rate of unemployment in the immediate trading area
9. Changes in store policy and procedure
10. Conditions of supply and demand in the marketplace

The estimate of sales for the forthcoming buying period is usually based on past sales with allowances for changes in business conditions as well as actions taken by competition. The impact of economic conditions, unemployment, and fashion trends may modify planned sales figures as well.

The buyer who is anticipating the addition of new merchandise to already existing merchandise categories may find it difficult to estimate sales even for a relatively short selling season. Therefore, the buyer may exercise caution by purchasing only a few units, simply to test consumer reaction. This type of hand-to-mouth buying may result in quickly running out of stock and will create a shallow type of merchandising assortment. However, this method of testing new items may be better than taking costly markdowns or having leftover and obsolete stock. Or, if an item is an expensive one, samples may be purchased, with special orders being placed as sales are made.

The buyer must also remember that a careful estimate of sales may vary with the type of stock as well as from one seasonal period to another. For example, a buyer of fashion goods or perishable goods may require careful estimates, since excessive purchases will result in large markdowns or in spoilage. On the other hand, staple goods purchased in excess may result in larger than necessary inventories, with inventory capital tied up for a longer period of time. However, in periods of price fluctuations, particularly in periods of falling prices, overestimates of sales for staple goods may lead to significant losses in inventory.

When considering the estimated sales from one seasonal selling period to another, the buyer must consider the nature of the selling season. For example, Christmas has traditionally been the retailer's largest and most profitable selling season. Therefore, sales estimates are usually higher for that period than for the spring season, Mother's Day, or Independence Day.

Merchandise On Hand and On Order
A third important factor the buyer should consider when determining the quantity of goods to order is the amount of merchandise on hand and on order.

Information as to the merchandise on hand may be obtained in the following ways: (1) observations and counts and (2) up-to-date inventory records. Observations and counts are self-explanatory. The buyer, the assistant buyer, or sales personnel will actually observe and count the merchandise that remains on the selling floor as well as that in the stockroom. This method is commonly used by small retailers, since their inventory is limited in size as compared to the inventory found in the large department store. A perpetual inventory system may be used in large retail stores whereby, through the use of a computerized system, the buyer is kept constantly informed as to the color, size, style, and price of each unit of merchandise remaining in stock, not only in the main store, but in each branch or twig store or in each store unit. As a result of the perpetual inventory system, the buyer is provided with an up-to-the-minute picture of stock conditions.

Information regarding merchandise on order may be obtained from the buyer's own records. It is relatively simple to determine the unfilled orders, since the buyer's records generally include duplicate copies of every unfilled order placed with vendors or manufacturers. As you recall, this file will be found in the buyer's purchase journal.

Desired Merchandise at the End of a Particular Period

A final important factor the buyer should consider when determining the quantity to buy is the planned or desired stock at the end of the particular selling period. The following conditions may determine whether or not the buyer decides to build up a large end-of-period stock or reduces the end-of-period inventory:

1. Sales trend—have marketing surveys indicated an increase or decrease in demand for the product?
2. Popularity of the fashion—has the item become an accepted fashion that will remain in style several seasons, or has it become a fad, which will only remain one or two seasons?
3. Stage in the product life cycle—is the product in the growth stage? The maturation stage? The obsolescence stage?
4. Price fluctuations in the marketplace—has the wholesale price fluctuated? Has there been an increase in price? A decrease in price?
5. Availability of supplies and materials—are manufacturers able to procure materials and supplies to meet production schedules? Have there been shortages in materials? In supplies?
6. What types of goods remain in stock? If staple goods, can they be stored for several seasons? If fashion goods, will they go out of style or become obsolete if stored over a period of time? If seasonal goods, will they be popular next season?
7. Type of retail institution—if a discount house, can the buyer afford

to have leftovers and costly markdowns? If a department store, can the merchandise be sent to branch stores? If a small retailer, can he afford to tie up his capital?

8. Supply conditions—can the vendor deliver the merchandise as scheduled?
9. Availability of discounts—will quantity discounts be available? If so, are they worth the risk?
10. A new item? If the merchandise that remains is new on the market, is this the result of consumer resistance? Poor store promotion? A poor product?

All of these factors must be taken into consideration when the buyer determines the desired or planned stock at the end of the particular period. Not only does the buyer need to plan merchandise for the beginning of a new selling period, but merchandise must be on hand at the end of a period so that it will be available for use at the beginning of the next period, and so on. For example, merchandise that remains at the end of the Christmas season will continue to be sold at the beginning of the winter season; however, it may be sold as "an inventory clearance" or "special after-Christmas sale" or "a January white sale."

Preparing for the Buying Trip

Buying in the market requires careful planning before the buying trip is scheduled. Approximately one to two weeks in advance, plans will be summarized regarding purchases by classifications, price lines, styles, sizes, and colors. Plans will be made concerning the merchandise needs of each branch store of a department-store operation, and for individual departments if a small business. (As you recall, the buyer for a chain operation is centrally located in the market; therefore, the need for a special buying trip is eliminated.)

The department-store buyer or the owner-manager will go to the market with a buying plan that will include a list of basic stock items and goods that will tie in to other store offerings, and with money to be used for purchasing new items and special merchandise offerings. The amount of money kept in reserve for specials and new items, however, will depend on the merchandising policies of the store. Often the merchandise manager likes to be kept informed about such matters, since he is responsible for coordinating the merchandising offerings as to present stock conditions, past sales, actual sales, expected sales, the open-to-buy in units, and the open-to-buy at retail (see Figure 10.5).

Once the buyer has supplied all the information necessary, the merchandise manager will evaluate the need for a buying trip and offer suggestions and guidance based on his or her own experiences in the trade markets. Thus, the buying plan will meet the needs and wants of store customers and reflect the image of the department and the store.

The Market Agenda

The procedure followed by the buying specialist will depend upon the type and size of the retail operation. The list that follows will outline the market agenda used by most department-store buyers and small business owner-managers.

1. Determine the period of the season for which you are buying. Are you buying for the beginning of the season? Have you returned to the market to replenish the merchandise assortment? Are you seeking special promotion merchandise?

2. Determine the number of days you wish to spend in the market. Usually more time is required if you intend to view a new seasonal line; less time (three to five days) is required if you are seeking fresh styles to liven up the assortment or special promotional goods.

3. Announce your arrival and your wants in advance to your store's resident buying office. If your store belongs to a resident buying office, call the buyer's arrival office and inform personnel of the day and date of your arrival. Contact your resident buyer and inform him or her of your particular interests and merchandising needs.

4. Visit stores in the market center that are selling your particular line of merchandise. These store visits are usually made on the first or second day of the buying trip to provide background information before visiting merchandise resources.

Figure 10.5. An example of a buying plan. A buying plan for the coming season, in this case, back-to-school and fall, will provide information regarding present stock conditions, past sales, actual sales, expected sales, the open-to-buy in units, and the open-to-buy at retail. Once the buying plan is formulated, the need for a buying trip to the wholesale market is determined.

5. Talk to other store buyers who are selling the same or similar lines of merchandise to determine those factors that have led to successful selling.

6. Inform merchandise resources of the day and date of your market visit. Call various merchandise resources you wish to visit so that arrangements may be made to view manufacturers' lines, examine samples, and gain information about best sellers for the coming season.

Season BACK-TO-SCHOOL	Planned Sales	ADD planned BOM stock	SUBTRACT on hand 7/31	SUBTRACT on order 7/31	OPEN-TO-BUY, in units	OPEN-TO-BUY, retail
August	24	48	– 16	– 0	56	$1,675
September	48	12	– 0	– 0	12	359.10
October	12	0	– 0	– 0	0	0
November	0	0	– 0	– 0	0	0
FALL MERCHANDISE						
August	12	48	– 0	– 0	48	$1,438
September	0	12	– 0	– 0	12	359.10
October	36	0	– 0	– 0	0	0
November	48	36	– 0	– 0	36	1,078

7. Visit magazine editors to determine the amount and type of cooperative advertising available.

8. Contact primary producers such as fiber, leather, and fabric houses. Primary manufacturers may provide information regarding current fashion trends, popular textures, fabrics, and colors, and successful merchandise resources.

9. Participate actively in buying clinics. If you belong to a resident buying office, buying clinics may be arranged. In these clinics you will have an opportunity to study market trends, economic conditions, and supply conditions, and examine new and innovative patterns of distribution.

10. Discuss current fashion trends with fashion specialists. Manufacturers, resident buying offices, and fashion magazines will provide fashion specialists who will inform you of current trends, popular styles and colors, emerging trends, popular fads, and so forth.

11. Allow time to visit new merchandise resources, as well as the small manufacturers, to seek new items, the unique, and the unusual. In other words, leave no stone unturned while in the market center.

The Rewards of Conscientious Planning

It is very important for the buying specialist to do all the necessary planning and paperwork before leaving the retail store to go to the market center. If the buyer works carefully and conscientiously, he or she will arrive in the wholesale market with the information and guidance necessary to ensure a successful, possibly even a prosperous, buying trip. As a result of proper planning, the buyer will focus attention on the business at hand, save time, energy, and money, and be more productive.[7]

Chapter Summary

The retail buyer must be presented with a clear set of merchandising policies to stock the kind of merchandise that will sell and thus make a profit for the store. As a result of experience, the buyer is aware of the product lines for which he or she is responsible and the price ranges in which to buy them. The buyer knows the advantages and disadvantages of private or store brands as well as the degree of influence reflected in national brands. The buyer is aware of the standards of quality and good taste that will govern his or her selections and knows the requirements for meeting and beating competition in the marketplace. The buyer is aware of the importance of proper timing, particularly when introducing new items, and is alert to the requirements of the seasonal selling cycle. Within particular product lines, the buyer is aware of the variety of products available, the products' life cycle, and the amount of profit that may result. The buyer has been advised as to inventory limitations, the breadth and depth of the assortment, and the importance of combining breadth and depth to obtain a balanced assortment. The buying specialist will also buy foreign merchandise to obtain a larger markup, provide the unusual and different, add prestige and leadership to the store, and meet the challenge of direct competition.

Part 2 of this chapter emphasizes a very important aspect of buying—knowing how much to buy. To buy the proper quantity of merchandise, a good retail buyer must give close attention to details and must plan. The buyer must consider the period for which purchasing is done, estimate sales for the period, merchandise on hand and on order, and the desired merchandise at the end of a particular period. With this information in hand, as well as information regarding the kind of merchandise to buy, the retail buyer is now ready to plan the buying trip.

A buyer going to market finds it to his or her advantage to develop a carefully worked out buying plan that covers the specific items wanted for purchase. The amount intended for spending is based on open-to-buy, as well as other sources of information that have been discussed in this chapter. With this information available, the buyer is now in a position to start selecting sources of supply. In the next chapter we shall turn our attention to this topic.

Trade Terminology

DIRECTIONS: Briefly explain or discuss each of the following trade terms:

1. Merchandise quality
2. Product line
3. Assortment depth
4. Assortment breadth
5. Balanced assortment

6. Product mix
7. Buying committee
8. Hand-to-mouth buying
9. Speculative buying

Questions for Review and Study

1. Do you agree with the statement that a most important aspect of the buying-selling activity is knowing what merchandise to buy and in what quantities to purchase it? Do you agree that these two concepts are, perhaps, inseparable? Explain your answer.

2. As a men's shoe buyer, what factors would you consider as you assemble your merchandise assortment?

3. What is the correlation, if any, between price range and merchandise quality?

4. Do you agree that it is difficult to define "good taste"? How does the buyer use good taste in selecting the merchandise assortment?

5. What factors should the buyer consider when introducing a new item?

6. Define the following: assortment depth, assortment breadth, balanced assortment. What points should the buyer consider when determining the breadth and depth of the assortment?

7. Why is it advantageous for a buyer of fashion apparel to purchase foreign goods? Is it advantageous for the buyer of hard goods to purchase imported items?

8. As a buyer of expensive costume jewelry, what factors would you consider in determining the quantity of merchandise to purchase for resale?

9. How does the time period for which purchasing is done differ? Cite examples. What factors may influence the length of the selling period? Explain.

10. You are a buyer of women's fashion apparel. You have not decided whether you want to build a large end-of-period stock or slowly reduce your end-of-period inventory. What conditions should you consider when determining the amount of merchandise remaining at the end of the selling season?

11. Why must a buyer plan carefully before going to the wholesale market? Discuss five important duties the buyer will list on the market agenda.

Case Study Number One

For the last half hour you have been listening patiently to the merchandise manager talking about the importance of a good fashion image. He stated, among other things, that to maintain a fashion image it is often necessary to sacrifice quality when purchasing. He said that this is especially the case when the store finds it is necessary to get the most popular styles and the latest fads;

Quality vs. Image

that the store cannot wait for manufacturers of higher-priced merchandise to keep pace with the demand. The merchandise manager also stated that, to a large extent, store customers choose fashion over quality and price anyway. What do you think of these ideas? Be prepared in class to discuss the pros and cons of the manager's conclusions.

Case Study Number Two

White Bear—A White Elephant?

The Locker Room is a well-known medium-sized sporting-goods store located in a New England city, where Barbara Blenheim has been the buyer of ski wear for the past five years. Barbara's department has been operating on a very sound basis with respect to profit, volume, inventory turnover, and so forth. The department does an annual volume of approximately $450,000.

For the past five years Ms. Blenheim has conducted an end-of-season promotion on ski wear, which has always met with enormous success. Held in late February, the sale has usually grossed approximately $50,000 for the store each year.

This January White Bear, a well-known nationally advertised manufacturer of ski clothing and one of Ms. Blenheim's regular suppliers, has announced a reduction in price on all ski wear. White Bear has had a poor selling season due to bad weather and an overloaded inventory. When Barbara Blenheim first became aware of this situation, she realized that the White Bear company would offer the remaining line to her before anyone else in the area. She has been informed that she can have delivery within three days. The total cost of the merchandise will amount to $15,000, less 35 percent special discount. However, Ms. Blenheim is concerned that if she purchases additional merchandise and offers it at a reduced price during the month of January, which is still her peak selling period, it may affect the sale of her complete stock of ski wear, which has already been purchased at the regular prices. Furthermore, she fears that a preseason sale may affect the annual end-of-season sale, which she must offer. Barbara realizes, however, that if she turns down the White Bear offer, it will go to her competition. The advantages of purchasing the reduced line are many. However, there are disadvantages to consider. If you were Barbara Blenheim, how would you handle this situation?

Retailing Activities to Stimulate Student Interest and Participation

1. Interview the manager of an appliance store. Determine the product life cycle for portable dishwashers. Would the life cycle be the same for the standard models? Explain your answer.

2. Interview the manager of a small apparel business. Determine the product life cycle of a "classic-type" fashion; of a "fad-type" fashion. Would the product life cycle be the same? Explain.

3. Visit men's wear departments in a discount house; a traditional department store; a general merchandise chain. Compare the merchandise assortment of each with regard to the breadth and depth of the assortment at the beginning of a particular selling season and at the end of the season. Explain any similarities or differences you may note.

The Retail Student's Reference Library

REFERENCES

Appelbaum, Nat. *How to Improve Your Retail Fashion Fabrics Business.* New York: National Retail Merchants Association, 1970.

Beldon, Donald L. *The Role of the Buyer in Mass Merchandising.* New York: Chain Store Publishing Corporation, 1971.

The Buyer's Manual. New York: National Retail Merchants Association, 1970.

Drew-Bear, R. *Mass Merchandising: Revolution and Evolution.* New York: Fairchild Publications, Inc., n.d.

Ferguson, Frank. *Efficient Drug Store Management.* New York: Fairchild Publications, Inc., n.d.

Frank, Bertrand. *Progressive Apparel Production.* New York: Fairchild Publications, Inc., n.d.

Fried, Eleanor. *Is the Fashion Business Your Business?* New York: Fairchild Publications, Inc., 1970.

Gawne, Eleanor. *Fabrics for Clothing.* Peoria, Ill.: Charles A. Bennett Company, Inc., 1973.

Judelle, Beatrice. *The Fashion Buyer's Job.* New York: National Retail Merchants Association, 1971.

Leather Sales Tactics. New York: Leather Industries of America, n.d.

Leed, T. W., and German, G. A. *Principles of Good Merchandising.* New York: Chain Store Publishing Corporation, 1973.

Mullikin, Eleanor. *Selling Fashion Apparel.* Cincinnati: South-Western Publishing Company, 1971.

Profitable Merchandising of Men's Clothing. New York: National Retail Merchants Association, n.d.

Reeser, Clayton. *Management Functions and Modern Concepts.* Glenview, Ill.: Scott, Foresman & Company, 1973.

A Retailer Visits the Market. New York: Fairchild Publications, Inc., n.d.

Swimwear Merchandising. Washington, D.C.: National Education Association, n.d.

Taylor, C. G. *Merchandise Assortment Planning.* New York: National Retail Merchants Association, n.d.

To Multiply a Buyer. New York: National Retail Merchants Association, n.d.

Walker, H. S., and Mendelson, N. H. *Children's Wear Merchandiser.* New York: National Retail Merchants Association, n.d.

Women's Ready To Wear, 1970. Austin: University of Texas Press, 1970.

Zanetti, Giacomo. *Principles of Profitable Importing.* New York: National Retail Merchants Association, 1970.

References

1. John W. Wingate and J. Weiner, *Retail Merchandising* (Cincinnati: South-Western Publishing Company, 1963), pp. 176–178.
2. Donald L. Belden, *Role of the Buyer in Mass Merchandising* (New York: Chain Store Publishing Corporation, 1971), p. 44.
3. Ibid., p. 55.
4. Ibid., pp. 129–131.
5. *The Buyer's Manual* (New York: National Retail Merchants Association, 1970), p. 438.
6. Ibid., pp. 438–439.
7. Beatrice Judelle, *The Fashion Buyer's Job* (New York: National Retail Merchants Association, 1971), p. 80.

Working with Merchandise Resources

Photo courtesy of The Merchandise Mart (left) and The Apparel Center (right).

The Resources of Merchandise

11

Performance Objectives

Chapter Summary
Trade Terminology
Questions for Discussion and Review
Case Study Number One; Number Two
Retailing Activities to Stimulate Student Interest and Participation
Retail Student's Reference Library
References

PERFORMANCE
OBJECTIVES

As a result of reading this chapter the student should be able to accomplish the following:

1. Identify and define the main sources of merchandise.

2. Discuss five factors that are important when selecting merchandise resources.

3. Become aware of two methods used to make buying contacts.

4. Discuss in detail how vendors take the initiative and locate retail buyers.

5. Discuss in detail how retailers take the initiative and locate vendors.

6. Relate five major methods used by buyers when purchasing foreign goods.

7. Discuss eight methods of buying that may be used by retail buyers when purchasing goods in the domestic marketplace.

The Resources of Merchandise

Selecting Suitable Merchandise Resources

PART 1

Once the retail buyer has determined what merchandise to buy and what quantities are necessary to meet the anticipated needs of the store's clientele, he or she must locate sources of supply—or merchandise resources, as they are called in the retail trade. There are hundreds of vendors located in many markets, both at home and abroad, and literally hundreds of vendors in a given classification of merchandise. For example, some large-scale retailers and discount houses may stock as many as 50,000 different styles, sizes, or types of merchandise. A small retail store may stock from 5,000 to 7,000 different

Who Are They?

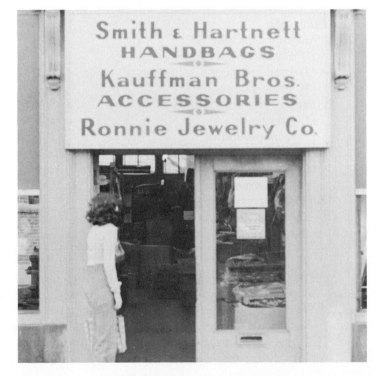

Figure 11.1. How does the buyer determine who will be a source of supply? The answer to this question as well as to others may be a result of the buyer's past experience while working with vendors.

items. For this reason, buyers, regardless of the size and type of the retail store, must keep constantly aware of sources of supply and must always be appraising new sources for the unusual and the unique. How does the buyer determine who will be the merchandise resources, and whether or not to purchase merchandise from a few vendors or from many vendors? Who will be the key resources?

The answers to these questions and others may be a result of the buyer's past experience while working with vendors and learning the major sources of supply. The purpose of this chapter, therefore, will be to: (1) identify and describe merchandise resources, (2) discuss factors in selecting merchandise resources, and (3) discuss how to make buying contacts. Part 2 will (1) discuss methods used in foreign buying, (2) describe various buying methods, and (3) discuss how various methods are used by retail buyers in different types and sizes of stores.

Main Merchandise Resources

Basically, there are three major sources of supply available to the buying specialist. They are: (1) middlemen, (2) manufacturers, and (3) farmers and growers.

The main merchandise resources available to the retail buyer are:

1. Middlemen
   a. Merchant middlemen
      (1) Service wholesalers
      (2) Limited-function wholesalers
      (3) Rack jobbers
   b. Nonmerchant middlemen
      (1) Brokers
      (2) Commission men
      (3) Selling agents
      (4) Manufacturer's agents (Manufacturer's representatives)
      (5) Auctions
2. Manufacturers
   a. Buying direct
3. Farmers or growers

Middlemen

Broadly speaking, *middlemen* may be defined as individuals or organizations who operate between producers and industrial or ultimate consumers. A synonym is the term *wholesaler,* who, as you recall from your basic marketing course, purchases goods from manufacturers in relatively large quantities and sells to retail merchants in substantially smaller quantities.[1] Usually, middlemen or wholesalers do not change the physical form of products but merely pass the goods through the distribution system. They may distribute as much as 75 percent of the merchandise handled by the drugstore trade and nearly 90 percent of the goods found in the hardware business. Middlemen may be classified into two broad categories: (1) merchant middlemen and (2) nonmerchant middlemen.

Merchant Middlemen

Merchant middlemen may be defined as wholesalers who take title or assume ownership by taking possession of goods they purchase for resale. Examples are service wholesalers, limited-function wholesalers, and rack jobbers.

Service Wholesalers. *Service wholesalers,* or "regular" wholesalers, assemble merchandise in relatively large quantities and sell it to retailers in substantially smaller quantities. A most important function of service wholesalers is to provide service to the buying specialist. They act as the retailer's buying agent, since they anticipate the needs of buyers, will go into the marketplace to obtain the merchandise, and have goods available when the buyer wants them. Not only does the service wholesaler perform the enormous task of assembling many different items; he or she also provides services such as advertising and promotion, transportation and storage, and the granting of credit. This type of wholesaling is especially valuable to the small and medium-sized retail store, since service wholesalers find it to their advantage to provide this type of buying specialist with advertising, transportation, storage, and financing services. For example, the buyer of a small children's wear business may seek a regular or service type of wholesaler because the small business cannot afford the kind of advertising necessary to compete with a local department store and therefore will arrange a cooperative advertising deal with the wholesaler. Or a small retailer may require special credit arrangements to meet the merchandising needs of the back-to-school or Christmas season. Department-store buyers, too, seek services that will enable them to meet the competition of discount houses and general-merchandise chains.

Limited-Function Wholesalers. *Limited-function* or "cash-and-carry" wholesalers are merchant middlemen who limit themselves to smaller stocks of fast-moving items and offer no credit or delivery service, thus reducing the cost of the wholesaling. In other words, they do not provide the variety of services offered by service or regular wholesalers. Large chain operations that are able to perform many of the wholesaler's service functions (warehousing, advertising, financing, and so forth) within their own firms will find it more economical to use this type of merchandise resource. For example, a variety-store chain may use a limited-service wholesaler to procure staple goods, store the merchandise in their own warehouse or distribution centers, and ship the merchandise to their various store units as needed. Department stores and small businesses also purchase goods from limited-function wholesalers. Since the cost of wholesaling is reduced, they can offer merchandise at a lower cost and pass the savings on to the department-store buyer or the owner-manager.

Rack Jobbers. Rack Jobbers are merchant middlemen who are wholesalers of nonfood items and who arrange with independent grocers and chain supermarkets to stock and maintain an assortment of goods on a rack in a particular location in each store. Rack jobbers usually work on a 25 to 33 percent markup, depending on the type of merchandise and the amount of competition. The rack jobber will select the merchandise and arrange displays when such actions are considered necessary. Rack jobbers have been primarily responsible for the introduction of nonfood items into supermarket chains. Note, for example, the wearing apparel and numerous kinds of housewares found on the shelves in your local supermarket! Even though some large operations such as Acme Markets, Inc., and Mayfair Markets have felt it more economical to take over the function of the rack jobber, many supermarket operators feel that as long as the rack jobbers provide nonfood items that are in demand, continue to provide good service, and meet competitive prices, they will continue to be widely used as merchandise resources. Also, the rack jobber

Figure 11.2. Rack jobbers provide nonfood items, for example, wearing apparel, to large chain supermarkets. (Courtesy of Pantry Pride/Food Fair Supermarkets.)

has the ability to scout the markets of wearing apparel and hard goods for interesting and unique types of merchandise; the food merchant does not have the time or the expertise to do this successfully.

Street Vendors. A new type of merchandise resource, the street vendor, offers a convenient yet unique assortment of goods. (See Figure 11.3.) They are usually located on street corners near major traffic intersections in metropolitan areas. These small business operators will set up tables, carts, or stands and sell such items as costume jewelry, handbags and leather items, hats and scarves, incense, books, and whatever else appeals to passersby. The street vendor will purchase merchandise from a wholesaler, usually located in the area. Recently, most cities have passed laws regulating their business activity. For example, laws have been passed controlling the number of vendors on a block and the amount of space between each vendor's stand. Also, some retail stores have complained that street vendors are offering merchandise that is in direct competition with store offerings. Most people, however, enjoy browsing and buying merchandise sold in the atmosphere of the "open-air" market.

Figure 11.3. The street vendor offers a convenient yet unique assortment of goods. (Photograph by Steve Hawkins.)

Nonmerchant Middlemen

Nonmerchant middlemen may be defined as those middlemen who do not take title or assume ownership by taking possession of goods they purchase for resale. These middlemen usually act in behalf of sellers by negotiating sales and performing other services for their principals. The nonmerchant middleman receives a fee for bringing buyer and seller together. Examples of nonmerchant middlemen are brokers, commission men, selling agents, manufacturer's agents, and auctions.

Brokers. Brokers are nonmerchant middlemen whose primary function is to bring buyers and sellers together. Large food chains will utilize the services of food brokers in grocery specialties, dry goods, fruits and vegetables, and other commodities. Merchandise brokers are also found in resident buying offices. They offer the brokerage service to small retailers interested in purchasing hardware, small appliances, furniture, jewelry, and men's and women's fashion apparel. (Review Chapter 4 on the resident buying office.)

Commission Men. Commission men are nonmerchant middlemen who handle merchandise by displaying the goods for resale in a central marketplace. Commission men also handle grocery specialties, dry goods, and fruits and vegetables. They differ from brokers in that they actually receive the merchandise that they display and sell. Commission men constitute a source of supply for large food retailers; they operate out of the central market, deduct their commissions and other fees from the proceeds of the sale, and remit the balance to their principals.

Selling Agents. Selling agents are independent businessmen who take over the entire sales function for their clients by offering advice on styling, extending financial aid, and making collections. Selling agents usually work for small manufacturers of piece goods or fashion apparel or for food specialists who are not large enough to organize their own sales forces. The owner-manager of a small retail outlet is visited by many selling agents, who come to the store and attempt to interest the owner in their merchandise offerings. This type of middleman gives the small retailers the opportunity to see a new line of goods and saves them time, energy, and money by making a trip to the central markets unnecessary. The small retailer is enabled to see merchandise samples and learn how they will tie in to the existing merchandise assortment.

Manufacturers' Agents. Manufacturers' agents, also called *manufacturers' representatives,* are nonmerchant middlemen who take over part of their clients' sales activities and have less authority over prices and terms of sale. Manufacturers' agents are also employed by small manufacturers of soft goods and food specialties, but they are restricted to smaller sales territories and for a variety of reasons may sell only part of their clients' lines. They, too, will call on the small business operator. Along with selling agents, they will also visit department-store buyers, specialty-store buyers, and central buyers of discount, variety, and general-merchandise chains.

Auctions. The *auction* is a type of nonmerchant buying, whereby goods are placed on display and sold quickly to the highest bidder. Auctions are an important source of supply for large supermarket retailers who must purchase fruits and vegetables. Since this kind of merchandise is perishable, the auction affords the opportunity of rapid sales and fast delivery. Proceeds from auctions will go to the shipper after commissions and other charges have been deducted. Small food retailers often buy fruits and vegetables from wholesalers who may have used the auction as their source of supply. The small grocer will usually not go directly to the auction, since he cannot afford to buy large amounts of merchandise, nor does he have the outlet to dispose of them. However, he may join with other small grocers and "pool" the buying activity to take advantage of quantity buying and develop buying power in the marketplace. This is the primary method used by the small grocer to meet the competition of the large food chains.

Manufacturers

Manufacturers are a second main merchandise resource used by retail buyers. A *manufacturer* may be defined as an individual or firm who engages in assembling goods for use by the ultimate consumer. Many retailers prefer to purchase their merchandise directly from the manufacturer, since this may save both time and money and often results in better service. Services offered by the manufacturer may include precise and accurate information regarding specific merchandise lines; advice on advertising and promotion; special assistance and sales training once the merchandise arrives in the store; and suggestions on display techniques and materials.

Direct Buying. Buying direct from the manufacturer affords the retailer other advantages. For example, the buyer of fashion apparel gets the merchandise more quickly, since middlemen are eliminated. Direct buying also affords opportunities to large-scale retailers who are seeking goods made according to their own specifications. For example, Sears, Montgomery Ward, and others are responsible for almost 90 percent of the product lines made to their own specifications. Discount houses, drug chains, department stores, and food operations are also buying on this basis. Also, many smaller retailers have joined together in buying pools. For example, hardware retailers, appliance and TV retailers, and fashion shops have grouped together to take advantage of lower net prices and reduced marketing costs.

Farmers and Growers

The farmer or grower is a third merchandise resource and is an important source of supply primarily to those in the food retailing field. Small food retailers often drive to local growers and purchase fruits and vegetables directly. Large chain retailers such as A & P may send out teams of buyers who actually follow the crops northward as they ripen and keep in constant communication with the central headquarters.

Factors in Selecting Merchandise Resources

Buyers usually prefer to work with a few key resources rather than with many, since a concentrated source of supply will encourage lower prices and better service. However, the concentration of key resources depends to a great extent on the buying power available, as well as upon the desire of the buyer to broaden market contacts by experimenting with new items and new resources.

The buyer will select resources on the basis of what they will do for the retail firm that he or she represents. Merchandise resources are evaluated on the basis of the amount of goods they supply and the profit potential the merchandise will yield the department and store. Buying specialists will maintain a diary on each vendor, which will contain notes of their dealings with each resource for each selling season. The diary may contain information such as:[2]

> Advertising allowances
> Total purchases for the year
> Total purchases for each season
> Purchases at cost and at retail
> Vendor returns
> Initial mark-on percentage
> Delivery and shipping problems
> Receiving and marking problems
> Number and amount of markdowns
> Special orders
> Number and amount of reorders
> Reliability as to delivery and service
> Methods of handling of complaints
> Prestige of line as compared to other store offerings
> Reliability as to merchandise quality
> Number and kind of merchandise defects
> Availability of promotional aids, assist to salespeople

This information will provide the department-store buyer, central buyer, resident buyer, and small-business manager with enough information regarding the amount and profit potential each resource has to contribute.

In most cases, a buyer's resources will show a fine record on those points felt to be of importance to the merchandiser. However, a buyer will often feel a need to add new merchandise resources to take advantage of new and different kinds of goods. How is this task accomplished? How does a buying specialist determine when to eliminate certain resources and start afresh with new ones?

There can be several reasons for change. A resource may permit quality standards to fall off; prices may be increased too high for the buyer to maintain a reasonable markup; or the vendor's line may prove unacceptable to a store's merchandising policies. For these and other reasons the buyer may give up a well-established resource and seek new ones. In consultation with merchandise managers and other store buyers, facts and opinions should be carefully weighed and checked. However, once the decision is made, the buying specialist should consider the factors in the list that follows when selecting merchandise resources.

When selecting merchandise resources
the buyer should consider the following:

Characteristics of the merchandise assortment
Quality   Brand   Availability   Price
Distinctiveness   Styling   Specifications

Competition
Merchandise offering ahead of competition

Method of procurement
Distribution policies   Delivery practices
Shipping quantities   Vendor dependability

Services available
Display units   Warranty   Trained sales force
Demonstrations   Repair   Missionary men

Pricing and terms of sale
Market price   EOM   Thirty days
Market-plus-price   Market-minus-price

Characteristics of the Merchandise Assortment

Characteristics that a buyer considers when inspecting the merchandise offerings are quality, price, distinctiveness, styling, brand, specifications, and availability. As you recall, these topics were discussed in detail in the previous chapter.

These characteristics must suit the preferences of a large segment of the store's clientele as well as have a special appeal to particular shoppers. For example, buyers of fashion goods must purchase goods from vendors who are usually "right on" during most fashion seasons, since hopping from vendor to vendor takes time and may lead to indifference on the part of the vendors. Vendors will learn of a store's likes and dislikes and the nature of the clientele they must cater to. Fashion-oriented resources can help the retail buyer in determining which merchandise lines will appeal to his store's clientele and

Figure 11.4. When selecting the merchandise assortment, characteristics such as quality, brand, price, and distinctiveness are considered.

maintain the fashion image of the store. On the other hand, the buyer of home furnishings must purchase merchandise from vendors who provide quality goods, are prepared to support guarantees, assist buyers in merchandise displays, and offer selling techniques to help stimulate sales.

Competition

Buyers will select those merchandise resources who are fairly successful in avoiding merchandise offerings that are in direct competition. They will look for merchandise that is different and distinctive and is original in style. The buyer will seek vendors who are able to offer such merchandise ahead of the competition. The buyer who is able to obtain goods at the beginning of the selling season is able to capture a good share of the market. His or her store or department will soon become known as the one that is "always first to come out with the newest and latest styles." However, the buyer must be aware of merchandise resources who will offer the same or similar goods to other merchants in the area. This practice may cause friction between the buyer and the resources and lead to a loss of sales to the store's competition.

Method of Procurement

Distribution policies, shipping quantities, delivery practices, and vendor dependability are other factors considered by retail buyers when determining who will be their source of supply. For example, a buyer will usually strive to obtain a line that is confined to his or her particular store. However, many vendors, especially those who make convenience goods, will have a policy of wide distribution. A buyer who needs this type of merchandise must make a choice. Also, buyers must concern themselves with vendors who ship only in gross lots or who ship only small quantities. For example, a buyer who needs quantity may be unable to patronize excellent but small resources that have neither the stock nor the manufacturing facilities to provide enough merchandise. Finally, dependability and reliability of vendors in meeting delivery dates is important. For example, if the buyer finds it difficult to anticipate sales far ahead or to finance or warehouse reserve stocks, quick delivery is vital. A buyer must select a vendor who is located nearby or who has a warehouse in a convenient location to ensure fast, dependable delivery service.

Services Available

Many vendors will take an active interest in their products by offering point-of-sale help. Most small stores and some large ones will take advantage of vendor offerings of display units, fixtures, signs, and other point-of-sale assists. Apart from display services, merchandise resources may train skilled demonstrators, offer warranty and repair service, train a sales force in product knowledge and selling techniques, set up in-store displays, and send out "missionaries" who will check stock and make out orders. (We will discuss this topic in detail in the next chapter.)

Pricing and Terms of Sale

All retail buyers are interested in the price lines and terms of sale offered by merchandise resources. However, the buyer must determine if the vendor's policy is to sell at the (1) market price, (2) market-plus price, or (3) market-minus price.

Market Price. The *market price* is the price established by consumers and competition alike. It is "whatever price the traffic will bear." A merchant will work on a particular markup percent, for example, 50%, 100%, or 300% (which is determined by the types of goods sold, amount of risk involved, and cost of operation), and must consider whether or not the cost of goods offered by the vendor will make it possible to meet the department's profit potential and maintain the store's markup policy.

Market-Plus Price. *Market-plus price* means that the vendor will ask a higher market price on the basis of the special and distinctive characteristics of the merchandise offerings. Usually buyers of boutique goods, specialty-store buyers, and buyers of better-priced merchandise will deal with such vendors. A higher markup percent is maintained by buyers who seek distinctive goods.

Market-Minus Price. *Market-minus price* refers to a vendor's policy of "underselling" by offering less service and less palatable products. Buyers who purchase goods from such vendors are usually seeking discount merchandise for the middle- to lower-income consumer.

Some vendors will maintain a steady price policy throughout the season (market price), offering clearances only toward the end of the season (market-minus price). Or some vendors will offer special price inducements at frequent intervals throughout the season.

In regards to terms of sale, the small retailer, particularly, is looking for merchandise resources who will grant end-of-month (EOM), thirty days, or longer. However, the buyer may decide that long terms may mean the loss of substantial discounts and perhaps lessen the opportunity for vendor assists. We will discuss pricing and terms of sale in the chapters that follow.

Making Contacts with Merchandise Resources

The buyer is often deluged with merchandise offerings; therefore, it is important to have a clear image of the merchandise that is wanted for resale. Such a clear image will help the buyer to select the items that will conform closely to the objectives formulated by the buying plan. A thorough understanding of this plan will assist the buyer when making final decisions, not only on the goods required but on those vendors who will best meet the store's needs. For example, a buyer of women's shoes may go to a shoe manufacturer's showroom and be confronted by forty different styles, in one or two price ranges, one classification, and three colors, and may have to select five styles. Or a buyer of boutique items may attend a special market showing where as many as two hundred vendors will locate on ten floors of a major hotel, all offering a variety of goods of different quality, price, style, and consumer appeal. The boutique buyer may have to inspect more than a thousand items to select sixty. In a houseware or jewelry show or at a furniture mart, the retail buyer must cover hundreds of vendors showing many lines of merchandise, usually all in the space of three to five days.

Since the retail buyer never seems to have enough time or money, he or she must seek those vendors who will accommodate the requirements of the store or department. Since time especially is of the essence, the buyer will usually make vendor contacts before entering the marketplace. Choice of one vendor over another is usually through a process of elimination. The buyer must consider all selection factors before making a final decision.

Buying contacts may be made in two ways: (1) vendors will take the initiative and contact retailers through the use of catalogs, price lists, and salespeople; or (2) retailers will take the initiative and contact vendors by visiting local and central markets and working through resident buying offices and by mail and telephone.

How to make buying contacts

1. The vendor takes the initiative
   Catalogs, price lists, salesmen
2. The retailer takes the initiative
   Visit local central markets; work through resident buying offices or by mail and telephone

---

The Vendor Takes the Initiative

Catalogs and Price Lists. Catalogs and price lists are issued both by manufacturers and wholesalers to provide information concerning their merchandise offerings at the time it is required by the retailer. However, these are used by retail buyers largely for the purchase of fill-in merchandise.

Some vendors will prepare catalogs mainly for use by small retailers located in remote or rural areas. This method of selling has proved successful, since the store does not have to invest in a large inventory and the consumer is willing to wait until the merchandise arrives.

Resident buying offices also prepare catalogs for use by their members. For example, a housewares catalog will describe all the items listed as well as giving the price. Price lists usually have less complete descriptions of the items offered for sale than those appearing in the catalog. Buyers of sewing notions, underwear, small appliances, kitchen utensils, housewares, toys, small leather goods, cleaning aids, closet accessories, laundry and ironing aids, hair goods, beauty supplies—the list is never-ending—will use catalogs and price lists to assist them in merchandise planning.

Salespeople. Using salespeople to call on prospective customers is perhaps the most important activity of vendors. Depending on the stock turnover of certain goods, a salesman or saleswoman may call on a buyer as often as once each week. This makes the practice of hand-to-mouth buying much easier for the buyer. Or, as in the case of drugs and hardware, the vendor's salesmen may contact their retailers daily by telephone to ensure proper stock maintenance. The manager of a small fashion apparel business will depend upon the manufacturer's salespeople because they will provide an opportunity for obtaining

seasonable merchandise and save time, effort, and money. The department-
store buyer will also use the services provided by the manufacturer's salesmen.

A disadvantage of this method, however, is the fact that purchasing
directly through salesmen does not give the buyer an opportunity to compare
the merchandise offerings with those of other manufacturers before placing the
order. The advantages of buying directly from salesmen perhaps outweigh this
disadvantage. For instance, when salesmen bring in samples, the buyer will
show the samples to his salespeople and merchandise manager and seek their
opinions. Also, since buying is done on the retailer's home ground, the buyer
may more adequately visualize how new lines of merchandise will work into
the existing lines. Also, the buyer can usually do a better job of buying, since
he or she has more time and can feel more at ease. This method of buying is
popular with retail businesses of many types and sizes. As you recall, the rack
jobber will visit food markets and small grocers for the primary purpose of
checking and maintaining the merchandise inventory.

The Retailer Takes the Initiative

Visiting Local Markets. If the vendor is located near the retailer, the
retailer will take the initiative and visit him. As previously mentioned, the
small food retailer will often find it advantageous to seek out local growers of
fruits and vegetables and other perishables. Large food retailers will send
buyers into local markets to take advantage of an ample supply of goods at
the best possible price. Retail buyers may also deal with limited wholesalers;
in this case, they will pay cash and take responsibility for transporting the
merchandise to the store. This practice is often used by buyers in small apparel
businesses, since it affords them the opportunity of getting merchandise ahead
of the competition and eliminates some delivery problems.

Visiting Central Markets. More and more buyers, even small retailers, are
going directly into the marketplace. Making direct market visits is one way of
being assured of getting the newest and best styles, the widest selections, and
the lowest prices. Also, it is the best way to make market contacts with new
merchandise resources who have limited selling organizations.

Usually the buyer will use the trip to the market for the purpose of getting
ideas as to what is available, the prices, terms of sale, and and delivery. A buyer
will do most of the actual ordering back in the store or central office, away from
high-pressure salesmen and with the opportunity to consult with staff members.

Resident Buying Offices. Resident buying offices are usually used by department stores and large chain operations. As you recall from reading chapter
4, the resident buyer functions as a merchandise consultant for client stores.
Among the many services offered, the resident buyer will arrange for manufac-

turers' showings, organize fashion shows, scout the marketplace for the best resources, seek the best prices, and utilize those vendors who are most reliable and dependable. Resident buying offices save a great deal of time and energy for member stores and, as a result of the growth and expansion or retail institutions, they have assumed increased importance in the buying-selling activity.

By Mail and Telephone. Staple merchandise is usually kept in stock through mail and telephone orders. The buyer may telephone the order by giving a purchase number and issuing a purchase order shortly thereafter.

Mail and telephone contacts are also used by small retailers for the reordering of fashion merchandise. Or the small retailer may refer to a catalog or price list and send orders to the vendor. The retailers who do this are usually isolated from the buying centers and frequently depend upon catalog descriptions of new goods. This method, however, creates the same difficulty for the buyer that the consumer has when ordering from a catalog. He does not actually see or feel the merchandise and does not have the vendor's formal acceptance or a firm delivery date.

Methods of Buying Merchandise

PART 2

As previously stated, a retail store will add imported goods to its merchandise assortment to obtain a larger markup, offer the unique and the different, and obtain the prestige often associated with imported merchandise. The following five channels of foreign buying may be used: (1) private import wholesalers; (2) foreign exporters or selling houses; (3) purchasing agents or commissionaires; (4) store-owned foreign buying offices; and (5) buying trips to foreign markets.

Selecting Foreign Merchandise Resources

Private Import Wholesalers

Private import wholesalers serve many sizes and types of retail stores that desire foreign products. Import wholesalers are middlemen who purchase samples of foreign products and in turn offer the goods to retailers through the use of catalogs and salespeople. Even though the goods procured from this type of foreign resource cost more than they would if a direct foreign contact were used, the buyer will find that the private wholesaler is a specialist in a particular merchandise category. Also, he or she will usually assume the risks involved in foreign buying as well as the financial responsibility.

Many small businesses use the private import wholesaler. For example, an owner-manager of a women's specialty shop may receive a catalog from a wholesaler who imports women's sweaters and knit accessories from Italy. The owner-manager may select the goods from the catalog or ask the importer to send a salesperson to the shop. The salesperson will show a wide range of samples of the stocks available and discuss quantity discounts, delivery terms, and methods of payment. When a retailer uses foreign merchandise resources, delivery dates and shipping methods are very important, due to the time and distance involved.

Foreign Exporters or Selling Houses

Foreign exporters are middlemen who export goods from a particular country. Often they will locate in the major market centers, such as New York City, where buying specialists may come to visit them in their showrooms and see samples of the various lines they represent. Depending on the size of the selling house, these foreign exporters may have a special import buying show before particular selling seasons to encourage buyers, especially from specialty stores and department stores, to purchase their goods. Foreign exporters will facilitate foreign buying since they are in a better position to understand market conditions and problems with shipping and supply and may communicate with buying sources almost daily. These exporters will also send catalogs or salespeople to retailers to inform them of the merchandise available for sale.

Purchasing Agents or Commissionaires

Purchasing agent is the title given to the individual who represents a foreign resident buying office under American management, whereas *commissionaire* is the title given to the individual who represents a foreign resident buying

Table 11.1. *A store is billed by a commissionaire from the Netherlands.*

Cut glass from Netherlands	18,159.00	gulden*	=	$ 7,350.00	U.S.
Discount	1,271.00	gulden	=	515.00	U.S.
(7%)	16,888.00	gulden	=	6,835.00	U.S.
Buying commission	2,533.00	gulden	=	1,025.00	U.S.
(15%)	19,421.00	gulden	=	7,860.00	U.S.
Packaging (1%)	194.20	gulden	=	78.00	U.S.
Consular invoice (13%)	2,525.00	gulden	=	1,022.00	U.S.
Total	22,140.00	gulden	=	$ 8,960.00	U.S.

*Present money rate of foreign exchange: 2.47 gulden = $1.00 U.S. dollar

office under foreign management. Foreign resident buying offices operate in much the same way as salaried resident buying offices in American cities. These offices assist buying specialists in selecting merchandise for resale. Foreign resident buying offices generally charge a percentage of the net foreign cost of the purchases they make, usually 7 to 8 percent. Some foreign buying offices also work with New York resident buying offices so that buyers from stores that belong to the buying office in New York may make use of the services of the commissionaire when abroad. A store may be billed by a commissionaire from the Netherlands, for example, as Table 11.1 illustrates.

Store-owned Foreign Buying Office

A foreign buying office may also be store-owned, that is, owned by a group of noncompeting stores, which will share expenses for the operation and maintenance of the foreign office. For example, the Associated Merchandising Corporation and the Associated Dry Goods Corporation maintain buying offices in London, and the Great Atlantic & Pacific Tea Company (A & P) has buying offices in Colombia and Brazil to purchase coffee beans. The association type of foreign buying office, like the association type of resident buying office, makes possible the exchange of information among member stores, provides ample opportunity for increased buying power for each member store, and gives each store control over the operation of the foreign buying office. Managers of foreign offices will make numerous visits to the stores they represent in this country. During these visits the foreign agent will determine the needs of individual stores and provide a wide assortment of samples for the inspection of various buying specialists. For example, a buyer for a wig department will discuss with the foreign buying specialist the availability of new styles of wigs and hairpieces, the costs of importing the merchandise, shipping and delivery terms, special and promotional goods, and so forth. In turn, the foreign specialist will inform the buyer of how well merchandise is or is not selling in different parts of the country and discuss popular styles and any problems encountered.

Buying Trips to Foreign Markets

The last method of purchasing foreign goods is for buying specialists, particularly chain and department-store buyers, to visit foreign merchandise resources personally. Usually, buyers of high-priced fashion apparel and accessories, giftware, and linens and related domestics will visit foreign markets. For example, a buyer of fashion goods may visit foreign markets late in the winter season and during the spring season to have the merchandise when required. A buyer of linens and domestics may visit foreign resources at least once a year. Today, buyers find it desirable to make direct contact with foreign resources because of the need to style foreign goods to meet the requirements set by American manufacturers.

The foreign buying trip, like the buying trip to domestic markets, requires careful and accurate planning. For example, the buyer of a better dresses department will draw up a foreign purchase plan, on which are listed the assortment of goods according to size, style, color, etc., the quantity to be purchased, the expected costs, terms and methods of shipping, delivery time, discounts available, and terms of sale. Often the buyer will tour several countries, in which case a separate plan should be made out for each resource visited. Once the foreign buying plan is developed, however, the buyer must plan the details of the buying trip—for example, the itinerary to be followed, the date of arrival in each country, the departure time, the hotel accommodations, and so forth. Planning will enable the store to keep in touch with the buyer and allow the foreign buying agent to prepare for the buyer's arrival. It will also ensure that the buyer's time is budgeted properly so that too much time is not spent with certain resources early in the trip, leaving too little time at the end for the new and unexpected.

While personal visits to foreign markets provide an opportunity to find the unique and the unusual, there are disadvantages. For example, while the buyer of better dresses is visiting foreign resources, the department tends to suffer. Problems may arise with regard to lost or delayed shipments, slow sellers, inadequacy of sales personnel, customer complaints about inferior goods, and so on.

A major objection to making trips abroad is the expense and time involved. Usually, however, the expense is compensated for by the profit increase resulting from purchasing foreign goods, and time spent may be minimized as the result of air travel.

Another objection is that it is difficult for the buyer to estimate needs. The goods in their foreign setting may possess glamour and excitement, but at home they may be found to be uninteresting or out of place with respect to the rest of the merchandise line. For example, a leather coat may look very luxurious against its native setting, however, when compared to American-made products the coat may look inferior.

Finally, when buyers go to foreign markets, there is a tendency to rush through the buying process, attempting to view as many different lines as possible and perhaps purchasing hastily due to tight buying schedules. Sometimes the time schedule is so tight that the buyer is not able to consult with

---

When will the buying specialist use the following foreign buying resources and methods?

Private import wholesaler
Foreign exporter or selling house
Purchasing agent or commissionaire
Store-owned foreign buying office
Buying trips to foreign markets

foreign craftsmen or smaller, less popular resources to find the best in foreign-made goods—goods that will meet the needs and tastes of the American consumer.

Beyond those factors already discussed, the buyer's job may be further compli-cated by the numerous methods of buying available. Since these methods may affect the development of the buying plan as well as the cost of doing business, buyers in all types and sizes of retail stores must be aware of sound buying practices. The buyer has the responsibility not only for procuring goods that meet the needs and wants of the store's customers but also for protecting the store's reputation. It is important to recognize the numerous advantages of following merchandising policies based on fair play and honesty, which help the buying specialist to develop and maintain a good reputation in the market-place and thus to be a successful and profitable retail merchant.

Methods of Buying

This spirit of sound buying practices should be followed in the procure-ment of goods, domestic and foreign, by the numerous methods of buying available.[3] These methods are: (1) regular buying; (2) buying job lots; (3) buying irregulars and seconds; (4) specification buying; (5) advance buying; (6) promotional buying; (7) consignment or memo buying; and (8) special-order buying.

A buying specialist may use the following buying methods

1. Regular buying
2. Buying job lots
3. Buying irregulars and seconds
4. Specification buying
5. Advance buying
6. Promotional buying
7. Consignment or memo buying
8. Special-order buying

Regular Buying

Regular buying, or buying goods at regular retail prices, is the method used by most buyers of fashion merchandise and staple goods. The buyer is assured of a normal delivery period of from two to four weeks, the usual discount of 2/10 net 30, extra dating whereby the buyer is given a specified number of extra days to pay the bill, a return privilege, and so forth. (Terms used in finance and credit will be discussed in detail in the next chapter.) The buyer will order goods he or she thinks will sell and then place reorders as soon as possible to keep an adequate supply of merchandise in stock at all times. For example, the fashion buyer of men's shirts will draw as much information as possible from salesmen who come to the store, from the representative in the market center (the resident buyer), and from personal visits to manufacturers.

While viewing a line, the buyer will take up each major classification in turn, for example, knit shirts, silk-screened shirts, or long-sleeved shirts, and within each subclass start with the highest price lines and work down to the lowest. Usually the fashion buyer will examine merchandise at the top of the line because better-priced merchandise will often be the first to show new colors and details, style trends, and new fashion ideas. As stated previously, buying fashion merchandise is more of an art than buying staple goods. The fashion buyer is limited by the season or selling period, which is usually only a few months. As noted in previous chapters, the past history of particular styles, fashion trends, and popular colors and patterns is often not of much assistance in determining consumer acceptance, since customer tastes may completely change with each new season. However, while the popularity of a new fashion style may be unknown at the beginning of the fashion season, the buyer is reasonably confident when planning purchases by price ranges and sizes. Past sales records are guides in making these decisions. On the other hand, initial orders of new styles of merchandise are often placed with little or no sales information. However, a good buyer will use the services of market experts and give close attention to the judgment of the merchandise manager as well as his or her own merchandising experience when determining the merchandise assortment.

The buyer of staple goods will also use the regular buying method when purchasing goods. However, most staple products or never-out goods may, with some seasonal variations, be purchased mechanically or automatically through the store's computer system. Once the buyer determines the composition of the merchandise assortment, the quantity, and the price range, adequate stock will be planned to minimize inventory "outs." As you recall from chapter 9, the amount to be purchased at any one time depends on sales estimates for the coming season, the quantity of goods on hand and on order, and the desired stock at the end of the selling season.

In some types of retail stores, for example, discount houses, there is a temptation to operate with minimum inventory and hand-to-mouth buying. As a result, a smaller investment is required, and money is available to broaden the merchandise assortment and add new lines of goods. The disadvantage of buying in this way is that unexpectedly large sales or slow deliveries may lead to the store's being out of stock, so that customers will shop elsewhere. On the other hand, a surplus of stock may result from the desire to take advantage of quantity discounts or special buys and lead to high markdowns and slow selling of goods. The quantity of goods on hand can be determined by stock reports. Usually, a stock count is required immediately prior to reordering to determine how much is needed.

The regular buying method requires the buying specialist of fashion goods and staple items to determine the maximum or total amount of goods on order and on hand. As you recall from our discussion in chapter 9, the following formula may be used when ordering fashion goods or staple items:

Maximum = (Reorder Period + Delivery Period) Rate of Sales + Reserve

    M   RP   DP   S   R

or

Maximum + (Lead Time) Rate of Sales + Reserve

   M   LT = RP + DP   S   R

Buying Job Lots

A *job lot* may be defined as an assortment of merchandise the vendor has been unable to sell at regular prices and is now offering at a reduced price per item. The buyer will not buy job lots unless the price is low enough to ensure that the entire lot will sell at a satisfactory markup.

Since the lot is an assortment of vendor leftovers of various styles, sizes, and colors, the buyer must be careful in determining how these items will fit into existing stock. For example, a department-store buyer of curtains and drapery accessories will purchase job lots for a special January clearance sale. The assortment may consist of limited color selections, out-of-season patterns and prints, extra wide panels, and limited styles and sizes. This assortment of leftovers will round out the end-of-season stock to make an interesting offering for bargain-hunting customers.

Many retail buyers will use the job-lot method of buying. The small business owner, the discounter, the specialty-store buyer, the chain buyer—all will shop the various trade markets seeking specials to pass on to their customers. However, the buyers must be certain the job lots they select will not lead to increased markdowns, lower the store's image of quality merchandise offerings, or detract from already existing lines of goods. He or she must not be talked into making purchases that will lead to lost sales. Often a buyer may purchase things he or she does not like to round out the assortment according to size, color, price, or whatever. It would be very unwise for a buyer to purchase only those goods that appealed to personal likes or dislikes. A good merchandiser will develop an awareness of what to look for and be quick to distinguish what customers' tastes are for both regular goods and special buys.

Buying Irregulars and Seconds

An *irregular* may be defined as an item that contains an imperfection or repair not visible to the naked eye. A *second* may be defined as an item that contains a more obvious damage or repair. This definition may also be applied to "thirds." Manufacturers will often have merchandise left over at the end of the selling season. To rid themselves of unwanted goods, they offer these items to buyers at reduced prices. Manufacturers may inform retail buyers of their offerings through trade-paper advertisements, by word of mouth, or through market representatives. (See Figure 11.5.) Many buyers will purchase these substandard units, since very often the performance or durability of the product remains unimpaired. The saving is passed on to the customer. Also, the values achieved are often greater than those of perfect goods that have been manufactured at a lower quality. However, some buyers will not purchase irregulars and seconds, since they feel their quality image may be damaged, while others will offer only limited amounts.

Figure 11.5. An example of a buyer's offer as advertised in a popular trade journal.

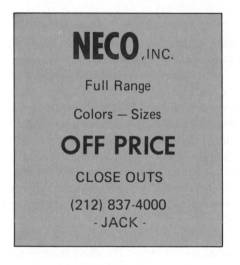

When shopping, you may notice that a special tag or ticket is affixed to a garment or product informing you that the item is an irregular or second; depending on the imperfection or the repair, the merchant will adjust the price accordingly. Perhaps you will find knit dresses or knit trousers that contain tiny pulls or snags. If the imperfection is hardly noticeable, you will purchase the item and take advantage of the lower price offering.

A vendor will offer irregulars and seconds at reduced prices to deplete his own stocks as well as to provide special buys to store merchants. However, the buyer must be certain that goods purchased will meet the demand flow, coordinate with assortments offered in his or her own as well as in other departments, and continue to maintain merchandising policies set forth by top store management. The buyer must consider the risks involved in offering imperfect goods at the end of the season, the markup, and the kind and amount of pulling power possessed by such items.

Specification Buying

Specification buying may be a request by a central buyer, a department-store buyer, or a resident buyer for minor changes in a product that has already been produced, or it may include specifications for production from raw materials to final package.

Today many stores urge their buyers to do specification buying instead of using national branded items. This method of buying enables the store to offer merchandise that is different from that offered by its competition and often of better quality at prices considerably lower than those asked for comparable national brands. Customers will benefit from this type of buying because they are provided a merchandise assortment that is distinctive and unique. For example, a central buyer for a general merchandise chain in consultation with top store managers may decide to sell tennis rackets under the name of the store. The sporting-goods buyer will carefully study the market, learn to know the product thoroughly, investigate the kinds of tennis rackets sold in other stores, and search for manufacturers who are willing and able to produce the product wanted. Once manufacturers are located, the buyer must specifiy the quantities required and the cost price he or she is willing to pay, and discuss other requirements that will make the product different from those already on the market. Manufacturers find specification buying advantageous because it provides an opportunity for year-round production, since large orders are usually placed well in advance of normal production requests. Also, since goods are produced in quantity, a discount is passed on to the central buyer, who in turn may take a normal or near-normal markup, depending on the competition from other stores.

On the other hand, the small business buyer may have to join with other small businesses and form buying pools to encourage a manufacturer to "tool up" or make minor changes in a product. The small business may have a more difficult time locating a manufacturer, since it does not have the buying power, that is, it does not have the ability to buy in large quantities as do chain operations or department stores. For this reason, you will usually not find a small business offering goods under its own private label.

Advance Buying

Advance buying is used primarily by buyers of staple goods. It permits the buyer to place orders in advance of the selling season; as an incentive, the buyer is offered a discount by the vendor. The buyer may in turn pass the savings on to customers; or, if the merchandise must be warehoused, the savings will be used to pay part of the cost of warehousing.

Advance buying ensures adequate delivery and a steady flow of merchandise. For example, the store manager of a variety chain is usually assured of a steady flow of goods because the central buyer has ordered merchandise in advance of the season. Since staple goods are never "out" and are always needed by store customers, the risk of purchasing in advance and placing goods in a warehouse is minimized. The central buyer may also arrange to have certain goods delivered to store units at various times to avoid having to handle all the merchandise at one time. The Christmas season is a good example. The central buyer may arrange with manufacturers to have Christmas-tree ornaments shipped either directly to individual store units during September, October, and November, or to have them sent directly to a distribution center, from which store managers may request them as they are needed.

The fashion buyer will also use advance buying. However, the buyer must be certain that the merchandise will not become out of style while it is in the warehouse. For example, a buyer of ladies' robes may wish to place advance orders to ensure a balanced stock of goods throughout a particular selling season, for example, Mother's Day. Usually, advance orders will be placed for already proved styles, classic lines, or basic types of soft goods. Fashion apparel buyers will place advance orders for special sales promotions, the Christmas season, the spring season, or whenever large amounts of goods are required.

Promotional Buying

Stores are always featuring special events and general sales promotions, and buyers are continuously seeking special purchases. If the store is having a pre-Easter Sale, the buyer will seek merchandise of a lower price that will appeal to customers interested in purchasing goods for the spring season, for example, children's shoes, women's spring coats, or paint and garden supplies. The buyer must be careful in calculating the amount of merchandise required for the sale. Previous sales records may provide some information; however, the buyer must also rely on previous experience with regular-line merchandise and personal knowledge of the consumer market. For example, a store may be having an Oriental promotion, and the buying specialists may be required to seek resources offering appropriate goods to feature during the event. A buyer of fashion goods may offer women's blouses with Oriental designs on silk fabric; a buyer of men's better sportswear may feature quilted jackets with mandarin collars; a buyer of loungewear and pajamas may offer two-piece silk pajamas, while a buyer of giftware may offer various imports that carry the Oriental influence.

Consignment or Memo Buying

In *consignment or memo buying,* the buyer and vendor agree that within a given period of time the buyer may return the merchandise to the vendor. This type of buying occurs when the merchandise is very expensive, when it is a new and high-risk item, or when the buyer feels the cost of the merchandise is too high. The agreement worked out between the vendor and the buyer is that the buyer will take the merchandise on consignment or on memorandum.

With this method of buying, the vendor may show his merchandise, for example, jewelry, in a showcase located in the jewelry department of the retail store. Once the merchandise is sold, the store takes title and pays the vendor. The cost of merchandise ordered by this method is usually higher than that of merchandise ordered by other methods; therefore, the store does not usually gain the same percent of markup. However, if the goods are not sold, the buyer has risked very little, since he has no money invested in the stock. We will discuss this topic in detail in Chapter 13.

Special-Order Buying

A store may offer an individualized service whereby customers may order special merchandise. In this case, the buyer must "special order," that is, place orders with the vendor indicating a particular color, size, or style. Since this service (*special-order buying*) takes time in order placement, checking, and receiving, as well as additional costs from the vendor, it is primarily used by full-service stores. Also, stores offering limited selections in color, size, and style may use this method of buying and make almost as many sales as those offering larger merchandise selections. The overall savings in small inventories will often more than compensate for the extra cost charged by the vendor.

A small business will use this buying method to provide a special service to persons who are good steady customers. This is one method a small business may use to meet competition. Department stores and specialty shops, especially those dealing in men's and women's fashion apparel, will also special order for certain customers. For example, a men's wear buyer may place an order for a customer who wants a suit in size 44 extra long. Or a buyer in the women's better suit department may special order a smaller size jacket rather than break up a suit ensemble. Special orders may be placed by the buyer of handbags and leather goods whereby a monogramming and initialing service is made available; thus, something unique and interesting has been added to an otherwise ordinary merchandise assortment.

The buying specialist will soon learn that selecting merchandise to implement the buying plan is basically a process of elimination. The "perfect item," the "best seller," the "sure winner" is not likely simply to declare itself the season's best seller. More often the buyer must seek it out and discover it from among the many items that are almost right. Before purchasing goods for resale, the buyer, department manager, or store manager must have a clear image of what is wanted and needed by the store's clientele. The purchaser must work within the guidelines set forth by the store's merchandising team and follow established procedures. Thus, the buying methods discussed will be used to provide merchandise assortments that will prove profitable to the department as well as to the store as a whole.

Review the buying methods discussed
1. Regular buying 2. Buying job lots 3. Buying irregulars and seconds 4. Specification buying 5. Advance buying 6. Promotional buying 7. Consignment or memo buying 8. Special-order buying
How will each method be used by the following buying specialists?
The toy buyer in a department store A buyer of boys' wear in a discount house A children's wear buyer in a small business The housewares buyer in a department store

Chapter Summary

Three major sources of supply are available to the retail buyer. The buyer must first determine which major source of supply will best suit the needs of the store or department. Once this decision is made, he must determine who will be the key resources, that is, where buying interests will be concentrated. This concentration on key resources depends to a great extent upon the buying power available, as well as upon the desire of the buyer to broaden market contacts by experimenting with new items and new resources. The buyer must weigh all the selection factors before making a decision as to the choice of merchandise resources. For example, the type of retail institution that he or she represents, the classification of merchandise bought, the competition in the marketplace, the buyer's own qualifications and past experiences and finally, his or her merchandise know-how—all will enter into the decision as to which merchandise resources will best suit the needs of the department or store, and thus make a profit.

The buyer may take the initiative and seek merchandise resources by visiting local markets, by going into the central marketplace, or by using the services of a resident buying office, which in turn may seek particular vendors.

Retail buyers will also use the mails and the telephone to contact vendors, particularly for reorders and follow-up.

Buying contacts may be made by the vendor, who may take the initiative and send catalogs and price lists to retailers interested in staple merchandise. The vendor may also send salesmen who will show samples and take orders. Using salesmen to call upon prospective customers is a most important activity of the vendor. This method of buying contact will often make the practice of hand-to-mouth buying much easier for the buyer, as well as ensuring proper stock maintenance.

Many types of retail institutions have also found it advantageous to purchase goods for resale from foreign resources. Resources may be contacted in much the same way as in the domestic market. For example, a buyer may seek information regarding foreign merchandise resources by contacting the resident buying office. Or foreign resources may send catalogs and price lists to prospective clients. In some cases, foreign offices will send salesmen who will display lines of merchandise and provide samples for their buyers. As a result of competition in the domestic market, retail buyers have turned to imported merchandise because such commodities provide an opportunity for a larger markup, create an atmosphere of the unusual and different, and add an image of prestige and leadership to a retail store.

Not only is a buyer's job complicated by the numerous lines of merchandise available and by the many sources from which information may be purchased and obtained, but also there are numerous methods of buying available. The buyer may use the regular methods of buying, buy job lots, buy irregulars and seconds, do specification buying, buy in advance, use promotional buying, seek consignment and memo buying, or use special-order buying. However, the methods used will depend upon the store's buying plan and the cost of doing business.

Trade Terminology

DIRECTIONS: Briefly explain or discuss each of the following trade terms:

1. Middlemen
2. Wholesalers
3. Merchant middlemen
4. Service wholesalers
5. Limited-function wholesaler
6. Rack jobbers
7. Nonmerchant middlemen
8. Brokers
9. Commission men
10. Selling agents
11. Manufacturers' Agents
12. Auctions
13. Manufacturers
14. Market price
15. Market-plus price
16. Market-minus price
17. Purchasing agent
18. Commissionaire
19. Job lot
20. Irregular
21. Second

Questions for Discussion and Review

1. Why is selecting a merchandise resource largely a process of elimination?

2. Distinguish between middlemen, manufacturers, and farmers and growers.

3. Explain how the buyer with a buying plan for small electric appliances determines who will be a source of supply.

4. How do you explain the fact that some retail buyers go to the central market frequently, while others go to the central market very little?

5. As a buyer of small leather accessories, you wish to expand your purchases of foreign goods. How would you accomplish this? Explain.

6. What are the major methods of making buying contacts? Explain each.

7. Why must a retail buyer give close consideration to the many methods of buying available?

8. What problems and responsibilities does a buyer who engages in buying job lots assume? Irregulars? Seconds and thirds? Consignment and memo buying?

9. Why do many retailers still use the services of middlemen as opposed to buying directly from manufacturers?

10. What advantages does special-order buying afford the retailer? The consumer?

Case Study Number One

Going to the Market A buyer for a men's shoe department in a small department store decided that he could increase sales volume by assessing new but related lines of merchandise. Since he did not use the services of a resident buying office, he had to make his own market contacts by visiting shoe manufacturers in the central market and by seeing sales representatives as they came to the store. He soon realized, however, that locating new merchandise resources was no easy task. He found that going to the market was very time-consuming and that his departmental duties and responsibilities began to suffer. Also, he was interested not only in adding new items but also imported goods.

Be prepared in class to discuss what advice you would offer the shoe buyer to help him locate new merchandise resources. How would he locate foreign merchandise resources?

Case Study Number Two

Monroe's is a large department store located in the Northwest. Mike Jackson, **The Better of Two**
the buyer of men's sweaters, was asked to make a special purchase of seventy dozen sweaters for a forthcoming storewide pre-Christmas sale. After the four-day sale, all merchandise that was not sold would be marked up to its original value. For this reason, Mike Jackson was directed by his merchandise manager not to purchase seconds, irregulars, odd prices and colors, etc. He was further instructed to maintain an initial markup of 45 percent on all special purchases, if possible.

After visiting several manufacturers, Mike Jackson determined that he had two suppliers from which to select his goods. The first supplier was one with whom he had been doing business with over the past year and with whose line he was familiar. This manufacturer, however, had a limited selection of styles, which he would offer at a special price. The buyer would have the option of selecting suitable colors and sizes, but style selection was limited and did not include best sellers. The cost price of the goods, however, would enable the buyer to maintain his initial markup goal of 45 percent.

The second merchandise resource was a manufacturer with whom Mike Jackson had not done business previously. Since the manufacturer was very anxious to secure Monroe's account, Mike Jackson was offered a one-time special price on seventy dozen sweaters. He was also given the opportunity of selecting the sizes, styles, and colors required from the manufacturer's complete line. However, the special price offered would only allow him to obtain an initial markup of 37 percent.

In your opinion, which supplier would offer Mike Jackson the best opportunity to obtain his merchandise goal?

Retailing Activities to Stimulate Student Interest and Participation

1. Prepare a short paper on the importance of selecting suitable merchandise resources. Refer to the Retailing Student's Reference Library for research references.

2. Select a leading retail department store in your local shopping area. Make an appointment with a buyer of staple goods to discuss the various methods of buying and how they are used by a buyer of staple goods. Interview the

buyer of fashion merchandise. Discuss the various methods of buying fashion goods. Compare and evaluate your findings.

3. Interview a store manager from a general merchandise chain like J. C. Penney, Sears, or Montgomery Ward. Discuss with the manager how specification buying is used in private brand development.

REFERENCES

The Retailing Student's Reference Library

Alpert, M. I. *Pricing Decisions.* Glenview, Ill.: Scott, Foresman & Company, 1971.

Applebaum, W., and Goldberg, R. *Brand Strategy in U.S. Food Marketing.* Boston: Harvard University Press, n.d.

Cahill, Jane. *Can a Smaller Store Succeed?* New York: Fairchild Publications, Inc., n.d.

Duncan, D. J., and Hermanson, R. H. *Retailing: Modern Concepts and Practices.* Homewood, Ill.: Learning Systems Company, 1970.

Ferguson, F. *Efficient Drug Store Management.* New York: Fairchild Publications, Inc., n.d.

Fine, I. B., Westing, J. H., and Zenz, G. J. *Purchasing Management.* New York: John Wiley & Sons, 1970.

Fried, Eleanor L. *Is the Fashion Business Your Business?* New York: Fairchild Publications, Inc., 1970.

Gold, E. B. *Dynamics of Retailing.* New York: Fairchild Publications, Inc., n.d.

Helfant, S., and Judelle, B. *Management Manual for Independent Stores.* New York: National Retail Merchants Association, n.d.

Hoffman, E., Buck, B. F., and Small, V. *Fairchild's Directory of Home Furnishings.* New York: Fairchild Publications, Inc., 1972.

Jimerson, H. C., and Rowe, K. L. *Communications in Marketing.* Hightstown: McGraw-Hill Book Company, 1971.

Judelle, B. *The Fashion Buyer's Job.* New York: National Retail Merchants Association, 1971.

Judelle, B., and Troxell, M. *Fashion Merchandising.* Hightstown: McGraw-Hill Book Company, 1971.

Kelley, P. C. *Variety Stores.* Washington, D.C.: Small Business Administration, n.d.

Mulhern, Helen. *Facts about Department Stores.* New York: National Retail Merchants Association, n.d.

Orbach, E., Ayal, I., and Jehiel, J. *Marketing a New Product.* New York: Macmillan Company, 1971.

Profitable Merchandising Techniques. New York: Fairchild Publications, Inc., 1970.

Promoting New Merchandising Areas. New York: Fairchild Publications, Inc., 1971.

Readings in Modern Retailing. New York: National Retail Merchants Association, 1970.

A Retailer Visits the Market. New York: Fairchild Publications, Inc., n.d.

Retailer's Guide to Buying Appliances. New York: National Retail Merchants Association, 1970.

Rice, J. W. *Furniture Retailing.* Washington, D.C.: Small Business Administration, n.d.

Ritter, Dorothy. *Hardware Retailing.* Washington, D.C.: Small Business Administration, n.d.

Robinson, J. W. *Gift and Art Shops.* Washington, D.C.: Small Business Administration, n.d.

Slom, S. *Profitable Furniture Retailing: For the Home Furnishing Markets.* New York: Fairchild Publications, Inc., n.d.

Taylor, C. G. *Merchandise Assortment Planning.* New York: National Retail Merchants Association, n.d.

Valentine, R. E. *Bookstore Operation.* Washington, D.C.: Small Business Administration, n.d.
Zanetti, Giacomo. *Principles of Profitable Importing.* New York: National Retail Merchants
    Association, 1971.

References

1. D. J. Duncan and C. F. Phillips, *Retailing Principles and Methods* (Homewood, Ill.: Richard
    D. Irwin, Inc., 1969), p. 307.
2. Beatrice Judelle, *The Fashion Buyer's Job* (New York: National Retail Merchants Association,
    1971), p. 79.
3. *The Buyer's Manual* (New York: National Retail Merchants Association, 1970), p. 75.

Services Offered by Merchandise Resources

12

Performance Objectives

PERFORMANCE
OBJECTIVES

As a result of reading this chapter the student should be able to accomplish the following:

1. Classify under major headings services offered by merchandise vendors.

2. Discuss the differences between personal and nonpersonal promotional aids.

3. List and define six selling aids offered by vendors.

4. Define the terms used in finance and credit.

5. Discuss six promotional allowances offered by vendors that reprice.

6. Explain three types of dealer helps and tell how they may be useful in attracting customer attention and interest.

7. Become aware of six types of consumer inducements used by retailers.

Services Offered by Merchandise Resources

Personal Promotion Aids

As mentioned previously, many retail buyers find it advantageous to do most of their business with a few key suppliers. There are a large number of merchandise resources located in the central market, with each handling many lines of merchandise; it would be confusing to have to work with so many vendors. Buyers have found that purchasing from only a few merchandise resources reduces the number of contacts, thus saving time and energy as well as minimizing adjustments that may arise from shipping errors. Consolidating orders with a few key resources has many advantages, too. Credit terms, adequate delivery, cash discounts, and liberal adjustment policies are but a few of the advantages that may result. Also, merchandise resources are willing to give a little extra attention to those buyers who they know will account for a significant portion of their business.

A Little Extra Attention

These advantages may occur in the form of vendor services. The scope and amount of services will vary from one vendor to another. The buyer must narrow the choice and eliminate those merchandise resources that will not best meet requirements.

The purpose of Part 1 of this chapter will be to discuss: (1) personal promotion aids; (2) types of vendor's selling aids; and (3) various types of promotional allowances that are available from vendors. Part 2 will discuss nonpersonal promotional aids. Topics to be considered are: (1) types of dealer helps available; (2) methods used to encourage consumers to buy; and (3) how nonpersonal promotional aids are used by various buying specialists.

When the buyer goes to the marketplace, he or she must be guided by past experience and judgment, as well as the knowledge that most merchandise resources have both the background and the incentive to provide fruitful assistance. An important responsibility of all buyers is to solicit every service to which the store is entitled that is available from the merchandise broker, wholesaler, rack jobber, vendor, and so forth. Sometimes a buyer may have to request a particular service, offer suggestions for additional services, or seek

Services Offered by Vendors

improvements on those services already available. Of course, the services offered to merchants will depend on the type of merchandise resource, the amount and nature of the business conducted between retailer and supplier, and the type of buyer-vendor relationship established. (This subject will be covered in detail in the next chapter.) Beatrice Judelle suggests that the following types of services may be available from merchandise resources:[1]

* Cash discounts at least equal to those prevailing in the trade
* Payment by the seller of some or all transportation costs
* Cooperative advertising arrangements
* Advertising aids, such as glossy photos (from which the store can have cuts made), copy suggestions, mats, broadcast scripts
* Special numbers and prices for store promotion
* Exclusive distribution
* Return and exchange privileges
* Allowances for mark-downs on the merchandise
* Participation in store fashion events by sending trunk shows, visiting fashion experts, other consumer attractions
* Materials or manpower to inform and stimulate the salespeople
* Assistance in stock counts and stock control
* Pre-ticketing
* Advance information on planned national advertising and possibility of mention of store name
* Back-up stock
* Precise information on fiber content, fur origin, and other requirements laid down by Government regulations.

For purposes of study, however, vendor services may be divided into two types. First, *personal promotional aids* are those services that directly affect the selling activity of the buyer; they include the vendor's selling aids and promotional allowances. Second, *nonpersonal promotional aids* are those services that directly influence the buying behavior of the consumer; they include dealers' helps and consumer inducements.

Services offered by vendors
Personal Promotion Aids 1. Vendor's selling aids 2. Promotional allowances Nonpersonal Promotion Aids 1. Dealer's helps 2. Consumer inducements

Vendor's Selling Aids   The following is a list of selling aids offered by vendors. However, it is important to remember that the buyer must determine if the services available are in the buyer's best interests, those of the retail organization, and those of the clientele.

Selling Aids Offered by the Vendor Are:	
1. Demonstrators	4. Exclusive distribution
2. Finance and credit	5. Markdown insurance
3. Return privilege	6. On memorandum

Demonstrators

Assistance from vendors in connection with personal selling is often welcomed by the retail buyer. In housewares and cosmetics, especially, vendors will often provide their client stores with demonstrators. These individuals will demonstrate the product to salespeople, pointing out product advantages, suggesting selling techniques, and relating pertinent merchandise facts that will help to sell the product. Also, demonstrators may actually demonstrate the item on the floor, showing store customers how to use a particular product to best advantage. In this case, resulting sales may be turned over to regular salespeople, or the demonstrator may actually complete the sale.

Demonstrators are usually used in departments where brand reputation is important. In this case, the department's selling costs are reduced since trained demonstrators are responsible for increasing department sales. However, a retail store must be careful when using demonstrators, especially if they are responsible for completing sales. For example, a customer may come to the department seeking an item, only to be misled by the demonstrator, who is "pushing" a particular brand. The customer may purchase the brand being promoted by the department only to be dissatisfied with the product later.

Usually, when a store decides to use demonstrators, it will place them through its personnel office. The purpose of this procedure is to have it clearly understood that demonstrators are employees of the store and thus subject to the store's merchandising policies and procedures. If this procedure is not followed, it may become difficult to get demonstrators to observe store regulations. The small business, on the other hand, does not use demonstrators, since the cost of their services is not in proportion to the volume of purchases made by the owner-manager. As a result, the small business manager will seek an alternate service from vendors, for example, displays that can help sell merchandise.

Finance and Credit

A second important service offered by many vendors is finance and credit. Most retail buying is accomplished on an open-account basis, with 30 days allowed from date of the invoice until payment. Often a discount is allowed if the bill is paid in a shorter period of time, such as ten days. There are particular terms the student should become familiar with, since this information is necessary in order placement and receiving and in vendor negotiations. The list of credit terms that follows will also be discussed in subsequent chapters.

Advanced Dating. In the case of advanced dating, the invoice is dated from a specified future date, not from the designated invoice date. For example, the invoice covering a shipment of towels made on October 15 may have terms of 2/10 net 30 as of December 1. This arrangement will give the buyer until January 1 to pay the bill. This technique will provide a store that is inadequately financed with an opportunity to sell merchandise before paying for it.

Anticipation. An extra discount is taken for paying an invoice in advance of the cash discount date. This is usually done by those store buyers who have ready cash available. The buyer will deduct interest, usually at the rate of 6 percent a year, for the number of days of prepayment.

Cash Discount. A reduction in price is allowed by the vendor for prompt payment. The common practice is to allow the retail buyer 10 days from the invoice date. For example, if the goods are shipped on August 5, with terms of 2/10 net 30, the invoice must be paid on August 15 to earn a discount of 2 percent. The entire amount is due on September 4.

COD Dating. Cash on Delivery terms state that merchandise may be sold for cash on delivery. However, nearly all retail stores have achieved a credit rating that permits them to buy on credit.

Consignment. Merchandise sold on consignment does not become the property of the buyer, but remains the property of the seller. Unsold goods are returned to the vendor.

Dating. This refers to the length of time the seller will extend credit to the store buyer. For example, the vendor may state net 30 or net 60, which signifies that the bill must be paid within thirty days or sixty days of the invoice date.

EOM. End of Month states that the time for payment is calculated from the end of the month in which the invoice is dated and the merchandise shipped, and not from the invoice date. For example, if dresses are shipped on May 5, they do not have to be paid for until a specified number of days after May 31. In ready-to-wear EOM is a typical term.

Extra Dating. The buyer is given a specified number of extra days in which to pay the bill and to earn the discount. For example, instead of 30 days, the buyer may be granted 60 extra days, giving a total of 90 days, or 120 days, giving a total of 150 days. Additional days may also be extended to enable a buyer to earn a discount, for example, 2/10–90 extra.

If the goods are shipped on September 10, with terms of 2/10 net 90, the invoice must be paid on September 20 to earn a discount of 2 percent. The entire amount is due on December 8.

Floor Plan. The vendor will turn an assortment of merchandise over to the store buyer, who in return signs a trust receipt. The title will remain with the vendor, and the store buyer agrees to make payment as he makes sales. This finance plan is commonly used to finance stocks of expensive merchandise such as major appliances. If payments are made to the retail store on credit sales, this will include turning over the customer paper to the seller or his agent which may be a bank or finance company.

Proximo Dating. This is a common credit term, a synonym for EOM dating.

Regular Dating. This means that the length of time for which the vendor will extend credit is calculated from the date of the invoice. For example, "net 30" signifies that the billed amount is due within 30 days of the invoice date.

Postdating. This is also referred to as advanced dating.

ROG. This term is commonly granted to retailers who are some distance from the market. Receipt of goods means that the date of payment is based on the date the goods are received by the store, rather than the date of shipment or the invoice date.

Loading the Invoice. This term describes a practice used by retailers whereby the amount of the retailer's invoice is increased to permit a larger cash discount than is normally available at the supplier's going rate. Thus, the department or store will increase the amount of the invoice received from the supplier by a certain percentage and charge the department the increased or loaded price. For example, a supplier will send a store a bill (invoice) for the amount of $200 with a 2 percent discount if the bill is paid within 10 days (2 percent net 30). However, the store has a standard policy that requires an 8 percent discount for bills paid within 10 days. The store will take the usual 2 percent discount, or $4, from the invoice cost of $200, which leaves an adjusted invoice of $196 ($200–$4). To achieve the 8 percent discount, the store will load the invoice cost of $196 by dividing it by 92 percent (100%–8%), which gives a loaded invoice price of $213, or 8 percent of $213 gives an invoice cost of $196.

Return Privilege

The return privilege is a third important service offered by merchandise resources. The vendor in some instances will agree to take back the merchandise if it is not sold within a specified period of time. In this case, the risk of markdown is carried by the vendor. The return privilege may take on two forms: consignment selling, whereby the store acts as an agent for the vendor, and selling with the privilege of return. Unlike consignment selling, sale with return privilege signifies that the title passes to the store buyer when the goods are shipped, yet the vendor will take back the unsold portion of the stock within a specified time period. A contractual agreement is made between vendor and buyer whereby the vendor continues to assume a contractual obligation to take back the unsold portion of the goods.

Both buyer and seller must understand the return privilege and its implication if good buyer-vendor relations are to exist. For example, if a small business owner buys goods on consignment from the supplier, the vendor or manufacturer has complete control over the retail price charged store customers. On the other hand, if the store manager purchases goods from a supplier with a return privilege, the retailer may sell at any price he chooses. Also, if the supplier refuses to take back consignment goods, the store manager is under no obligation to pay for the goods; however, he is responsible for keeping them safe. If the store manager discovers the supplier will not accept the goods under the terms of the return privilege, the store is legally responsible to the vendor for the price of the merchandise; however, the store manager may sue for losses incurred as a result of the failure of the supplier to take back the merchandise.

The return privilege is a device used by most retail stores to shift the risk of selling back to the vendor. Therefore, since the risk of markdown is carried by the vendor or supplier, the buyer's maintained markup is equivalent to the initial markup.

Often consignment selling and sale with return privilege are used by buying specialists as a form of price concession to obtain sales that would not be available otherwise. For example, a department-store buyer may refuse to pay a price of $30 on a dozen items; however, the buyer may agree to the price if he or she need pay only for the merchandise sold at a realistic markup and can have a return privilege contract with the supplier. The vendor may agree to this arrangement if he or she is selling new merchandise or is getting rid of old stock, which may require a large markdown unless sold under these conditions. A disadvantage of this method to the supplier is that it may foster excessive returns of unsold merchandise, especially if the supplier is not in a position to insist upon the retailer providing adequate advertising and promotional coverage for the product line.

On Memorandum

On memorandum is a term used in connection with a consignment sale or a sale with the return privilege. The specific details of the memorandum will determine its significance. For example, in the fine jewelry trade (in contrast to costume jewelry), it is understood that the title remains with the supplier and that the retail buyer receiving the merchandise is responsible either to sell the merchandise and account for the sales or to return the merchandise to the vendor.[2] Specific details of the memorandum are determined by the buyer and the supplier.

Exclusive Distribution

Vendors may control the distribution of their merchandise by dictating the resale price to the store buyer. You can see how consignment selling was found to be a legal method of achieving this end. The store was an agent, since it did not take title to the merchandise and therefore had to abide by the regulations set by the merchandise resource. It was soon found, however, that few vendors who desired to control retail prices would sell under a resale contract, which is legal in most states. Also, federal law does not allow the merchant to enter into such arrangements if they are considered to be part of a conspiracy with other merchants or suppliers to restrain trade or to monopolize the marketplace.

Markdown Insurance

Markdown insurance is a relatively new form of risk bearing assumed by vendors and is developing particularly in the area of women's fashion apparel. Buyers are requesting that manufacturers guarantee them against markdowns, which are usually necessary late in the season. Store buyers are asking that manufacturers reimburse them for half the amount of markdowns they find necessary to take. Many vendors are resisting such demands, since the general consensus of opinion is that such a practice will lead to careless buying and to increases in the cost of distribution.

Promotional Allowances

Often, to ensure maximum cooperation between the buyer and the seller, promotional services, the second type of personal promotional aid, are offered by vendors. Such services may take the form of (1) advertising allowances, (2) preferred selling space, (3) free display material, (4) unit packaging, (5) price decline guarantees, and (6) merchandise deals.

Promotional Allowances That Reduce Price Offered by Vendors

1. Advertising allowances
2. Preferrred selling space
3. Free display material
4. Unit packaging
5. Price decline guarantees
6. Merchandise deals

Advertising Allowances

Many consumers are unaware that most retail store advertisements are paid for either in part or wholly by merchandise resources. These resources seek increased cooperation in the sale of their merchandise from retailers at the point of sale. Cooperative advertising is a service offered by suppliers who arrange with retail stores to share advertising expenses. This is a most important promotional tool. Estimates reveal that over $500 million annually is spent on cooperative advertising and that more than 30 percent of the total advertising costs of department stores are supplied by cooperative advertising allowances.[3]

The federal government forbids discrimination in the giving and receiving of advertising. Advertising allowances must be offered to all retailers on proportionately equal terms. Large retail stores will receive the largest cooperative advertising allowances; however, the allowance must have a proportional relationship to the advertising services performed. The federal government further states that the buying specialists for large retail organizations have a greater responsibility than small shop owners to be aware of discrimination. The following is an example of a discrimination case in the handling of cooperative advertising allowances cited by Donald Belden, an expert in the field of mass merchandising.[4]

The Fred Meyer Case and Its Implications. In 1963 the government took action against Fred Meyer, Inc., a chain of food outlets on the Pacific Coast, charging discrimination in the handling of cooperative advertising allowances. The case went to the Supreme Court, whose decision was then subject to interpretation and the issuance of guidelines by the Federal Trade Commission. Substantially, these guidelines held that a supplier of promotional allowances is as responsible for giving these monies to the indirect customers of wholesalers as he is to his direct customers. In other words, the smallest independent retailer, buying entirely through a wholesaler and having no direct dealings with the manufacturer, must be treated in the same way as a mass merchandiser. While admitting that these payments should be based on the volume of purchases by a retailer, the ruling requires that all retailers be explicitly informed of the details of the offer to earn the monies. Affected are all forms of merchandising assistance such as advertising, prizes, catalogs, display helps, contests, and demonstrations. The manufacturer's plan must be fair to all customers. Its availability must be known to all customers. If the basic plan is not usable by all customers, an alternative plan must be made available. The plan must be clearly understood, and the supplier must see to it that payments under the plan are equal.

An advertising allowance is offered by the vendor in which he agrees to pay part or all of the cost of a retailer's advertisement for a particular product. The justification for advertising allowances lies in the fact that the manufacturer may obtain additional business as a result of the advertising efforts of the retail store. If an agreement is worked out, the buyer may then deduct the manufacturer's advertising allowance from the invoice.

Most advertising allowances were originally intended for the retailer's newspaper advertising. However, recent trends have been for many retail stores to contract with manufacturers for allowances for radio and television advertising or for magazine space. Also, manufacturers have not only been charged for space in the advertising media, but also for overhead in the store's advertising department.

The advantages of cooperative advertising are many. The retail store is able to meet competition from large chain operations as well as reducing the cost of maintaining its own advertising department. A small store may obtain better copy and art work as a result of the experience of the cooperating advertiser. On the other hand, the cooperating advertiser may be assured adequate and complete advertising that the retail store's budget may not permit. He or she may also pressure the store into selling new products as well as maintaining already existing lines. Figure 12.1 is an example of an advertisement provided by a shoe manufacturer to a retail department store.

There are also disadvantages to cooperative advertising. The store may have a tendency to promote only merchandise that includes an advertising allowance, rather than goods that are of top quality and in demand. Certain lines of merchandise may be given more selling space than they deserve. Also, the type of layout and copy insisted upon by the vendor may not be in keeping with the image of the store or its established standards. A major disadvantage for the manufacturer is that the allowance provided may not be used for advertising by the store, or at least not used effectively. Often advertising allowances are used as price-cutting devices. As the Fred Meyer case illustrates, the difficulty in making advertising allowances proportionately equal has presented problems to buyers and sellers alike. The Federal Trade Commission is continuously investigating complaints of discrimination and unfair dealings in regard to the use of advertising allowances.

Figure 12.1. An example of an advertisement provided by a shoe manufacturer to a retail store. (Courtesy of Brown Shoe Company.)

AS-621 • SPIRE   Size: 3 col. x 9-1/2 inches (399 lines)

Preferred Selling Space

A second type of promotional allowance offered by vendors is preferred selling space. That is to say, the retail buyer will offer preferred selling space to the vendor, and in return will be granted an allowance from the regular price. For example, the merchandise may be given a special window treatment or perhaps will be assigned space near the check-out counter. In many types of stores, especially variety stores and food markets, the value of each display area has been charted; thus, a vendor may be provided with preferred space with the assurance of an increased sales volume. The small business, especially in the hard-goods and drug fields, will take advantage of allowances offered by vendors for preferred selling space. The small business operator will place certain items alongside the cash register, on corner aisles, in the shop window, and in other effective display areas. Usually the merchandise is stable in nature and constitutes convenience items and impulse goods that are readily purchased by customers.

Free Display Material

A third type of promotional service from the vendor is the provision of free display material. Counter exhibits, window displays, elaborate signs, and sometimes "giveaways" are frequently available to the store buyer for the asking. Display material often costs vendors considerable amounts of money; however, they feel that the additional sales produced by it are well worth the expense. The buyer must use such material with caution and restraint, however. A window containing nothing but vendor materials may distract from the image of the store. Display materials offered by merchandise resources are often the results of the creative efforts of advertising agencies and thus do not reflect the image of a particular store. Sometimes the display materials are large and elaborate and the results are impractical, especially for the small retailer.

Unit Packaging

Unit packaging is another service the seller may assume through special arrangement with the store buyer. Articles are packed by the seller in units suitable for resale in the retail store. Buyers in the home furnishings and appliance fields are particularly interested in special packaging. Competition in these areas has fostered more interesting, exciting, and convenient packaging designs. The vendor will offer his merchandise in new materials, use bolder graphics, emphasize new sizes, and develop new opening and closing devices just to promote his product over the competition. The buyer is often able to obtain this service at no extra charge, since it will add to the salability of the product (see Figure 12.2). Also, special packing services can be eliminated by the store, and the risk of loss through breakage, repacking, and unpacking may be avoided.

The Packaging Committee of the Association of General Merchandise

Figure 12.2. Unit packaging offers many advantages to retailers. The buyer is often able to obtain this service at no extra charge, since it will add to the salability of the product.

Chains has issued the *Guide to Better Variety Packaging,* which contains a checklist for better self-selection packaging.[5] It includes the following considerations for the consumer-oriented buyer:[6]

* Does the package have quick eye-appeal?
* Are design and color in keeping with the item?
* Does the package possess individuality?
* If part of a line, are packages matched and coordinated?
* Is printed matter clear—is lettering uncluttered?
* Are all sides used for informative selling?
* Does packaging tell clearly what is inside?
* If more than one of a kind, is quantity stated?
* Is size specified—with age and weight measurements where practical?
* Is kind of material plainly indicated?
* Are required government specifications visible?
* Are directions for use clear and specific?
* Are there instructions for maintenance, laundering, cleaning?
* Are there simple, adequate assembly instructions?
* Is packaging material the most up-to-date available?
* Can customers examine merchandise without tearing the package?

Price Decline Guarantees

When seasonal merchandise is ordered well in advance, it is often possible to obtain special guarantees against price declines. For example, if a buyer agrees to purchase merchandise from a vendor in September when seasonally he does not need the goods until January, he will be guaranteed protection from a price decline during the time period involved. For example, if the buyer purchases the goods at $7 and the price in January is $6, the vendor will credit or refund the store $1 for each article the buyer has on hand January 1. The vendor will agree to this arrangement to secure orders during the off-season so that he can continue plant operation.

Merchandise Deals

In merchandise deals, goods are given free by the vendor if the buyer orders in quantity or performs a promotional service. For example, a buyer for stationery may be offered two dozen pencils free with an order of ten dozen boxes of deluxe writing paper. Merchandise deals are offered by manufacturers to induce buyers to purchase "tie-in" merchandise or some other merchandise made by the manufacturer. Usually, the small business will attempt to secure merchandise deals to stimulate merchandise offerings and thus build sales. For example, the owner-manager of a men's wear shop may purchase fifty units of men's shirts and be offered a deal of one dozen ties to coordinate with the shirts. The shop owner is pleased to get "a little something for nothing," and the vendor is satisfied to have stimulated sales for a line of shirts. Store managers, however, must be careful when accepting such offers, since they must be certain there is a market to sell the goods as well as the merchandise accompanying the items.

Personal promotional aids may include:

I. Vendors' selling aids
Demonstrators
Finance and credit
Return privilege

Exclusive distribution
Markdown insurance
On memorandum

II. Promotional allowances
Advertising allowances
Preferred selling space
Free display material

Unit packaging
Price decline guarantees
Merchandise deals

Review how each will affect the selling activity of buying specialists

---

Nonpersonal Promotional Aids

PART 2

Nonpersonal promotional aids are welcomed by the buyer because they are useful in attracting customer attention and interest. Since nonpersonal promotional aids are those services that directly influence the buying behavior of the

Dealer Helps

customer, they will be classified as follows: (1) dealer helps and (2) consumer inducements.

Dealer helps are a type of nonpersonal promotional aid

Examples are:
1. Packaging
2. Labeling
3. Price ticketing

Packaging

After World War II, improvements in the art of packaging, as well as the trend toward self-service, led retail buyers to recognize that many products take on more value and have more consumer appeal when they appear in well-designed, attractive packages. Also, good packaging can save selling time on the part of the sales personnel. This is especially true in merchandise that in itself has little eye appeal. For example, staple goods such as hardware, tools, auto accessories, kitchen utensils, and stationery are unaffected by fashion seasons. They are not sought for their fashion appeal but for their utilitarian appeal. The vendors then, will provide prepackaging to make the items more interesting. They usually have the facilities as well as the expertise to do so.

The vendors will also provide unit packaging. For example, they will supply tennis balls three to a package or light bulbs two to a package. Since the vendors are first to see changes in unit quantities as well as trends in packaging designs, they are excellent sources of information in this area.

New techniques in packaging have also helped to eliminate problems resulting from shoplifting. For example, small items such as cosmetics and candy are packaged into containers that cannot be easily concealed. Packaging will also protect merchandise from being damaged or soiled. For example, men's shirts and women's blouses are packed in clear cellophane bags. Perishables, such as meats and dairy products, are packaged to provide the consumer with adequate visual inspection as well as easy storage.

Well-designed packaging will attract customer attention and will act as a silent salesperson for the merchandise it contains. The buyer who considers packaging from the point of view of the customer will analyze and study the packaging as well as the contents, considering the following factors:

- Will the package design protect the merchandise while it is in transit, in storage, on the selling floor, and carried home by the customer?
- Will the package design conserve storage space and fit into existing merchandise display fixtures?

- Does the packaging make the merchandise too heavy or bulky to ship or carry?
- Does the packaging provide selling appeal?
- Will the packaging protect the merchandise from pilferage and shoplifting?
- Is the merchandise clearly identified?
- Will the packaging provide an opportunity for the customer to inspect the merchandise?
- Does the package contain required care and labeling information?
- How is the package opened? Is it functional?
- Apart from holding merchandise, what other uses does the packaging serve?

Labeling

Labeling is a nonpersonal selling aid of growing importance today. (See Figure 12.3.) Readying merchandise for resale is an important vendor service, which

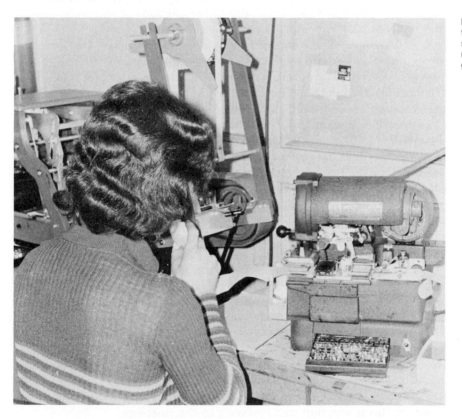

Figure 12.3. Labeling and ticketing, important vendor services, are types of nonpersonal selling aids growing in popularity today.

involves not only packaging but also labeling. In some cases the package may serve as the label; however, products that are not unit packaged, such as clothing, need labels. Labels are usually attached directly to the merchandise; if this is done by the vendor, the label emphasizes the brand name and provides little factual information. However, consumers have demanded product information to assist them in buying, and the federal government has developed trade practice regulations requiring that labels show the fiber content, the percent of fiber used, and instructions for washing and care. (Review the Fair Packaging and Labeling Act, discussed in chapter 1.) Every buyer should be interested in working with suppliers and the government toward providing consumer protection as well as preventing dissatisfaction, which would foster consumer ill will and thus affect the store's image.

The buyer should carefully study a product presented by a vendor and determine if the printed message contained on the package or on the label contains all necessary information. The buyer must be able to determine the ingredients, fiber content, or whatever in determining merchandise value in relation to costs. If important details are missing or unimportant details are exaggerated, the buyer should call this to the attention of the vendor, and if still in doubt, should consult the store's legal counsel.

For example, in the area of housewares and appliances, the consumer needs to know how much service he or she can expect to derive from a product and what alternatives are available if the product does not perform as expected. The manufacturer and the buyer will provide this information to sell the merchandise. They will spell out the guarantee in words that do not leave them open to unfair and unjust claims for repair, refund, or replacement. The Federal Trade Commission further offers definite recommendations in this area. It states that the guarantee should be a genuine attempt to protect the consumer rather than the manufacturer. The buyer and the manufacturer should check for the following information: the name of the guarantor, products or parts covered by the guarantee, length of the guarantee period, how the customer will secure action if not satisfied, matching of all statements in the guarantee, ease of reading of the guarantee, and the guarantee's location in an obvious place.[7]

Labels, therefore, have two primary functions: (1) they provide salespeople with specific information about the features of the garment, and (2) they assist the customer in making a selection, especially if the retail store carries several quality lines of a particular product.

It is in the best interest of the retail buyer to negotiate for labels that will best satisfy the store's and the client's needs, especially in such matters as size, appearance, type, and amount. The buyer should arrange with the vendor that all merchandise information be included on one label that is attached at a central point. Some vendors may attach three to five labels to each garment; however, this is unsightly and confusing to the customer.

Price Ticketing

To purchase merchandise, the consumer needs specific price information. This information is placed on the merchandise in the form of a label, as just discussed, or on a price ticket, which is either attached directly to the merchandise or placed near the product.

Price tickets are also provided by vendors, which is called preticketing. The Association of General Merchandise Chains has been working on preticketing of merchandise items by suppliers before shipping goods to retailers. This organization is also attempting to develop a standard reorder ticket that can be inserted in the product's container or bin or attached by a string or pin to a wide variety of items.[8] A preticketing service would eliminate heavy costs of ticketing now assumed by many retailers.

Buyers of soft goods and fashion apparel have begun to make demands on the seller by insisting that price tickets include such information as purchase date, department and classification number, manufacturer or vendor number, size, color, season, style number, cost price, and retail price. The buyer insists that this job can best be accomplished by the vendor, who can do the job more cheaply and effectively.

Many kinds of price tickets or tags are used for marking products. Gummed labels and pin tickets, whether machine-attached or hand-attached, are usually the cheapest and fastest forms of ticketing. However, whether to use a label, a string ticket, or a handwritten ticket depends upon the kind of merchandise to be marked. For example, string tags are usually used on clothing; merchandise with a hard surface is usually marked with gummed labels; and pin tickets are used on products that pinholes will not damage.

Not all merchandise needs to be marked, particularly where personal selling is used rather than self-service. For example, low-priced, fast-selling staples are not individually marked. Instead they are sold from containers, shelves, trays, or bins that are marked with the price. In self-service stores, however, each individual item is usually marked. For example, in supermarkets, discount houses, low-margin retail stores and variety stores, individual items are marked so that neither the customer nor the cashier performing the check-out process will have problems in attempting to determine the correct price.

Consumer Inducements

Not only do manufacturers provide selling assistance to retail buyers to influence a consumer purchase, but they will also attempt to influence the consumer directly. For example, the vendor will provide certain inducements to influence the consumer to buy a certain brand of television, a particular flavor of toothpaste, a certain size of soap powder. Such attempts on the part of the manufacturer may interfere with normal business activities; therefore, they require cooperation between the vendor and the retail buyer.

The following examples of consumer inducement may be used: (1) premiums, (2) coupons, (3) contests, (4) deals, (5) trading stamps, and (6) sampling.

Consumer inducements offered by vendors	
1. Premiums	4. Deals
2. Coupons	5. Trading stamps
3. Contests	6. Sampling

Premiums

A *premium* may be defined as an article of value or "gift" that can be obtained by the consumer for a nominal price after the advertised item has been purchased. The consumer may be required to tear off the label or box top and send it to the manufacturer with a small sum of money. A method often used by cosmetic companies is to offer, for example, a beauty face cream for $1.50 with a minimum $6.00 purchase.

The premium is a common selling device used by vendors. The retailer usually has no hand in the advertising or promotion, since the manufacturer will advertise the merchandise nationally. However, the store may be forced to warehouse and distribute the premium as well as the advertised merchandise. The Robinson-Patman Act prohibits the use of premiums as a form of price discrimination among competing retailers. It also prohibits deceptive advertising that calls a premium "free" if the cost of the article is included in the purchase price of the article sold in connection with it.

An example of a common type of premium is a two-for-one sale in a dress shop, whereby the customer will purchase one dress at the regular price to obtain a second dress at a drastically reduced rate. This is a very popular method of selling today. A gasoline station may offer free glassware with each full tank of gasoline; a supermarket may offer an opportunity to purchase a place setting of china or silverware at a reduced price with each $25 order; or a small variety store may offer fingernail polish with a 1¢ sales allowance whereby the customer will purchase two bottles of nail polish for the price of one bottle plus 1¢.

Coupons

The *coupon* is an award granted by the manufacturer or vendor for purchasing his product. Usually the objective of the manufacturer is to grant the consumer an indrect price cut that will help make the merchandise a leader in that particular market. The consumer may receive a coupon through house-to-house distribution, by mail, by cutting it out of the newspaper, at the store, or in the packaged product (see Figure 12.4). The coupon usually has a value stated in cents and may be used instead of cash in the purchase of particular branded products. The retailer is expected to accept coupons instead of cash

Figure 12.4. An example of coupons that have been sent through the mail and distributed in the store (restaurant). (Courtesy of Dante's Inferno, Philadelphia, Pa.)

and in turn to hand them in to the vendor for redemption. The vendor will usually grant the retailer a small commission for handling coupons and for waiting for the money.

Sometimes the coupon is a device used by vendors to force the buyer to carry merchandise that is not already in stock. For example, a can of coffee may contain a coupon worth 25¢; however, the coupon may have to be redeemed for a product not carried by the store. If enough customers return to the store seeking the article, the retailer may decide to stock it.

Contests

A third device used by vendors is the consumer contest. The *contest* usually offers expensive prizes and usually requires that the consumer present evidence of purchase to qualify. It may also require the customer to elaborate upon the advantages of the product and its value in relation to competition. The store buyer is often required to provide entry blanks and information. Sometimes the store's sales personnel may also receive a prize along with the winning contestant. Some stores may stage contests and offer a variety of prizes. For example, a department store may offer a sewing course and then offer a prize to the participant who sews the best garment, as well as to those who take second and third place. Usually, those who enter the contest will purchase the material and sewing notions from the store's piece goods department. Or a store may offer contests in cooking, painting, woodworking, table setting, and so forth. Participants in these contests, too, will usually purchase the required materials or tools from the store offering the contest.

Deals

A *deal* may best be defined as a temporary special retail price offered to store customers. For example, the vendor may band two items together; instead of selling one article for 39¢, the store may sell "two for 66¢." This offers an obvious advantage to the store's clientele; however, the buyer makes a lower profit. Also, merchandise that is not banded together will not sell until the deal is over.

Trading Stamps

Trading stamps are given to a consumer with each purchase of merchandise. The number of stamps received is based upon the cost of the merchandise. For example, a consumer may receive 10 trading stamps if the article costs $1.

Technically speaking, trading stamps are not offered by vendors; however, they definitely influence the consumers as they decide on their purchases. Trading-stamp companies such as S & H Green Stamps, Blue Chip, Top Value Plaid Stamps, and Gold Bond sell stamps to retail stores and provide the premium merchandise for which the stamps are redeemed. The premium merchandise may be distributed through cooperating stores or through stamp redemption centers where the merchandise is on display.

Trading stamps became a popular customer inducement during the 1950s and even more so during the 1960s. They were commonplace in supermarkets, gasoline stations, drugstores, discount houses, and even in garden and supply centers. Customers accepted them wholeheartedly, and stores found them to be builders of repeat patronage.

During the early 1970s, however, trading stamps declined as a popular customer inducement. Since retail stores had to pay for the stamps, their cost was included in the retailer's markup price. As a result of competition, fuel shortages, and supply conditions in general, customers sought lower prices. As a result, many retail stores gave up trading stamps to lower the price of their merchandise. For example, one retail merchant's ad read, "No More Stamps or Other Gimmicks—Only Quality Merchandise and Lower Prices."

It is important that the buyer become acquainted with vendor policy regarding such activity. No action should be taken without first considering

Figure 12.5. Trading stamps will influence the customer as he or she decides on purchases. (Courtesy of the Sperry and Hutchinson Company, New York, N.Y.)

the interests of the store and the customers and his or her duties and obligations as a buyer.

Trading stamps offer many advantages to retail buyers. They are not offered by vendors or manufacturers but by companies dealing specifically with this type of consumer protection. The trading-stamp inducement plan has been found to be especially suited to convenience goods, those goods which consumers expect to have readily available in a handy location. However, retailers who handle shopping goods, those products for which a consumer will accept no substitutes, have not been convinced of the advantages of the trading stamp plan.

Sampling

Sampling is a frequently used method of reaching customers directly, especially in food markets, cosmetic counters in retail stores, and drugstores. For example, a food merchant will offer free samples of cheese, meat products, candy, or a new type of gourmet food. The customer is given an opportunity to taste and smell the food and as a result may purchase the item. Cosmetic departments will offer lipstick, cologne, perfume, nail polish, and so forth to give the shopper an opportunity to try the product. Samples are found in many merchandise areas and often help customers to decide on a purchase. The sample may be given out in the store or may be sent through the mail to potential customers.

Nonpersonal promotional aids will directly influence the buying behavior of the retail customer. They may be classified as:

I. Dealer helps	II. Consumer inducements	
Packaging	Premiums	Deals
Labeling	Coupons	Trading stamps
Price ticketing	Contests	Sampling

Review how each will affect the selling activity of buying specialists.

Chapter Summary

Personal promotional aids are those services offered by vendors that will directly affect the selling activity of the buyer. Such services may take the form of vendor's selling aids—the use of demonstrators, the availability of finance and credit, a return privilege, controlled distribution, markdown insurance, and memorandum buying. Promotional allowances are also offered to the retail buyer. Such allowances are used to ensure maximum cooperation between the buyer and the seller. They may take the form of advertising allowances, preferred selling space, free display material, unit packaging, price decline guarantees, and merchandise deals.

   The buyer may negotiate for price adjustments through specific credit arrangements such as discounts, dating, and floor planning or achieve price concessions through special promotional allowances. Whatever method is used, the buyer must be certain that such buying techniques are in his or her best interest, that of the retail store and, of course, that of the customers.

   Nonpersonal promotional aids are welcomed by the buyer, since they are useful in attracting customer attention and interest. They may be classified as (1) dealer helps and (2) consumer inducements. Dealer helps may come in the form of packaging, labeling, and price ticketing.

   Packaging may add value and attractiveness to a product. Good packaging may help minimize problems with shoplifting, protect merchandise from being damaged or soiled, and provide easy storage for retailer and consumer alike.

Labeling is a nonpersonal selling aid of growing importance. Labels have two primary functions: (1) they provide salespeople with specific information about the features of the garment, and (2) they assist the customer in making a selection, especially if the retail store carries several quality lines of a particular product.

Not only is the consumer provided information through the use of labeling but also by price ticketing. Price tickets may be attached directly to the product or placed near the merchandise. The many types available include gummed labels, pin tickets, string tickets, and many variations. Not all merchandise needs to be marked, particularly where personal selling is used. On the other hand, self-service requires that each individual item be marked, since this will assist the cashier in performing his or her job at the check-out counter.

Not only do vendors provide selling assistance to retail buyers, but they will also attempt to influence the consumer directly. Consumer inducements may include (1) premiums, (2) coupons, (3) contests, (4) deals, (5) trading stamps, and (6) sampling. Such devices as premiums, coupons, contests, and deals place a degree of pressure on the retail buyer to stock the merchandise offered in substantial quantity.

Trade Terminology

DIRECTIONS: Briefly explain or discuss each of the following trade terms:

1. Personal promotional aids
2. Nonpersonal promotional aids
3. Advanced dating
4. Anticipation
5. Cash discount
6. C.O.D. dating
7. Consignment
8. Dating
9. End-of-month
10. Extra dating
11. Floor plan
12. Proximo dating
13. Regular dating
14. Postdating
15. ROG
16. Loading the invoice
17. On memorandum
18. Premium
19. Coupon
20. Contest
21. Deal
22. Trading stamps

Questions For Discussion and Review

1. What questions should the buyer ask when considering the types of services offered by merchandise resources?

2. Under what major classifications may vendor services to the buyer be analyzed?

3. What types of retail stores gain the most by offering trading stamps? Why?

4. What methods are used by merchandise resources to extend credit to buyers?

5. What is cooperative advertising? Cite five examples from your local newspaper.

6. Other than advertising allowances, what forms of promotional allowances are offered by merchandise resources?

7. From the customer's point of view, what are the advantages and disadvantages of a store's using demonstrators provided by suppliers?

8. Name six kinds of inducements used by vendors to influence the consumer directly. Select three examples from your local newspaper. Explain how each is used by the retail store to increase customer traffic.

9. What is the difference between buying on consignment and buying with a return privilege?

10. What is floor planning? What types of retail stores favor the floor-planning method?

Case Study Number One

Too Many Suppliers?   You have been promoted to the position of furniture buyer in a rather large department. After working there for only a few weeks, you realize that a large number of sales representatives are interested in seeing you. When you check back through the department's invoices, you notice that orders have been sent to as many as forty different manufacturers. You check with the assistant buyer and learn that the previous buyer's policy was to order from as many different sources as possible. The previous buyer argued that this policy enabled the store to offer a wide choice of merchandise. Your predecessor also felt that if merchandise ran short, it was always possible to find a supplier. Will you follow the same buying policy in selecting vendors? Be prepared in class to explain your answer.

Case Study Number Two

Cape Cod is the manufacturer of Ship Side Rainwear, which is sold by a number of specialty shops and exclusive sporting-goods stores along the New England coast. The rainwear retails for about $125, and most of the full rain suits sell for $250. The product has long been recognized as a leader in the marketplace for quality, style, and prestige.

Is Cape Cod all Wet?

Cape Cod advertises in the leading boating magazines and various fashion periodicals. To promote the Cape Cod name and label further, the company participates in major boat shows and other sporting activities.

In recent years, however, it has become evident that more and more stores are removing the Cape Cod label and replacing it with their own labels. Jim Walker, president of the Cape Cod manufacturing company, is disturbed by this. He believes that, if the stores are permitted to continue this practice, Cape Cod rainwear will lose its prestige and status in the marketplace, which will lead to a decrease in sales. At a meeting with his sales representatives, it is decided that to protect the Cape Cod label, the company will have to adopt a policy that obliges store accounts to feature and promote the label.

What methods may be used to stimulate an interest in the Cape Cod label?

Retailing Activities to Stimulate Student Interest and Participation

1. Interview the store manager of a variety chain operation; a specialty chain; a department-store branch. Prepare a list of questions based on the topic "the kind of vendor services available to encourage customers to buy." How will the services available differ with each store? How will they be similar?

2. Interview the owner-manager of a hardware store; a specialty shop. What forms of dealer helps are used by each store? What kinds of problems has each store manager had to deal with when seeking dealer helps?

3. You have been asked to write a term paper on the topic "Does the small retailer get the same advantages from vendors as the large store?" Referring to the books listed in The Retail Student's Reference Library, develop an outline of the important points you wish to emphasize.

REFERENCES

The Retail Student's Reference Library

Belden, Donald L. *The Role of the Buyer in Mass Merchandising.* New York: Chain Store Publishing Corporation, 1971.

The Buyer's Manual. New York: National Retail Merchants Association, 1970.

Cahill, Jane. *Can a Smaller Store Succeed?* New York: Fairchild Publications, Inc., n.d.

China and Glassware Merchandiser. New York: National Retail Merchants Association, n.d.

Cohen, Richard L. *The Footwear Industry.* New York: Fairchild Publications, Inc., n.d.

Creative Men's Wear Retailing. New York: Fairchild Publications, Inc., n.d.

Duncan, D. J., and Hermanson, R. H. *Retailing: Modern Concepts and Practices.* Homewood, Ill.: Learning Systems Company, 1970.

Essentials of Merchandising. Albany: State University of New York Press, n.d.

Ferguson, F. *Efficient Drug Store Management.* New York: Fairchild Publications, Inc., n.d.

Fried, Eleanor. *Is the Fashion Business Your Business?* New York: Fairchild Publications, Inc., 1970.

Gillespie, Karen. *Apparel and Accessories for Women, Misses and Children.* Washington, D.C.: U. S. Government Printing Office, n.d.

Gold, E. B. *Dynamics of Retailing.* New York: Fairchild Publications, Inc., n.d.

Jimerson, H. C., and Rowe, K. L. *Communication in Marketing.* Hightstown: McGraw-Hill Book Company, 1971.

Judelle, Beatrice. *The Fashion Buyer's Job.* New York: National Retail Merchants Association, 1970.

Kelley, P. C. *Variety Stores.* Washington, D.C.: U. S. Government Printing Office, n.d.

Logan, W. B., and Moon, H. M. *Facts about Merchandising.* Englewood Cliffs, N.J.: Prentice-Hall, Inc., n.d.

Moller, W. C., and Wilemon, D. L. *Marketing Channels: A Systems Viewpoint.* Homewood, Ill.: Richard D. Irwin, Inc., 1971.

Mulhern, Helen. *Facts about Department Stores.* New York: National Retail Merchants Association, n.d.

Profitable Merchandising Techniques. New York: Fairchild Publications, Inc., 1970.

Readings in Modern Retailing. New York: National Retail Merchants Association, 1970.

Reich, E., Feldman, R., and Levy, L. *Basic Retailing and Distribution.* New York: Pitman Publishing Corporation, 1970

A Retailer Visits the Market. New York: Fairchild Publications, Inc., n.d.

Rice, J. W. *Furniture Retailing.* Washington, D.C.: U. S. Government Printing Office, n.d.

Ritter, Dorothy. *Hardware Retailing.* Washington, D. C.: U.S. Government Printing Office, n.d.

Robinson, J. W. *Gift and Art Shops.* Washington, D. C.: U. S. Government Printing Office, n.d.

Slom, S. *Profitable Furniture Retailing: For the Home Furnishings Markets.* Fairchild Publications, Inc., n.d.

Taylor, C. G. *Merchandise Assortment Planning.* New York: National Retail Merchants Association, n.d.

References

1. Beatrice Judelle, *The Fashion Buyer's Job* (New York: National Retail Merchants Association, 1971), pp. 81–82.
2. J. W. Wingate and J. S. Friedlander, *The Management of Retail Buying* (Englewood Cliffs, N.J.: Prentice-Hall, Inc., 1963), p. 319.

3. Donald L. Belden, *The Role of the Buyer in Mass Merchandising* (New York: Chain Store Publishing Corporation, 1971), p. 191.
4. Ibid., p. 192.
5. Ibid., p. 62.
6. *Packaging Digest,* July, 1969, p. 5.
7. Belden, *Role of the Buyer,* p. 189.
8. Ibid., p. 89.

Developing Good Buyer-Vendor Relations

13

Performance Objectives

PERFORMANCE OBJECTIVES

As a result of reading this chapter, the student should be able to accomplish the following:

1. Explain five activities important to the negotiation process.

2. Define four kinds of discounts and allowances available to the buyer from the vendor.

3. Become aware of two important factors a buyer must consider when determining transportation and storage.

4. Discuss four terms used in transportation (FOB).

5. Learn the importance of the buyer's order form, the necessity of properly filling out the order form, and the legal responsibilities involved.

6. List seven kinds of orders that may be placed by a buyer.

7. Discuss guidelines a buyer should observe when negotiating with a vendor.

8. Understand the circumstances that dictate when a buyer may return merchandise to a vendor.

9. Define legal contract.

10. List five trade practices that must be observed by vendors and buyers when writing and accepting an order.

11. Discuss ten practices that may cause friction between vendors and buyers.

12. Become aware of the policies that should be established to ensure the development of good buyer-vendor relations.

Developing Good Buyer-Vendor Relations

The Buyer's Responsibility to the Vendor

Early Encounters

Early merchandise resources considered retail buyers, especially buyers for chain-store operations, a threat to the existence of the traditional method of distribution, whereby goods were sold to middlemen, who in turn sold them to individual store buyers. Manufacturers were reluctant to sell to merchandisers, even to the largest of them. Manufacturers especially slow to break away from traditional distribution patterns were those in the drug, houseware, appliance, and food lines. The result was that early buyers had to seek suppliers who were unwilling to sell to them. Later, however, as chain-store buying and discounting became more popular, merchandise resources found it difficult to resist the opportunity for profit that resulted from the increased volume.

During the early days of retailing the store buyer often had difficulties in determining what he would or would not purchase for resale. Manufacturers had not yet fully developed the complete lines of merchandise they carry today. A buyer would purchase one item at a time or purchase closeouts or lots. Highly competitive bargaining over single units of merchandise was not uncommon. It was soon realized, however, that such chaotic conditions could not continue if retail distribution in the United States were to prosper and meet the demands of an ever-increasing population.

Eventually, a teamwork approach to buyer-vendor relations was developed. This led to a modification of trade practices that allowed both buyer and vendor the freedom of creativity and expression, yet ensured fair play for both. The purpose of Part 1, therefore, will be to discuss the buyer's responsibility to the vendor. Topics considered are (1) steps in the negotiation process, (2) order placement, (3) the kinds of orders available, and (4) some hints for retail buyers. Part 2 will discuss the vendor's responsibility to the buyer. Topics to be discussed are (1) the conduct of the vendor, (2) legal aspects of the buyer's order, (3) causes of friction between vendors and buyers, and (4) establishment of good vendor-buyer relations.

The Negotiation Process

The *negotiation process* involves the mutual discussion and agreement between the retail buyer and the merchandise resources to terms of various business transactions. It is the bargaining activity that occurs between the buyer and the seller over certain goods and services. As you recall, the seller may be a manufacturer, a wholesaler, a vendor, or a manufacturer's representative.

The size of the retail institution will greatly influence both the purchasing potential of the buyer and the willingness of the vendor to grant concessions. For example, a buyer from a small women's apparel shop would have less influence in the negotiation process for more than 2 percent cash discount than would a buyer of women's apparel in a department store.

The negotiation process provides an opportunity for the buyer to implement a most important store objective: profit maximization. A variety of activities involved in the process will help the buyer meet this objective. Chief among the negotiating activities are: (1) buying authority, (2) securing discounts and allowances, (3) arranging transportation and storage, (4) establishing the terms of sale, and (5) seeking price guarantees.

Chief activities involved in the negotiation process

1. Buying authority
2. Securing discounts and allowances
3. Arranging transportation and storage
4. Establishing the terms of sale
5. Seeking price guarantees

Buying Authority

When the buyer is employed by the retail store, he or she is given the authority to act in behalf of that store as a duly authorized agent and will represent the firm in dealings with merchandise resources. However, a buyer for curtains and draperies cannot place orders for sporting equipment or for towels and linens, but can only purchase for the department for which hired.

The authority delegated to the buyer by the retail firm is important to the negotiation process. The merchandise resource is aware that contracts placed and signed by the buyer and merchandise manager are valid and will be honored by the retail firm involved.

As the representative or agent of the retail store, the buyer has certain responsibilities, which are listed as follows:

1. To be loyal and act in good faith in the best interest of the retail organization.
2. To act in person—that is, the buyer must do the purchasing himself —unless permitted to appoint another individual to act on his or her behalf.
3. To work with reasonable care, effort, and skill.

4. To follow all lawful instructions; that is, to abide by any special instructions that require a countersignature.
5. To render an accounting for all merchandise belonging to the retail organization and for all activities performed in the store's behalf.
6. To give the retail organization an account of all purchases made and money spent.
7. To turn over all profits received and to make no personal profit.

Figure 13.1. Buyers represent the retail store in dealings with merchandise resources. They are given the authority to act in behalf of the store as duly authorized agents.

Securing Discounts and Allowances

A second activity involved in the negotiation process is securing discounts and allowances. A *discount* or *allowance* may be defined as any reduction in the list or quoted price given to the retailer by the merchandise resource. There are four kinds of discounts and allowances available to the retail buyer. They are (1) quantity discount, (2) seasonal discount, (3) trade discount, and (4) cash discount. The formulas used to calculate each of the following will be discussed in the next chapter.

Discounts and allowances available to the retail buyer from merchandise resources

1. Quantity discounts
2. Seasonal discounts
3. Trade discounts
4. Cash discounts

Quantity Discount. May be defined as a reduction from list price given to buyers purchasing in unusually large quantities. It may be stated in terms of a percentage reduction or in the form of free goods. For example, a manufacturer of women's hosiery may offer a "1 dozen free with 10 dozen purchased" deal or a 15 percent discount for purchasing 10 dozen stockings. Manufacturers often use quantity discount to encourage the retailer not only to purchase from them but to purchase larger quantities. The buyer must be careful not to be misled by such attractive offerings, since this may lead to overbuying.

Seasonal Discount. May be defined as a reduction in list price granted to the retail buyer for purchasing goods during the off-season. Certain kinds of goods are in demand only at particular times of the year. For example, ski clothing is in demand during the winter and bathing suits during the summer. Vendors will offer discounts to retailers to encourage them to order as well as accept delivery of goods during the off-season. As a result, vendors can continue a minimum production schedule while the buyer assumes the added expense of warehousing the goods until the season arrives. The retailer, however, is compensated for additional warehousing expenses and added investment cost by the price reduction that has been granted by the vendor. Seasonal discounts may run as high as 10 or 20 percent. To take advantage of these discounts, the buyer must anticipate requirements far in advance. Along with the price advantage, the merchandise is likely to be more carefully checked, packed, and delivered. It may also be more carefully made.

Trade Discount. May be defined as a reduction in price granted to a certain category or trade of customer to cover the costs of a particular trading function. The trade discount is granted in addition to a quantity discount. Trade discount is usually not a form of price concession but a method of quoting prices based on list prices. For example, in some trades it is an accepted practice for a manufacturer to quote a list price that may approximate the actual retail price. The retail buyer may then be granted a trade discount of 50 percent off the list price. The discount is high enough to cover the buyer's markup for expenses, risk, and profit. However, some manufacturers distort the list price. In this case, the retailer will offer the merchandise at a price far below the list price and still make an adequate markup. For example, a clock may be listed at $90.00 but be sold to a buyer for $32.50. The buyer then resells the clock at $69.95 but advertises it as a "gigantic bargain."

Cash Discount. May be defined as a reduction in list price granted to the retail buyer if the buyer pays within a specified period of time. The time period is usually expressed as a certain number of days after the invoice date. Take, for example, cash discount terms of 2/10 net 30. The buyer may take a cash discount of 2 percent by paying within ten days after the invoice date. The cash discount is taken after all other discounts are deducted. For example, the buyer deducts the trade, quantity, and/or seasonal discount before deducting the cash discount. This type of discount is often granted by merchandise resources to encourage the buyer to pay bills within a specified time period. As a result, the supplier is enabled to invest the money and in turn take advantage of discounts offered by merchandise resources.

Arranging Transportation and Storage

Arranging transportation and storage is a third important negotiating activity. When considering such arrangements, the buyer should ask himself or herself two important questions: (1) Who is to pay for the cost of transportation? (2) Who is to own the merchandise and be responsible for it while it is en route?

Important factors when determining transportation and storage
1. Who is to pay for the cost of transportation? The buyer? The vendor? 2. Who is to own the merchandise and be responsible for it while it is en route? The buyer? The vendor?

Transportation terms offered by the vendor may take any one of the following forms: (1) FOB factory, (2) FOB destination, (3) FOB shipping point, (4) FOB destination, charges reversed, (5) FOB factory, freight prepaid.

FOB (Free on board) Factory. This agreement states that the buyer will pay all transportation costs and will own the goods from the moment they are shipped.

FOB Destination. This agreement states that the seller is to pay all transportation costs and is to own the merchandise until it arrives at the retail store.

FOB Shipping Point. In this agreement the seller pays any crating necessary for sending the goods to the place at which they are to be turned over to a transportation company.

FOB Destination, Charges Reversed. Such an agreement means that the seller will own the goods until they get into the retail store; however, the buyer agrees to pay the transportation charges.

FOB Destination, Freight Prepaid. This agreement means the goods are to become the possession of the buyer as soon as they are shipped; however, the seller will pay freight charges.

In addition to determining the form of FOB, the retail buyer must determine the method of shipment. The main methods are railroad freight, railway express, motor freight, parcel post, air express, air freight, and truck-rail. The truck-rail method is a combination whereby merchandise is loaded into a trailer and hauled by truck to a railroad siding, where the entire trailer is lifted onto a flatcar. Once the goods arrive at the destination, the trailer is removed and transported by truck to the warehouse or directly to the store.

Time and cost are two important elements the buyer must consider when determining methods of transportation and storage. For example, a buyer of large quantities of staple goods may achieve lower unit rates by concentrating his purchases and by using less expensive methods of shipment. However, if the merchandise is needed quickly, as is often the case with fashion goods, faster methods of transportation are generally used.

How will the terms of transportation assist the buyer during the negotiation activity?

FOB factory
FOB destination
FOB shipping point
FOB destination, charges reversed
FOB destination, freight prepaid

Establishing the Terms of Sale

The fourth important activity in the negotiation process is the establishment of the terms of sale. As was mentioned in the previous chapter, the terms of sale are often offered to the retail buyer in the form of vendor services. In our earlier discussion, we mentioned various forms of dating and the different types of discounts available. For example, the term 2/10, net 30 means that a 2 percent discount may be taken within a ten-day period and that payment of the bill is due thirty days from the date of the invoice. The retail buyer will usually consider an invoice dating more favorable if the period during which discounts may be taken and/or payment may be made is a long one. However, vendors usually want payment as soon as possible. For this reason the buyer should carefully review the types of dating available when making finance and credit arrangements.

Seeking Price Guarantees

Seeking price guarantees is a fifth activity necessary to the negotiation process. The retail buyer may seek a guarantee from the vendor to protect him against possible future price fluctuations. For example, a buyer may ask for a seasonal discount along with a price guarantee. The vendor may be willing to make concessions to obtain early orders from buyers. The price guarantee is fairly common for seasonal merchandise because the vendor is eager to encourage the buyer to place early orders. Or the vendor may use the price guarantee along with the quantity discount to encourage buyers of staple goods to place especially large orders. The guarantee is of particular interest to those retail buyers who must carry a complete line of manufacturer's goods, since there is a substantial inventory investment. The price guarantee is most desirable during economic periods when the market price is uncertain.

Once the buyer determines the merchandise assortment and negotiates the terms and conditions of sale, he is ready to go on to the next step, that is, to fill out the buyer's order form.

Placing the Order

In the past, the sales contract was relatively simple and the negotiations were relatively uninvolved. However, with increased sales activity, more and more care was taken to assure the buyer that merchandise ordered would be received in good condition and according to the prearranged specifications.

A buyer may order merchandise by telephone or in person. Such an agreement is legally binding up to an amount of $50 in most states. However, since many retail buyers are acting as agents of stores and oral orders may prove uncertain and unreliable, it is a practical necessity for retail stores to place written orders.

The order form, then, becomes a most important document, since it contains all details of the business transaction. Although every retail store has its own order form, they all basically contain the same information. Both the front and the back of the order form constitute the legal contract when signed by both the buyer and the vendor. The following information should be contained on the front of the buyer's order form:

- Name and address of the retail organization
- The order number
- The date

BASIC TRADE PROVISIONS

Adopted by the NRMA for inclusion in an order form, specifically or by reference.

1. It is mutually agreed and understood that all the terms and conditions set forth on this Order are satisfactory unless the Seller notifies Purchaser to the contrary, before shipment is made, within 15 days from the date of this order.

2. Purchaser may not cancel this Order for any reason before date for completion of delivery; cancellation after date for completion of delivery shall be effective only upon Purchaser's written notice to Seller, but shall not be effective with respect to any shipments made by the Seller within three (3) working days after receipt of such notice.

3. No returns of merchandise shall be made except for defects therein, or for non-conformity with some material provision of this Order. Where defects are discoverable upon reasonable inspection, or where non-conformity is claimed, such returns shall be made within five (5) working days after the receipt of goods affected. The Purchaser shall send the Seller a separate written notice, setting forth the nature of the defects or non-conformity claimed, prior to or simultaneously with the return. Seller may replace such returned merchandise, provided such replacement is made within five days after the last permissible delivery date.

4. In the event of the material interruption of the business of either the Seller or Purchaser by reason of fire, war, Act of God, governmental action, or strikes which materially affect the performance of this contract, the party so affected may cancel the order for such merchandise as has not been delivered, upon notice to the other party, notwithstanding any other provisions herein.

5. In the event that the Seller should be unable to manufacture, or determine not to manufacture, any style contained in this Order, he shall immediately notify the Purchaser to that effect and thereupon the Seller shall not be liable for non-delivery of such merchandise. Purchaser shall, however, accept delivery and pay for all other merchandise.

6. Seller shall have the right, from time to time, on any unfilled portion of this contract, to limit any credit to be extended hereunder or to require payment before delivery.

7. Any controversy or claim rising out of or relating to any of the provisions of this Order shall be settled by arbitration in accordance with the rules of the American Arbitration Association. For any purpose relating to this arbitration clause or an award rendered hereunder, the Purchaser and Seller consent to the jurisdiction of the Courts of the State in which the Seller has his principal place of business, and any legal process or paper may be served outside of such State by registered mail, or by personal service, provided that a reasonable time for appearance is allowed. Purchaser and Seller further consent that service in accordance herewith shall be sufficient to confer upon the Court jurisdiction in personam over the Purchaser and Seller.

8. No modification of the terms of this agreement shall be effective unless stated in writing, and no waiver by either party of any default shall be deemed a waiver of any subsequent default.

- Department or store ordering the merchandise
- Delivery date
- Cancellation date
- Terms and dating
- Method of transportation
- FOB point
- Place of delivery
- Complete description of the merchandise: style, quantity, color, unit price, total price
- Authorized signatures

The back of the order form usually contains stipulations concerning arrangements whereby the vendor is legally held responsible when he accepts the order from the buyer. The *Basic Trade Provisions* formulated by the National Retail Merchants Association appear on the reverse side of most buyer order forms. These provisions and the information contained on the front of the order form constitute a legal contract when signed by the store's authorized agent, the buyer, and accepted by the seller. (See Figure 13.2.)

The buyer is also concerned with other details such as the method of invoicing, method of packaging, and the method of labeling for distribution

DEPT. 62		Hecker's						PURCHASE ORDER NO. 17411				

Portland, Oregon 97200

TERMS *2/10 Net 30*

DATE *3 / 18 / 19 77*

TO *TRIM LINE*

ADDRESS *1401 BROADWAY, NEW YORK CITY*

SHIP VIA *U.P.S.*   SHIP AS READY BY *4 / 30 / 77* OR CANCEL _____

STYLE	QUAN.	DESCRIPTION	CLR.	INSERT SIZES HERE					COST		RETAIL		TOTAL RET.	
1506	5	Navy Blue - Trim J.S.	06	10	12	14	16	18	14	99	29	95	149	75
1586	10	Pant Suit - Terry Tou	03	10	12	14	16	18	18	95	32	95	329	50
1701	6	Tops - V-Neck	01	S	M	L			5	95	9	95	59	70
1840	18	Jeans - Trim	04	12	14				9	95	18	-	324	-

MERCHANDISE MANAGERS APPROVAL BY *Francis McNeil*

Figure 13.3. An example of a buyer's order form used by a women's specialty shop.

to branch stores, other units of the company, or various departments within the store. This information is also specified on the front and back of the buyer's order form (see Figure 13.3).

Kinds of Orders

There are seven kinds of orders that may be placed by the buying specialist. They are listed as follows:

1. Regular orders. Regular stock orders are placed by the buyer directly with the vendor. They give complete specifications regarding time, amount, and shipment.
2. Reorders. These are orders for goods previously purchased.
3. Open orders. These are orders placed by the resident buying office whereby the resident buyer fills in the name of the vendor believed to be best suited to fill the merchandise requirements of the store.
4. Advance orders. These are regular orders that are placed in advance of immediate need.
5. Special orders. These are orders placed by the buyer for merchandise units to meet the needs of an individual customer or a few customers.
6. Back orders. These are orders placed by the buyer for shipments or parts of shipments that were not filled on time by the vendor.
7. Blanket orders. These are orders placed by the buyer for merchandise for all or part of a season. The order does not indicate details such as shipping, dates, size, finish, color, etc. The buyer will place a requisition against these orders as the merchandise is needed.

Since the order form is a legal agreement between the retail firm and the merchandise resource, it is important for the buyer to fill it out carefully. When writing orders the buyer should observe the following rules:

1. Use the order form provided by the retail store.
2. If an oral order has been placed, confirm it immediately by filling out an order form.
3. It is usually best if the buyer writes out his or her own order form; however, some retail buyers will permit the manufacturer's representative to do so.
4. Always check the order carefully before signing it.
5. Write out specifications and directions carefully and precisely.
6. Put all agreements or any special arrangements in writing.

By observing pre-established rules concerning the writing of the order form, the buyer will facilitate the follow-up procedure. Follow-up is usually the task of the assistant buyer or department head. Order forms written legibly and accurately will enable the assistant to communicate better with vendors regarding merchandise shipments, terms of sale, and order specifications.[1]

Some Hints for Retail Buyers

Whether a new buyer or "an old pro," there are guidelines the buyer should observe when negotiating with vendors. They are listed in Table 13.1.[2]

Don't Be Unreasonable

The buyer should not expect unreasonable concessions from the vendor or manufacturer. For example, a buyer who takes advantage of a vendor by returning merchandise when he or she has no legal right to do so will only encourage the ill will of the vendor, who may eventually ignore the buyer when specials or job lots are available. However, certain circumstances may dictate when merchandise may be returned to the vendor. Once the buyer has taken title to the goods, they should not be returned unless:

1. The merchandise received fails to meet the sample specifications.
2. The merchandise arrives too early or too late in terms of the promised date.
3. Merchandise quantity, style, or color is not as ordered.
4. The terms of sale on the invoice differ from those agreed upon during the negotiation process.

To avoid the tendency on the part of some buyers to take advantage of vendors and manufacturers, many large retail stores require that cancellations of orders and merchandise returns be approved by the merchandise manager. The vendor should not suffer because a retail buyer used poor judgment in buying.

Table 13.1. *Some hints to the retail buyer.*

DO'S	DON'TS
1. Notify the resident buying office when you will be in the market. The resident buyer will help you determine the market's best sellers before you buy.	1. Seek unreasonable concessions from vendors.
2. Seek the opinion of others. Consult with your merchandise manager, other buyers, salespeople and assistants as well as merchandise resources.	2. Avoid playing the "bluff" game.
3. Study all merchandise units carefully and critically. Consider fabric quality, performance, texture, and construction. Ask questions.	3. Pretend to be a "know it all." Ask the vendor for help.
4. Look for goods which will become fast moving items and provide a steady re-order business.	4. Try to redesign the manufacturer's merchandise. Suggest detail changes which will help both you and the manufacturer to sell the goods.
5. Carefully check past sales records before determining quantity and price.	5. Unfairly cancel merchandise.
6. Visit all manufacturers before making a final decision.	6. Accept personal favors and thus become obligated.
7. Fill out the order form at home where you can think clearly and away from pressure.	7. Try and pass your buying "mistakes" on to the vendor.
8. When purchasing bargains, be sure the merchandise will be suitable to the entire line.	8. Put in unfair damage or shortage claims.

The Vendor's Responsibility to the Buyer

PART 2

The Conduct of the Vendor

It goes without saying that the vendor or manufacturer has certain obligations to the buyer. For example, the vendor has the responsibility of offering the same *opportunities* for price concessions to small retailers as he does to buyers for large retail operations (this point was discussed at length in Chapter 12).

This, however, does not mean that vendors must offer the same *prices* to all buyers. Lower prices and concessions must be based on the specific quantities ordered, as well as the conditions of the terms of sale. Any buyer, therefore, placing orders for specified quantities and conditions of purchase is entitled to similar concessions on proportionately equal terms.

The vendor has the responsibility of fair play when dealing with the buyer. A vendor should not "ship short," that is, the specified amount of merchandise should be shipped. He or she should not ship unordered merchandise or include extra goods in the hope that the buyer will accept and pay for the whole shipment. A vendor who continually engages in this type of activity not only breaks the contractual agreement but also soon develops a reputation among store buyers for being unreliable and lacking good business conduct.

Legal Aspects of the Buyer's Order

It is important to remember that, *once the vendor accepts the order, the contract has been made.* Vendors who offer merchandise for sale and who accept orders from retail buyers complete the cycle that forms the legal contract. A *legal contract* may be defined as an order that has been properly filled out, signed, and accepted by the vendor. Since the buyer's order is an agreement containing a promise enforceable by law, the laws of contract require that the buyer and the vendor observe the trade practices listed in Table 13.2 when writing and accepting the order.[3]

It is important to remember that both the buyer and the vendor must follow established trade practices and customs, since their observance will affect legal decisions regarding the validity of the order. The buyer must be aware of and understand his legal rights, and the actions of both parties must be governed by the principles of good business conduct and fair dealing.

Table 13.2. *Trade practices that must be observed by the vendor and the buyer.*

1. The order must be established for a lawful purpose
   The sale of merchandise
2. The order is made by competent parties
   Both parties must be over 21 years of age, sane, competent, and not enemies.
3. Contains an offer and an acceptance
   The buyer offered money in payment and the offer was accepted by the vendor.
4. Entails a consideration
   The buyer promises to give up money. The vendor promises to give up goods; or, a payment is actually made.
5. There is a meeting of the minds
   Both the buyer and the vendor agree that the order is reasonable and acceptable.

The following is a list of practices that may cause friction between vendors and buyers:[4]

Causes of friction between vendors and buyers
1. Returns and adjustments
2. Cancellations
3. Shipping problems
4. Special order and minimum orders
5. Price maintenance
6. Selling competitors and exclusives
7. Fashion piracy
8. Advancing seasons
9. Substitutions
10. Failure to follow instructions

Returns and Adjustments

Some retail buyers may return unsold merchandise at the end of the season for credit without the consent of the vendor, and when they have no legal right to do so. For example, the merchandise may have been damaged by rough handling in the store, or it may have been returned by customers to the store for a refund. Some buyers may return goods that are slightly soiled and expect the vendor to replace them. The buyer is not legally justified in making such returns unless he and the vendor have agreed in writing that such goods may be returned and will be accepted for credit.

Vendors may agree to take back merchandise, particularly if the retail store is a good customer. On the other hand, some vendors may refuse to accept legitimate returns or to make adjustments when they themselves are responsible or at fault. Such practices will cause friction and lead to poor vendor-buyer relations. If objectionable practices become excessive, the buyer may seek another vendor, or the vendor may drop the buyer's account.

Cancellations

A cancellation policy should be agreed upon between vendors and buying specialists. The following list is representative of conditions under which orders may be cancelled:

1. When merchandise is not shipped by the final due date specified on the buyer's order form
2. When the vendor or manufacturer receives a cancellation notice from the buyer

ORDER CANCELLATION

DEPT. _428 –_

DATE _10 - 16 - 77_   No. 27336   VENDOR COPY
515-28 (REV. 5-73)

STORE(S) TO BE NOTIFIED	
PHILADELPHIA	☒
WILMINGTON	☐
WYNNEWOOD	☐
WESTCHESTER	☐
JENKINTOWN	☐
MOORESTOWN	☐
KING OF PRUSSIA	☐
HARRISBURG	☐
READING	☐
OXFORD VALLEY	☐
SPRINGFIELD	☐

GENTLEMEN:

THIS IS A ☒ SINGLE STORE CANCELLATION

☐ MULTI STORE CANCELLATION

RAMIE SPORTSWEAR

BROADWAY

NEW YORK, NEW YORK

John Wanamaker

P.O. BOX 7497
THIRTEENTH AND MARKET STREETS
PHILADELPHIA, PENNSYLVANIA 19101

YOU ARE HEREBY NOTIFIED THAT THE STYLE NUMBERS ON THE ORDERS LISTED BELOW
ARE CANCELLED. THIS CANCELLATION IS EFFECTIVE IMMEDIATELY UPON RECEIPT.

STORE NAME	ORDER #	STYLE #	UNIT PIECE DOZ GROSS	QUANTITY	UNIT COST	EXTENDED COST	UNIT RETAIL	EXTENDED RETAIL	MONTH OF DELIVERY
J.W.	5601	72	UNIT	24	6.50	—	13.00	—	NOV
	5614	18	UNIT	10	8.50		17.00	—	NOV
		TOTALS		24		—		—	

REASON FOR CANCELLATION _LATE SHIPMENT_
BUYER SIGNATURE _H. L. Bachman_   MDSE OFFICE _SPORTSWEAR_

**REMOVE THIS STUB
BEFORE MAILING**

Figure 13.4. An example of an order cancellation. (Courtesy of John Wanamaker Department Store, Philadelphia, Pa.)

3. When the vendor changes merchandise specifications or other conditions of the order
4. When there is mutual agreement between the vendor and the buyer regarding merchandise cancellations
5. When the merchandise manager's approval is obtained

Figure 13.4 is an example of an order cancellation used by a department store to notify a vendor that the style numbers on the orders listed are cancelled.

Shipping Problems

Early, late, or split shipments can cause friction between vendors and buyers. If, for example, the buyer has limited storage space, it may be impossible to accept merchandise before the time designated on the order. Also, early shipments require earlier payment unless the vendor or manufacturer provides for extra dating. If a buyer does not want an early shipment of goods, this should be stated in writing on the order form: for example, "Do not deliver before October 1."

Late shipments also cause problems for buyers. They may find themselves with an inadequate assortment of merchandise, which may cause their customers to shop elsewhere. Or the buyer may be "stuck" with out-of-season goods. A telephone call or a letter from a vendor explaining the situation would help the buyer plan more effectively and eliminate costly markdowns.

Split shipments often are an unusual hardship for the vendor as well as the buyer. A manufacturer or a vendor who is not able to fill an entire order as specified may make a partial shipment on the designated delivery date with a notation that the remainder will be shipped at a later date. However, when the unfilled portion arrives, the buyer may refuse to accept the merchandise, even though he or she has not previously notified the vendor of intention to reject the goods.

Special Orders and Minimum Orders

A retail buyer may wish to place special orders with a vendor, especially if the buyer carries a limited stock of merchandise. Special orders enable buyers to provide for individual needs of customers while eliminating the necessity for carrying a large assortment of goods. On the other hand, special orders are costly for manufacturers to handle; therefore, they dislike working on them. To discourage special orders, a manufacturer may charge an extra handling fee, which retailers object to rather strongly.

Some buyers use the "hand-to-mouth principle" when ordering merchan-

Figure 13.5. An example of a special order form. (Courtesy of John Wanamaker Department Store, Philadelphia, Pa.)

dise, whereby they buy in small quantities those goods they can sell within a short period of time; therefore, some manufacturers charge extra for minimum orders. This practice also causes friction between vendors and buyers. Figure 13.5 is an example of a special order placed by a salesperson, which in turn will be forwarded to the vendor by the buyer.

Price Maintenance

Failure on the part of some buyers to follow the vendor's policy of price maintenance is a fifth cause of friction. Problems may arise as a result of some retailers' policy of price cutting. That is, they will sell the merchandise at a price lower than the manufacturer's suggested retail price. Many vendors insist that their accounts may sell their merchandise only if the retail buyer agrees to maintain the manufacturer's suggested retail price. If this policy is not followed, retail buyers may seek other vendors and manufacturers. Also, the vendor may refuse to sell in future to a buyer violating this policy.

Selling Competitors and Exclusives

For the most part, a manufacturer will not sell special lines of merchandise to buyers from retail stores that are in direct competition with one another. However, to increase volume, a manufacturer may sell identical merchandise to those traditionally not associated with the selling of such goods. For example, a manufacturer of women's stockings may sell his product to a manufacturer of soap or detergent to be available in return for the coupon attached to the box of soap. Some retail buyers may see this as a threat to product sales. Buyers may seek to have agreements established preventing the selling of identical goods in such nontraditional ways to more than one company.

Exclusive agreements may be arranged between vendors and buyers. The purpose of an exclusive agreement is primarily to protect the buyer from having the same goods offered for sale to his competition. Also, such an agreement will ensure the vendor of full coverage of his lines in a store that will best merchandise his product.

Fashion Piracy

Fashion piracy is a matter of concern among vendors themselves. However, occasionally a retail buyer will copy a vendor's sample or hold out a sample and seek another manufacturer to reproduce the article. Buyers and vendors must establish policies prohibiting such practices.

Advancing Seasons

Competition has promoted the practice of advancing seasons, whereby both vendors and buyers cut prices before a season is over and while an active consumer demand still exists. Usually, the next season's line is promoted before the period of normal consumer demand. Often, however, such premature markdowns cause unnecessary losses to both vendors and buyers. Individual vendors or buyers may find it to their immediate advantage to act ahead of the competition. However, there is a need for a general but flexible agreement between vendors and buyers as to the proper time to institute seasonal clearance and offer new seasonal merchandise.

Substitutions

Often a vendor will have to send the buyer substitutes for the original merchandise offered. For example, in the fashion goods trade a manufacturer is frequently unable to obtain unlimited quantities of certain fabrics or color combinations. When the manufacturer receives a reorder, he fills it with merchandise that follows as closely as possible the original merchandise specifications. The manufacturer should notify the buyer of the substitution and get permission to ship the merchandise; however, the rush of business and the desire of buyers to receive merchandise, even though it is different from the shipment ordered, makes this difficult.

Failure to Follow Instructions

Finally, friction between vendors and buyers is caused by failure to follow instructions. For example, a vendor may add greatly to the cost of transportation by failing to follow shipping instructions. This has led retail stores to compare shipments with shipping instructions and charge back to the vendor the added cost caused by failure to follow the instructions provided. The vendor must remember that additional shipping charges will increase the cost of goods, thus lowering the buyer's profit.

Needless to say, vendors and buyers can supply long lists of complaints against each other. However, most problems arise because some vendors and some buyers are thoughtless about their responsibilities. The vendor and the buyer must remember that each is responsible for actively promoting and protecting a company's image. Problems and complaints that reflect on the image of the vendor's or the buyer's company will eventually prove costly and lead to a serious loss of business. It is important to both parties that mutual confidence and respect become more evident than distrust or disrespect. Each must effectively communicate with the other, respect the other's business policies, and attempt to understand the other's potentials and problems. Both should work together in mutual agreement and understanding.

Establishing Good Vendor-Buyer Relations

The following policies should be considered to ensure the establishment and maintenance of good vendor-buyer relations:[5]

1. Be as loyal to a good vendor as he is expected to be to the buyer.
2. Never discontinue business without sufficient cause and only when mutual discussions and criticisms have failed to produce desired results.
3. Be fair and honest when considering one another's offerings.
4. Make all commitments definite and precise.

5. Do not partake in commercial bribery, that is, accept or offer gifts, rewards, and commissions.
6. Continuously improve trade relations through education, self-regulation and government regulation.
7. Represent the best interests of the company at all times.
8. Do not take unfair advantage of one another.
9. Become thoroughly knowledgeable of the merchandise line you represent.
10. Work hard to establish and maintain a good working relationship.

Chapter Summary

The activities that occur during the negotiation process are very important to buyer and vendor alike. The buyer has the responsibility of ethically representing his retail organization to the vendor, securing discounts and allowances, arranging transportation and storage, establishing the terms of sale, and seeking price guarantees. This interchange between buyer and vendor occurs before the order is written and signed.

There are several kinds of orders that may be placed by the buyer. They are: (1) regular orders, (2) reorders, (3) open orders, (4) advance orders, (5) special orders, (6) back orders, and (7) blanket orders.

The order form is a most important document, since it contains all details of the business transaction. Because it is a legal agreement between the retail firm and the merchandise resource, it is important for the buyer to fill it out carefully. By observing the rules concerning the writing of the order form, the buyer will facilitate the follow-up procedure and assist in establishing communications between the store and the vendor.

Retail buyers should not expect unreasonable concessions during the negotiation process. They must observe certain guidelines or "do's and don'ts" when dealing with vendors and manufacturers.

Vendors have certain obligations to retail buyers. Once the vendor accepts an order from the buying specialist, a legal contract has been made. Since the buyer's order is an agreement containing a promise enforceable by law, the laws of contract require that the vendor and the buyer observe specific trade practices when writing and accepting the order.

Although the vendor and the buyer must follow established trade practices, problems may arise that may cause friction between them. Causes of friction are: (1) returns and adjustments, (2) cancellations, (3) shipping problems, (4) special orders and minimum orders, (5) price maintenance, (6) selling competitors and exclusives, (7) fashion piracy, (8) advancing seasons, (9) substitutions, and (10) failure to follow instructions.

Most problems arise because some buyers and some vendors are thoughtless about their responsibilities. It is important for each to remember that he or she carries the good name and reputation of the company in all dealings. Problems and complaints that reflect on the image of the vendor or the buyer will eventually prove costly and lead to a serious loss of business. Both the vendor and the buyer should establish policies that will ensure the establishment and maintenance of good vendor-buyer relations.

Trade Terminology

DIRECTIONS: Briefly explain or discuss each of the following trade terms:

1. Negotiation process
2. Discount or allowance
3. Quantity discount
4. Seasonal discount
5. Trade discount
6. Cash discount
7. FOB factory
8. FOB destination
9. FOB shipping point
10. FOB destination, charges reversed
11. FOB destination, freight prepaid
12. Legal contract

Questions for Discussion and Review

1. What is the negotiation process? Name five activities involved and explain the importance of each.

2. Discuss the seasonal discount from the point of view of (1) the retail buyer, (2) the vendor, and (3) the consumer.

3. As the retail firm's representative, the buyer has certain responsibilities. Name five of these, and explain how each is important in developing good buyer-vendor relations.

4. Why is the buyer's order considered to be a most important document?

5. What kind of information is usually found on the order form?

6. What is meant by the statement, "Once the vendor accepts the order, the contract has been made?"

7. What rules and recommendations should the buyer observe when filling out the order?

8. What kinds of orders may be placed by the buying specialist?

9. Referring to "Some Hints for Retail Buyers," what guidelines would you suggest to help the new buyer when negotiating with the vendor?

10. What trade practices should be observed by the vendor and the buyer when writing and accepting the order?

11. What are some important causes of friction between vendors and buyers?

12. Consider each of the ten policies that should be followed by vendors and buyers. What suggestions can you offer to improve upon these policies?

Case Study Number One

A Cause of Friction

You are a buyer of men's shirts and have just been informed by the stockboy that only three of the five styles of shirts you have ordered have arrived in the stockroom. The storewide sale that is planned to begin in two days has already been advertised, and the advertisement specifies that all five styles of men's shirts will be on sale. The vendor is located approximately 150 miles away and, due to a shipper's strike, the merchandise will take longer than usual to arrive. You must attend a meeting with the merchandise manager to discuss final plans for the sale. Since your assistant buyer is out to lunch and your meeting is to take place in five minutes, you must outline directions to the assistant buyer to call the manufacturer and attempt to straighten out the problem. List on a separate piece of paper the information you would want the assistant buyer to obtain for you. How would you solve this problem?

Case Study Number Two

An Exclusive Arrangement

Judy Haines had been a most successful buyer of ladies' shoes and boots in a leading department store located in a large city in the Pacific Northwest. The boot line was Judy's favorite, and she developed an excellent sense of where to buy, how much to buy, and how to get the best markup. In most cases, Judy was able to eliminate competition by purchasing the supplier's complete stock.

Recently, however, Judy had taken over a new position as ladies' shoe buyer for Muskas department store, located in a large city in Alaska. When Judy arrived in Alaska, she found that Muskas's former buyer had purchased a substantial supply of shoes and boots from many different merchandise resources and, in particular, a number of styles of boots. She also discovered that many styles and sizes of boots had not sold in more than a year. This situation had to be corrected if Judy was to have a profitable department.

Thinking back on her previous method of doing business, Judy decided to call upon her old supplier, Reindeer Boot Manufacturing Company, and see if it could supply all the department's needs in boots. If this were possible, she would take the position that the supplier would get all of Muskas's boot business. However, for this to occur, the boot manufacturer would have to be competitive in price and not sell to other retail stores within a 50-mile radius. Judy found that Reindeer had never had much business in Alaska and was very anxious to enter into such an arrangement. The agreement would increase Reindeer's boot business by 400 percent.

With the agreement in hand, Judy now presented her idea to the merchandise manager for final approval. The merchandise manager, however, had a decision to make. Should he go along with this new and progressive buyer and take on a new and exclusive line of ladies' boots, or should he maintain present store buying principles?

How would you handle this situation?

Retailing Activities to Stimulate Student Interest and Participation

1. Prepare a short paper on the importance of good buyer-vendor relations. Refer to The Retail Student's Reference Library for selected references.

2. Select a small retail business in your local shopping area. Make an appointment with the store manager to discuss various methods of buying. Determine how they are used by the entrepreneur during the buying process.

3. Interview a buyer of fashion goods in a department store. Discuss the importance of understanding the Basic Trade Provisions as formulated by the National Retail Merchants Association. Cite specific examples.

The Retail Student's Reference Library   REFERENCES

Belden, Donald L. *The Role of the Buyer in Mass Merchandising.* New York: Chain Store Publishing Corporation, 1971.

Duncan, D. J., and Hermanson, R. H. *Retailing: Modern Concepts and Practices.* Homewood, Ill.: Learning Systems Company, 1970.

Fine, I. B., Westing, J. H., and Lenz, G. J. *Purchasing Management.* New York: John Wiley & Sons, 1970.

Freeman, H., and Logan, William B. *Merchandising Mathematics.* Hightstown: McGraw-Hill Book Company, 1973.

Fried, Eleanor. *Is the Fashion Business Your Business?* New York: Fairchild Publications, Inc., 1970.

Gillespie, Karen R., and Hecht, Joseph C. *Retail Business Management.* Hightstown: McGraw-Hill Book Company, 1970.

Gold, E. B. *Dynamics of Retailing.* New York: Fairchild Publications, Inc., n. d.

Helfant, S., and Judelle, B. *Management Manual for Independent Stores.* New York: National Retail Merchants Association, n. d.

Hoffman, E., Buck, B. F., and Small, V. *Fairchild's Directory of Home Furnishings.* New York: Fairchild Publications, Inc., 1972.

Johnston, John Wallis. *The Department Store Buyer.* Austin: University of Texas Press, n. d.

Judelle, Beatrice. *The Fashion Buyer's Job.* New York: National Retail Merchants Association, 1971.

Judelle, B., and Troxell, M. *Fashion Merchandising.* Hightstown: McGraw-Hill Book Company, 1971.

Kelley, P. C. *Variety Stores.* Washington, D.C.: U.S. Government Printing Office, n. d.

Kiernan, Gladys M. *Retailer's Manual of Laws and Regulations.* New York: Research Company of America, 1971.

Kissel, Irwin R., and Grun, Ann K. *How to Handle Claims and Returns.* Hightstown: McGraw-Hill Book Company, 1973.

Profitable Merchandising Techniques. New York: Fairchild Publications, Inc., 1970.

Promoting New Merchandising Areas. New York: Fairchild Publications, Inc., 1971.

Rachman, David J. *Retail Management Strategy: Selected Readings.* New York: Prentice-Hall, Inc., 1970.

Readings in Modern Retailing. New York: National Retail Merchants Association, 1970.

A Retailer Visits the Market. New York: Fairchild Publications, Inc., n. d.

Rice, J. W. *Furniture Retailing.* Washington, D.C.: U.S. Government Printing Office, n. d.

Ritter, Dorothy. *Hardware Retailing.* Washington, D.C.: U.S. Government Printing Office, n. d.

Robinson, J. W. *Gift and Art Shops.* Washington, D.C.: U.S. Government Printing Office, n. d.

Taylor, C. G. *Merchandise Assortment Planning.* New York: National Retail Merchants Association, n.d.

References

1. J. W. Wingate and Joseph S. Friedlander, *The Management of Retail Buying* (Englewood Cliffs, N.J.: Prentice-Hall, Inc., 1963), pp. 334–337.

2. Donald L. Belden, *The Role of the Buyer in Mass Merchandising* (New York: Chain Store Publishing Corporation, 1971), pp. 22–23.

3. Karen R. Gillespie and Joseph C. Hecht, *Retail Business Management* (Hightstown: McGraw-Hill Book Company, 1970), p. 178.

4. Wingate and Friedlander, *Management of Retail Buying,* pp. 348–351.

5. Belden, *Role of the Buyer,* pp. 22–24.

Preparing Merchandise for Resale

SECTION 4

Pricing Merchandise for Resale

14

Performance Objectives

PART 1

Determining the Wholesale Price

Obtaining the Best Possible Value

A Thorough Knowledge of Prices

Price Guessing
Price Memorization
Price Buildup

Elements in the Wholesale Price

Wholesale or Quoted Price
Wholesale Discounts
Transportation and Shipping Costs

Legal Aspects of Pricing

Anti-price Discrimination Laws
Unfair Practice Laws
Fair Trade Laws

PART 2

Determining the Retail Price

An Important Selection Factor

Important Factors to Consider

Internal Factors
External Factors
Other Factors

Chapter Summary
Trade Terminology
Questions for Discussion and Review
Case Study Number One; Number Two
Retailing Activities to Stimulate Student Interest and Participation
The Retail Student's Reference Library
References

PERFORMANCE
OBJECTIVES

As a result of reading this chapter, the student should be able to accomplish the following:

1. Recall three techniques used by a buyer to develop a thorough knowledge of prices.

2. Prepare a list of sources used by buyers to obtain price information.

3. Define wholesale price; retail price.

4. Discuss three important elements included in the wholesale price.

5. List five kinds of discounts offered to a retail buyer by merchandise resources.

6. Explain quantity discount; seasonal discount; cash discount; series discount.

7. Give examples of transportation and shipping costs.

8. Identify three major price laws that have been passed to protect both the retailer and the consumer.

9. Identify three major factors to consider when determining the retail price.

10. Define markup; markdown.

11. Write the markup formula; the markdown formula.

Pricing Merchandise for Resale

Determining the Wholesale Price

Part 1

As you recall from earlier chapters, two very important responsibilities of the retail buyer are to obtain a profit for the store and to serve the needs and wants of the store's customers. To accomplish these two tasks, the buying specialist must obtain the best values possible when negotiating with merchandise resources. This means familiarizing himself or herself with the price offerings of various merchandise resources who carry the particular line of goods wanted.

Obtaining the Best Possible Value

The capable buyer, as a result of past experience, will know when he or she is paying too much for merchandise. Upon close inspection, the buyer will be able to approximate the cost price, or the price to be paid to the vendor, as well as estimating the retail price, or the price the goods will be sold for in the retail store. How does the buyer develop this thorough knowledge of prices? Part 1 of this chapter will discuss (1) developing a thorough knowledge of prices, (2) determining elements in the wholesale price, and (3) understanding the legal aspects of pricing. Part 2 will discuss how the retail price is determined. Topics to be considered are (1) the importance of the retail price in merchandise selection, (2) various factors in pricing for retail, and (3) formulas used to determine the retail price.

The following three techniques may be used by all types of buyers to assist them in developing a thorough knowledge of prices. They are: (1) price guessing, (2) price memorization, and (3) price buildup.

A Thorough Knowledge of Prices

Price Guessing
Before the buying specialist can begin price negotiations with merchandise resources, he should accumulate a vast amount of price information. The sources of price information are too numerous to list completely; they may include conversations with vendors and manufacturers' representatives, examination of merchandise in his or her own department (see Figure 14.1) and of similar merchandise offered by the competition, trade journals, catalogs and

Figure 14.1. Before this buying specialist can begin price negotiations, she must accumulate a vast amount of price information. One source of price information is the merchandise offerings in her own department.

price lists, and conversations with others in the trade. As a result of accumulating price information, the buyer will soon develop a remarkable skill in price guessing and be able to place prices upon merchandise wherever it is to be seen, in retail stores, manufacturers' showrooms, or as samples displayed by salespeople. Sources of price information used by buyers are:

1. Merchandise offerings in the buyer's own store
2. Merchandise offerings of competitors
3. Trade journals
4. Catalogs and price lists
5. Conversations

What other sources of price information are available?

Price Memorization

Once the buyers learn the cost prices offered by vendors and the retail prices of similar goods offered in retail stores, they memorize them. The buyers will also remember price changes as reported by trade journals or vendors. They have the ability to build up a storehouse of memorized prices based upon careful and close concentration on price information and close attention to price changes in the marketplace.

Price Buildup

A third technique used by buyers in developing a thorough knowledge of prices is the ability to estimate manufacturers' expenses. If the buyers can estimate the cost of materials used in the manufacturing of the product and the manufacturer's operating expenses, they are better able to evaluate the fairness of the manufacturer's quoted price. Using this method, the buyer may determine whether or not the vendor or manufacturer is attempting to make too much profit. Or, if the goods offered are priced too low, there is a possibility that the merchandise is of poor quality, of poor workmanship, or that the finished product may not be a good seller.

How will the following techniques help the buyer develop a thorough knowledge of prices?

Price Guessing

The buyer is enabled to place prices upon merchandise wherever and whenever seen.

Price Memorization

The buyer will remember prices seen in the marketplace and price changes as reported by trade journals and vendors.

Price Buildup

The buyer will estimate the manufacturer's cost of materials and operating expenses to determine the fairness of the manufacturer's quoted price.

Elements in the Wholesale Price

Wholesale price may be defined as the price paid for goods purchased from merchandise resources, for example, vendors, manufacturers, or suppliers. Since price negotiation is a very important responsibility of the buyer, he or she must be aware of three elements that are included in the wholesale price. They are: (1) wholesale or quoted price, (2) wholesale discounts, and (3) transportation and shipping costs.

Wholesale or Quoted Price

While most buying is done at the wholesale price or quoted price, the capable buyer is always attempting to secure the lowest price possible. A successful buyer is usually a skilled trader. If it seems that the vendor's price is too high, that the value of the purchase does not equal the quality, that production costs are unfair, that the season indicates a lower price, or that there are unusual conditions of sale, the buyer will negotiate with the vendor or manufacturer for a price concession. However, a smart buyer will be careful not to press for rock-bottom prices unless such a bid can be justified. A buyer who habitually makes unsupported demands on merchandise resources will develop a reputation throughout the trade. Sellers will find considerable satisfaction in quoting higher than normal prices to this buyer, whose job will become unnecessarily difficult. Generally, a buyer will enter the marketplace intent on purchasing the right goods at the right time and at the right amount, rather than on saving a few dollars on the purchase price. The store buyer will have ample opportunity to obtain price concessions when buying *special merchandise,* that is, goods offered not for quality appeal but for price appeal.

Wholesale Discounts

There are five kinds of discounts offered a retail buyer by merchandise resources. They are: (1) trade discounts, (2) quantity discounts, (3) seasonal discounts, (4) cash discounts, and (5) series discounts. As you recall from previous readings, discounts are offered to buyers in the form of vendor aids. In this chapter we will discuss how discounts are formulated.

Five kinds of discounts offered by merchandise resources to retail buyers are:

1. Trade discounts or functional discounts
   A reduction in price given to certain trade customers to cover costs involved in performing particular trade functions
2. Quantity discounts
   A discount offered to retail buyers to encourage large-quantity purchases
3. Seasonal discounts
   A reduction in wholesale price granted to buyers to encourage off-season buying
4. Cash discounts
   A reduction in price given to a retail buyer when a cash payment is made within a certain date specified on the invoice
5. Series discounts or chain discounts
   A series of discounts granted to the buyer to stimulate a greater volume of business

---

Trade Discount. It is important to remember that trade discounts are usually not considered a form of price concession but rather a method of quoting prices based on list prices. For example, a manufacturer may list prices in a catalog that are often suggested retail prices or "offering prices." A retailer may be granted a trade discount perhaps 25 percent off the list price. Also, a manufacturer may use the trade discount as a method of changing the prices of all the merchandise in his line. For example, the manufacturer's catalog may list as many as 1,000 items. Rather than reprinting the catalog with new prices, the manufacturer will send a notice to buyers informing them that the former 25 percent trade discount is changed to 25 percent and 10 percent, thus the buyer is granted an additional 10 percent discount. Or, if merchandise prices need to be increased, the vendor may issue new price lists informing the trade of a reduction in discount.

A supplier may sell to service wholesalers, drop-shipment wholesalers (wholesalers who ship directly to retail stores), chain-store buyers, resident buyers, and small independent retailers, and may offer a 50 percent trade discount to all wholesalers, chain buyers, and resident buyers; 40 percent to drop-shipment wholesalers; and 25 percent to the small independents. The trade discount bears no relationship to the amount of goods purchased at any given time period. It may be given in addition to other discounts, for example, the quantity discount.[1]

The trade discount offered to buyers will vary for a number of reasons. First, the vendor's cost of selling to a small independent retailer as opposed to a chain-store buyer may vary significantly. It is less costly for a vendor to sell 5,000 units of his product to a single chain buyer than it is to sell the same quantity to 300 small independent retailers. Second, variations in trade discounts may differ as a result of the buyer's operating costs. By way of illustration, the cost of selling to wholesalers and discount buyers may be the same. However, the wholesaler may have lower operating costs as compared to the discount buyer, who must ship and warehouse the merchandise throughout a region or territory. Thus, if both the wholesaler and the discounter buy at the same price, the discounter can be undersold and may withdraw from the sale of the goods offered by the vendor. To prevent this situation from occurring, the vendor will offer the discounter a larger trade discount.[2]

Trade discounts may be computed as follows:

A vendor may offer a 50% trade discount to chain-store buyers, wholesalers, and resident buyers.

Thus:

List Price Per Unit (suggested retail price)	$50.00
Less 50% (trade discount)	− 25.00
(50% of $50.00 = $25.00)	$25.00

A vendor may offer a 40% trade discount to drop-shipment wholesalers. Thus:

List Price Per Unit (suggested retail price)	$50.00
Less 40% (trade discount)	− 20.00
(40% of $50.00 = $20.00)	$30.00

A vendor may offer a 25% trade discount to small independent retailers. Thus:

List Price Per Unit (suggested retail price)	$50.00
Less 25% (trade discount)	− 12.50
(25% of $50.00 = $12.50)	$37.50

A vendor may offer a 25% trade discount and an additional 10% trade discount to buyers.
Thus:

List Price Per Unit (suggested retail price)	$50.00
Less 25% (trade discount)	− 12.50
	37.50
Less 10% (additional trade discount)	− 3.75
	$33.75

Quantity Discount. The quantity discount is offered by vendors to encourage retail buyers to make large quantity purchases. For example, a buyer who agrees to purchase 500 units of merchandise instead of 300 units may be given a 10 percent reduction in the wholesale price. However, the buyer must be aware that quantity discounts may lead to overbuying and hence must carefully weigh the advantages and disadvantages of quantity purchases and be certain that the additional units of merchandise will make a profit for the department and thus for the store.

A quantity discount may be computed as follows:

A vendor may offer a 10% quantity discount if the buyer purchases 500 units of stock instead of 300 units.
Thus:

Wholesale Price	$500.00
Less 10% (quantity discount)	− 50.00
(10% of $500.00 = $50.00)	$450.00

As you recall, a quantity discount may also be stated in the form of "free" merchandise given to the buying specialist. For example, a wholesaler of gourmet food may offer a 1-case-free-with-15-cases-purchased deal for food buyers who wish to make purchases for the Christmas season.

Seasonal Discount. The seasonal discount is a percentage reduction in wholesale price or list price granted by suppliers to buyers to encourage off-season buying. Since many kinds of staple merchandise are in demand only during particular seasons throughout the year—for example, air conditioners, skiing equipment, Christmas ornaments, and bathing suits—vendors will offer discounts to encourage buyers to anticipate their needs in advance of the season. Vendors find it good business to offer seasonal discounts because off-season orders enable them to stabilize production activities on a year-round basis, rather than being swamped with orders during particular seasons. Also, the buyer may gain not only a price concession, but also goods manufactured during the off-season months, which are more carefully produced, marked, and packaged. However, once again the buyer must carefully anticipate needs because, if the merchandise does not sell, there is the problem of storage and warehousing expenses as well as the problem of merchandise becoming out of style. A seasonal discount may range from 10 percent to 40 percent, depending on the type of retail store and the nature of the goods.

Seasonal discounts may be computed as follows:

A vendor may offer a 40% seasonal discount to a toy buyer to encourage the buyer to place orders and to accept delivery in June rather than wait until August.
Thus:

List Price	$175.00
Less 40% (seasonal discount)	– 70.00
(40% of $175.00 = $70.00)	$105.00

A vendor may offer a 30% seasonal discount to a buyer of lawn supplies to encourage the buyer to place orders and to accept delivery in December rather than wait until February.
Thus:

List Price	$85.00
Less 30% (seasonal discount)	–25.50
(30% of $85.00 = $25.50)	$59.50

A vendor may offer a 10% seasonal discount to a buyer of children's shoes to encourage the buyer to place orders and accept delivery in March rather than waiting until June.
Thus:

List Price	$15.00
Less 10% (seasonal discount)	– 1.50
(10% of $15.00 = $1.50)	$13.50

Cash Discount. A cash discount is a reduction in price given by a vendor to a retailer when a cash payment is made within a certain time period specified on the invoice. For example, 2/10 net 30 will allow the buyer a 2 percent discount if he pays the bill promptly. It must be remembered, however, that often a period of several days from the date of the invoice elapses before the merchandise is received. The cash discount may still be granted because payment need be made only within the stated period of the terms of sale. Cash discounts are taken after trade discounts, quantity discounts, and seasonal discounts.

There are other forms of cash discount. For example, a vendor may send an invoice (bill) with terms of 2/10 net 30 extra, whereby the 2 percent cash discount is extended for a thirty-day period in addition to the ten-day period, which gives a total of forty days from the invoice date. Or a vendor may send an invoice (bill) with terms of 2/10 EOM, whereby the 2 percent cash discount period runs for ten days following the end of the month (EOM) in which the goods were purchased. If, for example, a purchase was made on September 1 with terms of 2/10 EOM, the 2 percent discount could be taken any time through October 10.

Cash discounts may be computed as follows:

A vendor may send an invoice (bill) with terms of 2/10 net 30. Thus:

Amount of Invoice	$250.00
2/10 net 30	− 5.00
(2% cash discount if paid within ten days)	$245.00
(2% of $250.00 = $5.00)	

However, if payment is not made within the ten days, it is customary for the buyer to wait twenty days longer and pay the total invoice price at that time, thus the terms are usually stated on the invoice as 2/10 net 30.

A vendor may send an invoice (bill) with terms of 2/10 net 30 extra. Thus:

Amount of Invoice	$250.00
2/10 net 30 extra	− 5.00
(2% cash discount is extended for	$245.00
a thirty-day period, in addition to	
ten days, which gives a total of	
forty days)	

A vendor may send an invoice (bill) with terms of 2/10 EOM. Thus:

Amount of Invoice	$250.00
	– 5.00
2/10 EOM	$245.00
(2% cash discount period runs for ten days following the end of the month [EOM] in which goods were purchased)	

Series Discount. A *series discount* or *chain discount* may be defined as a series of discounts granted by the merchandise resource to the retail buyer. Extra discounts are granted to secure the business of a particular retail store or to stimulate a greater volume of business. It is important to remember that in taking a series discount, the discount is taken from the cost price and then on from the preceding price. For example, if the series discount is 10/30/20 percent, these are *not* added together to equal 60 percent.

A series discount may be computed as follows:

A vendor may offer a series discount of 10 percent, 30 percent, 20 percent. Thus:

List Price	$50.00
Less 10% (trade discount)	5.00
Cost Price	$45.00
Less 30% (extra trade discount)	13.50
	$31.50
Less 20% (quantity discount)	6.30
Net Price	$25.20

Transportation and Shipping Costs

The method of transportation as well as the method of shipping will also affect the cost of goods purchased from merchandise resources. Usually, the vendor or manufacturer will quote the selling price of goods (wholesale price) at the point of production. Or the buyer may purchase goods from a middleman, a warehouse, or a limited-function wholesaler. In most instances, the buyer will pay the entire cost of transportation and will also assume responsibility for damage and all other costs while the merchandise is en route to the retail store. (Review the terms used in transportation and shipping, discussed in the previous chapter.)

Review the elements included in the wholesale price

1. Wholesale or quoted price
   A capable buyer is able to secure the lowest price possible.
2. Wholesale discounts
   Discounts will enable the buyer an opportunity for a reduction in goods.
3. Transportation and shipping costs
   The buyer must determine who is going to pay for transportation and shipping.
Why are the elements of the wholesale price important?

Legal Aspects of Pricing

The major purpose of government regulation of business is to promote the public welfare, benefit the economy as a whole, and protect the small business enterprise. The laws passed by Congress that affect business are wide-ranging and often complex. Also, each state in which a business operates has laws regulating business conduct. The objective of this section will be to discuss the impact of government's influence on retail businesses through: (1) price discrimination laws, (2) unfair trade practice laws, and (3) fair trade laws. Also, the student should review federal legislation, as presented in Chapter 1 under "Response to Governmental Changes."

The government influences business through
Anti-price discrimination laws Unfair trade practice laws Fair trade laws

Anti-price Discrimination Laws

In 1914 the Clayton Act was passed, which outlawed price discrimination, exclusive and tying contracts, intercorporate stockholdings, and interlocking directorates. It is quite specific in forbidding certain practices. The principal provisions of the Clayton Act include:[3]

Section 2, which makes it unlawful for sellers to discriminate in price among different purchasers of commodities either directly or indirectly, and among different purchasers of commodities of like grade, quality, or quantity, whether the commodities are sold for use, resale, or consumption.

Section 3, which prohibits sellers from making tying contracts that prevent purchasers from dealing with the seller's competition, on the condition that the purchaser shall not deal in the commodity of a competitor.

Section 7 prohibits any corporation from acquiring shares of stock or assets of a competing corporation where the effect may be substantial to lessen competition or tend to create a monopoly.

Section 8 disallows interlocking boards of directors in competing corporations, except banks, banking associations, common carriers, and trust companies where one has capital accounts of $1 million or more.

In 1936 the Robinson-Patman Act revised Section 2 of the Clayton Act, which dealt with price discrimination. This act was written to make the price-discrimination provisions of the Clayton Act more flexible, as well as giving increased protection to smaller retailers. The Robinson-Patman Act forbade a vendor selling in interstate trade to give a lower price to one buyer than to another under the following circumstances:[4]

1. If the commodities offered to the buyers are of the same grade and quality.
2. If the sale of goods at unreasonably low prices would substantially lower competition, tend to create a monopoly or injure or destroy competition with a vendor or buyer or the customers of either.
3. If a broker's commission, which is, in effect, a reduction in price when an independent broker is not employed, is paid.
4. If advertising and promotional allowances are given on purchases made by large-volume retailers that are not available on "proportionally equal terms" to smaller competitive retailers.

Unfair Trade Practice Laws

In 1890 Congress passed the Sherman Antitrust Act in order that business organizations might operate in a free-enterprise economy without restraint of trade from other firms. Many smaller businesses and stockholders had been injured by the abusive and aggressive practices of larger businesses, which led to monopolistic and collusive practices in restraint of trade.

In 1914 Congress passed the Federal Trade Commission Act to strengthen the Sherman Antitrust Act. A federal agency called the Federal Trade Commission (FTC) was organized to police the antitrust laws. The powers of the commission dealt with Section 5 of the Act, which declared unfair or deceptive methods of competition unlawful. Other duties of the FTC included investigation of alleged restraint of trade and of discriminatory practices or other attempts at unfair competition, as well as the enforcement of acts forbidding such practices. In 1938 the Wheeler-Lee Act amended Section 5 of the Federal Trade Commission Act.

Fair Trade Laws

Small businesses had been active in securing protective legislation at the state level. By 1937 most states had followed California's lead and passed fair trade legislation. These laws permitted manufacturers or distributors of branded products in open competition to sign a contract with the retailer establishing the minimum retail price for which the merchandise would be sold to the consumer. These fair trade laws, however, were applicable only in intrastate commerce. The Miller-Tydings Act, which was passed in 1937 as an amendment to the Sherman Act, legalized the practice in interstate commerce (where manufacturers and retailers or wholesalers were in different states).

In 1952 Congress passed the McGuire Act, which permitted states to include nonsigner clauses in their resale price maintenance laws. The nonsigner clause states that all retailers in a state are bound by resale price agreements as long as one retailer in the state agrees to sign the contract.

Today, fair trade laws are not popular with consumers or retailers because such laws do not provide the retailer with an opportunity to meet competitive prices or changes in consumer demand. A number of large manufacturers have abandoned fair trade pricing policies. However, certain products, such as cosmetics and drugs, are still subject to resale price maintenance laws in some states. Figure 14.2 shows a recent piece of federal legislation regarding fair trade laws.

Figure 14.2. A recent piece of federal legislation regarding fair trade laws. Source: *The Merchant,* published by the Pennsylvania Retailers Association, 1975.

FTC Ruling on "Fair Trade"

The Federal Trade Commission recently declared illegal a technique used by manufacturers to maintain prices in "signer-only" fair trade states.

The FTC said manufacturers cannot prohibit wholesalers in non-fair-trade states from transshipping to discounters in fair-trade areas — particularly "signer-only" states.

The decision thus makes it legal for a distributor in a state like Alabama, for example, which has no fair trade law, to transship to discounters in Pennsylvania or Georgia, which have "signer-only" provisions.

It means that discounters in the 20 "signer-only" states may cut prices on fair trade items if they can obtain them from suppliers in the 14 "free trade" states.

The "signer-only" states are Arkansas, Colorado, Florida, Georgia, Idaho, Indiana, Iowa, Kentucky, Louisiana, Massachusetts, Michigan, Minnesota, New Mexico, Oklahoma, Oregon, **Pennsylvania**, South Carolina, South Dakota, Washington, and West Virginia.

There are no fair trade laws in the District of Columbia, Puerto Rico, and 14 "free-trade" states — Alabama, Alaska, Hawaii, Kansas, Montana, Mississippi, Missouri, Nebraska, Nevada, Rhode Island, Texas, Utah, Vermont and Wyoming.

PART 2

Determining the Retail Price

An Important Selection Factor

Not only is the retail buyer responsible for determining the wholesale price or cost price of merchandise; he is also responsible for determining the retail price. The *retail price* may be defined as the first price at retail that is placed on merchandise by the retailer regardless of later sales or other special-event prices. The retail price of an item becomes an important factor during the consumer selection process. If the retail price is too high, the consumer may not purchase the item because he or she "cannot afford it" or can purchase the merchandise elsewhere for a lower price. If the product is priced too low, the consumer may become suspicious of product quality.

There are three major groups of factors the buying specialist should consider when determining the retail price. First, there are certain internal factors, such as pricing objectives of the retail firm, the cost of goods sold, price maintenance contracts, and business expenses; second, there are a number of external factors, such as consumer demand, competition, and state and federal laws; third, there are other important factors such as the markup formula, price linings, one-price and varying-price policy, prestige pricing, odd pricing, leader pricing, and markdowns. Each will be explained in detail in the following pages.

Important Factors to Consider

Internal Factors

The buyer should give consideration to internal factors that may affect pricing decisions. Important internal factors are:

Pricing Objectives. The pricing policies of the retail business should be carefully considered, since an effective pricing policy is directly related to the overall objectives of the retail organization. Top management will usually determine pricing objectives, which in turn are communicated to the buyer or store manager. With pricing objectives in mind, a good retailer attempts to maximize profits on a long-term basis, although not necessarily to maximize profits on every item sold. For example, a boy's denim jacket may cost the buyer $4.50 and may be sold at retail for $6.00, a markup of 33⅓ percent. However, a cotton suede jacket costing the buyer $10.00 may be sold at retail for $14.00, a markup of 40 percent. Better-quality merchandise, less competition, and greater consumer demand may make the higher markup necessary. A buyer considering long-term objectives must realize that profit maximization depends on a variety of factors, including those that follow.

Cost of Goods Sold. The retail buyer must consider the price paid for merchandise when establishing the retail price. For example, a vendor may sell a certain type of sweater for $4.95 to two retailers in the same trading area, yet one of these retailers may sell the sweater at a higher markup. Both, however, will build the retail price from the cost of the merchandise ($4.95), using the cost price as a base when determining the retail price. As you recall from reading Part 1 of this chapter, all elements of the wholesale or cost price should be considered when determining the retail price, such as discounts and transportation and shipping costs.

Price Maintenance Contracts. If the retail buyer is purchasing from manufacturers of fair trade items, he is usually obligated by contract to sell the merchandise at a predetermined minimum price. In most cases, the buyer will not price the merchandise above the minimum price, since this may lead to a loss of sales and loss of customers to the competition.

Business Expenses. The buyer must also consider various business expenses when determining the retail price. You will recall that fixed costs are costs that usually remain constant and do not vary with the rate of sales. Examples of fixed costs are rent, utilities, taxes, and insurance. The buyer must also consider variable costs, which are costs that vary or change with the sales volume. Examples of variable costs may include commissions paid to salespeople or salaries paid to salespeople and stockpeople, clerks, and other supportive personnel.

External Factors

The buyer should give consideration to external factors that may affect pricing decisions. Important external factors are:

Consumer Demand. A retail buyer may learn through experience that certain customers are interested in merchandise that sells at a particular price. He finds that a number of customers consider the price attractive enough for sufficient quantities to be purchased for resale. So long as enough customers demand a particular product, the buyer will obtain the best value the market has to offer and sell the product to consumers at the going price.

Figure 14.3. The retail buyer will learn through experience that customers are interested in merchandise that sells at a particular price.

Competition. The retail buyer must give consideration to the price of the same or similar items offered by the competition. Most stores will attempt to meet competitive prices; however, some retail stores, due to high overhead and other expenses, are forced to charge a higher price. To compensate for the higher markup, the store will offer additional services such as free delivery, a variety of credit arrangements, and a flexible return policy. If, however, the price of the merchandise has been predetermined by the manufacturer, the retailer and his competition have very little to do with the pricing.

Federal and State Laws. The buyer must pay close attention to various state and federal laws when determining the retail price. As we learned in Part 1 of this chapter, retail buyers must be thoroughly knowledgeable about laws dealing with price discrimination (Robinson-Patman Act), unfair trade practice laws (Federal Trade Commission Act), and fair trade laws (Miller-Tydings Act, McGuire Amendment). Compliance with these laws is a most important consideration when determining a firm's pricing policies.

Other Factors

Markup Formula. You will recall that the amount a retail buyer adds to the wholesale or cost price in determining the retail price is called a markup. The markup equation may be written as follows:

$$\text{Retail Price} = \text{Cost Price} + \text{Markup}$$
$$\$5 \quad = \quad \$4 \quad + \quad \$1$$

Markup may be expressed as the difference between the cost price and the retail price. The markup equation may also be written as follows:

$$\text{Markup} = \text{Retail Price} - \text{Cost Price}$$
$$\$1 \quad = \quad \$5 \quad - \quad \$4$$

Markup may be used to determine the cost price; the cost of goods sold equals the retail price minus the markup price. The equation may be written as follows:

$$\text{Cost Price} = \text{Retail Price} - \text{Markup}$$
$$\$4 \quad = \quad \$5 \quad - \quad \$1$$

To provide an easy working tool, markup is usually expressed as a percent. Markup percent can be figured as a percent of the retail price or of the cost price. Since the retail method of inventory is prevalent in large stores, the markup percent figured on the retail price is most common; the cost method of calculating is considered relatively old-fashioned. The markup equation as expressed in percent may be written as follows:

$$\frac{\text{Markup \%}}{\text{Retail Price}} = \frac{\text{Markup}}{\text{Retail Price}} = \frac{\$1.00}{\$5.00} = 20\% \text{ of retail price}$$

$$\frac{\text{Markup \%}}{\text{Cost Price}} = \frac{\text{Markup}}{\text{Cost Price}} = \frac{\$1.00}{\$4.00} = 25\% \text{ of cost price}$$

In merchandising, the markup percent is calculated as a percent of the retail price because all operating costs and profit or loss are determined as a percentage of net sales. The student will notice that the markup percent of retail price is less than the markup percent of cost price. This is often considered an advantage, since customers associate a high markup with a high profit. It is also important to remember that most of the markup reflects store overhead and expenses.

An additional factor, not part of the formula, is needed to solve markup problems. This factor is known as the *cost percent,* which is found by deducting the markup percent from the retail percent (100%). Since cost price plus markup equals retail dollars, the cost percent plus the markup percent equals the retail percent, which is also 100%. Therefore, given a markup percent of 45, and knowing that the retail percent is 100, we find that the cost percent is 55.

1. Given: Cost price $300   Retail price $500
   Find: Markup %

$$\text{Markup Percent} = \frac{\text{Retail Price} - \text{Cost Price}}{\text{Retail Price}}$$

$$= \frac{\$500 - \$300}{\$500} = \frac{\$200}{\$500}$$

$$= 40\%$$

2. Given: Cost Price $325   Markup % 35
   Find: Retail Price (remember: cost % = 100% − Markup %)

$$\text{Retail Price} = \frac{\text{Cost Price}}{\text{Cost \%}}$$

$$= \frac{\$325}{65\%}$$

$$= \$500$$

3. Given: Retail price $325   Markup % 35
   Find: Cost price

Cost Price = (100% − Markup %) Retail Price
$$= (100\% - 35\%) \$325$$
$$= \$211.25$$

4. Given: Retail price $500   Cost price $300
   Find: Cost %

$$\text{Cost \%} = \frac{\text{Cost Price}}{\text{Retail Price}}$$

$$= \frac{\$300}{\$500}$$

$$= 60\%$$

Price Lining. Price lining is a common pricing practice used by many retail buyers whereby the buyer does not attempt to price merchandise at all possible prices but predetermines the retail price at which an assortment of merchandise will be carried.

For example, a store buyer will create a stock assortment by considering the price lines to be carried and the depth of the merchandise assortment offered at various price ranges. The number of price lines depends on the consumer income bracket the buyer wishes to attract as well as the types of goods offered for sale. Price lines may cover a variety of styles, sizes, and fabrics, which will appeal to customers in a particular income bracket.

Price range refers to the spread of the price line carried from the lowest to the highest price carried (for example, $5 to $35). *Price zone* refers to a series of price lines that are likely to appeal to one group of customers. When more than two price lines are inventoried, a price zone situation exists. Thus, price zones can be referred to as:[5]

Promotional	Low Price Zone	For Example	$5.00
Mass Volume	Medium Price Zone	For Example	$10, $25, $35
Prestige	High Price Zone	For Example	$40, $50, $60

Price lining offers the buyer a number of advantages when attempting to price merchandise for resale. Advantages of price lining are listed in the chart that follows.[6]

1. It facilitates selling by simplifying customer choice during the selection process.
2. A wide assortment of goods may be offered at popular-selling price lines.
3. Buying becomes simplified, since the range of wholesale costs is limited.
4. It results in a favorable turnover and decreased markdowns, and reduces size of stock.

5. Stock control is simplified.
6. Marking costs are decreased.

One-Price–Varying-Price Policy. This method of pricing is used by many retailers. Under the *one-price policy,* the same price is charged to all consumers who purchase merchandise in the same quantities under similar circumstances. A major advantage of the one-price policy is that consumer "bargaining" is eliminated. Also, the one-price policy does not foster preferential treatment of one consumer over another. In contrast to the one-price policy, the buyer may follow a *varying-price policy* whereby a consumer seeking to purchase merchandise at a lower price will bargain with the retailer until an agreement has been reached. For example, if a buyer is anxious to make a sale, he may allow the consumer to find some fault with the merchandise and mark down the price of the item to compensate for the fault.

Prestige Pricing, Odd Pricing, Leader Pricing. In *prestige pricing,* a high-price policy is followed for particular kinds of merchandise that appeal to the prestige- or status-minded consumer. Stores that have a high-fashion image or carry status-type merchandise follow this method of pricing. *Odd pricing* is a psychological method of pricing. Instead of pricing an item at $1, the price is set at 99¢. The use of an odd number creates the illusion of a lower price and often increases sales. *Leader pricing* involves the offering of a well-known brand of merchandise at a special low price. The primary objective of this method is to attract consumers into a store in the hope that they will purchase additional merchandise as well as higher-priced goods. If a well-known brand of merchandise is offered at a price below the buyer's cost, the merchandise is termed a *loss leader.*

Markdowns. As stated earlier, a reduction in price from the original retail price is called a *markdown.* Here is an example of the markdown equation:

Original Retail Price	$5.00
− Markdown Price	−$4.00
Dollar Markdown	$1.00

Markdown is the difference between the original retail price and the markdown price. The markdown percent equation may be expressed as in the following example:

$$\text{Markdown \%} = \frac{\text{Dollar Markdown}}{\text{Markdown Price}} = \frac{\$1.00}{\$4.00} = 25\%$$

Markdowns are expressed as a percentage of net sales, not as a percentage of original retail price.

The buyer will use a markdown as a method for stimulating sales and cleaning out remaining slow-moving merchandise. However, the markdown percent must be carefully determined to appeal to the consumer. For example, a blouse marked down to $9.00 from $10.00 (10% markdown) may have little sales appeal, whereas if the same blouse were marked down to $5.00 (50% markdown), the consumer would think of it as "a real bargain."

Review the following:

When determining the retail price, the buyer should consider:

Internal factors

1. Pricing objectives of the firm
2. The cost of goods sold
3. Price maintenance contracts
4. Business expenses

External factors

1. Consumer demand
2. Competition
3. Federal and state laws

Other factors

1. Markup formula
2. Price linings
3. One-price–varying-price policy
4. Prestige pricing, odd pricing, leader pricing
5. Markdowns

How will this information assist the buying specialist when determining the retail price?

Chapter Summary

There are three techniques a buyer may use in developing a thorough knowledge of prices: (1) price guessing, (2) price memorization, and (3) price buildup. The wholesale price may be defined as the price paid for goods purchased from merchandise resources such as vendors or manufacturers. Since price negotiation is a very important responsibility of the retail buyer, he or she must be aware of three elements that are included in the wholesale price: (1) the wholesale or quoted price, (2) wholesale discounts, and (3) transportation and shipping costs.

The major purpose of government regulation of business is to promote the public welfare, benefit the economy as a whole, and protect the small business enterprise. The government has had an influence on retail businesses through price discrimination laws such as the Clayton Act and the Robinson-Patman Act; through unfair trade practice laws such as the Sherman Antitrust Act, the Federal Trade Commission Act, and the Wheeler Act; and through fair trade laws such as the Miller-Tydings Act and the McGuire Act.

Not only is the buyer responsible for determining the wholesale or cost price of merchandise; he or she is also responsible for determining the retail price. There are three major factors that the buyer should consider when determining the price of goods for resale. First, there are certain internal factors such as pricing objectives of the business, the cost of goods sold, price maintenance contracts, and business expenses; second, there are external factors such as demand, competition, and state and federal laws; and third, other important factors are the markup formula, price lining, one-price and varying-price policy, prestige pricing, odd pricing, leader pricing, and markdowns.

The student should remember that pricing policies of a retail business can vary widely. The techniques presented in this chapter, however, are basic approaches used by most retailers when determining retail price.

Trade Terminology

DIRECTIONS: Briefly explain or discuss each of the following trade terms:

1. Wholesale price
2. Special merchandise
3. Series discount or chain discount
4. Retail price
5. Cost percent
6. Price lining
7. Price range
8. Price zone
9. One-price policy
10. Varying-price policy
11. Prestige pricing
12. Odd pricing
13. Leader pricing
14. Loss leader

Questions for Discussion and Review

1. Explain three techniques that may be used by a retail buyer in developing a thorough knowledge of pricing.

2. There are several sources of price information available to the retail buyer. Other than those mentioned, name five sources that a buyer may consult when determining the best price.

3. Discuss three important elements that must be included when determining the wholesale price.

4. Define the following terms: quantity discount, series discount, trade discount.

5. How can transportation and shipping costs increase the cost of goods sold?

6. Define the following terms: price lining, varying-price policy, leader pricing.

7. What is a markdown? A dollar markdown? Calculate the markdown percent when the dollar markdown is $1 and the markdown price is $5.

8. What is a markup? Calculate the markup percent when the markup is $5, the cost price is $25, and the retail price is $9. Why do retailers calculate the markup percent as a percent of the retail price?

9. Briefly outline the major provisions of the Robinson-Patman Act.

10. Explain the important factors a buyer should consider when determining the retail price.

Case Study Number One

As the sportswear buyer for a men's specialty store, you are aware that **Special Buys** turtleneck sweaters priced at $19.95 have sold extremely well during the months of December and January. Meanwhile, the vendor has offered you a special buy on the same turtleneck sweater in an assortment of sizes and colors. If you purchase the sweaters, you must decide whether you will sell the goods at the same price as before and make even a higher markup, or sell the sweaters for less and include them in the special promotion sale that is to be held the last week of February. How would you price the merchandise? Why? What problems may you encounter by purchasing seasonal merchandise towards the end of the season? Be prepared to explain your answers in class.

**Problems with
Competition**

Case Study Number Two

O'Brien's was a well-established medium-sized department store located in a
Midwestern city. The store would not be considered a discount house; however, some of its high-fashion merchandise was sold at cut-rate or discount
prices. O'Brien's felt this pricing policy permitted it to draw customers from
several income brackets as well as providing an opportunity to sell staple goods
at a full markup. One of the fashion items discounted by O'Briens was the
Lucky Lucy handbag. Since O'Brien's did an excellent job of advertising, it
became the top merchandiser for the Lucky Lucy manufacturing company.

   Harriet MacMillan was the buyer of handbags and leather accessories at
Albright's department store, located in the same city. She had handled Lucky
Lucy merchandise for the past five years and had always merchandised the
goods successfully. She had always expressed a great deal of confidence in
Lucky Lucy handbags and had gone so far as to tell the saleswomen in her
department that there was not a better handbag manufacturer in the country.
Harriet had been selling the handbags at full price, and had lately found that
sales were falling off. When she investigated the problem, she discovered that
O'Brien's was discounting the handbags up to 30%. Harriet was aware that
most of Albright's customers did not shop at O'Brien's; however, she did feel
that O'Brien's heavy advertising campaign had directly contributed to a loss
of sales in her department.

   Harriet decided to call Lucky Lucy's sales representative and attempt to
persuade the company not to sell to O'Brien's at such a low price, or at least
to have Lucky Lucy talk to O'Brien's about selling the merchandise at list
price. When Harriet spoke to the sales representative, she was informed that
O'Brien's was at present Lucky Lucy's biggest customer. She was also told that
perhaps Albright's should lower its price to meet competition, or that perhaps
she should increase her purchases to take advantage of quantity discounts.

   If you were Harriet MacMillan, how would you handle this situation?

Retailing Activities to Stimulate Student Interest and Participation

1. Prepare a paper on the topic "How does the retailer price for profit?" Refer
   to The Retail Student's Reference Library for selected references.

2. Interview the store manager of a small grocery business; a supermarket
   chain. Select ten items sold by each business. Find out how each business
   manager determines the markup price of the various items you have selected. What kinds of expenses are incurred by each? What are the risks?

3. Select five types of businesses in your local area, for example, a department store, a variety chain, a boutique, a shoe store, a women's specialty shop, or a men's specialty store. Interview the department manager or assistant buyer and determine the price policy used by each type of store. For example, find out whether the store uses prestige pricing, odd pricing, loss leaders, a one-price policy, or a varying-price policy. Attempt to determine the reasons for the stores' using various methods of pricing.

The Retail Student's Reference Library

Alpert, Mark I. *Pricing Decisions.* Glenview, Ill.: Scott, Foresman & Company, 1971.

Basic Trade Provisions. New York: National Retail Merchants Association, n.d.

Bear-Dres, Robert. *Mass Merchandising: Revolution & Evolution.* New York: Fairchild Publications, Inc., n.d.

Belden, Donald L. *The Role of the Buyer in Mass Merchandising.* New York: Chain Store Publishing Corporation, 1971.

The Buyer's Manual. New York: National Retail Merchants Association, 1970.

Curran, Ward S. *Principles of Financial Management.* Hightstown: McGraw-Hill Book Company, 1970.

Fairchild's Financial Manual of Retail Stores. New York: Fairchild Publications, Inc., 1971.

Judelle, Beatrice. *The Fashion Buyer's Job.* New York: National Retail Merchants Association, 1971.

Leed, T. W., and German, G. A. *Principles of Good Merchandising.* New York: Chain Store Publishing Corporation, 1973.

Lewis, R. D., and Lewis, J. N. *What Every Retailer Should Know about the Law.* New York: Fairchild Publications, Inc., n.d.

Mason, R. *College Mathematics: With Applications in Business and Economics.* Homewood, Ill.: Learning Systems Company, 1971.

Merchandising Arithmetic for Retail Training. New York: National Retail Merchants Association, 1971.

Meyer, J. S., and Harling, E. L. *Merchandise Control and Budgeting.* New York: National Retail Merchants Association, 1970.

Stocking, Jessie. *Fundamentals of Buying.* Kent, Ohio: Kent State University, n.d.

Telchin, C. S., and Helfant, S. *Planning Your Store for Maximum Sales and Profits.* New York: National Retail Merchants Association, n.d.

314 Ways to Run a Better More Profitable Store. New York: National Retail Merchants Association, n.d.

To Multiply a Buyer. New York: National Retail Merchants Association, n.d.

Trading Stamps and Their Impact on Food Prices. Washington, D.C.: U.S. Department of Agriculture, n.d.

Walker, Herbert, and Mendelson, Nathaniel H. *Children's Wear Merchandiser.* New York: National Retail Merchants Association, n.d.

Watson, Donald S. *Price Theory and Its Uses.* Boston: Houghton Mifflin Company, n.d.

Weiss, E. B. *The Decline of the Store Buyer.* New York: Doyle, Dane, Bernbeck, Inc., n.d.

Wingate, Isabel. *Buying for Retail Stores.* Washington, D.C.: U.S. Government Printing Office, n.d.

References

1. D. J. Duncan and C. F. Phillips, *Retailing Principles and Methods* (Homewood, Ill.: Richard D. Irwin, Inc., 1970), pp. 343–344.
2. Ibid.
3. *The Clayton Act,* 1914, Federal Trade Commission, Washington, D.C.
4. *The Robinson-Patman Act,* 1936, Federal Trade Commission, Washington, D.C.
5. *Retail Mathematics Manual* (Philadelphia: Strawbridge & Clothier Department Store, 1970), pp. 37–40.
6. Ibid.

The Buyer and the Communication Process

15

Performance Objectives

PERFORMANCE
OBJECTIVES

As a result of reading this chapter, the student should be able to accomplish the following:

1. List nonpersonal selling devices that may be used by a buyer to communicate with customers indirectly.

2. Define advertising, sales promotion, publicity.

3. Discuss several reasons why a retail buyer will advertise.

4. Define promotional advertising, institutional advertising, combination advertising.

5. Outline the psychological steps that must be followed when planning advertising.

6. List six steps that should be followed when planning an advertising campaign.

7. Identify four activities included in sales promotion.

8. Define personal selling.

9. Discuss three types of retail personal selling.

10. Outline the activities performed by a buyer when managing sales personnel.

11. Explain the duties and responsibilities of sales personnel.

12. Discuss six steps that should be followed during the selling process.

13. Outline the importance of different management techniques.

14. Identify problems encountered by new sales personnel.

The Buyer and the Communication Process

Advertising and Sales Promotion

PART 1

The retail buyer will make every effort to offer a combination of goods and services that will appeal to potential customers. However, for the customer to become aware of such offerings, the store executive must develop methods of sending messages or communicating with his trading area. He must relate price, products, service, and store image in such a way that customers will be motivated to purchase goods from a particular store or department.

The Importance of Effective Communication

To influence customers to take a desired action, the buyer must be able to send messages that contain a proper balance of information and persuasion. Customers need to know what specials are available, what styles are in season, the location of the store, what the store hours are, the features of particular products, and so on.

Since effective communication will stimulate and create demand, buying specialists must be aware of those activities that are used in the communication process. The purpose of Part 1 of this chapter, therefore, will be to (1) discuss the importance of effective communication and the role of nonpersonal selling; (2) identify the main type of retail advertising; (3) discuss the psychological aspects of advertising; and (4) determine how advertising is planned and the importance of ethics in advertising. Part 2 will discuss (1) the importance of personal selling; (2) various types of personal selling; (3) the buyer's job in managing retail salespeople; and (4) the duties and responsibilities of sales personnel.

Nonpersonal selling is a method of communicating with customers indirectly. Information about a store is communicated through nonpersonal selling devices such as advertising, sales promotion, publicity, word of mouth, packaging, and vending machines. Since many types of nonpersonal selling devices are used by store buyers in various combinations, each will be discussed in detail.

The Role of Nonpersonal Selling

Advertising

Advertising may be defined as a set of activities that involves the presentation of a mass message, called an advertisement, about a product, a service, or an idea; and the message is paid for by an identified sponsor.[1] According to the American Marketing Association, advertising may be defined as "any paid form of nonpersonal presentation and promotion of ideas, goods, or services by an identified sponsor."[2]

Since a store spends the greatest portion of its promotion budget on advertising, a buyer has the responsibility for planning advertising that will reach a large number of people. Primarily, advertising is used by the buyer to: (1) bring customers into the store; (2) motivate them to make purchases; and (3) build good will for the retail store. *It is important to remember that the prime objective of advertising is to attract potential customers to the store.* There are other reasons why buying specialists, department managers, or store managers will use this method to communicate with the trading area. The following list is representative of why retailers advertise.

1. To attract customers to the store
2. To motivate customers to make purchases
3. To build good will for the store
4. To introduce new products, fashions, and services
5. To stimulate and create demand for products and services
6. To build a favorable store image
7. To show new applications of a product
8. To develop a list of potential customers
9. To assist the salesperson through preselling
10. To increase mail and telephone orders
11. To maintain store name, trademark, or product before the public
12. To keep customers satisfied with previous purchases

The Main Types of Retail Advertising

For purposes of study, there are three types of retail advertising: (1) promotional advertising, (2) institutional advertising, and (3) a combination of promotional and institutional advertising.

Promotional Advertising

Promotional advertising may be defined as direct-action advertising whose primary objective is to bring customers into the store to purchase specific items of merchandise. This is the most popular type of advertising used by buying specialists and may take any one of the following three forms:

1. Regular-price advertising. Merchandise is offered at regular prices; however, consumer appeal is based on the product's characteristics and desirability.
2. Sale-price advertising. Merchandise is offered at a sale price or as a special. Consumer appeal is based on the opportunity to save.
3. Clearance-sale advertising. Merchandise is offered at a lower price; however, the prime objective is to move out slow-moving inventory, broken and odd assortments, obsolete goods, and irregulars and seconds.

In this type of advertising one or more items are featured at regular, sale, or special prices with the primary objective that of increasing store traffic, since the merchandise offered is available only for a limited time period. The increase in store traffic will usually boost the sales of regular-priced goods. See Figure 15.1.

For example, a ladies' wear factory outlet may advertise merchandise that

Figure 15.1. An example of promotional advertising.

Look what $5 will buy!

Super tops at super savings!
Misses' short sleeve solid polyester tunics and shirts. Printed polyester and arnel pant tops. Machine washable. Sizes S,M,L and 32 to 38.
Plus sizes, reg. 6.99, $5 and $6

G74-10-817   3 x 7¼" Special

Figure 15.2. Examples of
prestige advertising from
various departments in a
well-known jewelry store.
(Courtesy of Bailey Banks &
Biddle, Philadelphia, Pa.)

has been left over from a previous season with consumer appeal based on the
opportunity to save while selecting from "fantastic" bargains. Or a discount
house will advertise special discounts on seasonal merchandise.

Institutional Advertising

Institutional advertising may be defined as indirect-action advertising; the
primary objective is to create good will for the store, build confidence in its
merchandise and services, and establish customer loyalty. There are two forms
of institutional advertising.

Prestige advertising. This type of institutional advertising aims to attract
present and prospective customers by the store's ability to offer the latest styles,
designs, and materials, as well as maintaining past traditions. Figure 15.2
illustrates examples of prestige advertising.

Service Advertising. This type of institutional advertising seeks to attract
present and prospective customers by calling attention to the store's various
services and facilities, which make it a desirable place to shop. In service
advertising no merchandise is advertised, no special sale is mentioned, and no
attempt is made to build immediate customer traffic. However, this type of
advertisement is attempting to build good will for the store by showing that
it has a pleasant shopping atmosphere, offers a variety of services, and is
concerned about the welfare of its customers. See Figure 15.3.

Figure 15.3. An example of
an institutional advertisement.
(Courtesy of Lord & Taylor,
New York, N.Y.) See facing
page.

A Combination of Promotional and Institutional Advertising

Combination retail advertising is a method whereby institutional and promotional approaches are blended together in the same advertisement. For example, merchandise in competing stores is often so similar that merchandise advertising in itself is not enough to draw customers to that particular store. By blending the prestige characteristics of the store in the advertisement, the product is made to take on the characteristics of the store, thus making it appear different from that carried by its competition.

Under what circumstances will the retail buyer use the following types of advertising?		
Promotional Advertising	Institutional Advertising	Combination Advertising
Regular price Sale price Clearance sale	Prestige Service	Promotional and Institutional

The Psychological Aspect of Advertising

As you learned in chapter 6, psychological studies of the emotions and drives of people have greatly influenced the use of advertising as an effective communications device. Such studies suggest that people may act on three levels: (1) on the conscious level, where people know why they perform certain acts; (2) on the subconscious level, where people know why they perform certain acts but do not admit the real reason for their actions; and, (3) on the unconscious level, where individuals act in a certain way but do not know the reason. A review of chapter 6 will further suggest that appeals to emotional drives are more effective than those aimed at reason.

Since the buyers are responsible for assisting in the planning and promotion of advertisements for their departments or the store as a whole, they must also be aware of certan psychological steps that every advertisement must contain: (1) attracting attention; (2) developing interest; (3) creating desire; (4) securing action. The student will note that these psychological steps are also applicable to personal selling, which will be discussed in Part 2 of this chapter.

Attracting Attention

For the advertisement to meet its objective, that is, to bring customers into the store to purchase merchandise, it must attract the attention of the customer. For example, the use of illustrations, vivid use of colors, unusual lettering, bold print, or unusual or decorative spacing are just some of the techniques that may be used to attract the attention of the customer. Psychological studies have also shown that attention must be secured before a message can be communicated to the customer.

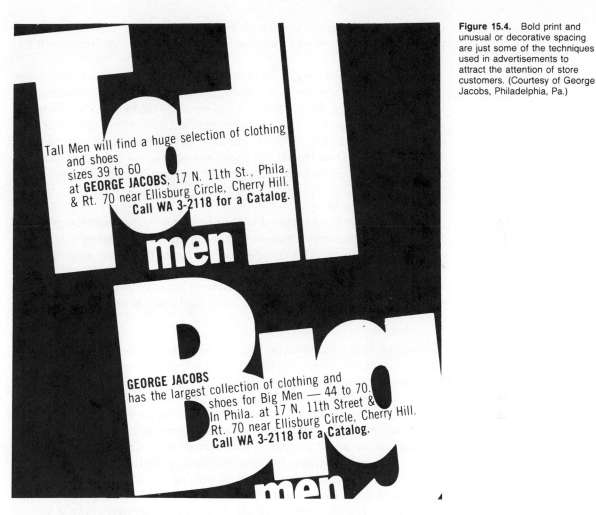

Developing Interest

Once the customer's attention is attracted by the advertisement, interest must be aroused. Since people are usually interested in matters that relate to themselves, merchandise that fullfills their needs and wants will interest them. Thus, the advertisement should relate products to the needs of customers for them to develop an interest. Also, merchandise descriptions should be simply written, in nontechnical language.

Creating Desire

Desire for particular products is created by appealing to both emotional and rational desires. As you recall from reading chapter 6, people may buy from such motives as hunger, security, pride, attracting the opposite sex, and a desire for comfort, economy, and dependability, to name but a few. The type of goods being advertised and the kind of customers to be reached will determine which buying motive or motives are used to create a desire or need for the product.

For example, Figure 15.1 seeks to create a desire for the particular items advertised through the appeal to reason. If the reader of the advertisement is interested in savings, she will hurry in and purchase the blouses that are being offered at "super savings." Also, an advertisement may inform the reader that the items are offered for a limited time only and after that time there will be "no rainchecks." Thus, the ads will appeal to budget-conscious customers who are seeking bargains and who desire to get the most for their money.

Securing Action

The desired action should result if all the preparatory steps have been carefully followed. The action may involve a visit to the store, a mail order, a telephone call, or the filling out of a coupon. The customer must take some kind of desired action if merchandise is to be sold. For example, in the type of advertisement illustrated in Figure 15.1, customers are encouraged to hurry in to make their purchases, since no coupon or mail order is provided.

Planning Advertising for Your Department or Store

If you own your own business, you will have the responsibility of planning advertising for the entire store. If the budget permits, you may seek the services of an advertising agency; however, usually you will have to plan the store's ads, and perhaps seek the advice and assistance of your employees throughout the planning process. One of the advantages of working for a large retail business such as a department store, a discount house, a general-merchandise chain, or a specialty store, is that you have a well-trained group of professionals to assist you in planning advertising for your particular department. It is important, however, for you to understand how advertising plans are developed so that you may constructively contribute to the overall planning process. Thus, whether you are the owner-manager of a small retail business or a buying specialist for one or more departments, consideration should be given to the following six steps when planning an advertising campaign: (1) setting specific objectives; (2) identifying a theme; (3) establishing a budget; (4) selecting merchandise to promote; (5) selecting the media; and (6) preparing the advertisement.

Setting Specific Objectives

Those individuals usually responsible for planning advertising in a large retail operation are the sales promotion manager, the fashion copywriter, the fashion illustrator, the fashion coordinator, and the display manager. These promotion executives will determine advertising objectives for the store as a whole. Advertising objectives may be based on a long-term plan (yearly objectives) or on

---

Consideration should be given to the following when planning an ad campaign:

---

1. Setting specific objectives
2. Identifying a theme
3. Establishing a budget
4. Selecting merchandise to promote
5. Selecting the media
6. Preparing the advertisement

---

a short-term basis (daily or weekly objectives). Objectives must determine *who* will be the target market and *what* is to be accomplished.

The promotion team will review last year's sales promotion efforts and lay out a program based on this year's suggested objectives. Once the plan has been approved by top store executives, programs are developed for each department individually. These plans may be based on three-month or six-month periods, depending upon the store's advertising policy. At this point the buyer may be requested to submit a tentative schedule of what he or she would like to promote. Later, as the season progresses, the merchandise manager and the promotion division will develop a plan for each department to ensure that overall coordinated promotional efforts are maintained.

The buyer will develop a preliminary outline of the promotions he or she would like to have during particular selling seasons. The outline will include a review of the previous year's sales promotion activities, the costs involved, and the results of previous promotions. Also, suppliers will run sales promotion activities; thus, the buyer must consider the department's immediate goals as well as those of the division and the store as a whole. According to Beatrice Judelle, thought should also be given to commitments already made or under consideration such as:[3]

- storewide and divisional events in which you participate
- commitments to resources with whom you have program merchandising arrangements
- special needs of individual branches, such as participation in local community events
- special offerings and clearances of your nationally advertised brands, in which you will participate
- editorial credits and other forms of tie-in with consumer publications
- cooperative advertising available to you
- other helps from outside sources: tie-ins with national advertising campaigns of resources; opportunities to have speakers, shows, and demonstrations brought to the store by resources or publications; opportunities to tie in with consumer magazine promotional themes, etc.

With this kind of information, the buyer can work out a tentative schedule of promotions for the department and thus provide a guide for the store's promotional team.

Identifying a Theme

The second step when planning an advertising campaign is to identify a theme. The *advertising theme* will determine *how* the objectives can be accomplished. It will describe the benefits the consumer will receive by purchasing the advertised product and by shopping in a particular store. For example, a buying theme may read, "Inflation Fighters—Prices Good thru Sunday, April 13th —Shop As Late As 10 P.M."

The advertising theme used by individual departments or the store as a whole will depend upon the merchandising policies of the store, the target market, the kinds of merchandise to be advertised, and the store's overall promotional objectives. For example, a fashion department will use a number of promotional approaches that best suit the needs of its customers. Emphasis may be on trends, prestige, feelings of security or insecurity, and so forth. The fashion theme may use fashion shows, clinics (for example, teen-age model and charm clinics), special cosmetic demonstrations, designer fashion shows, or the opportunity to meet an important author, celebrity, or rock star. For some fashion departments, the advertising theme may emphasize the availability of certain styles at moderate or budget prices.

The buyer of hard goods will also use a variety of advertising themes geared to the needs of the customers. For example, the buyer of hardware and paints may use "Fix Up, Paint Up, and Clean Up" as an ad theme during the spring of the year. A buyer of furniture may use "Dress up Your Living Room for the Holidays" as an incentive to encourage consumer spending. Or the home-appliances buyer may use "Beat the Heat and Save" as an ad theme for selling air conditioners before the selling season begins.

Establishing a Budget

The third important step when planning an advertising campaign is to prepare a budget. Since advertising is usually the second or third largest expense, next to payroll and overhead, it must be planned with the utmost care. As you recall from previous readings, certain monies have already been allotted to each department for the cost of its advertising. The buyer will be consulted during the initial planning stages, and thus should be aware of the following four steps in planning the advertising budget:

1. Analyzing last year's sales figures as well as the figures of the previous selling season and setting a realistic sales goal
2. Referring to past years' advertising budgets to determine how much advertising will be necessary to meet departmental sales goals as well as those of the store as a whole

3. Determining the sales contribution of each department and deciding what merchandise lines to promote
4. Planning advertising expenditure based on a month-to-month and then a day-to-day schedule. Special consideration should be given to heavy-selling seasons such as Christmas; special promotions such as inventory clearance sales; special events such as Washington's birthday; and night openings, such as those that occur from Thanksgiving to Christmas.

The buyer must have a general idea of costs to make tentative promotional plans for the department, evaluate cooperative advertising offers, and estimate expected advertising costs in return for various kinds of tie-in promotions. Store management will usually allot a percentage of planned sales to each department when planning the advertising budget. The cost of advertising is based on storewide considerations and the merchandising objectives of the individual departments.

Selecting Merchandise to Promote

The fourth step to consider when planning the advertising campaign is selecting the right merchandise. The buyer and the advertising department will work together in determining which goods will be selected for promotion. They must decide what goods will appeal to the most customers. *Selecting the "right" products to advertise is a single most important factor in store promotion.* The buyer must be aware that all merchandise in the store cannot be advertised, since this would mean an increase in advertising expenses without a propor-

Table 15.1. *Selecting the right products to advertise.*

Selecting the Right Products to Advertise	
Merchandise that *Should* be Advertised	Merchandise that *Should Not* be Advertised
1. Fast-selling, popular items that are in demand	1. Old and obsolete goods
2. New fashion items	2. Limited-quantity merchandise
3. New and unusual merchandise	3. Merchandise that cannot be quickly reordered
4. Exclusive and distinctive goods	4. Goods not in stock when the advertisement appears
5. Special-occasion merchandise	5. Goods previously advertised and still in stock
6. Merchandise with distinct price appeal	6. Merchandise that has not been promoted to salespeople
7. Convenience goods	7. Merchandise that does not meet store standards of price and quality
8. Private or store brands	
9. National brands	
10. Related lines of merchandise	

tional sales increase. The buyer must select representative items that will bring the largest number of people to his department and create the most good will. The list in Table 15.1 is representative of those goods that should be considered for store promotion, as well as of those items that should not be given promotional consideration.

When the buyer is requested to provide information to the advertising division for planned advertising, the following procedure should be carried out:

1. Selecting the merchandise to be featured. The selection will be based on the factors previously discussed.
2. Filling out the appropriate forms sent to the buyer by the ad department. As Figure 15.5 illustrates, the buyer should supply factual information about the merchandise, including price, size, material, and color range. Information regarding special features such as how the article is to be worn, its fashion importance, its brand name or designer, fabric care, type of occasion for which it is to be worn, and whatever else the customer needs to know, should also be supplied. The buyer of hard goods should also supply complete information about the merchandise to be promoted.

The buyer should also brief salespeople about the promotional activities of the department. It is important to build enthusiasm about the merchandise and, in turn, get that enthusiasm across to the sales staff. The buyer, store manager, or department manager should inform salespeople of:

1. Merchandise to be advertised, when it is to be advertised, and where —for example, store windows, displays, the media
2. Special features of the merchandise that should be emphasized by salespersons
3. The fashion message used to promote the goods
4. When and where the promotion will occur—at what dates and in what store units, departments, or branches
5. How other department merchandising activities will tie in
6. How storewide promotional activities will relate to this promotion
7. Important features or fashion emphasis to point out to customers
8. Anticipated questions regarding the merchandise advertised
9. Customer reactions to merchandise advertised
10. Reactions of sales personnel to the merchandise promoted

Most buyers realize that feedback received from sales personnel on a department's advertising promotion is vitally important. Feedback will help the buyer determine how effective promotional efforts have been. Also, the buyer will post copies of the advertisement in the department, send copies to the branches or store units, make certain that merchandise is in stock or on

Dept. No.	Indicate by "X"	Newspaper Preferred
Amount Involved in Promotion:	Special Purchase	Inquirer
	Reduced Price	
	Clearance	Bulletin
2-Day Sales Expected:	Regular Stock at Usual Price	
	Size of ad requested	Space Cost:
Ad to appear _____Day of Wk._____	Number of Illustrations	Old New
_____ Month Date		

Description of Merchandise to be Advertised

Price, Size, Material, Color Range: _____

Special Features: _____

Window Requested   _____

Posters   _____

Direct Mail   _____

Other   _____

I hereby certify that all the above statements are true and that every fact which vitally affects the truth of this advertisement has been included.

3 copies of this form must be okayed by Merchandise Manager and Comparison Office.

_____
Buyer

_____
Date

Then

Original stays in Advertising Dept.

OK   _____
Mdse. Mgr.

_____
Date

Duplicate stays in Comparison Office

Triplicate stays in Buyer's Office

OK   _____
Comp. Off.

_____
Date

Received by:

_____
Adv. Dept.   Date

This Sheet, together with a sample of the merchandise, is due in the Advertising Department _____ days in advance.

Figure 15.5. An example of a form sent by the advertising department to the buyer. The buyer is required to supply all factual information. (Courtesy of John Wanamaker Department Store, Philadelphia, Pa.)

the floor when required, possibly arrange for salespeople to wear the advertised items while working, and constantly check sales results as the promotion is in progress.

Selecting the Media

The fifth step to consider when planning the advertising campaign is selecting the media. The media selected for carrying the advertising message to the public are usually determined by the advertising department. The choice of which medium to use is dependent upon: (1) what is to be advertised; (2) the trading area of the store; (3) the medium used by competition; (4) the particular selling season; (5) the type of customers to be reached; and (6) the amount of money available.

Usually the best advertising a retail store can have is "word-of-mouth" advertising. This is not a type of medium because the store does not pay for time or space. However, it is very instrumental in building prestige and good will for the store.

The list in Table 15.2 is self-explanatory and is representative of various types of media used to advertise merchandise.

Table 15.2.   *Media used to carry messages to the public.*

Media Used to Carry Messages to the Public	
Television	Handbills
Radio	Billboards
Newspapers	Signs
Magazines	Exhibits
Direct mail	Posters
Announcements	Leaflets
Pamphlets	Package inserts
Displays	

A small business will usually advertise in local newspapers, since its customers are drawn from the immediate trade area. Also, this is less expensive than advertising in the large metropolitan newspapers. On the other hand, the large chain operation will advertise in metropolitan newspapers on a daily and weekend basis, as well as nationally. Department stores may advertise on local television stations as well as in the newspapers, especially on the weekends. Department stores will also use leaflets and pamphlets, which may be inserted in billings sent to charge-account customers. As you can see, retailers will use a variety of advertising media, depending on their sales promotion objectives and the amount of money available for advertising.

Preparing the Advertisement

The last step to consider when planning the advertising campaign is the actual preparation of the ad. Even though this is the responsibility of the advertising department and its staff of capable professionals, the following information will help the buyer better understand the total advertising procedure. There are five major parts of an advertisement. Each will be discussed as follows:

1. The Headline. The *headline* in an advertisement must attract the attention of the public, it must arouse interest, and it must lead the reader to read the entire ad. Popular headlines are: "Last Sales Day before Christmas," "Spring Clearance Sale," "Gigantic Inventory Reductions," "Founder's Day Sale," "Fire Sale," "Warehouse Sale," "Liquidation Sale," and so forth.

2. The Illustration. The *illustration* or picture will attract attention to the whole advertisement as well as developing the reader's interest in the product. The illustration may show women's nylon jackets with special features such as front zipper closings, fur-lined hoods, tie belts, and fancy top-stitching. Or the illustration may show portable AM/FM radios and describe special features such as carrying case, antenna, pocket size, regular size, or whatever.

3. The Copy. The *copy* constitutes the language of the ad. Using dialog in advertising provides detailed information about the product and helps the **consumer see a need for the product, which in turn leads to the appropriate** action. Usually, the buyer is consulted when writing the copy to make sure that all required and correct information is used. For example, the copy for the women's nylon coats may read: "The perfect winter jackets. They'll keep you warm all winter without adding a lot of weight. A fantastic buy at our regular price. At 30% off, these jackets are the buy of the season. Sizes 10 to 18. Winter's coming, hurry!" Or the advertisement for the AM/FM portable radios may read: "Pocket radio with telescopic whip FM antenna. AFC, carry strap. Great Father's Day gift, hurry while they last!"

4. The Layout. The *layout* is the arrangement of the ad. Layout should be so arranged as to lead the eye of the reader in regular sequence to the other parts of the advertisement. This will take the reader through the psychological steps of developing interest, creating desire, and securing action.

5. The Signature Plate. The store's *signature plate* is usually the emblem, trademark, symbol, or distinctive print that immediately identifies the store to the public. The signature plate is usually placed near the top or bottom of the advertisement, and close to the store name is the address of the store, the location of branch stores, and the store's slogan.

Review the following:

The headline
The illustration
The copy
The layout
The signature plate

How will a knowledge of the major parts of an advertisement help the buying specialist understand the total advertising procedure?

Ethics in Advertising

Advertising has been primarily responsible for increased mass production, lower prices, and higher standards of living. It has been considered as an educational tool used to inform the public about the great variety of goods and services available to them so they may make intelligent buying decisions. However, when advertising to the public, the buyer has the responsibility for giving information that is true and will not prove misleading.

The Federal Trade Commission (FTC) has been primarily responsible for controlling deceptive advertising practices in interstate commerce. The Commission is particularly responsible for retail businesses that sell across state lines and for the advertising of products that come under the Federal Textile Products Identification Act. Stores must disclose, in advertisements and on signs, the names of the generic fibers from which the advertised products are made, and textile fibers must be stated in order of their weight in the item. The Federal Trade Commission is also responsible for the advertising ethics of television. One rule is that substitutions may not be used simply to give a visual effect on the screen; for example, shaving cream may not be used as whipped cream. The Federal Communications Commission (FCC) is responsible for putting pressure on television stations not to accept deceptive advertisements for broadcasting.

Review how the following information will assist the buyer when planning advertising for a particular department or the store as a whole:

1. The primary objective of advertising
2. Reasons why retail buyers will advertise
3. Main types of retail advertising
4. Psychological aspects of advertising
5. Six steps involved in planning an ad

Sales promotion is the second type of nonpersonal selling used by all types of buying specialists to sell merchandise. *Sales promotion* may be defined as any promotional activity other than advertising, publicity, and personal selling that attracts the public to a retail store to stimulate purchasing and make a profit for the store. Thus, sales promotion will include the following types of activities: (1) display; (2) stamps, coupons, and labels; (3) sampling and demonstrations; and (4) special events.

Sales Promotion—A Type of Nonpersonal Selling

Display

A good merchandise presentation or display will reinforce a store's advertising campaign. Display is considered an important selling device because it provides a visual presentation of what is available for sale and will assist customers in making buying decisions. A buyer may use two types of display: (1) the window display, and (2) the interior display. Usually, the store's display or promotion department will decorate store windows to promote a price, a merchandising theme, a product line, or a store image. In a small business, the owner-manager or the assistant will decorate store windows. Regardless of who does the work, window displays are designed to attract attention and draw people into the store. Once the customer comes into the store or department, interior displays should be designed to encourage customers to try the products sold by that particular department.

Since the importance of the first impression cannot be overlooked, the buyer or department manager must carefully plan merchandise presentations. For example, the department-store buyer will give careful consideration to the type of customer who comes to the department, since the customer may or may not be similar to those served in other departments throughout the store. The buyer, especially a buyer for a specialty department such as a bridal shop, a boutique, a women's large-size or half-size department, or a teen department, should present merchandise displays that emphasize the unique qualities of the merchandise available for sale. A buyer for a small business should develop a merchandise presentation that projects the store's overall image as well as the self-image of those who patronize a particular department.

A buyer of fashion goods in particular has a responsibility for providing merchandise displays that will invite customers into the department and thus stimulate sales. For example, a good display will help the customer visualize herself wearing the fashion look that is being promoted during a particular fashion season. The buyer for a boutique-type department may wish to emphasize a new fabric or color. Thus, many displays, especially at the entrance to the department, will feature the new color or fabric in a variety of applications. Or the boutique buyer may feature a certain style that he or she feels will be popular throughout the season.

The buyer of staple goods will also use merchandise displays to encourage consumer spending. For example, the buyer of stereo equipment may emphasize price and quality throughout various display presentations; a toy buyer

Figure 15.6. Display is considered an important selling device because it provides a visual presentation of what is. available for sale. Good displays will assist customers in making buying decisions.

may present movable displays, for example, a display of an electric train set that features the interesting characteristics of the product. A buyer of sewing notions may display buttons, threads, patches, and pins and needles on the counter to provide ease of selection and perhaps encourage impulse puying.

The responsibility for good merchandise displays rests with the buyer in a department-store operation; a department manager in a branch operation; a store manager in a chain store; and the owner-manager in a small business. Since good merchandise presentation is one of the least expensive yet most powerful forms of selling available, the time and energy spent on displays that communicate with store customers are very important.[4]

Stamps, Coupons, and Labels

Trading stamps are often offered to customers as a premium for shopping in a particular store. They have been found to build customer loyalty to the store and thus lead to an increase in sales volume. Trading stamps are considered a promotional device because they are associated with the store name and are an additional cost to the retailer. During periods of economic difficulty, however, other forms of promotion may be considered whereby prices may be lowered or services increased. For example, trading stamps declined in popularity during the mid-1970s due to an inflationary economy. However, many retailers have since added this promotion incentive to meet competition and encourage customers to shop in their particular retail establishments. Food markets, gasoline stations, drugstores, and some small businesses have found the use of trading stamps to be a popular sales promotion device.

Coupons may be distributed in newspaper advertisements or as handouts. They are still very popular today and are used to stimulate sales volume, introduce new products, or to sell a particular item. Food markets, particularly, use this promotional device since customers will redeem the coupons while going through the checkout line.

Labels carry the name of the store or the store's private brand and the name of the manufacturer or distributor. Labels are found in fashion goods as well as in hard goods. They serve as promotional devices because they continuously remind the consumer of the place where he or she purchased the merchandise as well as of the store's image and good-will policy.

Sampling and Demonstrations

Sampling and demonstrations, the third type of sales promotion activity, give the customer an opportunity to experience the particular product. A sample may be a miniature of the real thing, for example, a bar of soap. A demonstration may permit the customer to try out or actually use the product before purchasing. Both will help stimulate sales because they actually involve the customer by appealing to the senses. A manufacturer may provide the buyer with samples as well as demonstrators to help stimulate sales activity (Review Chapter 12).

Special Events

The last type of sales promotion activity, special events, will be used by many buying specialists to promote good will and increase customer traffic. The nature and extent of the special event depends on the kind of retail store, the size of the trading area, and the nature of the competition. Special events may include fashion shows, historic events, ethnic promotions, or civic events.

> Review the following types of sales promotion activities
>
> Display
> Stamps, coupons, and labels
> Sampling and demonstrations
> Special events
>
> How will each type of sales promotion activity attract customers to the store?

Publicity, Word of Mouth, Packaging, Vending Machines

Publicity is a third type of nonpersonal selling used by merchants. *Publicity* may be defined as the presentation of goods or services in a nonpersonal way both outside and within the retail establishment. Most publicity is paid for by the store, although some is free. For example, a small business may receive "free" publicity when it supports the local basketball or baseball team by providing uniforms. A department store will receive publicity when it presents a fashion show to senior citizens; a variety store will receive publicity when it provides toys and games for a children's Christmas party.

Word of mouth, the fourth type of nonpersonal selling, is primarily responsible for building store image and good will. If the consumer is satisfied with his purchases, he will tell his friends and neighbors. If he is dissatisfied, he will also communicate this feeling to those around him. Word of mouth, even though not directly paid for by the store, is a valuable store promotion activity.

Packaging is the fifth type of promotional device. In recent years more attention has been given to product packaging by manufacturers and by retailers. Today, well-designed packaging is important both to stores where display must carry a major part of the sales task and to retail stores that rely primarily on sales help. Well-designed packaging offers many advantages to the buyer. As you recall from our discussion on the buyer's responsibility in packaging in Chapter 12, good packaging will attract customer attention, stimulate interest in the product, protect the merchandise, make the product available in proper quantity and size, reflect the use of the product, and make displays more attractive and effective.

One of the fastest-growing types of nonpersonal selling is the automatic vending machine, the sixth type of promotion. It is found to be a useful method for both in-store and out-of-store selling. Vending machines are suitable for the sale of soft drinks and snacks within the store and are also located in front of some retail stores to dispense goods after hours. Vending machines have proved successful in areas where it is not economical to maintain a personal sales force on a routine basis. For example, a cafeteria may be operated entirely by means of vending-machine units that contain hot and cold sandwiches, confections, soup, coffee, fruit juices, milk, snack goods, and other prepared meals. If such is the case, the term *venditeria* can be used to describe the serving area. Vending machines have proven successful in selling not only food items but also fashion accessories (lipsticks, perfumes, combs) and hard goods (screwdrivers, games, puzzles, balloons, kites).

Nonpersonal selling is a method of communicating with customers indirectly

---

Review the following types of nonpersonal selling devices. How are they used by the buying specialist?

Advertising
Sales promotion
Publicity
Word of mouth
Packaging
Vending machines

Retail Personal Selling

PART 2

The consumer who enters a store, other than a self-service establishment, expects to be greeted by salespeople. Since sales personnel have direct contact with customers, they are very important to the retail business. A good salesperson, therefore, should have a proper attitude toward selling and possess the art and skill of modern selling techniques. The salesperson must know the merchandise thoroughly, know the store's selling system to avoid errors, and be aware of the store's merchandising policies and objectives. He or she must be aware of the needs and wants of the customers and be able to communicate to them the merchandise assortment provided by the store. Personal selling is still used by many retail establishments, especially department stores and specialty shops, since direct contact with store customers proves to be a most effective merchandising technique.

    During the last few years, however, the importance of the retail salesperson has been diminishing. Many retail stores have turned to self-service in an effort to cut selling costs; others have been virtually forced to it because of increasing competition and difficulty in keeping good sales help. Discount

The Importance of Personal Selling

houses and vending machines, in particular, have thrived in the absence of sales help. However, during healthy economic periods, customers tire of the impersonality of self-service and turn toward full-service stores.

The Types of Personal Selling

Personal selling, broadly defined, includes wholesale selling or contact selling, since the seller usually contacts the customer, and retail selling, where the customer usually approaches the retail store. In the part of this chapter that follows, we will discuss the role of the retail salesperson and the responsibility of the buyer in retail selling.

There are three types of retail personal selling: (1) house-to-house selling; (2) mail and telephone selling; and (3) over-the-counter selling. A discussion of each follows.

House-to-House Selling

House-to-house selling is still a very popular type of retail personal selling. A salesperson representing a store or a company will personally call on customers at their homes. The business organization may hold periodic sales drives, give demonstrations, or send representatives who offer advice on interior decorat-

Figure 15.7. House-to-house selling is still a very popular type of retail personal selling. A salesperson representing a company—in this example, Avon—will personally call at the home of one of the customers. (Courtesy of Avon Products, Inc., New York, N.Y.)

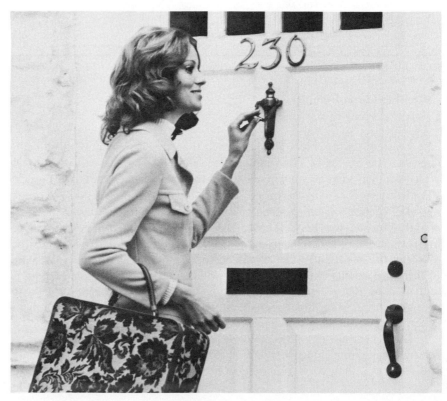

ing or provide some other service. As you recall from reading Chapter 1, house-to-house selling is used primarily to sell staple items that offer convenience and comfort to customers.

Mail and Telephone Selling

Mail and telephone selling is also very popular. For example, a department store or a general-merchandise chain will advertise that mail and telephone orders will be accepted for special advertised products and will provide a special department to answer telephone calls and receive mail orders. Once the orders are received, information is sent to the particular departments involved, and sales personnel will make certain that customers receive their merchandise. Mail and telephone selling is especially popular during the Christmas season. Most major retailers will print special catalogs for the Christmas season to induce customers to make purchases.

Over-the-Counter Selling

Over-the-counter selling takes place in most retail stores, unless they are self-service operations, and is performed by salespeople. Unlike retail order taking, where the salesperson does not assist the customer during the decision-making process, over-the-counter selling will help the consumer reach a decision regarding the merchandise. Since over-the-counter selling is so important to the successful and profitable operation of the retail store, the remaining sections of this chapter will be devoted to this topic. However, by way of review, you will recall that the selling activity is a responsibility of the department-store buyer and the small business owner-manager, since the buying-selling activity is a combined responsibility. In the chain operation, you will recall, the selling responsibility is primarily that of the store manager and his staff, with the buying activity performed by central buyers.

Managing Retail Salespeople

Regardless of the type and size of the retail operation, the responsibility for guiding and directing the sales staff is an important one. Whether the buyer specialist is managing a small business, a department store, or a chain operation, he or she has certain tasks to perform to ensure that personal selling is successful. The following activities are performed when managing sales personnel: (1) sales force planning; (2) recruitment and selection; (3) induction and training; (4) scheduling; (5) compensation; and (6) supervision.

The role of the buying specialist in sales management	
1. Sales force planning	4. Scheduling
2. Recruitment and selection	5. Compensation
3. Induction and training	6. Supervision

Sales Force Planning

When planning the sales force, consideration should be given to store image, the type of clientele the store must cater to, store policies and practices, and the type of department. Attention should also be given to the characteristics of salespeople and how they will match against the characteristics of the store's customers. For example, if the department caters to prejunior and junior sizes, it would be unwise to employ salespeople who cannot relate to the youth market. Or if the department sells sporting goods and equipment, and the salesperson does not play various sports or is not interested in sporting activities, selling attempts would prove unsuccessful and lead to a loss of sales.

Sales force planning will also include the budgeting of salespeople required on a full-time basis as well as on a part-time basis. For example, the sales force may be increased during particular seasons, such as Christmas, Easter, and special sales promotion periods such as Valentine's Day, Father's Day, or Mother's Day. Additional part-time help may be required during the evening hours or on weekends, since full-time people are not available.

Recruitment and Selection

The buying specialist will usually work with the store's personnel office when recruiting and selecting the sales staff. He or she will send a requisition to the personnel director in charge of sales, and, in turn, potential candidates will be sent to the buyer or department head to be interviewed. The selection process may consist of a brief interview or may be more complex, consisting of several interviews with various store executives, psychological testing, and a physical examination. The buyer is usually interested in the candidate's past work experience, educational background, merchandising attitude, ability to get along with people, and the ability to lead as well as follow orders. Figure 15.8 is an example of an employee rating form that measures characteristics important in retail selling.

Induction and Training

If the retail store has its own training division, new employees will be introduced formally into the organization. They will be provided with useful and accurate information about the retail store, the policies that will affect them, and the services that may be provided for their benefit. Besides the induction program, the employee may be subject to specific training that will relate to the job he is assuming. Specific job training will provide information on successful selling techniques, operation of the cash register, wrapping and packaging merchandise, telephone sales, team selling, and customer relations. Once the new employee has completed the training program, he is sent to a particular department, where he will receive additional training or on-the-job training. Here, the new salesperson is usually assigned a sponsor who will give special instructions on the specific operations of the department. Figure 15.9 is an example of the kind of information given new employees.

Name	Dept.	Emp. No.	Salary	Last Increase	Amount	Tenure Date	Position	Store
Annual Follow-Up		Rated By		Date		Interviewed By		Date
Increase	New Salary		Effective Date	Approved By	Date	Personnel Dept. Approval		Date

	Excellent	Very Good	Good	Average	Unsatisfactory
I. PERSONAL CHARACTERISTICS					
1. Self control-maintains poise under pressure.	☐	☐	☐	☐	☐
2. Analytical mind-disects problems, sets correct priorities.	☐	☐	☐	☐	☐
3. Creativeness-has imagination. Produces new ideas.	☐	☐	☐	☐	☐
4. Initiative-self starting.	☐	☐	☐	☐	☐
5. Motivation and drive-has goals, enthusiasm and sence of urgency.	☐	☐	☐	☐	☐
II. MANAGEMENT ABILITIES					
1. Administration-organizes work and delegates intelligently.	☐	☐	☐	☐	☐
2. Control-knows status of activities under his supervision.	☐	☐	☐	☐	☐
3. Planning-develops programs for future events.	☐	☐	☐	☐	☐
4. Communication-effectively and concisely conveys his thoughts to people at all levels.	☐	☐	☐	☐	☐
5. Leadership-motivates subordinates. Receives a high degree of cooperation.	☐	☐	☐	☐	☐
6. Executive attitude-makes decisions promptly, objectively and accepts responsibility for his decisions.	☐	☐	☐	☐	☐

Figure 15.8. An example of an employee rating form.

Scheduling

Before scheduling additional sales help, it is important to be certain that the level of service, which presumably grows as more salespeople are hired, is not less than the costs resulting from salespeople's wages. Systematic scheduling requires that certain factors be considered, such as the amount of customer

Figure 15.9. An example of
the kind of information provided
by the store's personnel
department to new employees.
(Courtesy of John Wanamaker
Department Store, Philadelphia,
Pa.)

traffic during particular store hours, the amount of time a salesperson spends
performing particular tasks, the department sales volume, the average number
of transactions per salesperson, and consumer spending patterns. When arranging work schedules, the buyer, department head, or store manager should
consider employee preferences regarding hours of work, days off, and vacation
periods.

Compensation

The compensation is the salary paid to salespeople and is determined by store
policy. According to retailers and other observers, however, a basic cause of
personal selling problems is the relatively low pay. As a result, the supply of
applicants is reduced. Often those who become sales employees do so only until
they find a higher-paying position, while others who will accept a sales position
are often poorly motivated. To help offset this problem, some retail stores offer
incentive programs for the purpose of improving the quality of retail selling.
Incentive programs may take the form of contests, commissions, bonuses, and
special employee shopping days.

Supervision

As a supervisor, the buying specialist should give frequent encouragement and praise as well as constructive criticism to the sales staff. Sales employees should be informed of department standards, and be given the proper supervision to avoid problems on the selling floor. The following section will discuss in detail the duties and responsibilities of sales personnel as instructed by the buyer and other store executives.

During the induction and training process, the buyer has the responsibility for instructing new sales personnel on the following: (1) department standards and routines; (2) housekeeping duties; (3) display techniques; (4) stock control methods; (5) assisting customers; (6) handling complaints; (7) preventing waste and losses: pilferage and shoplifting; and (8) developing good selling techniques.

Duties and Responsibilities of Sales Personnel

The buyer should instruct new sales personnel on

1. Department standards and routines
2. Housekeeping duties
3. Display techniques
4. Stock control methods
5. Assisting customers
6. Handling complaints
7. Preventing waste and losses: pilferage and shoplifting
8. Developing good selling techniques

Department Standards and Routines

The buyer, assistant buyer, or department head will provide the new sales employee with information regarding department standards. For example, the proper dress regulation that will reflect the image of the store and that of the department will be emphasized, as well as the importance of the "right" retail attitude. The buying specialist will assist the new recruit in learning and understanding store routines such as the check-in procedure when he arrives on the job and when he takes his lunch period, and department routines regarding break time, shopping privileges, and the store's lay-away system. Since well-motivated salespeople will sell effectively, it is important to give them the facts about the department as a whole, the merchandise offered for sale, and the store's overall merchandising policies. As a fashion buyer, you will soon learn there is no better way to sell fashion goods than through well-motivated, well-trained, and well-informed sales personnel. Needless to say, the same applies to the buyer of hard goods. Through well-informed sales personnel, the buyer of patio furniture, for example, will get the selling message through to customers, and in return the buyer will get customer reactions to the merchandise offered for sale.

All salespeople, whether new on the job or old-timers, need constant training and motivation. A wise buyer will recognize good performers and continuously encourage and assist them on the job.

Housekeeping Duties

Sales personnel must also be informed of their responsibilities regarding maintenance and general housekeeping duties. The salesperson is usually responsible for keeping merchandise properly organized, neat, and attractive. A sloppy and disorganized merchandise presentation will lead to confusion for customer and salesperson alike and thus minimize department efficiency. A primary responsibility of a buyer specialist, therefore, is to teach salespeople about the presentation of the merchandise assortment and what benefits it will bring to the store's customers. For example, if you run a fashion department, you will point out to the salesgirl what merchandise will coordinate with goods offered in other departments. However, fashion goods must be presented in an orderly, neat manner if the customer is to interpret the fashion message properly. For example, salespeople should be instructed on how to fold merchandise, refill empty cases or bins, check that each item is in its proper location, report any sizes, styles, prices, or colors that are running low, and so forth. The buyer may instruct the assistant or department head to show salespeople how to organize packaged merchandise samples. Also, senior salespeople may be instructed by the store manager or buyer to teach new, part-time, or temporary salespeople about department housekeeping duties and routines.

Display Techniques

As you have learned from Part 1 of this chapter, displays are used to promote and sell merchandise. The new salesperson should know something about color, texture, line, and design. Displays should be attractive enough to draw customer attention and should create a desire on the part of the customer to purchase the product. The salesperson should be aware that good displays should be kept fresh and clean and changed frequently. A display may show goods used in a particular way or coordinated with related lines of merchandise. The buyer of men's better-priced shirts may arrange merchandise displays that present, for example, goods with a high markup, items that invite the purchase of related items, classic styles, or new merchandise. The buyer should communicate the fashion message to salespeople so they may relate the information to store customers. Also, if the display becomes soiled or damaged, the salesperson may arrange a new merchandise presentation that will continue to emphasize the fashion message.

Stock Control Methods

Sales personnel are very instrumental in assisting the buyer or store manager in stock control methods. Usually, a salesperson is assigned a portion of stock and is responsible for the counting and control of the stock, both in the stockroom and on the selling floor. The salesperson will let the buyer or the assistant know when merchandise is ready for reorder and how much reserve stock is available by taking daily or weekly inventories. The salesperson is also provided with a list of slow-selling merchandise and is asked to report on the amount of merchandise on hand and the price for which the merchandise is selling.

Assisting Customers

Assisting and directing customers is a most important responsibility of the salesperson. Often, the consumer will enter the retail establishment without knowing exactly where to go to purchase specific items. The salesperson should be courteous, attentive, and patient when directing customers. A salesperson who does not know where a particular item may be found should volunteer to find someone who does. Nothing is more annoying to a customer than to be directed from one department to the next, only to realize that the merchandise sought is not carried by the store.

Personal customer attention is a service provided by special stores, most small businesses, and department stores. Specialty shops, especially those catering to the middle and upper income levels, will emphasize personal selling by offering fewer merchandise displays, since they require sales personnel to show the merchandise personally to customers and assist them in making purchases.

Handling Complaints

Many times the salesperson is required to handle complaints and adjustments. This calls for a great deal of patience and tact. The salesperson should become familiar with the products he or she sells to know how to make merchandise adjustments. He must develop an understanding of consumer problems if he is to make a satisfactory adjustment and continue to maintain good customer relations.

Many retailers have discovered, however, that salespeople need assistance in handling consumer complaints. Thus, many stores will instruct their sales personnel to send customers to the service manager or adjustment counter. As a result, salespeople can go about their job of selling, customers are taken care of more efficiently and effectively, and the store continues to have happy, well-satisfied customers.

Preventing Waste and Losses: Pilferage and Shoplifting

Good salespeople will help prevent waste and losses and thus keep store expenses down. The salesperson can prevent waste and loss by keeping goods clean, handling merchandise carefully, avoiding overselling that may lead to complaints and returns, and being careful not to damage fixtures, merchandise, and store property.

As you recall, when there is a discrepancy between book inventory figures and physical inventory figures and the physical inventory is less than the book inventory, there is a stock shortage. Salespeople can further assist the retailer in controlling stock shortages by carefully receiving and checking merchandise when it enters the department, properly recording any broken or missing items, and carefully weighing and measuring merchandise.

However, pilferage (employee theft) and shoplifting (consumer theft) still continue to be the leading cause of merchandise waste and loss. Today there is increased attention to both problems. According to one report, shoplifting is growing at the rate of 20 percent a year, with stock shortages estimated at $4.5 billion a year. For some retail stores, especially self-service operations, inventory losses are as high as 3 or 4 percent of sales.[5] It is also believed that employee dishonesty may be a bigger source of inventory shrinkage than many realize. For example, one report suggests that employee dishonesty accounts for about 70 percent of inventory shortages, shoplifting 15 percent, and book-keeping errors approximately 15 percent.[6]

Some factors that contribute to both pilferage and shoplifting are poor inventory controls, inadequate shipping and receiving procedures, and poor display techniques. To remedy these problems, many stores have: (1) employed the services of security guards; (2) improved lighting in stockrooms and shipping areas; and (3) placed alarms in stairways, entrances and exits, and throughout various departments.

Developing Good Selling Techniques

Salespeople should also be taught selling techniques that will assist them when waiting on store customers. Selling techniques that should be learned by salespeople are listed in the chart that follows.

Selling techniques that should be learned by the salesperson
1. Approaching and greeting the customer 2. Determining customer needs and wants 3. Effectively presenting the merchandise 4. Answering objections 5. Closing the sale 6. Maintaining customer good will

Figure 15.10. A knowledge of good selling techniques will assist the salesperson when waiting on store customers.

Approaching and Greeting the Customer. The salesperson should prepare himself or herself and the department surroundings before the customer enters the store. He or she should have a neat appearance, be knowledgeable about stock, be aware of department and store advertising, provide appealing merchandise displays, and learn the name, background, and interests of specific customers. Once the customer enters the store, the salesperson should approach and greet the shopper with confidence and a friendly and sincere desire to be of service. It is important that the customer be welcomed with a pleasant greeting and be made to feel appreciated by the salesperson and the retail store. If this is accomplished properly, the sales transaction is off to a good start. Often, however, salespeople gather in groups to converse and as a result neglect, if not ignore, the customer. Those in charge must correct this situation by proper instruction and supervision.

Determining Customer Needs and Wants. The second step in the selling process is determining customer needs and wants. After the customer has been properly greeted, his or her needs and wants should be defined. This task is usually easy for staple items, since they are asked for by brand name; however, fashion merchandise is more difficult. The salesperson must carefully size up the customer through a few well-phrased questions relating to customer needs.

The salesperson will receive valuable guides from the customer's dress, manner, and reaction to the merchandise displayed. By eliminating as quickly as possible those articles that do not meet the customer's needs, the salesperson may then concentrate on those that prove interesting. Salespersons must be careful not to judge customer interests and purchasing power by their own tastes and desires. Such a mistake will only irritate and annoy the customer and lead to a loss in sales if not a loss in good will.

Effectively Presenting the Merchandise. Once the customer's needs are known, the salesperson is ready for the third step in the selling process, that of effectively presenting the merchandise for sale. The following five points should be considered when presenting merchandise:

1. Knowledge of the location of goods in the department or in the stockroom
2. Wise selection of merchandise
3. Displaying the merchandise properly
4. Pointing out the important characteristics or selling points of the item
5. Developing skill and confidence when making a sales presentation

Answering Objections. Answering objections is the most difficult step in the selling process. There are two types of objections which a salesperson will experience: (1) genuine objections based on sincere reasons for failure to purchase, and (2) excuses designed to conceal the real reason for failure to take action. Genuine objections are usually easier to answer because they are based on definite obstacles, whereby excuses may not in all cases genuinely reflect the opinions of the customer. Therefore, they provide no logical basis to which the salesperson may react. There are certain general rules which may prove helpful to a salesperson when attempting to answer objections. They are listed as follows:

1. Anticipate objections and incorporate them into the presentation.
2. Never argue with a customer, since this will only aggravate and annoy both parties concerned. Customers are valuable to a store, and it is best not to prove a point only to lose a potential shopper.
3. Understand customers' objections by not condescending to them or belittling their questions.
4. Tactfully and confidently handle customer objections.
5. Encourage the customer to raise genuine questions.
6. Avoid mentioning competition and their merchandise. If the customer mentions them, then speak of them briefly and courteously.

Closing the Sale. If objections have been properly handled and adequately answered, closing the sale, the fifth step in the selling process, will occur without particular attention being given to it by the customer. Often, however, the salesperson does not close the sale. The salesperson, especially a new one, may make one or more of the following mistakes when closing the sale:

1. Hurrying the customer in making a decision
2. Failing to assist the customer during merchandise selection
3. Not answering objections, real or otherwise, confidently and intelligently
4. Emphasizing unimportant and irrelevant selling points
5. Being too confident a salesperson
6. Using high-pressure techniques to force action
7. Assuming the customer is aware of all product characteristics
8. Acting discourteously or disappointed when customers fail to purchase

Maintaining Customer Good Will. The last step in the selling process is to maintain customer good will after the sale is made. The customer will remember a store that employs courteous and friendly salespeople who are genuinely interested in the customers. Even if no sale has been made, the customer should be made to feel at home and feel that his or her interest was appreciated. Such an approach on the part of salespeople will make friends for the store and for themselves as well as increase store patronage and continue to maintain good will.

Regardless of the size and type of retail operation, the buying specialist or manager should develop management techniques that will guide and direct sales personnel. For example, a department-store buyer may send informal memos to salespeople telling them of a forthcoming store promotion, new items that have been added to the merchandise assortment, fashion trends, special events, or whatever. Also, the buyer will contact the department or group manager in each branch store and send out similar kinds of information. Or the buyer may contact senior sales personnel and ask them to instruct new and part-time salespeople on stock conditions, sales promotions, advertising specials, and so forth. A central buyer, for example, a buyer for a women's discount chain, may send fashion clippings, publications, news bulletins, or samples to store managers and ask each to communicate items of importance to individual department supervisors or managers. The supervisors or managers, in turn, may post the information on bulletin boards and hold informal meetings before the store opens to discuss new arrivals, slow sellers, or "hot" items. The buyer for a boutique or specialty shop may hold special fashion seminars; permit sales personnel to view the lines of manufacturers' representatives who visit the department or store, to view films, or to listen to tapes;

Good Management Techniques: Communicating with Salespeople; The Department Meeting

and provide demonstrators to show salespeople how to use certain products. The small business owner may post fashion photos, newspaper clippings, store ads, and other pertinent information on a bulletin board. Since the business is small, it is usually easier for the owner-manager to brief salespeople continuously on changes in merchandise offerings, special sales, new merchandising policies, the activities of competition, and so forth.

In most large stores, however, the most popular management technique used to reach salespeople is the department meeting. Department meetings are usually held once a week. The advantages are many. Salespeople are provided an opportunity to exchange views; meet new people, especially part-timers and temporary full-time help; and have personal contact with the buyer and the assistant, and the department manager, store manager, or store owner, depending on the nature of the organization.

Some objections to holding department meetings are that they may become too routine, lack good planning and organization, do not always include the entire staff, and become dull and uninteresting. Thus, when planning interesting and informative department meetings, you as a buyer should consider the following activities:

1. Determine the purpose or objective of the meeting. What points are you trying to get across? For example, a discussion on new style trends? New fibers? New packaging methods?
2. Determine how you will introduce the subject matter; how you will arouse interest. For example, if a new style trend is predicted for the coming season, you may introduce the topic by describing various events that have fostered its development.
3. Determine how you will develop your presentation. For example, you may wish to show fashion photos, slides, or a movie to illustrate your discussion of new fashion trends further.
4. Determine how you will summarize the meeting. Once you have completed the presentation, you may wish to provide salespeople with illustrated leaflets that describe how the new fashion trend will be worn and accessorized.
5. Determine how you will follow up on your meeting to ensure that your message got across. You may observe sales personnel to determine whether or not they understood the message you were trying to convey; you may check sales figures for increases; or you may hold another meeting and retrain to secure the proper action.

Most buyers will develop a variety of management techniques that they have found to be successful when attempting to get messages across to salespeople. The buyer, or manager, or whoever, soon realizes that no one management technique can carry every message or reach all salespeople.[7]

Due to lack of confidence and lack of experience in selling and in getting along with others, the new salesperson (and sometimes the sales veteran) may encounter many difficulties when working on the selling floor. It should be recognized that salespeople may have problems in communicating with other salespeople, the assistant buyer, the sponsor, the department manager, or the buyer. The salesperson often has problems not because of lack of product knowledge or of selling ability, but because he or she has not adopted the right retail attitude. A salesperson who feels self-conscious and insecure may try to give the impression that he or she is superior; thus, a poor attitude may develop. This may also happen if one is overconfident about one's ability. A poor attitude may lead to a personality that antagonizes others and to irresponsibility toward department housekeeping duties; it may create customer ill will and lead to problems with co-workers. For example, a new salesperson may take advantage of fellow workers by waiting on customers out of turn or "grabbing" customers. Such a practice will cause much friction among salespeople and often will drive customers away. Store executives must be aware of these and other problems on the selling floor, such as shoplifting and pilferage, return sales, arguments, tardiness, and absenteeism.

Problems on the Selling Floor

Problems on the selling floor usually result from:

Poor retail attitude	Arguments
Shoplifting and pilferage	Tardiness
Return sales	Absenteeism

What methods can be used to help minimize problems on the selling floor?

The buyer and the assistant buyer have the responsibility of providing the direction and leadership as well as the kind of selling atmosphere that leads to effective selling. When this is accomplished, customers will be pleased with their shopping surroundings, and salespeople will become congenial in their working relationships with one another.

Chapter Summary

The buyer and other store executives must be able to communicate with or send messages to customers to make them aware of store offerings. Nonpersonal selling is a method of communicating with customers indirectly and includes such promotional devices as advertising, sales promotion, publicity, word of mouth, packaging, and vending machines.

The buyer will advertise for many reasons; however, the prime objective is to attract potential customers to the store. There are three types of retail advertising: promotional advertising, institutional advertising, and a combination of both. Psychological studies of the emotions and drives of people have greatly influenced the use of advertising. Such studies suggest that people may act on three levels. There are four psychological steps that every advertisement must contain: (1) attracting attention; (2) developing interest; (3) creating desire; and (4) securing action. The student will note that these psychological steps are also applicable in personal selling. There are six steps the buyer should follow when planning advertising: (1) setting specific objectives; (2) identifying a theme; (3) establishing a budget; (4) selecting merchandise to promote; (5) selecting the media; and (6) preparing the advertisement. When preparing the advertisement, the buyer will work with the advertising department, which consists of copywriters and artists. The advertisement uses five major parts: headline, illustration, copy, layout, and signature plate. The buyer should practice good ethics in advertising. The Federal Trade Commission (FTC) has been primarily responsible for controlling deceptive advertising practices in interstate commerce.

Sales promotion, the second type of promotional device, may be defined as any promotional activity other than advertising, publicity, and personal selling that attracts the public to a retail store to stimulate purchasing and thus makes a profit for the store. The student should review the following sales promotion activities: (1) display; (2) stamps, coupons, and labels; (3) sampling and demonstrations; and (4) special events. Publicity, word of mouth, packaging, and use of vending machines are also effective sales promotion activities.

Personal selling, broadly defined, includes wholesale selling or contact selling, since the seller usually contacts the customer, and retail selling, where the customer usually approaches the store. There are three types of retail personal selling: (1) house-to-house selling; (2) mail and telephone selling; and (3) over-the-counter selling. The buyer performs certain activities when managing sales personnel. Such activities include planning of the sales force, recruitment and selection of the sales staff, induction and training, scheduling, compensation, and supervision. Sales personnel have many duties and responsibilities to perform when working in a retail store. Responsibilities include learning department standards and routines, keeping the department maintained and organized, keeping displays fresh and clean and changed frequently, following department stock control procedures, assisting and directing customers, handling complaints, preventing waste and losses, and developing good selling techniques. There are certain well-defined selling techniques that should be learned by the salesperson. They are: (1) approaching and greeting the customer; (2) determining the customer's needs and wants; (3) effectively presenting the merchandise; (4) answering objections; (5) closing the sale; and (6) maintaining customer good will.

The buying expert will develop and use different management techniques when reaching salespeople. The most popular of these is the department meeting. As a result of inexperience and a lack of confidence, the new salesperson may encounter many difficulties when working on the selling floor. The buyer and the assistant buyer have the responsibility of providing the direction and leadership as well as the kind of selling atmosphere that leads to effective selling.

Trade Terminology

DIRECTIONS: Briefly explain or discuss each of the following trade terms:

1. Nonpersonal selling
2. Advertising
3. Promotional advertising
4. Institutional advertising
5. Combination retail advertising
6. Advertising theme
7. Headline
8. Illustration
9. Copy
10. Layout
11. Signature plate
12. Sales promotion
13. Publicity
14. Personal selling

Questions for Discussion and Review

1. What is the primary objective of retail advertising? Retail buyers will advertise for many reasons. List five and explain why each is important.

2. How does institutional advertising differ from the promotional type? Which type is used most by the retail buyer? Why?

3. Scan the local newspaper and select examples of the following: prestige advertising, sale price advertising, service advertising. How do they differ?

4. There are certain psychological steps that must be followed when planning advertising. What are they? Select an advertisement from the local newspaper and determine whether or not the advertisement employed each of the psychological steps named.

5. Once the buyer becomes familiar with the types of retail advertising and its important psychological implications, he or she is ready to plan. What six steps should the buyer follow when planning an advertising campaign? Explain.

6. In your opinion, what is the most popular medium used to carry messages to the public? Cite specific examples.

7. Interview the advertising manager of your local TV station. Determine how an advertising program is developed using the TV medium. Also, include a discussion of the rules and regulations set forth by the Federal Communication Commission (FCC) and its role in preventing deceptive advertising.

8. What is meant by the term "sales promotion"? Select three examples of sales promotion activities and relate how each will stimulate purchasing and help make a profit for the store.

9. Interview the display director of a traditional department store and of a discount house. How will display techniques differ? How will they be similar? Explain.

10. Define personal selling. Do you consider the role of the salesperson important to the operation of a discount house? A specialty store? A variety store?

11. Review the special forms of sales promotion that have been used in your community. What have been the results of these efforts?

12. What management techniques are used by buyers to reach salespeople? What steps are followed when setting up a department meeting?

13. Discuss the salesperson's responsibility for effective personal selling. What is the obligation of the buyer and the assistant buyer in connection with this activity?

14. Many problems are encountered by the new salesperson in beginning a sales career. Review those listed in this chapter. What other problems would you add to the list? Why?

Case Study Number One

Mrs. Weed and Her Companion

You have been working six months as a salesperson in the Early American department of a leading furniture specialty store. The previous day you showed Mrs. Weed and a companion a dining-room set. You recall the frustration you felt when you attempted to point out specific features of the furniture only to be contradicted by Mrs. Weed's highly critical companion. Throughout the sales presentation, Mrs. Weed heeded her companion's opinion and, as a result, she left without making a buying decision. She did state, however, that she would return the following day to make her final decision. Today, as you see Mrs. Weed coming toward your department, you shudder slightly when you see Mrs. Weed's friend trailing her. Once again you prepare yourself for a no-sale meeting. What assumptions would you make about the fact that the customer is returning for a second time? Be prepared in class to discuss how you could close the sale this time.

Case Study Number Two

Ed Long was a recent college graduate who joined the executive training program of Hopkins Department Store. Part of Ed's job consisted of working in the area of men's suits for a three-month period to learn sales floor supervision. Ed worked on a salary basis and was expected to make sales on a noncommission basis.

The Old-Timer and the New Recruit

Richard Smith was a salesman in the men's suits department and had worked at Hopkins for the past twenty years. He worked on a commission basis and over the years had made an adequate salary, enough to support himself, his wife, and two children. Mr. Smith's success as a salesman could be attributed to his positive attitude towards his job and his ability as a salesman. He had many old customers who would ask for him when they came to the department.

Troubles began, however, when Mr. Smith discovered that Ed Long was handling customers who previously had been buying from him. After all, Ed was young, very enthusiastic, and had a good sales personality. Mr. Smith was getting older and was starting to lose the "old sales spark" that had successfully carried him along for many years.

Mr. Smith complained to the department manager that, since Ed was an executive trainee and worked on a straight salary, he should not be placed in a sales-commission department. He also stated that Ed was impulsive, discourteous, and greedy—that he was out only to make a name for himself at the expense of the regular sales help.

When the department manager discussed the situation with Ed, Ed told him that the sales staff (especially Mr. Smith) were envious of his position and of his ability to succeed in merchandising. Ed further stated that he was confused about how he was supposed to get sales experience when people were complaining about his waiting on customers. The department manager informed Ed that he was to continue working as he had been but to attempt to consider the needs of the full-time sales staff. The manager reminded Ed that he was also responsible for teaching and training salespeople and for providing a pleasant work environment.

As a result of this conversation, Ed decided to stay in the background and let Mr. Smith take over. However, after several weeks the department manager noted that Ed had undergone a change in attitude and was definitely losing interest in his job. In fact, Ed finally informed the manager that he was losing his enthusiasm for merchandising and was very uncertain about his responsibilities.

If you were Ed's department manager, how would you remedy this situation?

Retailing Activities to Stimulate Student Interest and Participation

1. Interview the display manager of a department store; a boutique; a men's specialty shop. Prepare a list of questions based on the topic "How do you plan in-store displays and window displays for the coming season?" Are there similarities in the methods used in each type of store? How do they differ?

2. Prepare a paper on the topic "Why is a knowledge of salesmanship important to the retail buyer?" Refer to The Retail Student's Reference Library for selected references.

3. Select five types of media that may be used by a small business, a department store, and a variety chain operation to advertise their products. What kind of advertising (promotional, institutional, or combination) is used by each? Why do you suppose the retailers use these particular media to advertise their merchandise?

REFERENCES

The Retail Student's Reference Library

Agee, W., Ault, P., and Emery, E. *Introduction to Mass Communications.* New York: Dodd, Mead & Company, 1971.

Antrim, William. *Advertising.* Hightstown: McGraw-Hill Book Company, 1970.

Ashman, R. D., and Ernest, J. W. *Salesmanship Fundamentals.* Hightstown: McGraw-Hill Book Company, 1973.

Barnhill, J. A. *Sales Management: Contemporary Perspectives.* Glenview, Ill.: Scott, Foresman & Company, 1970.

Bern, Ronald L., and Greenberg, Herbert M. *The Successful Salesman.* Philadelphia: Auerbach Publishers Inc., 1972.

Burton, P. W., and Miller, R. J. *Advertising Fundamentals.* Scranton, Pa.: International Textbook Company, 1970.

Degenshein, Joan, and Stern, Naomi. *Successful Cosmetic Selling.* New York: Chain Store Publishing Corporation, 1971.

Diamant, Lincoln. *The Anatomy of Television Commercials.* New York: Hastings House Publishers, Inc., 1970.

Dommermuth, W. P., Kernan, J. B., and Sommers, M. S. *Promotion: An Introduction Analysis.* Hightstown: McGraw-Hill Book Company, 1970.

Engel, J. F., Larson, C. M., and Talarzyk, W. W. *Cases in Promotional Strategy.* Homewood, Ill.: Richard D. Irwin, Inc., 1971.

Hartzler, F. E. *Retail Salesmanship.* Hightstown: McGraw-Hill Book Company, 1970.

Hatchett, Melvin. *Merchandise Display.* Austin: University of Texas Press, 1972.

How To Plan and Prepare Newspaper Ads. Indianapolis: National Retail Hardware Association, n.d.

Isolating and Measuring the Effects of Magazine Advertising. New York: Magazine Publishers Association, 1972.

Jacobs, L. W. *Advertising and Promotion for Retailing.* Glenview, Ill.: Scott, Foresman & Company, 1972.

Judelle, Beatrice. *The Fashion Buyer's Job.* New York: National Retail Merchants Association, 1971.

Kirkpatrick, C. A. *Salesmanship.* Cincinnati: South-Western Publishing Company, 1971.

Kirkpatrick, C. A., and Littlefield, J. E. *Advertising.* Boston: Houghton Mifflin Company, 1970.

Krieger, Murray. *1973 Merchandising Planbook and Sales Promotion Calendar.* New York: National Retail Merchants Association, 1973.

Levy, Sidney. *Promotional Behavior.* Glenview, Ill.: Scott, Foresman & Company, 1971.

Mauger, E. M. *Modern Display Techniques.* New York: Fairchild Publications, Inc., 1972.

Minsky, Betty Jane. *Gimmicks for Making Money in Retailing.* New York: Fairchild Publications, Inc., n.d.

NRMA Instant Promotions. New York: National Retail Merchants Association, n.d.

Obermeyer, E. *The Myth of Trade Advertising.* New York: Fairchild Publications, Inc., n.d.

Ocko, J. Y. *Retail Advertising Copy: The How, the What, the Why.* New York: National Retail Merchants Association, 1971.

Rowe, Frank A. *Display Fundamentals.* Cincinnati: Display Publishing Company, 1970.

Steinberg, Jules. *Customers Don't Bite: Selling with Confidence.* New York: Fairchild Publications, Inc., 1972.

Tif, Jenkins. *Planning the Advertising Campaign.* New York: Macmillan Company, 1971.

References

1. D. J. Duncan and C. F. Phillips, *Retailing Principles and Methods* (Homewood, Ill.: Richard D. Irwin, Inc., 1970), pp. 519–520.
2. *Journal of Marketing,* October 1948, p. 205.
3. Beatrice Judelle, *The Fashion Buyer's Job* (New York: National Retail Merchants Association, 1971), p. 107.
4. Ibid., p. 120.
5. "Stores Find It's Not Easy to Stop Thieves—Pros or Amateurs," *Wall Street Journal,* October 11, 1971, pp. 1–15.
6. "Leary's High Pay Position at A & S Hailed as Pace Setter," *Women's Wear Daily,* September 9, 1970, p. 6.
7. Judelle, *The Fashion Buyer's Job,* pp. 38–39.

Glossary of Trade Terms Used in Merchandise Buying

---

advanced dating   the invoice is dated from a specified future date, not from the designated invoice date.

advertising   a set of activities that involves the presentation of a mass message about a product, a service, or an idea; the message is paid for by an identified sponsor.

advertising theme   benefits the consumer will receive by purchasing the advertised product and by shopping in a particular store.

allowance   a term used synonymously with *discount*.

anticipation   an extra discount is given for paying an invoice in advance of the cash discount date.

assistant buyer   an individual who has been selected for his or her managerial potential and is capable of assuming the managerial functions of the department in the absence of the buyer.

associated office   a resident buying office owned and operated by a group of stores that controls it.

assortment breadth   characteristic of an inventory assortment offering a large number of different categories or classifications but not a large stock of any one style.

assortment depth   characteristic of an inventory assortment offering limited versions of proved popular styles.

auction   a type of nonmerchant buying whereby goods are placed on display and sold quickly to the highest bidder.

automatic open-to-buy   a plan whereby a predetermined portion of funds is allotted to the central buyer after the coming months' purchases have been planned, with the balance allotted to the store manager.

balanced assortment   an inventory assortment using both assortment breadth and depth.

billing record   a term used synonymously with *purchase journal*.

book method of inventory   the record of stock that should be on hand in view of what has been purchased and what has been sold. The record of what should be left is called the *closing book inventory*.

bottom-up planning   planning for a specific department, whether it be located in one store or in many selling units.

boutique   a French word that means "shop"; usually used for a women's fashionable specialty shop or department.

broker   nonmerchant middleman whose primary function is to bring buyers and sellers together.

business objective   the goals toward which the management activities of the business establishment are directed.

business policies   guidelines providing management with a frame of reference for decision making that is consistent with planned objectives.

buying   the purchase of consumer goods in relatively large or wholesale quantities for subsequent resale in smaller (retail) lots to the ultimate consumer.

buying committee   a three- to eight-person committee that acts in behalf of a single buyer and assists in decision-making policies regarding the procurement of specific merchandise categories.

capital budget   a plan for the investment of assets that will last longer than a year. It contains a list of future investment projects, with a justification for each proposal listed next to each item on the list.

cash budget   an estimate of the retail business' cash receipts and cash disbursements for a specified period of time.

cash discount   a reduction in list price is allowed by the vendor for prompt payment. The common practice is to allow the retail buyer 10 days from the invoice date.

cash on delivery (COD) dating   cash on delivery terms state that merchandise may be sold with the agreement that cash will be paid when the merchandise is delivered.

central buying   the centralization of all buying activities from a central headquarters that is located in the market center and in which the authority and responsibility for the selection and purchase of merchandise is limited to buyers of particular merchandise categories.

central merchandise plan   a form of central buying whereby the central buying authority assumes complete responsibility for the merchandise plan, for the buying of the assortment of goods, pricing, warehousing, and distribution to the many store units.

chain discount   a term used synonymously with *series discount.*

chain store   an organization with two or more centrally owned and managed outlets that operate on the same plane of distribution and handle same or similar lines of merchandise.

chain-owned office   a term used synonymously with *syndicated office.*

classic styles   those styles that remain in good taste over a long period of time.

classification   the subdividing by the buyer of each general line of merchandise into subdivisions.

classification control   refers to the use of dollar control based upon classifications of related types of merchandise within individual departments.

classification merchandising   a term used synonymously with *classification control.*

combination retail advertising   a method whereby institutional promotional approaches are blended together in the same advertising.

commissionaire   the title given to the individual who represents a foreign resident buying office under foreign management.

commission men   nonmerchant middlemen who handle merchandise by displaying the goods for resale in a central marketplace.

commission office   this type of independent office receives its remuneration directly from the manufacturer or vendor it represents and is found primarily in the fashion apparel trade.

comparison shopping bureau   a special bureau whose objective is to shop competing stores and determine if the competition is selling the same merchandise at the same price and quality or merchandise of inferior quality at a lower price.

consignment   merchandise sold on consignment does not become the property of the buyer but instead remains the property of the seller.

contest   a competition offering expensive prizes; usually requires that the consumer presents evidence of purchase to qualify.

control standards   represent a business firm's objectives and goals.

convenience goods   those goods consumers expect to have readily available at a convenient location.

copy   constitutes the language of the ad.

cost method of inventory   goods are recorded at cost price, and the ending inventory values are determined by actually counting the merchandise in stock and recording values at cost prices.

cost of goods sold   amount of money paid for merchandise sold during a particular period covered by the profit-and-loss statement.

coupon   an award granted by the manufacturer or vendor for purchasing his product. May be used to purchase an item at a lower price.

dating   the length of time the seller will extend credit to the store buyer.

deal   a temporary special retail price offered to store customers.

departmental control   refers to the use of dollar control on a departmental basis.

departmentalized specialty store   a departmentalized retail store that concentrates its merchandise offerings in one broad category such as fashion apparel or home furnishings.

departmentalizing   organizing different activities and functions into departments or compartments, with individuals assigned to each department to see that the various activities and functions are carried out.

department-store buying   a term used synonymously with *local buying.*

detail   the design lines that are held within a silhouette.

discount   any reduction in the list or quoted price given to the retailer by the merchandise resource.

discount department store   a departmentalized retail store that offers hard goods and major appliances along with fashion apparel and soft goods, but at discount or cut-rate prices.

disposable personal income (DPI)   the income persons have available for saving or spending, and the most useful measure of income for retailers. Disposable personal income may be determined by subtracting personal taxes from personal income.

dollar control   the amount of dollars at retail prices that is invested in the merchandise inventory.

economic buying motive   a term used synonymously with *rational buying motive.*

emotional buying motive   involves little logical thought. Such buying decisions come from feelings rather than from thinking or rationalizing.

employee discount   a reduction from the retail price granted to store employees.

end of month (EOM)   end of month states that the time for payment is calculated from the end of the month in which the invoice is dated and the merchandise shipped, and not from the invoice date.

extra dating   the buyer is given a specified number of extra days in which to pay the bill and to earn the discount.

fad   a minor fashion that has been adopted by a group of people for a short period of time. A fad is usually taken up with exaggerated zeal and quickly abandoned.

fashion   a distinctive method of expression that has been accepted and adopted by a number of people at a given time in a particular consumer market.

fashion coordinator   an individual who is responsible for promoting the sale of fashion merchandise throughout the entire store.

fashion cycle   fashion goes through a series of six stages to complete a life cycle. The stages are: rise, acceptance or rejection, consumer popularization, mass-production, decline in popularity, and abandonment of the fashion.

fashion department   a department that sells feminine outer apparel and accessories.

fashion goods   new merchandise that appeals to consumers for a short period of time and has a relatively short life cycle.

fashion trend   the direction in which a style or fashion is moving.

first-in-first-out method (FIFO)   under the FIFO method of inventory evaluation, larger profits result during periods of rising prices because higher values are placed on ending inventories than on the merchandise on hand at the beginning of the year.

fixed-fee office   a term used synonymously with *salaried office.*

floor plan   the vendor turns an assortment of merchandise over to the store buyer, who in return signs a trust receipt. The title will remain with the vendor, and the store buyer agrees to make payment as he makes sales.

free on board (FOB) destination   an agreement in which the seller is to pay all transportation costs and is to own the merchandise until it arrives at the retail store.

free on board (FOB) destination, charges reversed   the seller will own the goods until they get into the retail store; however, the buyer agrees to pay the transportation charges.

free on board (FOB) destination, freight prepaid   goods are to become the possession of the buyer as soon as they are shipped; however, the seller will pay freight charges.

free on board (FOB) factory   an agreement that the buyer will pay all transportation costs and will own the goods from the moment they are shipped.

free on board (FOB) shipping point   an agreement that the seller pays any crating necessary to the place at which the goods are to be turned over to a transportation company.

functional departmentalization   activities of a similar nature are grouped together in the same department.

general-merchandise chain   offers merchandise in the soft goods and fashion apparel lines, as well as in the hard goods or staple goods area.

geographical departmentalization   activities are departmentalized on a territorial or geographical basis.

good taste   implies a knowledge of the proper use of materials, of design, and of color.

gross margin   the amount of profit before operating costs are deducted.

gross national product (GNP)   represents the total output of goods and services produced in a year.

group buying   a method of buying in which a number of stores participate to secure a better price, ensure high standards of quality, and obtain goods more readily.

hand-to-mouth buying   the practice of limiting orders to immediate needs and ordering goods for immediate delivery rather than well in advance.

haute couture   refers to an expensive original style created by a French fashion designer or manufacturer in limited editions for a group of people considered leaders of fashion.

headline   the line of an advertisement that must attract the attention of the public, arouse interest, and lead the reader into reading the entire ad.

heterogeneous staples   a group of staple goods that are alike but are not identical.

high fashion   high-priced fashion goods, usually created by a famous designer in limited editions and bought by an elite group of consumers who are the first to accept the new style.

homogeneous staples   a group of staple goods that are identical, that is, they are all of the same size, color, fabric, and style.

illustration   an illustration or picture will attract attention to the whole advertisement and develop the reader's interest in the product.

income   is measured in money and is derived from producing and selling goods or services in the marketplace.

income statement   a term used synonymously with *profit-and-loss statement.*

independent buying office   a privately owned and operated resident buying office that continuously seeks stores as clients.

initial markup   also called the *mark-on* or *original markup*, this is the difference between the cost price and the retail price of goods.

institutional advertising   indirect-action advertising whose primary objectives are to create good will for the store, build confidence in its merchandise and services, and establish customer loyalty.

irregular   an item that contains an imperfection or repair not obviously visible to the naked eye.

job lot   an assortment of merchandise the vendor has been unable to sell at regular prices and is now offering at a reduced price per item.

journal   a term used synonymously with *trade paper.*

last-in-first-out method (LIFO)   the LIFO method assumes that those goods purchased recently are sold first.

layout   the arrangement of the ad.

leader pricing   the offering of a well-known brand of merchandise at a special low price.

legal contract   an order that has been properly filled out, signed, and accepted by the vendor.

limited-function wholesalers   also called "cash-and-carry" wholesalers. Merchant middlemen who limit themselves to smaller stock of fast-moving items and offer no credit or delivery service, thus reducing the cost of wholesaling.

loading the invoice   a practice whereby the amount of the retailer's invoice is increased (loaded) to permit a larger cash discount than is normally available at the supplier's going rate.

local buying   a method of buying that is accomplished by a retail specialist who works out of the main store and procures the necessary merchandise for the main store and its various branches and twigs.

loss leader   occurs when a well-known brand of merchandise is offered at a price below the buyer's cost.

maintained markup   the difference between the cost price and the final retail price.

manufacturer   an individual or firm who engages in the assembling or "putting together" of goods for use by the ultimate consumer.

manufacturers' agents   nonmerchant middlemen who take over part of their client's sales activities and have less authority over prices and terms of sale.

manufacturers' representatives   a term used synonymously with *manufacturers' agents.*

markdown   a reduction in price from the original retail price.

markdown percent   the difference between the net dollar markdown and original retail price divided by net sales.

marketing   the system that links the markets of production with markets of demand.

mark-on   a term used synonymously with *initial markup.*

markup   the difference between the cost price and the retail price of an item.

markup percent   the difference between the retail price and the cost price divided by the retail price.

mass fashion   a style or design that is mass-produced at a moderate price and is widely accepted by the majority of consumers.

membership group   a composition of people that the individual looks to when formulating concepts, beliefs, opinions, and attitudes. Reference groups may be organized according to age, sex, religion, ethnic membership, occupation, income, life-style, or likes and dislikes.

merchandise broker   a term used synonymously with *commission office.*

merchandise budget   a budget planned by the buyer (local or central) along with other store executives. It is a plan that forecasts specific merchandising activities for a department or store for a specified period of time.

merchandise control   the maintenance of a stock of merchandise that is adjusted to the needs of consumers and prospective consumers.

merchandise inventory   merchandise that is available for sale to the ultimate consumer.

merchandise manager   the individual usually found at the head of the merchandising division.

merchandise overage   occurs when the physical inventory is more than the book inventory.

merchandise quality   the best or finest material available, or superior to that of lesser quality or standards.

merchandise scrambling   the overlapping of one or more lines of different types of merchandise in a given type of retail store.

merchandise shortage   occurs when the physical inventory is smaller than the book inventory.

merchandising   the planning and supervision involved in marketing a particular merchandise or service at the places, times, and prices, and in the quantities that will best serve to realize the marketing objectives of the business.

merchant middlemen　wholesalers who take title or assume ownership by taking possession of goods they purchase for resale.

middlemen　individuals or organizations who operate between producers and industrial or ultimate consumers.

model stock　the desired assortment of stock broken down according to predictable factors such as classification, price, material, color, and size, based on consumer demand.

national income (NI)　the sum of the total amount earned by employees, proprietors' income, corporate profits, rental income, and net interest for a given year.

negotiation process　involves the mutual discussion of, and agreement between the retail buyer and the merchandise resources to, terms of various business transactions.

net profit　may be determined by deducting operating expenses from gross margin.

net sales　the difference between gross sales (all the sales that were made) and customer adjustments or returns.

never-out goods　a term used synonymously with *staple goods.*

new item　an item that introduces certain new and different characteristics not yet available in merchandise of a similar type.

nonmerchant middlemen　middlemen who do not take title or assume ownership by taking possession of goods they purchase for resale.

nonpersonal promotional aids　those services that will directly influence the buying behavior of the consumer; includes dealer's helps and consumer inducements.

nonpersonal selling　a method of communicating with customers indirectly.

nonstore retailing　a retailing transaction that may occur without the customers' actually visiting the store.

odd pricing　a psychological method of pricing. Instead of pricing an item at $1.00, the price is set at 99¢.

one-price policy　the same price is charged to all consumers who purchase merchandise in the same quantities under similar circumstances.

one-stop concept　boasts of providing all the merchandise needed under one roof.

on memorandum　a term used in connection with a consignment sale or a sale with the return privilege.

operating expenses　these may be classified as *direct expenses* (those paid out directly for the benefit of the department) and *indirect expenses* (those that serve the whole store).

operating profit　that part of the gross margin that remains after operating expenses have been deducted.

operating statement　a term used synonymously with *profit-and-loss statement.*

operations budget　a forecast of expected sales along with expected costs for a specified time period.

original markup　a term used synonymously with *initial markup.*

patronage motives　may be emotional or rational; explain why a consumer purchases products or services from one retail store rather than another.

periodic inventory system　a method of inventory that derives sales from inventory and purchase data by adding opening inventory and purchases and subtracting the sum of the closing inventory and markdowns, periodically or at certain intervals.

perpetual inventory system　a system where sales information is derived from sales and purchase records that record merchandise on hand in view of what has been received and what has been sold at regular intervals such as every day, week, or month.

personal income (PI)　may be calculated by first subtracting from national income the undistributed corporate profits, taxes on profits, and social security taxes, then adding all transfer payments (payments unrelated to current production, such as Social Security benefits and pensions).

personal promotional aids   those services that will directly affect the selling activity of the buyer; include vendor's selling aids and promotional allowances.

personal selling   includes wholesale selling or contact selling, since the seller usually contacts the customer, and retail selling, where the customer usually approaches the retail store.

physical inventory   the actual counting and recording of the merchandise or stock on hand at a specified time, together with the cost or retail price of each item.

physical inventory system   a figure for net sales is obtained by adding the former physical inventory to the purchases received from vendors and subtracting the ending physical inventory.

postdating   a term used synonymously with *advanced dating.*

premium   an article of value or "gift" that can be obtained by the consumer for a nominal price after the consumer purchases the advertised item.

prestige pricing   a high-price policy is followed for particular kinds of merchandise that appeal to the prestige- or status-minded consumer.

price agreement plan   a form of central buying whereby a central buyer will work with vendors and manufacturers and agree on the retail price, color, size, style, and assortment of staple types of merchandise as well as on the terms of shipping.

price-line control   refers to the use of dollar control based upon a single retail price.

price lining method   the buyer does not attempt to price merchandise at all possible prices but predetermines the retail price at which an assortment of merchandise will be carried.

price range   the spread of price line from the lowest to the highest price carried, for example, $5 to $25.

price zone   a series of price lines that are likely to appeal to one group of customers.

private resident buying office   some large retail organizations maintain their own private buying offices in major market centers such as New York City.

procedures   the necessary steps that must be followed to implement a given policy. A *rule* is a statement that must be obeyed; a *guide* is a statement that recommends an action be taken and is not necessarily mandatory.

product line   a broad category of products having reasonably similar characteristics and similar end uses.

product-line departmentalization   organizing a business enterprise according to the various types and kinds of merchandise that it sells.

product mix   all the products and services offered for sale.

profit-and-loss statement   a summary of the transactions conducted by a business during a specific period of time such as one month, six months, or a year, which shows the relationship that has prevailed for the period among amount of sales, cost of goods sold, and expenses.

promotional advertising   direct-action advertising, whereby the primary objective is to bring customers into the store to purchase specific items of merchandise.

proximo   a term used synonymously for end of month (EOM).

publicity   communication to the public about goods or services in a nonpersonal way both outside and within the retail establishment.

purchase journal   a record that contains invoices providing information on department transfers, vendor returns, short shipments, damages, lost merchandise, and other claims.

purchasing agent   the title given to the individual who represents a foreign resident buying office under United States management.

quantity discount   a reduction from list price given to buyers purchasing in unusually large quantities.

rack jobbers   middlemen who are wholesalers of nonfood items and who arrange with independent grocers and chain supermarkets to stock and maintain an assortment of goods on a rack in a particular location in each store.

rational buying motive involves man's ability to reason or learn and to make the most effective use of limited resources.

receipt of goods (ROG) means that the date of payment is based on the date the goods are received by the store rather than the date of shipment or invoice date.

reference group a term used synonymously with *membership group.*

regular dating the length of time the vendor will extend credit, calculated from the date of the invoice.

resident buyer a buying specialist who works in the capacity of advisor or assistant to those stores that the resident buying office represents and who is responsible for all phases of merchandising and promotion.

resident buying office an outside agency whose primary responsibility and specialization is coverage of the various trade markets it represents. (See *resident buyer.*)

retail buyer the key individual within the retail institution; responsible for providing merchandise that will meet the needs of the consumers.

retail consumer an individual who attempts to satisfy his physical and psychological needs and wants through the use of goods and services.

retailing provides the consumer with the merchandise assortment at the right price and at the right time; the last stage of the marketing process.

retail institution the trading center or marketplace that provides for the last activity in the marketing process.

retail method of inventory a combination of the cost method of inventory with the book method of inventory at retail prices.

retail price the first price at retail, which is placed on merchandise by the retailer regardless of later sales or other special event prices; the cost price of an item plus the markup.

retail reduction the allowance for the difference between the original retail value of merchandise and the actual final sales value of the merchandise; consists of three major factors: merchandise shortages and overages, employee discounts and discounts for other special groups, and markdowns.

salaried office the salaried office is paid a fixed fee directly from the client store it represents.

sales promotion any promotional activity other than advertising, publicity, and personal selling that attracts the public to a retail store, stimulates purchasing, and makes a profit for the store.

seasonal discount a reduction in list price granted to the retail buyer for purchasing goods during the off-season.

seasonal goods merchandise that is in demand only at certain times of the year or for particular seasons of the year.

second an item that contains obvious damage or repair.

selling agents nonmerchant middlemen who are independent businessmen and take over the entire sales function for their clients by offering advice on styling, extending financial aid, and making collections.

series discount a series of discounts granted by the merchandise resource to the retail buyer.

service wholesalers also called "regular" wholesalers. They assemble merchandise in relatively large quantities and sell it to retailers in substantially smaller quantities.

shopping goods those products for which a consumer will accept no substitute and about which the consumer does not have a thorough product knowledge.

signature plate the emblem, trademark, symbol, or distinctive print that immediately identifies the store to the public.

silhouette the overall shape or contour of a costume; the basic ingredient, which changes slightly with each new season.

social classes   groups of people who share the same income bracket and the same goals and attitudes towards life.

special merchandise   goods offered not for their quality appeal but instead for their price appeal.

specialty goods   products for which the consumer will usually accept only a well-known brand and of which the consumer has full knowledge.

speculative buying   the decision to purchase goods based on an expected rise or fall in price level.

staple goods   goods that should always be in stock, since they are demanded by consumers year in and year out.

store-owned office   a resident buying office that is owned by the store or stores it represents and is organized to provide buying services for those stores.

style   the characteristic that makes one fashion different from another.

style-out technique   a method used to detect trends in customer preferences.

syndicated office   a syndicated resident buying office; differs from the associated buying office in that it is a division of a corporation that owns a chain of department stores.

tickler file   a system that serves as a reminder and is arranged to bring items to timely attention.

top-down planning   the planning of general, overall sales activity based on economic trends, environmental conditions, and changes in store policies.

trade discount   a reduction in price granted to a certain category or trade of customer to cover the costs of a particular trading function.

trade paper   a publication containing information that is of importance and interest to people dealing with a specific trade or line.

trading stamps   stamps given to a consumer with each purchase, which can eventually be exchanged for merchandise.

traditional department store   a retail store that employs 25 or more people and is engaged in selling merchandise in the areas of home furnishings, fashion apparel, and linens and dry goods.

twig store   representative of one line of merchandise or one price line carried by a main store. It is usually found in or near a major shopping center.

unit control   an organized method of recording the individual units or pieces of merchandise found in the inventory.

varying-price policy   policy whereby a consumer seeking to purchase merchandise at a lower price will bargain with the retailer until an agreement has been reached.

warehouse and requisition plan   a form of central buying whereby the central buyer arranges for the initial stock assortment and has it shipped to the individual stores.

wholesale price   the price paid for goods purchased from merchandise resources, for example, vendors, manufacturers, or suppliers.

wholesalers   a term used synonymously with *middlemen.*

Merchandise Mathematical Formulas Used By Buying Specialists and Their Assistants

---

sales = opening inventory + purchases − closing inventory and markdowns

actual or net sales = derived sales ÷ (100% + shortage percentage)

indirect expenses = department expenses − cost of goods sold − direct expenses

net sales = gross sales − customer adjustments and returns

cost of goods sold = opening inventory + purchase costs + cost of shipping

gross cost of goods sold = opening inventory + purchase costs + shipping costs − closing inventory (cost value)

net cost of goods sold = opening inventory + purchase costs + shipping costs
= total cost of goods sold − closing inventory
= gross cost of goods sold − cash discounts

gross margin = net sales − net cost of goods sold

net profit = gross margin − operating expenses

beginning of the month (BOM) stock = planned sales for the month + (average stock at retail − average monthly sales)

the percentage − variation (or deviation) method:
beginning of the month (BOM) stock = average $\dfrac{\text{yearly sales}}{\text{turnover}}$ X

$$\left[\tfrac{1}{2} \left(1 + \frac{\text{sales for month}}{\text{average monthly sales}}\right) \right]$$

weeks supply method = 52 weeks ÷ desired stock turn

stock-sales ratio method:
beginning of the month (BOM) stock = planned monthly sales volume X planned BOM stock-sales ratio

stock-sales ratio = $\dfrac{\text{beginning stock}}{\text{sales}}$

stock turn retail basis = $\dfrac{\text{net sales}}{\text{average stock at retail price}}$

stock turn cost basis = $\dfrac{\text{cost of goods sold}}{\text{average cost of stock}}$

stock turn unit basis = $\dfrac{\text{number of units sold}}{\text{average number of units in stock}}$

average inventory = $\dfrac{\text{sum of all inventories in a period}}{\text{number of inventories}}$

merchandise shortage = book inventory – physical inventory

merchandise overage = physical inventory – book inventory

$$\text{employee discount percent} = \frac{\text{employee discounts for month}}{\text{net sales}}$$

markdown = original retail price – markdown price

$$\text{markdown percent} = \frac{\text{net dollar markdown}}{\text{net sales}}$$

$$\text{markup percent at retail} = \frac{\text{markup}}{\text{retail price}}$$

maintained markup = cost price – final retail price

net profit = gross margin – total operating expenses

planned purchases = planned sales + planned reductions
   + planned end of month stock
= total need for month
   – beginning-of-the-month (BOM) stock

open-to-buy = planned purchases – merchandise on order

maximum (total amount of staple goods to be on order and on hand) = (reorder period + delivery period) rate of sales + reserve

OR

maximum = (lead time) rate of sales + reserve

unit open-to-buy = maximum – (on-hand orders + outstanding orders)

99–100% protection against reserve depletion:
   reserve = $2.3 \times \sqrt{\text{(lead time)}}$ sales

when 95% protection is adequate to maintain a maximum reserve level:
   reserve = $1.6 \times \sqrt{\text{(lead time)}}$ sales

maximum or total amount of fashion goods and home furnishings to be on order and on hand:
   maximum = reorder period + delivery period $\times$ rate of sales + reserve

OR

   maximum = lead time $\times$ rate of sales + reserve

trade discount = list price per unit $\times$ suggested retail price – trade discount

quantity discount = wholesale price – quantity discount

seasonal discount = list price – seasonal discount

cash discount = amount of invoice – terms

series discount = list price – trade discount – extra trade discount – quantity discount

retail price = cost price + markup

markup = retail price – cost price

cost price = retail price – markup

$$\text{markup percent} = \frac{\text{retail price} - \text{cost price}}{\text{retail price}}$$

retail price = $\dfrac{\text{cost price}}{\text{cost percent } (100\% - \text{markup } \%)}$

cost price = $(100\% - \text{markup } \%)$ retail price

cost percent = $\dfrac{\text{cost price}}{\text{retail price}}$

INDEX